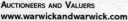

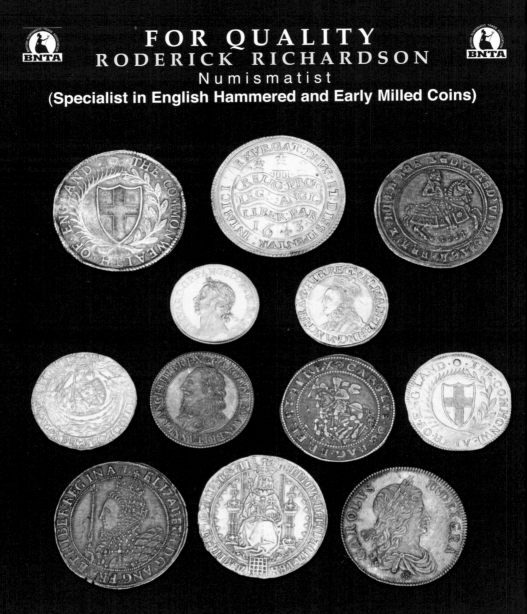

A SELECTION OF COINS FROM STOCK

Many more gold, silver and copper coins on main list from £1 upwards.

HAMMERED GOLD .... On List

£5 & £2 PIECES .... On List

GUINEAS
1673 EF ABU ......................P.O.A
1679 CHS II NEF...................P.O.A
1698 Will III GF/NVF 975
1779 NVF/VF 450
1785 VF 450
1787 Nice EF 650
1788 GVF 425
1793 Nice ABT UNC 750
1794 Nice BU 895

SOVEREIGNS
1818 Nice GVF+ ...................P.O.A
1820 VF 595
1820 Fine 495
1820 VF 495
1821 NVF/VF 550
1822 VF 575
1825 B. Hd. NVF/VF...............495
1825 EF Laur. Hd....................P.O.A
1825 Bare Head Nice NEF 675
1826 NVF/VF 495
1826 Nice BU .......................P.O.A
1827 NVF...............................450
1829 NVF/VF 495
1830 NEF 750
1830 VF 550
1835 NEF/EF .........................P.O.A
1836 BU Nice ........................P.O.A

Victoria 1837 – 1887
Young Head Shield Rev.
1838 Sov GVF+/NEF ..............P.O.A
1838 VF 875
1842 NVF/VF 295
1842 GVF+ 350
1843 GVF+ 350
1843 GVF 325
1845 NVF...............................295
1846 GVF 325
1846 Sov EF+ 595
1846 GVF+ 350
1846 ABT BU/BU....................750
1847 EF 395
1847 VF+ 325
1847 GVF+ 350
1849 VF Rare 295
1849 Nice NEF 450
1850 Nice EF 495
1851 ABU 395
1851 NEF 325
1851 NEF Nice 375
1852 NEF/EF 325
1852 ABU 375
1853 BU 495
1853 NEF 295
1853 EF+ 350
1853 ABU 350
1853 GVF 275
1854 ABT EF 375
1854 ABU/BU.........................495

1855 EF 325
1857 NEF/EF 295
1857 Nice EF 350
1858 VF.................................350
1860 GVF+ 295
1861 VF+ 275
1861 EF/NEF 325
1861 ABT BU/BU....................375
1862 EF 295
1863 ABU DN1 325
1864 NEF 295
1864 EF 325
1866 Sydney GVF+ 495
1866 GVF+ D.29 275
1868 GVF+ 295
1869 ABU/BU 350
1870 Sydney GVF+ 495
1871 S GVF 260
1871 L BU..............................350
1872 L ABU/BU 325
1872 L VF 250
1872 L EF 275
1873 L EF 295
1873 L ABU/BU 450
1875 S GVF+...........................295
1878 S EF 295
1878 S ABU/BU......................350
1879 S VF+ 275
1884 S EF/ABU 325
1885 S NEF/EF 295
1886 S ABT BU 350

1887–2011 .... On List

1/2 SOVEREIGNS .... On List

USA GOLD .... On List

FOREIGN GOLD .... On List

CROWNS
1658 Cromwell Vir.UNC/UNCP.O.A
1658 Cromwell GVF+ .............P.O.A
1662 Rose Bel Dtd Edge Fine.....175
1662 Rose Bel Dtd Edge GF......250
1666 Fine 350
1671 GF 125
1682/1 Fine 125
1687 Jms II BU .......................P.O.A
1687 Jms II VF Nice 650
1691 W+Mary VF+ .................P.O.A
1696 GF 125
1697 Fine ..............................P.O.A
1700 Nice GVF+......................850
1723 Geo I SSC EF ..................P.O.A
1732 EF Nice Tone ..................P.O.A
1741 Nice GVF+......................950
1743 Sup. Vir. UNC Lov. Tone P.O.A
1751 GEM ABT UNC Lov. Col.P.O.A
1790 C-Mark Doll Oval AUNC/UNC
....850
1799 C-Mark Doll Octag. Nice EF.995
1804 BE Doll EF Nice Lov. Tone.395
1804 BE DON GVF+..................240
1818 LIX GEM UNC Nice Tone 595

1818 LVIII UNC Nice Tone........450
1820 LX UNC Lt. Tone Rare......495
1820 2/1 GEM UNC LC R.AR.3..775
1831 Pl. Edge UNC Nice Tone . POA
1844 Nice NEF/EF....................350
1844 BU GEM .........................P.O.A
1844 EF 450
1845 GVF+/NEF 175
1845 ABT EF 295
1845 Small date EF/AUNC 595
1847 Gothic Nice UNC ..........P.O.A
1847 Y. Hd, Superb UNC ........P.O.A
1847 EF Lov. Col......................495
1847 Nice GVF 195
1887 BU (1889 Head) 150
1888 Wide Date Supb. UNC 750
1889 BU GEM 110
1889 NEF.................................45
1890 GVF+ 40
1890 BU 195
1890 UNC Nice Tone................225
1891 Fine/GF 22
1892 ABU 125
1892 BU GEM 250
1893 LVI VF 30
1893 LVI BU Lt. Tone 250
1893 LVII GVF+ 75
1893 LVI Sup. UNC....................395
1893 LVI NEF 65
1893 LVII EF 175
1893 LVII NVF/VF.......................50
1894 LVIII ABU 350
1894 LVII Sup. UNC 495
1894 LVII BU 395
1894 LVIII BU 350
1895 LVIII BU 375
1895 LIX BU Lt. Tone 275
1896 LX VF 30
1896 LX GVF+ 50
1896 LX VF 32
1896 LX ABT BU 195
1896 LX BU 295
1896 LX NEF 50
1896 LX Nice BU 295
1897 LXI NVF 28
1897 LX NEF/EF 90
1897 LX UNC.............................195
1897 LXI BU 225
1897 LXI ABU............................125
1897 LXI EF Nice Tone 85
1897 LXI Nice GVF 55
1897 LXI NEF/EF 75
1900 LXIII GVF 40
1900 LXIII EF Lt. Tone 135
1900 LXIV NVF/VF 32
1900 LXIV BU............................295
1900 LXIV BU GEM.....................395
1902 GF 65
1927 Proof Sup FDC 250
1928 Supb. BU 395
1928 BU GEM 395
1929 UNC 395

1929 Nice BU 385
1929 UNC Toned 350
1929 NEF/EF 240
1930 Nice BU 425
1930 BU 395
1931 ABT BU 325
1931 EF/AU Lt. Tone 295
1931 GVF+ 295
1932 BU GEM 850
1933 BU 375
1934 ABT EF ............................P.O.A
1934 Pr. UNC 15 known .........P.O.A
1935 - 2006 ....On List

HALF CROWNS
Eliz. I MM I EF S2583. .............P.O.A
CHS I Vir. EF for issue 650
Jms I GF S2666 MM Lis 395
1668/4 F/GF............................250
1670 GF 195
1673 Nice VF+ 495
1676 NF 375
1677 Nice AUNC.....................P.O.A
1685 JMS II GF 295
1685 JMS II GEM Vir. UNC ...P.O.A
1685 Nice NVF 395
1687 VF+1st Bust 850
1687 Jms II ABT VF 575
1689 GVF 1st Bust 350
1689 NVF.................................175
1690 NEF ...............................P.O.A
1693 W+Mary GVF+ S.3435 495
1693 Nice GVF 475
1698 UNC Nice Tone 950
1698 Nice UNC Lov. Col 995
1708 A/UNC Nice Plain Rev ....P.O.A
1708 Plain EF Lt. Tone 595
1708 Plumes VF 250
1712 GVF/NEF Nice Tone 350
1715 GVF Nice 950
1731 Vir. EF. 650
1736 GVF 595
1741 A/UNC Nice 950
1743 Superb Mint, Pr. like .......P.O.A
1745 LIMA Nice AUNC Lov. Col.495
1745 Lima GEM ABT UNC 675
1745 Roses VF+.......................195
1746 Lima NVF/VF 95
1750 Sup. UNC. Lov. Col .......P.O.A
1751 GEM UNC Lov. Col .......P.O.A
1791 CM 1/2 Doll Nef Rare 495

1817 - 1967 ....On List
FLORINS............................On List
SHILLINGS.......................On List
SIXPENCES ....On List
GROATS ....On List
SILVER 3d ....On List
BRASS 3d ....On List
MAUNDY SETS, ODDS....On List
PENNIES/BRONZE COINS On List
USA SILVER DOLLARS..On List

"THE I.A.P.N. dealer, your guide to the world of numismatics"

"More than one hundred of the world's most respected coin dealers are members of the I.A.P.N. (International Association of Professional Numismatists). I.A.P.N. members offer the collector an exceptional selection of quality material, expert cataloguing, outstanding service, and realistic pricing. The I.A.P.N. also maintain the International Bureau for the Suppression of Counterfeit Coins (I.B.S.C.C.) which, for a fee can provide expert opinions on the authenticity of coin submitted to it. A booklet listing the name, address and specialities of all I.A.P.N. members is available without charge by writing to the I.A.P.N. Secretariat". Jean-Luc Van der Schueren, 14, Rue de la Bourse, B-1000, Bruxelles.

Tel: +32–2–513 3400   Fax: +32–2–512 2528   E-mail: iapnsecret@compuserve.com   Web site: http://www.iapn-coins.org

AUSTRALIA
DOWNIES COINS Pty Ltd, PO Box 888, Abbotsford, VIC. 3067
NOBLE NUMISMATICS Pty Ltd, 169 Macquarie Street, SYDNEY NSW 2000

AUSTRIA
HERINEK, Gerhard, Josefstädterstrasse 27, A–1082 WIEN

BELGIUM
FRANCESCHI & Fils, B, 10, Rue Croix-de-Fer, B–1000 BRUXELLES
VAN DER SCHUEREN, Jean-Luc, 14, Rue de la Bourse, B–1000 BRUXELLES

CANADA
WEIR LTD., Randy, PO Box 64577, UNIONVILLE, Ontario, L3R 0M9

EGYPT
BAJOCCHI JEWELLERS, 45 Abdel Khalek Sarwat Street, 11511 CAIRO

FRANCE
BOURGEY, Sabine, 7, Rue Drouot, F–75009 PARIS
BURGAN NUMISMATIQUE—Maison Florange, 8, Rue du 4 Septembre, F–75002, PARIS
GUILLARD, Patrick, Eurl, B. P. 41, F–75261 Paris Cedex 06
LA PARPAIOLLE, 10 rue Bernex – B. P. 30006, F–13191, Cedex 20, MARSEILLE
MAISON PLATT SA, 49, Rue de Richelieu, F–75001, PARIS
NUMISMATIQUE et CHANGE DE PARIS, 3, Rue de la Bourse, F–75002 PARIS
O.G.N., 64, Rue de Richelieu, F–75002 PARIS
POINSIGNON-NUMISMATIQUE, 4, Rue des Francs Bourgeois, F–67000 STRASBOURG
SAIVE NUMISMATIQUE, 18, rue Dupont des Loges, F–57000, METZ
VINCHON-NUMISMATIQUE, 77, Rue de Richelieu, F–75002 PARIS

GERMANY
DILLER, Johannes, Postfach 70 04 29, D–81304 MÜNCHEN
FRITZ RUDOLF KÜNKER GmbH & Co. KG, Gutenbergstrasse 23, D–49076 OSNABRUCK
GORNY & MOSCH, GIESSENER MÜNZHANDLUNG GmbH, Maximiliansplatz 20, D–80333 MÜNCHEN
GERHARD HIRSCH Nachfolger, Promenadeplatz 10/II, D–80333 MÜNCHEN
JACQUIER,Paul-Francis, Honsellstrasse 8, D–77694 KEHL am RHEIN
KAISER MÜNZFACHGESCHAFT, Mittelweg 54, D–60318 FRANKFURT
KRICHELDORF Nachf., H. H. Günter-stalstrasse 16, D–79100 FREIBURG i.Br.
KURPFÄLZISCHE MÜNZENHANDLUNG—KPM, Augusta-Anlage 52, D–68165 MANNHEIM
LEIPZIGER Münzhandlung und Auktion, Nikolaistrasse 25, D–04109, LEIPZIG
MANFRED OLDING MÜNZEN-HANDLUNG, Goldbreede 14, D–49078, OSNABRÜCK
MEISTER Münzenhandlung, Moltkestrasse 6, D–71634 LUDWIGSBURG
MÜNZEN-UND MEDAILLEN-HANDLUG STUTTGART, Charlottenstrasse 4, D–70182 STUTTGART
NEUMANN GmbH, Ernst, Watteplatz 6, D–89312, GÜNZBURG
NUMISMATIK LANZ, Luitpoldblock-Maximiliansplatz 10, D–80333 MÜNCHEN
PEUS NACHF., Dr. Busso Bornwiesenweg 34, D–60322 FRANKFURT/M,
Münzhandlung RITTER GmbH Postfach 24 01 26, D–40090 DÜSSELDORF
TIETJEN + CO, Spitalerstrasse 30, D–20095 HAMBURG
WESFÄLISCHE AUKTIONSGESELLSCHAFT oHG, Nordring 22, D–59821, ARNSBERG

HUNGARY
NUMISMATICA EREMBOLT, Vörösmarty Tèr 6, HG–1051, BUDAPEST

ITALY
BARANOWSKY s.a.s, Via del Corso 184, I–00187, ROMA
CRIPPA NUMISTMATIQUE s.a.s., Via Cavalieri del S. Sepolcro 10, I–20121 MILANO
DE FALCO, Corso Umberto 24, I–80138 NAPOLI
FALLANI, Via del Babuino 58a, I–00187, ROMA
GIULIO BERNARDI, Casella Postale 560, I–34 121 TRIESTE
PAOLUCCI NUMISMATICA s.a.s., Via San Francesco 154, I–35121 PADOVA
RANIERI Numismatica srl, Sign. Marco Ranieri, I–BOLOGNA
RINALDI & Figlio, O.,Via Cappello 23 (Casa di Giulietta), I–37121 VERONA
VARESI Numismatica s.a.s., Alberto Varesi, Viale Montegrappa 3, 27100 PAVIA

IRELAND
I.C.E. Ltd, Charter House, 5 Pembroke Row, DUBLIN 2

JAPAN
DARUMA INTERNATIONAL GALLERIES, 2–16-32-701, Takanawa, Minato-ku, JP-TOKYO 108-0074
WORLD COINS, 1-15-5, Hamamatsu-cho, Minato-Ku, TOKYO 105-0013

MONACO
EDITIONS VICTOR GADOURY, 57 rue Grimaldi, "Le Panorama", MC–98000

THE NETHERLANDS
MEVIUS NUMISBOOKS Int. BV Oosteinde 97, NL 7671 VRIEZENVEEN
SCHULMAN BV, PO Box 346, NL–1400 AH BUSSUM
VERSCHOOR MUNTHANDEL, Postbus 5803, 3291 AC STRIJEN
WESTERHOF, Trekpad 38–40, NL–8742 KP, Burgwerd

NORWAY
OSLO MYNTHANDEL AS, Postboks 2745, Solli, N–0204, OSLO

POLAND
ANTYKWARIAT NUMIZMATYCZNY, ul. Zelazna 67, pawilon 22, 00-871 WARSZAWA

PORTUGAL
NUMISPORTO LDA, Av. Combatentes Grande Guerra 610 LJ6, P–4200-186 PORTO

SPAIN
AUREO & CALICO, Plaza del Angel 2, E-08002 BARCELONA
CAYON, JANO S.L., Calle Orfila 10, E–28010 MADRID
SEGARA, Plaza Mayor 26, E–28012, MADRID
Jesús VICO S.A., Jorge Juan n-83, Duplicado, E - 28009 MADRID

SWEDEN
NORDLINDS MYNTHANDEL AB, ULF, Karlavagen 46, PO Box 5132, S–102 43 STOCKHOLM

SWITZERLAND
ADOLPH HESS A. G Postfach 7070, CH-8023, ZÜRICH
HESS—DIVO AG, Postfach 7070, CH-8023, ZÜRICH
LHS NUMISMATIK, Post-fach 2553, CH - 8022, ZÜRICH
NOMOS AG, Zähringerstrasse 27, 8001 ZÜRICH
NUMISMATICA ARS CLASSICA AG, Postfach 2655, CH–8022 ZÜRICH
NUMISMATICA GENEVENSIS SA, 1 Rond-point de Plainpalais, CH–1205 GENEVE

THAILAND
HOUSE OF THE GOLDEN COIN, 193/119 Moo 10, South Pattaya Road, Nongprue Banglamung, CHONBURI 20230

UNITED KINGDOM
BALDWIN & SONS LTD., A.H., 11 Adelphi Terrace, LONDON WC2N 6BJ
PAUL DAVIES LTD, PO Box 17, ILKLEY, West Yorkshire LS29 8TZ
DIX NOONAN WEBB, 16 Bolton Street, Piccadilly, LONDON W1J 8BQ
CHRISTOPHER EIMER, PO Box 352, LONDON NW11 7RF
FORMAT OF BIRMINGHAM LTD Burlington Court, 18 Lower Temple Street, BIRMINGHAM B2 4JD
KNIGHTSBRIDGE COINS, 43 Duke Street. St. James's, LONDON SW1Y 6DD
RASMUSSEN Mark, PO Box 42, BETCHWORTH RH3 7YR
RUDD, Chris, PO Box 222, Aylsham, NORFOLK NR11 6TY
SAVILLE, Douglas, Chiltern Thameside, 37c St Peters Avenue, Caversham, READING RG4 7DH
SPINK & SON LTD, 69, Southampton Row, Bloomsbury, LONDON WC1B 4ET
WILKES, Tim, PO Box 150, Battle, TN33 0FA

UNITED STATES OF AMERICA
BERK, LTD., 31 North Clark Street, CHICAGO, IL. 60602
BULLOWA, C.E. COINHUNTER, Suite 2112, 1616 Walnut Street, PHILADELPHIA, PA 19103
CEDERLIND Tom, P. O. BOX 1963, PORTLAND, OR 97207
CLASSICAL NUMISMATIC GROUP INC, PO Box 479, LANCASTER, PA 17608
COIN AND CURRENCY INSTITUTE INC, PO Box 1057, CLIFTON, NJ 07014
DAVISSON'S LTD, COLD SPRING, MN 56320–1050
DUNIGAN, Mike, 5332 Birchman, Fort Worth, TX 76107
FREEMAN & SEAR, PO Box 641352, LOS ANGELES, CA 90064–6352
FROSETH INC., K.M., PO Box 23116, MINNEAPOLIS, MN 55423
GILLIO INC. - GOLDMÜNZEN INTERNATIONAL 8 West Figueroa Street, SANTA BARBARA, CA. 93101
HARVEY, Stephen, PO Box 3778, BEVERLEY HILLS, CA 90212
JENCEK, John, 205 De Anza Blvd. No. 119, SAN MATEO, CA 94402
KERN, Jonathan K. Co., 441, S. Ashland Avenue, LEXINGTON, KY 40502–2114
KOVACS, Frank L., PO Box 7150, CORTE MADERA, CA 94976
KREINDLER, B&H, 236 Altessa Blvd, MELVILLE, NY 11747
MALTER GALLERIES Inc., 17003 Ventura Blvd., ENCINO, CA 91316
MARGOLIS, Richard, PO Box 2054, TEANECK, NJ 07666
DMITRY MARKOV COINS & MEDALS, PO Box 950, NEW YORK, NY 10272
MILCAREK, Dr. Ron, PO Box 1028, GREENFIELD, MA 01302
PEGASI Numismatics, PO. Box 131040 ANN ARBOR, MI. 48113
PONTERIO & ASSOCIATES, a division of Bowers & Merena, 18061 Fitch, IRVINE, CA. 92614-6018
RARCOA INC, 6262 South Route 83, WILLOWBROOK, IL 60514
WILLIAM M. ROSENBLUM RARE COINS, PO Box 785, LITTLETON, CO. 80160–0785
SEDWICK, Daniel Frank, LLC, 2180 North Park Avenue, Suite 200, Winter Park, FL. 32789
HLS STACKS Rare Coins, 18 Arlington Lane, BAYVILLE, N.Y.11709
STEPHEN ALBUM RARE COINS, P.O. Box 7386, Santa Rosa, CA. 95407
STEPHENS Inc., Karl, PO Box 3038, FALLBROOK, CA 92088
SUBAK Inc., 79 West Monroe Street, Room 1008, CHICAGO, IL 60603
TELLER NUMISMATIC ENTERPRISES, 16055 Ventura Blvd., Suite 635, ENCINO, CA 91436
WADDELL, Ltd., Edward J., PO Box 3759, FREDERICK, MD 21705–3759
WORLD-WIDE COINS OF CALIFORNIA, PO Box 3684, SANTA ROSA, CA 95402

VENEZUELA
NUMISMATICA GLOBUS, Apartado de Correos 50418, CARACAS 1050–A

~ Visit our website at www.iapn-coins.org ~

8

THE

COIN
YEARBOOK
2012

Edited by
John W. Mussell, FRGS
and the Editorial Team of COIN NEWS

ISBN–978–1–870192–33–0

Published by
TOKEN PUBLISHING LIMITED
Orchard House, Duchy Road, Heathpark, Honiton, EX14 1YD
Telephone: 01404 46972   Fax: 01404 44788
e-mail: info@tokenpublishing.com. Website: http://www.tokenpublishing.com

Printed in Great Britain by Polestar, Exeter

CONTENTS

FOREWORD

F OR the third year running I start the COIN YEARBOOK with talk of the wider financial markets; unless
you have been living on another planet you will have heard the endless doom and gloom in the media
regarding the continuing economic situation across the globe and cannot help but have noticed that
things are far from settled out there. The wider world doesn't generally have as much of an effect on the
hobby of numismatics as it does on other spheres of life—after all, those who collect coins do, by their very
nature, have some spare cash and so are not perhaps as directly influenced by the rising prices and financial
turmoil as those whose disposable income is less. However, it would be a foolish man who ignored the wider
world completely and there is no doubt that as the "slow-down/credit crunch/recession/depression/insert
woeful name for it here" carries on, the effects ARE being felt in the coin hobby. True the collectors are still
there and still buying, the shows are as busy as ever and good stock still as hard to come by, the auctions
continue to break records and to all intents and purposes everything is as it should be in our hobby. But that
doesn't mean the outside world isn't encroaching, nor indeed that the current situation won't have an impact
for years to come.

The main issues are as they have always been—the problem of precious metal prices and the money
brought into the hobby by investors. Whilst silver took a bit of a tumble in mid-2011 the price has returned
to near record highs and of course the price of gold has continued an inexorable rise, standing at nearly 50%
higher than it was a year ago—that is a staggering increase and as we go to press with this book (September
2011) it shows no sign of stopping. Many of you will of course wonder what, if any affect, the bullion prices
will have on numismatics as a whole. After all, the people who accumulate the Krugerrands, Maple Leaves
and Britannias are not necessarily the same people who collect gold Ryals, long cross pennies, or Gothic
Crowns. But nevertheless the price of precious metals does have an impact and many of you will have noticed
that it is being reflected in the price you pay at auction or at fairs. The coins you buy may not be bullion but
the precious metal market is such that any item made of those metals will increase in price regardless of
whether it has another value not linked to bullion—that's just the way things are. And then there are those
items whose "other value", i.e. its value as a collectable, is less than its scrap value. Those items—the pre-1947
and pre-1920 silver, the "standard" sovereigns of the 20th century, have all seen their value as lumps of metal
(as opposed to coins) increase massively as they get hoovered up by the bullion dealers, melted down and
turned into bars to be sold on as investment pieces and this in itself is proving a problem.

Many collectors around today will have started back in the 1940s and 50s by sorting through their
pocket change to find the rare dates or to complete their sets; since 1971 and decimalisation that has been
impossible on a day to day basis but that doesn't mean that new collectors don't behave in the same way—it
is just that rather than sorting through their pockets they instead search on-line, at auction and in the dealers'
trays at fairs in order to try to complete their date runs. Unfortunately as more and more of the early shillings
and sixpences, etc., gain a value that bears no relation to their numismatic rarity, so it won't be long before we
find that new collectors are simply unable to find those last few dates they are desperate to acquire—dates
once so common that are now simply no longer with us having succumbed to the melting pots. This can only
be a bad thing. At the moment there are still enough of the 34 million 1918 shillings originally minted around
for it not to be a problem, but if the value of silver keeps climbing who knows…? Already we are seeing the
"ordinary" sovereigns becoming more and more hard to come by. When once a Victorian or Edward Sovereign
could be found on any dealer's table, today you have to hunt. They are still there but not in the quantities they
were—how long before they aren't seen at all?

Of course few would mourn the loss of a few of the early decimal sovereigns but how long, I wonder,
before even those from the 1970s are keenly sought after? Once something is melted down it is lost to the
world of numismatics forever and whilst we may scoff at the idea that the once ubiquitous "Vicky Sov" or

silver sixpence from the reign of George V may one day disappear for good, it is worth noting that whilst this precious metal rise continues 1000s of coins are lost forever every day and the "outside world" really does have an impact on our hobby.

The other major "outside influence" is investment money. We always try to steer clear of the idea of coins as an investment, preferring instead to love them and covet them for their numismatic appeal rather than simply their value but there can be no denying the fact that a great deal of money coming into coins today is there purely because they do seem, at the moment, to be an excellent investment. This isn't simply because of the bullion prices but rather because more traditional forms of investments: stocks, shares and the like, just aren't as attractive as once they were and those with money, be they private individuals or fund managers, have started to look elsewhere for returns. Investors are not, in themselves, a major problem—after all, whilst they may not have the numismatic nous that some long term collectors may have and won't ever look at the coins in the same way as the die-hards in the hobby, that doesn't mean they don't often grow to love their acquisitions—and of course the money they pump into the hobby benefits us all as it allows dealers more liquidity to buy new stock. Of course, too much interest from investors inevitably pushes the price of coins up and collectors never like that. But conversely nor do they like to see the price go down, as then their collections become devalued"—and that is where the real problem with investment money comes in. Investors don't love their coins like true collectors do, often seeing them like any other commodity and, like any other commodity they are happy to sell them off the moment the market gets a little shaky. This in turn leads to prices falling and before you know it prices across the board have slumped as was seen with the stamp hobby in the early 1980s. It hasn't happened to coins yet and to be honest I don't think it will but it is always worth remembering, whether you are a seasoned numismatist or simply buying this new COIN YEARBOOK to work out where to put your money, that actually coins are far more than just an investment: they are fascinating pieces of history and if those who saw them as commodities would but realise it the return they give to those who are truly interested far outweighs the monetary gains they may bring.

Money does play a part in this hobby (if you'll excuse the pun), of course it does—that is why we do our best every year to bring the COIN YEARBOOK as up to date as possible. There will always be variations of course—the aforementioned price of precious metals may well mean that some of the coins listed here will change dramatically in value over the next 12 months but sadly we just can't predict which ones or which way they'll vary! Other coins won't be subject to such wide swings, they have a price dictated by their interest as a collectable not a bullion item, and as such we like to think that the prices given here for those are a true reflection of the current market situation and will remain so for some time. In order to get to these prices we take averages from dealers' lists and websites as well as from auction results and, whilst grading is a subjective issue that will always affect individual prices, we like to think that as a rule what is printed here is pretty much what you would pay for that coin anywhere in the UK. We haven't just relied on "averages" though—we have had a number of acknowledged experts in their field check and double check the Yearbook and as ever we are indebted to them. In particular we would like to thank Patrick Mackenzie for his work on the decimals, Roy Norbury of West Essex Coins for checking the Milled section, Elizabeth Cottam and Chris Rudd for their input and help with the Celtic Section, Mike Vosper for his work on the Roman Section, Stephen Mitchell of Studio Coins for the Hammered coinage, Charles Riley for working on the medals section, Declan O'Kelly and Andrew Auld for their contributions to the Irish section and Nick Swabey for his help with the Maundy sets and oddments. This year we are particularly grateful to David Stuart for giving his expertise and assisting with fully upgrading the Scottish coin guide and of course we are indebted to the many collectors and dealers who share their knowledge with us and help us keep this YEARBOOK and of course our related magazine COIN NEWS, at the forefront of the hobby.

MARKET review

JOHN ANDREW takes a look at what has been an outstanding year for numismatics at auction

The UK's 2010–11 auction season will go down in history as outstanding. There have never been so many sales over Coinex—there were a dozen in London before the show opened. Throughout the season the demand for top quality English material continued to be frenzied with a small group of bidders all equally determined to obtain the best that was on offer. The result was prices that only a few years ago would have been the stuff of dreams. In many aspects there are two parallel markets at the present moment with the one for choice rarities being in a different world to items that are ordinary. The mundane run-of-the-mill material is not flying out of the trays with such gusto. Indeed, items that are not quite "there" are struggling.

Islamic coins break new ground

The demand for overseas material is certainly also buoyant for choice rarities and it is for one particular sale that the 2010–11 season will be remembered. This was held by Morton & Eden on April 4, 2011. It is probably the smallest coin auction that London has ever seen—a mere 81 lots. Nevertheless, it established new record prices for both a gold and a silver Islamic coin; a new record for a coin selling at auction in the UK; set a new record for a numismatic auction in London (it totalled £6,685,800) and perhaps many more records as well. The top price was £3.72 million, making it the second most expensive coin ever sold at auction. The record is still held by the 1933 double eagle sold by Sotheby's in New York during July 2002 for US$7.59 million (then about £4.8 million).

"Lot 12 made a good price!" was quite an understatement from Tom Eden after the sale. The star of the auction was an Umayyad gold dinar dated 105h (AD 723). What makes this one of the rarest and most highly prized of all Islamic gold coins is that the gold from which it was struck was obtained from a mine owned by the Caliph himself.

This is signified from the text in the reverse field that reads Ma'din Amir al-Mu 'minin. Although the exact significance of this is still debated the general gist is "a mine belonging to the Caliph". Such coins are known as "Dinars from the Mine of the Commander of the Faithful". The additional words, bi'l-Hijaz, which translate as "in the Hejaz", indicate that the mine was located in a region in the west of present-day Saudi Arabia. This is the

This Umayyad gold dinar dated 105h (AD 723) sold for a record £3.72 million.

first Islamic coin and indeed, probably the first dated object, to mention a location within the present Kingdom of Saudi Arabia.

Stephen Lloyd, explained, "The site of the mine itself has been identified as Ma`din Bani Sulaim, located northwest of the Holy City of Mecca. Gold has been mined there for thousands of years, and the site is still worked today. Remarkably, mediaeval Arab writers record that the Caliph bought a piece of land in this area, containing at least one gold mine, almost exactly when these coins were made." But why mention the source of the metal from which it was struck? As our conversation progressed, it was clear that no one had yet come up with a definitive answer, but one could make reasoned suggestions. It could be to distinguish the Caliph's private resources from the public treasury. But scholars have also noted a connection between the dates of these coins and the years when the Caliph personally led the pilgrimage to Mecca. He would have passed near the mine. Did he have a travelling mint to strike these dinars from the "Mine of the Commander of the Faithful?" Were the coins given as gifts, or were they used as currency on the pilgrimage?

The coins are fascinating. We will probably never get the answers to all the questions that they raise. However, one thing is sure—they are extremely rare. Including the coin offered at this sale, there are believed to be 10 or 11 dated 105h, but none has appeared at public auction until this sale. Almost all of these are held in museum or institutional collections and are in good condition. An example dated 106h is rumoured to exist, but to date it remains unpublished. Morton & Eden estimated the piece at £300,000–400,000. There was strong interest in the piece with at least four bidders in the room, but the auction house had never dreamed that it might sell for £3.72 million. A member of the London trade purchased this extremely fine piece on behalf of a European collection.

An earlier gold dinar "From the Mine of the Commander of the Faithful" was also offered. Dated 92h, it does not bear the additional words bi'l-Hijaz—"in the Hejaz", found on the piece dated 105h. Only one other example has appeared at public auction. That was in 1999 and it sold for £308,000. Described as having "minor marks on obverse, extremely fine", the cataloguer estimated it at £250,000–300,000. Including this coin, eight coins dated 91 or 92h are known. There

are rumours of a similar coin dated 89h, but this has not been published. A Middle Eastern buyer purchased it for £648,000.

However, lot 12 was not the only surprise in the sale as an Umayyad silver dirham struck in Oman in 90h also brought an astonishing price. Umayyad dirhams from Oman are the earliest Islamic coins struck in the Arabian Peninsula, and also the first dated objects to preserve the name Oman. Only two dates are known: 81h and 90h, and just a few specimens are recorded in total. At first sight, the calligraphy on this piece is surprising for a coin struck in Oman. By the time that it was issued, two distinct regional styles of lettering on Umayyad dirhams had developed. Mints in the East (broadly speaking Iran and Iraq) generally used a more angular style, characterised by lam-alifs resembling an X with a closed base. The relatively few dirham mints active in the North and West continued the more rounded style established at Damascus, where the bottom loop of the lam-alif is less triangular and the uprights curve up towards the vertical. Interestingly, this dirham is stylistically linked with the Western rather than the Eastern group, in spite of Oman's geographical proximity to the Iranian coast. The piece was estimated at £20,000–30,000, but sold to the same collection which had purchased the 105h dinar for £1.08 million. This is a new record for an Islamic silver coin.

However, it was not just the great rarities that generated surprises. A revolutionary period silver dirham issued by Abu Muslim at Balkh in 130h was offered. Apart from minor double striking it is otherwise in very fine state. The coin is very rare, but an estimate of £1,800–2,200 was considered reasonable. The piece sold to a private Middle Eastern buyer for £78,000. An Umayyad dirham supposedly issued at Fil in 80h (the conventional reading of this mint name, but the correct interpretation may be different) was offered in good very fine condition. This is an extremely rare coin, which was estimated at £3,500–4,000—it sold to the same collection which purchased the 105h dinar for £102,000.

Overseas interest in British material

On September 30, 2010, St James's Auctions had a sale entirely devoted to patterns and proofs. This included the Mitchell-Davis Collection that was formed in the States over the past six to seven years. The most staggering result was for an with excellent eye appeal". Not unreasonably it was offered with an estimate of £24,000–26,000. It sold for a hammer price of £114,000, which is £133,950 with the Premium. The coin will be leaving the UK and heading East—not the Far East—but to Russia.

At Dix Noonan Webb (DNW) on September 29, 2010, an Edward VIII pattern sixpence by T. H. Paget and K. Gray was offered with an estimate of £15,000–20,000. Apart from a few minimal hairlines and marks, it is otherwise "brilliant as struck and toned". Needless to say, examples of this coin are of the highest rarity. The piece was contested to £40,800. The buyer was from Japan. Meanwhile back at St James's on September 30 the rarest of the 17th century guineas attracted an overseas buyer. The piece is a gem, a 1664 example with the elephant below Charles II's piece. With an excellent provenance, the famous Bridgewater House Collection started by John, the second Earl of Bridgewater (1622–86), this proof-like piece is in brilliantr mint state. It sold for £58,750.

New records for English and British coins

The season saw many new records being set for coins native to our island. At DNW on September 29 a 1656 Cromwell gold broad was offered. Apart from some hairlines, the piece is in good extremely fine condition and is brilliant. The estimate was set at an undemanding £8,000–10,000. Although both the auction house and the room considered it would exceed its top estimate, no one anticipated that it would sell for £28,320, a new record for the coin.

The highlight of this sale was a Henry VII sovereign, an extremely rare coin. Although it

An undated pattern crown in gold featuring a large young head of Queen Victoria. It sold for a hammer price of £114,000

undated pattern crown in gold featuring a large young head of Queen Victoria upon its obverse, while its reverse features a lion-topped crowned arms over a central Order of the Garter supported by a lion and unicorn, all within a wreath of oak and laurel. The coin is not listed in *English Pattern Trial and Proof Coins in Gold 1547–1968* by Messrs Wilson and Rasmussen, but a silver version is listed in *English Silver Coinage since 1649*, but no one can recall ever seeing an example. The coin was auctioned at the Plymouth Auction Rooms in April 2008. Had this not been known, it is doubted whether it would have been realised that the piece was from the celebrated Murdoch Collection sold in 1903–4. It was acquired together with another 30 gold pattern coins and restrikes from the Murdoch sale by an Evan Roberts. We know nothing of him. After his death these coins passed down the family until a descendant based in Devon decided to dispose of them at a local auction house in Plymouth.

At the Murdoch sale this coin, together with a uniface gold halfcrown sold for a hammer price of £7 17s 6d (£7.875). In the Murdoch catalogue, the coins are listed under Unofficial Gold Issues. In the Plymouth catalogue both pieces were described as being patterns by L. C. Lauer for Adolph Weyl and were offered in separate lots. These realised hammer prices of £16,500 and £5,000 respectively. St James's Auctions make no reference to Lauer and Weyl, but state that the piece is exceedingly rare, adding as a note, "the gold striking appears to be unique". Apart from faint hairlines, the piece is virtually as struck and is "beautifully preserved

This extremely rare Henry VII sovereign was contested to £192,000— more than twice the estimate.

may not have been the first issued (it is a type V) the piece is a stunner. It is a very majestic coin and artistically it is regarded as one of the high points of English numismatics. Furthermore, it is beautifully struck on a full round flan and is in extremely fine condition. The cataloguer gave it an estimate of £70,000–90,000, but was no doubt hoping for more. The piece was contested to £192,000. Stephen Fenton of Knightsbridge Coins and St James's Auctions bought it.

The outstanding feature of Spink's Coinex sales was the number of quality pre-decimal proof sets offered. The top price here was for an 1839 set of the 15 coins from the Una and the Lion £5 to the copper farthing (and also included the Maundy). Apart from a few very light hairlines, the coins are practically in mint state and were offered in a contemporary black shagreen case. It sold for £69,100, but VAT at 17.5 per cent was payable on both the hammer price and the Premium. A 1937 four-coin gold set commanded £6,770 and the corresponding silver and base metal set £744. These all set new records for standard sets.

A Roman surprise

At Morton & Eden's on November 11, the surprise was a Roman aureus of Maximinus I struck at Rome in AD 235. Strangely, he never set foot in the Eternal City himself. While the silver coinage of this Emperor is plentiful, his gold coinage is extremely rare. When this piece was auctioned at Sotheby's in New York in 1990, the cataloguer stated that it was only the third example to have been auctioned since 1979. On that occasion it realised a hammer price of US$6500, then about £3,780. Twenty years later, Morton & Eden's estimate of £40,000–60,000

A Roman aureus of Maximunus I struck at Rome in AD 235 sold for £195,500.

looked optimistic. When it was sold in 1990, the coin was part of the extremely large Nelson Bunker Hunt Collection that was being sold over several sales. Such a large offering could have softened prices a little, but not dramatically. The most likely explanation is that it just got missed. The coin has a fine portrait, is struck on a broad flan and apart from a few minor marks, is in about extremely fine state. So was the estimate on the high side? The coin sold for nearly three times the top estimate at £195,500! A European collector, bidding against telephone bidders and internet buyers, purchased the coin.

Indian coins shine

The biggest surprise at Baldwin's sale on September 28 was when a 1939 Bombay mint rupee was offered. It was no ordinary issue, but was a trial for the security edge that was introduced to the regular coinage the following year. A few experimental coins were struck in 1939 before the edge had been approved. Pridmore privately commented that only five examples were struck. The cataloguer not unreasonably set the estimate at £4,000–5,000—after all, it was only a very fine rupee with a different edge. After a battle royal the piece sold for a staggering £27,140. Major Fred Pridmore would never have anticipated Indian rarities rising to such dizzy heights.

At Spink's on December 1, two properties of Indian coins were offered. The first belonged to an Indian Prince, while the second was an old British collection. The market for Indian material is specialised and given the fact the sale featured an extremely rare gold 5-mohurs of the Mughal ruler Akbar (1556–1605), as well as other rarities, it attracted all the Indian collectors. The 5-mohurs was estimate at £12,000–15,000 in good very fine state. No one could recall one being offered before and the presale "chatter" was that it could have realised £25,000, perhaps £50,000 or as much as £100,000. The consensus was that it would reach a high price, but as to what no one knew. There was a battle for it, the final fight being between a phone bidder and an established collector in the room. The room won with a bid of £125,000, which is £150,000 with the Premium.

English hammered gold and British bronze and Chinese soar

At Spink the following day some stunning English hammered gold was offered and the hammer prices matched: £150,000, £100,000,

This rare Henry VII type IV sovereign in very fine state sold at the hammer price of £150,000.

Russian sparkles

Top dog at Baldwin's on September 28 was a gold 37½ roubles of 1902. Apart from light hairlines and marks this rarity is in extremely fine state. It was fiercely contested, the hammer falling at £50,000 or £59,000 with the Premium. The interest in an Ivan the Terrible (1533–84) gold half kopeck surprised the cataloguer. Apart from being holed and plugged, the piece, which looks a little like a squashed shirt button, is otherwise in good very fine condition. It is the coin actually illustrated in Friedberg's *Gold Coins of the World*. The piece was given a very undemanding estimate of £600–800. This is an extremely rare coin and it was contested to £4,720.

A new record for a modern UK proof set

Appropriately in the year when the historical drama *The King's Speech* starring Colin Firth as George VI became a box office hit, coins of the monarch's reign made auctioneering history at Baldwin's in May 2011. On offer was one of only two known proof sets struck with an experimental finish specifically to be used for the pre-production promotions of the coins struck for the King's Coronation. When the designs were in their gestation in 1936, numismatic photography was in its infancy. The reflective properties of the gold coins made it impossible to obtain a clear image of each denomination.

To overcome the problem, the Royal Mint successfully experimented with matt finishes produced from a sand-blasting process to generate these pre-productions coins which were used to advertise the new coins to the public. This set would have been one of the first to be produced solely for that purpose. Unlike the other existing set, this one is in its original case. This differs from the standard 20th century UK proof sets as the coins as the housing is blue-black as opposed to cream.

Apart from being toned, the coins are "as struck". The set sold at its lower estimate—£106,200. It was acquired by a bidder in the room representing an American client. This is a new world auction record for a George VI numismatic item. The lot was exceptionally well catalogued with a five page entry in the catalogue. In addition to the page description and image of the cased set. The notes extended to two pages. In addition there were two pages of "Important Dates relating to the 1937 Matt Proof Set", which in reality was

£140,000, a couple of £82,000s and an £85,000 with plenty more selling for five-figure sums. Top price was for a Henry VII (1485–1509) type IV sovereign offered with an estimate of £50,000–60,000. This very rare piece sold is in good very fine state. It sold for £150,000 hammer, which is £180,000 with the Premium.

Meanwhile at London Coin Auctions on December 5 and 6 top of the British coins was an 1882 bronze penny without the H. Graded by the Coin Grading Service (CGS) as EF 60, it will be appreciated that examples are very rare in this state. Indeed, the example offered in the Bamford sale graded as "about fine, reverse better". The example offered here is probably the finest example available. The vendor purchased the coin from Spink in the 1980s for £450 and was hoping to see his buy sell for 10 times this sum. Much to his surprise, the hammer fell at £9,500, which is £11,115 with the Premium.

Prior to 2000, it is believed that bullion proof sets were not issued in China, but were marketed elsewhere, mainly in the US. A 1995 500-yuan was offered at this event. This is a bimetallic gold/silver coin with a 5-ounce gold centre and a 2-ounce silver ring. Only 199 were issued. The piece was estimated at bullion—£3,500–4,000. A 1996 example, which had a mintage of 108, was also offered with the same estimate. There were Chinese bidders in the room as well as commission bids and one Chinese bidder on the phone. The bidding rose to £25,000 and continued nonchalantly to a hammer price of £36,000 and £34,000 respectively, which is £39,780 and £37,440 with the Premium.

One of the two known matt proof sets struck for George VI. The set sold for £106,200.

Interest in the provinces

only partially true—most of the entries featured noteworthy news stories from 1937. Nevertheless, it was well done and interesting.

Most of the UK's numismatic auctions take place in the capital, but it must not be forgotten that good sales are also held out of town. September saw a landmark sale for Lockdales—its 80th auction. The event featured the collection of Norwich Mint and other hammered coins and tokens formed by the late Trevor Wherrett. An active member of the Rochford Hundred and the Essex Numismatic Societies. One of his major projects of the 1970s was a film titled *Essex: Its Coins*. It is hoped to transfer this to a digital format so that it may be shown again. However, his real love was the coins of Norwich. The sale attracted collectors of this mint as well as his old friends from Essex.

Highlight's from the Wherrett Collection include an excessively rare William II (1087–1100) voided cross type struck at Norwich by the moneyer Howorth. The piece is thought to be one of two known of this moneyer and type. This is a full round coin. Its reverse is very slightly off centre and the obverse is a little weak, but otherwise it is in good fine/nearly very fine state and has a

dark tone. The piece sold for £2,460.

In October there were some interesting sovereigns at Warwick & Warwick in the Midlands. Top price here was for an 1874 shield back sovereign struck from die 32. In nearly very fine/ good very fine condition it sold for double expectations at £3,450. A shield back sovereign struck at Melbourne in 1880 was offered in good fine/very fine state. It sold for £1,495, a strong price. An 1889 Sydney mint variety was offered with the JEB (the engraver's initials) being straight on the truncation with the D:G (for Dei Gratia) in the obverse legend being further away than usual from the crown. In fine/ good fine, the piece sold for a tad below estimate at £2,185. However, another colonial sovereign, a 1913 Ottawa mint example was contested. This is in about uncirculated state it commanded £1,380. A 1923 South Africa proof sovereign described as being FDC sold for £1,725. The most sought after of this series was in fact for a fractional sovereign. An 1835 die error half-sovereign with the obverse being struck from a die for the sixpence generated considerable interest. In good very fine condition the piece sold for nearly double its estimate at £2,415.

1874 shield back sovereign struck from die 32, sold for double expectations at £3,450.

Despite choice rarities selling at unprecedented levels, it is still possible to form an interesting coin collection of good material without having to spend a King's Ransom. Do your homework and scan dealers' lists, stock and websites. Look at what is coming up at auction and if you can, attend sales. I well remember being taken on holiday by my parents to Llandudno in the early 1960s. Although still at primary school, I was keenly interested in coins. One of the jewellers/antique shops sold coins and was taken to browse the stock and see if there was anything I could spend my modest pocket money upon. My parents got into conversation with the owner who said, "Coins have risen so much in value recently that they are really becoming unaffordable". If that shop owner is still alive, I wonder what he would make at today's prices — from memory sovereigns were less than £4 a piece and of course Victorian bronze pennies and pre-1919 sterling silver and pre-1947 .500 fine silver was still in circulation.

Remember, the real fun in collecting is the hunt for material. Its acquisition is almost an anti-climax.

IMPORTANT NOTE: Unless otherwise stated, the above prices are inclusive of the Buyers' Premium. In other words they are the hammer price plus the Premium.

MUSEUM *archive*

Every month in COIN NEWS we are privileged to feature one of the rare items from the Royal Mint's own private Museum at Llanstrisant. The collection represents one of the most impressive numismatic collections in the world, featuring outstanding rarities alongside the currency we all use in our every day lives. Here we have chosen a few of the items we have featured as a "snap shot" of the Museum's treasures.

Great Seal of the Realm

While new coins and medals are designed and issued fairly regularly, the need for a new Great Seal of the Realm occurs much less frequently but in 2000 just such a need arose. One of the first considerations was whether or not to continue the thousand-year tradition of depicting the monarch enthroned on one side and on horseback on the other. Since the Queen no longer attends the Trooping the Colour ceremony on horseback, there was a feeling that a different solution should be sought and it was decided to use the Royal Arms instead of an equestrian portrait.

The artist chosen was James Butler, a Royal Academician and one of the foremost sculptors of his generation who has built a reputation for creating major figurative pieces. The plaster model illustrated of the Royal Arms reverse of the Seal shows his free and vigorous style of sculpting and, at close to a metre in diameter, to reduce it down to the 16cm of the actual Seal presented some interesting technical challenges. James Butler's original artwork was regarded as a triumph from the start and it is so well regarded that it still hangs in the Royal Mint's Board Room.

Elizabeth I fine sovereign

The fine sovereign of Elizabeth I pictured here was purchased from the London coin dealer Lincoln for the Royal Mint Museum on February 9, 1914. It is a handsome coin and is one of only two sovereigns of Elizabeth's reign in the collection, but its significance for the Museum extends beyond the addition of a new type of Tudor sovereign.

In August 1913 William Hocking was appointed as the first Curator and Librarian of the Museum, in large part as recognition of his substantial contribution evidenced through the publication a few years before of his two-volume catalogue of the collection. His responsibility for the Museum having thus been recognised, he thought it appropriate to set up a new system of recording additions and an Accessions Register was duly established in 1914, the first entry being this fine sovereign of Elizabeth I. From that time on funds were made available for further additions under Hocking's direction and as a result a number of rare and interesting items now have a home in the Museum.

Matthew Boulton secured the contract to make and supply regal copper coins at the end of the 18th century and, as readers of COIN NEWS will know, the progress towards an agreed design generated a number of pattern pieces. Prominent artists, such as Nathaniel Dance Holland, provided Boulton with help in securing a contemporary treatment of Britannia and the result, as is evident from the piece illustrated here, was dignified and very well composed.

The coin is one of several hundred that were given to the Royal Mint from the estate of Sarah Sophia Banks, the assiduous collector of the late 18th century. She made it her business to cultivate relations with individuals and organisations who could be of help in enhancing her collection and through her brother, Sir Joseph Banks, her interest in coins would have been well known to Boulton. He certainly supplied Miss Banks with new, unusual and rare pieces resulting from the domestic and overseas orders he secured for his Soho Mint. Her collection, as well as being historical, was therefore a distinctive record of what was being produced at Soho at that time and the presence of such coins in the Royal Mint Museum collection today fills what might otherwise have been an unfortunate gap.

The first coinage of Tower Hill

Having been based in the Tower of London for over 500 years the Royal Mint moved to new purpose-built premises on Tower Hill in 1810 and the first coinage to be struck there was for the East India Company. They were copper pice for Prince of Wales's Island, now Penang, and the specimen shown here is an ordinary striking from that initial run.

Copper coins for the East India Company had formerly been produced by Matthew Boulton at Soho and it came as something of a disappointment to the Birmingham Mint that the newly refurbished and equipped Royal Mint was turning its attention to copper as well as to silver and gold coins. The move to Tower Hill was a major turning point for the Royal Mint and this relatively ordinary coinage is important because it is symbolic of that new beginning.

Joseph Fry Medal
by Eric Gill

A number of celebrated artists have designed coins and medals for the Royal Mint but it is to be regretted that Eric Gill, despite being invited to submit artwork for a number of projects, was never as successful as he might have been. One such instance was the commission to design a medal to mark the bicentenary of the firm J S Fry & Sons Ltd.

Gill insisted on carving the design himself as a conscious statement of his allegiance to traditional engraving skills. It was an issue about which he expressed himself with some passion in the knowledge that his approach could well exclude him from seeing designs through to struck pieces. The boxwood carving, with its elegant lettering and the easy grace of its portrait, is a beautiful object in its own right but Royal Mint officials at the time, while praising its charm, questioned its technical suitability. The commission eventually went to Harold Youngman but what we are left with is an original Gill carving thoughtfully conceived and exquisitely realised.

Decimal trial piece

Forty years ago Britain's currency was decimalised and it is appropriate to mark the anniversary by looking at an item from the Royal Mint Museum made during the period of the changeover. A pattern 50 pence piece dated 1969 bearing an arrangement of the Royal Arms by Christopher Ironside is in the Museum collection. Despite its being an attractive design, opinion sided in the end with the idea of using Britannia but before an actual treatment of the chosen theme had been determined it looks as if the trial piece illustrated here was produced.

With its reverse taken from a pre-decimal halfpenny but including the denomination 50, and dated 1968 on the obverse, it is certainly an odd combination of elements that nevertheless might have served a purpose in helping to visualise what a Britannia 50 pence would look like. It is one of the more unusual items from an outstanding collection of trial and pattern pieces built up during the years leading to February 15, 1971 when Britain finally adopted a decimal currency.

The World coins you can trust.

GUARANTEED

NGC fully guarantees the authenticity of every World and US coin it certifies, something no other grading company can offer. Look for our name on the world's greatest coins — synonymous with security, accuracy and greater desirability in the marketplace.

www.NGCcoin.com

MONARCHS *of England*

Here we list the Kings and Queens from Anglo-Saxon times to the present, with the dates of their rule. Before Eadgar became the King of all England the country had been divided up into small kingdoms, each with their own ruler.

ANGLO-SAXON KINGS

The Anglo-Saxon monarchs ruled over the various kingdoms which existed in England following the withdrawal of the Romans in the 5th century AD. The most prominent kingdoms in the land were Kent, Sussex, Wessex, Mercia and Northumbria. Each kingdom produced its own coinage but in 973 Eadgar introduced a new coinage that became the standard for the whole of the country.

Eadgar (959–975)
Edward the Martyr (975–978)
Aethelred II (978–1016)
Cnut (1016–1035)
Harold I (1035–1040)
Harthacanut (1035–1042)
Edward the Confessor (1042–1066)
Harold II (1066)

NORMAN KINGS

The Normans came to Britain from their native France following the establishment of a kingdom in Sicily and southern Italy. An expedition led by the powerful Duke William of Normandy culminated in the battle of Hastings in 1066 where he defeated Harold II and was proclaimed King of All England. Their influence spread from these new centres to the Crusader States in the Near East and to Scotland and Wales in Great Britain, and to Ireland. Today their influence can be seen in their typical Romanesque style of architecture.

William I (1066–1087)
William II (1087–1100)
Henry I (1100–1135)
Stephen (1135–1154)

PLANTAGENETS

The Plantagenet kings of England were descended from the first House of Anjou who were established as rulers of England through the Treaty of Wallingford, which passed over the claims of Eustace and William, Stephen of Blois's sons, in favour of Henry of Anjou, son of the Empress Matilda and Geoffrey V, Count of Anjou.

Henry II (1154–1189)
Richard I (1189–1199)
John (1199–1216)
Henry III (1216–1272)
Edward I (1272–1307)
Edward II (1307–1327)
Edward III (1327–1377)
Richard II (1377–1399)

HOUSE OF LANCASTER

The House of Lancaster, a branch of the English royal House of Plantagenet, was one of the opposing factions involved in the Wars of the Roses, the civil war which dominated England and Wales during the 15th century. Lancaster provided England with three Kings

Henry IV (1399–1413)
Henry V (1413–1422)
Henry VI (1422–1461) and again 1470

HOUSE OF YORK

The House of York was the other branch of the House of Plantagenet involved in the disastrous Wars of the Roses. Edward IV was descended from Edmund of Langley, 1st Duke of York, the fourth surviving son of Edward III.

Edward IV (1461–1483 and again 1471–83)
Richard III (1483–1485)

TUDORS

The House of Tudor was an English royal dynasty that lasted 118 years, from 1485 to 1603. The family descended from the Welsh courtier Owen Tudor (Tewdwr). Following the defeat of Richard III at Bosworth, the battle that ended the Wars of the Roses, Henry Tudor, 2nd Earl of Richmond, took the throne as Henry VII.

Henry VII (1485–1509)
Henry VIII (1509–1547)
Edward VI (1547–1553)
Mary (1553–1558)
Philip & Mary (1554–1558)
Elizabeth I (1558–1603)

STUARTS

The House of Stuart ruled Scotland for 336 years, between 1371 and 1707. Elizabeth I of England's closest heir was James VI of Scotland via her grandfather Henry VII of England, who was founder of the Tudor dynasty. On Elizabeth's death, James Stuart ascended the thrones of England and Ireland and inherited the English claims to the French throne. The Stuarts styled themselves "Kings and Queens of Great Britain", although there was no parliamentary union until the reign of Queen Anne, the last monarch of the House of Stuart.

James I (1603–1625)
Charles I (1625–1649)
The Commonwealth (1653–1658)
Charles II (1660–1685)
James II (1685–1688)
William III & Mary (1688–1694)
William III (1694–1702)
Anne (1702–1714)

HOUSE OF HANOVER

The House of Hanover was a Germanic royal dynasty which ruled the Duchy of Brunswick-Lüneburg and the Kingdom of Hanover. George Ludwig ascended to the throne of the Kingdom of Great Britain and Ireland through the female line from Princess Elizabeth, sister of Charles I.

George I (1714–1727)
George II (1727–1760)
George III (1760–1820)
George IV (1820–1830)
William IV (1830–1837)
Victoria (1837–1901)

HOUSES OF SAXE-COBURG-GOTHA AND WINDSOR

The name Saxe-Coburg-Gotha was inherited by Edward VII from his father Prince Albert, the second son of the Duke of Saxe-Coburg-Gotha and husband of Victoria. During World War I the name was changed to Windsor to avoid the Germanic connotatiion.

Edward VII (1901–1910)
George V (1910–1936)
Edward VIII (1936)
George VI (1936–1952)
Elizabeth II (1952–)

Leading the way in Numismatics

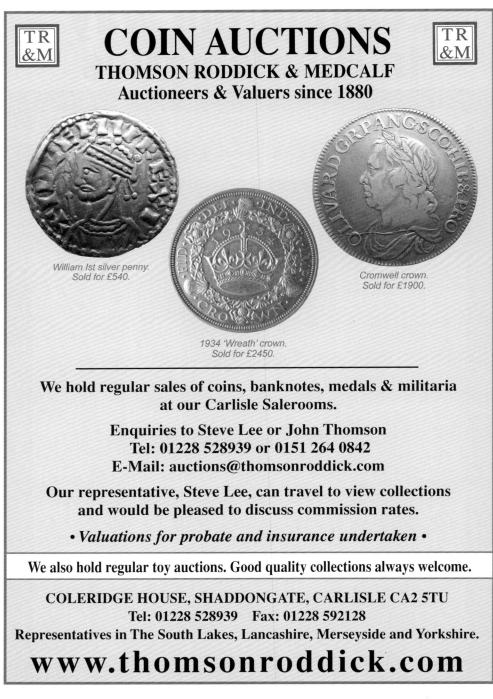

St James's Auctions

We are now seeking consignments for our 2012 auctions

Edward VI Sovereign
Another world record price £34,075

0% Commission*

There are no hidden costs, you get the entire hammer price!
Photography and insurance free of charge.

Generous advances available at no extra cost.

For enquiries and to consign contact:
St James's Auctions (Knightsbridge Coins-Stephen Fenton)
43 Duke Street, St James's, London SW1Y 6DD
Tel: 020 7930 7597 / 7888 / 8215 Fax: 020 7930 8214
E-mail: info@stjauctions.com   www.stjauctions.com

* This applies to individual lots over £1,000

THE LONDON 2012
Olympic 50p programme

In January 2009 the Royal Mint launched one of the most ambitious coin projects of modern times. Following the success of the open competition to design the six circulating coins from the 1p to the 50p (won by Matthew Dent with his "Jigsaw" design that we can find everyday) another competition was announced to find designers for no fewer than 29 commemorative coins for the London 2012 Olympics. The idea was that the Royal Mint was going to produce not one generic "sporting" coin to mark the Games but rather was planning to issue a whole series of special 50p pieces, each featuring one Olympic or Paralympic sport or, as in the case of athletics, "aquatics" equestrian events and others, one sport that represents a larger genre. Never before had such a large scale design project been undertaken by the Mint and the fact that it was open to everybody gave it immense appeal. The first inkling the public had of the plans for the new coins was when it was announced that one lucky viewer of the children's television programme Blue Peter would be guaranteed to have a design accepted thus ensuring that for the first time in British numismatic history a child under the age of 12 would have their design on a circulating coin. Children were able to take part in the wider competition too but the Blue Peter element meant that a guaranteed winner would come from the under 12s. In the end the winning design for the Blue Peter coin came from 9-year-old Florence Jackson who beat over 17,000 other entrants with her "High Jump" coin. The next youngest designer

was 16-year-old Theo Crutchley-Mack with his portrayal of Olympic cycling. The competition itself closed in April 2009 with 27 designers successfully managing to capture 29 sports in numismatic form. Two designers, Natasha Ratcliffe (Handball, Wheelchair Rugby) and Jonathon Oliffe (Aquatics, Gymnastics) were lucky enough to have two of their designs chosen. Whilst there were some familiar numismatic names in the list of successful artists (such as Bruce Rushin—designer of the "Technology" £2 coin and now the Sailing 50p) many others were completely unknown in the world of coin design. As might be expected most winners were from an artistic profession with animators, illustrators, sculptors and designers all submitting designs that caught the judges' eye but others, like the radiologist Ruth Summerfield (fencing), delivery driver Shane Abery (boxing), crop advisor Piotr Powaga (archery) and former body builder and wrestler now policeman Rob Shakespeare (weightlifting), simply had an interest in art or indeed in the sport they chose to depict.

It was first thought that the coins would be issued one a month for 29 months, in a similar fashion to the hugely successful US States Quarters programme, however the logistics of such distribution and the number of 50p coins needed in circulation at any one time meant that instead of such a regimented roll out the first coins started appearing in the autumn of 2010 and even now as we go to press with the COIN YEARBOOK 2012 (September 2011) not all, it seems, are to be found in change. By the time the Olympics rolls around in August it is anticipated that all will be "out there" although whether we get to see them all is another matter. Already those that do surface in change are being squirrelled away by collectors keen to "get the set" so don't be surprised if you aren't lucky enough to be able to secure all 29. Uncirculated versions are available in special presentation packs (as are precious metal versions) for those determined to get their hands on all 29 but for the collector half the fun of the hobby is being able to track such things down oneself rather than simply purchasing them en masse however the interest in this hugely ambitious roll out means that there are a great many people hunting a relatively small number of coins, usually around 1,000,000 but in the case of ones like the cycling coin just 400,000—so keep checking your change.

The sports depicted, and the designers of the relevant coins are:

Aquatics: Jonathon Olliffe (see also gymnastics)
Archery : Piotr Powaga
Athletics: Florence Jackson
Badminton: Emma Kelly
Basketball: Sarah Payne
Boccia: Justin Chung
Boxing: Shane Abery
Canoeing: Timothy Lees
Cycling: Theo Crutchley-Mack
Equestrian: Thomas Babbage
Fencing: Ruth Summerfield

Football: Neil Wolfson
Goalball: Jonathon Wren
Gymnastics: Jonathon Olliffe (see also aquatics)
Handball: Natasha Ratcliffe (see also wheelchair rugby)
Hockey: Robert Evans
Judo: David Cornell
Modern Pentathlon: Daniel Brittain
Rowing: Davey Podmore
Sailing: Bruce Rushin

Shooting: Pravid Dewdhory
Table Tennis: Alan Linsdell
Tae Kwondo: David Gibbons
Tennis: Tracy Baines
Triathlon: Sarah Harvey
Volleyball: Daniela Boothman
Weightlifting: Rob Shakespeare
Wheelchair Rugby: Natasha Ratcliffe (see also handball)
Wrestling: Roderick Enriquez

Not shown to scale

VIEW *of the bay*

WILLIAM McCREATH offers some advice when it comes to the internet

In the thirteen years that I've been registered on eBay the number of numismatic items listed has grown enormously as has the variety of items on offer, from the very common to the very rare and everything in-between, they will all appear as some time or another. eBay is a very rich hunting ground for those who are interested in items that are off the beaten track, countermarked coins, tokens, error coins and notes, old contemporary counterfeits etc., the variety on offer simply can't be found in any other one place. Buying these types of items holds few dangers for bidders as they are often in low grade but still desirable so it's difficult to go wrong with a little caution. Very rare countermarked coins can be found where the seller is unaware of how rare they are which can give the informed collector the chance to bag a real bargain, for example Spanish American dollars counter stamped by Scottish merchants that can be worth over £1,000 can turn up unrecognised by the seller.

Bidding on mainstream items is entirely a different matter however and extreme caution has to be exercised along with doing some homework before bidding. If a seller regularly lists nothing but "high grade" coins or notes a collector should be asking themselves, where does the seller get their stock from, especially if they seem to be happy to frequently sell at "bargain" prices, it's astounding that this question does not even cross the mind of many collectors as they merrily bid away snapping up what they see as bargain after bargain from the same seller. A few other sellers have now jumped on this bandwagon as they see this seller doing very well, one bad apple etc. A large percentage of coins listed are overgraded, no surprise perhaps, coins in no better than fine condition can be found listed as being EF, or commonly a somewhat vague "high grade", which should be a red flag for prospective bidders. So many bidders seem happy to buy grossly overgraded coins that a dishonest seller could make handsome profits buy buying accurately graded VF coins from leading dealers to be sold on eBay as EF, I hope that there is not now a rush of crooks following this suggestion. A silver coin that appears to have original lustre may have been "dipped" which can sometimes gives them a matt appearance so watch out for this especially if the majority of a sellers silver coins have this look. Coins that to an experienced collector look to have been cleaned or even harshly polished can still find inexperienced happy buyers, hopefully a regular reader of Coin News will know better. I would recommend completely ignoring the stated grade, including coins that have been "slabbed", and grade from the photographs and if they are of poor quality then do not bid as the seller is possibly trying to hide something, good quality digital cameras are now not expensive so there is no excuse for dark or fuzzy pictures. If a seller has the items that they have sold hidden as "private" in their feedbacks, thus making it impossible to find out what the item was, they may have a good reason for hiding this information so they should perhaps be avoided. Unfortunately a 100% positive feedback record for a seller no longer counts for as much as it once did as inexperienced buyers now appear to be in the majority so they give positives to bad sellers when they should be giving strong negatives. One buyer gave feedback of just "VF" when the coin they bought had been described as "EF" but they still gave a positive, a negative would have acting as a warning to other collectors.

Recommending to never to bid on a coin from a seller in China might be considered extreme, and perhaps unfair to honest sellers in that country, but there are huge numbers of fake coins being made in China for sale to collectors and some are very convincing. They range from 1977 crowns that are dated 1877 to USA trade dollars, some sell for suitably low prices but some sell for £100's of pounds to soon to be disappointed buyers. As they are being made on an industrial scale the fakes will by now outnumber the genuine population of some rare coins so buy from sellers in China only if the item is cheap and the postage charge not extortionate and you enjoy a gamble with long odds. A "Northumberland" shilling for sale by a seller in China will not be genuine, the fact that so many are for sale is a bit of a giveaway but they still receive bids.

It's not all depressing news when it comes to the mainstream numismatic items listed on eBay but good news can be thin on the ground. It may be possible to find a few sellers who do accurately grade the coins they list for sale and if that few are found use should be made of eBay's "saved sellers" feature. The chance of a bargain can be had when a seller offers a rare variety that they don't recognise, just hope that you are one of just a few that have and bid at the last possible moment but not more that you are prepared to pay. Placing a very high last minute "must have" bid is a very risky business because if another bidder does likewise the winning bid could be close to your maximum. Very rare notes or first or last serial number notes can also be found where the seller is unaware of their status, there are many active banknote collectors on eBay so there may be some competition but a last minute bid may win the day.

"Buy the book before the coin, and read it" is advice that's often given to beginners, and very sound advice it is. Collectors may not consider eBay as a source of reference material but they should. In addition to the usual well known standard references very often

auction catalogues can be found, and with a bit of luck complete with prices realised. For a specialist collector an auction catalogue containing their speciality can be a mine of information that's not available in any other single publication. There is a subsection for publications in the coins section but a search in the general "books" category for your chosen subject may reveal addition items. Numismatic ephemera is worth searching for as a gem or two might be found, Decimal Currency Board booklets and leaflets from the 1960s and 70s, old dealers list, old magazines, old banking letters perhaps signed by a high ranking bank official whose printed signature appeared on notes, there are many other possibilities.

There is always a large variety of cheques listed on eBay, or checks if the seller is in North America so if searching for your home town search for it with "cheque" and "check". Cheque collectors will be spoilt for choice and from time to time prices can be in the region of £50 for a single old cheque as well as a few pounds or less. Old savings banks can be of interest to both coin and banknote collectors and the sturdy metal "home safe" types turn up regularly sometimes unused in the original cardboard box. Finding one with a key could be useful as most that contain a few coins have no key, which was retained by the bank, and there could be a rare date penny in there.

In the not too distant future it may become near impossible to find accurately graded coins and notes on eBay as more and more good sellers give up selling there. They find it frustrating to get a low price for their accurately graded coins, achieving just Fine prices for VF coins, while bad sellers find it easy to get high prices for their overgraded coins, achieving EF prices for VF coins. Some long term eBay coin sellers who used to offer accurately graded coins that sold for fair prices are now offering overgraded coins, a case of, "if you can't beat them, join them". It's getting closer to the stage where the only people buying "high grade" coins and notes off eBay are those who have no idea of how an accurately graded coin or note should look, a knowledgeable collector has little chance of bidding success if many are willing to pay EF money for VF coins or notes. I often wonder if the buyers of these overgraded coins and notes have had a shock when they try to sell them at a coin fair to dealers who recognise their true grade.

ASK!

ASK YOURSELF AT LEAST SOME OF THESE QUESTIONS BEFORE BIDDING ON A NUMISMATIC ITEM ON EBAY . . .

How can a seller have an-unending supply of old notes or coins that are claimed to be high grade?

How can a seller afford to frequently sell at below a likely dealer's buying price if the coins they offer are accurately graded?

Why does a seller keep some information private?

Do really I want to buy from a seller who describes every item they list as "rare" even if it's very common?

Why are this seller's coin photographs always dark or fuzzy or too small?

Do I really want that "rare" coin from a seller in China?

If you are considering placing a large bid amount spend some time on-line looking at photographs of similar coins in dealers' lists and in auction catalogues as this can give a very good idea if the coins on eBay are overgraded or not, they probably will be. Some dealers have an archive on their web site of coins sold or auctioned over many years which is a useful resource.

First time eBay bidders should perhaps start off by bidding on low cost items, place low bids just the get the feel of it, but beware, it will probably lead to eBay addiction with bids getting ever higher and when that elusive item that has been searched for for decades comes along, and it will eventually, costly bidding fever may strike.

The fact that there are now non gold UK coins regularly fetching over £1,000 is an indication that more and more sellers now consider eBay to be a serious alternative to the long established traditional auction houses. The large buyer and seller premiums that are added by them, over 40% in total when VAT is included, may drive sellers to eBay in ever increasing numbers. One seller has recently begun to list, "over the next year or so", his entire banknote collection. It will be interesting to watch how well he does, if he does as well as would be as expected this should be of concern to the auction houses. Will there come a time when only exceptionally rare items are consigned to the large auction houses and their currently thick auction catalogues will begin to slim down? Their very high commission charges may kill the goose that has been laying golden eggs for many years. As the popularity of selling rare and expensive coins on eBay increases the profits of the tradition numismatic auction houses will decrease. Will they be forced to reduce the commonly applied very high buyer's premium of 20%, which in effect reduces the amount of money received by sellers as bidders allow for this extra 20% when deciding on their maximum bid, in an attempt to tempt sellers back from eBay?

DATES *on coins*

The vast majority of modern coins bear the date prominently on one side. In most cases dates are expressed in modified Arabic numerals according to the Christian calendar and present no problem in identification. There have been a few notable exceptions to this general rule, however. Morocco, for example, has used European numerals to express dates according to the Moslem calendar, so that a coin dated 1321 actually signifies 1903. Dates are almost invariably written from left to right—even in Arabic script which writes words from right to left. An exception, however, occurred in the Philippines quarto of 1822 where the date appeared as 2281, and the "2"s back to front for good measure.

	ARABIC-TURKISH	CHINESE, JAPANESE KOREAN, ANNAMESE (ORDINARY)	CHINESE, JAPANESE KOREAN, ANNAMESE (OFFICIAL)	INDIAN	SIAMESE	BURMESE
1	𝟏	一	壹	၅	๑	၁
2	٢	二	貳	੨	๒	၂
3	٣	三	叁	੩	๓	၃
4	٤	四	肆	੪	๔	၄
5	٥	五	伍	੫	๕	၅
6	٦	六	陸	੬	๖	၆
7	٧	七	柒	੭	๗	၇
8	٨	八	捌	੮	๘	၈
9	٩	九	玖	੧	๙	၉
0	٠			੦	๐	၀
10	١٠	十	拾		๙๐	
100	١٠٠	百			๙๐๐	
1000	١٠٠٠	千				

Dates in Roman numerals have been used since 1234 when this practice was adopted by the Danish town of Roskilde. Such Roman numerals were used sporadically throughout the Middle Ages and in later centuries and survive fitfully to this day. This was the system used in England for the first dated coins, the gold half-sovereigns of Edward VI struck at Durham House in 1548 (MDXLVIII). This continued till 1550 (MDL) but thereafter Arabic numerals were used, beginning with the half-crown of 1551. Notable exceptions of more recent times include the Gothic coinage of Queen Victoria (1847–87).

The first coin with the date in European numerals was a plappart of St Gallen, Switzerland dated 1424, but this was an isolated case. In 1477 Maria of Burgundy issued a guldiner which bore a date on the reverse, in the form of two pairs of digits flanking the crown at the top. The numerals in this instance were true Gothic, an interesting transition between true Arabic numerals and the modified Arabic figures now used in Europe. The Tyrolese guldengroschen of 1484–6 were the first coins to be regularly dated in European numerals and thereafter this custom spread rapidly.

For the numismatist, the problem arises when coins bear a date in the numerals of a different alphabet or computed according to a different era. Opposite is a table showing the basic numerals used in different scripts. The various eras which may be found in coin dates are as listed and explained opposite.

Hijra

The era used on Moslem coins dates from the flight of Mohammed from Mecca to Medina on July 15, 622 and is often expressed as digits followed by AH (Anno Hegirae). Moslems employ a lunar calendar of twelve months comprising 354 11/30 days. Tipu Sultan of Mysore in 1201 AH (the fifth year of his reign) introduced a new era dating from the birth of Mohammed in AD 570 and using a luni-solar system. Tipu also adopted the Hindu cycle of sixty years (the Tamil Brihaspate Cycle), but changed this two or three years later, from Hijra to Muludi.

Afghan coins used the lunar calendar until 1920 and during 1929–31, but at other times have used the solar calendar. Thus the Democratic Republic began issuing its coins in SH 1358 (1979).

To convert an AH date to the Christian calendar you must translate the Arabic into European numerals. Taking an Arabic coin dated 1320, for example, first deduct 3% (to convert from the Moslem lunar year to our solar year). This gives 39.6 which, rounded up to the nearest whole number, is 40. Deduct 40 from 1320 (1280), then add 622. The answer is 1902.

There have been a few notable exceptions. Thus the Khanian era of Ilkhan Ghazan Mahmud began on 1st Rajab 701 AH (1301). This era used a solar calendar, but was shortlived, being confined to coins of Mahmud and his nephew Abu Said down to year 34 (1333).

The era of Tarikh Ilahi was adopted by the Mughal emperor Akbar in the thirteenth year of his reign (922 AH). This era dated from his accession on 5th Rabi al-Sani 963 AH (February 19, 1556). The calendar had solar months and days but no weeks, so each day of the month had a different name. This system was used by Akbar, Jahangir and Shah Jahan, often with a Hijra date as well.

Saphar

The era of the Caesars began on January 1, 38 BC and dated from the conquest of Spain by Augustus. Its use on coinage, however, seems to have been confined to the marabotins of Alfonso VIII of Castile and was expressed in both Latin and Arabic.

Samvat

The era of Vikramaditya began in 57 BC and was a luni-solar system used in some Indian states. Coins may be found with both Samvat and Hijra dates. Conversion to the Christian date is simple; merely subtract 57 from the Samvat to arrive at the AD date.

Saka

This originated in the southwestern district of Northern India and began in AD 78. As it used the luni-solar system it converts easily by adding 78 to the Saka date.

Nepal

Nepalese coins have used four different date systems. All coins of the Malla kings were dated in Nepal Samvat (NS) era, year 1 beginning in 881. This system was also used briefly by the state of Cooch Behar. Until 1888 all coins of the Gurkha dynasty were dated in the Saka era (SE) which began in AD 78. After 1888 most copper coins were dated in the Vikram Samvat (VS) era from 57 BC. With the exception of some gold coins struck in 1890 and 1892, silver and gold coins only changed to the VS era in 1911, but now this system is used for all coins struck in Nepal. Finally, dates in the Christian era have appeared on some commemorative coins of recent years.

Ethiopian

This era dates from August AD 7, so that EE 1885 is AD 1892. Ethiopian dates are expressed in five digits using Amharic numerals. The first two are the digits of the centuries, the third is the character for 100, while the fourth and fifth are the digits representing the decade and year. On modern coins dates are rendered in Amharic numerals using the Christian era.

Thailand

Thai coins mainly use the Buddhist era (BE) which dates from 543 BC, but some coins have used dates from the Chula-Sakarat calendar (CS) which began in AD 638, while others use a Ratanakosind Sok (RS) date from the foundation of the Chakri dynasty in AD 1781.

Hebrew

The coins of Israel use the Jewish calendar dating from the beginning of the world (Adam and Eve in the Garden of Eden) in 3760 BC. Thus the year 1993 is rendered as 5753. The five millennia are assumed in dates, so that only the last three digits are expressed. 735 therefore equates with AD 1975. Dates are written in Hebrew letters, reading from right to left. The first two characters signify 400 and 300 respectively, totalling 700. The third letter denotes the decades (lamedh = 30) and the fourth letter, following the separation mark (") represents the final digit (heh = 5). The Jewish year runs from September or October in the Christian calendar.

Dates from the creation of the world

This system was also used in Russia under Ivan IV. The dating system Anno Mundi (AM) was established by the Council of Constantinople in AD 680 which determined that the birth of Christ had occurred in 5508 AM. Ivan's coins expressed the date as 7055 (1447).

Dynastic dates

The system of dating coinage according to regnal years is a feature of Chinese and Japanese coins. Chinese coins normally have an inscription stating that they are coins of such and such a reign period (not the emperor's name), and during the Southern Sung dynasty this was joined by the numeral of the year of the reign. This system was continued under the republic and survives in Taiwan to this day, although the coins of the Chinese Peoples Republic are dated in western numerals using the Christian calendar.

Early Japanese coins bore a reference to the era (the title assumed by each emperor on his accession) but, like Chinese coins, could not be dated accurately. From the beginning of the Meiji era (1867), however, coins have included a regnal number. The Showa era, beginning in 1926 with the accession of Hirohito, eventually ran to sixty-three (expressed in western numerals on some denominations, in Japanese ideograms on others) to denote 1988, although the rest of the inscription was in Japanese characters.

Dynastic dates were used on Korean milled coins introduced in 1888. These bore two characters at the top Kae Kuk (founding of the dynasty) followed by quantitative numerals. The system dated from the founding of the Yi dynasty in 1392. Curiously enough, some Korean banknotes have borne dates from the foundation of the first dynasty in 2333 BC.

Iran adopted a similar system in 1975, celebrating the 15th anniversary of the Pahlavi regime by harking back to the glories of Darius. The new calendar dated from the foundation of the Persian Empire 2535 years earlier, but was abolished only three years later when the Shah was overthrown.

Political eras

France adopted a republican calendar in 1793 when the monarchy was abolished. Coins were then inscribed L'AN (the year) followed by Roman numerals, but later Arabic numerals were substituted. This continued to the year 14 (1806) but in that year the Emperor Napoleon restored the Christian calendar. The French system was emulated by Haiti whose coins dated from the revolution of 1803. The date appeared as AN followed by a number until AN 31 (1834) on some coins; others had both the evolutionary year and the Christian date from 1828 until 1850 (AN 47). Coins with a date in the Christian calendar appeared only in 1807–9 and then from 1850 onwards.

Mussolini introduced the Fascist calendar to Italy, dating from the seizure of power in October 1922. This system was widely employed on documents and memorials, but was first used on silver 20 lire coins of 1927 and then only in addition to the Christian date and appearing discreetly as Roman numerals. Subsequently it was extended to gold 50 lire and 100 lire coins in 1931 and the subsidiary coinage in 1936, being last used in the year XXI (1943).

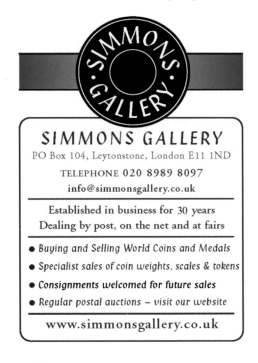
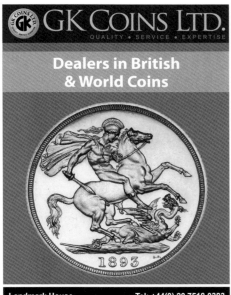

COIN TERMS *glossary*

In this section we list all the terms commonly encountered in numismatics or in the production of coins.

Abbey Coins Medieval coins struck in the abbeys, convents and other great religious houses which were granted coinage rights. These coins were often used also by pilgrims journeying from one monastery to another.

Abschlag (German for "discount") A *restrike* from an original die.

Accolated Synonym for *conjoined* or *jugate* and signifying two or more profiles overlapping.

Acmonital Acronym from *Aciaio Monetario Italiano*, a stainless steel alloy used for Italian coins since 1939.

Adjustment Reduction of metal in a *flan* or *blank* to the specified weight prior to striking, accomplished by filing down the face. Such file marks often survived the coining process and are occasionally met with in coins, especially of the 18th century.

Ae Abbreviation for the Latin *Aes* (bronze), used for coins made of brass, bronze or other copper alloys.

Aes Grave (Latin for heavy bronze) Heavy circular coins first minted at Rome in 269 BC.

Aes Rude (Latin for rough bronze) Irregular lumps of bronze which gradually developed into ingots of uniform shape and were the precursors of coins in Rome.

Aes Signatum (Latin for signed bronze) Bronze ingots of regular size and weight, bearing marks of authority to guarantee their weight (289–269 BC).

Agonistic (Greek) Term for coins issued to commemorate, or pertaining to, sporting events.

Alliance Coinage struck by two or more states acting together and having common features of design or inscription.

Alloy Coinage metal composed of two or more metallic elements.

Altered Deliberately changed, usually unofficially, with the aim of increasing the numismatic value of a coin, medal or note. This applies particularly to dates, where a common date may be altered to a rare date by filing or re-engraving one of the digits.

Aluminium (American *Aluminum*) Silvery lightweight metal, developed commercially in the late 19th century for commemorative medals, but used for tokens and emergency money during the First World War and since 1940 widely used in subsidiary coinage.

Aluminium-bronze Alloy of aluminium and copper. Hard-wearing and gold-coloured, it is now widely used in tokens and subsidiary coinage.

Amulet Coin or medal believed to have talismanic qualities, such as warding off disease and bad luck. Many Chinese and Korean pieces come into this category. See also *Touchpiece*.

Androcephalous Heraldic term for creatures with a human head.

Anepigraphic Coins or medals without a legend.

Annealing Process of heating and cooling applied to metal to relieve stresses and prepare it for striking into coins.

Annulet Small circle often used as an ornament or spacing device in coin inscriptions.

Antimony Brittle white metal, chemical symbol *Sb*, virtually impractical as a coinage metal but used for the Chinese 10 cents of Kweichow, 1931. Alloyed with tin, copper or lead, it produces the white metal popular as a medallic medium.

Antoniniani   Silver coins minted in Imperial Rome. The name derives from the Emperor Caracalla (Marcus Aurelius Antoninus) in whose reign they were first struck. The silver content was progressively reduced and by the last issue (AD 295) they were reduced to *billon*.

Ar   Abbreviation for Latin *Argentum* (silver), used for coins struck in this metal.

Assay Mark   Mark applied to a medal struck in precious metal by an assayer or assay office as a guarantee of the fineness of the metal.

Assignat   Type of paper money used in France 1789–96, representing the land assigned to the holders.

Attribution   Identification of a coin by characteristics such as issuing authority, date or reign, mint, denomination, metal, and by a standard reference.

Au   Abbreviation for *aurum* (Latin for gold), denoting coins of this metal.

AU   Abbreviation for "About Uncirculated", often found in catalogues and dealers' lists to describe the condition of a numismatic piece.

Autodollar   Name given to the silver yuan issued by Kweichow, 1928, and having a contemporary motor car as the obverse motif.

Auxiliary Payment Certificate   Form of paper money intended for use by American military personnel stationed in overseas countries. See also *Baf* and *Scrip*.

Babel Note   Nickname given to the paper money of the Russian Socialist Federated Soviet Republic (1919) because it bore the slogan "workers of the world unite" in seven languages, a reference to the biblical tower of Babel.

Baf   Acronym from British Armed Forces, the popular name for the vouchers which could only be exchanged for goods in service canteens from 1945 onwards.

Bag Mark   Minor scratch or abrasion on an otherwise uncirculated coin, caused by coins in mint bags knocking together.

Banknote   Form of paper money issued by banks and usually promising to pay the bearer on demand in coin of the realm.

Barbarous   Imitation of Greek or Roman coins by the Celtic and Germanic tribes who lived beyond the frontiers of the civilised world.

Base   Non-precious metals or alloys.

Bath Metal   Inferior bronze alloy, named after the English city where it was used for casting cannon. Used by William Wood of Bristol for Irish and American tokens and by Amos Topping for Manx coins of 1733/4.

Beading   Ornamental border found on the raised rim of a coin.

Behalfszahlungsmittel   German term for auxiliary payment certificates used in occupied Europe from 1939 to 1945.

Bell Metal   Alloy of copper and tin normally used for casting bells, but employed for the subsidiary coinage of the French Revolutionary period.

Billon   Silver alloy containing less than 50 per cent fine silver, usually mixed with copper. In Spain this alloy was known as *vellon*.

Bi-metallic   Coins struck in two separate metals or alloys. Patterns for such coins exist from the 19th century but actual coins with a centre of one metal surrounded by a ring of another did not appear till 1982 (Italy, San Marino and Vatican). Canada introduced coins with a tiny plaque inset in a second metal (1990). See also *Clad, Plugged* and *Sandwich*.

Bi-metallism   Monetary system in which two metals are in simultaneous use and equally available as legal tender, implying a definite ratio between the two. A double standard of gold and silver, with a ratio of 16:1, existed till the mid-19th century.

Bingle   American term for a trade token, more specifically the US government issue of tokens for the Matacuska, Alaska colonization project, 1935.

Birthday Coins   Coins celebrating the birthday of a ruler originated in Roman Imperial times, notably the reigns of Maximianus (286–305) and Constantinus I (307–37). Birthday talers were issued by many German states, and among recent examples may be cited coins marking the 70th, 80th and 90th birthdays of Gustaf Adolf VI of Sweden, 80th and 90th birthday coins from the British Commonwealth for the Queen Mother, and coins honouring Queen Elizabeth, the Duke of Edinburgh and the Prince of Wales.

2011 coin from the British Virgin Islands celebrating HM Queen Elizabeth's 85th birthday

Bit   Term denoting fragments of large silver coins, cut up and circulating as fractional values. Spanish dollars were frequently broken up for circulation in the American colonies and the West Indies. Long bits and short bits circulated at 15 and 10 cents respectively, but the term came to be equated with the Spanish real or eighth peso, hence the American colloquialism "two-bit" signifying a quarter dollar.

Black Money   English term for the debased silver deniers minted in France which circulated freely in England until they were banned by government decree in 1351.

Blank   Piece of metal, cut or punched out of a roller bar or strip, and prepared for striking to produce coins. Alternate terms are *flan* and *planchet*.

Blundered Inscription   Legend in which the lettering is jumbled or meaningless, indicating the illiteracy of the tribes who copied Greek and Roman coins.

Bonnet Piece   Scottish gold coin, minted in 1539–40. The name is derived from the obverse portraying King James V in a large, flat bonnet.

Bon Pour   French for "good for", inscribed on Chamber of Commerce brass tokens issued in 1920–7 during a shortage of legal tender coinage.

Bouquet Sou   Canadian copper token halfpenny of 1837 deriving its name from the nosegay of heraldic flowers on the obverse.

Box Coin   Small container formed by *obverse* and *reverse* of two coins, hollowed out and screwed together.

Bracteate   (Latin *bractea*, a thin piece of metal) Coins struck on blanks so thin that the image applied to one side appears in reverse on the other. First minted in Erfurt and Thuringia in the 12th century, and later produced elsewhere in Germany, Switzerland and Poland till the 14th century.

Brass   Alloy of copper and zinc, widely used for subsidiary coinage. The term was also formerly used for bronze Roman coins, known numismatically as first, second or third brass.

Breeches Money   Derisive term given by the Royalists to the coinage of the Commonwealth, 1651, the conjoined elongated oval shields on the reverse resembling a pair of breeches.

Brockage   Mis-struck coin with only one design, normal on one side and *incuse* on the other. This occurs when a coin previously struck adheres to the die and strikes the next blank to pass through the press.

Broken Bank-note   Note issued by a bank which has failed, but often applied more generally to banknotes which have been demonetised.

Bronze   Alloy of copper and tin, first used as a coinage metal by the Chinese c. 1000 BC. Often used synonymously with copper, though it should be noted that bronze only superseded copper as the constituent of the base metal British coins in 1860.

Bull Neck   Popular term for the coins of King George III, 1816–17.

Bullet Money   Pieces of silver, *globular* in shape, bearing various *countermarks* and used as coins in Siam (Thailand) in the 18th and 19th centuries.

George III bullneck shilling

Bullion   Precious metal in bars, ingots, strip or scrap (i.e. broken jewellery mounts, watch-cases and plate), its weight reckoned solely by weight and fineness, before being converted into coin.

Bullion Coin   A coin struck in platinum, gold or silver, whose value is determined solely by the prevailing market price for the metal as a commodity. Such coins do not generally have a nominal face value, but include in their inscriptions their weight and fineness. Good examples of recent times include the Krugerrand (South Africa), the Britannia (UK), the Maple Leaf (Canada), Libertad (Mexico), the Nugget (Australia) and the Eagle (USA).

Bun Coinage   British coins of 1860–94 showing Queen Victoria with her hair in a bun.

Bungtown Coppers   Derisive term (from Anglo-American slang *bung*, to swindle or bribe) for halfpence of English or Irish origin, often counterfeit, which circulated in North America towards the end of the colonial period.

Carat   (American *Karat*) Originally a unit of weight for precious stones, based on carob seeds (ceratia), it also denotes the fineness or purity of gold, being 1/24th part of the whole. Thus 9 carat gold is .375 fine and 22 carat, the English sovereign standard, is .916 fine. Abbreviated as ct or kt.

Cartwheel   Popular term for the large and cumbersome penny and twopenny pieces of 1797 weighing one and two ounces, struck by Matthew Boulton at the Soho Mint, Birmingham.

Cased Set   Set of coins in mint condition, housed in the official case issued by the mint. Formerly leather cases with blue plush or velvet lining were used, but nowadays many sets are encapsulated in plastic to facilitate handling.

Cash   (from Portuguese *caixa*, Hindi *kasu*). Round piece of bronze or brass with a square hole in the centre, used as subsidiary coinage in China for almost 2000 years, till the early 12th century. In Chinese these pieces were known as *Ch'ien* or *Li* and strung together in groups of 1000 were equivalent to a silver tael.

Cast Coins Coins cast from molten metals in moulds. This technique, widespread in the case of early commemorative medals, has been used infrequently in coins, the vast majority of which are struck from *dies*. Examples of cast coins include the Chinese cash and the Manx coins of 1709.

Check A form of *token* given as a means of identification, or issued for small amounts of money or for services of a specific nature.

Cheque (American *Check*) A written order directing a bank to pay money.

Chop (Hindi, to seal). Countermark, usually consisting of a single character, applied by Chinese merchants to precious metal coins and ingots as a guarantee of their weight and fineness. Coins may be found with a wide variety of chop marks and the presence of several different marks on the same coin considerably enhances its interest and value. See also *Shroff mark*.

Christmas Coins issued as Christmas gifts date from the Middle Ages when the Venetian Doges struck *Osselle* as presents for their courtiers. In modern times, however, the custom has developed only since the late 1970s, several countries having issued attractive coins at Christmas since then.

Cistophori (Greek for chest bearing) a generic term for the coins of Pergamum with an obverse motif of a chest showing a serpent crawling out of the half-opened lid. Cistophori became very popular all over Asia Minor in the 3rd and 2nd centuries BC and were struck also at mints in Ionia, Phrygia, Lydia and Mysia.

Clad Coins Coins with a core of one alloy, covered with a layer or coating of another. US half dollars from 1965 to 1970, for example, had a core of 21 per cent silver and 79 per cent copper, bonded to outer layers of 80 per cent silver and 20 per cent copper. More recently, however, coins usually have a body in a cheap alloy, with only a thin cladding of a more expensive material, such as the British 1p and 2p coins of stainless steel with a copper cladding, introduced late in 1992.

Clash Marks Mirror image traces found on a coin which has been struck from a pair of dies, themselves damaged by having been struck together without a blank between.

Clipped Coins Precious metal coins from which small amounts have been removed by clipping the edges. It was to prevent this that *graining* and *edge inscriptions* were adopted.

Cob Crude, irregularly shaped silver piece, often with little more than a vestige of die impressions, produced in the Spanish American mints in the 16th–18th centuries.

Coin Piece of metal, marked with a device, issued by government authority and intended for use as money.

Collar Retaining ring within which the *dies* for the *obverse* and *reverse* operate. When the *blank* is struck under high pressure between the dies the metal flows sideways and is formed by the collar, taking up the impression of *reeding* or *edge inscription* from it.

Commemorative Coin, medal, token or paper note issued to celebrate a current event or the anniversary of a historic event or personality.

Communion Token Token, cast in lead, but later struck in pewter, brass, bronze or white metal, issued to members of a congregation to permit them to partake of the annual communion service in the Calvinist and Presbyterian churches. John Calvin himself is said to have invented the communion token in 1561 but they were actually referred to in the minutes of the Scottish General Assembly in 1560. Later they were adopted by the Reformed churches in many parts of Europe. They survived in Scotland till the early years of this century. Each parish had its own tokens, often bearing the names or initials of individual ministers, with dates, symbols and biblical texts.

Conjoined Term denoting overlapped profiles of two or more rulers (e.g. William and Mary).

Contorniate (from Italian *contorno*, edge). Late 4th and 5th century Roman bronze piece whose name alludes to the characteristic grooving on the edges.

Contribution Coins Coins struck by Bamberg, Eichstatt, Fulda and other German cities in the 1790s during the First Coalition War against the French Republic. The name alludes to the fact that the bullion used to produce the coins necessary to pay troops was raised by contribution from the Church and the public.

Convention Money Any system of coinage agreed by neighbouring countries for mutual acceptance and interchange. Examples include the Amphictyonic coins of ancient Greece, and the Austrian and Bavarian talers and gulden of 1753–1857 which were copied by other south German states and paved the way for the German Monetary union.

Copper Metallic element, chemical symbol *Cu*, widely used as a coinage medium for 2,500 years. Pure or almost pure copper was used for subsidiary coinage in many countries till the mid-19th century, but has since been superseded by copper alloys which are cheaper and more durable: *bronze* (copper and tin), *brass* (copper and zinc), *Bath metal* or *bell metal* (low-grade copper and tin), *aluminium-bronze* (copper and aluminium), *potin* (copper, tin, lead and silver) or *cupro-nickel* (copper and nickel). Copper is also alloyed with gold to give it its reddish hue, and is normally alloyed with silver in coinage metals. When the copper exceeds the silver content the alloy is known as *billon*.

Copperhead Popular term for a copper *token* about the size and weight of an American cent which circulated in the USA during the Civil War (1861–65) during a shortage of subsidiary coinage. Many different types were produced, often of a political or patriotic nature.

Coppernose Popular name for the debased silver shillings of Henry VIII. Many of them were struck in copper with little more than a silver wash which tended to wear off at the highest point of the obverse, the nose on the full-face portrait of the king.

Counter A piece resembling a coin but intended for use on a medieval accountancy board or in gambling. See also *jeton*.

Counterfeit Imitation of a coin, token or banknote intended for circulation to deceive the public and defraud the state.

Countermark Punch mark applied to a coin some time after its original issue, either to alter its nominal value, or to authorise its circulation in some other country.

Cowrie Small shell (*Cypraea moneta*) circulating as a form of primitive currency from 1000 BC (China) to the present century (East and West Africa) and also used in the islands of the Indian and Pacific Oceans.

Crockard Debased silver imitation of English pennies produced in the Netherlands and imported into England in the late 13th century. Edward I tried to prevent their import then, in 1299, allowed them to pass current as halfpennies. As they contained more than a halfpennyworth of silver this encouraged their trading in to be melted down and they disappeared from circulation within a year. Sometimes known as *pollards*. See also *Lushbourne*.

Crown Gold Gold of 22 carat (.916) fineness, so called on account of its adoption in 1526 for the English gold crown. It has remained the British standard gold fineness ever since.

1837 Cumberland Jack

Cumberland Jack Popular name for a counter or medalet of sovereign size, struck unofficially in 1837 in brass. The figure of St George was replaced by the Duke of Cumberland on horseback with the inscription "To Hanover" a reference to the unpopular Duke of Cumberland, uncle of Queen Victoria, who succeeded to the Hanoverian throne since Victoria, as a female, was debarred by Salic law from inheritance.

Cupellation (Latin *cupella*, a little cup). Process by which gold and silver were separated from lead and other impurities in their ores. A cupel is a shallow cup of bone-ash or other absorbent material which, when hot, absorbs any molten material that wets its surface. Lead melts and oxidises with impurities into the cupel, whereas gold and silver remain on the cupel. Cupellation is also used in assaying the fineness of these precious metals.

Cupro-nickel Coinage alloy of 75 per cent copper and 25 per cent nickel, now widely used as a base metal substitute for silver. A small amount of zinc is added to the alloy in modern Russian coins.

Currency Coins, tokens, paper notes and other articles intended to pass current in general circulation as money.

Current Coins and paper money still in circulation.

Cut Money Coins cut into smaller pieces to provide correspondingly smaller denominations. The cross on many medieval coins assisted the division of silver pennies into halfpence and farthings. Spanish dollars were frequently divided into *bits* which themselves became units of currency in America and the West Indies.

Darlehnskassen (German for "state loan notes"). Paper money issued during the First World War in an abortive bid to fill the shortage of coinage in circulation. These low-denomination notes failed to meet demand and were superseded by local issues of small *Notgeld* in 1916.

Debasement The reduction in the precious metal content of the coinage, widely practised since time immemorial by governments for economic reasons. British coins, for example, were debased from sterling (.925 fine) silver to .500 in 1920 and from silver to cupro-nickel in 1947.

Decimalisation A currency system in which the principal unit is subdivided into ten, a hundred, or a thousand fractions. Russia was the first country to decimalise, in 1534 when the rouble of 100 kopeks was introduced, but it was not till 1792 that France adopted the franc of 100 centimes and 1793 when the USA introduced the dollar of 100 cents. Most European countries decimalised their currency in the 19th century. Britain toyed with the idea, introducing the florin or tenth of a pound in 1849 as the first step, but did not complete the process till 1971. The last countries to decimalise were Malta and Nigeria, in 1972 and 1973 respectively.

Demidiated Heraldic term to describe the junction of two armorial devices, in which only half of each is shown.

Demonetisation The withdrawal of coins or paper money from circulation and declaring them to be worthless.

Device Heraldic term for the pattern or emblem on coins or paper notes.

Die Hardened piece of metal bearing a mirror image of the device to be struck on one side of a coin or medal.

Die Proof An impression, usually pulled on soft carton or India paper, of an *intaglio* engraving of a banknote, usually taken during the progress of the engraving to check the detail. Banknote proofs of this nature usually consist of the portrait or some detail of the design, such as the border, rather than the complete motif.

Dodecagonal Twelve-sided, a term applied to the nickel-brass threepence of Great Britain, 1937–67.

1954 dodecagonal threepence

Dump Any primitive coin struck on a very thick *flan*, but more specifically applied to the circular pieces cut from the centre of Spanish dollars, countermarked with the name of the colony, a crown and the value, and circulated in New South Wales at 15 pence in 1813. See *Holey Dollar*.

Duodecimal Currency system based on units of twelve, i.e. medieval money of account (12 denarii = 1 soldo) which survived in Britain as 12 pence to the shilling as late as 1971.

Ecclesiastical Coins Coins struck by a religious authority, such as an archbishop, bishop, abbot, prior or the canons of a religious order. Such coins were common in medieval times but survived as late as the early 19th century, the bishops of Breslau (1817) and Gurk (1823) being the last prelates to exercise coinage rights. Coins were struck by authority of the Pope at Rome till 1870 but since 1929 coinage has been struck at the Italian state mint on behalf of the Vatican.

Edge Inscription Lettering on the edge of a coin or medal to prevent clipping. Alluding to this, the Latin motto *Decus et Tutamen* (an ornament and a safeguard) was applied to the edge of English milled coins in the reign of Charles II.

Edge Ornament An elaboration of the *graining* found on many milled coins to prevent clipping, taking the form of tiny leaves, florets, interlocking rings, pellets and zigzag patterns. In some cases the ornament appears between layers of more conventional reeding.

EF Abbreviation for Extremely Fine.

Effigy An image or representation of a person, normally the head of state, a historical personage, or an allegorical figure, usually on the *obverse* or "heads" side of a coin or medal.

Electrotype A reproduction of a coin or medal made by an electrolytic process.

Electrum Alloy of gold and silver, sometimes called white gold, used for minting the staters of Lydia, 7th century BC, and other early European coins.

Elongated Coin An oval *medalet* created by passing a coin, such as an American cent, between rollers under pressure with the effect of squeezing it out and impressing on it a souvenir or commemorative motif.

Emergency Money Any form of money used in times of economic and political upheaval, when traditional kinds of currency are not available. Examples include the comparatively crude silver coins issued by the Royalists during the *Civil War* (1642–49), *obsidional* money, issued in time of siege, from Tyre (1122) to Mafeking (1900), the *Notgeld* issued by many German towns (1916–23), *encased money*, *fractional currency*, *guerrilla notes*, *invasion*, *liberation* and *occupation money* from the two World Wars and minor campaigns. Among the more recent examples may be cited the use of sweets and cheques in Italy (1976–77) and the issue of coupons and vouchers in many of the countries of the former Soviet Union pending the introduction of their own distinctive coins and notes.

Enamelled Coins Coins decorated by enamelling the obverse and reverse motifs in contrasting colours was an art practised by many jewellers in Birmingham and Paris in the 19th century, and revived in Europe and America in the 1970s.

Encased Money Postage and revenue stamps enclosed in small metal and mica-faced discs, circulated as small change in times of emergency. The practice was invented by John Gault, a Boston sewing-machine salesman, during the American Civil War (1862). The face of the stamp was visible through the transparent window, while the back of the disc was embossed with firms' advertisements. This practice was revived during and after the First

World War when there was again a shortage of small coins. Encased stamps have also been recorded from France, Austria, Norway, Germany and Monaco. See also under *Stamp Money*.

Engrailing Technical term for the close serrations or vertical bars round the edge of a coin, applied as a security device.

Engraving The art of cutting lines or grooves in plates, blocks or dies. Numismatically this takes the form of engraving images into the face of the dies used in striking coins, a process which has now been almost completely superseded by *hubbing* and the use of *reducing machinery*. In the production of paper money, *intaglio* engraving is still commonly practised. In this process the engraver cuts the design into a steel die and the printing ink lies in the grooves. The paper is forced under great pressure into the grooves and picks up the ink, and this gives banknotes their characteristic ridged feeling to the touch. Nowadays many banknotes combine traditional intaglio engraving with multicolour lithography or photogravure to defeat the would-be counterfeiter.

Epigraphy The study of inscriptions, involving the classification and interpretation of coin legends, an invaluable adjunct to the study of a coin series, particularly the classical and medieval coins which, in the absence of dates and mintmarks, would otherwise be difficult to arrange in chronological sequence.

Erasion The removal of the title or effigy of a ruler from the coinage issued after his or her death. This process was practised in imperial Rome, and applied to the coins of Caligula, Nero and Geta, as part of the more general practice of *damnatio memoriae* (damnation of the memory) ordered by the Senate.

Error Mistakes on coins and paper money may be either caused at the design or engraving stage, or as a result of a fault in the production processes. In the first category come mis-spellings in legends causing, in extreme cases, *blundered inscriptions*, or anachronisms or inaccuracies in details of the design. In the second, the most glaring error is the mule caused by marrying the wrong dies. Faulty alignment of dies can cause obverse and reverse to be out of true. Although many coins are issued with obverse and reverse upside down in relation to each other, this can also occur as an error in coins where both sides should normally be facing the same way up. Other errors caused at the production stage include striking coins in the wrong metal or with the wrong *collar* thus creating a different edge from the normal.

Essay (From the French *essai*, a trial piece). The term is applied to any piece struck for the purposes of examination, by parliamentary or financial bodies, prior to the authorisation of an issue of coins or paper money. The official nature of these items distinguishes them from *patterns*, which denote trial pieces often produced by mints or even private individuals bidding for coinage contracts.

Evasion Close copy or imitation of a coin, with sufficient deliberate differences in the design or inscription to avoid infringing counterfeit legislation. A good example is the imitation of Sumatran coins by European merchants, inscribed SULTANA instead of SUMATRA.

Exergue Lower segment of a coin or medal, usually divided from the rest of the *field* by a horizontal line, and often containing the date, value, ornament or identification symbols.

Exonumia Generic term for numismatic items not authorised by a government, e.g. *patterns*, *tokens*, *medalets* or *model coins*.

F Fine

Face The surface of a coin, medal or token, referred to as the *obverse* or the *reverse*. The corresponding faces of a paper note are more correctly termed *verso* and *recto*, but the coin terms are often used instead.

Facing Term for the portrait, usually on the obverse, which faces to the front instead of to the side (profile).

Fantasy Piece of metal purporting to be the coinage of a country which does not exist. Recent examples include the money of Atlantis and the Hutt River Province which declared its independence of Western Australia.

FDC Abbreviation for *Fleur de Coin*, a term denoting the finest possible condition of a coin.

Fiat Money Paper notes issued by a government but not redeemable in coin or bullion.

Field Flat part of the surface of a coin or medal, between the *legend*, the *effigy* and other raised parts of the design.

Fillet Heraldic term for the ribbon or headband on the effigy of a ruler or allegorical figure.

Find Term applied to an archaeological discovery of one or more coins. A large quantity of such material is described as a *hoard*.

Flan Alternative name for *blank* or *planchet*, the piece of metal struck between dies to produce a coin or medal.

Forgery An unauthorised copy or imitation, made with the intention of deceiving collectors. Forgeries intended to pass current for real coins or notes are more properly called *counterfeits*.

Fractional Currency   Emergency issue of small-denomonation notes by the USA in 1863–5, following a shortage of coins caused by the Civil War. This issue superseded the *Postage Currency* notes, but bore the inscription "Receivable for all US stamps", alluding to the most popular medium of small change at that time. Denominations ranged from 3c to 50c.

Franklinium   Cupro-nickel alloy developed by the Franklin Mint of Philadelphia and used for coins, medals and gaming tokens since 1967.

Freak   An *error* or *variety* of a non-recurring type, usually caused accidentally during production.

Frosting   Matt surface used for the high relief areas of many proof coins and medals, for greater contrast with the mirrored surface of the field.

Funeral Money   Imitations of banknotes, used in China and Latin America in funeral ceremonies.

Geat (Git)   Channel through which molten metal is ducted to the mould. Cast coins and medals often show tiny protrusions known as geat marks.

Ghost   Faint image of the design on one side of a coin visible on the other. Good examples were the British penny and halfpenny of George V, 1911–27, the ghosting being eliminated by the introduction of a smaller effigy in 1928.

Globular   Coins struck on very thick *dumps* with convex faces. The term is applied to some Byzantine coins, and also the *bullet money* of Siam (Thailand).

Godless   (or *Graceless*) Epithet applied to any coin which omits the traditional reference to the deity, e.g. the British florin of 1849 which omitted D.G. (*Dei Gratia*, "by the Grace of God").

Gold   Precious metal, chemical symbol and numismatic abbreviation *Au*, from the *Latin Aurum*, used as a coinage medium from the 7th century BC till the present day. The purity of gold is reckoned in *carats* or a decimal system. Thus British gold sovereigns are 22 carat or .916 fine. Medieval coins were 23.5 carat or .995 fine, and some modern bullion coins are virtually pure gold, denoted by the inscription .999. Canadian maple leaves are now struck in "four nines" gold and bear the inscription .9999.

Goodfor   Popular name for token coins and *emergency money* made of paper or card, from the inscription "Good for" or its equivalent in other languages (e.g. French *Bon pour* or Dutch *Goed voor*) followed by a monetary value. They have been recorded from Europe, Africa and America during times of economic crises or shortage of more traditional coinage.

Gothic Crown   Popular name for the silver crown issued by the United Kingdom (1847–53), so-called on account of its script (more properly Old English, rather than Gothic).

Grain   The weight of a single grain of wheat was taken as the smallest unit of weight in England. The troy grain was 1/5760 of a pound, while the avoirdupois grain was 1/7000 pound, the former being used in the weighing of precious metals and thus employed by numismatists in weighing coins. A grain is 1/480 troy ounce or 0.066 gram in the metric system.

Graining   Term sometimes used as a synonym for the *reeding* on the edge of milled coins.

Gripped Edge   Pattern of indentations found on the majority of American cents of 1797, caused by the milling process. Coins of the same date with a plain edge are rather scarcer.

Guerrilla Money   Money issued in areas under the control of guerrillas and partisans during wartime range from the *veld ponds* of the Boers (1900–2) to the notes issued by the Garibaldi Brigade in Italy and the anti-fascist notes of Tito's forces in Yugoslavia. The most prolific issues were those produced in Luzon, Mindanao and Negros Occidental by the Filipino resistance during the Japanese occupation (1942–5).

Guilloche   French term signifying the intricate pattern of curved lines produced by the rose engine and used as a security feature in the production of banknote, cheques, stocks and share certificates.

Gun Money   Emergency coinage of Ireland (1689 –91) minted from gunmetal, a type of bronze used in the casting of cannon. All denominations of James II, from the sixpence to the crown, normally struck in silver, were produced in this base metal.

Irish gun money

Gutschein   German word for voucher or coupon, denoting the paper money used aboard ships of the Imperial Navy during the First World War. The last issue was made at Scapa Flow, 1918–19, during the internment of the High Seas Fleet.

Hammered   Term denoting coins produce by the traditional method of striking a *flan* laid on an anvil with a hammer. A characteristic of hammered coins is their uneven shape which tended to encourage *clipping*. This abuse was gradually eliminated by the introduction of the screw press in the 15th century and the mechanisation of coining processes in the course of the 16th and 17th centuries.

Hard Times Token Copper piece the size of the large cent, issued in the USA, 1834–44, during a shortage of coins caused by the collapse of the Bank of the United States, the panic of 1837 and the economic crisis of 1839, the landmarks in the period known as the Hard Times. Banks suspended *specie* payments and the shortage of coinage was filled by tradesmen's tokens. Many of these were more in the nature of satirical *medalets* than circulating pieces.

Hat Piece Alternative name for the *bonnet piece* of James VI of Scotland, 1591.

Hell Notes Imitation paper money used in Chinese funeral ceremonies and buried with the dead to pay for services in the next world.

Hoard Accumulation of coins concealed in times of economic or political upheaval and discovered, often centuries later. Under English common law, such hoards are subject to th law of *treasure trove* if they contain precious metal.

Hog Money Popular name for the early coinage of Bermuda, issued about 1616. The coins were minted in brass with a silver wash and circulated at various values from twopence to a shilling. They derived their name from the hog depicted on the obverse, an allusion to the pigs introduced to the island in 1515 by Juan Bermudez.

Holed Term denoting two different categories: (a) coins which have been pierced for suspension as a form of jewellery or talisman, and (b) coins which have a hole as part of their design. In the latter category come the Chinese *cash* with a square hole, and numerous issues of the 19th and 20th centuries from many countries, with the object of reducing weight and metal without sacrificing overall diameter.

Holey Dollar Spanish silver peso of 8 reales with the centre removed. The resultant ring was counter-marked "New South Wales" and dated 1813, with "Five Shillings" on the reverse, and placed into circulation during a shortage of British coin. The centre, known as a *dump*, was circulated at 15 pence.

Hub Heavy circular piece of steel on which the *die* for a coin or medal is engraved. The process of cutting the die and transferring the master die, by means of intermediary *punches*, to the die from which the coins will be struck, is known as hubbing. Soft steel is used in the preliminary process, and after the design has been transferred, the hub is hardened by chemical action.

Hybrid Alternative name for a *mule*.

Imitation Money Also known as play money or toy money, it consists of coins and notes produced for games of chance (like Monopoly), children's toy shops and post offices, as tourist souvenirs, or for political satire (e.g. the shrinking pound or dollar). See also *funeral money*, *hell notes*, *model coins* and *skit notes*.

Imprint Inscription on a paper note giving the name of the printer.

Incuse Impression which cuts into the surface of a coin or medal, as opposed to the more usual raised relief. Many of the earliest coins, especially those with a device on one side only, bear an incuse impression often in a geometric pattern. An incuse impression appears on one side of the coins, reflecting the image on the other side. Few modern coins have had an incuse design, notable examples being the American half and quarter eagle gold coins of 1908–29 designed by Bela Pratt. Incuse inscriptions on a raised rim, however, are more common, and include the British *Cartwheel* coins of 1797 and the 20p coins since 1982.

Inflation Money Coins produced as a result of inflation date back to Roman times when bronze minimi, little bigger than a pinhead, circulated as denarii. Nearer the present day inflation has had devastating effects on the coinage and banknotes of Germany (1921–3), Austria (1923), Poland (1923), Hungary (1945–6), Greece (1946) and many Latin American countries since the 1980s. Hungary holds the record for the highest value of any note ever issued — one thousand million adopengos, which is written as 20,00 0,000,000,000,000,000,000,000 pengos.

Ingot Piece of precious metal, usually cast in a mould, and stamped with the weight and fineness. though mainly used as a convenient method of storing bullion, ingots have been used as currency in many countries, notably Russia and Japan.

Inlay Insertion into the surface of a coin or medal of another substance for decorative effect. e.g. Poland Amber Trade Routes 20zl (amber), Isle of Man Queen Mother centenery (pearl) and various coins incorporating rubies or diamonds.

Intaglio Form of *engraving* in which lines are cut into a steel die for the recess-printing of banknotes.

Intrinsic The net metallic value of a coin, as distinguished from the nominal or face value.

Iron Metal, chemical symbol *Fe* (from Latin *Ferrum*), used as a primitive form of currency from classical times onwards. Iron spits (obeliskoi) preceded the obol as the lowest unit of Greek coinage, a handful of six spits being worth a drachma (from *drassomai*, "I grasp"). Cast iron coins were issued in China as a substitute for copper *cash*. Many of the emergency token issues of Germany during the First World War were struck in iron. Iron coins were issued by

Bulgaria in 1943. See also *Steel*.

Ithyphallic (Greek for "erect penis"). Term descriptive of coins of classical Greece showing a satyr.

Janiform Double profiles back to back, after the Roman god Janus.

Jeton (From French *jeter*, to throw). Alternative term for *counter*, and used originally on the chequerboard employed by medieval accountants. Nuremberg was the most important centre for the production of medieval jetons, often issued in lengthy portrait series. In modern parlance the term is often synonymous with *token*, though more specifically confined to pieces used in vending equipment, parking meters, laundromats, telephones and urban transport systems in many European countries. Apart from security, removing the temptation of vandals to break into the receptacles, the main advantage of such pieces is that they can be retariffed as charges increase, without any alteration in their design or composition, a method that is far cheaper than altering costly equipment to take larger coins.

Jubilee Head The effigy of Queen Victoria by Joseph Boehm adopted for British coinage after the 1887 Golden Jubilee.

Victoria Jubilee head florin

Jugate (From Latin *jugum*, a yoke). Alternative to *accolated* or *conjoined* to denote overlapping profiles of rulers.

Key Date Term describing the rarest in a long-running series of coins with the dates changed at annual intervals.

Kipperzeit German term meaning the time of clipped money, denoting the period during and after the Thirty Years War (1618–48) in which debased and clipped money was in circulation.

Klippe Rectangular or square pieces of metal bearing the impression of a coin. Coins of this type were first struck in Sweden in the 16th century and were subsequently produced in many of the German states. The idea has been revived in recent years as a medium for striking commemorative pieces.

Knife Money Cast bronze pieces, with an elongated blade and a ring at one end to facilitate stringing together in bunches, were used as currency in China from the 9th century BC until the 19th century.

Chinese knife money

Kreditivsedlar (Swedish for "credit notes"). The name given to the first issue of paper money made in the western world. Paper money of this type was the brainchild of Johan Palmstruch at Riga in 1652, but nine years elapsed before it was implemented by the Stockholm Bank. The notes were redeemable in copper *platmynt*.

Laureate Heraldic term for a laurel wreath, often framing a state emblem or shown, in the Roman fashion, as a crown on the ruler's forehead.

Leather Money Pieces of leather embossed with an official device have been used as money on various occasions, including the sieges of Faenza and Leiden and in the Isle of Man in the 15th and 16th centuries. Several towns in Austria and Germany produced leather tokens during and after the First World War.

Legal Tender Coins or paper money which are declared by law to be current money and which tradesmen and shopkeers are obliged to accept in payment for goods or services. (See *Money and the Law*).

Legend The inscription on a coin or medal.

Liberation Money Paper money prepared for use in parts of Europe and Asia, formerly under Axis occupation. Liberation notes were used in France, Belgium and the Netherlands in 1944–5, while various Japanese and Chinese notes were overprinted for use in Hong Kong when it was liberated in 1945. Indian notes overprinted for use in Burma were issued in 1945–6 when that country was freed from Japanese occupation.

Ligature (From Latin *ligatus*, bound together). Term denoting the linking of two letters in a *legend*, e.g. Æ and Œ.

Long Cross Coinage Type of coinage introduced by King Henry III in 1247, deriving its name from the reverse which bore a cross whose arms extended right to the edge to help safeguard the coins against *clipping*. This remained the style of the silver penny, its fractions and multiples, till the reign of Henry VII, and vestiges of the long cross theme is seen in the silver coins throughout the remaining years of the Tudor period.

Love Token A coin which has been altered by smoothing one or both surfaces and engraving initials, dates, scenes, symbols of affection and messages thereon.

Lushbourne   English word for base pennies of inferior silver, said to have emanated from Luxembourg, from which the name derived. These coins were first minted under John the Blind who adopted the curious spelling of his name EIWANES in the hope that illiterate English merchants might confuse it with EDWARDVS and thus be accepted as coin issued in the name of Edward III.   Lushbournes were also minted by Robert of Bethune, William I of Namur and the bishops of Toul during the mid-14th century.

Lustre   The sheen or bloom on the surface of an uncirculated coin resulting from the centrifugal flow of metal caused by striking.

Magnimat   Trade name used by VDM (*Verein Deutscher Metallwerke*) for a high-security alloy containing copper, nickel and magnetised steel. First used for the 5 deutschemark coin of 1975, it has since been adopted for other high-value coins in Germany and other countries.

Manilla   Copper, bronze or brass rings, sometimes shaped like horseshoes and sometimes open, with flattened terminals, used as currency in West Africa until recent years.

Matrix   Secondary die for a coin or medal, produced from the master die by means of an intermediate punch. In this way dies can be duplicated from the original cut on the reducing machine.

Matt or Matte   Finely granulated surface or overall satin finish to proof coins, a style which was briefly fashionable at the turn of the century. The Edward VII proof set of 1902 is a notable example. In more recent years many issues produced by the Franklin Mint have been issued with this finish.

Maundy Money   Set of small silver coins, in denominations of 1, 2, 3 and 4 pence, distributed by the reigning British monarch to the poor and needy on Maundy Thursday. The custom dates back to the Middle Ages, but in its present form, of distributing pence to as many men and women as the years in the monarch's age, it dates from 1666. At first ordinary silver pennies and multiples were used but after they went out of everyday use distinctive silver coins were produced specifically for the purpose from the reign of George II (1727–60) onwards. For centuries the ceremony took place in Westminster Abbey but since 1955 other venues have been used in alternate years.

Medal   (French *medaille*, Italian *medaglia*, from Latin *metallum*). A piece of metal bearing devices and legends commemorating an event or person, or given as an award. Military medals date from the 16th and 17th centuries, but were not generally awarded to all ranks till the 19th century. Commemora-tive medals can be traced back to Roman times, but in their present form they date from the Italian Renaissance when there was a fashion for large cast portrait medals.

Medalet   A small medal, generally 25mm or less in diameter.

Medallion   Synonym for medal, but usually confined to those with a diameter of 50mm or more.

Milling   Process denoting the mechanical production of coins, as opposed to the handmade technique implied in *hammering*. It alludes to the use of watermills to drive the machinery of the screw presses and blank rollers developed in the 16th century. As the even thickness and diameter of milled coins permitted a security edge, the term milling is popularly, though erroneously, used as a synonym for *graining* or *reeding*.

Mint   The place in which coins and medals are produced. Mint condition is a term sometimes used to denote pieces in an uncirculated state.

Mint Set   A set of coins or medals in the package or case issued by the mint. See also *year set*.

Mintmark   A device appearing on a coin to denote the place of minting. Athenian coins of classical times have been recorded with up to 40 different marks, denoting individual workshops. In the 4th century AD the Romans adopted this system to identify coins struck in provincial mints. This system was widely used in the Middle Ages and survives in France and Germany to this day. Initials and symbols are also used to identify mints, especially where the production of a coin is shared between several different mints. From 1351 onwards symbols were adopted in England to denote periods between trials of the *Pyx*, and thus assist the proper chronological sequence of coins, in an era prior to the adoption of dating. These mintmarks continued into the 17th century, but gradually died out as the use of dates became more widespread. See also *countermark* and *privy mark*.

Mionnet Scale   Scale of nineteen diameters covering all sizes of coins belonging to the classical period, devised by the French numismatist, Theodore-Edme Mionnet (1770–1842) during the compilation of his fifteen-volume catalogue of the numismatic collection in the Bibliotheque Nationale in Paris.

Mirror Finish   The highly polished surface of proof coins.

Misstrike   A coin or medal on which the impression has been struck off-centre.

Model Coin Tiny pieces of metal, either reproducing the designs of existing coins (used as play money by children) or, more specifically, denoting patterns produced by Joseph Moore and Hyam Hyams in their attempts to promote an improved subsidiary coinage in 19th century Britain. These small coins were struck in bronze with a brass or silver centre and were designed to reduce the size of the existing cumbersome range of pence, halfpence and farthings.

Modified Effigy Any coin in which the profile on the obverse has been subtly altered. Examples include minor changes in the Victorian Young Head and Old Head effigies and the George V profile by Sir Bertram Mackennal.

Money Order Certificate for a specified amount of money, which may be transmitted by post and encashed at a money order office or post office. This system was pioneered by Britain and the United States in the early 19th century and is now virtually worldwide. The term is now confined to certificates above a certain value, the terms *postal order* and *postal note* being used for similar certificates covering small amounts.

Mule Coin whose obverse is not matched with its official or regular reverse. Mules include the erroneous combination of dies from different reigns, but in recent years such hybrids have arisen in mints where coins for several countries are struck. Examples include the Coronation Anniversary crowns combining Ascension and Isle of Man dies and the 2 cent coins with Bahamas and New Zealand dies. *Restrikes* of rare American coins have been detected in which the dated die has been paired with the wrong reverse die, e.g. the 1860 restrike of the rare 1804 large cent.

Mute An *anepigraphic* coin, identifiable only by the devices struck on it.

Nail Mark Small indentation on ancient coins. The earliest coins of Asia Minor developed from the electrum *dumps* which merchants marked with a broken nail as their personal guarantee of value, the ancient counterpart of the *chop* marks used in China and Japan.

NCLT Coins Abbreviation for "Non Circulating Legal Tender", a term devised by modern coin catalogues to denote coins which, though declared *legal tender*, are not intended for general circulation on account of their precious metal content or superior finish.

Nicked Coin Coin bearing a tiny cut or nick in its edge. Silver coins were tested by this method, especially in the reign of Henry I (1100–35) when so many base silver pennies were in circulation. Eventually people refused to accept these nicked coins a problem which was only overcome when the state decreed that all coins should have a nick in them.

Nickel Metallic element, chemical symbol *Ni*, a hard white metal relatively resistant to tarnish, and extensively used as a cheap substitute for silver. It was first used for the American 5 cent coin in 1866, hence its popular name which has stuck ever since, although nowadays the higher denominations are minted in an alloy of copper and nickel. Although best known as a silver substitute, nickel was widely used in Jamaica (1869–1969) for halfpence and pennies and in British West Africa for the tiny 1/10th pennies (1908–57). Pure nickel was used for French francs and German marks, but usually it is alloyed with copper or zinc to produce *cupro-nickel* or nickel brass.

Notaphily Hybrid word from Latin *nota* (note) and Greek philos (love), coined about 1970 to denote the branch of numismatics devoted to the study of paper money.

Notgeld German word meaning emergency money, applied to the *tokens*, in metals, wood, leather and even ceramic materials, issued during the First World War when coinage disappeared from circulation. These tokens were soon superseded by low-denomination paper money issued by shops and businessmen in denominations from 10 to 50 pfennige and known as *kleine Notgeld* (small emergency money). These notes were prohibited in September 1922 but by that time some 50,000 varieties are thought to have been issued. Inflation raced out of control and the government permitted a second issue of local notes, known as *large Notgeld*, as the denomi-nations were in thousands, and latterly millions, of marks. Some 3,600 types appeared in 1922 and over 60,000 in 1923 alone. These mementoes of the German hyperinflation ceased to circulate in 1924 when the currency was reformed.

Numismatics The study of coins, medals and other related fields, a term derived from the Latin *numisma* and Greek *nomisma* (money).

Obsidional Currency (From Latin *obsidium*, a siege). Term for *emergency money* produced by the defenders of besieged towns and cities. These usually took the form of pieces of silver plate, commandeered for the purpose, crudely marked with an official device and the value. Instances of such seige coinage have been recorded from the 12th to the 19th centuries.

Obverse The "heads" side of a coin or medal, generally bearing the effigy of the head of state or an allegorical figure.

Off Metal Term denoting a piece struck in a metal other than the officially authorisied or issued alloy. This originally applied to *patterns* which were often struck in lead or copper instead of gold and silver as trial pieces or to test the dies; but in recent years it has applied to collectors' versions, e.g. proofs in platinum, gold or silver of coins normally issued in bronze or cupro-nickel.

Overdate   One or more digits in a date altered by superimposing another figure. Alterations of this kind, by means of small punches, were made to dated dies so that they could be used in years other than that of the original manufacture. Coins with overdates invariably show traces of the original digit.

Overstrike   Coin, token or medal produced by using a previously struck pieces as a flan. The Bank of England dollar of 1804 was overstruck on Spanish pieces of eight, and examples showing traces of the original coins are worth a good premium.

Paduan   Name given to imitations of medals and bogus coins produced in Italy in the 16th century, and deriving from the city of Padua where forgeries of bronze sculpture were produced for the antique market.

Patina   Oxidation forming on the surface of metallic objects. So far as coins and medals are concerned, this applies mainly to silver, brass, bronze and copper pieces which may acquire oxidation from the atmosphere, or spectacular patination from salts in the ground in which they have been buried. In extreme forms patina leads to verdigris and other forms of rust which corrode the surface, but in uncirculated coins it may be little more than a mellowing of the original *lustre*. Coins preserved in blue velvet presentation cases often acquire a subtle toning from the dyes in the material.

Pattern   Piece resembling a coin or medal, prepared by the mint to the specifications or on the authorisation of the coin-issuing authority, but also applied to pieces produced by mints when tendering for coinage or medal contracts. Patterns may differ from the final coins as issued in the type of alloy used (*off metal*) but more often they differ in details of the design.

Pellet   Raised circular ornament used as a spacing device between words and abbreviations in the *legend* of coins and medals. Groups of pellets were also used as ornaments in the angles of the cross on the reverse of English silver pennies.

Piece de Plaisir   (French for "fancy piece"). Term given to coins struck in a superior precious metal, or to a superior finish, or on a much thicker flan than usual. See *off metal*, *piedfort* and *proof*.

Piedfort (Piefort)   Piece struck with coinage dies on a *flan* of much more than normal thickness. This practice originated in France in the late 16th century and continues to the present day. In recent years it has been adopted by mints in Britain and other countries as a medium for collectors' pieces.

Pile   Lower die incorporating the obverse motif, used in striking coins and medals. See also *trussel*.

Planchet   French term used as an alternative for *blank* or *flan*.

Plaque or **Plaquette**   Terms sometimes used for medals struck on a square or rectangular flan.

Plaster   Cast taken from the original model for a coin or medal sculpted by an artist, and used in modern reducing machines in the manufacture of the master *die*.

Plated Coins   Coins stuck in base metal but given a wash of silver or some other precious metal. This expedient was adopted in inflationary times, from the Roman Republic (91 BC) till the Tudor period. American cents of 1943 were struck in steel with a zinc coating, and more recently *clad* coins have produced similar results.

Platinum   The noblest of all precious metals, platinum has a higher specific gravity than gold and a harder, brighter surface than silver. Until an industrial application was discovered in the mid-19th century, it was regarded as of little value, and was popular with counterfeiters as a cheap substitute for gold in their forgeries which, with a light gold wash, could be passed off as genuine. It was first used for circulating coins in Russia (the chief source of the metal since 1819) and 3, 6 and 12 rouble coins were mined at various times between 1828 and 1845. In recent years platinum has been a popular metal for limited-edition proof coins.

Platmynt   (Swedish for "plate money"). Large copper plates bearing royal cyphers and values from half to ten dalers produced in Sweden between 1643 and 1768. They represented laudable attempts by a country rich in copper to produce a coinage in terms of its silver value, but the net result was far too cumbersome to be practical. The weight of the daler plate, for example, ranged from 766 grams to 1.1kg, and special carts had to be devised to transport them!

Plugged Coins   Coins struck predominantly in one metal, but containing a small plug of another. This curious practice may be found in the farthings of Charles II (1684–85) and the halfpenny or farthings of James II (1685–87), which were struck in tin, with a copper plug, to defeat forgers.

Porcelain Money   Tokens made of porcelain circulated in Thailand from the late 18th century till 1868. The Meissen pottery struck tokens in 1920–22 as a form of small *Notgeld*, using reddish-brown Bottger stoneware and white *bisque* porcelain. These ceramic tokens circulated in various towns of Saxony.

Postage Currency Small paper notes in denominations of 5, 10, 25 and 50 cents, issued by the US federal government in 1862–63, were thus inscribed and had reproductions of postage stamps engraved on them — five 5c stamps on the 25c and five 10c stamps on the 50c notes. The earliest issue even had perforations in the manner of stamps, but this unnecessary device was soon done away with. See also *stamp money*.

Postal Notes or Orders Low-value notes intended for transmission by post and encashable at post offices. Introduced by Britain in 1883, they were an extension of the earlier *money order* system, and are now issued by virtually every country.

Potin (French for pewter). Alloy of copper, tin, lead and silver used as a coinage metal by the Celtic tribes of eastern Gaul at the beginning of the Christian era.

Privy Mark Secret mark incorporated in the design of a coin or medal to identify the minter, or even the particular die used. The term is also used more loosely to denote any small symbol or initials appearing on a coin other than a *mint mark*, and is sometimes applied to the symbols associated with the trial of the *Pyx* found on English coins.

Prize Coins Coins of large size and value struck primarily as prizes in sporting contests. this principle dates from the late 5th century BC when Syracuse minted decadrachms as prizes in the Demareteian Games. The most notable example in modern times is the lengthy series of talers and five-franc coins issued by the Swiss cantons since 1842 as prizes in the annual shooting festivals, the last of which honoured the Lucerne contest of 1939.

Profile A side view of the human face, widely used as a coinage effigy.

Proof Originally a trial strike testing the *dies*, but now denoting a special collectors' version struck with dies that have been specially polished on *flans* with a mirror finish. Presses operating at a very slow speed, or multi-striking processes, are also used.

Propaganda Notes Paper money containing a political slogan or a didactic element. During the Second World War forgeries of German and Japanese notes were produced by the Allies and additionally inscribed or overprinted with slogans such as "Co-Prosperity Sphere—What is it worth?" (a reference to the Japanese occupied areas of SE Asia). Forged dollars with anti-American propaganda were airdropped over Sicily by the Germans in 1943 and counterfeit pounds with Arabic propaganda over Egypt in 1942–43. Various anti-communist organisations liberated propaganda forgeries of paper money by balloon over Eastern Europe during the Cold War period.

Provenance Mark Form of *privy mark* denoting the source of the metal used in coins. Examples include the plumes or roses on English coins denoting silver from Welsh or West of England mines, and the elephant or elephant and castle on gold coins denoting bullion imported by the African Company. Coins inscribed VIGO (1702–03) or LIMA (1745–46) denote bullion seized from the Spaniards by Anglo-Dutch privateers and Admiral Anson respectively. Other provenance marks on English coins include the letters EIC and SSC, denoting bullion imported by the East India Company or the South Sea Company.

Pseudo Coins Derisory term coined in recent years to signify pieces of precious metal, often struck in *proof* versions only, aimed at the international investment market. Many of these pieces, though bearing a nominal face value, are not *legal tender* in the countries purporting to issue them and in many cases they go straight from the overseas mint where they are produced to coin dealers in America and western Europe, without ever appearing in the so-called country of origin. See also *NCLT coins*.

Punch or Puncheon Intermediate *die* whereby working dies can be duplicated from the master die, prior to the striking of coins and medals.

Pyx Box in which a specimen from every 15 pounds troy weight of gold and every 60 pounds of silver minted in England is kept for annual trial by weight and assay. Many of the *mintmarks* on English coins of the 14th–17th centuries were in use from one trial to the next and still exist today and can therefore be used to date them.

Reducing Machinery Equipment designed on the pantographic principle for transferring the image from a *plaster* to a *hub* and reducing it to the size of the actual coin or medal. The image is transferred by means of a stylus operating rather like a gramophone needle, but working from the centre to the outer edge.

Reeding Security edging on coins, consisting of close vertical ridges. As a rule, this appears all round the edge but some coins, e.g. New Zealand's 50c (1967) and the Isle of Man's £1 (1978) have segments of reeding alternating with a plain edge, to help blind and partially sighted persons to identify these coins.

Re-issue A coin or note issued again after an extended lapse of time.

Relief   Raised parts of the *obverse* and *reverse* of coins and medals, the opposite of *incuse*.

Remainder   A note from a bank or issuing authority which has never been circulated, due to inflation, political changes or bank failure. Such notes, some-times in partial or unfinished state (e.g. missing serial numbers or signatures), are generally unloaded on to the numismatic market at a nominal sum and provide a good source of inexpensive material for the beginner.

Restrike   Coin, medal or token produced from *dies* subsequent to the original use. Usually restrikes are made long after the original and can often be identified by marks caused by damage, pitting or corrosion of the dies after they were taken out of service.

Retrograde   Term describing inscriptions running from right to left, or with the letters in a mirror image, thought to arise from unskilled die-cutters failing to realise that inscriptions have to be engraved in negative form to achieve a positive impression.   Retrograde inscriptions are common on ancient Greek coins, but also found on Roman and Byzantine coins.

Reverse   The side of a coin or medal regarded as of lesser importance; in colloquial parlance, the "tails" side.

Saltire   Heraldic term for a cross in the shape of an X.

Sandwich   Coin *blank* consisting of thin outer layers in one alloy bonded to a core in another. See *clad coins*.

Sceat   (Anglo-Saxon for "treasure", or German *Schatz*). Money of account in Kent early in the 7th century as the twelfth part of a shilling or Merovingian gold tremissis. As a silver coin, it dates from about AD 680–700 and weighed about 20 grains, putting it on par with the Merovingian denier or penny. Sceats spread to other parts of England in the 8th century but tended to decline in weight and value, but from about 760 it was gradually superseded by the silver penny minted under Offa and his successors.

Silver sceat, circa 710-760

Scissel   The clippings of metal left after a *blank* has been cut. Occasionally one of these clippings accidentally adheres to the blank during the striking process, producing characteristic crescent-shaped flaws on the finished coin.

Scrip   Paper money of restricted validity or circulation, e.g. *Bafs* and other military scrip used in canteens and post exchanges.

Scyphate   (Greek *scypha*, a skiff or small boat). Byzantine coin with a concave *flan*.

Sede Vacante   (Latin for "Vacant See"). Coins struck at *ecclesiastical mints* between the death of a prelate and the election of his successor are often thus inscribed.   This practice originated at Rome in the 13th century.

Seignorage or Seigneurage   Royalty or percentage paid by persons bringing *bullion* to a mint for conversion into coin, but nowadays synonymous with the royalty paid by mints in respect of the precious metal versions of coins sold direct to collectors.   It arises from the medieval right of the king to a small portion of the proceeds of a mint, and amounted to a tax on moneying.   It has also been applied to the money accruing to the state when the coinage is re-issued in an alloy of lesser fineness, as, for example, the debased sovereigns of Henry VIII in 20 instead of 23 carat gold, the king's treasury collecting the difference.

Series   Term applied to sets of medals of a thematic character, which first became fashionable in the early 18th century. Jean Dassier pioneered the medallic series in the 1720s with his set of 72 medals portraying the rulers of France till Louis XV.   The idea was developed by J. Kirk, Sir Edward Thomason, J. Mudie and A. J. Stothard in Britain, and by Moritz Fuerst and Amedee Durand in Europe.   The fashion died out in the 19th century, but has been revived in America and Europe since 1964.

Serrated   Having a notched or toothed edge, rather like a cogwheel. Coins of this type, struck in *electrum,* an alloy of silver and gold, are known from Carthage in the 2nd century BC, and some silver denarii of Rome in the 2nd century AD also come into this category.

Sexagesimal System   Monetary system in which the principal unit is divided into 60 parts. The oldest system in the Western world was based on the gold talent of 60 minae and the mina of 60 shekels.   In medieval Europe 60 groschen were worth a fine mark; in England from 1551, the silver coinage was based on the crown of 60 pence, and in the south German states till 1873 the gulden was worth 60 kreuzers.

Shin Plasters   Derisory term originally applied to the Continental currency notes issued during the American War of Independence, the fractional currency of the Civil War period and also the low-denomination notes of Canada between 1870 and 1935, but often applied indiscriminately to any other low-denomination, small-format notes.

Henry II Short Cross Penny

Short Cross Coinage   Term for the silver coinage introduced by Henry II in 1180 and minted till 1247 at which time it was replaced by the *Long Cross* type. The termination of the arms of the cross on the reverse well within the circumference encouraged the dishonest practice of *clipping*.

Shroff Mark   A *countermark* applied by Indian bankers or merchants to attest the full weight and purity of coins. See also *chop*.

Siege Money   See *Obsidional Currency*

Silver   Precious metal, chemical symbol *Ag*, numismatic abbreviation *Ar*, from Latin *Argentum*, widely used as a coinage metal from the 6th century BC to the present day.

Sterling silver denotes an alloy of .925 fine silver with .075 copper. Fine silver alloys used over the past 2,500 years have ranged from .880 to .960 fine, but base silver has also been all too common. British coins from 1920 to 1946 were struck in .500 fine silver, while alloys of lesser fineness are known as *billon* or *vellon*. Silver alloyed with gold produces a metal called *electrum*, used for the earliest coinage of the western world, the staters of Lydia in the 7th century BC. Since 1970 silver as a medium for circulating coinage has almost virtually disappeared, yet the volume of silver coins for sale to collectors has risen considerably in recent years.

Skit Note   Piece of paper masquerading as a banknote. It differs from a *counterfeit* in that its design parodies that of a genuine note, often for political, satirical or advertising reasons. Others were produced as April Fools' Day jokes or a form of Valentine (e.g. the Bank of Lovers). In recent years they have been produced as advertising gimmicks, or as coupons permitting a discount off the list price of goods.

Slug   Popular name for the $50 gold pieces produced by private mints in California in the mid-19th century. The term is also applied nowadays to *tokens* intended for use in gaming machines.

Spade Guinea   Name given to the guineas of George III issued between 1787 and 1799 because the shield on the reverse design resembled the shape of a spade. In Victorian times the spade guinea was extensively copied in brass for gaming counters.

Spade Money   Cast bronze pieces resembling miniature spades and other agricultural implements, used as money and derived from the actual implements which had previously been used in barter. Often referred to as *Pu* or *Boo* money.

Specie   Financial term denoting money in the form of precious metals (silver and gold), usually struck as coin, as opposed to money in the form of paper notes and bills of exchange. It occurs in the name of some European coins (e.g. *speciedaler*, *speciestaler* and *speciesducat*) to denote the use of fine silver or gold.

Specimen   Generally used to denote a single piece, but more specifically applying to a coin in a special finish, less than *proof* in quality but superior to the general circulating version. It also denotes paper notes intended for circulation between banks or for press publicity and distinguished from the generally issued version by zero serial numbers, punch holes or a security endorsement.

Spintriae   Metal tokens produced in Roman imperial times, with erotic motifs, thought to have been tickets of admission to brothels.

Spit   Copper or iron rod used as a primitive form of currency in the Mediterranean area. The Greek word *belos* meant a spit, dart or bolt, and from this came the word *obolos* used for a coin worth a 6th of a drachma.

Stamp Money   Both postage and revenue (fiscal) stamps have circulated as money during shortages of coins, from the American Civil War onwards. *Encased postage stamps* were used in the USA, 1861–62, before they were superseded by *Postage Currency* notes, but the same expedient was adopted by many countries during and immediately after the First World War. Stamps affixed to special cards have circulated as money in Rhodesia (now Zimbabwe) in 1900, the French colonies and Turkey during the First World War, in Spain during the Civil War (1936–39) and the Philippines during the Second World War. Stamps printed on thick card, with an inscription on the reverse signifying their parity with silver coins, were issued in Russia (1917–18) and also in Armenia, the Crimea and the Ukraine (1918–20). During the Second World War Ceylon (now Sri Lanka) and several Indian states issued small money cards with contemporary stamps printed on them.

Steel   Refined and tempered from *iron*, and used in chromed or stainless versions as a coinage metal in the 20th century. Zinc-coated steel cents were issued by the USA (1943) but in the form known as *acmonital* (nickel steel) it has been extensively used by Italy since 1939. Other alloys of nickel and steel have been used for coins of the Philippines (1944–45) and Roumania since 1963. Chrome steel was used by France for 5 centime coins in 1961–64. Copper-clad steel is now extensively used for subsidiary coins formerly struck in bronze.

Sterling Word of uncertain origin denoting money of a standard weight and fineness, and hence the more general meaning of recognised worth. The traditionally accepted derivation from the Easterlings, north German merchants who settled in London in the 13th century and produced silver pennies of uniform fineness, is unlikely as the term has been found in documents a century earlier. A more plausible explanation is from Old English *steorling* ("little coin with a star"), alluding to Viking pennies with this device, or even as a diminutive of *stater*. Sterling silver denotes silver of .925 fineness.

Stone money from the Pacific island of Yap

Stone Money Primitive currency in the form of large stone discs, used in West Africa in the pre-colonial period, and in the Pacific island of Yap (now Micronesia) as recently as 1940.

Striation A pattern of alternate light and dark parallel marks or minute grooves on the surface of a coin or medal. In the latter case it is sometimes done for textural effect, but in coins it may result from faulty *annealing*. Deliberate ridging of the surface, however, was a distinctive feature of Japanese *koban* and *goryoban* coins of 1736–1862.

Styca Name given to the debased silver *sceats* of Northumbria in the 8th century.

Tael Chinese unit of weight corresponding to the European ounce and sometimes referred to as a liang. It was a measure of silver varying between 32 and 39 grams. In the 19th century it served as *money of account*, 100 British or Mexican trade dollars being worth 72 tael. The term has also been loosely applied to the Chinese silver yuan, although this was worth only .72 tael, or 7 mace and 2 candareens (10 candareens = 1 mace; 10 mace = 1 tael).

Thrymsa Early Anglo-Saxon gold coin based on the Merovingian tremissis or third-solidus, current in Kent, London and York about AD 63–75.

Tical Unit of weight in Thailand, first appearing as coins in the form of crudely shaped *bullet money* current from the 14th till the late 19th centuries. When European-style coins were introduced in 1860 the word was retained as a denomination (32 solot = 16 atts = 8 peinung or sio = 4 songpy or sik = 2 fuang= 1 salung or quarter-tical. The currency was decimalised in 1909 (100 satangs = 1 tical), and the tical was superseded by the baht about 1950.

Tin Metallic element, chemical symbol Sn (from Latin *Stannum*). Because of its unstable nature and tendency to oxidise badly when exposed to the atmosphere, it is unsatisfactory as a coinage metal, but has been used on several occasions, notably in Malaya, Thailand and the East Indies. In was also used for British halfpence and farthings, 1672–92.

Token Any piece of money whose nominal value is greater than its intrinsic value is, strictly speaking, a token or promise. Thus most of the coins issued since 1964 can be regarded in this light, but numismatists reserve the term for a piece of limited validity and circulation, produced by tradesmen, chambers of commerce and other organisations during times of a shortage of government coinage. The term is also loosely applied to metal tickets of admission, such as *communion tokens*, or *jetons* and *counters* intended for games of chance. Tokens with a nominal value may be produced for security reasons to lessen the possibility of theft from milk bottles, vending machines, telephones, parking meters and transport facilities. Tokens exchangeable for goods have been issued by co-operative societies and used in prisons and internment camps in wartime. In addition to the traditional coinage alloys, tokens have been produced in ceramics, plastics, wood, stout card, leather and even rubber, in circular, square or polygonal shapes.

Tombac Type of brass alloy with a high copper content, used in coinage requiring a rich golden colour. It is, in fact, a modern version of the *aurichalcum* used by the Romans. It was used for the Canadian 5-cent coins of 1942–43, while 5- and 10-pfennig coins of Germany have a tombac cladding on a steel core.

Touchpiece Coin kept as a lucky charm, but more specifically the medieval gold angel of England which was worn round the neck as an antidote to scrofula, otherwise known as king's evil, from the belief that the reigning monarch possessed the power of healing by touch. The ceremony of touching for king's evil involved the suspension of an angel round the victim's neck, hence the prevalence of these coins pierced for suspension.

Trade Coins Coins widely used as a medium of international trade, often far beyond the boundaries of the country issuing them. The earliest examples were the Aiginetan turtles and Athenian tetrdrachms of the classical period. In the Middle Ages the English *sterling* was widely prized on account of its silver purity. Arab dinars and Italian florins were popular as gold coins in late-medieval times, while the British gold sovereign has been the preferred gold coin of modern times. The Maria Theresa silver thaler of Austria, with its date frozen at 1782, has been minted widely down to the present time for circulation in the Near and Middle East as a trade coin. Trade dollars were minted by Britain, the USA, the Netherlands and Japan to compete with the Spanish, and later the Mexican, peso or 8-reales coins as a trading medium in the Far East.

Transport Tokens Coin-like pieces of metal, plastic or card, issued by companies and corporations to employees and exchangeable for rides on municipal transport systems, date from the mid-19th century. In more recent times similar tokens have been used in many countries to activate turnstiles in buses, trams and rapid-transit railway systems.

1914 Treasury Note

Treasury Note Paper money worth 10 shillings or one pound, issued by the British Treasury on the outbreak of the First World War when *specie* payments were suspended, and continuing till 1928 when the Bank of England took over responsibility for note-issuing.

Treasure Trove Articles of precious metal concealed in times of economic or political upheaval and discovered years (often centuries) later are deemed by law to be treasure trove (from the French word *trouve*, found). For further details see *Money and the Law*.

Victoria veiled head

Trial Plate Plate of the same metal as the current coinage against which the fineness and quality of the coins produced are compared and tested.

Troy Weight System of weights derived from the French town of Troyes whose standard pound was adopted in England in 1526. It continued in Britain till 1879 when it was abolished, with the exception of the troy ounce and its decimal parts and multiples, which were retained for gold, silver, platinum and precious stones. The troy ounce of 480 grains is used by numismatists for weighing coins.

Truncation Stylised cut at the base of a coinage effigy, sometimes containing a die number, engraver's initials or *mintmark*.

Trussel Reverse die in *hammered* coinage, the opposite of the *pile*.

Type Principal motif on a coin or medal, enabling numismatists to identify the issue.

Type Set A set of coins comprising one of each coin in a particular series, regardless of the actual date of issue.

Uncirculated Term used in grading coins to denote specimens in perfect condition, with original mint lustre. In recent years the term "Brilliant Uncirculated" has been adopted (abbreviated as BUnc or BU) both to indicate the condition of a coin, and, by The Royal Mint, to indicate the standard to which some coins are minted, being a standard between Circulation and Proof.

Uniface Coin with a device on one side only.

Vecture Term (mainly US) for a *transport token*.

Veiled Head The effigy of Queen Victoria by Thomas Brock adopted for British coinage after 1893—often referred to as the "Old Head" coinage.

Veld Pond (Dutch for "field pound"). Gold coin struck by the Boer guerrillas at Pilgrims Rest in 1902, in imitation of the British sovereign.

VF Abbreviation for Very Fine, used to describe the state of a coin or medal.

VG Abbreviation for Very Good.

Vignette Strictly speaking the pictorial element of a paper note shading off into the surrounding unprinted paper rather than having a clearly defined border or frame; but nowadays applied generally to the picture portion of a banknote, as opposed to portrait, armorial or numeral elements.

Vis-à-Vis (French for "face to face"). Term describing coins with double portraits of rulers, their profiles or busts facing each other. A good example is the English coinage of Philip and Mary, 1554–58.

Wampum Barter currency of the North American Indians, composed of shells of *Venus mercenaria* strung together to form belts or "fathoms" worth 5 shillings. Wampum were tariffed variously from three to six to the English penny in the American colonies till 1704.

Wire Money Primitive currency of the Maldive Islands in the form of lengths of silver wire known as lari, from which the modern currency unit *laree* is derived. The term was also applied to English coins of the 18th century in which the numerals of value were exceptionally thin, resembling wire.

Wooden Coins Thin pieces of wood used as tokens are known from many parts of China and Africa, and as small *Notgeld* from Austria and

Germany during World War I. Wooden nickels is the name given to tokens of a commemorative nature, widely popular in the USA since 1930.

Young Head Profile of Queen Victoria sculpted by William Wyon for the Guildhall Medal of 1837 and subsequently utilised for British coins struck from 1837 to 1860 (copper) and 1887 (silver and gold).

Zinc Metallic element, chemical symbol *Zn*, widely used, with copper, as a constituent of brass. Alloyed with copper to form *tombac*, it was used for Canadian 5-cent coins (1942–43) and, coated on steel, it was used for American cents (1943). Zinc was used for *emergency coinage* in Austria, Belgium, Luxembourg and Germany (1915–18) and in Germany and German-occupied countries during World War II. Since then alloys of copper, nickel and zinc have been used for coinage in Eastern Europe.

1938 wooden nickel

Australian Government

Royal Australian Mint

AUSTRALIAN MINTMARKS

marks of distinction

MINTMARKS *of the world*

The following is a list of the initials and symbols denoting mints. In many cases, notably the Royal Mint, no mintmark was used on either British coins or those struck on behalf of other countries. Conversely many countries have only used one mintmark, that of one or other of the leading private mints.

It should be noted that the mintmarks of the main private mints have been recorded on the coins of the following countries:

H (Heaton, later the Birmingham Mint):
Australia, Bolivia, British Honduras, British North Borneo, British West Africa, Bulgaria, Canada, Ceylon, Chile, Colombia, Costa Rica, Cyprus, Dominican Republic, East Africa, Ecuador, Egypt, El Salvador, Finland, French Indochina, Great Britain, Greece, Guatemala, Guernsey, Haiti, Hong Kong, Iran, Israel, Italy, Jamaica, Jersey, Liberia, Malaya and British Borneo, Mauritius, Mombasa, Mozambique, Newfoundland, Nicaragua, Poland, Roumania, Sarawak, Serbia, Siam, Straits Settlements, Uruguay and Venezuela.

FM (Franklin Mint, Philadelphia): Bahamas, Belize, British Virgin Islands, Cayman Islands, Cook Islands, Guyana, Jamaica, Liberia, Malaysia, Malta, Panama, Papua New Guinea, Philippines, Solomon Islands, Trinidad and Tobago.

PM (Pobjoy Mint, Sutton, Surrey): Ascension, Bosnia, Cook Islands, Gibraltar, Isle of Man, Liberia, Macau, Niue, Philippines, St Helena, Senegal, Seychelles, Tonga and Tristan da Cunha.

ALBANIA
L	London
R	Rome
V	Valona

ARGENTINA
BA	Buenos Aires
Bs	Buenos Aires
B.AS	Buenos Aires
JPP	Jose Policarpo Patino
M	Mendoza
PNP	Pedro Nolasco Pizarro
PP	Pedro Nolasco Pizarro
PTS	Potosi
R	Rioja
RA	Rioja
SE	Santiago del Estero
SoEo	Santiago del Estero
TN	Tucuman

AUSTRALIA
A	Perth
D	Denver
H	Heaton (1912–16)
I	Bombay (1942–43)
I	Calcutta (1916–18)
M	Melbourne
P	Perth
PL	Royal Mint, London
S	Sydney
S	San Francisco (1942–43)
Dot before and after PENNY and I on obverse	Bombay (1942–43)
Dot before and after HALFPENNY and I on obverse	Bombay (1942–43)
Dot before and after PENNY	Bombay (1942–43)
Dot after HALFPENNY	Perth
Dot before SHILLING	Perth (1946)
Dot above scroll on reverse	Sydney (1920)
Dot below scroll on reverse	Melbourne (1919–20)
Dot between designer's initials KG	Perth (1940–41)
Dot after AUSTRALIA	Perth (1952–53)

AUSTRIA

A	Vienna (1765–1872)
AH–AG	Carlsburg, Transylvania (1765–76)
AH–GS	Carlsburg (1776–80)
A–S	Hall, Tyrol (1765–74)
AS–IE	Vienna (1745)
AW	Vienna (1764, 1768)
B	Kremnitz (1765–1857)
B–L	Nagybanya (1765–71)
B–V	Nagybanya (1772–80)
C	Carlsburg (1762–64)
C	Prague (1766–1855)
C–A	Carlsburg (1746–66)
C–A	Vienna (1774–80)
CG–AK	Graz (1767–72)
CG–AR	Graz (1767)
C–K	Vienna (1765–73)
CM	Kremnitz (1779)
CVG–AK	Graz (1767–72)
CVG–AR	Graz (1767)
D	Graz (1765–72), Salzburg (1800–09)
E	Carlsburg (1765–1867)
EC–SK	Vienna (1766)
EvM–D	Kremnitz (1765–74)
EvS–AS	Prague (1765–73)
EvS–IK	Prague (1774–80)
F	Hall (1765–1807)
FH	Hall
G	Graz (1761–63)
G	Gunzburg (1764–79)
G	Nagybanya (1766–1851)
G–K	Graz (1767–72)
G–R	Graz (1746–67)
GTK	Vienna (1761)
H	Hall (1760–80)
H	Gunzburg (1765–1805)
H–A	Hall (1746–65)
H–G	Carlsburg (1765–77)
H–S	Carlsburg (1777–80)
IB–FL	Nagybanya (1765–71)
IB–IV	Nagybanya (1772–80)
IC–FA	Vienna (1774–80)
IC–IA	Vienna (1780)
IC–SK	Vienna (1765–73)
I–K	Graz (1765-67)
I–K	Vienna (1767)
IZV	Vienna (1763–65)
K	Kremnitz (1760–63)
K–B	Kremnitz (1619–1765)
K–D	Kremnitz (1765)
K–M	Kremnitz (1763–65)
M	Milan (1780–1859)
N	Nagybanya (1780)
N–B	Nagybanya (1630–1777, 1849)
O	Oravicza (1783–1816)
P	Prague (1760–63)
P–R	Prague (1746–67)
PS–IK	Prague (1774–80)
S	Hall (1765–80), Schmollnitz (1763–1816)

S–C	Gunzburg (1765–74)
SC–G	Gunzburg (1765)
S–F	Gunzburg (1775–80)
S–G	Gunzburg (1764–65)
S–IE	Vienna (1745)
SK–PD	Kremnitz (1774–80)
TS	Gunzburg (1762–88)
V	Venice (1805–66)
VC–S	Hall (1774–80)
VS–K	Prague (1774–80)
VS–S	Prague (1765–73)
W	Vienna (1748–63)
W–I	Vienna (1746–71)

BAHAMAS
FM	Franklin Mint
JP	John Pinches

BELGIUM
A	Vienna
B	Kremnitz
C	Prague
E	Carlsburg
F	Hall
G	Nagybanya
H	Gunzburg
hand	Antwerp
lion	Bruges

BELIZE (British Honduras)
FM	Franklin Mint
H	Heaton (1912–16)

BOLIVIA
H	Heaton (1892–1953)
P, PTR, PTS	Potosi

BRAZIL
A	Berlin (1913)
B	Bahia (1714–1831)
C	Cuiaba (1823–33)
G	Goias (1823–33)
M	Minas Gerais (1823–28)
P	Pernambuco
R	Rio de Janeiro (1703–1834)
RS	Rio de Janeiro (1869)
SP	Sao Paulo (1825–32)

BRITISH NORTH BORNEO (Sabah)
H	Heaton (1882–1941)

BRITISH WEST AFRICA
G	JR Gaunt, Birmingham
H	Heaton, Birmingham (1911–57)
K	King's Norton
KN	King's Norton
SA	Pretoria

BULGARIA

A	Berlin
BP	Budapest
Heaton	Heaton, Birmingham (1881–1923)
KB	Kormoczbanya
cornucopia	Paris
thunderbolt	Poissy

CANADA

C	Ottawa
H	Heaton (1871–1907)
maple leaf	Ottawa (on coins struck after the year inscribed on them)

CENTRAL AMERICAN REPUBLIC

CR	San Jose (Costa Rica)
G	Guatemala
NG	Guatemala
T	Tegucigalpa (Honduras)

CEYLON

H	Heaton (1912)

CHILE

A	Agustin de Infante y Prado (1768–72)
AJ	The above and Jose Maria de Bobadilla (1800–01)
D	Domingo Eizaguirre
DA	Domingo Eizaguirre and Agustin de Infante (1772–99)
BFF	Francisco Rodriguez Brochero
FJJF	Brochero and Jose Maria de Bobadilla (1803–17)
H	Heaton (1851)
J	Jose Larraneta (1749–67)
So	Santiago
VA	Val Distra

COLOMBIA

A	Paris
B	Bogota
BA	Bogota
B.B	Bogota
H	Heaton (1912)
M	Medellin
NR	Nuevo Reino
NoRo	Nuevo Reino
P	Popayan
PN, Pn	Popayan
SM	Santa Marta

COSTA RICA

CR	San Jose (1825–1947)
HBM	Heaton (1889–93)
S	San Domingo
SD	San Domingo

COURLAND

ICS	Justin Carl Schroder

IFS	Johan Friedrich Schmickert

CYPRUS

H	Heaton (1881–2)

DENMARK

FF	Altona
KM	Copenhagen Altona (1842)
crown	Copenhagen
heart	Copenhagen
orb	Altona (1839–48)

Other letters are the initials of mintmasters and moneyers

DOMINICAN REPUBLIC

HH	Heaton (1888–1919)

EAST AFRICA

A	Ackroyd & Best, Morley
H	Heaton (1910–64)
I	Bombay
K	Kynoch (IMI)
KN	King's Norton
SA	Pretoria

ECUADOR

BIRMᴹH	Heaton (1915)
BIRMING-HAM	Heaton (1899–1900, 1928)
D	Denver
H	Heaton (1890, 1909, 1924–5)
HEATON BIRMING-HAM	Heaton (1872–95)
HF	Le Locle
LIMA	Lima
Mo	Mexico
PHILA	Philadelphia
QUITO	Quito
SANTIAGO	Santiago de Chile

EGYPT

H	Heaton (1904–37)

EL SALVADOR

CAM	Central American Mint, San Salvador
H	Heaton (1889–1913)
Mo	Mexico
S	San Francisco

FIJI

S	San Francisco

FINLAND

H	Heaton (1921)
heart	Copenhagen (1922). Since then coins have been struck at Helsinki without a mintmark.

Initials of mintmasters:

S	August Soldan (1864–85)	A	Clausthal, Hannover (1832–49)
L	Johan Lihr (1885–1912)	AE	Breslau, Silesia (1743–51)
S	Isaac Sundell (1915–47)	AGP	Cleve, Rhineland (1742–43)
L	V. U. Liuhto (1948)	AK	Dusseldorf, Julich-Berg (1749–66)
H	Uolevi Helle (1948–58)	ALS	Berlin (1749)
S	Allan Soiniemi (1958–75)	B	Bayreuth, Franconia (1796–1804)
SH	Soiniemi & Heikki Halvaoja	B	Breslau, Silesia (1750–1826)
	(1967–71)	B	Brunswick, Brunswick (1850–60)
K	Timo Koivuranta (1977, 1979)	B	Brunswick, Westphalia (1809–13)
KN	Koivuranta and Antti Neuvonen (1978)	B	Dresden, Saxony (1861–72)
KT	Koivuranta and Erja Tielinen (1982)	B	Hannover, Brunswick (1860–71)
KM	Koivuranta and Pertti Makinen (1983)	B	Hannover, East Friesland (1823–25)
N	Reino Nevalainen (1983)	B	Hannover, Hannover (1821–66)
		B	Hannover, Germany (1866-78)

FRANCE

A	Paris (1768)	B	Regensburg, Regensburg (1809)
AA	Metz (1775–98)	B	Vienna, Germany (1938–45)
B	Rouen (1786–1857)	BH	Frankfurt (1808)
B	Beaumont le Roger (1943–58)	B–H	Regensburg, Rhenish Confederation
BB	Strasbourg (1743–1870)		(1802–12)
C	Castelsarrasin (1914, 1942–46)	C	Cassel, Westphalia (1810–13)
CC	Genoa (1805)	C	Clausthal, Brunswick
CL	Genoa (1813–14)	C	Clausthal, Westphalia (1810–11)
D	Lyons (1771–1857)	C	Dresden, Saxony (1779–1804)
G	Geneva (1796–1805)	C	Frankfurt, Germany (1866–79)
H	La Rochelle (1770–1837)	CHI	Berlin (1749–63)
L	Limoges (1766–1837)	CLS	Dusseldorf, Julich-Berg (1767–70)
K	Bordeaux (1759–1878)	D	Aurich, East Friesland (1750–1806)
L	Bayonne (1761–1837)	D	Dusseldorf, Rhineland (1816–48)
M	Toulouse (1766–1837)	D	Munich, Germany (1872)
MA	Marseilles (1787–1857)	E	Dresden, Germany (1872–87)
N	Montpellier (1766–93)	E	Koenigberg, East Prussia (1750–98)
O	Riom	E	Muldenhutte, Germany (1887–1953)
P	Dijon	EC	Leipzig, Saxony (1753–63)
Q	Perpignan (1777–1837)	EGN	Berlin (1725–49)
R	Royal Mint, London (1815)	F	Dresden, Saxony (1845–58)
R	Orleans (1780–92)	F	Magdeburg, Lower Saxony (1740–1806)
T	Nantes (1739–1835)	F	Cassel, Hesse-Cassel (1803–07)
U	Turin (1814)	F	Stuttgart, Germany (1872)
V	Troyes	FW	Dresden, Saxony (1734–63)
W	Lille (1759–1857)	G	Dresden, Saxony (1833–44, 1850–54)
X	Amiens (1740)	G	Glatz, Silesia (1807–09)
&	Aix en Provence (1775)	G	Karlsruhe, Germany (1872)
9	Rennes	G	Stettin, Pomerania (1750–1806)
cow	Pau (1746–93)	GK	Cleve (1740–55)
flag	Utrecht (1811–14)	GN	Bamberg, Bamberg
crowned R	Rome (1811–14)	H	Darmstadt, Germany (1872–82)
thunderbolt	Poissy (1922-24)	H	Dresden, Saxony (1804–12)
star	Madrid (1916)	HK	Rostock, Rostock (1862–64)

In addition, French coins include symbols denoting the privy marks of Engravers General (Chief Engravers since 1880) and Mint Directors.

I	Hamburg, Germany (1872)
IDB	Dresden, Prussian occupation (1756–59)
IEC	Dresden, Saxony (1779–1804)
IF	Leipzig, Saxony (1763–65)
IGG	Leipzig, Saxony (1716–34, 1813–32)

GERMANY

The first name gives the location of the mint, and the second the name of the country or state issuing the coins.

		J	Hamburg, Germany (1873)
		J	Paris, Westphalia (1808–09)
		L	Leipzig, Saxony (1761–62)
A	Amberg, Bavaria (1763–94)	MC	Brunswick, Brunswick (1813–14, 1820)
A	Berlin (1850)	PM	Dusseldorf, Julich-Berg (1771–83)
		PR	Dusseldorf, Julich-Berg (1783–1804)

S	Dresden, Saxony (1813–32)
S	Hannover, Hannover (1839–44)
S	Schwabach, Franconia (1792–94)
SGH	Dresden, Saxony (1804–12)
ST	Strickling, Blomberg (1820–40)

GREAT BRITAIN

A	Ashby (1645)
B	Nicolas Briot (1631–39)
B	Bridgnorth (1646)
B	Bristol (1696)
Br	Bristol (1643–45)
C	Chester (1696)
CARL	Carlisle (1644–45)
CC	Corfe Castle (1644)
CHST	Chester (1644)
CR	Chester (1644)
E	Southwark (1547–49)
E	Exeter (1696)
E	Edinburgh (1707–13)
E*	Edinburgh (1707–09)
H	Heaton, Birmingham (1874–1919)
HC	Hartlebury Castle (1646)
K	London (1547–49)
KN	King's Norton
N	Norwich (1696)
OX	Oxford (1644–45)
OXON	Oxford (1644)
PC	Pontefract (1648–49)
SC	Scarborough (1644–45)
SOHO	Birmingham (1797–1806)
T	Canterbury (1549)
TC	Bristol (1549)
WS	Bristol (1547–49)
Y	Southwark (1551)
boar	Shrewsbury (1643–44)
book	Aberystwyth (1638–42)
bow	Durham House (1548–49)
castle	Exeter (1644–45)
crown	Aberystwyth Furnace (1648–49)
plume	Shrewsbury (1642)
plume	Oxford (1642–46)
plume	Bristol (1643–46)

Other symbols and marks on the hammered coins of Great Britain are usually referred to as Initial Marks. Complete listings of these marks appear in a number of specialist publications.

GREECE

A	Paris
B	Vienna
BB	Strasbourg
H	Heaton (1921)
K	Bordeaux
KN	King's Norton
owl	Aegina (1828–32)
owl	Athens (1838-55)
thunderbolt	Poissy

GUATEMALA

CG	Guatemala City (1733-76)
G	Guatemala City (1776)
H	Heaton (1894–1901)
NG	Nueva Guatemala (1777)

GUERNSEY

H	Heaton (1855–1949)

HAITI

A	Paris
HEATON	Heaton (1863)

HONDURAS

A	Paris (1869–71)
T	Tegucigalpa (1825–62)

HONG KONG

H	Heaton (1872–1971)
KN	King's Norton

HUNGARY

A	Vienna
B	Kremnitz
BP	Budapest
CA	Vienna
G	Nagybanya
GN	Nagybanya
GYF	Carlsburg
HA	Hall
K	Kremnitz
KB	Kremnitz
NB	Nagybanya
S	Schmollnitz
WI	Vienna

INDIA

B	Bombay (1835-1947)
C	Calcutta (1835-1947)
I	Bombay (1918)
L	Lahore (1943-45)
M	Madras (1869)
P	Pretoria (1943-44)
diamond	Bombay
dot in diamond	Hyderabad
split diamond	Hyderabad
star	Hyderabad

IRAN

H	Heaton (1928–29)

IRAQ

I	Bombay

ISRAEL

H	Heaton (1951–52)
star of David	Jerusalem

ITALY AND STATES

B	Bologna

B/I	Birmingham (1893–4)
FIRENZE	Florence
H	Heaton (1866–67)
KB	Berlin
M	Milan
N	Naples
OM	Strasbourg
R	Rome
T	Turin
V	Venice
ZV	Venice
anchor	Genoa
eagle head	Turin

JAMAICA

C	Ottawa
FM	Franklin Mint
H	Heaton (1882–1916)

JERSEY

H	Heaton (1877)

KENYA

C/M	Calcutta
H	Heaton (1911–64)

LIBERIA

B	Berne
FM	Franklin Mint
H	Heaton (1896–1906)
PM	Pobjoy Mint

LIECHTENSTEIN

A	Vienna
B	Berne
M	Munich

LUXEMBOURG

A	Paris
H	Gunzburg
anchor	Paris
angel	Brussels
caduceus	Utrecht
double eagle	Brussels
sword	Utrecht

MALAYSIA

B	Bombay
FM	Franklin Mint
H	Heaton (1955–61)
I	Calcutta (1941)
I	Bombay (1945)
KN	King's Norton
W	James Watt, Birmingham

MAURITIUS

H	Heaton (1877–90)
SA	Pretoria

MEXICO

A, As	Alamos
C, CN	Culiacan
CA, CH	Chihuahua
Ce	Real del Catorce
D, Do	Durango
Eo	Tlalpam
GA	Guadalajara
GC	Guadelupe y Calvo
Go	Guanajuato
Ho	Hermosillo
M, Mo	Mexico City
Mo	Morelos
MX	Mexico City
O, OA, OKA	Oaxaca
Pi	San Luis Potosi
SLPi	San Luis Potosi
TC	Tierra Caliente
Z, Zs	Zacatecas

MONACO

A	Paris
M	Monte Carlo
clasped hands	Cabanis
thunderbolt	Poissy

MOZAMBIQUE

H	Heaton (1894)
R	Rio

NETHERLANDS AND COLONIES
Austrian Netherlands (1700-93)

H	Amsterdam
S	Utrecht
W	Vienna
hand	Antwerp
head	Brussels
lion	Bruges

Kingdom of the Netherlands

B	Brussels (1821–30)
D	Denver (1943–45)
P	Philadelphia (1941–45)
S	Utrecht (1816–36)
S	San Francisco (1944–45)
Sa	Surabaya
caduceus	Utrecht

NICARAGUA

H	Heaton (1880–1916)
NR	Leon de Nicaragua

NORWAY

hammers	Kongsberg

PANAMA

CHI	Valcambi
FM	Franklin Mint

PERU

AREQ, AREQUIPA	Arequipa
AYACUCHO	Ayacucho
CUZCO, Co	Cuzco
L, LM, LR	Lima
LIMAE	Lima
PASCO	Pasco
Paz, Po	Pasco
P	Lima (1568-70)
P	Philadelphia
S	San Francisco

PHILIPPINES

BSP	Bangko Sentral Pilipinas
D	Denver (1944–45)
FM	Franklin Mint
M, MA	Manila
PM	Pobjoy Mint
S	San Francisco (1903–47)
5 point star	Manila

POLAND

AP	Warsaw (1772–74)
CI	Cracow (1765–68)
EB	Warsaw (1774–92)
EC	Leipzig (1758–63)
FF	Stuttgart (1916–17)
FH	Warsaw (1815–27)
FS	Warsaw (1765–68)
FWoF	Dresden (1734–64)
G	Cracow (1765–72)
H	Heaton (1924)
IB	Warsaw (1811–27)
IGS	Dresden (1716–34)
IP	Warsaw (1834–43)
IS	Warsaw (1768–74)
JGG	Leipzig (1750–53)
JS	Warsaw (1810–11)
KG	Warsaw (1829–34)
MV, MW	Warsaw
arrow	Warsaw (1925–39)
Dot after date	Royal Mint (1925)
8 torches	Paris (1924)

ROUMANIA

B	Bucharest (1879–85)
C	Bucharest (1886)
H	Heaton (1867–1930)
HUGUENIN	Le Locle
J	Hamburg
KN	King's Norton
V	Vienna
W	Watt, Birmingham
thunderbolt	Poissy

RUSSIA

AM	Annensk (1762–96)
BM	Warsaw (1825–55)
bM	St Petersburg (1796)
C–M	Sestroretsk (1762–96)
CM	Souzan (1825–55)
E–M	Ekaterinburg (1762–1810)
KM	Kolpina (1810)
K–M	Kolyvan (1762–1810)
MM, M–M	Moscow (1730–96)
MMD	Moscow (1730–96)
MW	Warsaw (1842–54)
NM	Izhorsk (1811–21)
SP	St Petersburg (1798–1800)
SPB	St Petersburg (1724–1915)
SPM	St Petersburg (1825–55)
T–M	Feodosia (1762–96)

SAN MARINO

M	Milan
R	Rome

SIAM

(Thailand)	H Heaton (1898)

SOUTH AFRICA

SA	Pretoria

SPAIN

B	Burgos
B, BA	Barcelona
Bo	Bilbao
C	Catalonia
C	Cuenca
C	Reus
CA	Zaragoza
G	Granada
GNA	Gerona
LD	Lerida
J, JA	Jubia
M, MD	Madrid
P	Palma de Majorca
PpP, PL, PA	Pamplona
S, S/L	Seville
Sr	Santander
T, To, Tole	Toledo
TOR:SA	Tortosa
V, VA, VAL	Valencia
crowned C	Cadiz
crowned M	Madrid
aqueduct	Segovia
crowned shield	Tarragona
pomegranate	Granada
quartered shield	Palma
scallop	Coruna
stars:	
3 points	Segovia
4 points	Jubia
5 points	Manila
6 points	Madrid
7 points	Seville (1833)
8 points	Barcelona (1838)
wavy lines	Valladolid

SURINAM

P	Philadelphia
S	Sydney
caduceus	Utrecht

COIN *inscriptions*

This alphabetical listing is confined to inscriptions found on coins, mainly in the form of mottoes or of a commemorative nature. Names of rulers are, for the most part, excluded. Where the inscription is in a language other than English a translation is given, followed by the name of the issuing country or authority in parentheses.

A Deo et Caesare From God and the Emperor (Frankfurt).

A Domino Factum est Istud et est Mirabile in Oculis Nostris This is the Lord's doing and it is marvellous in our eyes (England, Mary).

A Solo Iehova Sapientia From God alone comes true wisdom (Wittgenstein).

Ab Inimicis Meis Libera Me Deus Free me from enemies (Burgundy).

Ad Legem Conventionis According to the law of the Convention (Furstenberg).

Ad Normam Conventionis According to the standard of the Convention (Prussia).

Ad Palmam Pressa Laeturo Resurgo Pressed to the palm I rise more joyfully (Wittgenstein).

Ad Usam Luxemburgi CC Vallati For the use of the besieged Luxembourgers (Luxembourg siege coins).

Adiuva Nos Deus Salutaris Noster Help us, O God, our Saviour (Lorraine).

Adventus Optimi Principis The coming of the noblest prince (Papacy).

Aes Usibus Aptius Auro Bronze in its uses is more suitable than gold (Brazil).

Aeternum Meditans Decus An ornament intended for all time (Alencon).

Aliis Inserviendo Consumor I spend my life devoted to others (Brunswick-Wolfenbuttel).

Alles Mit Bedacht All with reflection (Brunswick).

Amor Populi Praesidium Regis The love of the people is the king's protection (England, Charles I).

Ang Fra Dom Hib & Aquit (King) of England and France, Lord of Ireland and Aquitaine (England, Edward III).

Anno Regni Primo In the first year of the reign (Britain, edge inscription on crowns).

Apres les Tenebres la Lumiere After the shadows, the light (Geneva).

Archangelus Michael Archangel Michael (Italy, Grimoald IV).

Ardua ad Gloriam Via Struggles are the way to glory (Waldeck).

Arte Mea Bis Iustus Moneta Lud Iust By my art I am twice the just coin of King Louis (France, 1641).

Aspera Oblectant Wild places delight (Nassau-Weilburg).

Aspice Pisas Sup Omnes Specio Behold the coin of Pisa, superior to all (Pisa).

Audiatur Altera Pars Let the other part be heard (Stavelot).

Auf Gott Trawe Ich In God I trust (Brunswick).

Ausen Gefaesen der Kirchen und Burger From the vessels of the Church and citizens (Frankfurt siege, 1796).

Auspicio Regis et Senatus Angliae By authority of the king and parliament of England (East India Company).

Auxilio fortissimo Dei With the strongest help of God (Mecklenburg).

Auxilium de Sanctio Aid from the sanctuary (Papacy).

Auxilium Meum a Dno Qui Fecit Celum e Terram My help comes from God who made heaven and earth (Portugal).

Beata Tranquillatis Blessed tranquillity (Rome, Licinius II).

Beatus Qui Speravit in dom Blessed is he who has hoped in the Lord (Mansfeld).

Benedic Haereditati Tuae Blessings on your inheritance (Savoy).

Benedicta Sit Sancta Trinitas Blessed be the Holy Trinity (Albon).

Benedictio Domini Divites Facit The blessing of the Lord makes the rich (Teschen).

Benedictus Qui Venit in Nomine Domini Blessed is he who comes in the name of the Lord (Flanders).

Beschaw das Ziel Sage Nicht Viel Consider the matter but say little (Quedlinburg).

Besser Land und Lud Verloren als ein Falscher Aid Geschworn   Better to lose land and wealth than swear a false oath (Hesse).

Bey Gott ist Rath und That   With God is counsel and deed (Mansfeld).

Britanniarum Regina   Queen of the Britains (Britain, Victoria).

Britt Omn Rex   King of all the Britains (i.e. Britain and the overseas dominions) (Britain, 1902–52).

Cal et Car Com de Fugger in Zin et Norn Sen & Adm Fam   Cajetan and Carl, Counts of Fugger in Zinnenberg and Nordendorf, Lords and Administrators of the Family (Empire, Fugger).

Candide et Constanter   Sincerely and steadfastly (Hesse-Cassel).

Candide sed Provide   Clearly but cautiously (Osterwitz).

Candore et Amore   With sincerity and love (Fulda).

Candore et Constantia   With sincerity and constancy (Bavaria).

Capit Cath Ecclesia Monasteriensis   Chapter of the Cathedral Church of Munster (Munster).

Capit Eccle Metropolit Colon   Chapter of the Metropolitan Church of Cologne (Cologne).

Capitulum Regnans Sede Vacante   Chapter governing, the See being vacant (Eichstadt).

Carola Magna Ducissa Feliciter Regnante   Grand Duchess Charlotte, happily reigning (Luxembourg).

Carolus a Carolo   Charles (I) to Charles (II) (England).

Cedunt Prementi Fata   The fates yield to him who presses (Ploen, Hese-Cassel).

Charitate et Candore   With charity and sincerity (East Frisia).

Charta Magna Bavariae   The Great Charter of Bavaria (Bavaria).

Christo Auspice Regno   I reign under the auspices of Christ (England, Charles I).

Christus Spes Una Salutis   Christ is our one hope of salvation (Cleve).

Chur Mainz   Electoral Principality of Mainz (Mainz).

Circumeundo Servat et Ornat   It serves and decorates by going around (Sweden).

Civibus Quorum Pietas Coniuratione Die III Mai MDCCXCI Obrutam et Deletam Libertate Polona Tueri Conabatur Respublica Resurgens   To the citizens whose piety the resurgent commonwealth tried to protect Poland overturned and deprived of liberty by the conspiracy of the third day of May 1791 (Poland).

Civitas Lucemborgiensis Millesimum Ovans Expletannum   Completing the celebration of a thousand years of the city of Luxembourg (Luxembourg).

Civium Industria Floret Civitas   By the industry of its people the state flourishes (Festival of Britain crown, 1951).

Cluniaco Cenobio Petrus et Paulus   Peter and Paul from the Abbey of Cluny (Cluny).

Comes Provincie Fili Regis Francie   Court of Provence and son of the King of France (Provence).

Communitas et Senatus Bonon   City and senate of Bologna (Bologna).

Concordia Fratrum   The harmony of the brothers (Iever).

Concordia Patriae Nutrix   Peace, the nurse of the fatherland (Waldeck).

Concordia Res Parvae Crescunt   Little things increase through harmony (Batavian Republic).

Concordia Res Parvae Crescunt, Discordia Dilabuntur   By harmony little things increase, by discord they fall apart (Lowenstein-Wertheim-Virneburg).

Concordia Stabili   With lasting peace (Hildesheim).

Confidens Dno Non Movetur   He who trusts in God is unmoved (Spanish Netherlands).

Confidentia in Deo et Vigilantia   Trust in God and vigilance (Prussian Asiatic Company).

Confoederato Helvetica   Swiss Confederation (Switzerland)

Conjuncto Felix   Fortunate in his connections (Solms).

Conservator Urbis Suae   Saviour of his city (Rome, 4th century).

Consilio et Aequitate   With deliberation and justice (Fulda).

Consilio et Virtutis   With deliberation and valour (Hesse-Cassel).

Constanter et Sincere   Steadfastly and sincerely (Lautern).

Crescite et Multiplicamini   Increase and multiply (Maryland).

Cristiana Religio   Christian religion (Germany, 11th century).

Crux Benedicat   May the cross bless you (Oldenburg).

Cuius Cruore Sanati Sumus   By His sacrifice are we healed (Reggio).

Cultores Sui Deus Protegit   God protects His followers (England, Charles I).

Cum Deo et Die (Jure)   With God and the day (Wurttemberg).

Cum Deo et Jure   With God and the law (Wurttemberg).

Cum Deo et Labore   With God and work (Wittgenstein).

Cum His Qui Orderant Pacem Eram Pacificus   With those who order peace I was peaceful (Zug).

Curie Bonthon to so Doulo   Protect his servant, o Lord (Byzantine Empire).

Custos Regni Deus   God is the guardian of the kingdom (Naples and Sicily).

Da Gloriam Deo et Eius Genitrici Marie   Give glory to God and His mother Mary (Wurttemberg).

Da Mihi Virtutem Contra Hostes Tuos   Give me valour against mine enemies (Netherlands, Charles V).

Dat Wort is Fleis Gworden   The word is made flesh (Muster).

Date Caesaris Caesari et Quae Sunt Dei Deo   Render unto Caesar the things that are Caesar's and unto God the things that are God's (Stralsund).

De Oficina . . .   From the mint of . . . (France, medieval).

Decreto Reipublicae Nexu Confoederationis Iunctae Die V Xbris MDCCXCII Stanislao Augusto Regnante   By decree of the state in conjunction with the joint federation on the fifth day of December 1792, Stanislaus Augustus ruling (Poland).

Decus et Tutamen   An ornament and a safeguard (Britain, pound).

Deducet Nos Mirabiliter Dextera Tua   Thy right hand will guide us miraculously (Savoy).

Denarium Terrae Mariae   Penny of Maryland (Maryland).

Deo Conservatori Pacis   To God, preserver of peace (Brandenburg-Ansbach).

Deo OM Auspice Suaviter et Fortiter sed Luste nec Sibi sed Suis   Under the auspices of God, greatest and best, pleasantly and bravely but justly, not for himself but for his people (Speyer).

Deo Patriae et Subditio   For God, fatherland and neighbourhood (Mainz).

Der Recht Glaubt In Ewig Lebt   Who believes in right will live in eternity (Linange-Westerburg).

Der Rhein ist Deutschlands Strom Nicht Deutschlands Grenze   The Rhine is Germany's River not Germany's Frontier.

Deum Solum Adorabis   You will venerate God alone (Hesse).

Deus Constituit Regna   God establishes kingdoms (Ni jmegen).

Deus Dat Qui Vult   God gives to him who wishes (Hanau-Munzenberg).

Deus et Dominus   God and Lord (Rome, 3rd century).

Deus in Adiutorium Meum Intende   God stretch out in my assistance (France).

Deus Providebit   God will provide (Lowenstein-Wertheim-Virneburg).

Deus Refugium Meum   God is my refuge (Cleve).

Deus Solatium Meum   God is my comfort (Sweden).

Dextera Domini Exaltavit Me   The right hand of God has raised me up (Modena, Spain).

Dextra Dei Exalta Me   The right hand of God exalts me (Denmark).

Dieu et Mon Droit   God and my right (Britain, George IV).

Dilexit Dns Andream   The Lord delights in St Andrew (Holstein).

Dilexit Dominus Decorem Iustitiae   The Lord is pleased with the beauty of justice (Unterwalden).

Dirige Deus Gressus Meos   O God, direct my steps (Tuscany, Britain, Una £5).

Discerne Causam Meam   Distinguish my cause (Savoy).

Divina Benedictiae et Caesarea Iustitia   Sacrifice of blessings and imperial justice (Coblenz).

Dn Ihs Chs Rex Regnantium   Lord Jesus Christ, King of Kings (Rome, Justinian II).

Dns Ptetor Ms Z Lib'ator Ms   The Lord is my protector and liberator (Scotland, David II).

Dominabitur Gentium et Ipse   He himself will also be lord of the nations (Austrian Netherlands).

Domine Conserva Nos in Pace   O Lord preserve us in peace (Basle, Mulhausen).

Domine Elegisti Lilium Tibi   O Lord Thou hast chosen the lily for Thyself (France, Louis XIV).

Domine ne in Furore Tuo Arguas Me   O Lord rebuke me not in Thine anger (England, Edward III).

Domine Probasti Me et Congnovisti Me   O Lord Thou hast tested me and recognised me (Mantua).

Domini est Regnum   The Kingdom is the Lord's (Austrian Netherlands).

Dominus Deus Omnipotens Rex   Lord God, almighty King (Viking coins).

Dominus Mihi Adiutor   The Lord is my helper (Spanish Netherlands).

Dominus Providebit   The Lord will provide (Berne).

Dominus Spes Populi Sui   The Lord is the hope of his people (Lucerne).

Donum Dei ex Fodinis Vilmariens   A gift of God from the Vilmar mines (Coblenz).

Duce Deo Fide et Justicia   By faith and justice lead us to God (Ragusa).

Dum Praemor Amplior   I increase while I die prematurely (Savoy).

Dum Spiro Spero   While I live, I hope (Pontefract siege coins).

Dum Totum Compleat Orbem   Until it fills the world (France, Henri II).

Dura Pati Virtus   Valour endures hardships (Saxe-Lauenburg).

Durae Necessitatis   Through force of necessity (Bommel siege, 1599).

Durum Telum Necessitas   Hardship is a weapon of necessity (Minden).

Dux et Gubernatores Reip Genu   Duke and governors of the republic of Genoa (Genoa).

E Pluribus Unum   One out of more (USA).

Eccl S. Barbarae Patronae Fodin Kuttenbergensium Duo Flor Arg Puri   The church of St Barbara, patron of the Kuttensberg mines, two florins of pure silver (Hungary).

Een en Ondelbaer Sterk   One and indivisible (Batavian Republic).

Eendracht Mag Macht   Unity makes strength (Belgium, South African Republic).

Einigkeit Recht und Freiheit   Union, right and freedom (Germany).

Electorus Saxoniae Administrator   Elector and administrator of Saxony (Saxony).

Elimosina Alms (France, Pepin).

Ep Fris & Ratisb Ad Prum Pp Coad Aug Bishop of Freising and Regensburg, administrator of Pruem, prince-provost, co-adjutant bishop of Augsburg (Trier).

Equa Libertas Deo Gratia Frat Pax in Virtute Tua et in Domino Confido I believe in equal liberty by the grace of God, brotherly love in Thy valour and in the Lord (Burgundy).

Equitas Iudicia Tua Dom Equity and Thy judgments O Lord (Gelderland).

Espoir Me Conforte Hope comforts me (Mansfeld).

Espreuve Faicto Par Lexpres Commandement du Roy Proof made by the express commandment of the King (France, piedforts).

Et in Minimis Integer Faithful even in the smallest things (Olmutz).

Ex Auro Argentes Resurgit From gold it arises, silver again (Sicily).

Ex Auro Sinico From Chinese gold (Denmark).

Ex Flammis Orior I arise from the flames (Hohenlohe-Neuenstein-Ohringen).

Ex Fodinis Bipontio Seelbergensibus From the Seelberg mines of Zweibrucken (Pfalz-Birkenfeld).

Ex Metallo Novo From new metal (Spain).

Ex Uno Omnis Nostra Salus From one is all our salvation (Eichstadt, Mulhouse).

Ex Vasis Argent Cleri Mogunt Pro Aris et Focis From the silver vessels of the clergy of Mainz for altars and for hearths (Mainz).

Ex Visceribus Fodinse Bieber From the bowels of the Bieber mine (Hanau-Munzenberg).

Exaltabitur in Gloria He shall be exalted in glory (England, quarter nobles).

Exemplum Probati Numismatis An example of a proof coin (France, Louis XIII piedforts).

Exemtae Eccle Passau Episc et SRI Princ Prince Bishop of the freed church of Passau, prince of the Holy Roman Empire (Passau).

Expectate Veni Come, o expected one (Roman Britain, Carausius).

Extremum Subidium Campen Kampen under extreme siege (Kampen, 1578).

Exurgat Deus et Dissipentur Inimici Eius Let God arise and let His enemies be scattered (England, James I).

Faciam Eos in Gentem Unam I will make them one nation (England, unites and laurels).

Faith and Truth I will Bear unto You (UK £5, 1993).

Fata Consiliis Potiora The fates are more powerful than councils (Hesse-Cassel).

Fata Viam Invenient The fates will find a way (Gelderland).

Fecit Potentiam in Brachio Suo He put power in your forearm (Lorraine).

Fecunditas Fertility (Naples and Sicily).

Fel Temp Reparatio The restoration of lucky times (Rome, AD 348).

Felicitas Perpetua Everlasting good fortune (Rome, Constantius II).

Felix coniunctio Happy Union (Brandenburg-Ansbach).

Fiat Misericordia Tua Dne Let Thy mercy be O Lord (Gelderland).

Fiat Voluntas Domini Perpetuo Let the goodwill of the Lord last for ever (Fulda).

Fidei Defensor Defender of the Faith (Britain).

Fidelitate et Fortitudine With fidelity and fortitude (Batthanyi).

Fideliter et Constanter Faithfully and steadfastly (Saxe-Coburg-Gotha).

Fidem Servando Patriam Tuendo By keeping faith and protecting the fatherland (Savoy).

Filius Augustorum Son of emperors (Rome, 4th century).

Fisci Iudaici Calumnia Sublata The false accusation of the Jewish tax lifted (Rome, Nerva).

Florent Concordia Regna Through harmony kingdoms flourish (England, Charles I and II).

Fortitudo et Laus Mea Dominu Fortitude and my praise in the Lord (Sardinia).

Free Trade to Africa by Act of Parliment (*Sic*) (Gold Coast).

Friedt Ernehrt Unfriedt Verzehrt Peace nourishes, unrest wastes (Brunswick).

Fulgent Sic Littora Rheni Thus shine the banks of the Rhine (Mannheim).

Fundator Pacis Founder of peace (Rome, Severus).

Gaudium Populi Romani The joy of the Roman people (Rome, 4th century).

Gen C Mar VI Dim Col USC & RAMAI Cons & S Conf M General field marshal, colonel of the only dragoon regiment, present privy councillor of both their sacred imperial and royal apostolic majesties, and state conference minister (Batthanyi).

Gerecht und Beharrlich Just and steadfast (Bavaria).

Germ Hun Boh Rex AAD Loth Ven Sal King of Germany, Hungary and Bohemia, Archduke of Austria, Duke of Lorraine, Venice and Salzburg (Austria).

Germ Jero Rex Loth Bar Mag Het Dux King of Germany, Jerusalem, Lorraine and Bar, Grand Duke of Tuscany (Austrian Netherlands).

Germania Voti Compos Germany sharing the vows (Brandenburg-Ansbach).

Gloria ex Amore Patriae Glory from love of country (Denmark).

Gloria in Excelsis Deo Glory to God in the highest (France, Sweden).

Gloria Novi Saeculi The glory of a new century (Rome, Gratian).

God With Us (England, Commonwealth).

Godt Met Ons God with us (Oudewater).

Gottes Freundt der Pfaffen Feindt God's friend, the Pope's enemy (Brunswick, Christian).

Gratia Dei Sum Id Quod Sum   By the grace of God, I am what I am (Navarre).

Gratia Di Rex   By the grace of God, king (France, 8th century).

Gratitudo Concivibus Exemplum Posteritati   Gratitude to fellow Citizens, an example to posterity (Poland).

Gud och Folket   God and the people (Sweden).

Hac Nitimur Hanc Tuemur   With this we strive, this we shall defend (Batavian Republic).

Hac Sub Tutela   Under this protection (Eichstadt).

Haec Sunt Munera Minerae S Antony Eremitae   These are the rewards of the mine of St Antony the hermit (Hildesheim).

Hanc Deus Dedit   God has given this (Pontefract siege coins).

Hanc Tuemur Hac Nitimur   This we defend, by this we strive (Batavian Republic).

Has Nisi Periturus Mihi Adimat Nemo   Let no one remove these (Letters) from me under penalty of death (Commonwealth, edge inscription).

Henricus Rosas Regna Jacobus   Henry (united) the roses, James the kingdoms (England and Scotland, James VI and I).

Herculeo Vincta Nodo   Bound by a Herculean fetter (Savoy).

Herr Nach Deinem Willen   O Lord Thy will be done (Palatinate, Erbach).

Herre Gott Verleich Uns Gnade   Lord God grant us grace (Brunswick).

Hic Est Qui Multum Orat Pro Populo   Here is he who prays a lot for the people (Paderborn).

Hir Steid te Biscop   Here is represented the bishop (Gittelde).

His Ventis Vela Levantur   By these winds the sails are raised up (Hesse-Cassel).

Hispaniarum Infans   Infante of Spain and its dominions (Spain).

Hispaniarum et Ind Rex   King of Spain and the Indies.

Hispaniarum Rex   King of Spain (Spain).

Hoc Signo Victor Eris   With this sign you will be victor (Rome, Vetranio).

Honeste et Decenter   Honestly and decently (Nassau-Idstein).

Honi Soit Qui Mal y Pense   Evil to him who evil thinks (Britain, George III).

Honni Soit Qui Mal y Pense   (Hesse-Cassel).

Hospitalis et S Sepul Hierusal   Hospital and Holy Sepulchre of Jerusalem (Malta).

Hun Boh Gal Rex AA Lo Wi et in Fr Dux   King of Hungary, Bohemia and Galicia, Archduke of Austria, Dalmatia, Lodomeria, Wurzburg and Duke in Franconia (Austria).

Hung Boh Lomb et Ven Gal Lod III Rex Aa   King of Hungary, Bohemia, Lombardo-Venezia, Galicia, Lodomeria and Illyria, Archduke of Austria (Austria).

Ich Dien   I serve (Aberystwyth 2d, UK 2p).

Ich Getrawe Got in Aller Noth   I trust in God in all my needs (Hesse-Marburg).

Ich Habe Nur Ein Vaterland und das Heisst Deutschland   I have only one fatherland and that is called Germany (Germany).

Ielithes Penniae   Penny of Gittelde (Gittelde, 11th century).

Iesus Autem Transiens Per Medium Illorum Ibat   But Jesus, passing through the midst of them, went His way (England, Scotland, Anglo-Gallic).

Iesus Rex Noster et Deus Noster   Jesus is our king and our God (Florence).

Ihs Xs Rex Regnantium   Jesus Christ, King of Kings (Byzantine Empire).

Ihsus Xristus Basileu Baslie   Jesus Christ, King of Kings (Byzantine Empire).

Imago Sanch Regis Illustris Castelle Legionis e Toleto   The image of Sancho the illustrious king of Castile, Leon and Toledo.

In Casus Per Vigil Omnes   In all seasons through vigil (Wertheim).

In Deo Meo Transgrediar Murum   In my God I shall pass through walls (Teschen).

In Deo Spes Mea   In God is my hope (Gelderland).

In Domino Fiducia Nostra   In the Lord is our trust (Iever).

In Equitate Tua Vivificasti Me   In thy equity Thou hast vivified me (Gelderland).

In God We Trust   (USA).

In Hoc Signo Vinces   In this sign shalt thou conquer (Portugal).

In Honore Sci Mavrici Marti   In honour of the martyr St Maurice (St Maurice, 8th century).

In Manibus Domini sortes Meae   In the hands of the Lord are my fates (Mainz siege, 1688–9).

In Memor Vindicatae Libere ac Relig   In memory of the establishment of freedom and religion (Sweden).

In Memoriam Conjunctionis Utriusque Burgraviatus Norice   In memory of the union of both burgraviates in peace (Brandenburg-Ansbach).

In Memorian Connub Feliciaes Inter Princ Her Frider Carol et Dub Sax August Louis Frider Rodas D 28 Nov 1780 Celebrati   In memory of the most happy marriage between the hereditary prince Friedrich Karl and the Duchess of Saxony Augusta Louisa Frederika, celebrated on 28 Nov 1780 (Schwarzburg-Rudolstadt).

In Memorian Felicisssimi Matrimonii   In memory of the most happy marriage (Wied).

In Memoriam Pacis Teschinensis   Commemorating the Treaty of Teschen (Brandenburg-Ansbach).

In Nomine Domini Amen   In the name of the Lord amen (Zaltbommel).

In Omnem Terram Sonus Eorum   In to all the land their shall go sound (Chateau Renault, Papal States).

In Silencio et Spe Fortitudo Mea   In silence and hope is my fortitude (Brandenburg-Kustrin).

In Spe et Silentio Fortitudo Mea   In hope and silence is my fortitude (Vianen).

In Te Domine Confido   In you O Lord I place my trust (Hesse).

In Te Domine Speravi   In You, O Lord, I have hoped (Gurk).

In Terra Pax   Peace in the land (Papacy).

In Via Virtuti Nulla Via   There is no way for virtue on the way. (Veldenz).

Ind Imp, Indiae Imperator, Imperatrix   Emperor (Empress) of India (Britain).

India Tibi Cessit   India has yielded to thee (Portuguese India).

Infestus Infestis   Hostile to the troublesome (Savoy).

Inimicos Eius Induam Confusione   As for his enemies, I shall clothe them in shame (Sardinia, England, Edward VI).

Insignia Capituli Brixensis   The badge of the chapter of Brixen (Brixen).

Isti Sunt Patres Tui Verique Pastores   These are your fathers and true shepherds (Papacy).

Iudicium Melius Posteritatis Erit   Posterity's judgment will be better (Paderborn).

Iure et Tempore   By right and time (Groningen).

Iusques a Sa Plenitude   As far as your plenitude (France, Henri II).

Iuste et Constanter   Justly and constantly (Paderborn).

Iustirt   Adjusted (Hesse-Cassel).

Iustitia et Concordia   Justice and harmony (Zurich).

Iustitia et Mansuetudine   By justice and mildness (Bavaria, Cologne).

Iustitia Regnorum Fundamentum   Justice is the foundation of kingdoms (Austria).

Iustitia Thronum Firmat   Justice strengthens the throne (England, Charles I).

Iustus Non Derelinquitur   The just person is not deserted (Brandenburg-Calenberg).

Iustus Ut Palma Florebit   The just will flourish like the palm (Portugal).

L Mun Planco Rauracorum Illustratori Vetustis-simo   To L Municius Plancus the most ancient and celebrated of the Rauraci (Basle).

Landgr in Cleggov Com in Sulz Dux Crum   Landgrave of Klettgau, count of Sulz, duke of Krumlau (Schwarzburg-Sonderhausen).

Latina Emeri Munita   Latin money of Merida (Suevi).

Lege et Fide   By law and faith (Austria).

Lex Tua Veritas   Thy law is the truth (Tuscany).

Liberta Eguaglianza   Freedom and equality (Venice)

Libertad en la Ley   Freedom within the law (Mexico).

Libertas Carior Auro   Freedom is dearer than gold (St Gall).

Libertas Vita Carior   Freedom is dearer than life (Kulenberg).

Libertas Xpo Firmata   Freedom strengthened by Christ (Genoa).

Liberte, Egalite, Fraternite   Liberty, equality, fraternity (France).

Lucerna Pedibus Meis Verbum Est   Thy word is a lamp unto mine feet (England, Edward VI).

Lumen ad Revelationem Gentium   Light to enlighten the nations (Papacy).

L'Union Fait la Force   The union makes strength (Belgium)

Macula Non Est in Te   There is no sin in Thee (Essen).

Magnus ab Integro Saeculorum Nascitur Ordo   The great order of the centuries is born anew (Bavaria).

Mandavit Dominus Palatie hanc Monetam Fiert   The lord of the Palatine ordained this coin to be made (Balath).

Manibus Ne Laedar Avaris   Lest I be injured by greedy hands (Sweden).

Mar Bran Sac Rom Imp Arcam et Elec Sup Dux Siles   Margrave of Brandenburg, archchamberlain of the Holy Roman Empire and elector, senior duke of Silesia (Prussia).

Maria Mater Domini Xpi   Mary mother of Christ the Lord (Teutonic Knights).

Maria Unxit Pedes Xpisti   Mary washes the feet of Christ (France, Rene d'Anjou).

Mater Castrorum   Mother of fortresses (Rome, Marcus Aurelius).

Matrimonio Conjuncti   Joined in wedlock (Austria).

Me Coniunctio Servat Dum Scinditur Frangor   The relationship serves me while I am being torn to pieces (Lowenstein-Wertheim).

Mediolani Dux   Duke of Milan (Milan).

Mediolani et Man   Duke of Mantua and Milan (Milan).

Memor Ero Tui Iustina Virgo   I shall remember you, o maiden Justina (Venice).

Merces Laborum   Wages of work (Wurzburg).

Mirabilia Fecit   He wrought marvels (Viking coinage).

Misericordia Di Rex   King by the mercy of God (France, Louis II).

Mo Arg Ord Foe Belg D Gel & CZ   Silver coin of the order of the Belgian Federation, duchy of Guelder-land, county of Zutphen (Guelderland).

Moneta Abbatis   Coin of the abbey (German ecclesiastical coins, 13th–14th centuries).

Moneta Argentiae Ord Foed Belgii Holl   Silver coin of the federated union of Belgium and Holland (Batavian Republic).

Mo No Arg Con Foe Belg Pro Hol   New silver coin of the Belgian Federation, province of Holland (Holland).

Mo No Arg Pro Confoe Belg Trai Holl   New silver coin of the confederated Belgian provinces, Utrecht and Holland (Batavian Republic).

Mon Lib Reip Bremens   Coin of the free state of Bremen (Bremen).

Mon Nova Arg Duc Curl Ad Norma Tal Alb   New silver coin of the duchy of Courland, according to the standard of the Albert thaler (Courland).

Mon Nov Castri Imp   New coin of the Imperial free city of . . . (Friedberg).

Moneta Bipont   Coin of Zweibrucken (Pfalz-Birkenfeld-Zweibrucken).

Monet Capit Cathedr Fuld Sede Vacante   Coin of the cathedral chapter of Fulda, the see being vacant (Fulda).

Moneta in Obsidione Tornacensi Cusa   Coin struck during the siege of Tournai (Tournai, 1709).

Moneta Livosesthonica   Coin of Livonia (Estonia).

Moneta Nov Arg Regis Daniae   New silver coin of the king of Denmark (Denmark).

Moneta Nova Ad Norman Conventionis   New coin according to the Convention standard (Orsini-Rosenberg).

Moneta Nova Domini Imperatoris   New coin of the lord emperor (Brunswick, 13th century).

Moneta Nova Lubecensis   New coin of Lubeck.

Moneta Nova Reipublicae Halae Suevicae   New coin of the republic of Hall in Swabia.

Moneta Reipublicae Ratisbonensis   Coin of the republic of Regensburg.

Nach Alt Reichs Schrot und Korn   According to the old empire's grits and grain (Hesse).

Nach dem Conventions Fusse   According to the Convention's basis (German Conventionsthalers).

Nach dem Frankf Schlus   According to the Frankfurt standard (Solms).

Nach dem Schlus der V Staend   According to the standard of the union (Hesse).

Navigare Necesse Est   It is necessary to navigate (Germany).

Nec Aspera Terrent   Nor do difficulties terrify (Brunswick).

Nec Cito Nec Temere   Neither hastily nor rashlly (Cambrai).

Nec Numina Desunt   Nor is the divine will absent (Savoy).

Nec Temere Nec Timide   Neither rashly nor timidly (Danzig, Lippe).

Necessitas Legem Non Habet   Necessity has no law (Magdeburg).

Nemo Me Impune Lacessit   No one touches me with impunity (UK, Scottish pound edge inscription).

Nihil Restat Reliqui   No relic remains (Ypres).

Nil Ultra Aras   Nothing beyond the rocks (Franque-mont).

No Nobis Dne Sed Noi Tuo Da Gloriam   Not to us, o Lord but to Thy name be glory given (France, Francis I).

Nobilissimum Dom Ac Com in Lipp & St   Most noble lord and count in Lippe and Sternberg (Schaumburg-Lippe).

Nomen Domini Turris Fortissima   The name of the Lord is the strongest tower (Frankfurt).

Non Aes Sed Fides   Not bronze but trust (Malta).

Non Est Mortale Quod Opto   What I desire is not mortal. (Mecklenburg).

Non Mihi Sed Populo   Not to me but to the people (Bavaria).

Non Relinquam Vos Orphanos   I shall not leave you as orphans (Papacy).

Non Surrexit Major   None greater has arisen (Genoa, Malta).

Nullum Simulatum Diuturnum Tandem   Nothing that is feigned lasts long (Wittgenstein).

Nummorum Famulus   The servant of the coinage (England, tin halfpence and farthings).

Nunquam Retrorsum   Never backwards (Brunswick-Wolfenbuttel).

O Crux Ave Spes Unica   Hail, o Cross, our only hope (England half-angels, France, Rene d'Anjou).

O Maria Ora Pro Me   O Mary pray for me (Bavaria).

Ob Cives Servatos   On account of the rescued citizens (Rome, Augustus).

Oculi Domini Super Iustos   The eyes of the Lord look down on the just (Neuchatel).

Omnia Auxiliante Maria   Mary helping everything (Schwyz).

Omnia Cum Deo   Everything with God (Reuss-Greiz).

Omnia cum Deo et Nihil Sine Eo   Everthing with God and nothing without Him (Erbach).

Omnis Potestas a Deo Est   All power comes from God (Sweden).

Opp & Carn Dux Comm Rittb SCM Cons Int & Compi Mareschal   Duke of Troppau and Carniola, count of Rietberg, privy councillor of his sacred imperial majesty, field marshal (Liechtenstein).

Opp & Carn . . . Aur Velleris Eques   Duke of Troppau . . . knight of the Golden Fleece (Liechtenstein).

Opportune   Conveniently (Savoy).

Optimus Princeps   Best prince (Rome, Trajan).

Opulentia Salerno   Wealthy Salerno (Siculo-Norman kingdom).

Pace et Iustitia   With peace and justice (Spanish Netherlands).

Pacator Orbis   Pacifier of the world (Rome, Aurelian).

Palma Sub Pondere Crescit   The palm grows under its weight (Waldeck).

Pater Noster   Our Father (Flanders, 14th century).

Pater Patriae   Farther of his country (Rome, Caligula).

Patria Si Dreptul Meu   The country and my right (Roumania).

Patrimon Henr Frid Sorte Divisum   The heritage of Heinrich Friedrich divided by lot (Hohenlohe-Langenberg).

Patrimonia Beati Petri   The inheritance of the blessed Peter (Papacy).

Patrona Franconiae Patron of Franconia (Wurzburg).

Pax Aeterna Eternal peace (Rome, Marcus Aurelius).

Pax et Abundantia Peace and plenty (Burgundy, Gelderland).

Pax Missa Per Orbem Peace sent throughout the world (England, Anne).

Pax Petrus Peace Peter (Trier, 10th century).

Pax Praevalet Armis May peace prevail by force of arms (Mainz).

Pax Quaeritur Bello Peace is sought by war (Commonwealth, Cromwell).

Pecunia Totum Circumit Orbem Money goes round the whole world (Brazil).

Per Aspera Ad Astra Through difficulties to the stars (Mecklenburg-Schwerin).

Per Angusta ad Augusta Through precarious times to the majestic (Solms-Roedelheim, a pun on the name of the ruler Johan August).

Per Crucem Tuam Salva Nos Christe Redemptor By Thy cross save us, O Christ our Redeemer (England, angels).

Per Crucem Tuam Salva Nos Xpe Redemt By Thy cross save us, O Christ our Redeemer (Portugal, 15th century).

Perdam Babillonis Nomen May the name of Babylon perish (Naples).

Perennitati Iustissimi Regis For the duration of the most just king (France, Louis XIII).

Perennitati Principis Galliae Restitutionis For the duration of the restoration of the prince of the Gauls (France, Henri IV).

Perfer et Obdura Bruxella Carry on and stick it out, Brussels (Brussels siege, 1579–80).

Perpetuus in Nemet Vivar Hereditary count in Nemt-Ujvar (Batthanyi).

Pietate et Constantia By piety and constancy (Fulda).

Pietate et Iustitia By piety and justice (Denmark).

Plebei Urbanae Frumento Constituto Free distribu-tion of grain to the urban working-class established (Rome, Nerva).

Pleidio Wyf Im Gwlad True am I to my country (UK, Welsh pound edge inscription).

Plus Ultra Beyond (the Pillars of Hercules) (Spanish America).

Point du Couronne sans Peine Point of the crown without penalty (Coburg).

Pons Civit Castellana The bridge of the town of Castellana (Papacy).

Populus et Senatus Bonon The people and senate of Bologna (Bologna).

Post Mortem Patris Pro Filio For the son after his father's death (Pontefract siege coins).

Post Tenebras Lux After darkness light (Geneva).

Post Tenebras Spero Lucem After darkness I hope for light (Geneva).

Posui Deum Adiutorem Meum I have made God my helper (England, Ireland, 1351–1603).

Praesidium et Decus Protection and ornament (Bologna).

Prima Sedes Galliarum First see of the Gauls (Lyon).

Primitiae Fodin Kuttenb ab Aerari Iterum Susceptarum First results dug from the Kuttenberg mines in a renewed undertaking (Austria).

Princps Iuventutis Prince of youth (Roman Empire).

Pro Defensione Urbis et Patriae For the defence of city and country (France, Louis XIV).

Pro Deo et Patria For God and the fatherland (Fulda).

Pro Deo et Populo For God and the people (Bavaria).

Pro Ecclesia et Pro Patria For the church and the fatherland (Constance).

Pro Fausio PP Reitur VS For happy returns of the princes of the Two Sicilies (Naples and Sicily).

Pro Lege et Grege For law and the flock (Fulda).

Pro maximo Dei Gloria et Bono Publico For the greatest glory of God and the good of the people (Wurttemberg).

Pro Patria For the fatherland (Wurzburg).

Propitio Deo Secura Ago With God's favour I lead a secure life. (Saxe-Lauenburg).

Protector Literis Literae Nummis Corona et Salus A protection to the letters (on the face of the coin), the letters (on the edge) are a garland and a safeguard to the coinage (Commonwealth, Cromwell broad).

Protege Virgo Pisas Protect Pisa, O Virgin (Pisa).

Provide et Constanter Wisely and firmly (Wurttem-berg).

Providentia et Pactis Through foresight and pacts (Brandenburg-Ansbach).

Providentia Optimi Principis With the foresight of the best prince (Naples and Sicily).

Proxima Fisica Finis Nearest to natural end (Orciano).

Proxima Soli Nearest to the sun (Modena).

Pulcra Virtutis Imago The beautiful image of virtue (Genoa).

Pupillum et Viduam Suscipiat May he support the orphan and the widow (Savoy).

Quae Deus Conjunxit Nemo Separet What God hath joined let no man put asunder (England, James I).

Quem Quadragesies et Semel Patriae Natum Esse Gratulamur Whom we congratulate for the forty-first time for being born for the fatherland (Lippe-Detmold).

Qui Dat Pauperi Non Indigebit Who gives to the poor will never be in need (Munster).

Quid Non Cogit Necessitas To what does Necessity not drive. (Ypres).

Quin Matrimonii Lustrum Celebrant They celebrate their silver wedding (Austria, 1879).

Quocunque Gesseris (Jeceris) Stabit Whichever way you throw it it will stand (Isle of Man).

Quod Deus Vult Hoc Semper Fit   What God wishes always occurs. (Saxe-Weimar).

Reconduntur non Retonduntur   They are laid up in store, not thundered back (Savoy).

Recta Tueri   Defend the right (Austria).

Recte Constanter et Fortiter   Rightly, constantly and bravely (Bavaria).

Recte Faciendo Neminem Timeas   May you fear no one in doing right. (Solms-Laubach).

Rector Orbis   Ruler of the world (Rome, Didius Julianus).

Rectus et Immotus   Right and immovable (Hesse).

Redde Cuique Quod Suum Est   Render to each that which is his own (England, Henry VIII).

Redeunt antiqui Gaudia Moris   There return the joys of ancient custom (Regensburg).

Reg Pr Pol et Lith Saxon Dux   Royal prince of Poland and Lithuania and duke of Saxony (Trier).

Regia Boruss Societas Asiat Embdae   Royal Prussian Asiatic Society of Emden (Prussia).

Regier Mich Her Nach Deinen Wort   Govern me here according to Thy word (Palatinate).

Regnans Capitulum Ecclesiae Cathedralis Ratisbonensis Sede Vacante   Administering the chapter of the cathedral church at Regensburg, the see being vacant (Regensburg).

Regni Utr Sic et Hier   Of the kingdom of the Two Sicilies and of Jerusalem (Naples and Sicily).

Religio Protestantium Leges Angliae Libertas Parliamenti   The religion of the Protestants, the laws of England and the freedom of Parliament (England, Royalists, 1642).

Relinquo Vos Liberos ab Utroque Homine   I leave you as children of each man (San Marino).

Restauracao da Independencia   Restoration of inde-pendence (Portugal, 1990).

Restitutor Exercitus   Restorer of the army (Rome, Aurelian).

Restitutor Galliarum   Restorer of the Gauls (Rome, Gallienus).

Restitutor Generis Humani   Restorer of mankind (Rome, Valerian).

Restitutor Libertatis   Restorer of freedom (Rome, Constantine).

Restitutor Orbis   Restorer of the world (Rome, Valerian).

Restitutor Orientis   Restorer of the east (Rome, Valerian).

Restitutor Saeculi   Restorer of the century (Rome, Valerian).

Restitutor Urbis   Restorer of the city (Rome, Severus).

Rosa Americana Utile Dulci   The American rose, useful and sweet (American colonies).

Rosa Sine Spina   A rose without a thorn (England, Tudor coins).

Rutilans Rosa Sine Spina   A dazzling rose without a thorn (England, Tudor gold coins).

S Annae Fundgruben Ausb Tha in N Oe   Mining thaler of the St Anne mine in Lower Austria (Austria).

S Ap S Leg Nat Germ Primas   Legate of the Holy Apostolic See, born Primate of Germany (Salzburg).

S Carolus Magnus Fundator   Charlemagne founder (Munster).

S. Gertrudis Virgo Prudens Niviella   St Gertrude the wise virgin of Nivelles (Nivelles).

SI Aul Reg Her & P Ge H Post Mag   General hereditary postmaster, supreme of the imperial court of the hereditary kingdom and provinces (Paar).

S. Ian Bapt F. Zachari   St John the Baptist, son of Zachary (Florence).

S. Kilianus Cum Sociis Francorum Apostoli   St Kilian and his companions, apostles to the Franks (Wurzburg).

S. Lambertus Patronus Leodiensis   St Lambert, patron of Liege (Liege).

Sac Nupt Celeb Berol   For the holy matrimony celebrated at Berlin (Brandenburg-Ansbach).

Sac Rom Imp   Holy Roman Empire (German states).

Sac Rom Imp Provisor Iterum   Administrator of the Holy Roman Empire for the second time (Saxony).

Salus Generis Humani   Safety of mankind (Rome, Vindex).

Salus Patriae   Safety of the fatherland (Italy).

Salus Populi   The safety of the people (Spain).

Salus Provinciarum   Safety of the provinces (Rome, Postumus).

Salus Publica Salus Mea   Public safety is my safety (Sweden).

Salus Reipublicae   The safety of the republic (Rome, Theodosius II).

Salus Reipublicae Suprema Lex   The safety of the republic is the supreme law (Poland).

Salvam Fac Rempublicam Tuam   Make your state safe (San Marino).

Sanctus Iohannes Innoce   St John the harmless (Gandersheim).

Sans Changer   Without changing (Isle of Man).

Sans Eclat   Without pomp (Bouchain siege, 1711).

Sapiente Diffidentia   Wise distrust (Teschen).

Scutum Fidei Proteget Eum / Eam   The shield of faith shall protect him / her (England, Edward VI and Elizabeth I).

Secundum Voluntatem Tuam Domine   Your favourable will o Lord (Hesse).

Securitati Publicae   For the public safety (Brandenburg-Ansbach).

Sede Vacante   The see being vacant (Papal states, Vatican and ecclesiastical coinage).

Sena Vetus Alpha et W Principum et Finis   Old Siena alpha and omega, the beginning and the end (Siena).

Senatus Populus QR   Senate and people of Rome (Rome, 1188).

Si Deus Nobiscum Quis Contra Nos   If God is with us who can oppose us (Hesse).

Si Deus Pro Nobis Quis Contra Nos   If God is for us who can oppose us (Roemhild).

Sieh Deine Seeligkeit Steht Fest Ins Vaters Liebe   Behold thy salvation stands surely in thy Father's love (Gotha).

Signis Receptis   When the standards had been recovered (Rome, Augustus).

Signum Crucis   The sign of the cross (Groningen).

Sincere et Constanter   Truthfully and steadfastly (Hesse-Darmstadt).

Sit Nomen Domini Benedictum   Blessed be the name of the Lord (Burgundy, Strasbourg).

St T X Adiuto Reg Iste Domba   Let it be to you, o Christ, the assistant to the king of Dombes (Dombes).

Sit Tibi Xpe Dat q'tu Regis Iste Ducat   May this duchy which Thou rulest be given to Thee, O Christ (Venice, ducat).

Sit Unio Haec Perennis   May this union last for ever (Hohenlohe-Langenberg).

Sola Bona Quae Honesta   The only good things are those which are honest (Brunswick).

Sola Facta Deum Sequor   Through deeds alone I strive to follow God (Milan).

Soli Deo Honor et Gloria   To God alone be honour and glory (Nassau).

Soli Reduci   To him, the only one restored (Naples and Sicily).

Solius Virtutis Flos Perpetuus   The flower of Virtue alone is perpetual (Strasbourg).

Spes Confisa Deo Nunquam Confusa Recedit   Hope entrusted in God never retreats in a disorderly fashion (Lippe).

Spes Nr Deus   God is our hope (Oudenarde siege, 1582).

Spes Rei Publicae   The hope of the republic (Rome, Valens).

Strena ex Argyrocopeo Vallis S Christoph   A New Year's gift from the silver-bearing valley of St Christopher (Wurttemberg, 1625).

Sub His Secura Spes Clupeus Omnibus in Te Sperantibus   Under these hope is safe, a shield for all who reside hope in Thee (Bavaria).

Sub Pondere   Under weight (Fulda).

Sub Protectione Caesarea   Under imperial protection (Soragna).

Sub Tuum Praesidium Confug   We flee to Thy protection (Salzburg).

Sub Umbra Alarum Tuarum   Under the shadow of Thy wings (Iever, Scotland, James V).

Subditorum Salus Felicitas Summa   The safety of the subjects is the highest happiness (Lubeck).

Sufficit Mihi Gratia Tua Domine   Sufficient to me is Thy grace, o Lord (Ploen).

Supra Firmam Petram   Upon a firm rock (Papacy).

Susceptor Noster Deus   God is our defence (Tuscany).

Sydera Favent Industriae   The stars favour industry (Furstenberg).

Sylvarum Culturae Praemium   Prize for the culture of the forest (Brandenburg-Ansbach).

Tali Dicata Signo Mens Fluctuari Nequit   Consecrated by such a sign the mind cannot waver (England, Henry VIII George noble).

Tandem Bona Caus Triumphat   A good cause eventually triumphs (Dillenburg).

Tandem Fortuna Obstetrice   With good luck ultimately as the midwife (Wittgenstein).

Te Stante Virebo   With you at my side I shall be strong (Moravia).

Tene Mensuram et Respice Finem   Hold the measure and look to the end (Burgundy).

Tert Ducat Secular   Tercentenary of the duchy (Wurttemberg).

Thu Recht Schev Niemand   Go with right and fear no one (Saxe-Lauenburg).

Tibi Laus et Gloria   To Thee be praise and glory (Venice).

Timor Domini Fons Vitae   The fear of the Lord is a fountain of life (England, Edward VI shillings).

Tout Avec Dieu   Everything with God (Brunswick, 1626).

Traiectum ad Mosam   The crossing of the Maas (Maastricht).

Transvolat Nubila Virtus   Marriageable virtue soon flies past (Grueyeres).

Travail, Famille, Patrie   Work, family, country (Vichy France).

Triumphator Gent Barb   Victor over the barbarian people (Byzantine Empire, Arcadius).

Tueatur Unita Deus   May God guard these united (Kingdoms) (England, James I; Britain, 1847).

Turck Blegert Wien   Vienna besieged by the Turks (Vienna, 1531).

Tut Mar Gab Pr Vid de Lobk Nat Pr Sab Car et Aug Pr de Lobk   Regency of Maria Gabriela, widow of the prince of Lobkowitz, born princess of Savoy-Carignan, and August prince of Lobkowitz (Lobkowitz).

Tutela Italiae   The guardianship of Italy (Rome, Nerva).

Ubi Vult Spirat   He breathes where he will (Papacy).

Ubique Pax   Peace everywhere (Rome, Gallienus).

Union et Force   Union and strength (France).

Urbe Obsessa   The city under siege (Maastricht).

Urbem Virgo Tuam Serva   Protects thy city o virgin (Mary) (Strasbourg).

USC & RAM Cons Int Gen C Mar & Nob Praet H Turmae Capit   Privy councillor of both their holy imperial and royal apostolic majesties, general field marshal and captain of the noble praetorian Hungarian squadrons (Eszterhazy).

Veni Luumen Cordium   Come light of hearts (Vatican).

Veni Sancte Spiritus   Come Holy Ghost (Vatican).

Verbum Domini Manet in Aeternum   The word of the Lord abides forever (Hesse-Darmstadt, Veldenz).

Veritas Lex Tua   The truth is your law (Salzburg).
Veritas Temporis Filia   Truth is the daughter of time (England and Ireland, Mary Tudor).
Veritate et Labore   By truth and work (Wittgenstein).
Veritate et Iustitia   By truth and justice (German states).
Victoria Principum   The victory of princes (Ostrogoths).
Videant Pauperes et Laetentur   Let the poor see and rejoice (Tuscany).
Virgo Maria Protege Civitatem Savonae   Virgin Mary Protect the city of Savona (Savona).
Viribus Unitis   With united strength (Austria).
Virtute et Fidelitate   By virtue and faithfulness (Hesse-Cassel).
Virtute et Prudentia   With virtue and prudence (Auersperg).
Virtute Viam Dimetiar   I shall mark the way with valour (Waldeck).
Virtutis Gloria Merces   Glory is the reward of valour (Holstein-Gottorp).
Vis Unita Concordia Fratrum Fortior   United power is the stronger harmony of brothers (Mansfeld).

Visitavit Nos Oriens ex Alto   He has visited us arising on high (Luneburg).
Vivit Post Funera   He lives after death (Bremen).
Vota Optata Romae Fel   Vows taken for the luck of Rome (Rome, Maxentius).
Vox de Throno   A voice from the throne (Papacy).
Was Got Beschert Bleibet Unerwert   What God hath endowed leave undisturbed
Wider macht und List Mein Fels Gott Ist   Against might and trickery God is my rock (Hesse-Cassel).
Xpc Vincit Xpc Regnat   Christ conquers, Christ reigns (Scotland, Spain).
Xpc Vivet Xpc Regnat Xpc Impat   Christ lives, Christ reigns, Christ commands (Cambrai).
Xpe Resurescit   Christ lives again (Venice).
Xpistiana Religio   Christian religion (Carolingian Empire).
Xps Ihs Elegit me Regem Populo   Jesus Christ chose me as king to the people (Norway).
Zelator Fidei Usque ad Montem   An upholder of the faith through and through (Portugal).
Zum Besten des Vaterlands   To the best of the fatherland (Bamberg).

ABBREVIATIONS COMMONLY USED TO DENOTE METALLIC COMPOSITION	
Cu	Copper
Cu/Steel	Copper plated Steel
Ag/Cu	Silver plated copper
Ae	Bronze
Cu-Ni	Cupro-Nickel
Ni-Ag	Nickel Silver (note-does not contain silver)
Brass/Cu-Ni	Brass outer, Cupro-Nickel inner
Ni-Brass	Nickel-Brass
Ag	Silver
Au/Ag	Gold plated silver
Au	Gold
Pl	Platinum

CARE of coins

There is no point in going to a great deal of trouble and expense in selecting the best coins you can afford, only to let them deteriorate in value by neglect and mishandling. Unless you give some thought to the proper care of your coins, your collection is unlikely to make a profit for you if and when you come to sell it. Housing your coins is the biggest problem of all, so it is important to give a lot of attention to this.

Storage

The ideal, but admittedly the most expensive, method is the coin cabinet, constructed of air-dried mahogany, walnut or rosewood *(never oak, cedar or any highly resinous timber likely to cause chemical tarnish)*. These cabinets have banks of shallow drawers containing trays made of the same wood, with half-drilled holes of various sizes to accommodate the different denominations of coins. Such cabinets are handsome pieces of furniture but, being largely handmade, tend to be rather expensive. Occasionally good specimens can be picked up in secondhand furniture shops, or at the dispersal of house contents by auction, but the best bet is still to purchase a new cabinet, tailored to your own requirements. Only plantation-grown Honduras mahogany is used to resolve any environmental concerns.

Peter Nichols Cabinets of East Sussex (telephone 01424 436682, www.coincabinets.com) are a specialist manufacturer of display and storage systems who have also been producing coin and medal cabinets to suit every need for more than a quarter of a century. They can produce a cabinet to fit into a wall safe or some other form of security box. They can match existing work, and thus replicate cabinets which you may already be using, or even produce designs to suit your specific requirements. A nice touch is that all the products in the Nichols repertoire take their names from Elizabethan mint-marks.

Nichols produces a wide range of cabinets from the seven-tray Pheon all the way up to the massive 40-tray specials designed for the British Museum. All cabinets are fitted with double doors. Prices start at around £80 and go up to about £350 for the thirty-tray Coronet. They are not cheap, but

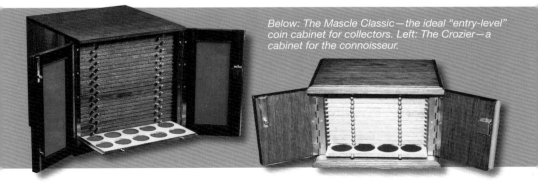

Below: The Mascle Classic—the ideal "entry-level" coin cabinet for collectors. Left: The Crozier—a cabinet for the connoisseur.

The Diplomat, Abafil's plush flagship of the portable Diplomat range.

you have the satisfaction of acquiring exquisite examples of the cabinet maker's craft.

Spink & Son are distributors for the Abafil series manufactured in Milan. These cases are of stout wooden construction covered with simulated leather and lined with red plush. The trays to fit the cases are also manufactured in wood lined with plush although a less expensive lined plastic alternative is also available. The Diplomat range is designed primarily for secure transportation, but the Mini-diplomat makes a good static cabinet, and can take up to three trays holding a maximum of 241 coins, while the Custom case holds 14 de luxe or 20 standard trays and will house up to 1,500 coins. Even cheaper is the Mignon case holding up to 105 coins, ideally suited for carrying in a briefcase or travel bag.

An excellent compromise is provided by a number of firms who manufacture coin trays in durable, felt-lined materials with shallow compartments to suit the various sizes of coins. Most of these trays interlock so that they build up into a cabinet of the desired size, and there are also versions designed as carrying cases, which are ideal for transporting coins.

The popular and extensive Lighthouse range is available from The Duncannon Partnership, 4 Beaufort Road, Reigate, RH2 9DJ (telephone 01737 244222, www.duncannon. co.uk) or Token Publishing Ltd (telephone 01404 44167, www.tokenpublishing.com). This range includes a wide variety of cases and albums for the general

Adding on to the stacking Lindner range is easy.

collector in basic or de luxe styles as required, as well as printed albums for the specialist. Their cases, including the popular aluminium range, are manufactured to the highest standards, lined with blue plush which displays any coin to its best advantage. The red-lined single trays come in deep or standard size and make an ideal cabinet when stacked together or housed in their attractive aluminium case, which is available separately. The trays themselves come with a variety of compartments for every size of coin. Their complete range can be viewed on-line.

The extensive Lindner range is supplied in the UK by Prinze Publications of 3A Hayle Industrial Park, Hayle, Cornwall TR27 5JR (telephone 01736 751914, www.prinz.co.uk or from Token Publishing Ltd telephone 01404 44167, www.tokenpublishing. com). Well-known for their wide range of philatelic and numismatic accessories, but these include a full array of coin boxes, capsules, carrying cases and trays . The basic Lindner coin box is, in fact, a shallow tray available in a standard version or a smoked glass version. These trays have a crystal clear frame, red felt inserts and holes for various diameters of coins and medals. A novel feature of these trays is the rounded insert which facilitates the removal of coins from their spaces with the minimum of handling. These boxes are designed in such a manner that they interlock and can be built up into banks of trays, each fitted with a draw-handle and sliding in and out easily. Various types of chemically inert plastic capsules and envelopes have been designed for use in combination with plain shallow trays, without holes drilled. Lindner also manufacture a range of luxury cases lined in velvet and Atlas silk with padded covers and gold embossing on the spines, producing a most tasteful and elegant appearance.

Safe Albums of 16 Falcon Business Park, 38 Ivanhoe Road, Finchampstead, Berkshire RG40 4QQ (telephone 0118 932 8976, www. safealbums.co.uk) are the UK agents for the German Stapel-Element, a drawer-stacking system with clear plasticiser-free trays that fit into standard bookshelves. The sliding coin compartments, lined with blue velvet, can be angled for display to best advantage. Stackable drawers can be built up to any height desired. A wide range of drawer sizes is available, with compartments suitable for the smallest coins right up to four-compartment trays designed for

Safe's cabinet combines elegance with security.

very large artefacts such as card-cases or cigarette cases. The Mobel-Element cabinet is a superb specialised cabinet constructed of the finest timber with a steel frame and steel grip bars which can be securely locked. It thus combines elegance with security and is the ideal medium for the most valuable coins and medals.

There are also various storage systems, such as Coindex, which operate on the principle of narrow drawers in which the coins are stored in envelopes of chemically-inert plastic. A strip across the top holds a little slip giving a brief description, catalogue number and the price of each coin.

The Sydney Museum in Australia, for example, keeps its coins in manila envelopes stored in plastic lunch-boxes which seemed to do the job pretty well!

Coin Albums

When coin collecting became a popular hobby in the 1960s, several firms marketed ranges of coin albums. They had clear plastic sleeves divided into tiny compartments of various sizes and had the merit of being cheap and taking up little room on a bookshelf.

They had several drawbacks, however, not the least being the tendency of the pages to sag with the weight of the coins, or even, in extreme cases, to pull away from the pegs or rings holding them on to the spine. They required very careful handling as the coins could easily fall out of the top row as the pages were turned. The more expensive albums had little flaps that folded over the top of the coin to overcome this problem.

Arguably the worst aspect of these albums was the use of polyvinyl chloride (PVC) in the construction of the sleeves. Collectors soon discovered to their horror that this reacted chemically with their coins, especially those made of silver, causing a rather disgusting yellow slime to adhere to the coins' surface. I shudder to think how many fine collections were ruined as a result, or of the countless coins that required highly expert treatment in a bid to restore them to as near the original condition as possible.

Fortunately the lesson has been learned and the coin albums now on the market are quite safe. Lighthouse and Lindner offer a wide range of albums designed to house coins, medals or banknotes. The old problem about sagging pages is overcome by the use of a multi-ring binding welded to a very stout spine, while the sleeves contain neither Styrol nor PVC and will not affect any metals at all. In addition to pages with pockets of uniform size, the Karat range of albums operates on a slide principle which enables the user to insert vertical strips of different sizes on the same page, so that the coins of one country or series, or perhaps a thematic

Albums are a convenient way to transport your coins.

display of coins from different countries, can be displayed side by side.

Safe Albums offer a wide range of albums in the Coinholder System and Coin-Combi ranges. These, too, offer the choice of fixed pages with uniform-sized pockets, or interchangeable sliding inserts for different sizes side by side.

Token Publishing Ltd stock a complete and varied range of coin accessories from magnifying glasses to coin albums. To find out more, simply log onto www.tokenpublishing.com or call 01404 44167 for an up-to-date illustrated, colour catalogue.

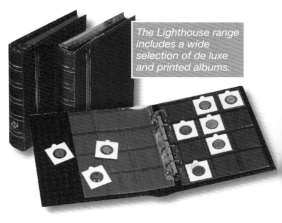

The Lighthouse range includes a wide selection of de luxe and printed albums.

CLEANING *coins*

This is like matrimony—it should not be embarked on lightly. Indeed, the advice given by the magazine *Punch* in regard to marriage is equally sound in this case—don't do it! It is far better to have a dirty coin than an irretrievably damaged one. Every dealer has horror stories of handling coins that previous owners have cleaned, to their detriment. The worst example I ever saw was a display of coins found by a metal detectorist who "improved" his finds by abrading them in the kind of rotary drum used by lapidarists to polish gemstones. If you really must remove the dirt and grease from coins, it is advisable to practise on coins of little value.

Warm water containing a mild household detergent or washing-up liquid will work wonders in removing surface dirt and grease from most coins, but silver is best washed in a weak solution of ammonia and warm water—one part ammonia to ten parts water. Gold coins can be cleaned with diluted citric acid, such as lemon juice. Copper or bronze coins present more of a problem, but patches of verdigris can usually be removed by careful washing in a 20 per cent solution of sodium sesquicarbonate. Wartime coins made of tin, zinc, iron or steel can be cleaned in a 5 per cent solution of caustic soda containing some aluminium or zinc foil or filings, but they must be rinsed afterwards in clean water and carefully dried. Cotton buds are ideal for gently prising dirt out of coin legends and crevices in the designs. Soft brushes (with animal bristles—*never* nylon or other artificial bristles) designed for cleaning silver are most suitable for gently cleaning coins.

Coins recovered from the soil or the sea bed present special problems, due to chemical reaction between the metals and the salts in the earth or sea water. In such cases, the best advice is to take them to the nearest museum and let the professional experts decide on what can or should be done.

Both Lindner and Safe Albums offer a range of coin-cleaning kits and materials suitable for gold, silver, copper and other base alloys respectively. Safe (living up to their name) also provide a stern warning that rubber gloves should be worn and care taken to avoid breathing fumes or getting splashes of liquid in your eyes or on your skin. Obviously, the whole business of cleaning is a matter that should not be entered into without the utmost care and forethought.

POLISHING: A WARNING

If cleaning should only be approached with the greatest trepidation, polishing is definitely *out!* Beginners sometimes fall into the appalling error of thinking that a smart rub with metal polish might improve the appearance of their coins. Short of actually punching a hole through it, there can hardly be a more destructive act. Polishing a coin may improve its superficial appearance for a few days, but such abrasive action will destroy the patina and reduce the fineness of the high points of the surface.

Even if a coin is only polished once, it will never be quite the same again, and an expert can tell this a mile off.

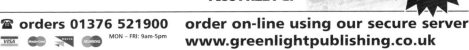

CELTIC *coinage of Britain*

Celtic coins were the first coins made in Britain. They were issued for a century and a half before the Roman invasion, and possibly a little later in some areas. They were issued by 11 tribal groups or administrative authorities situated southeast of a line from the Humber to the Severn. In this short article Celtic specialist CHRIS RUDD introduces this increasingly popular area.

The earliest coins were uninscribed and often abstract in design. Later ones carried the names of local leaders and tribal centres, and in the southeast became increasingly Roman in style, sometimes copying classical images quite closely.

Most Celtic coins were struck between two dies on flans of gold, silver, billion and bronze. Some were cast in strip moulds in tin-rich bronze alloy called "potin".

Because the Celts wrote no books and left no written records of their activities, little is known about the people and places behind their coins. Who made them? When? Where? And why? These are questions that are still largely unanswered, except in the very vaguest terms. Celtic cataloguers talk about gold quarters, silver units and silver minims. But the truth is we don't even know what the Celts themselves called their coins.

British Celtic coins are among the most fascinating ever fashioned and perhaps the least familiar to the average collector because of their rarity. Like the Celts themselves, Celtic coin designs are wild, free flowing, flamboyant and full of fun. Yes, Celtic moneyers had a great sense of humour!

Celtic coins bear a vast variety of gods and goddesses, armed warriors, chariot wheels, hidden faces, decapitated heads, suns, moons, stars, thunderbolts, floral motifs, magic signs and phallic symbols. Plus a menagerie of antelopes, bears, boars, bulls, cocks, crabs, cranes, dogs, dolphins, ducks, eagles, hares, all kinds of horses (some with wings, some with human heads, many with three tails, a few breathing fire), goats, lions, lizards, owls, rams, rats, ravens, snakes, stags, starfish,

worms and wolves. Not to mention dragons, griffins, hippocamps, sphinxes and ram-horned serpents.

Ask any metal detectorist how many Celtic coins he or she has found and you will immediately realise they are rarer than Roman coins in this country—at least a thousand times rarer on average. This is because far fewer Celtic coins were minted, in smaller runs, over a much shorter time span. Though some may have been made as early as 80 BC, the majority of British Celtic coins were struck from 54 BC to AD 43; barely 100 years of production, and most of that seems to have been sporadic.

However, the greater rarity of Celtic coins doesn't mean they are necessarily more costly than other ancient coins: in fact, they are often cheaper. You see, in the coin market, demand determines price.

Method that may have been used for striking Celtic coins (drawing by Simon Pressey).

The more collectors that want a coin, the higher its price.

A recent survey revealed "worldwide there may be no more than 150 regular private collectors of Celtic coins, buying on average one or more coins per month". Whereas there are literally thousands of people collecting the other major series of ancient and medieval coins. That is why Celtic coins are still comparatively less costly than Greek, Anglo-Saxon and English hammered coins. The Celtic market is smaller, though expanding. For example a very fine Celtic gold stater typically costs half the price

of a Greek gold stater or an English gold noble of comparable quality and rarity. The price differential can be even more dramatic at major international auctions. But the disparity is diminishing as more and more collectors are beginning to appreciate the hitherto unrecognised beauty, scarcity and good value of British Celtic coins. So now could be a good time to start collecting Celtic coins, before their prices begin climbing more steeply.

Thirty years ago collecting British Celtic coins was a rich man's hobby and understanding them was the lonely pursuit of a few scholarly

Eleven tribal groups minted coins in late Iron Age Britain, c. 80 BC–AD 45. The boundaries shown here are guesstimates, not actual, and often follow rivers, many of which are still known by their Celtic names.

Silver unit attributed to King Esuprastus of the Eceni, whose death resulted in the revolt of Queen Boudica, AD 60 (drawn four times actual size by Susan White).

numismatists. Today, thanks to the popularity of metal detecting, Celtic coins are more plentiful and almost everyone can afford to collect them. Most ancient coin dealers sell Celtic coins, some for as little as £20 each, and you will always find a few trays of them at every coin fair.

British Celtic coins are also easier to study today, thanks to the publication of some excellent books on the subject. The Celtic collector's bible is *Celtic Coinage of Britain* by Robert D. Van Arsdell (Spink, 1989)—well researched, well written, well illustrated, always quoted in dealers' catalogues, often controversial when dates are discussed and hopefully to be republished soon in a revised edition. For the dedicated Celtic devotee *British Iron Age Coins in the British Museum* by Richard Hobbs (British Museum Press, 1996) is an invaluable companion volume to Van Arsdell—more cautious, less speculative.

By far the best introductory book is *Celtic Coinage in Britain* by Dr Philip de Jersey (Shire Archaeology, 1996) who manages the Celtic Coin Index, a photographic record of over 31,000 British coins at the Institute of Archaeology, Oxford. In plain language Dr Philip de Jersey explains how Celtic coins and the images they carry can reveal information on the political, economic and social life of the Celts. *Celtic Coinage in Britain* contains clear twice-size photos of over a hundred Celtic coins, some of them rarely seen before. It gives the names, addresses and phone numbers of the museums in England, Scotland and Wales with the best and most accessible collections of Celtic coins.

In short, if you want to know more about British Celtic coins, *Celtic Coinage in Britain* is where you start reading and keep reading. This is the best little book ever written about British Celtic coins and and unfortunately is now out of print. How should you start collecting British Celtic coins? First, get a few of the commoner uninscribed types from each of the 11 tribal areas, aiming for the highest grade you can comfortably afford. Then you may wish to get an inscribed coin of each of the main rulers. You would also be well advised to acquire some Gaulish coins at the same time, because many British coins were influenced by Gallic prototypes.

How much do British Celtic coins cost? Very little, considering how scarce they are. Types with legends usually cost more than those without and top quality bronze is frequently more pricey than top quality silver (which may surprise you) because silver is commoner and generally survives better after 2,000 years underground.

Chris Rudd is a well-known dealer who specialises in Celtic coins.

COLLECTING
ancient coins

Ancient coins differ from most other series which are collected in Britain in that every piece has spent the major part of the last two thousand years in the ground. As **JOHN CUMMINGS**, dealer in ancient coins and antiquities explains here, the effect that burial has had on the surface of the coin determines more than anything else the value of a particular piece. With more modern coins, the only things which affect price are rarity and grade. There may be a premium for coins exhibiting particularly fine tone, or with outstanding pedigrees, but an 1887 crown in "extremely fine" condition has virtually the same value as every other piece with the same grade and of the same date. With ancient coins the story is very different.

A large number of different criteria affect the price of an ancient coin. Factors affecting prices can be broken down into several categories:

Condition

The most important factor by far in determining price. Ancient coins were struck by hand and can exhibit striking faults. Value suffers if the coin is struck with the designs off-centre, is weakly struck, or if the flan is irregular in shape. Many of the Celtic tribes issued coins of varying fineness and those made from low quality gold or silver are worth less than similar specimens where the metal quality is better. Conversely, coins on exceptional flans, particularly well struck, or with fine patinas command a premium.

Many ancient coins have suffered during their stay in the ground. It must be borne in mind that the prices given in the price guide are for uncorroded, undamaged examples. A Roman denarius should be graded using the same criteria as those used for grading modern coins. The surfaces must be good, and the coin intact. The fact that the coin is 2,000 years old is irrelevant as far as grading is concerned. Coins which are not perfectly preserved are certainly not without value, however, the value for a given grade decreases with the degree of fault.

Rarity

As with all other series, rare coins usually command higher prices than common ones. A unique variety of a small fourth century Roman bronze coin, even in perfect condition, can be worth much less than a more worn and common piece from an earlier part of the empire. In the Celtic series, there is an almost infinite variety of minor types and a unique variety of an uninscribed type will rarely outbid an inscribed issue of a known king.

Historical and local significance

Types which have historical or local interest can command a price far above their scarcity value. Denarii of the emperor Tiberius are believed to have been referred to in the New Testament and command a far higher price than a less interesting piece of similar rarity. Similarly, pieces which have British reverse types such as the "VICT BRIT" reverse of the third century AD are more expensive than their scarcity would indicate. The 12 Caesars remain ever popular especially in the American market and this affects prices throughout the world. In the Celtic series, coins of Cunobelin or Boudicca are far more popular than pieces which have no historical interest but which may be far scarcer.

Reverse types

All Roman emperors who survived for a reasonable time issued coins with many different reverse types. The most common of these usually show various Roman gods. When a coin has an unusual reverse it always enhances the value. Particularly popular are architectural scenes, animals, references to Judaism, and legionary types.

Artistic merit

The Roman coinage is blessed with a large number of bust varieties and these can have a startling effect on price. For example, a common coin with the bust facing left instead of right can be worth several times the price of a normal specimen. Like many of the emperors, the coinage of Hadrian has a large number of bust varieties, some of which are extremely artistic and these, too, can command a premium.

The coinage used in Britain from the time of the invasion in AD 43 was the same as that introduced throughout the Empire by the emperor Augustus around 20 BC. The simple divisions of 2 asses equal to one dupondius, 2 dupondii equal to 1 sestertius, 4 sestertii equal to one denarius and 25 denarii equal to one aureus continued in use until the reformation of the coinage by Caracalla in AD 214.

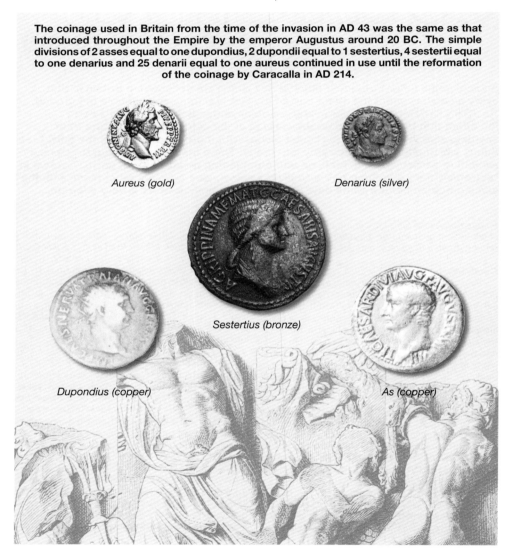

Aureus (gold)

Denarius (silver)

Sestertius (bronze)

Dupondius (copper)

As (copper)

introducing
HAMMERED
coinage

The hammered currency of medieval Britain is among some of the most interesting coinage in the world. The turbulent history of these islands is reflected in the fascinating changes in size, design, fineness and workmanship, culminating in the many strange examples that emanated from the strife of the Civil War.

The Norman Conquest of England in 1066 and succeeding years had far-reaching effects on all aspects of life. Surprisingly, however, it had little impact on the coinage. William the Conqueror was anxious to emphasise the continuity of his reign, so far as the ordinary people were concerned, and therefore he retained the fabric, size and general design pattern of the silver penny. Almost 70 mints were in operation during this reign, but by the middle of the 12th century the number was reduced to 55 and under Henry II (1154–89) it fell to 30 and latterly to only eleven. By the early 14th century the production of coins had been centralised on London and Canterbury, together with the ecclesiastical mints at York and Canterbury. The silver penny was the principal denomination throughout the Norman period, pieces cut along the lines of the cross on the reverse continuing to serve as halfpence and farthings.

Eight types of penny were struck under William I and five under his son William Rufus, both profiles (left and right) and facing portraits being used in both reigns allied to crosses of various types. Fifteen types were minted under Henry I (1100–35), portraiture having now degenerated to crude caricature, the lines engraved on the coinage dies being built up by means of various punches. Halfpence modelled on the same pattern were also struck, but very sparingly and are very rare.

On Henry's death the succession was contested by his daughter Matilda and his nephew Stephen of Blois. Civil war broke out in 1138 and continued till 1153. Stephen controlled London and its mint, but Matilda and her supporters occupied the West Country and struck their own coins at Bristol. Several of the powerful barons struck their own coins, and there were distinct regional variants of the regal coinage. Of particular interest are the coins

Silver pennies of, from left to right, William I, William Rufus, Henry I and Stephen.

struck from obverse dies with Stephen's portrait erased or defaced, believed to date from 1148 when the usurper was under papal interdict.

Peace was restored in 1153 when it was agreed that Matilda's son Henry should succeed Stephen. On the latter's death the following year, Henry II ascended the throne. Coins of Stephen's last type continued to be minted till 1158, but Henry then took the opportunity to overhaul the coinage which had become irregular and sub-standard during the civil war. The new "Cross Crosslet" coins, usually known as the Tealby coinage (from the hoard of over 5,000 pennies found at Tealby, Lincolnshire in 1807), were produced at 30 mints, but when the recoinage was completed this number was reduced to a dozen. The design of Henry's coins remained virtually the same throughout more than two decades, apart from minor variants. Then, in 1180, a new type, known as the Short Cross coinage, was introduced. This was a vast improvement over the poorly struck Cross Crosslet coins and continued without alteration, not only to the end of the reign of Henry II in 1189, but throughout the reigns of his sons Richard (1189–99) and John (1199–1216) and the first half of the reign of his grandson Henry III (1216–46). Throughout that 66 year period, however, there were minor variations in portraits and lettering which enable numismatists to attribute the HENRICUS coins to specific reigns and periods.

"Tealby" type penny (top), and "Short Cross" penny of Henry II.

The style and workmanship of the Short Cross coinage deteriorated in the reign of Henry III. By the 1220s coin production was confined to the regal mints at London and Canterbury, the sole exception being the ecclesiastical mint maintained by the Abbot of Bury St Edmunds.

Halfpence and farthings were briefly struck in 1221–30, though halfpence are now extremely rare and so far only a solitary farthing has been discovered.

By the middle of this reign the coinage was in a deplorable state, being poorly struck, badly worn and often ruthlessly clipped. In 1247 Henry ordered a new coinage and in this the arms of the cross on the reverse were extended to the rim as a safeguard against clipping. This established a pattern of facing portrait and long cross on obverse and reverse respectively that was to continue till the beginning of the 16th century. Several provincial mints were re-activated to assist with the recoinage but they were all closed down again by 1250, only the regal mints at London and Canterbury and the ecclesiastical mints at Durham and Bury St Edmunds remaining active.

"Long Cross" pennies of Henry III (top), and Edward I.

In 1257 Henry tentatively introduced a gold penny (worth 20 silver pence and twice the weight of a silver penny). The coin was undervalued and soon disappeared from circulation.

The Long Cross coinage of Henry III continued under Edward I till 1279 when the king introduced a new coinage in his own name. The penny continued the style of its predecessors, though much better designed and executed; but new denominations were now added. Henceforward halfpence and farthings became a regular issue and, at the same time, a fourpenny coin known as the groat (from French *gros*) was briefly introduced (minting ceased in 1282 and was not revived till 1351). Due to the centralisation of coin production the name of the moneyer was now generally dropped, although it lingered on a few years at Bury St Edmunds. The provincial mints were again revived in 1299–1302 to recoin the lightweight foreign imitations of pennies which had flooded in from the Continent.

The coinage of Edward II (1307–27) differed only in minor respects from that of his father, and a similar pattern prevailed in the first years of Edward III. In 1335 halfpence and farthings below the sterling fineness were struck. More importantly, further attempts were made to introduce gold coins. In 1344 the florin or double

Pre-Treaty Noble of Edward III which contained reference to France in the legend.

leopard of six shillings was introduced, along with its half and quarter. This coinage was not successful and was soon replaced by a heavier series based on the noble of 80 pence (6s. 8d.), half a mark or one third of a pound. The noble originally weighed 138.5 grains but it was successively reduced to120 grains, at which weight it continued from 1351. During this reign the protracted conflict with France known as the Hundred Years' War erupted. Edward III, through his mother, claimed the French throne and inscribed this title on his coins. By the Treaty of Bretigny (1361) Edward temporarily gave up his claim and the reference to France

Noble of Edward IV, issued before he was forced to abandon the throne of England.

was dropped from the coins, but when war was renewed in 1369 the title was resumed, and remained on many English coins until the end of the 18th century. The silver coinage followed the pattern of the previous reign, but in 1351 the groat was re-introduced and with it came the twopence or half-groat. Another innovation was the use of mintmarks at the beginning of the inscriptions. Seven types of cross and one crown were employed from 1334 onwards and their sequence enables numismatists to date coins fairly accurately.

The full range of gold (noble, half-noble and quarter-noble) and silver (groat, half-groat, penny, halfpenny and farthing) continued under Richard II (1377–99). Little attempt was made to alter the facing portrait on the silver coins, by now little more than a stylised caricature anyway.

Noble of Henry IV which was reduced in weight due to the shortage of gold.

Under Henry IV (1399–1413) the pattern of previous reigns prevailed, but in 1412 the weights of the coinage were reduced due to a shortage of bullion. The noble was reduced to 108 grains and its sub-divisions lightened proportionally. The penny was reduced by 3 grains, and its multiples and sub-divisions correspondingly reduced. One interesting change was the reduction of the fleur de lis of France from four to three in the heraldic shield on the reverse of the noble; this change corresponded with the alteration in the arms used in France itself. The Calais mint, opened by Edward III in 1363, was closed in 1411. There was no change in the designs used for the coins of Henry V (1413–22) but greater use was now made of mintmarks to distinguish the various periods of production. Coins were by now produced mainly at London, although the episcopal mints at Durham and York were permitted to strike pennies.

The supply of gold dwindled early in the reign of Henry VI and few nobles were struck after 1426. The Calais mint was re-opened in 1424 and struck a large amount of gold before closing finally in 1440. A regal mint briefly operated at York in 1423–24. Mintmarks were now much more widely used and tended to correspond more closely to the annual trials of the Pyx. The series of civil upheavals known as the Wars of the Roses erupted in this period.

In 1461 Henry VI was deposed by the Yorkist Earl of March after he defeated the Lancastrians at Mortimer's Cross. The Yorkists advanced on London where the victor was crowned Edward IV. At first he continued the gold series of his predecessor, issuing nobles and quarter-nobles, but in 1464 the weight of the penny was reduced to 12 grains and the value of the noble was raised to 100 pence (8s. 4d.).The ryal or rose-

Groat of Richard III (1483–85).

noble of 120 grains, together with its half and quarter, was introduced in 1465 and tariffed at ten shillings or half a pound. The need for a coin worth a third of a pound, however, led to the issue of the angel of 80 grains, worth 6s. 8d., but this was initially unsucessful and very few examples are now extant. The angel derived its name from the figure of the Archangel Michael on the obverse; a cross surmounting a shield appeared on the reverse.

In 1470 Edward was forced to flee to Holland and Henry VI was briefly restored. During this brief period (to April 1471) the ryal was discontinued but a substantial issue of angels and half-angels was made both at London and Bristol. Silver coins were struck at York as well as London and Bristol, the issues of the provincial mints being identified by the initials B or E (Eboracum, Latin for York). Edward defeated the Lancastrians at Tewkesbury and deposed the luckless Henry once more. In his

second reign Edward struck only angels and half-angels as well as silver from the groat to halfpenny. In addition to the three existing mints, silver coins were struck at Canterbury, Durham and the archiepiscopal mint at York. Mintmarks were now much more frequent and varied. Coins with a mark of a halved sun and rose are usually assigned to the reign of Edward IV, but they were probably also struck in the nominal reign of Edward V, the twelve-year-old prince held in the Tower of London under the protection of his uncle Richard, Duke of Gloucester. Coins with this mark on the reverse had an obverse mark of a boar's head, Richard's personal emblem. The brief reign of Richard III (1483–5) came to an end with his defeat at Bosworth and the relatively scarce coins of this period followed the pattern of the previous reigns, distinguished by the sequence of mint marks and the inscription RICAD or RICARD.

In the early years of Henry VII's reign the coinage likewise followed the previous patterns, but in 1489 the first of several radical changes was effected, with the introduction of the gold sovereign of 20 shillings showing a full-length portrait of the monarch seated on an elaborate throne. For reverse, this coin depicted a Tudor rose surmounted by a heraldic shield. A similar reverse appeared on the ryal of 10 shillings, but the angel and angelet retained previous motifs. The silver coins at first adhered to the medieval pattern, with the stylised facing portrait and long cross, but at the beginning of the 16th century a large silver coin, the testoon or shilling of 12 pence, was introduced and adopted a realistic profile of the king, allied to a reverse showing a cross surmounted by the royal arms. The same design was also used for the later issue of groat and half groat.

First coinage Angel of Henry VIII which retained the traditional 23.5 carat fineness.

This established a pattern which was to continue till the reign of Charles I. In the reign of Henry VIII, however, the coinage was subject to considerable debasement. This led to the eventual introduction of 22 carat (.916 fine) gold for the crown while the traditional 23 1/2 carat gold was retained for the angel and ryal. This dual system continued until the angel was discontinued at the outset of the Civil War in 1642; latterly it had been associated with the ceremony of touching for "King's Evil" or scrofula, a ritual used by the early Stuart monarchs to bolster their belief in the divine right of kings.

Under the Tudors and Stuarts the range and complexity of the gold coinage increased, but it was not until the reign of Edward VI that the silver series was expanded. In 1551 he introduced the silver crown of five shillings, the first English coin to bear a clear date on the obverse. Under Mary dates were extended to the shilling and sixpence.

The mixture of dated and undated coins continued under Elizabeth I, a reign remarkable for the range of denominations—nine gold and

The magnificent second coinage Rose-Ryal of James I (1603–25).

eight silver. The latter included the sixpence, threepence, threehalfpence and threefarthings, distinguished by the rose which appeared behind the Queen's head.

The coinage of James I was even more complex, reflecting the king's attempts to unite his dominions. The first issue bore the legend ANG: SCO (England and Scotland), but from 1604 this was altered to MAG: BRIT (Great Britain). This period witnessed new denominations, such as the rose-ryal and spur-ryal, the unite, the Britain crown and the thistle crown, and finally the laurel of 20 shillings and its sub-divisions.

In the reign of Elizabeth experiments began with milled coinage under Eloi Mestrell. These continued sporadically in the 17th century, culminating in the beautiful coins struck by Nicholas Briot (1631–39). A branch mint was established at Aberystwyth in 1637 to refine and coin silver from the Welsh mines. Relations between King and Parliament deteriorated in the reign of Charles I and led to the Civil War (1642). Parliament controlled London but continued to strike coins in the King's name. The Royalists struck coins, both in pre-war and new types, at Shrewsbury, Oxford, Bristol, Worcester, Exeter, Chester, Hereford and other Royalist strongholds, while curious siege pieces were pressed into service at Newark, Pontefract and Scarborough.

After the execution of Charles I in 1649 the Commonwealth was proclaimed and gold and silver coins were now inscribed in English instead of Latin. Patterns portraying Cromwell and a crowned shield restored Latin in 1656. Plans for milled coinage were already being considered before the Restoration of the monarchy in 1660. Hammered coinage appeared initially, resuming the style of coins under Charles I, but in 1662 the hand-hammering of coins was abandoned in favour of coins struck on the mill and screw press. The hammered coins of 1660–62 were undated and bore a crown mintmark, the last vestiges of medievalism in British coinage.

COIN *grading*

Condition is the secret to the value of virtually anything, whether it be antiques, jewellery, horses or second-hand cars—and coins are certainly no exception. When collecting coins it is vital to understand the recognised standard British system of grading, i.e. accurately assessing a coin's condition or state of wear. Grading is an art which can only be learned by experience and so often it remains one person's opinion against another's, therefore it is important for the beginner or inexperienced collector to seek assistance from a reputable dealer or knowledgeable numismatist when making major purchases.

The standard grades as used in the Price Guide are as follows:	
UNC	**Uncirculated** A coin that has never been in circulation, although it may show signs of contact with other coins during the minting process.
EF	**Extremely Fine** A coin in this grade may appear uncirculated to the naked eye but on closer examination will show signs of minor friction on the highest surface.
VF	**Very Fine** A coin that has had very little use, but shows signs of wear on the high surfaces.
F	**Fine** A coin that has been in circulation and shows general signs of wear, but with all legends and date clearly visible.
Other grades used in the normal grading system are:	
BU	**Brilliant Uncirculated** As the name implies, a coin retaining its mint lustre.
Fair	A coin extensively worn but still quite recognisable and legends readable.
Poor	A coin very worn and only just recognisable.
Other abbreviations used in the Price Guide are:	
Obv	**Obverse**
Rev	**Reverse**
Other abbreviations, mintmarks, etc. can be identified under the appropriate section of this Yearbook.	

Help Your Coins Make the Grade

Since 1986, Professional Coin Grading Service (PCGS) has evaluated more than 22 million coins from around the world, with a total declared value of more than 24 billion USD. Using our established 70-point grading scale and world-class grading experts, your coins receive the most accurate, universally trusted grades possible.

With PCGS grades behind them, your coins will realize their true worth in the marketplace. PCGS means confidence for buyers and sellers alike. And for your convenience, we offer our grading center in Paris to better serve the European Numismatic Community.

For more information on PCGS and the Paris grading center, visit **www.pcgsglobal.com**. To request a FREE, wallet-sized coin grading guide (pictured here) that compares the 70-point PCGS grading scale to traditional European grading scales, contact us at **info@pcgsglobal.com**.

PCGS

The Grading Standard for 25 Years

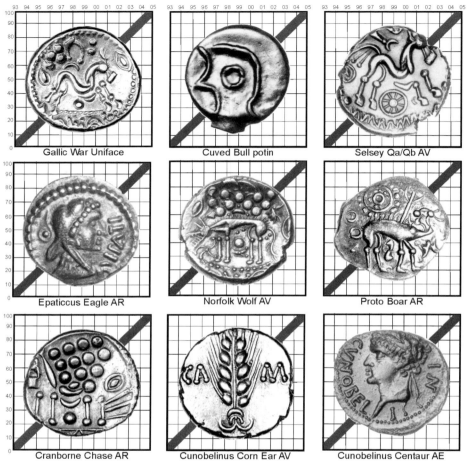

Schema of average percentage increments of retail values of selected commoner types of Late Iron Age coins monitored 1993-2005 with annual fluctuations flattened out. Source: EC Retail Review 8/05.

Up and up, year after year.

A recent review indicates that during the past dozen years many Celtic coins have doubled in value, particularly top-grade gold and bronze. If you would like to know more about Celtic coins - how to collect them and why they can be such an attractive long term investment - talk to the people who specialise exclusively in Celtic coins and who give you a double your money back guarantee of authenticity. Chris Rudd, PO Box 222, Aylsham, Norfolk NR11 6TY. *Tel*: **01263 735 007** *Fax*: 01263 731 777 *Email*: liz@celticcoins.com

Chris Rudd
First choice for choice Celtic

A SIMPLIFIED PRICE GUIDE TO
ANCIENT COINS
USED IN BRITAIN

PART I
Celtic

The prices given in this section are those that you would expect to pay from a reputable dealer and not the prices at which you could expect to sell coins.

The list below, which has been generously provided by Celtic coin dealer Chris Rudd, contains most of the commonly available types: a full comprehensive guide is beyond the scope of this book. Prices are for coins with good surfaces which are not weakly struck or struck from worn dies. Examples which are struck from worn or damaged dies can be worth considerably less. Particularly attractive examples of bronze Celtic coins command a very high premium. Where a price is given for an issue of which there are many varieties, the price is for the most common type. The illustrations are representative examples only and are not shown actual size.

UNINSCRIBED COINAGE

	F	VF	EF
GOLD STATERS			
Gallo-Belgic A	£700	£1750	£5500
Gallo-Belgic E (Ambiani)	£200	£300	£600
Chute type	£200	£300	£600
Cheriton type			
normally rather "brassy" metal	£250	£450	£850
Corieltavi (various types)	£200	£400	£850
Norfolk "wolf" type			
fine gold	£250	£450	£1250
brassy gold	£150	£300	£650
very debased	£100	£200	£400
Whaddon Chase types	£250	£450	£1250
Wonersh type	£250	£450	£1750
Eceni (various types)	£300	£500	£1250
Remic type	£250	£400	£750
Dobunni	£250	£500	£1250

Cheriton Smiler gold stater

	F	VF	EF
GOLD QUARTER STATERS			
North Thames types	£200	£300	£500
North Kent types	£200	£300	£500
Eceni	£150	£250	£400
Sussex types	£125	£200	£350
Dobunni	£175	£300	£550
SILVER COINAGE			
North Thames types	£100	£175	£325
South Thames types	£100	£175	£325
Durotriges full stater			
fine silver	£75	£175	£300
base silver	£25	£55	£150
Durotriges small silver	£20	£35	£75
Dobunni	£75	£125	£275

(Note—Most examples are for base coins as better quality items are appreciably higher)

Cranborne Chase silver stater

	F	VF	EF
Corieltavi	£45	£100	£200
Eceni ("crescent" types)	£30	£75	£150
Eceni ("Norfolk god" types)	£50	£100	£250
Armorican Billon staters	£75	£150	£400

POTIN COINAGE

Kent	£20	£50	£120

BRONZE COINAGE

Durotriges debased stater	£25	£55	£100
Durotriges cast bronzes	£60	£120	£200
North Thames types. Various issues from:	£40	£100	£400

Hengistbury cast bronze

INSCRIBED CELTIC COINAGE

ATREBATES & REGNI

Commios
stater	£550	£1500	£2850
silver unit	£75	£150	£300
silver minim	£60	£120	£250

Tincomarus
stater	£450	£850	£2000
quarter stater	£150	£250	£450
silver unit	£75	£140	£275
silver minim	£60	£120	£175

Tincomarus gold stater

Eppillus
quarter stater	£150	£235	£500
silver unit	£75	£145	£300
bronze			Rare

Verica
stater	£275	£550	£1250
quarter stater	£155	£275	£425
silver unit	£55	£150	£250
silver minim	£50	£120	£225

Epaticcus
stater	£1000	£2000	£4000
silver unit	£50	£100	£265
silver minim	£55	£110	£275

Caratacos
silver unit	£165	£320	£465
silver minim	£110	£220	£325

Verica gold stater

CANTIACI

Dubnovellaunos
stater	£300	£575	£1250
silver unit	£130	£210	£500
bronze unit	£55	£150	£350

Vosenos
stater	£1000	£2500	£5000
quarter stater	£275	£585	£1200
silver unit	£135	£285	£650

Sam
silver unit	£175	£350	£750
bronze unit	£100	£250	£500

Eppillus
stater	£1000	£2000	£4250
quarter stater	£145	£255	£500
silver unit	£65	£145	£350
bronze unit	£55	£125	£450
bronze minim	£85	£150	£275

Amminus
silver unit	£155	£320	£650
silver minim	£110	£215	£450
bronze unit	£80	£155	£500

Solidu
silver unit	£500	£1000	£2250
silver minim	£500	£1000	£1500

Vosenos gold quarter stater

	F	VF	EF

DUROTRIGES
Crab

silver	£155	£320	£650
silver minim	£100	£250	£400

TRINOVANTES
Addedomaros

stater	£300	£550	£1000
quarter stater	£175	£350	£600
bronze	£30	£65	£150

Dubnovellaunos

stater	£275	£475	£1000
quarter stater	£175	£350	£575
bronze unit	£55	£130	£450

Addedomaros gold stater

CATUVELLAUNI
Tasciovanos

stater	£250	£450	£1250
quarter stater	£150	£250	£475
silver unit	£80	£165	£375
bronze unit	£55	£135	£350
bronze half unit	£55	£135	£275

Sego

stater	£1000	£3000	£4000
quarter stater	£600	£1750	£3000
silver unit	£250	£500	£1000
bronze unit	£80	£200	£400

Dias

silver unit	£100	£200	£400
bronze unit	£50	£150	£400

Rues

bronze unit	£50	£150	£400

Tasciovanos gold stater

Andoco

stater	£350	£550	£1500
quarter stater	£210	£420	£755
silver unit	£155	£400	£750
bronze	£85	£215	£355

Cunobelin

stater	£250	£500	£1250
quarter stater	£150	£275	£450
silver unit	£85	£165	£360
bronze unit	£65	£145	£320

AGR

quarter stater	£600	£1500	£3000
silver unit	£500	£1000	£2000

Cunobelinus gold stater

DOBUNNI
Anted

stater	£350	£700	£1500
silver unit	£55	£120	£300

Eisu

stater	£450	£750	£1500
silver unit	£55	£125	£325

Catti

stater	£275	£550	£1500

Comux

stater	£800	£1650	£3500

Corio

stater	£275	£550	£1500
quarter stater	£200	£355	£625

Boduoc

stater	£1000	£2250	£3000
silver unit	£200	£500	£850

Catti gold stater

ECENI	F	VF	EF
Cani Duro			
silver unit...	£110	£265	£550
Anted			
stater...	£425	£1000	£2500
silver unit...	£35	£65	£185
silver half unit....................................	£45	£95	£200
Ecen			
silver unit...	£40	£75	£185
silver half unit....................................	£45	£95	£200
Saenu			
silver unit...	£65	£125	£285
Aesu			
silver unit...	£65	£125	£285
Esuprastus			
silver unit...	£420	£1,000	£1850
Ale Scavo			
silver unit...	£355	£765	£1550

Ale Scavo silver unit

CORIELTAVI			
Cat			
silver unit...	£400	£1000	£2000
Vep			
stater...	£450	£1000	£2500
silver unit...	£75	£150	£300
Aunt Cost			
stater...	£275	£575	£1000
silver unit...	£85	£185	£315
silver half unit....................................	£85	£160	£300
Esuprasu			
stater...	£350	£675	£1250
silver unit...	£155	£310	£550
Vep Corf			
stater...	£450	£1000	£2150
silver unit...	£80	£185	£300
silver half unit....................................	£100	£215	£450
Dumno Tigir Seno			
stater...	£800	£2000	£3500
silver unit...	£100	£185	£500
Volisios Dumnocoveros			
stater...	£350	£675	£1250
silver unit...	£100	£185	£475
silver half unit....................................	£100	£185	£450
Volisios Dumnovellaunos			
stater...	£310	£725	£1550
silver half unit....................................	£150	£335	£655
Volisios Cartivellaunos			
stater	£1000	£2000	£4000
silver half unit....................................	£300	£620	£1150
Latios Ison			
stater...	£1000	£2000	£4000
silver unit...	£155	£420	£1150

Vep CorF gold stater

Dumno Tigir Seno gold stater

*Illustrations by courtesy of
Chris Rudd*

A SIMPLIFIED PRICE GUIDE TO
ANCIENT COINS USED IN BRITAIN

PART II

Roman Britain

The list below has been generously provided by coin dealer Mike Vosper. These prices are for the most common types unless otherwise noted. In most cases, especially with large bronze coins, the price for coins in extremely fine condition will be <u>much</u> higher than the price for the same coin in very fine condition as early bronze coins are seldom found in hoards and perfect, undamaged examples are rarely available.

The illustrations provided are a representative guide to assist with identification only.

REPUBLICAN COINAGE 280–41 BC

	FROM F	VF	EF
Republican			
Quadrigatus (Janus/Quadriga)	£110	£395	£1150
Victoriatus (Jupiter/Victory)	£35	£95	£340
Denarius (Roma/Biga)	£20	£85	£315
Denarius (other types)	£30	£85	£400
Denarius (Gallic warrior, L. Hostilius			
Saserna)	£350	£950	£4000
Quinarius	£25	£70	£285
Cast Aes Grave, As	£185	£575	—
Struck As/Semis/Litra	£60	£195	—
Struck Triens/Quadrands	£50	£145	—

Gnaeus Pompey Junior

IMPERATORIAL COINAGE 49–27 BC

Pompey the Great			
Denarius (Hd. of Pompilius/Prow)	£125	£365	£1600
Scipio			
Denarius (Jupiter/Elephant)	£65	£220	£800
Cato Uticensis			
Quinarius (Bacchus/Victory)	£45	£125	£445
Gnaeus Pompey Junior			
Denarius (Roma/Hispania)	£95	£275	£925
Sextus Pompey			
Denarius (his bust)	£275	£695	£2700
Denarius (other types)	£180	£550	£2300
As	£160	£475	—
Julius Caesar			
Aureus	£850	£2500	£8000
Denarius ("elephant" type)	£100	£350	£1150
Denarius (Caesar portrait)	£350	£1200	£4600
Denarius (heads of godesses)	£100	£325	£1450

Julius Caesar

	FROM F	VF	EF
Brutus			
Denarius (his portrait/EID MAR)	£20000	£60000	£230000
Denarius (others)	£140	£400	£1725
Cassius			
Denarius..	£120	£350	£1300
Ahenobarbus			
Denarius	£375	£1400	£4850
Mark Antony			
Denarius ("Galley" type)	£75	£200	£1050
Denarius (with portrait)	£100	£350	£1650
Denarius (other types)	£70	£275	£1350
Mark Antony & Lepidus			
AR quinarius	£65	£185	£850
Mark Antony & Octavian			
AR denarius	£175	£600	£2300
Quninarius	£55	£165	£750
Mark Antony & Lucius Antony			
AR denarius	£335	£800	£3225
Mark Antony & Octavia			
AR Cistophorus	£225	£650	£2875
Cleopatra VII & Mark Antony			
AR denarius	£900	£3000	£14000
Fulvia			
AR quinarius	£125	£350	£1600
Octavian (later known as Augustus)			
Gold Aureus	£1100	£3500	£14500
Denarius	£125	£375	£1850
Quinarius (ASIA RECEPTA)	£40	£120	£575
Octavian & Divos Julius Caesar			
AE sestertius	£275	£1500	—

Brutus

Mark Antony & Octavian

IMPERIAL COINAGE—Julio-Claudian Dynasty 27BC–69 AD

	FROM F	VF	EF
Augustus			
Gold Aureus (Caius & Lucius Caesar)	£1000	£3000	£13000
AR Cistophorus.................................	£225	£750	£3000
Denarius (Caius & Lucius Caesar)	£60	£175	£800
Denarius (other types)	£65	£215	£1050
AR quinarius	£60	£160	£750
Sestertius (large SC)	£135	£395	£1850
Dupondius or as (large SC)..............	£60	£170	£700
Quadrans	£18	£50	£200
Divus Augustus (struck under Tiberius)			
As	£70	£195	£1000
Augustus & Agrippa			
Dupondius (Crocodile rev)	£70	£195	£1000
Livia			
Sestertius or Dupondius	£195	£595	£3500
Gaius Caesar			
AR denarius	£350	£1500	£3450
Tiberius			
Aureus (Tribute penny)	£1000	£3000	£8000
Denarius (Tribute penny)	£70	£225	£775
Sestertius	£195	£595	£3000
Dupondius	£160	£550	£2500
As	£70	£200	£825
Drusus			
Sestertius...	£275	£900	£4250
As (Large S C)...................................	£75	£210	£1000
Caligula			
Denarius (rev. portrait)	£450	£1400	£5500
Sestertius (PIETAS & Temple)	£300	£2000	£4850
As (VESTA).......................................	£90	£350	£1185

Augustus

Tiberius

	FROM F	VF	EF
Agrippa (struck under Caligula)			
As...	£60	£200	£800
Germanicus (struck under Caligula or Claudius)			
As (Large S C)	£70	£210	£900
Agrippina Senior (struck under Caligula)			
Sestertius (Carpentum)....................	£500	£1650	£6850
Nero & Drusus (struck under Caligula)			
Dupondius (On horseback, galloping)	£180	£700	£2950
Claudius			
Aureus ("DE BRITANN" type)	£1100	£4000	£8450
Denarius as above	£400	£1500	£5750
Didrachm as above	£350	£1000	£4500
Denarius other types	£325	£900	£3750
Sestertius	£175	£550	£2875
Dupondius	£60	£210	£1000
As	£55	£155	£800
Quadrans	£20	£60	£265
Irregular British Sestertius................	£30	£85	£400
Irregular British As	£22	£60	£285
Claudius & Agrippina Junior or Nero			
Denarius	£375	£1500	£5000
Nero Cludius Drusus (struck under Claudius)			
Sestertius	£200	£650	£2985
Antonia (struck under Claudius)			
Dupondius	£120	£425	£1725
Britannicus			
Sestertius	£10500	£37000	—
Nero			
Aureus	£500	£3200	£10000
Denarius	£95	£260	£1250
Sestertius	£155	£550	£2875
Sestertius (Port of Ostia)	£1100	£4750	£25500
Dupondius	£85	£250	£1150
As	£50	£150	£725
Semis	£42	£115	£545
Quadrans	£22	£55	£260
Civil War			
Denarius	£170	£500	£2300
Galba			
Denarius	£100	£340	£1600
Sestertius	£220	£675	£3795
Dupondius	£175	£500	£2300
As	£110	£325	£1600
Otho			
Denarius	£200	£600	£2645
Vitellius			
Denarius	£95	£300	£1325
Sestertius	£1000	£3000	£13750
Dupondius	£400	£1100	£5175
As	£195	£595	£2765

Caligula

Agrippina Senior

Claudius

Nero

IMPERIAL COINAGE—Flavian Dynasty 69–96 AD

Vespasian			
Aureus	£800	£2600	£11500
Denarius	£35	£90	£325
Denarious (IVDAEA)	£80	£225	£1000
Sestertius	£190	£595	£4500
Dupondius	£70	£210	£1150
As	£55	£200	£1095
Titus			
Aureus...	£800	£2300	£10750
Denarius as Caesar	£40	£120	£525
Denarius as Augustus	£45	£135	£575

Galba

	FROM F	VF	EF
Sestertius	£135	£475	£2250
Dupondius	£55	£185	£800
As	£50	£170	£750
As (IVDAEA CAPTA)	£160	£500	£2350
Julia Titi			
Denarious	£190	£595	£2500
Domitian			
Aureus	£800	£2200	£10500
Cistophorus	£115	£375	£1600
Denarius as Caesar	£35	£85	£400
Denarius as Augustus	£25	£65	£300
Sestertius	£95	£330	£1000
Dupondius	£35	£110	£1500
As..	£45	£120	£550
Ae Semis	£35	£90	£425
Ae Quadrands	£25	£70	£285
Domitia			
Cistophorus	£235	£695	£2400

Titus

Domitian

IMPERIAL COINAGE—Adoptive Emperors 96–138 AD

	FROM F	VF	EF
Nerva			
Aureus	£1850	£5200	£23000
Denarius	£60	£125	£550
Sestertius	£155	£500	£2500
Sestertius (Palm-tree)	£500	£1600	£750
Dupondius	£75	£225	£1000
As	£55	£170	£800
Trajan			
Aureus	£800	£2000	£7350
Denarius	£25	£55	£275
Denarius (Trajan's Column)	£45	£130	£575
Sestertius	£65	£215	£1000
Sestertius (Dacian rev.)	£70	£250	£1150
Dupondius or as	£35	£95	£455
Ae Quadrands	£25	£65	£250
Plotina, Marciana or Matidia			
Denarius	£425	£1400	£4750
Hadrian			
Aureus	£800	£2500	£10350
Cistophourus	£100	£450	£1500
Denarius (provinces)	£45	£165	£575
Denarius other types	£25	£75	£300
Sestertius	£80	£235	£1000
Sertertius (RETITVTORI province types)	£135	£420	£2000
Sestertius (Britannia std)	£2600	£9000	—
Dupondius or As	£35	£120	£565
As (Britannia std).............................	£170	£575	—
Ae Semiis or Quadrands..................	£30	£90	£425
Eygpt. Alexandrian Billon Tetradrachm	£30	£85	£475
Sabina			
Denarius	£35	£85	£400
Sestertius	£115	£350	£1725
As or Dupondius	£75	£195	£875
Aelius Ceasar			
Denarius	£75	£225	£1000
Sestertius	£145	£450	£2250
As or Dupondius	£65	£190	£850

Nerva

Trajan

Hadrian

	FROM F	VF	EF

IMPERIAL COINAGE—The Antonines 138–193 AD

Antoninus Pius

Aureus	£600	£1575	£7500
Denarius	£18	£50	£245
Sestertius Britannia seated	£465	£1350	£6750
Sestertius other types	£45	£145	£700
As – Britannia rev.	£65	£195	£1000
Dupondius or As other types	£30	£70	£345

Antoninus Pius

Antoninus Pius & Marcus Aurelius

Denarius (bust each side)	£32	£95	£445

Diva Faustina Senior

Denarius	£18	£47	£235
Sestertius	£38	£145	£700
As or Dupondius	£25	£75	£365

Marcus Aurelius

Aureus	£650	£1750	£8550
Denarius as Caesar	£18	£55	£285
*Denarius as Augustus	£17	£50	£255
Sestertius	£45	£150	£600
As or Dupondius	£25	£75	£375

Marcus Aurelius

Faustina Junior

Denarius	£18	£50	£265
Sestertius	£40	£175	£850
As or Dupondius	£28	£85	£400

Lucius Verus

Denarius	£20	£65	£285
Sestertius	£55	£185	£800
As or Dupondius	£30	£85	£310

Lucilla

Denarius	£20	£65	£285
Sestertius	£55	£175	£800
As or Dupondius	£30	£95	£380

Commodus

Aureus	£825	£2500	£10000
Denarius as Caesar	£28	£75	£285
Denarius as Augustus	£18	£50	£250
Sestertius	£45	£140	£720
Sestertius (VICT BRIT)	£95	£365	£1600
As or Dupondius	£22	£85	£375

Faustina Junior

Crispina

Denarius	£22	£75	£300
Sestertius	£68	£225	£925
As or Dupondius	£32	£110	£475

IMPERIAL COINAGE—The Severan Dynasty 193–235 AD

Pertinax

Denarius	£225	£645	£2875
Sestertius	£475	£1600	£9200

Didius Julianus

Denarius	£395	£1200	£5000
Sestertius or Dupondius	£325	£1000	£5650

Lucius Verus

Manlia Scantilla or Didia Clara

Denarius	£395	£1200	£5450

Pescennius Niger

Denarius	£295	£850	£4000

Clodius Albinus

Denarius as Caesar........................	£45	£140	£600
Denarius as Augustus	£85	£255	£1000
Sestertius	£295	£920	£2525
As	£80	£245	£4250

Commodus

	FROM F	VF	EF
Septimius Severus			
Aureus	£800	£2300	£9500
Aureus (VICT BRIT)	£1000	£3250	£1400
Denarius (Mint of Rome)	£15	£45	£190
Denarius (Mints of Emesa & Laodicea)	£15	£45	£195
Denarius (LEG XIII)	£25	£85	£400
Denarius (VICT BRIT)	£25	£90	£400
Sestertius other types	£75	£240	£1200
Sestertius (VICT BRIT)	£395	£1200	£5750
Dupondius or as.............................	£50	£160	£775
Dupondius or As (VICT BRIT)	£125	£365	£1725
Julia Domna			
Denarius	£15	£45	£175
Sestertius	£75	£230	£1250
As or Dupondius	£50	£160	£725
Caracalla			
Aureus (VICT BRIT)	£1200	£3400	£16000
Denarius as Caesar...........................	£14	£45	£200
Denarius as Augustus	£14	£45	£185
Denarius (VICT BRIT)	£30	£95	£375
Antoninianus	£30	£75	£345
Sestertius	£90	£295	£1325
Sestertius (VICT BRIT)	£300	£845	£4250
Dupondius or As	£50	£165	£700
Dupondius or As (VICT BRIT)...........	£100	£300	£1325
Plautilla			
Denarius	£25	£70	£400
Geta			
Denarius as Caesar	£18	£45	£200
Denarius as Augustus	£20	£70	£300
Denarius (VICT BRIT)	£30	£95	£425
Sestertius......................................	£125	£350	£1665
Sestertius (VICT BRIT)	£230	£775	£3450
Dupondius or as	£75	£230	£1000
As (VICT BRIT)	£120	£340	£1435
Macrinus			
Antoninianus	£90	£275	£1200
Denarius	£30	£120	£420
Sestertius	£175	£345	£3000
Diadumenian			
Denarius	£55	£175	£450
Dupondius or As.............................	£125	£395	£2000
Elagabalus			
Aureus	£1000	£3200	£14000
Antoninianus	£20	£65	£275
Denarius	£15	£35	£175
Sestertius	£100	£320	£1400
Dupondius or As	£60	£175	£775
Julia Paula			
Denarius	£30	£95	£410
Aquilla Severa			
Denarius	£55	£165	£745
Julia Soaemias			
Denarius	£28	£75	£295
Dupondius or As	£65	£225	£1000
Julia Maesa			
Denarius	£15	£65	£200
Sestertius	£85	£300	£1400
Severus Alexander			
Aureus	£575	£1700	£7250
Denarius as Caesar...........................	£65	£185	£895
Denarius as Augustus......................	£12	£35	£150
Sestertius	£35	£100	£425
Dupondius or As	£25	£90	£365

Septimus Severus

Julia Domna

Geta

Macrinus

Elagabalus

Julia Maesa

	FROM F	VF	EF
Orbiana			
Denarius	£58	£185	£750
As	£90	£325	£1500
Julia Mamaea			
Denarius	£14	£45	£175
Sestertius	£35	£105	£475

IMPERIAL COINAGE—Military Anarchy 235–270 AD

	FROM F	VF	EF
Maximinus I			
Denarius	£12	£45	£145
Sestertius, Dupondius or As	£30	£125	£450
Diva Paula			
Denarius	£110	£320	£1025
Maximus Caesar			
Denarius	£50	£150	£575
Sestertius	£50	£160	£565
Gordian I & II, Africanus			
Denarius	£300	£1000	£3600
Sestertius	£375	£1100	£4500
Balbinus & Pupienus			
Antoninanus	£60	£195	£600
Denarius	£55	£185	£575
Gordian III			
Antoninianus	£5	£20	£75
Denarius	£9	£35	£110
Sestertius or As	£22	£85	£320
Tranquillina			
Common Colonial	£30	£110	£425
Philip I			
Antoninianus "Animal"			
Lion, stag, antelope, wolf & twins ...	£14	£50	£175
Other Antoninianus	£5	£20	£65
Sestertius, Dupondius or As	£25	£90	£300
Otacilla Severa			
Antoninianus	£8	£25	£75
Antoninianus "Hipo"	£16	£60	£195
Sestertius	£25	£85	£325
Philip II			
Antoninianus	£7	£20	£85
Antoninianus "Goat"	£16	£65	£195
Sestertius, Dupondius or As	£27	£85	£350
Pacatian			
Antoninianus	£1350	£4000	—
Trajan Decius			
Antoninianus	£6	£20	£75
Antoninianus (DIVI series Augustus, Trajan etc)	£30	£85	£285
Double Sestertius	£190	£600	£2500
Sestertius, Dupondius or As	£27	£85	£350
Herennius Etruscilla			
Antoniniaus	£7	£25	£75
Sestertius, Dupondius or As	£30	£100	£375
Herennius Etruscus			
Antoninianus	£16	£50	£175
Sesterius, Dupondius or As	£55	£185	£650
Hostilian			
Antoninianus as Caesar	£28	£90	£300
Antoninianus as Augustus	£65	£220	£700
Trebonianus Gallus			
Antoninianus...................................	£7	£25	£75
Sestertius or As	£25	£95	£300
Volusian			
Antoninianus...................................	£9	£35	£95
Sestertius..	£28	£95	£375

Orbiana

Julia Mamaea

Diva Paula

Gordian III

Trajan Decius

Hostilian

117

	FROM F	VF	EF
Aemilian			
Antoninianus	£45	£135	£450
Valerian I			
Antoninianus	£6	£25	£75
Sestertius & As	£45	£150	£550
Diva Mariniana			
Antoninianus	£35	£120	£425
Gallienus			
Silver Antoninianus	£8	£25	£75
AE Antoninianus	£4	£20	£75
Ae Antoninianus (Military bust)	£8	£24	£85
AE Antoninianus (Legionary)	£50	£200	—
Ae Sestertius	£40	£140	£575
Ae Denarius	£45	£125	£450
Saloninus			
Ae Antoninianus	£6	£18	£65
Valerian II			
Billon Antoninianus	£10	£35	£125
Saloninus			
Antoninianus	£12	£45	£135
Macrianus & Quietus			
Billon Antoninianus	£35	£110	£350
Regalianus or Dryantilla			
Billon Antoninianus	£1600	£6000	—
Postumus			
Silver Antoninianus	£7	£25	£85
Ae Antoninianus	£5	£25	£75
Radiated sestertius	£45	£175	£695
Laelianus			
Ae Antoninianus	£95	£285	£1000
Marius			
Ae Antoninianus	£35	£110	£375
Victorinus			
Ae Antoninianus	£5	£20	£75
Tetricus I & II			
Ae Antoninianus	£5	£20	£85
Claudius II Gothicus			
Ae Antoninianus	£4	£25	£75
Egypt, Alexandrian Billon tetradrachm	£5	£25	£75
DIVO Ae Antoninianus	£5	£25	£70
Quintillus			
Ae Antoninianus	£13	£42	£140

Postumus

Aurelian

Severina

IMPERIAL COINAGE—The Illyrian Emperors—270–285 AD

Aurelian			
Ae Antoninianus	£6	£25	£95
Ae Denarius	£18	£65	£225
Vabalathus & Aurelian			
Ae Antoninianus (bust both sides)	£23	£65	£250
Vabalathus			
Ae Antoninianus	£300	£600	—
Severina			
Ae Antoninianus	£12	£45	£165
Ae As	£35	£100	£400
Zenobia			
Eygpt, Alexandrian Billon Tetradrachm	£600	£2000	—
Tacitus			
Ae Antoninianus	£15	£35	£150
Florian			
Ae Antoninianus	£35	£85	£325

Tacitus

Florian

	FROM F	VF	EF
Probus			
Gold Aureus	£1000	£2800	£7500
Ae Antoninianus	£6	£25	£100
Antoninianus (military or imp. Busts RIC G or H)	£9	£32	£140
Antoninianus (Other military or imp NOT BUSTS G or H)	£15	£50	£200
Antoninianus (VICTOR GERM rev.) ..	£11	£35	£135
Egypt, Alexandrian Billon tetradrachm	£2	£15	£50
Carus			
Ae Antoninianus	£13	£40	£175
Numerian			
Ae Antoninianus	£12	£38	£165
Carinus			
Ae Antoninianus	£11	£35	£150
Magna Urbica			
Ae Antoninianus	£50	£170	£625
Julian of Pannonia			
Ae Antoninianus	£200	£675	£2500

Diocletian

IMPERIAL COINAGE — The Tetrarchy 285–307 AD

	FROM F	VF	EF
Diocletian			
Gold Aureus	£595	£1850	£6250
AR Argenteus	£85	£276	£775
Ae Antoninianus & Radiates	£7	£25	£95
Ae Follis (London Mint)	£12	£45	£150
As above with LON mint mark	£100	£295	£925
Ae Follis (other mints)	£18	£30	£100
Ae Follis (Imperial bust)...................	£23	£75	£275
Maximianus			
AR Argenteus	£85	£260	£300
Ae Follis (London mint)	£12	£45	£150
Ae Follis (other mints)	£8	£30	£95
Ae Follis (MONETA rev.)	£10	£35	£120
Carausius			
Aureus	£6000	£18000	–
Denarius	£250	£800	£2750
Ae Antoninianus (PAX).....................	£22	£75	£345
As above but full silvering	£30	£105	£450
Legionary Antoninianus	£70	£200	£910
Expectate Veni Antoninianus	£90	£280	–
In the name of Diocletian or Maximian	£30	£100	£485
Allectus			
Aureus	£6800	£24000	–
Ae Antoninianus	£25	£85	£400
As above but full silvering	£40	£125	£550
Quinarius	£25	£90	£375
Constantius I			
AR Argenteus	£90	£285	£750
Ae Follis (London Mint)	£12	£45	£150
Ae Follis (other mints)	£8	£30	£95
Ae Follis (SALVS rev.)	£11	£40	£125
Ae 4 (Lion or Eagle)	£9	£30	£105
Galerius			
Ae Follis (London mint)	£12	£35	£120
Ae Follis (other mints)	£7	£25	£90
Galeria Valeria			
Ae Follis	£28	£80	£260
Severus II			
Ae Follis (London mint)	£33	£100	£345
Ae Follis (other mints)	£27	£85	£275
Ae Radiate	£15	£50	£145
Ae Denarius	£25	£85	£275
Maximinus II			
Ae Follis (London mint)	£12	£40	£145

Maximianus

Carausius

Severus II

Maximinus II

	FROM F	VF	EF
Ae Follis (other mints)	£5	£18	£75
Ae Radiate	£8	£28	£95
Maxentius			
Ae Follis	£8	£30	£100
Romulus			
Ae Follis	£40	£135	£500
Licinius I			
Billon Argenteus	£60	£195	£675
Ae Follis (London mint)	£7	£25	£75
Ae Follis (other mints)	£6	£18	£55
AE3	£5	£18	£65
Licinius II			
AE3	£7	£25	£75
Alexander or Martinian			
AE	£1350	£4500	—

Licinius II

IMPERIAL COINAGE—Family of Constantine 307–350 AD

Constantine I			
Billon Argenteus	£50	£160	£575
Ae Follis (London mint)	£8	£25	£95
As above—helmeted bust	£13	£42	£135
Ae Follis (other mints) as Caesar	£12	£50	£175
Ae Follis (other mints) as Augustus	£4	£15	£60
AE3	£4	£15	£65
AE3 (London mint)	£7	£25	£95
AE3 (SARMATIA rev)	£10	£35	£145
Urbs Roma / Wolf & twins AE3/4	£4	£18	£70
Constantinopolis AE3/4	£3	£15	£60
Fausta & Helena			
AE3 (London mint)	£50	£150	£500
AE3 (other mints)	£14	£45	£140
Theodora			
AE4	£7	£25	£95
Crispus			
AE3 (London mint)	£8	£30	£95
AE3	£7	£20	£75
Delmatius			
AE3/4	£12	£40	£135
Hanniballianus Rex			
AE4	£80	£235	£850
Constantine II			
AE3 (London mint)	£8	£25	£75
AE3	£5	£18	£55
AE3/4	£2	£10	£30
Constans			
AE2 (centenionalis)	£9	£28	£80
AE3 (half centenionalis)	£5	£20	£55
AE4	£2	£10	£30
Constantius II			
Gold Solidus	£185	£460	£1450
Siliqua	£23	£75	£225
AE2 (or centenionalis)	£7	£25	£90
AE3 (or half centenionalis)	£4	£15	£60
AE3 (London mint)	£20	£65	£235
AE3	£2	£8	£35

Constantine I

Constantine II

Magnentius

IMPERIAL COINAGE—Late period to the collapse of the Empire 350 AD to end

Magnentius			
Gold Solidus	£525	£1700	£5750
Silver Siliqua	£200	£790	£2875
Double centenionalis	£45	£185	£750
Centenionalis	£12	£50	£195
Decentius			
Double centenionalis	£65	£235	£950
Centenionalis	£17	£60	£235

Vetranio

	FROM F	VF	EF
Vetranio			
AE2 (centenionalis)	£30	£110	£400
AE3 (half centenionalis)	£27	£95	£300
Nepotian			
AE2 (centenionalis)	£1850	£5800	—
Constantius Gallus			
AE2 (centenionalis)	£11	£35	£120
AE3 (half centenionalis)	£5	£18	£75
Julian II			
Siliqua	£23	£70	£225
AE1	£40	£120	£425
AE3 (helmeted bust)	£8	£28	£90
Anonymous, Serapis + Jupiter AE3	£195	£550	—
Jovian			
AE1	£65	£210	£675
AE3	£12	£40	£120
Valentinian I			
Sold Solidus	£120	£300	£775
Silver Milliarense...........................	£165	£520	£1600
Siliqua	£25	£80	£200
AE3	£5	£18	£55
Valens			
Gold Solidus	£120	£290	£775
Silver Milliarense...........................	£190	£585	£1800
Siliqua	£22	£75	£230
AE3	£5	£18	£65
Procopius			
AE3	£45	£130	£485
Gratian			
Silver Milliarense...........................	£165	£520	£1600
Siliqua	£24	£75	£235
AE3	£4	£18	£65
AE4	£3	£14	£50
Valentinian II			
Solidus	£160	£400	£1000
Siliqua	£25	£75	£250
AE2	£10	£28	£95
AE4	£2	£10	£45
Theodosius I			
Solidus	£160	£410	£1000
Siliqua	£28	£90	£250
AE2	£10	£35	£110
AE3	£8	£30	£95
Aelia Flaccilla			
AE2	£28	£90	£300
AE4	£15	£45	£150
Magnus Maximus			
Solidus (AVGOB)	£4800	£12500	—
Solidus	£700	£2000	£5000
Siliqua	£30	£95	£300
Siliqua (AVGPS)	£700	£2000	—
AE2	£18	£65	£200
Flavius Victor			
Silver Sliqua	£100	£310	£875
AE4	£30	£95	£300
Eugenius			
Silver Siliqua	£110	£335	£1000
Arcadius			
Gold Solidus....................................	£110	£310	£700
Silver Siliqua	£25	£85	£250
Silver Half-siliqua	£90	£275	£800
AE2	£10	£30	£90

Julian II

Jovian

Valentinian I

Valens

Theodosius I

Arcadius

	FROM F	VF	EF
AE4	£2	£12	£50
Eudoxia			
AE3	£25	£65	£220
Honorius			
Gold Solidus	£110	£280	£700
Silver Siliqua	£30	£90	£275
AE4	£5	£20	£60
Constantine III			
Silver Siliqua	£100	£320	£925
Theodosius II			
Gold Solidus	£110	£275	£700
Johannes			
AE4	£110	£435	—
Valentinian III			
Gold Soldius..................................	£110	£280	£650
AE4	£25	£90	£300

Honorius

Theodosius II

Ae = bronze; AE 1, 2, 3, 4 = bronze coins in descending order of size.

Illustrations by courtesy of Classical Numismatic Group/Seaby Coins.

 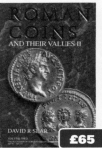 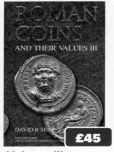 

A SIMPLIFIED PRICE GUIDE TO

ENGLISH
HAMMERED COINS

PART I

959–1485

INTRODUCTION

We have taken our starting point for hammered coin prices back to the Anglo-Saxon reign of Edgar; who could reasonably claim to be the first king of All England. Also it is from this time onwards that we start to get regular "portraits" as well as moneyers and mints on most issues. This gives a total of eight rulers to the list of kings prior to the Norman Conquest and most of these have coin issues that can be purchased quite reasonably. It is also worth pointing out here that of course coins had previously been struck in England for approximately 1000 years prior to our listings by Celtic, Roman and earlier Saxon rulers, details of which can be found in more specific publications.

PRICING

The prices given in the following pages are intended to be used as a "Pocket book guide" to the values of the *most common* coins within any denomination of any one reign. The price quoted is what a collector may expect to pay for such a piece in the condition indicated. For more detailed information we recommend the reader to one of the many specialist publications.

GRADING

The prices quoted are for three different grades of condition: Fine (F), Very Fine (VF) and Extremely Fine (EF). A "Fine" coin is assumed to be a fairly worn, circulated, piece but with all or most of the main features and lettering still clear. "Very Fine" is a middle grade with a small amount of wear and most details fairly clear. For this edition we have included the prices for coins in Extremely Fine condition where appropriate, although very few hammered coins actually turn up in this grade (i.e. nearly mint state with hardly any wear). In some instances the prices quoted are theoretically based and are only included to provide a guide. It is important to note that on all hammered coins the very nature of striking, i.e. individually, by hand, means hammered coinage is rarely a straight grade and when listed by a dealer the overall condition will often be qualified by terms such as: *weak in parts, struck off-centre, cracked or chipped flan, double struck,* etc. When applicable the price should be adjusted accordingly.

HISTORY

Below the heading for each monarch we have given a few historical notes as and when they apply to significant changes in the coinage.

EDGAR (First King of All England)
(959–975)

	F	VF	EF
Edgar Penny, non portrait (2 line inscription)	£250	£550	—

EDWARD THE MARTYR
(975–978)

	F	VF	EF
Edward, Penny, Portrait	£1300	£3500	—

AETHELRED II
(978–1016)

	F	VF	EF
Aethelred II, Penny, last small cross type (First hand type illustrated)	£150	£280	£600

CNUT
(1016–1035)

	F	VF	EF
Cnut, Penny (short cross type) (*Quatrefoil type illustrated*)	£135	£240	£500

HAROLD I
(1035–40)

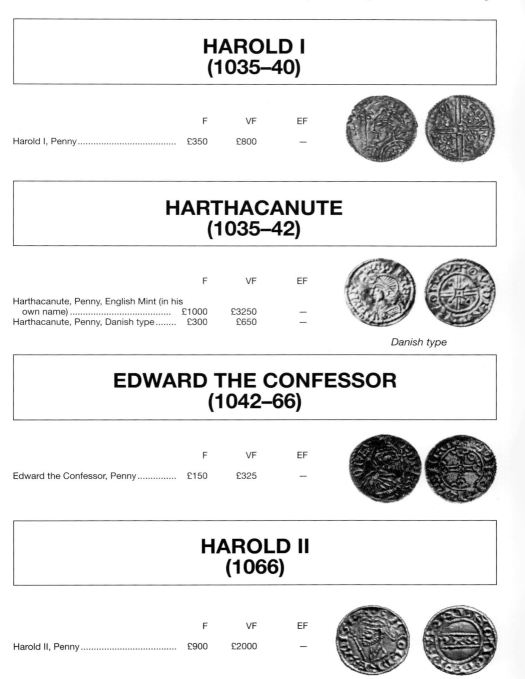

	F	VF	EF
Harold I, Penny	£350	£800	—

HARTHACANUTE
(1035–42)

	F	VF	EF
Harthacanute, Penny, English Mint (in his own name)	£1000	£3250	—
Harthacanute, Penny, Danish type	£300	£650	—

Danish type

EDWARD THE CONFESSOR
(1042–66)

	F	VF	EF
Edward the Confessor, Penny	£150	£325	—

HAROLD II
(1066)

	F	VF	EF
Harold II, Penny	£900	£2000	—

WILLIAM I
(1066–87)

The Norman Conquest had very little immediate effect on the coinage of England. The Anglo-Saxon standard of minting silver pennies was very high and the practice of the moneyer putting his name and mint town on the reverse continued as before, except with William's portrait of course. It is worth noting here that non-realistic, stylised portraits were used until the reign of Henry VII.

There are eight major types of pennies of which the last, the PAXS type, is by far the commonest.

	F	VF	EF
William I, Penny	£275	£500	£1000

WILLIAM II
(1087–1100)

Very little change from his father's reign except that five new types were issued, most of which were much more crudely designed than previous, all are scarce.

	F	VF	EF
William II, Penny	£750	£1750	—

HENRY I
(1100–35)

There are fifteen different types of penny for this reign of which the last two are the most common. Most issues are of a very poor standard both in workmanship and metal, the prices reflect a poor quality of issue.

	F	VF	EF
Henry I, Penny	£175	£475	—

STEPHEN
(1135–54)

This is historically a very complicated time for the coinage, mainly due to civil war and a consequential lack of central control in the country which resulted in very poor quality and deliberately damaged pieces. Coins were struck not only in the name of Stephen and his main rival claimant Matilda but also by their supporters. The commonest issue is the "Watford" type; so named, as are many issues, after the area in which a hoard was found.

	F	VF	EF
Stephen, Penny	£275	£700	—

HENRY II
(1154–89)

There were two distinct issues struck during this reign. The first, Cross and Crosslets or "Tealby" coinage (named after Tealby in Lincolnshire), continued to be very poorly made and lasted 20 years. However, in 1180 the new and superior "Short Cross" issue commenced, being issued from only twelve major towns.

	F	VF	EF
Henry II, Penny, Tealby	£100	£285	—

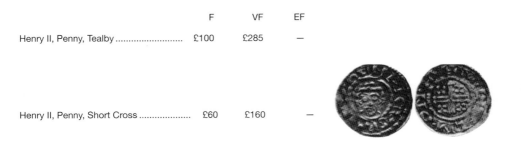

	F	VF	EF
Henry II, Penny, Short Cross	£60	£160	—

RICHARD I
(1189–1199)

There were no major changes during this reign, in fact pennies continued to be struck with his father Henry's name throughout the reign. The coins struck under Richard tend to be rather crude in style.

	F	VF	EF
Richard I, Penny	£85	£250	—

JOHN
(1199–1216)

As with his brother before him, there were no major changes during the reign of King John, and pennies with his father's name were struck throughout the reign, although they tended to be somewhat neater in style than those struck during the reign of Richard I.

	F	VF	EF
John, Penny......................................	£50	£140	£275

HENRY III
(1216–72)

The coinage during Henry III's reign continued as before with the short cross issue. However, in 1247 a new long cross design was introduced to prevent clipping. This design was to last in one form or another for many centuries. A gold penny is known with a throned monarch on the obverse.

	F	VF	EF
Henry III, Penny, Short Cross	£30	£100	£225
Henry III, Penny, Long Cross	£25	£60	£140

EDWARD I
(1272–1307)

After a few years of issuing similar pieces to his father, in 1279 Edward I ordered a major re-coinage. This consisted of well-made pennies, halfpennies and farthings in relatively large quantities, and for a brief period a groat (four pence) was produced. The pennies are amongst the most common of all hammered coins.

	F	VF	EF
Edward I (and Edward II)			
Groat (often damaged).....................	£3000	£7500	—
Penny..	£25	£50	£175
Halfpenny...	£20	£70	£225
Farthing..	£20	£65	£200

Edward I penny

EDWARD II
(1307–1327)

The coinage of Edward II differs in only a very few minor details from that of Edward I and are of similar value for the common types.

EDWARD III
(1327–77)

This was a long reign which saw major changes in the coinage, the most significant being the introduction of a gold coinage (based on the Noble, valued at 6s 8d, and its fractions) and a regular issue of a large silver groat (and half groat). The mints were limited to a few episcopal cities but coins of English type were also struck in the newly-acquired Calais.

	F	VF	EF
Gold			
Noble	£700	£1750	£3250
Half Noble	£425	£1150	£2350
Quarter Noble	£285	£550	£1000
Silver			
Groat	£50	£170	£700
Half Groat	£30	£110	£350
Penny	£30	£90	£250
Half Penny	£25	£70	£185
Farthing	£30	£100	£235

Gold Noble

RICHARD II
(1377–1399)

The denominations continued during this reign much as before. However, coins are quite rare mainly due to the lack of bullion gold and silver going into the mints, mainly because of an inbalance with European weights and fineness.

	F	VF	EF
Gold			
Noble	£850	£2300	—
Half Noble	£900	£3000	—
Quarter Noble	£425	£950	—
Silver			
Groat	£465	£1600	—
Half Groat	£265	£775	—
Penny	£70	£250	—
Half Penny	£45	£140	—
Farthing	£130	£375	—

Gold Noble

HENRY IV
(1399–1413)

Because of the continuing problems with the scarcity of gold and silver the coinage was reduced in weight in 1412, towards the end of the reign. All coins of this reign are quite scarce.

	F	VF
Gold		
Noble	£1700	£4600
Half Noble	£2000	£6000
Quarter Noble	£700	£1750
Silver		
Groat	£2400	£6500
Half Groat	£800	£2250
Penny	£375	£1000
Half Penny	£300	£700
Farthing	£750	£2000

Noble

HENRY V
(1413–22)

Monetary reform introduced towards the end of his father's reign in 1412 improved the supply of bullion and hence coins of Henry V are far more common. All of the main denominations continued as before.

	F	VF	EF
Gold			
Noble	£850	£2250	£4250
Half Noble	£700	£2000	–
Quarter Noble	£350	£750	£1400
Silver			
Groat	£185	£550	–
Half Groat	£140	£375	–
Penny	£40	£150	–
Half Penny	£35	£115	–
Farthing	£350	£850	–

Groat

HENRY VI
(1422–61 and again 1470–71)

Although there were no new denominations during these reigns (see Edward IV below), Henry's first reign saw eleven different issues, each for a few years and distinguished by privy marks, i.e. crosses, pellets, annulets, etc.

HENRY VI *continued*

	F	VF	EF
Gold			
First reign—			
Noble	£750	£2000	£4000
Half Noble	£600	£1500	£2750
Quarter Noble	£280	£625	£1100
2nd reign—			
Angel	£1600	£3750	—
Half Angel	£3000	£8000	—
Silver			
Groat	£50	£130	£275
Half Groat	£35	£100	£240
Penny	£30	£110	£250
Half Penny	£25	£70	£160
Farthing	£100	£280	—

Noble

EDWARD IV
(1461–70 and again 1471–83)

The significant changes during these reigns were the replacement of the noble by the rose ryal (and revalued at 10 shillings) and the introduction of the angel at the old noble value. We also start to see mint-marks or initial marks appearing, usually at the top of the coin, they were used to denote the period of issue for dating purposes and often lasted for two to three years.

	F	VF	EF
Gold			
Ryal	£700	£1750	£3000
Half Ryal	£675	£1650	£2750
Quarter Ryal	£400	£925	£1650
Angel	£650	£1700	£3000
Half Angel	£600	£1500	—
Silver			
Groat	£55	£150	£425
Half Groat	£50	£165	£400
Penny	£30	£110	£275
Half Penny	£25	£100	—
Farthing	£300	£875	—

Angel

RICHARD III
(1483–85)

The close of the Yorkist Plantagenet and Medieval period come together at this time. There are no new significant numismatic changes but most coins of Richard whilst not really rare, continue to be very popular and priced quite high.

	F	VF	EF
Gold			
Angel	£3250	£8500	—
Half Angel	£5000	£14000	—
Silver			
Groat	£700	£1800	—
Half Groat	£1000	£2800	—
Penny	£400	£1000	—
Half Penny	£325	£800	—
Farthing	£1300	£3500	—

Groat

PART II

Among the more significant features of the post-Renaissance period as it affected coinage is the introduction of realistic portraiture during the reign of Henry VII. We also have a much wider and varied number of new and revised denominations, for example eleven different gold denominations of Henry VIII and the same number of silver for Elizabeth I. Here we only mention the introduction or changes in the main denominations, giving a value for all of them, once again listing the commonest type.

HENRY VII
(1485–1509)

The gold sovereign of 20 shillings makes its first appearance in 1489 as does the testoon (later shilling) in about 1500. The silver penny was re-designed to a rather crude likeness of the sovereign.

	F	VF	EF
Gold			
Sovereign	£22500	£60000	—
Ryal	£25000	£65000	—
Angel	£650	£1600	—
Half Angel	£600	£1400	—
Silver			
Testoon 1/-	£14000	£27500	—
Groat	£70	£185	£500
Half Groat	£40	£120	£300
Penny	£40	£110	£250
Half Penny	£25	£85	—
Farthing	£340	£1000	—

Profile Groat

HENRY VIII
(1509–47)

After a long initial period of very little change in the coinage, in 1526 there were many, with an attempt to bring the gold/silver ratio in line with the continental currencies. Some gold coins only lasted a short time and are very rare. The crown (in gold) makes its first appearance. Towards the end of the reign we see large issues of debased silver coins (with a high copper content) bearing the well-known facing portrait of the ageing King. These tend to turn up in poor condition.

Gold			
Sovereign	£4400	£15000	—
Half Sovereign	£800	£2350	—
Angel	£675	£1600	£2750
Half Angel	£600	£1450	£2400
Quarter Angel	£625	£1600	—
George Noble	£8000	£22500	—
Half George Noble	Rare	Rare	—
Crown of the rose	Rare	Rare	—
Crown of the double rose	£600	£1600	£2400
Half Crown of the double rose	£500	£1150	—
Silver			
Testoon 1/-	£850	£3500	—
Groat	£125	£300	£750
Half Groat	£50	£150	£450
Penny	£50	£150	£275
Half Penny	£35	£100	—
Farthing	£275	£725	—

Gold Sovereign

EDWARD VI
(1547–53)

Some of the coins struck in the first few years of this short reign could really be called Henry VIII posthumous issues as there is continuity in both name and style from his father's last issue. However, overlapping this period are portrait issues of the boy King, particularly shillings (usually poor quality coins). This period also sees the first dated English coin (shown in Roman numerals). In 1551 however, a new coinage was introduced with a restored silver quality from the Crown (dated 1551) down to the new sixpence and threepence.

	F	VF	EF
Gold			
Sovereign (30s)	£5000	£15000	—
Half Sovereign	£1450	£4250	—
Crown	£1650	£5000	—
Half Crown	£1350	£3800	—
Angel	£8750	£25000	—
Half Angel	—	—	—
Sovereign (20s)	£3500	£10000	—
Silver			
Crown	£900	£2400	—
Half Crown	£700	£1750	—
Shilling	£125	£425	£1650
Sixpence	£130	£500	—
Groat	£750	£2650	—
Threepence	£200	£800	—
Half Groat	£575	£1200	—
Penny	£70	£250	—
Half Penny	£175	£650	—
Farthing	£1000	£3000	—

Crowned bust half sovereign

MARY
(1553–54)

The early coins of Mary's sole reign are limited and continue to use the same denominations as Edward, except that the gold ryal was reintroduced.

	F	VF
Gold		
Sovereign (30s)	£5000	£14000
Ryal	£20000	—
Angel	£2000	£4500
Half Angel	£3000	£8500
Silver		
Groat	£150	£475
Half Groat	£700	£2000
Penny	£600	£1900

Groat

PHILIP & MARY
(1554–58)

After a very short reign alone, Mary married Philip of Spain and they technically ruled jointly (although not for very long in practise) until her death. After her marriage we see both her and Philip on the shillings and sixpences.

	F	VF
Gold		
Angel	£4000	£13000
Half Angel	£8000	—
Silver		
Shilling	£425	£1700
Sixpence	£425	£1600
Groat	£150	£500
Half Groat	£450	£1350
Penny	£90	£250

Shilling

ELIZABETH I
(1558–1603)

As might be expected with a long reign there are a number of significant changes in the coinage which include several new denominations—so many in silver that every value from the shilling downwards was marked and dated to distinguish them. Early on we have old base Edward VI shillings countermarked to a new reduced value (not priced here). Also due to a lack of small change and the expense of making a miniscule farthing we have a new threehalfpence and threefarthings. Finally we see the beginnings of a milled (machine produced) coinage for a brief period from 1561–71.

	F	VF	EF
Gold			
Sovereign (30s)	£4500	£13000	—
Ryal (15s)	£12500	£30000	—
Angel	£900	£2500	—
Half Angel	£850	£2300	—
Quarter Angel	£775	£2000	—
Pound (20s)	£2250	£6750	—
Half Pound	£1250	£3500	—
Crown	£875	£2500	—
Half Crown	£825	£2350	—
Silver			
Crown	£1400	£3650	—
Half Crown	£1150	£2600	—
Shilling	£120	£385	£1150
Sixpence	£60	£190	£750
Groat	£85	£250	£650
Threepence	£40	£140	£385
Half Groat	£35	£100	£275
Threehalfpence	£45	£165	—
Penny	£35	£100	£200
Threefarthings	£80	£235	—
Half Penny	£40	£100	£165

Shilling

JAMES I
(1603–25)

Although the size of the gold coinage remains much the same as Elizabeth's reign, the name and weight or value of the denominations have several changes, i.e. Pound = Sovereign = Unite = Laurel. A new four shilling gold coin (thistle crown) was introduced. A number of the silver coins now have their value in Roman numerals on the coin. Relatively few angels were made from this period onwards and they are usually found pierced.

	F	VF	EF
Gold			
Sovereign (20s)	£1775	£6000	—
Unite	£600	£1450	£2650
Double crown/half unite	£350	£925	£2000
Crown	£250	£600	£1450
Thistle Crown	£275	£675	£1500
Half Crown	£220	£525	—
Rose Ryal (30s)	£2650	£7500	—
Spur Ryal (15s)	£5000	£13500	—
Angel (pierced)	£800	£1750	—
Half Angel (Unpierced)	£2250	£6500	—
Laurel	£575	£1425	£2650
Half Laurel	£475	£1000	£2000
Quarter Laurel	£250	£575	£1400
Silver			
Crown	£750	£1850	—
Half Crown	£300	£775	—
Shilling	£75	£240	—
Sixpence	£60	£215	—
Half Groat	£25	£60	£110
Penny	£20	£55	£100
Half Penny	£15	£40	£65

Halfcrown

CHARLES I
(1625–49)

This reign is probably the most difficult to simplify as there are so many different issues and whole books have been produced on this period alone. From the beginning of the King's reign and throughout the Civil War, a number of mints operated for varying lengths of time, producing both regular and irregular issues. The Tower mint was taken over by Parliament in 1642 but before this a small quantity of milled coinage was produced alongside the regular hammered issues. The Court then moved to Oxford from where, for the next three years, large quantities of gold and silver were struck (including rare triple unites and large silver pounds). The most prolific of the provincial mints were those situated at Aberystwyth, York, Oxford, Shrewsbury, Bristol, Exeter, Truro, Chester and Worcester as well as some smaller mints mainly situated in the West Country. Among the more interesting coins of the period are the pieces struck on unusually-shaped flans at Newark and Pontefract whilst those towns were under siege. As many of the coins struck during the Civil War were crudely struck on hastily gathered bullion and plate, they provide a fascinating area of study. The prices indicated below are the minimum for the commonest examples of each denomination irrespective of town of origin.

	F	VF	EF
Gold			
Triple Unite (£3)	£12000	£32500	—
Unite	£625	£1500	—
Double crown/Half unite	£425	£1100	—
Crown	£250	£575	—
Angel (pierced)	£800	£2250	—
Angel (unpierced)	£2350	£7750	—
Silver			
Pound (20 shillings—Oxford)	£2500	£7250	—
Half Pound (Shrewsbury)	£1450	£3250	—
Crown (Truro, Exeter)	£450	£1000	—
Half Crown	£60	£200	—
Shilling	£50	£175	£775
Sixpence	£55	£185	£700
Groat	£75	£200	£475
Threepence	£60	£175	£425
Half Groat	£25	£70	£160
Penny	£20	£65	£150
Half Penny	£15	£30	£65

Triple unite

Oxford Halfcrown

Above: Newark siege shilling.

THE COMMONWEALTH
(1649–60)

After the execution of Charles I, Parliament changed the design of the coinage. They are simple non- portrait pieces with an English legend.

	F	VF	EF
Gold			
Unite	£1700	£4000	—
Double crown/Half unite	£850	£2350	—
Crown	£825	£2250	—
Silver			
Crown	£775	£1825	£5000
Half Crown	£275	£700	£2500
Shilling	£185	£475	£1650
Sixpence	£170	£450	£1400
Half Groat	£40	£125	£300
Penny	£40	£125	£300
Halfpenny	£35	£90	£175

Crown

CHARLES II
(1660–85)

Although milled coins had been produced for Oliver Cromwell in 1656–58, after the Restoration of the monarchy hammered coins continued to be produced until 1663, when the machinery was ready to manufacture large quantities of good milled pieces.

	F	VF	EF
Gold			
Unite	£1325	£3800	—
Double crown/Half unite	£950	£2800	—
Crown	£1075	£3250	—
Silver			
Half Crown	£275	£825	—
Shilling	£175	£550	—
Sixpence	£150	£500	—
Fourpence	£35	£100	£180
Threepence	£30	£100	£170
Twopence	£25	£60	£110
Penny	£35	£85	£130

Halfcrown

In These Troubled Times, When You Sell Your Collection, How Can You be Sure You Will get Paid?

By dealing with one of Britain's oldest, largest, friendliest and most financially secure coin dealers, Coincraft.

Coincraft has been helping collectors for the past 54 years. We own the freehold of our building, just across the street from the British Museum and have been here for the past 33 years. Our company balance sheet is extremely strong, as we have always reinvested our profits into the company.

At Coincraft we will buy everything that you have for sale, not just the cream. Unlike auction houses, you will not have to wait months for your material to come up for sale and then have any unsold lots returned to you. Over 90% of the offers we make, are accepted.

When we agree a price, we pay you on the spot, no waiting for an auction, no giving your material on approval. You want to sell, we want to buy and we pay you immediately. In these troubled times, isn't it nice to know that you are dealing with friendly people who are also financially strong enough to pay you instantly?

A COMPREHENSIVE PRICE GUIDE
TO THE COINS OF

THE
UNITED KINGDOM
1656–2011
including

England, Scotland,
Isle Of Man,
Guernsey, Jersey, Alderney,
also Ireland

When referring to this price guide one must bear a number of important points in mind. The points listed here have been taken into consideration during the preparation of this guide and we hope that the prices given will provide a true reflection of the market at the time of going to press. Nevertheless, the publishers can accept no liability for the accuracy of the prices quoted.

1. "As struck" examples with flaws will be worth less than the indicated price.
2. Any coin which is particularly outstanding, with an attractive natural toning or in superb state will command a much *higher* price than that shown.
3. These prices refer strictly to the British market, and do not reflect outside opinions.
4. Some prices given for coins not seen in recent years are estimates based on a knowledge of the market.
5. In the case of coins of high rarity, prices are not generally given.
6. In the listing, "−" indicates, where applicable, one of the following:
    a. Metal or bullion value only
    b. Not usually found in this grade
    c. Not collected in this condition
7. Proof coins are listed in FDC under the UNC column.
8. All prices are quoted in £ sterling, exclusive of VAT (where applicable).

FIVE GUINEAS

	F	VF	EF
CHARLES II (1660–85)			
1668 First bust	£2000	£4750	£13000
1668 — Elephant	£2200	£4500	£12500
1669 —	£2000	£5000	—
1669 — Elephant	£2000	£5000	—
1670 —	£2200	£4500	£13000
1670 Proof	—	—	£75000
1671 —	£2200	£4500	£13000
1672 —	£2200	£4500	£13000
1673 —	£2200	£4500	£13000
1674 —	£2500	£5000	£14500
1675 —	£2200	£4500	£13000
1675 — Elephant	£2300	£5250	—
1675 — Elephant & Castle	£3000	£6000	£18000
1676 —	£2250	£5000	£13500
1676 — Elephant & Castle	£2400	£5200	£15000
1677 —	£2000	£4500	£12000
1677/5 — Elephant		Extremely rare	
1677 — Elephant & Castle	£2400	£5000	£14500
1678/7 — 8 over 7	£2000	£4500	£13000
1678/7 — Elephant & Castle	£2500	£5500	£15000
1678/7 Second Bust	£2000	£5000	£12500
1679 —	£1900	£4750	£12000
1680 —	£2000	£4500	£12500
1680 — Elephant & Castle	£2500	£6000	£15000
1681 —	£2000	£4500	£13000
1681 — Elephant & Castle	£2500	£5500	£15000
1682 —	£1900	£4500	£12000
1682 — Elephant & Castle	£2000	£5000	£13000
1683 —	£1900	£4500	£12500
1683 — Elephant & Castle	£2400	£5500	£15000
1684 —	£2000	£5000	£13000
1684 — Elephant & Castle	£2000	£4750	£13000

Charles II

	F	VF	EF
JAMES II (1685–88)			
1686	£2400	£6000	£15000
1687	£2200	£5000	£13500
1687 Elephant & Castle	£2200	£5000	£13500
1688	£2300	£5500	£14000
1688 Elephant & Castle	£2500	£5500	£15000

	F	VF	EF
WILLIAM AND MARY (1688–94)			
1691	£2000	£4500	£13000
1691 Elephant & Castle	£2000	£4750	£13000
1692	£2000	£4500	£12000
1692 Elephant & Castle	£2100	£5000	£13500
1693	£2000	£4500	£13000
1693 Elephant & Castle	£2200	£4750	£14000
1694	£2000	£5250	£14000
1694 Elephant & Castle	£2200	£4800	£14500

	F	VF	EF
WILLIAM III (1694–1702)			
1699 First bust	£2200	£5000	£14000
1699 — Elephant & Castle	£2500	£5750	£16000
1700 —	£2400	£5000	£15000
1701 Second bust "fine work"	£2200	£5000	£12500

William & Mary

	F	VF	EF
ANNE (1702–14)			
Pre-Union with Scotland			
1703 VIGO below bust	£27500	£65000	£200000
1705	£3000	£6000	£22000
1706	£2750	£6000	£20000
Post-Union (different shields)			
1706	£2200	£4750	£14000
1709 Narrow shields	£2400	£5000	£14000
1711 Broader shields	£2400	£5000	£14500
1713 —	£2500	£5250	£15000
1714 —	£2500	£5250	£15000
1714/3	£2500	£5250	£15000
GEORGE I (1714–27)			
1716	£2250	£5500	£16000
1717	£2500	£6000	£17500
1720	£2700	£7000	£18000
1726	£2200	£5500	£16000
GEORGE II (1727–60)			
1729 Young head	£2600	£4700	£12000
1729 — E.I.C. below head	£1800	£4500	£11000
1731 —	£2500	£5000	£15000
1735 —	£2500	£5000	£15000
1738 —	£2200	£5000	£14000
1741	£2000	£4000	£12000
1741/38 41 over 38	£2000	£4000	£12500
1746 Old head, LIMA	£2000	£4000	£12000
1748 —	£2000	£4000	£11500
1753 —	£2000	£4500	£12000
GEORGE III (1760–1820)			
1770 Patterns	—	—	£140000
1773	—	—	£135000
1777	—	—	£125000

Anne

IMPORTANT NOTE:

The prices quoted in this guide are set at August 2011 with the price of gold at £1150 per ounce and silver £25 per ounce—market fluctuations can have a marked effect on the values of modern precious metal coins.

TWO GUINEAS

	F	VF	EF

CHARLES II (1660–85)

	F	VF	EF
1664 First bust	£1050	£2750	£6500
1664 — Elephant	£1000	£2500	£6000
1665 —		Extremely rare	
1669 —		Extremely rare	
1671 —	£1250	£4000	£11000
1675 Second bust	£1200	£4000	£8000
1676 —	£1000	£4000	—
1676 — Elephant & Castle	£1200	£3500	£7250
1677 —	£1000	£3500	£6750
1677 — Elephant & Castle		Extremely rare	
1678/7 —	£1100	£3000	£6250
1678 — Elephant	£1200	£3000	£7250
1678 — Elephant & Castle	£1100	£3000	£7250
1679 —	£1100	£3500	£6500
1680 —	£1100	£3500	£7000
1681 —	£1000	£2750	£6000
1682 — Elephant & Castle	£1150	£3500	£7200
1683 —	£1000	£3000	£6250
1683 — Elephant & Castle	£1500	£3500	£8000
1684 —	£1100	£3750	£7000
1684 — Elephant & Castle	£1100	£3750	£7500

Charles II

JAMES II (1685–88)

	F	VF	EF
1687	£1200	£3500	£8500
1688/7	£1250	£4000	£9000

WILLIAM AND MARY (1688–94)

	F	VF	EF
1691 Elephant & Castle		Extremely rare	
1693	£1100	£3000	£8000
1693 Elephant & Castle	£1500	£3000	£9500
1694 — 4 over 3	£1200	£3000	£9000
1694/3 Elephant & Castle	£1200	£3000	£9000

James II

WILLIAM III (1694–1702)

	F	VF	EF
1701 "fine work"	£1400	£4000	£8000

ANNE (1702–14)

	F	VF	EF
1709	£950	£2400	£6250
1711	£950	£2200	£6250
1713	£950	£2500	£6250
1714/3	£1000	£2500	£6500

GEORGE I (1714–27)

	F	VF	EF
1717	£900	£2200	£6000
1720	£900	£2200	£6000
1720/17	£950	£2300	£6250
1726	£900	£2000	£5750

Anne

GEORGE II (1727–60)

	F	VF	EF
1733 Proof only FDC		Extremely Rare	
1734 Young head 4 over 3	£1000	£2500	—
1735 —	£700	£1500	£4000
1738 —	£700	£1200	£2400
1739 —	£700	£1200	£2400
1739 Intermediate head	£750	£1250	£2400
1740 —	£750	£1250	£2400
1748 Old head	£750	£1250	£3000
1753 —	£800	£1750	£4000

GEORGE III (1760–1820)

	F	VF	EF
1768 Patterns only		—	Extremely Rare
1773 Patterns only		—	Extremely Rare
1777 Patterns only		—	Extremely Rare

George II

GUINEAS

CHARLES II (1660–85)

	F	VF	EF
1663 First bust	£2200	£6000	£22500
1663 — Elephant below	£1500	£4200	—
1664 Second bust	£1200	£3500	—
1664 — Elephant		Extremely rare	
1664 Third bust	£700	£2500	£7000
1664 — Elephant	£1000	£3000	£8000
1665 —	£650	£2200	£6500
1665 — Elephant	£1000	£3000	£8500
1666 —	£700	£2300	£6500
1667 —	£700	£2200	£6250
1668 —	£650	£2200	£6250
1668 — Elephant		Extremely rare	
1669 —	£700	£2750	£7000
1670 —	£700	£2500	£6500
1671 —	£700	£2200	£6250
1672 —	£700	£2500	£6500
1672 Fourth bust	£650	£2000	£5000
1673 Third bust	£800	£3000	—
1673 Fourth bust	£550	£2000	£5000
1674 —	£575	£2000	—
1674 — Elephant & Castle		Extremely rare	
1675 —	£700	£2200	£5000
1675 — CRAOLVS Error		Extremely rare	
1675 — Elephant & Castle	£700	£2000	£7000
1676 —	£500	£1600	£4650
1676 — Elephant & Castle	£650	£2000	£7000
1677 —	£500	£1600	£4500
1677/5 — Elephant 7 over 5		Extremely rare	
1677 — Elephant & Castle	£600	£2000	£6500
1678 —	£500	£1600	£4500
1678 — Elephant		Extremely rare	
1678 — Elephant & Castle	£750	£2500	—

Charles II, third bust

Charles II, fourth bust, elephant & castle below

	F	VF	EF
1679 —	£475	£1600	£4500
1679 — Elephant & Castle	£700	£2200	£7000
1680 —	£500	£1800	£5000
1680 — Elephant & Castle	£750	£2350	—
1681 —	£500	£1800	£5000
1681 — Elephant & Castle	£700	£2500	—
1682 —	£500	£1750	£5000
1682 — Elephant & Castle	£750	£2200	£7000
1683 —	£550	£1700	£5000
1683 — Elephant & Castle	£725	£2500	£7000
1684 —	£550	£1800	£5000
1684 — Elephant & Castle	£650	£2250	£7500

James II, first bust, elephant & castle below

JAMES II (1685–1688)

	F	VF	EF
1685 First bust	£550	£1800	£6000
1685 — Elephant & Castle	£650	£2200	£6500
1686 —	£625	£2000	£6500
1686 — Elephant & Castle		Extremely rare	
1686 Second bust	£600	£1900	£6250
1686 — Elephant & Castle	£700	£2500	£7000
1687 —	£550	£1800	£6000
1687 —Elephant & Castle	£650	£2300	£7000
1688 —	£525	£1800	£6000
1688 — Elephant & Castle	£600	£2400	£6750

WILLIAM AND MARY (1688–94)

James II, second bust

	F	VF	EF
1689..	£550	£1800	£6000
1689 Elephant & Castle	£550	£2000	£6000
1690..	£550	£2000	£6500
1690 GVLIFLMVS.....................................	£700	£2200	—
1690 Elephant & Castle	£700	£2200	£7000
1691..	£575	£1900	£5500
1691 Elephant & Castle	£550	£2000	£6000
1692..	£550	£2000	£6000
1692 Elephant	£900	£3000	£8500
1692 Elephant & Castle	£600	£2400	£6000
1693..	£550	£2000	£6000
1693 Elephant		Extremely rare	
1693 Elephant & Castle		Extremely rare	
1694..	£600	£2000	£6000
1694/3...	£600	£2000	£6000
1694 Elephant & Castle	£625	£2200	£6250
1694/3 Elephant & Castle............................	£625	£2200	£6250

WILLIAM III (1694–1702)

	F	VF	EF
1695 First bust	£500	£1700	£5000
1695 — Elephant & Castle	£800	£2600	£10000
1696 —	£550	£1800	£6000
1696 — Elephant & Castle		Extremely rare	
1697 —	£600	£1800	£6000
1697 Second bust	£500	£1700	£5500
1697 — Elephant & Castle	£1250	£4000	—
1698 —	£450	£1600	£5500
1698 — Elephant & Castle	£450	£1800	£5500
1699 —	£500	£1750	£5500
1699 — Elephant & Castle		Extremely rare	
1700 —	£450	£1600	£5000
1700 — Elephant & Castle	£1000	£3750	—
1701 —	£400	£1500	£5000
1701 — Elephant & Castle		Extremely rare	
1701 Third bust "fine work"............................	£725	£2750	£8000

William III, second bust

	F	VF	EF

ANNE (1702–1714)

	F	VF	EF
1702 (Pre-Union) First bust	£600	£2500	£5000
1703 — VIGO below	£8500	£25000	£55000
1705 —	£700	£2200	£5500
1706 —	£700	£2200	£5500
1707 —	£700	£2200	£5500
1707 — (Post-Union)	£600	£2000	£5000
1707 — Elephant & Castle	£750	£2500	£8000
1707 Second bust	£550	£1500	£4750
1708 First bust	£650	£2000	£5500
1708 Second bust	£500	£1300	£4000
1708 — Elephant & Castle	£800	£2200	£7000
1709 —	£450	£1300	£4000
1709 — Elephant & Castle	£800	£2200	£5000
1710 Third bust	£500	£1400	£3250
1711 —	£500	£1300	£3000
1712 —	£500	£1300	£3000
1713 —	£450	£1100	£2500
1714 —	£450	£1100	£2750
1714 GRATIΛ	£700	£1650	£3500

Anne, second bust

GEORGE I (1714–27)

	F	VF	EF
1714 First bust (Prince Elector)	£1100	£2850	£5750
1715 Second bust	£450	£1500	£3500
1715 Third bust	£450	£1500	£3500
1716 —	£500	£1500	£3500
1716 Fourth bust	£450	£1200	£3000
1717 —	£450	£1200	£3000
1718 —			Extremely rare
1719 —	£450	£1400	£3000
1720 —	£450	£1400	£3000
1721 —	£500	£1400	£3250
1721 — Elephant & Castle			Extremely rare
1722 —	£450	£1300	£3000
1722 — Elephant & Castle			Extremely rare
1723 —	£450	£1350	£3000
1723 Fifth bust	£450	£1200	£3000
1724 —	£450	£1300	£3300
1725 —	£450	£1250	£3000
1726 —	£400	£1250	£2900
1726 — Elephant & Castle	£1500	£4000	£11000
1727 —	£500	£1800	£5000

George I, third bust

GEORGE II (1727–60)

	F	VF	EF
1727 First young head, early large shield	£750	£2200	£6500
1727 — Larger lettering, early small shield	£600	£2000	£6000
1728 — —	£600	£2000	£6000
1729 2nd young head E.I.C. below	£700	£2400	£7000
1729 — Proof		Very	Rare
1730 —	£500	£1500	£4000
1731 —	£400	£1300	£3200
1731 — E.I.C. below	£700	£2500	£7000
1732 —	£700	£2500	£7000
1732 — E.I.C. below	£650	£2000	£6500
1732 — Larger lettering obverse	£400	£1350	£3500
1732 — — E.I.C. below	£600	£1700	£5000
1733 — —	£400	£1250	£2750
1734 — —	£400	£1250	£2750
1735 — —	£400	£1250	£2750
1736 — —	£400	£1300	£2700
1737 — —	£400	£1350	£3000

George II, 1759, old head, larger lettering

	F	VF	EF
1738 — —	£400	£1250	£3000
1739 Intermediate head	£400	£1000	£2600
1739 — E.I.C. below	£700	£2000	£6000
1740 —	£400	£1100	£5000
1741/39 —		Extremely rare	
1743 —		Extremely rare	
1745 — Larger lettering obv. Older bust	£425	£1200	£4000
1745 — LIMA below	£1000	£2750	£8000
1746 — (GEORGIVS) Larger lettering obv.	£400	£1300	£3000
1747 Old head, large lettering	£375	£800	£2400
1748 —	£375	£800	£2400
1749 —	£375	£800	£2400
1750 —	£375	£800	£2400
1751 — small lettering	£375	£800	£2400
1753 —	£375	£800	£2400
1755 —	£375	£800	£2400
1756 —	£375	£800	£2400
1758 —	£375	£800	£2500
1759 —	£375	£800	£2250
1760 —	£375	£800	£2000

George III first head

GEORGE III (1760–1820)

	F	VF	EF
1761 First head	£1200	£3000	£6000
1763 Second head	£1200	£3000	£5500
1764 —	£700	£3000	£5200
1765 Third head	£300	£500	£1200
1766 —	£300	£500	£1100
1767 —	£400	£700	£150
1768 —	£300	£500	£1100
1769 —	£300	£500	£1100
1770 —	£450	£600	£1750
1771 —	£300	£500	£1100
1772 —	£300	£500	£1100
1773 —	£300	£500	£1100
1774 Fourth head	£275	£400	£800
1775 —	£275	£400	£800
1776 —	£275	£400	£800
1777 —	£275	£400	£800
1778 —	£350	£700	£1600
1779 —	£275	£500	£900
1781 —	£250	£400	£900
1782 —	£240	£475	£925
1783 —	£300	£475	£950
1784 —	£270	£475	£900
1785 —	£270	£475	£900
1786 —	£270	£475	£900
1787 Fifth head, "Spade" reverse	£240	£425	£750
1788 —	£240	£425	£750
1789 —	£240	£425	£750
1790 —	£240	£425	£750
1791 —	£240	£425	£750
1792 —	£240	£425	£750
1793 —	£240	£425	£750
1794 —	£240	£425	£750
1795 —	£240	£425	£750
1796 —	£240	£425	£750
1797 —	£240	£425	£750
1798 —	£240	£425	£750
1799 —	£250	£450	£950
1813 Sixth head, "Military" reverse	£600	£1600	£2800

Fourth head

Fifth head, Spade reverse

Sixth "Military" head

(Beware of counterfeits of this series—many dangerous copies exist)

HALF GUINEAS

	F	VF	EF
CHARLES II (1660–85)			
1669 First bust	£350	£1000	£3750
1670 —	£300	£1000	£3250
1671 —	£400	£1100	£4000
1672 —	£400	£1100	£4000
1672 Second bust	£325	£900	£3500
1673 —	£450	£1300	£4000
1674 —	£500	£1600	£4000
1675 —	£500	£1600	£4000
1676 —	£325	£1000	£3250
1676 — Elephant & Castle	£675	£2400	—
1677 —	£325	£1000	£3250
1677 — Elephant & Castle	£600	£1600	—
1678 —	£400	£1100	£3500
1678 — Elephant & Castle	£500	£1500	£5000
1679 —	£370	£1000	£3000
1680 —	£400	£1750	—
1680 — Elephant & Castle		Extremely rare	
1681 —	£400	£1500	—
1682 —	£400	£1300	£3500
1682 — Elephant & Castle	£600	£1700	—
1683 —	£350	£900	£3250
1683 — Elephant & Castle		Extremely rare	
1684 —	£350	£900	£3250
1684 — Elephant & Castle	£500	£1500	£5000

Charles II, first bust

	F	VF	EF
JAMES II (1685–88)			
1686	£400	£1100	£3500
1686 Elephant & Castle	£800	£3750	£7000
1687	£400	£1300	£4000
1688	£400	£1300	£3800

	F	VF	EF
WILLIAM AND MARY (1688–94)			
1689 First busts	£475	£1800	£4000
1690 Second busts	£500	£1850	£4200
1691 —	£500	£1800	£4000
1691 — Elephant & Castle	£500	£1700	£4000
1692 —	£450	£1500	£3500
1692 — Elephant		Extremely rare	
1692 — Elephant & Castle	£450	£1600	£4000
1693 —		Extremely rare	
1694 —	£450	£1600	£3750

Williuam & Mary, first busts

	F	VF	EF
WILLIAM III (1694–1702)			
1695	£350	£800	£3000
1695 Elephant & Castle	£500	£1400	£4250
1696 —	£400	£950	£3000
1697 Larger Harp rev.	£500	£1400	£4250
1698	£500	£1200	£4000
1698 Elephant & Castle	£600	£1500	£3250
1699		Extremely rare	
1700	£275	£800	£2700
1701	£275	£800	£2700

William III, elephant & castle below bust

149

	F	VF	EF

ANNE (1702–14)

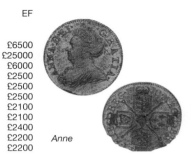

	F	VF	EF
1702 (Pre-Union)	£700	£2200	£6500
1703 VIGO below bust	£4800	£12000	£25000
1705	£600	£2000	£6000
1707 (Post-Union)	£300	£900	£2500
1708	£325	£900	£2500
1709	£300	£900	£2500
1710	£275	£750	£2100
1711	£275	£750	£2100
1712	£300	£800	£2400
1713	£275	£750	£2200
1714	£275	£750	£2200

Anne

GEORGE I (1714–27)

	F	VF	EF
1715 First bust	£400	£800	£2200
1717 —	£300	£650	£1750
1718 —	£300	£650	£1750
1719 —	£300	£650	£1750
1720 —	£325	£675	£1750
1721 —		Extremely rare	
1721 — Elephant & Castle		Extremely rare	
1722 —	£300	£600	£2000
1723 —	£350	£700	£2500
1724 —	£325	£700	£2200
1725 Second bust	£275	£500	£1500
1726 —	£275	£500	£1600
1727 —	£275	£500	£1750

George I, second bust

GEORGE II (1727–60)

	F	VF	EF
1728 Young head	£425	£1000	£3500
1729 —	£425	£1000	£3200
1729 — E.I.C.	£425	£1000	£3500
1730 —	£550	£2000	—
1730 — E.I.C.	£675	£2000	—
1731 —	£300	£950	£3000
1731 — E.I.C.		Extremely rare	
1732 —	£300	£900	£3000
1732 — E.I.C.		Extremely rare	
1733 —		Unknown	
1734 —	£300	£800	£2500
1735 —		Extremely rare	
1736 —	£300	£700	£3000
1737 —	£375	£800	£3000
1738 —	£300	£750	£2500
1739 —	£300	£750	£2500
1739 — E.I.C.		Extremely rare	
1740 Intermediate head	£375	£1000	£3000
1743 —		Extremely rare	
1745 —	£300	£900	£2850
1745 — LIMA	£800	£3500	—
1746 —	£275	£700	£2200
1747 Old head	£300	£700	£2200
1748 —	£250	£700	£1800
1749 —	£260	£650	£1750
1750 —	£260	£600	£1650
1751 —	£250	£600	£1600
1752 —	£250	£600	£1600
1753 —	£250	£600	£1600
1755 —	£250	£600	£1600
1756 —	£260	£800	£2000
1758 —	£300	£700	£2000

George II, young head

George II, old head

	F	VF	EF
1759 —	£260	£650	£1800
1760 —	£260	£650	£1800

GEORGE III (1760–1820)

	F	VF	EF
1762 First head	£450	£1250	£3000
1763 —	£600	£1500	£3750
1764 Second head	£200	£425	£950
1765 —	£400	£900	£2500
1766 —	£200	£425	£1000
1768 —	£220	£475	£1000
1769 —	£225	£475	£1000
1772 —		Extremely rare	
1773 —	£225	£425	£900
1774 —	£270	£550	£1600
1774 Third head		Extremely rare	
1775 —	£750	£1800	£4000
1775 Fourth head	£150	£275	£550
1775 — Proof		Extremely rare	
1776 —	£150	£250	£600
1777 —	£150	£250	£600
1778 —	£150	£250	£625
1779 —	£150	£325	£750
1781 —	£150	£300	£700
1783 —	£450	£1250	—
1784 —	£150	£300	£600
1785 —	£150	£300	£600
1786 —	£150	£300	£600
1787 Fifth head, "Spade" rev.	£145	£270	£575
1788 —	£145	£270	£575
1789 —	£145	£270	£600
1790 —	£145	£270	£575
1791 —	£145	£270	£575
1792 —	£500	£1600	—
1793 —	£145	£240	£525
1794 —	£145	£240	£525
1795 —	£170	£350	£725
1796 —	£145	£300	£550
1797 —	£145	£300	£550
1798 —	£145	£300	£550
1800 —	£270	£725	£1600
1801 Sixth head, Shield in Garter rev.	£145	£225	£400
1802 —	£145	£225	£400
1803 —	£145	£225	£400
1804 Seventh head	£145	£225	£400
1805		Extremely rare	
1806 —	£145	£225	£420
1808 —	£145	£225	£420
1899 —	£145	£225	£420
1810 —	£145	£225	£420
1811 —	£180	£350	£750
1813 —	£180	£350	£750

George III, second head

George III, fifth head, "spade" reverse

THIRD GUINEAS

GEORGE III (1760–1820)

DATE	F	VF	EF
1797 First head,date in legend	£90	£140	£325
1798 — —	£90	£140	£325
1799 — —	£90	£160	£350
1800 — —	£90	£140	£350
1801 Date under crown	£90	£140	£350
1802 —	£90	£140	£350
1803 —	£90	£140	£350
1804 Second head	£85	£140	£350
1806 —	£95	£150	£370
1808 —	£85	£140	£350
1809 —	£85	£140	£350
1810 —	£85	£140	£350
1811 —	£260	£500	£1350
1813 —	£150	£275	£750

George III, date in legend

George III, date under crown

QUARTER GUINEAS

GEORGE I (1714–27)

	F	VF	EF
1718	£150	£250	£550

GEORGE III (1760–1820)

	F	VF	EF
1762	£140	£325	£520

George I

FIVE POUNDS

GEORGE III (1760–1820)

DATE	Mintage	F	VF	EF	UNC
1820 (pattern only)		—		Extremely rare	

GEORGE IV (1820–30)

DATE	Mintage	F	VF	EF	UNC
1826 proof only		—	—	£8,000	£15,000

VICTORIA (1837–1901)

DATE	Mintage	F	VF	EF	UNC
1839 Proof Only (Una & The Lion) Many Varieties FDC £35,000 upwards					
1887	53,844	£1200	£1350	£1800	£2500
1887 Proof	797	—	—	—	£3500
1887 S on ground on rev. (Sydney Mint)				Excessively rare	
1893	20,405	£1200	£1400	£1900	£3000
1893 Proof	773	—	—	—	£4500

EDWARD VII (1902–10)

DATE	Mintage	F	VF	EF	UNC
1902	34,910	£1000	£1100	£1350	£1750
1902 Matt proof	8,066	—	—	—	£1500

DATE	MINTAGE	F	VF	EF	UNC

GEORGE V (1911–36)

1911 Proof only .... 2,812 — — — £3000

GEORGE VI (1937–52)

1937 Proof only .... 5,501 — — — £1800

Later issues are listed in the Decimal section.

TWO POUNDS

GEORGE III (1760–1820)

1820 (pattern only)............. — — — Extremely rare

GEORGE IV (1820–30)

1823 St George reverse..... — £750 £1000 £1600 £2500
1826 Proof only, shield reverse — — — — £7500

WILLIAM IV (1830–37)

1831 Proof only .... 225 — — — £6000

VICTORIA (1837–1901)

1887.................................. 91,345 £450 £550 £600 £725
1887 Proof......................... 797 — — — £1275
1887 S on ground of rev. (Sydney Mint) Excessively rare
1893.................................. 52,212 £450 £575 £800 £1400
1893 Proof......................... 773 — — — £1800

EDWARD VII (1902–10)

1902.................................. 45,807 £400 £500 £575 £775
1902 Matt proof................. 8,066 — — — £700

GEORGE V (1911–36)

1911 Proof only .... 2,812 — — — £1000

GEORGE VI (1937–52)

1937 Proof only .... 5,501 — — — £825
Later issues are listed in the Decimal section.

SOVEREIGNS

DATE	MINTAGE	F	VF	EF	UNC

GEORGE III (1760–1820)

DATE	MINTAGE	F	VF	EF	UNC
1817	3,235,239	£375	£600	£1400	£2500
1818	2,347,230	£375	£600	£1400	£2500
1819	3,574		Exceedingly rare		
1820	931,994	£375	£600	£1400	£2500

GEORGE IV (1820–30)

DATE	MINTAGE	F	VF	EF	UNC
1821 First bust, St George reverse	9,405,114	£325	£525	£1200	£2000
1821 — Proof	incl. above	—	—	—	£4500
1822 —	5,356,787	£325	£500	£1200	£2000
1823 —	616,770	£600	£1750	£4500	—
1824 —	3,767,904	£350	£600	£1500	£4000
1825 —	4,200,343	£550	£1300	£3250	£10000
1825 Second bust, shield reverse	incl. above	£325	£600	£1000	£2000
1826 —	5,724,046	£325	£600	£1000	£2000
1826 — Proof	—	—	—	—	£3250
1827 —	2,266,629	£325	£600	£1150	£2100
1828 —	386,182	£3500	£7250	£17500	—
1829 —	2,444,652	£350	£650	£1400	£2250
1830 —	2,387,881	£350	£650	£1400	£2250

George IV, shield reverse

WILLIAM IV (1830–37)

DATE	MINTAGE	F	VF	EF	UNC
1831	598,547	£450	£800	£1800	£3000
1831 Proof, plain edge	—	—	—	—	£3750
1832	3,737,065	£450	£800	£1800	£3000
1833	1,225,269	£450	£800	£1800	£3000
1835	723,441	£450	£800	£1800	£3000
1836	1,714,349	£450	£800	£1800	£3000
1837	1,172,984	£500	£700	£1800	£3000

Note—from the Victoria reign onwards, the prices of coins in lower grade will be subject to the bullion price of gold.

VICTORIA (1837–1901)

Many of the gold coins struck at the colonial mints found their way into circulation in Britain, for the sake of completeness these coins are listed here. These can easily be identified by a tiny initial letter for the appropriate mint which can be found below the base of the reverse shield or, in the case of the St George reverse, below the bust on the obverse of the Young Head issues, or on the "ground" below the horse's hoof on the later issues.

William IV

YOUNG HEAD ISSUES

Shield reverse
(Note—Shield back sovereigns in Fine/VF condition, common dates, are normally traded as bullion + a percentage)

DATE	MINTAGE	F	VF	EF	UNC
1838	2,718,694	£400	£950	£2000	£3800
1839	503,695	£800	£2500	£4500	£5500
1839 Proof, plain edge	—	—	—	—	£5000
1841	124,054	£2000	£3500	£10000	—
1842	4,865,375	£265	£275	£375	£600
1843	5,981,968	£265	£275	£375	£600
1843 "Narrow shield" variety	incl. above	£3000	£6000		
1844	3,000,445	£265	£275	£375	£600
1845	3,800,845	£265	£275	£375	£600
1846	3,802,947	£265	£275	£375	£600
1847	4,667,126	£265	£275	£375	£600

DATE	MINTAGE	F	VF	EF	UNC
1848	2,246,701	£265	£275	£300	£600
1849	1,755,399	£265	£275	£300	£600
1850	1,402,039	£265	£275	£300	£600
1851	4,013,624	£265	£275	£300	£600
1852	8,053,435	£265	£275	£300	£600
1853	10,597,993	£265	£275	£300	£600
1853 Proof	—	—	—	—	−£10000
1854 Incuse WW	3,589,611	£265	£275	£300	£600
1854 Surface raised WW	3,589,611	£265	£275	£750	£1500
1855	4,806,160	£265	£275	£300	£600
1856	8,448,482	£265	£275	£350	£600
1857	4,495,748	£265	£275	£300	£600
1858	803,234	£265	£275	£300	£600
1859	1,547,603	£265	£275	£300	£600
1859 "Ansell" (additional line on lower part of hair ribbon)	—	£500	£1200	£5000	—
1860	2,555,958	£265	£275	£285	£450
1861	7,624,736	£265	£275	£285	£450
1862	7,836,413	£265	£275	£285	£450
1863	5,921,669	£265	£275	£285	£425
1863 Die No 827 on Truncation...				Extremely rare	
1863 with Die number below shield	incl. above	£265	£275	£285	£475
1864 —	8,656,352	£265	£275	£285	£475
1865 —	1,450,238	£265	£275	£285	£475
1866 —	4,047,288	£265	£275	£285	£475
1868 —	1,653,384	£265	£275	£285	£475
1869 —	6,441,322	£265	£275	£285	£475
1870 —	2,189,960	£265	£275	£285	£475
1871 —	8,767,250	£265	£275	£285	£475
1872 —	8,767,250	£265	£275	£285	£475
1872 no Die number	incl. above	£265	£275	£285	£475
1873 with Die number	2,368,215	£265	£275	£285	£475
1874 —	520,713	£1375	£3000	£6000	—

M below reverse shield (Melbourne Mint)

1872	748,180	£275	£285	£300	£600
1873	—			Extremely rare	
1874	1,373,298	£275	£285	£300	£800
1879				Extremely rare	
1880	3,053,454	£500	£1200	£2750	£7000
1881	2,325,303	£265	£275	£300	£1100
1882	2,465,781	£265	£275	£285	£800
1883	2,050,450	£265	£300	£700	—
1884	2,942,630	£265	£275	£285	£600
1885	2,967,143	£265	£275	£285	£600
1886	2,902,131	£1800	£4000	£6000	£16000
1887	1,916,424	£500	£1200	£3500	£9000

The mint initial appears below the shield, i.e. "S" indicates that the coin was struck at the Sydney Mint

S below reverse shield (Sydney Mint)

1871	2,814,000	£265	£275	£300	£1000
1872	1,815,000	£265	£275	£300	£1200
1873	1,478,000	£265	£275	£300	£1200
1875	2,122,000	£265	£275	£300	£1200
1877	1,590,000	£265	£275	£300	£1200
1878	1,259,000	£265	£275	£300	£1200
1879	1,366,000	£265	£275	£300	£1200
1880	1,459,000	£265	£275	£300	£1500
1881	1,360,000	£265	£275	£300	£1500
1882	1,298,000	£265	£275	£300	£1200
1883	1,108,000	£265	£275	£300	£1000
1884	1,595,000	£265	£275	£300	£1000
1885	1,486,000	£265	£275	£300	£1000
1886	1,667,000	£265	£275	£300	£1000
1887	1,000,000	£265	£275	£300	£1000

DATE	MINTAGE	F	VF	EF	UNC

St George & Dragon reverse

DATE	MINTAGE	F	VF	EF	UNC
1871	incl. above	£265	£275	£285	£350
1872	incl. above	£265	£275	£285	£350
1873	incl. above	£265	£275	£285	£350
1874	incl. above	£265	£275	£285	£350
1876	3,318,866	£265	£275	£285	£350
1878	1,091,275	£265	£275	£285	£350
1879	20,013	£350	£850	£2500	—
1880	3,650,080	£265	£275	£285	£350
1884	1,769,635	£265	£275	£285	£350
1885	717,723	£265	£275	£285	£350

"M" below the horse's hoof above the date indicates that the coin was struck at the Melbourne Mint

M below bust on obverse (Melbourne Mint)

DATE	MINTAGE	F	VF	EF	UNC
1872	incl. above	£285	£500	£1100	£2750
1873	752,199	£265	£275	£285	£350
1874	incl. above	£265	£275	£285	£350
1875	incl. above	£265	£275	£285	£350
1876	2,124,445	£265	£275	£285	£350
1877	1,487,316	£265	£275	£285	£350
1878	2,171,457	£265	£275	£285	£350
1879	2,740,594	£265	£275	£285	£350
1880	incl. above	£265	£275	£285	£350
1881	incl. above	£265	£275	£285	£350
1882	incl. above	£265	£275	£285	£350
1883	incl. above	£265	£275	£285	£350
1884	incl. above	£265	£275	£285	£350
1885	incl. above	£265	£275	£285	£350
1886	incl. above	£265	£275	£285	£350
1887	incl. above	£265	£275	£285	£350

S below bust on obverse (Sydney Mint)

DATE	MINTAGE	F	VF	EF	UNC
1871	2,814,000	£265	£275	£285	£350
1872	incl. above	£265	£275	£285	£350
1873	incl. above	£265	£275	£285	£350
1874	1,899,000	£265	£275	£285	£350
1875	inc above	£265	£275	£285	£350
1876	1,613,000	£265	£275	£285	£350
1877	—			Extremely rare	
1879	incl. above	£265	£275	£285	£350
1880	incl. above	£265	£275	£285	£350
1881	incl. above	£265	£275	£285	£350
1882	incl. above	£265	£275	£285	£350
1883	incl. above	£265	£275	£285	£350
1884	incl. above	£265	£275	£285	£350
1885	incl. above	£265	£275	£285	£350
1886	incl. above	£265	£275	£285	£350
1887	incl. above	£265	£275	£285	£350

JUBILEE HEAD ISSUES

DATE	MINTAGE	F	VF	EF	UNC
1887	1,111,280	£265	£275	£285	£350
1887 Proof	797	—	—	—	£1250
1888	2,717,424	£265	£275	£285	£350
1889	7,257,455	£265	£275	£285	£350
1890	6,529.887	£265	£275	£285	£350
1891	6,329,476	£265	£275	£285	£350
1892	7,104,720	£265	£275	£285	£350

M on ground on reverse (Melbourne Mint)

DATE	MINTAGE	F	VF	EF	UNC
1887	940,000	£265	£275	£285	£350
1888	2,830,612	£265	£275	£300	£350
1889	2,732,590	£265	£275	£285	£350
1890	2,473,537	£265	£275	£285	£350
1891	2,749,592	£265	£275	£285	£350
1892	3,488,750	£265	£275	£285	£350
1893	1,649,352	£265	£275	£285	£350

Jubilee head type

DATE	MINTAGE	F	VF	EF	UNC
S on ground on reverse (Sydney Mint)					
1887	1,002,000	£265	£275	£400	£1000
1888	2,187,000	£265	£275	£285	£300
1889	3,262,000	£265	£275	£285	£300
1890	2,808,000	£265	£275	£285	£300
1891	2,596,000	£265	£275	£285	£300
1892	2,837,000	£265	£275	£285	£300
1893	1,498,000	£265	£275	£285	£300
OLD HEAD ISSUES					
1893	6,898,260	£265	£275	£285	£300
1893 Proof	773	—	—	—	£1500
1894	3,782,611	£265	£275	£285	£300
1895	2,285,317	£265	£275	£285	£300
1896	3,334,065	£265	£275	£285	£300
1898	4,361,347	£265	£275	£285	£300
1899	7,515,978	£265	£275	£285	£300
1900	10,846,741	£265	£275	£285	£300
1901	1,578,948	£265	£275	£285	£300
M on ground on reverse (Melbourne Mint)					
1893	1,914,000	£265	£275	£285	£300
1894	4,166,874	£265	£275	£285	£300
1895	4,165,869	£265	£275	£285	£300
1896	4,456,932	£265	£275	£285	£300
1897	5,130,565	£265	£275	£285	£300
1898	5,509,138	£265	£275	£285	£300
1899	5,579,157	£265	£275	£285	£300
1900	4,305,904	£265	£275	£285	£300
1901	3,987,701	£265	£275	£285	£300
P on ground on reverse (Perth Mint)					
1899	690,992	£265	£275	£350	£1250
1900	1,886,089	£265	£275	£285	£300
1901	2,889,333	£265	£275	£285	£300
S on ground on reverse (Sydney Mint)					
1893	1,346,000	£265	£275	£285	£300
1894	3,067,000	£265	£275	£285	£300
1895	2,758,000	£265	£275	£285	£300
1896	2,544,000	£265	£275	£285	£300
1897	2,532,000	£265	£275	£285	£300
1898	2,548,000	£265	£275	£285	£300
1899	3,259,000	£265	£275	£285	£300
1900	3,586,000	£265	£275	£285	£300
1901	3,012,000	£265	£275	£285	£300

Old head type

EDWARD VII (1902–10)

	MINTAGE	F	VF	EF	UNC
1902	4,737,796	£265	£275	£285	£300
1902 Matt proof	15,123	—	—	—	£300
1903	8,888,627	£265	£275	£285	£300
1904	10,041,369	£265	£275	£285	£300
1905	5,910,403	£265	£275	£285	£300
1906	10,466,981	£265	£275	£285	£300
1907	18,458,663	£265	£275	£285	£300
1908	11,729,006	£265	£275	£285	£300
1909	12,157,099	£265	£275	£285	£300
1910	22,379,624	£265	£275	£285	£300
C on ground on reverse (Ottawa Mint)					
1908 Satin finish Proof only	633			Extremely rare	
1909	16,300	£265	£275	£285	—
1910	28,020	£265	£275	£285	—

DATE	MINTAGE	F	VF	EF	UNC
M on ground on reverse (Melbourne Mint)					
1902	4,267,157	£265	£275	£285	£300
1903...	3,521,780	£265	£275	£285	£300
1904...	3,743,897	£265	£275	£285	£300
1905...	3,633,838	£265	£275	£285	£300
1906...	3,657,853	£265	£275	£285	£300
1907...	3,332,691	£265	£275	£285	£300
1908...	3,080,148	£265	£275	£285	£300
1909...	3,029,538	£265	£275	£285	£300
1910...	3,054,547	£265	£275	£285	£300
P on ground on reverse (Perth Mint)					
1902	3,289,122	£265	£275	£285	£300
1903...	4,674,783	£256	£275	£285	£300
1904...	4,506,756	£265	£275	£285	£300
1905...	4,876,193	£265	£275	£285	£300
1906...	4,829,817	£265	£275	£285	£300
1907...	4,972,289	£265	£275	£285	£300
1908...	4,875,617	£265	£275	£285	£300
1909...	4,524,241	£265	£275	£285	£300
1910...	4,690,625	£265	£275	£285	£300
S on ground on reverse (Sydney Mint)					
1902	2,813,000	£265	£275	£285	£260
1902 Proof....................................	incl. above			Extremely rare	
1903...	2,806,000	£265	£275	£285	£300
1904...	2,986,000	£265	£275	£285	£300
1905...	2,778,000	£265	£275	£285	£300
1906...	2,792,000	£265	£275	£285	£300
1907...	2,539,000	£265	£275	£285	£300
1908...	2,017,000	£265	£275	£285	£300
1909...	2,057,000	£265	£275	£285	£300
1910...	2,135,000	£265	£275	£285	£300

> **IMPORTANT NOTE:** The prices quoted in this guide are set at August 2011 with the price of gold at £1,150 per ounce and silver £25 per ounce—market fluctuations can have a marked effect on the values of modern precious metal coins.

GEORGE V (1911–36)

(Extra care should be exercised when purchasing as good quality forgeries exist of virtually all dates and mintmarks)

DATE	MINTAGE	F	VF	EF	UNC
1911...	30,044,105	£265	£275	£285	£300
1911 Proof....................................	3,764	–	–	–	£600
1912...	30,317,921	£265	£275	£285	£300
1913...	24,539,672	£265	£275	£285	£300
1914...	11,501,117	£265	£275	£285	£300
1915...	20,295,280	£265	£275	£285	£300
1916...	1,554,120	£265	£275	£285	£300
1917...	1,014,714	£1500	£3000	£6500	–
1925...	4,406,431	£265	£275	£285	£300
C on ground on reverse (Ottawa Mint)					
1911	256,946	£265	£275	£285	£300
1913...	3,715	£275	£300	£1200	–
1914...	14,891	£265	£275	£500	–
1916...	6,111			Extremely rare	
1917...	58,845	£265	£275	£285	£300
1918...	106,516	£265	£275	£285	£300
1919...	135,889	£265	£275	£285	£300
I on ground on reverse (Bombay Mint)					
1918...	1,295,372	£265	£265	£275	–
M on ground on reverse (Melbourne Mint)					
1911...	2,851,451	£265	£275	£285	£300
1912...	2,469,257	£265	£275	£285	£300
1913...	2,323,180	£265	£275	£285	£300
1914...	2,012,029	£265	£275	£285	£300
1915...	1,637,839	£265	£275	£285	£300
1916...	1,273,643	£265	£275	£285	£300
1917...	934,469	£265	£275	£285	£300
1918...	4,969,493	£265	£275	£285	£300

DATE	MINTAGE	F	VF	EF	UNC
1919	514,257	£265	£275	£300	£425
1920	530,266	£900	£1800	£3000	£5000
1921	240,121	£3000	£6000	£9000	£15000
1922	608,306	£2200	£4000	£7500	£16000
1923	510,870	£265	£275	£285	£300
1924	278,140	£265	£275	£285	£300
1925	3,311,622	£265	£275	£285	£300
1926	211,107	£265	£275	£285	£300
1928	413,208	£500	£900	£1500	£3000
1929	436,719	£500	£1000	£2000	£3500
1930	77,547	£265	£275	£285	£300
1931	57,779	£265	£275	£400	£625

P on ground on reverse (Perth Mint)

DATE	MINTAGE	F	VF	EF	UNC
1911	4,373,165	£265	£275	£285	£300
1912	4,278,144	£265	£275	£285	£300
1913	4,635,287	£265	£275	£285	£300
1914	4,815,996	£265	£275	£285	£300
1915	4,373,596	£265	£275	£285	£300
1916	4,096,771	£265	£275	£285	£300
1917	4,110,286	£265	£275	£285	£300
1918	3,812,884	£265	£275	£285	£300
1919	2,995,216	£265	£275	£285	£300
1920	2,421,196	£265	£275	£285	£300
1921	2,134,360	£265	£275	£285	£300
1922	2,298,884	£265	£275	£285	£300
1923	2,124,154	£265	£275	£285	£300
1924	1,464,416	£265	£275	£285	£300
1925	1,837,901	£265	£275	£285	£300
1926	1,313,578	£400	£750	£1500	£2500
1927	1,383,544	£265	£275	£285	£450
1928	1,333,417	£265	£275	£285	£300
1929	1,606,625	£265	£275	£285	£300
1930	1,915,352	£265	£275	£285	£300
1931	1,173,568	£265	£275	£285	£300

S on ground on reverse (Sydney Mint)

DATE	MINTAGE	F	VF	EF	UNC
1911	2,519,000	£265	£275	£285	£300
1912	2,227,000	£265	£275	£285	£300
1913	2,249,000	£265	£275	£285	£300
1914	1,774,000	£265	£275	£285	£300
1915	1,346,000	£265	£275	£285	£300
1916	1,242,000	£265	£275	£285	£300
1917	1,666,000	£265	£275	£285	£300
1918	3,716,000	£265	£275	£285	£300
1919	1,835,000	£265	£275	£285	£300

DATE	MINTAGE	F	VF	EF	UNC
1920	—		Excessively rare*		
1921	839,000	£400	£650	£1200	£1750
1922	578,000		Extremely rare		
1923	416,000		Extremely rare		
1924	394,000	£340	£625	£1000	£2000
1925	5,632,000	£265	£275	£285	£300
1926	1,031,050		Extremely rare		

SA on ground on reverse (Pretoria Mint)

1923	719	£500	£1000	£2250	£4500
1923 Proof	655		Extremely rare		
1924	3,184	—	£1750	£3750	—
1925	6,086,264	£265	£275	£285	£300
1926	11,107,611	£265	£275	£285	£300
1927	16,379,704	£265	£275	£285	£300
1928	18,235,057	£265	£275	£285	£300
1929	12,024,107	£265	£275	£285	£300
1930	10,027,756	£265	£275	£285	£300
1931	8,511,792	£265	£275	£285	£300
1932	1,066,680	£265	£275	£285	£300

GEORGE VI (1937–52)

1937 Proof only	5,501	—	—	£900	£1500

ELIZABETH II (1952–)

Pre Decimal Issues

1957	2,072,000	£265	£275	£285	£300
1958	8,700,140	£265	£275	£285	£300
1959	1,358,228	£265	£275	£285	£300
1962	3,000,000	£265	£275	£285	£300
1963	7,400,000	£265	£275	£285	£300
1964	3,000,000	£265	£275	£285	£300
1965	3,800,000	£265	£275	£285	£300
1966	7,050,000	£265	£275	£285	£300
1967	5,000,000	£265	£275	£285	£300
1968	4,203,000	£265	£275	£285	£300

*Later issues are included in the Decimal section. *In 2009 one sold for £415,000.*

HALF SOVEREIGNS

GEORGE III (1760–1820)

1817	2,080,197	£130	£160	£350	£800
1818	1,030,286	£130	£160	£350	£850
1820	35,043	£130	£160	£350	£800

GEORGE IV (1820–30)

1821 First bust, ornate shield reverse	231,288	£450	£1300	£2600	£4250
1821 — Proof	unrecorded	—	—	—	£4000
1823 First bust, Plain shield rev.	224,280	£130	£200	£400	£800
1824 —	591,538	£130	£200	£425	£800
1825 —	761,150	£130	£200	£425	£800
1826 bare head, shield with full legend reverse	344,830	£130	£200	£400	£800
1826 — Proof	unrecorded	—	—	—	£1500
1827 —	492,014	£130	£200	£400	£800
1828 —	1,224,754	£130	£200	£400	£900

DATE	MINTAGE	F	VF	EF	UNC

WILLIAM IV (1830–37)

1831 Proof only	unrecorded	—	—	—	£2300
1834..	133,899	£160	£340	£600	£1400
1835..	772,554	£160	£400	£500	£1250
1836..	146,865	£150	£300	£500	£1250
1836 obverse from 6d die	incl. above	£1000	£2500	£5000	—
1837..	160,207	£150	£300	£500	£1250

VICTORIA (1837–1901)

YOUNG HEAD ISSUES

Shield reverse

1838	273,341	£130	£135	£275	£900
1839 Proof only	1,230	—	—	—	£2250
1841..	508,835	£130	£135	£275	£900
1842..	2,223,352	—	—	£240	£600
1843..	1,251,762	£130	£135	£275	£700
1844..	1,127,007	£130	£135	£275	£600
1845..	887,526	£140	£450	£1500	£2750
1846..	1,063,928	£130	£135	£240	£650
1847..	982,636	£130	£135	£240	£650
1848..	410,595	£130	£135	£240	£650
1849..	845,112	—	£135	£240	£600
1850..	179,595	£130	£300	£600	£1500
1851..	773,573	—	£135	£240	£600
1852..	1,377,671	—	£135	£240	£600
1853..	2,708,796	—	£135	£240	£600
1853 Proof.................................	unrecorded	—	—	—	£6000
1854..	1,125,144		Extremely rare		
1855..	1,120,362	£130	£135	£220	£500
1856..	2,391,909	£130	£135	£220	£500
1857..	728,223	£130	£135	£220	£500
1858..	855,578	£130	£135	£220	£500
1859..	2,203,813	£130	£135	£220	£500
1860..	1,131,500	£130	£135	£220	£500
1861..	1,130,867	£130	£135	£220	£500
1862..	unrecorded	£500	£1400	£5000	—
1863..	1,571,574	£130	£135	£240	£500
1863 with Die number	incl. above	£130	£135	£240	£500
1864 —	1,758,490	£130	£135	£240	£500
1865 —	1,834,750	£130	£135	£240	£500
1866 —	2,058,776	£130	£135	£240	£500
1867 —	992,795	£130	£135	£240	£470
1869 —	1,861,764	£130	£135	£240	£470
1870 —	1,159,544	£130	£135	£240	£380
1871 —	2,062,970	£130	£135	£240	£380
1872 —	3,248,627	£130	£135	£240	£380
1873 —	1,927,050	£130	£135	£240	£380
1874 —	1,884,432	£130	£135	£240	£380
1875 —	516,240	£130	£135	£240	£380
1876 —	2,785,187	£130	£135	£240	£380
1877 —	2,197,482	£130	£135	£240	£380
1878 —	2,081,941	£130	£135	£240	£380
1879 —	35,201	£130	£135	£240	£380
1880 —	1,009,049	£130	£135	£240	£380
1880 no Die number	incl. above	£130	£135	£240	£380
1883 —	2,870,457	£130	£135	£240	£325
1884 —	1,113,756	£130	£135	£240	£325
1885 —	4,468,871	£130	£135	£240	£325

M below shield (Melbourne Mint)

1873..	165,034	£130	£150	£600	—
1877..	80,016	£130	£120	£450	—
1881..	42,009	£130	£200	£650	—
1882..	107,522	£130	£135	£600	—
1884..	48,009	£130	£135	£600	—

Date	Mintage	F	VF	EF	UNC
1885...	11,003	£130	£300	£1500	—
1886...	38,008	£130	£135	£1500	—
1887...	64,013	£150	£400	£1500	£4500

S below shield (Sydney Mint)

Date	Mintage	F	VF	EF	UNC
1871	180,000 (?)	£130	£135	£700	—
1872...	356,000	£130	£135	£700	—
1875...	unrecorded	£130	£135	£700	—
1879...	94,000	£130	£135	£900	—
1880...	80,000	£130	£400	£900	—
1881...	62,000	£130	£135	£900	—
1882...	52,000	£200	£700	£4000	£12000
1883...	220,000	£130	£135	£900	—
1886...	82,000	£130	£135	£900	—
1887...	134,000	£130	£135	£1100	£3750

JUBILEE HEAD ISSUES

Date	Mintage	F	VF	EF	UNC
1887...	871,770	£130	£135	£140	£160
1887 Proof..................................	797	£130	£135	—	£600
1890...	2.266,023	£130	£135	£140	£600
1891...	1,079,286	£130	£135	£140	£600
1892...	13,680,486	£130	£136	£140	£600
1893...	4,426,625	£130	£136	£140	£600

M below shield (Melbourne Mint)

Date	Mintage	F	VF	EF	UNC
1887	incl. above	£130	£136	£300	£600
1893...	110,024	£130	£140	£550	—

S below shield (Sydney Mint)

Date	Mintage	F	VF	EF	UNC
1887	incl. above	£130	£135	£280	£500
1889...	64,000	£130	£135	£280	—
1891...	154,000	£130	£135	£280	—

OLD HEAD ISSUES

Date	Mintage	F	VF	EF	UNC
1893...	incl. above	£130	£135	£140	£175
1893 Proof..................................	773	—	—	—	£625
1894...	3,794,591	£130	£135	£140	£175
1895...	2,869,183	£130	£135	£140	£175
1896...	2,946,605	£130	£135	£140	£175
1897...	3,568,156	£130	£135	£140	£175
1898...	2,868,527	£130	£135	£140	£175
1899...	3,361,881	£130	£135	£140	£175
1900...	4,307,372	£130	£135	£140	£175
1901...	2,037,664	£130	£135	£140	£175

M on ground on reverse (Melbourne Mint)

Date	Mintage	F	VF	EF	UNC
1893	unrecorded		Extremely rare		
1896...	218,946	£130	£135	£450	—
1899...	97,221	£130	£135	£450	—
1900...	112,920	£130	£135	£450	—

P on ground on reverse (Perth Mint)

Date	Mintage	F	VF	EF	UNC
1899...			Proof Unique		
1900	119,376	£130	£300	£550	—

S on ground on reverse (Sydney Mint)

Date	Mintage	F	VF	EF	UNC
1893...	250,000	£130	£135	£375	—
1897...	unrecorded	£130	£135	£350	—
1900...	260,00	£130	£135	£350	—

EDWARD VII (1902–10)

Date	Mintage	F	VF	EF	UNC
1902...	4,244,457	£130	£135	£140	£150
1902 Matt proof..........................	15,123	—	—	—	£150
1903...	2,522,057	£130	£135	£140	£150
1904...	1,717,440	£130	£135	£140	£150
1905...	3,023,993	£130	£135	£140	£150
1906...	4,245,437	£130	£135	£140	£150
1907...	4,233,421	£130	£135	£140	£150
1908...	3,996,992	£130	£135	£140	£150
1909...	4,010,715	£130	£135	£140	£150
1910...	5,023,881	£130	£135	£140	£150

DATE		F	VF	EF	UNC
M on ground on reverse (Melbourne Mint)					
1906	82,042	£120	£130	£150	£335
1907	405,034	£120	£130	£150	£285
1908	incl. above	£120	£130	£150	£335
1909	186,094	£120	£130	£150	£285
P on ground on reverse (Perth Mint)					
1904	60,030	£120	£130	£560	—
1908	24,668	£120	£130	£560	—
1909	44,022	£120	£130	£485	—
S on ground on reverse (Sydney Mint)					
1902	84,000	£120	£130	£140	£310
1902 Proof			Extremely rare		
1903	231,000				£260
1906	308,00	£120	£130	£140	£285
1908	538,000	£120	£130	£140	£285
1910	474,000	£120	£130	£140	£285

GEORGE V (1911–36)

		F	VF	EF	UNC
1911	6,104,106	£120	£130	£140	£150
1911 Proof	3,764	—	—	—	£310
1912	6,224,316	£120	£130	£140	£150
1913	6,094,290	£120	£130	£140	£150
1914	7,251,124	£120	£130	£140	£150
1915	2,042,747	£120	£130	£140	£150
M on ground on reverse (Melbourne Mint)					
1915	125,664	£120	£130	£140	£150
P on ground on reverse (Perth Mint)					
1911	130,373	£120	£130	£140	£210
1915	136,219	£120	£130	£140	£210
1918	unrecorded	£160	£410	£810	£1260
S on ground on reverse (Sydney Mint)					
1911	252,000	£120	£130	£140	£150
1912	278,000	£120	£130	£140	£150
1914	322,000	£120	£130	£140	£150
1915	892,000	£120	£130	£140	£150
1916	448,000	£120	£130	£140	£150
SA on ground on reverse (Pretoria Mint)					
1923 Proof only	655	—	—	—	£360
1925	946,615	£120	£130	£140	£150
1926	806,540	£120	£130	£140	£150

GEORGE VI (1937–52)

		F	VF	EF	UNC
1937 Proof only	5,501	—	—	—	£490

Later issues are included in the Decimal section.

IMPORTANT NOTE:

The prices quoted in this guide are set at August 2011 with the price of gold at £1,150 per ounce and silver £25 per ounce—market fluctuations can have a marked effect on the values of modern precious metal coins.

Krause Standard Catalogs ®

The reference books used by collectors and dealers throughout the world

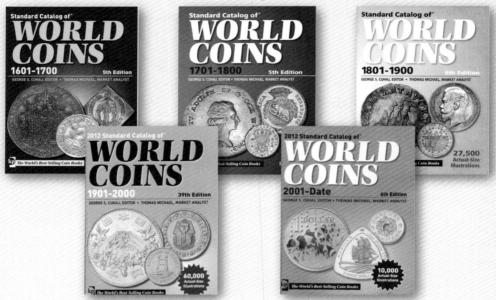

To world coin collectors the Krause series certainly needs no introduction. The Standard Catalog® of World Coins is now divided into five comprehensive volumes covering the 17th, 18th, 19th, 20th and 21st centuries. The Krause series is unique inasmuch that in these volumes just about every conceivable coin ever minted worldwide since 1601 has been catalogued and valued (in US$). These huge books are essential references for any coin collector.

Order your copies today and take advantage of our great postage rates if you order one volume or more.

WORLD COIN CATALOG® PRICE:

1601–1700	£58.99
1701–1800	£57.99
1801–1900	£47.99
1901–2000	£44.99
2001–Date	£25.99

These excellent books are essential references, however they are heavy. Postage costs are: £8* for 1 volume, £12* for 2 volumes, £15* for three volumes For four or more volumes please call for details.

These prices are UK/Europe/World surface only. For airmail please add an extra £7 to the above postage costs.

CROWNS

DATE	F	VF	EF	UNC

OLIVER CROMWELL

1658 8 over 7 (always)................................	£1800	£3500	£6000	—
1658 Dutch Copy		Extremely rare		
1658 Patterns. In Various Metals................		Extremely rare		

CHARLES II (1660–85)

1662 First bust, rose (2 varieties)	£250	£800	£4500	—
1662 — no rose (2 varieties).......................	£250	£800	£4500	—
1663 —	£240	£800	£4000	—
1664 Second bust	£200	£800	£4000	—
1665 —	£1350	—	—	—
1666 —	£225	£900	£4000	—
1666 — error RE.X for REX		Extremely rare		
1666 — Elephant below bust	£600	£2000	£12500	—
1667 —	£160	£500	£3000	—
1668/7 — 8 over 7......................................	£150	£550	—	—
1668 —	£150	£550	£3500	—
1669/8 — 9 over 8......................................	£350	£800	—	—
1669 —	£300	£1000	£4500	—
1670/69 — 70 over 69................................	£175	£1000	—	—
1670 —	£160	£600	£3500	—
1671..	£150	£600	£3000	—
1671 Third bust	£150	£600	£3000	—
1672 —	£150	£500	£3000	—
1673 —	£150	£500	£3000	—
1674 —		Extremely rare		
1675 —	£700	£2000	—	—
1675/3 —	£700	£2200	—	—
1676 —	£150	£550	£3000	—
1677 —	£140	£550	£3000	—
1677/6 — 7 over 6......................................	£175	£900	—	—
1678/7 —	£175	£900	—	—
1678/7 — 8 over 7......................................	£260	—	—	—
1679 —	£150	£600	£3000	—
1679 Fourth bust	£150	£600	£3000	—
1680 Third bust	£150	£800	£3500	—
1680/79 — 80 over 79................................	£175	£800	—	—
1680 Fourth bust	£160	£700	£3500	—
1680/79 — 80 over 79................................	£190	£1000	—	—
1681 —	£160	£600	£3000	—
1681 — Elephant & Castle below bust.......	£3000	£7500	—	—
1682/1 —	£160	£650	£3250	—
1682 — edge error QVRRTO for QVARTO .	£400	—	—	—
1683 —	£400	£1000	£4000	—
1684 —	£400	£1300	—	—

JAMES II (1685–88)

1686 First bust	£275	£800	£3800	—
1686 — No stops on obv	£350	£1400	—	—
1687 Second bust	£260	£600	£3400	—
1688/7 — 8 over 7......................................	£270	£800	—	—
1688 —	£260	£800	£3400	—

WILLIAM AND MARY (1688–94)

1691	£500	£1400	£4250	—
1692	£500	£1400	£4500	—
1692 2 over upside down 2.........................	£500	£1400	£4250	—

DATE	F	VF	EF	UNC

WILLIAM III (1694–1702)

DATE	F	VF	EF	UNC
1695 First bust	£100	£300	£1800	—
1696 —	£90	£275	£1600	—
1696 — no stops on obv.	£225	£400	—	—
1996 — no stops obv./rev.	£250	£400	—	—
1696 — GEI for DEI	£600	£1500	—	—
1696 Second bust				Unique
1696 Third bust	£90	£275	£1600	—
1697 —	£1200	£4000	£7500	—
1700 Third bust variety edge year DUODECIMO	£140	£550	£1750	—
1700 — edge year DUODECIMO TERTIO..	£140	£550	£1750	—

ANNE (1702–14)

DATE	F	VF	EF	UNC
1703 First bust, VIGO	£300	£900	£3500	—
1705 — Plumes in angles on rev.	£500	£1500	£5500	—
1706 — Roses & Plumes in angles on rev...	£160	£600	£2200	—
1707 — —	£160	£600	£2200	—
1707 Second bust, E below	£160	£500	£1800	—
1707 — Plain	£160	£500	£1800	—
1708 — E below	£160	£500	£1800	—
1708/7 — 8 over 7	£160	£800	—	—
1708 — Plain	£160	£600	£1800	—
1708 — — error BR for BRI			Extremely rare	
1708 — Plumes in angles on rev.	£180	£700	£2500	—
1713 Third bust, Roses & Plumes in angles on rev.	£180	£700	£2200	—

GEORGE I (1714–27)

DATE	F	VF	EF	UNC
1716	£525	£1500	£6000	—
1718 8 over 6	£525	£1500	£5000	—
1720 20 over 18	£525	£1500	£5000	—
1723 SSC in angles on rev. (South Sea Co.)	£525	£1500	£5000	—
1726	£525	£1500	£5250	—

GEORGE II (1727–60)

DATE	F	VF	EF	UNC
1732 Young head, Plain, Proof	—	—	£6000	
1732 — Roses & Plumes in angles on rev ..	£200	£700	£2300	—
1734 — —	£200	£700	£2300	—
1735 — —	£200	£700	£2300	—
1736 — —	£220	£700	£2300	—
1739 — Roses in angles on rev	£210	£600	£2300	—
1741 — —	£210	£600	£2300	—
1743 Old head, Roses in angles on rev	£200	£600	£2000	—
1746 — LIMA below bust	£200	£600	£2000	—
1746 — Plain, Proof	—	—	£4500	—
1750 — —	£350	£1000	£3000	—
1751 — —	£450	£1200	£3300	—

GEORGE III (1760–1820)

DATE	F	VF	EF	UNC
Dollar with oval counterstamp	£125	£400	£750	—
Dollar with octagonal counterstamp	£175	£500	£800	—
1804 Bank of England Dollar, Britannia rev.	£100	£225	£500	—
1818 LVIII	£40	£100	£250	£750
1818 LIX	£40	£100	£250	£750
1819 LIX	£40	£100	£250	£750
1819 LIX 9 over 8	£45	£150	£400	—
1819 LIX no stops on edge	£60	£150	£400	£950
1819 LX	£40	£100	£325	£850
1820 LX	£35	£100	£300	£750
1820 LX 20 over 19	£35	£200	£500	—

DATE	MINTAGE	F	VF	EF	UNC

GEORGE IV (1820–30)

1821 First bust, St George rev.

	MINTAGE	F	VF	EF	UNC
SECUNDO on edge	437,976	£40	£180	£700	£1500
1821 — — Proof	Incl above	£40	£180	—	£4000
1821 — — Proof TERTIO (error edge)	Incl above	£40	£180	—	£4000
1822 — — SECUNDO	124,929	£40	£180	£700	£1500
1822 — — TERTIO	Incl above	£40	£180	£700	£1500
1823 — Proof only				Extremely rare	
1826 Second bust, shield rev, SEPTIMO					
Proof only		—	—	£2000	£6000

WILLIAM IV (1830–37)

				UNC
1831 Proof only W.W. on truncation	—	—	£12500
1831 Proof only W. WYON on truncation	—	—	£14500
1834 Proof only	—	—	—£21000

VICTORIA (1837–1901)

YOUNG HEAD ISSUES

	MINTAGE	F	VF	EF	UNC
1839 Proof only	—	—	—	—	£6500
1844 Star stops on edge	94,248	£50	£260	£1200	£3000
1844 Cinquefoil stops on edge	incl. above	£50	£260	£1200	£3000
1845 Star stops on edge	159,192	£50	£260	£1200	£3000
1845 Cinquefoil stops on edge	incl. above	£50	£260	£1200	£3000
1847	140,976	£60	£275	£1300	£3500

GOTHIC HEAD ISSUES (Proof only)

	MINTAGE	F	VF	EF	UNC
1847 mdcccxlvii UNDECIMO on edge	8,000	£500	£900	£1750	£3000
1847 — Plain edge	—	—	—	—	£3500
1853 mdcccliii SEPTIMO on edge	460	—	—	—	£8000
1853 — Plain edge	—	—	—	—£11000	

JUBILEE HEAD ISSUES

	MINTAGE	F	VF	EF	UNC
1887	173,581	£20	£30	£60	£150
1887 Proof	1,084	—	—	—	£700
1888 Narrow date	131,899	£20	£35	£90	£240
1888 Wide date	incl above	£25	£60	£300	—
1889	1,807,224	£20	£30	£60	£150
1890	997,862	£20	£30	£70	£200
1891	556,394	£20	£30	£70	£200
1892	451,334	£20	£30	£80	£250

OLD HEAD ISSUES (Regnal date on edge in Roman numerals)

	MINTAGE	F	VF	EF	UNC
1893 LVI	497,845	£20	£45	£150	£375
1893 LVII	incl. above	£20	£45	£200	£425
1893 Proof	1,312	—	—	—	£600
1894 LVII	144,906	£20	£45	£175	£400
1894 LVIII	incl. above	£20	£45	£175	£400
1895 LVIII	252,862	£20	£45	£175	£400
1895 LIX	incl. above	£20	£45	£175	£400
1896 LIX	317,599	£20	£45	£175	£450
1896 LX	incl. above	£20	£45	£175	£400
1897 LX	262,118	£20	£45	£175	£400
1897 LXI	incl. above	£20	£45	£175	£450
1898 LXI	166,150	£20	£45	£175	£500
1898 LXII	incl. above	£20	£45	£175	£400
1899 LXII	166,300	£20	£45	£175	£400
1899 LXIII	incl. above	£20	£45	£175	£400
1900 LXIII	353,356	£20	£45	£175	£400
1900 LXIV	incl. above	£20	£45	£175	£400

Victoria, Jubilee head

DATE	MINTAGE	F	VF	EF	UNC

EDWARD VII (1901–10)

1902...	256,020	£55	£110	£175	£250
1902 "Matt Proof"	15,123	—	—	—	£235

GEORGE V (1910–36)

1927 Proof only	15,030	—	£100	£170	£260
1928...	9,034	£110	£160	£300	£500
1929...	4,994	£110	£160	£300	£500
1930...	4,847	£110	£160	£300	£500
1931...	4,056	£110	£160	£300	£500
1932...	2,395	£200	£400	£800	£1250
1933...	7,132	£110	£160	£300	£525
1934...	932	£800	£1600	£3500	£5000
1935 Jubilee issue. Incuse edge inscription	714,769	£15	£20	£30	£45
1935 — — error edge inscription	incl. above	—	—	—	£1500
1935 — Specimen in box............	incl. above	—	—	—	£60
1935 — Proof	incl. above	—	—	—	£175
1935 — Proof. Raised edge inscription	2,500	—	—	£175	£300
1935 — — fine lettering...............	incl. above	—	—	—	£1000
1935 — — error edge inscription	incl. above	—	—	—	£1500
1935 — Gold proof.....................	30	—	—	Extremely rare	
1936...	2,473	£170	£325	£600	£1000

GEORGE VI (1936–52)

1937 Coronation...........................	418,699	£18	£24	£38	£55
1937 Proof..................................	26,402	—	—	—	£60
1951 Festival of Britain, Proof-like	1,983,540	—	—	£4	£7

ELIZABETH II (1952–)

Pre-Decimal issues (Five Shillings)

1953	5,962,621	—	—	£3	£6
1953 Proof..................................	40,000	—	—	—	£20
1960...	1,024,038	—	—	£3	£6
1960 Polished dies......................	70,000	—	—	—	£9
1965 Churchill	19,640,000	—	—	—	£1

Later issues are listed in the Decimal section.

DOUBLE FLORINS

VICTORIA (1837–1901)

1887 Roman I	483,347	£15	£28	£50	£100
1887 Roman I Proof	incl. above	—	—	—	£400
1887 Arabic 1	incl. above	£15	£28	£50	£100
1887 Arabic 1 Proof....................	incl. above	—	—	—	£400
1888...	243,340	£15	£40	£80	£130
1888 Second I in VICTORIA an inverted 1	incl. above	£22	£45	£90	£340
1889...	1,185,111	£18	£28	£45	£130
1889 inverted 1...........................	incl. above	£25	£45	£90	£340
1890...	782,146	£15	£40	£60	£130

Patterns were also produced in 1911, 1914 and 1950 and are all extremely rare.

HALFCROWNS

DATE	MINTAGE	F	VF	EF	UNC

OLIVER CROMWELL

1656				Extremely rare	
1658		£1000	£1800	£3750	—
1658 Proof in Gold				Extremely rare	

CHARLES II (1660–1685)

1663 First bust		£150	£600	£3500	—
1663 — no stops on obv.		£200	£800	—	—
1664 Second bust		£250	£1200	£5000	—
1666 Third bust		£900	—	—	—
1666 — Elephant		£800	£3000	—	—
1667/4 — 7 over 4				Extremely rare	
1668/4 — 8 over 4		£300	£1500	—	—
1669 —		£400	£1600	—	—
1669/4 — 9 over 4		£250	£900	—	—
1670 —		£125	£500	£2500	—
1670 — MRG for MAG		£300	£1000	—	—
1671 —		£125	£450	£2500	—
1671/0 — 1 over 0		£150	£600	£2750	—
1672 — Third bust				Extremely rare	
1672 Fourth bust		£125	£500	£2500	—
1673 —		£125	£500	£2350	—
1673 — Plumes both sides				Extremely rare	
1673 — Plume below bust		£5000	£15000	—	—
1674 —		£140	£650	—	—
1675 —		£125	£400	£2000	—
1676 —		£125	£400	£1800	—
1676 — inverted 1 in date		£125	£400	£2000	—
1677 —		£125	£400	£1500	—
1678 —		£200	£800	—	—
1679 — GRATTA error				Extremely rare	
1679 —		£120	£400	£1800	—
1680 —		£160	£725	—	—
1681/0 — 1 over 0		£250	—	—	—
1681 —		£125	£450	£2000	—
1681 — Elephant & Castle		£3500	£10000	—	—
1682 —		£120	£450	£2750	—
1683 —		£120	£500	£2400	—
1683 — Plume below bust				Extremely rare	
1684/3 — 4 over 3		£275	£850	£4000	—

JAMES II (1685–1688)

1685 First bust		£220	£600	£2750	—
1686 —		£220	£600	£2750	—
1686/5 — 6 over 5		£220	£700	—	—
1686 — V over S		£225	£750	—	—
1687 —		£220	£650	£3000	—
1687/6 — 7 over 6		£300	£850	—	—
1687 Second bust		£200	£600	£3000	—
1688 —		£200	£600	£2500	—

WILLIAM AND MARY (1688–1694)

1689 First busts; first shield		£100	£350	£1600	—
1689 — — no pearls in crown		£100	£350	£1600	—
1689 — — FRA for FR		£160	£600	£2000	—
1689 — — No stop on obv		£100	£500	£1850	—
1689 — Second shield		£100	£350	£1500	—
1689 — — no pearls in crown		£100	£350	£1600	—
1690 —		£160	£700	£2600	—
1690 — — error GRETIA for GRATIA		£350	£1500	£4200	—
1691 Second busts		£150	£450	£2100	—
1692 —		£150	£450	£2100	—

DATE	MINTAGE	F	VF	EF	UNC
1693 —		£150	£450	£2000	—
1693 — 3 over inverted 3		£170	£625	£2500	—

WILLIAM III (1694–1702)

1696 First bust, large shields, early harp		£70	£240	£900	—
1696 — — — B (Bristol) below bust		£70	£240	£1000	—
1696 — — — C (Chester)..................................		£80	£325	£1100	—
1696 — — — E (Exeter)		£100	£400	£1300	—
1696 — — — N (Norwich)..............................		£90	£400	£1300	—
1696 — — — y (York)		£80	£350	£1500	—
1696 — — — — Scottish arms at date............				Extremely rare	
1696 — — ordinary harp		£80	£275	£1350	—
1696 — — — C		£110	£500	£1000	—
1696 — — — E...		£100	£500	£1000	—
1696 — — — N..		£150	£600	£2250	—
1696 — Small shields, ordinary harp		£70	£250	£900	—
1696 — — — B		£90	£300	£1000	—
1696 — — — C		£90	£300	£1200	—
1696 — — — E...		£100	£450	£2000	—
1696 — — — N..		£110	£450	£1500	—
1696 — — — y...		£100	£450	£1500	—
1696 Second bust				Only one known	
1697 First bust, large shields, ordinary harp		£75	£300	£1000	—
1697 — — — GRR for GRA				Extremely rare	
1697 — — — B		£80	£300	£1000	—
1697 — — — C		£80	£350	£1100	—
1697 — — — E...		£90	£350	£1100	—
1697 — — — N..		£100	£350	£1100	—
1697 — — — y...		£90	£350	£1100	—
1698 — —		£100	£350	£1200	—
1698/7 — — 8 over 7				Extremely rare	
1699 — —		£130	£425	£1600	—
1699 — — Scottish arms at date				Extremely rare	
1700 — —		£120	£375	£1300	—
1701 — —		£125	£400	£1350	—
1701 — — No stops on rev...............................		£150	£600	—	—
1701 — — Elephant & Castle below	Fair £2000				
1701 — — Plumes in angles on rev.		£230	£625	£2200	—

ANNE (1702–1714)

1703 Plain (pre-Union)......................................		£500	£2200	—	—
1703 VIGO below bust		£100	£340	£1100	—
1704 Plumes in angles on rev............................		£150	£500	£1600	—
1705 —		£120	£500	£1600	—
1706 Roses & Plumes in angles on rev.		£90	£350	£1200	—
1707 —		£80	£300	£1000	—
1707 Plain (post-Union).....................................		£80	£200	£850	—
1707 E below bust...		£80	£200	£850	—
1707 — SEPTIMO edge				Extremely rare	
1708 Plain..		£80	£250	£900	—
1708 E below bust...		£80	£250	£900	—
1708 Plumes in angles on rev............................		£90	£275	£1000	—
1709 Plain..		£75	£270	£800	—
1709 E below bust...		£220	£800	—	—
1710 Roses & Plumes in angles on rev.		£80	£325	£1000	—
1712 —		£80	£325	£1000	—
1713 Plain..		£80	£325	£1000	—
1713 Roses & Plumes in angles on rev.		£80	£325	£1000	—
1714 —		£80	£325	£1000	—
1714/3 4 over 3		£125	£500	—	—

GEORGE I (1714–1727)

1715 Roses & Plumes in angles on rev.		£450	£900	£3200	—
1715 Plain edge..				Extremely rare	
1717 —		£450	£900	£3200	—
1720 —		£425	£900	£3200	—
1720/17 20 over 17		£370	£800	£3000	—
1723 SSC in angles on rev.		£370	£800	£2750	—
1726 Small Roses & Plumes in angles on rev... .		£3500	£22000	—	—

DATE	MINTAGE	F	VF	EF	UNC

GEORGE II (1727–1760)

DATE	MINTAGE	F	VF	EF	UNC
1731 Young head, Plain, proof only..................		—	—	£4750	—
1731 — Roses & Plumes in angles on rev.........		£140	£400	£1350	—
1732 — —		£140	£400	£1350	—
1734 — —		£140	£400	£1350	—
1735 — —		£140	£400	£1350	—
1736 — —		£140	£400	£1350	—
1739 — Roses in angles on rev.		£140	£370	£1100	—
1741/39 — — 41 over 30		£150	£550	—	—
1741 — —		£140	£400	£1000	—
1743 Old head, Roses in angles on rev.		£75	£175	£700	—
1745 — —		£75	£175	£700	—
1745 — LIMA below bust..................................		£65	£160	£650	—
1746 — —		£65	£160	£650	—
1746/5 — — 6 over 5		£80	£220	£800	—
1746 — Plain, Proof		—	—	£1800	—
1750 — —		£200	£500	£1600	—
1751 — —		£225	£700	£2000	—

GEORGE III (1760–1820)

DATE	MINTAGE	F	VF	EF	UNC
1816 "Bull head"		—	£20	£75	£200	£450
1817 —	8,092,656	£20	£75	£200	£450
1817 "Small head"......................	incl. above	£20	£75	£200	£450
1818 —	2,905,056	£20	£75	£200	£450
1819/8 — 9 over 8......................	incl. above			Extremely rare	
1819 —	4,790,016	£20	£75	£200	£450
1820 —	2,396,592	£40	£130	£400	£950

GEORGE IV (1820–30)

DATE	MINTAGE	F	VF	EF	UNC
1820 First bust, first reverse........	incl. above	£25	£70	£250	£550
1821 — —	1,435,104	£25	£70	£250	£550
1821 — — Proof..........................	incl. above	—	—	—	£1500
1823 — —	2,003,760	£800	£2500	—	—
1823 — Second reverse..............	incl. above	£25	£70	£250	£500
1824 — —	465,696	£30	£80	£225	£600
1824 Second bust, third reverse .	incl. above			Extremely rare	
1825 — —	2,258,784	£25	£70	£180	£400
1826 — —	2,189,088	£25	£70	£180	£400
1826 — — Proof..........................	incl. above	—	—	—	£1250
1828 — —	49,890	£60	£150	£400	£900
1829 — —	508,464	£55	£130	£375	£875

WILLIAM IV (1830–37)

DATE	MINTAGE	F	VF	EF	UNC
1831...		—			Extremely rare	
1831 Proof (W.W. in script & block)		—	—	—	£1500
1834 W.W. in block......................	993,168	£30	£70	£250	£600
1834 W.W. in script......................	incl. above	£30	£70	£250	£600
1835...	281,952	£35	£80	£275	£650
1836...	1,588,752	£30	£70	£250	£600
1836/5 6 over 5	incl. above	£60	£125	£500	—
1837...	150,526	£40	£130	£475	£1000

VICTORIA (1837–1901)

YOUNG HEAD ISSUES

DATE	MINTAGE	F	VF	EF	UNC
1839 (two varieties)		—	£750	£2500	£6500	—
1839 Proof...................................		—	—	—	£3300
1840...	386,496	£40	£200	£600	£1350
1841...	42,768	£700	£1200	£3000	£6000
1842...	486,288	£50	£110	£500	£1200
1843...	454,608	£120	£300	£800	£2000
1844...	1,999,008	£40	£90	£450	£950
1845...	2,231,856	£40	£90	£450	£950
1846...	1,539,668	£50	£100	£475	£1000
1848 Plain 8................................	367,488	£90	£300	£1200	£3000
1848/6	incl. above	£70	£225	£700	£2250
1849...	261,360	£65	£150	£500	£1250
1849 Small date	incl. above	£80	£180	£700	£1400

DATE	MINTAGE	F	VF	EF	UNC
1850	484,613	£50	£120	£500	£1400
1853 Proof only	—	—	—	—	£3000
1874	2,188,599	£22	£60	£220	£500
1875	1,113,483	£22	£60	£220	£450
1876	633,221	£25	£60	£220	£500
1876/5 6 over 5	incl. above	£30	£60	£250	£500
1877	447,059	£22	£60	£220	£425
1878	1,466,323	£22	£60	£220	£425
1879	901,356	£25	£60	£250	£500
1880	1,346,350	£22	£60	£225	£400
1881	2,301,495	£22	£60	£225	£375
1882	808,227	£22	£60	£225	£400
1883	2,982,779	£22	£60	£225	£375
1884	1,569,175	£22	£60	£225	£375
1885	1,628,438	£22	£60	£225	£375
1886	891,767	£22	£60	£225	£380
1887	1,438,046	£22	£60	£225	£375

JUBILEE HEAD ISSUES

DATE	MINTAGE	F	VF	EF	UNC
1887	incl. above	£7	£12	£25	£60
1887 Proof	1,084	—	—	—	£225
1888	1,428,787	£10	£20	£45	£135
1889	4,811,954	£10	£18	£45	£120
1890	3,228,111	£10	£18	£60	£140
1891	2,284,632	£10	£18	£60	£140
1892	1,710,946	£10	£18	£65	£150

OLD HEAD ISSUES

DATE	MINTAGE	F	VF	EF	UNC
1893	1,792,600	£10	£20	£50	£95
1893 Proof	1,312	—	—	—	£200
1894	1,524,960	£12	£30	£75	£200
1895	1,772,662	£10	£25	£65	£150
1896	2,148,505	£10	£18	£55	£170
1897	1,678,643	£10	£18	£55	£150
1898	1,870,055	£10	£18	£55	£150
1899	2,865,872	£10	£18	£55	£150
1900	4,479,128	£10	£18	£55	£150
1901	1,516,570	£10	£18	£55	£150

DATE	MINTAGE	F	VF	EF	UNC

EDWARD VII (1901–10)

DATE	MINTAGE	F	VF	EF	UNC
1902	1,316,008	£10	£30	£80	£145
1902 "Matt Proof"	15,123	—	—	—	£160
1903	274,840	£175	£525	£1800	£4000
1904	709,652	£60	£225	£500	£1500
1905	166,008	£500	£1100	£4000	£7000
1906	2,886,206	£12	£45	£200	£800
1907	3,693,930	£12	£45	£200	£800
1908	1,758,889	£20	£75	£375	£900
1909	3,051,592	£12	£50	£300	£600
1910	2,557,685	£10	£40	£100	£400

GEORGE V (1910–36)

First issue

DATE	MINTAGE	F	VF	EF	UNC
1911	2,914,573	£8	£25	£60	£140
1911 Proof	6,007	—	—	—	£200
1912	4,700,789	£7	£18	£45	£150
1913	4,090,169	£8	£20	£70	£175
1914	18,333,003	£5	£12	£40	£65
1915	32,433,066	£5	£12	£35	£60
1916	29,530,020	£5	£12	£35	£60
1917	11,172,052	£6	£14	£40	£90
1918	29,079,592	£5	£12	£35	£65
1919	10,266,737	£8	£15	£45	£90

Second issue—debased silver

DATE	MINTAGE	F	VF	EF	UNC
1920	17,982,077	£3	£7	£20	£70
1921	23,677,889	£3	£7	£20	£60
1922	16,396,724	£4	£8	£22	£70
1923	26,308,526	£6	£8	£18	£45
1924	5,866,294	£12	£30	£80	£160
1925	1,413,461	£25	£70	£250	£700
1926	4,473,516	£8	£20	£40	£140

Third issue —Modified effigy

DATE	MINTAGE	F	VF	EF	UNC
1926	incl. above	£5	£12	£35	£80
1927	6,837,872	£5	£10	£30	£60

Fourth issue—New shield reverse

DATE	MINTAGE	F	VF	EF	UNC
1927 Proof	15,000	—	—	—	£70
1928	18,762,727	£5	£8	£18	£35
1929	17,632,636	£5	£8	£18	£35
1930	809,051	£10	£40	£250	£700
1931	11,264,468	£5	£8	£18	£35
1932	4,793,643	£5	£8	£22	£80
1933	10,311,494	£5	£8	£18	£40
1934	2,422,399	£5	£8	£50	£150
1935	7,022,216	£5	£8	£15	£22
1936	7,039,423	£5	£8	£15	£20

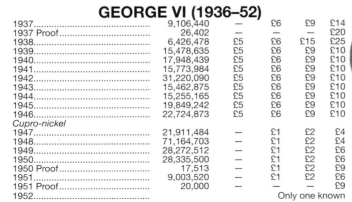

George V, fourth issue, new shield reverse

GEORGE VI (1936–52)

DATE	MINTAGE	F	VF	EF	UNC
1937	9,106,440	—	£6	£9	£14
1937 Proof	26,402	—	—	—	£20
1938	6,426,478	£5	£6	£15	£25
1939	15,478,635	£5	£6	£9	£10
1940	17,948,439	£5	£6	£9	£10
1941	15,773,984	£5	£6	£9	£10
1942	31,220,090	£5	£6	£9	£10
1943	15,462,875	£5	£6	£9	£10
1944	15,255,165	£5	£6	£9	£10
1945	19,849,242	£5	£6	£9	£10
1946	22,724,873	£5	£6	£9	£10

Cupro-nickel

DATE	MINTAGE	F	VF	EF	UNC
1947	21,911,484	—	£1	£2	£4
1948	71,164,703	—	£1	£2	£4
1949	28,272,512	—	£1	£2	£6
1950	28,335,500	—	£1	£2	£6
1950 Proof	17,513	—	£1	£2	£9
1951	9,003,520	—	£1	£2	£6
1951 Proof	20,000	—	—	—	£9
1952			Only one known		

DATE	MINTAGE	F	VF	EF	UNC

ELIZABETH II (1952–)

DATE	MINTAGE	F	VF	EF	UNC
1953	4,333,214	—	—	£1	£3
1953 Proof	40,000	—	—	—	£5
1954	11,614,953	—	£1	£5	£22
1955	23,628,726	—	—	£1	£6
1956	33,934,909	—	—	£1	£6
1957	34,200,563	—	—	£1	£6
1958	15,745,668	—	£1	£5	£22
1959	9,028,844	—	£1	£8	£25
1960	19,929,191	—	—	£1	£2
1961	25,887,897	—	—	—	£2
1961 Polished dies	incl. above	—	—	£1	£2
1962	24,013,312	—	—	—	£1
1963	17,625,200	—	—	—	£1
1964	5,973,600	—	—	—	£1
1965	9,778,440	—	—	—	£1
1966	13,375,200	—	—	—	£1
1967	33,058,400	—	—	—	—

FLORINS

VICTORIA (1837–1901)

YOUNG (CROWNED) HEAD ISSUES

"Godless" type (without D.G.—"Dei Gratia")

"Gothic" florin

	MINTAGE	F	VF	EF	UNC
1848 "Godless" Pattern only plain edge	—		Very rare		
1848 "Godless" Pattern only milled edge	—		Extremely rare		
1849	413,820	£20	£50	£170	£350

(Beware of recent forgeries)

"Gothic" type i.e. date in Roman numerals in obverse legend

"brit." in legend. No die no.

	MINTAGE	F	VF	EF	UNC
1851 mdcccli Proof	1,540		Extremely rare		
1852 mdccclii	1,014,552	£22	£60	£200	£450
1853 mdcccliii	3,919,950	£22	£55	£200	£475
1853 — Proof	incl. above	—	—	—	£2000
1854 mdcccliv	550,413	£500	£1200	—	—
1855 mdccclv	831,017	£25	£70	£225	£525
1856 mdccclvi	2,201,760	£25	£70	£225	£525
1857 mdccclvii	1,671,120	£25	£55	£225	£500
1858 mdccclviii	2,239,380	£22	£55	£225	£500
1859 mdccclix	2,568,060	£22	£55	£200	£500
1860 mdccclx	1,475,100	£35	£80	£250	£600
1862 mdccclxii	594,000	£175	£400	£1000	£2400
1863 mdccclxiii	938,520	£700	£1500	£3000	£6000

"brit" in legend. Die no. below bust

	MINTAGE	F	VF	EF	UNC
1864 mdccclxiv	1,861,200	£22	£55	£220	£475
1864 Gothic Piedfort flan	incl. above		Extremely rare		
1865 mdccclxv	1,580,044	£35	£70	£275	£625
1866 mdccclxvi	914,760	£35	£70	£275	£550
1867 mdccclxvii	423,720	£40	£100	£350	£700
1867—only 42 arcs in border	incl. above		Extremely rare		

"britt" in legend. Die no. below bust

	MINTAGE	F	VF	EF	UNC
1868 mdccclxviii	896,940	£30	£75	£300	£675
1869 mdccclxix	297,000	£30	£75	£300	£725
1870 mdccclxx	1,080,648	£20	£55	£200	£500
1871 mdccclxxi	3,425,605	£22	£55	£200	£500
1872 mdccclxxii	7,199,690	£22	£55	£175	£425
1873 mdccclxxiii	5,921,839	£22	£55	£200	£425
1874 mdccclxxiv	1,642,630	£22	£55	£200	£425
1874 — iv over iii in date	incl. above	£30	£70	£300	£600
1875 mdccclxxv	1,117,030	£20	£55	£200	£450
1876 mdccclxxvi	580,034	£35	£100	£350	£700
1877 mdccclxxvii	682,292	£25	£60	£200	£450
1877 — 48 arcs in border no W.W.	incl. above	£25	£60	£200	£450
1877 — 42 arcs	incl. above	£25	£60	£200	£450
1877 — — no die number	incl. above		Extremely rare		
1878 mdccclxxviii with die number	1,786,680	£20	£55	£200	£425

DATE	MINTAGE	F	VF	EF	UNC
1879 mdcccixxix no die no	1,512,247			Extremely rare	
1879 — 48 arcs in border	incl. above	£25	£60	£220	£450
1879 — no die number	incl. above			Extremely rare	
1879 — 38 arcs, no W.W..	incl. above	£20	£55	£200	£450
1880 mdccclxxx Younger portrait	—			Extremely rare	
1880 — 34 arcs, Older portrait ...	2,167,170	£24	£60	£200	£425
1881 mdccclxxxi — —	2,570,337	£20	£55	£190	£500
1881 — xxГi broken puncheon...	incl. above	£30	£70	£200	£450
1883 mdccclxxxiii — —	3,555,667	£20	£50	£170	£375
1884 mdccclxxxiv — —	1,447,379	£20	£50	£170	£375
1885 mdccclxxxv — —	1,758,210	£20	£50	£170	£375
1886 mdccclxxxvi — —	591,773	£20	£50	£170	£375
1887 mdccclxxxvii — —	1,776,903	£40	£110	£300	£625
1887 — 46 arcs........................	incl. above	£40	£110	£325	£650

JUBILEE HEAD ISSUES

1887	incl. above	£6	£14	£28	£55
1887 Proof	1,084	—	—	—	£200
1888	1,547,540	£7	£15	£45	£120
1889	2,973,561	£7	£15	£45	£120
1890	1,684,737	£10	£25	£80	£225
1891	836,438	£20	£60	£200	£425
1892	283,401	£30	£90	£300	£700

VICTORIA — OLD HEAD ISSUES

1893	1,666,103	£7	£16	£40	£85
1893 Proof	1,312	—	—	—	£225
1894	1,952,842	£10	£18	£70	£220
1895	2,182,968	£9	£25	£70	£200
1896	2,944,416	£7	£20	£55	£140
1897	1,699,921	£7	£20	£55	£140
1898	3,061,343	£7	£20	£55	£140
1899	3,966,953	£7	£20	£55	£140
1900	5,528,630	£7	£20	£55	£140
1901	2,648,870	£7	£20	£55	£140

EDWARD VII (1901–10)

1902	2,189,575	£8	£20	£55	£95
1902 "Matt Proof"	15,123	—	—	—	£120
1903	1,995,298	£10	£35	£120	£500
1904	2,769,932	£12	£40	£150	£475
1905	1,187,596	£60	£160	£600	£1500
1906	6,910,128	£10	£35	£130	£450
1907	5,947,895	£11	£35	£130	£450
1908	3,280,010	£18	£55	£350	£900
1909	3,482,829	£15	£50	£240	£700
1910	5,650,713	£14	£35	£100	£300

GEORGE V (1910–36)

First issue

1911	5,951,284	£6	£12	£40	£85
1911 Proof	6,007	—	—	—	£125
1912	8,571,731	£6	£15	£35	£125
1913	4,545,278	£10	£25	£50	£160
1914	21,252,701	£6	£18	£28	£60
1915	12,367,939	£7	£18	£26	£60
1916	21,064,337	£6	£18	£25	£60
1917	11,181,617	£87	£22	£35	£90
1918	29,211,792	£6	£18	£28	£90
1919	9,469,292	£8	£20	£40	£90

Second issue — *debased silver*

1920	15,387,833	£3	£12	£40	£85
1921	34,863,895	£3	£12	£40	£65
1922	23,861,044	£3	£12	£40	£65
1923	21,546,533	£3	£10	£30	£60
1924	4,582,372	£10	£30	£85	£220
1925	1,404,136	£25	£60	£250	£700
1926	5,125,410	£7	£22	£50	£125

Fourth issue — *new reverse*

1927 Proof only..........................	101,497	—	—	—	£90
1928	11,087,186	£3	£6	£14	£35

DATE	MINTAGE	F	VF	EF	UNC
1929	16,397,279	£3	£6	£15	£30
1930	5,753,568	£3	£6	£18	£40
1931	6,556,331	£3	£6	£15	£30
1932	717,041	£12	£30	£225	£600
1933	8,685,303	£3	£6	£16	£35
1935	7,540,546	£3	£6	£12	£25
1936	9,897,448	£3	£6	£12	£25

GEORGE VI (1936–52)

	MINTAGE	F	VF	EF	UNC
1937	13,006,781	£3	£4	£6	£10
1937 Proof	26,402	—	—	—	£10
1938	7,909,388	£5	£8	£15	£25
1939	20,850,607	£3	£4	£7	£9
1940	18,700,338	£3	£4	£7	£11
1941	24,451,079	£3	£4	£7	£9
1942	39,895,243	£3	£4	£7	£9
1943	26,711,987	£3	£4	£7	£9
1944	27,560,005	£3	£4	£7	£9
1945	25,858,049	£3	£4	£7	£9
1946	22,300,254	£3	£4	£7	£9
Cupro-nickel					
1947	22,910,085	—	—	£1	£3
1948	67,553,636	—	—	£1	£3
1949	28,614,939	—	—	£1	£5
1950	24,357,490	—	—	£2	£7
1950 Proof	17,513	—	—	£1	£9
1951	27,411,747	—	—	£2	£8
1951 Proof	20,000	—	—	—	£9

ELIZABETH II (1952–)

	MINTAGE	F	VF	EF	UNC
1953	11,958,710	—	—	—	£2
1953 Proof	40,000	—	—	—	£6
1954	13,085,422	—	—	£5	£25
1955	25,887,253	—	—	£1	£3
1956	47,824,500	—	—	£1	£3
1957	33,071,282	—	—	£4	£25
1958	9,564,580	—	—	£3	£20
1959	14,080,319	—	—	£4	£25
1960	13,831,782	—	—	£1	£4
1961	37,735,315	—	—	£1	£2
1962	35,147,903	—	—	£1	£2
1963	26,471,000	—	—	£1	£2
1964	16,539,000	—	—	£1	£2
1965	48,163,000	—	—	—	£1.50
1966	83,999,000	—	—	—	£1.50
1967	39,718,000	—	—	—	£1.50

SHILLINGS

OLIVER CROMWELL

		F	VF	EF	UNC
1658		£700	£1400	£2750	—
1658 Dutch Copy				Extremely rare	

CHARLES II (1660–85)

		F	VF	EF	UNC
1663 First bust		£110	£400	£1200	—
1663 — GARTIA error				Extremely rare	
1663 — Irish & Scottish shields transposed		£225	£800	—	—
1666 — Elephant below bust		£480	£1500	£6000	—
1666 "Guinea" head, elephant		£1800	£4500	—	—
1666 Second bust				Extremely rare	
1668 —		£100	£325	£1200	—
1668/7 — 8 over 7		£130	£400	—	—
1668 Second bust		£90	£320	£1200	—
1669/6 First bust variety				Extremely rare	
1669				Extremely rare	
1669 Second bust				Extremely rare	

DATE	F	VF	EF	UNC
1670 —	£140	£500	£1750	—
1671 —	£140	£500	£1750	—
1671 — Plume below, plume in centre rev.	£400	£1000	£3500	—
1672 —	£140	£550	£1750	—
1673 —	£140	£550	£1750	—
1673 — Plume below, plume in centre rev.	£350	£1100	£3500	—
1673/2 — 3 over 2	£175	£600	—	—
1674/3 — 4 over 3	£150	£550	—	—
1674 —	£150	£500	£2000	—
1674 — Plume below bust, plume in centre rev.	£350	£1100	£3500	—
1674 — Plume rev. only	£650	£2000	£4000	—
1674 Third bust	£400	£1500	—	—
1675 Second bust	£200	£800	—	—
1675/4 — 5 over 4	£210	£850	—	—
1675 — Plume below bust, plume in centre rev.	£350	£1100	£4000	—
1675 Third bust	£350	£1250	—	—
1675/3 — 5 over 3	£300	£1100	—	—
1676 Second bust	£125	£450	£1600	—
1676/5 — 6 over 5	£150	£550	—	—
1676 — Plume below bust, plume in centre rev.	£350	£1400	£4200	—
1677 —	£120	£475	£1600	—
1677 — Plume below bust	£700	£2200	£6000	—
1678 —	£140	£500	£1600	—
1678/7 — 8 over 7	£160	£700	—	—
1679 —	£125	£500	£1750	—
1679 — Plume below bust, plume in centre rev.	£350	£1100	£4000	—
1679 — Plume below bust	£650	£2000	£4000	—
1679 — 9 over 7	£160	£600	—	—
1680 —			Extremely rare	
1680 — Plume below bust, plume in centre rev.	£850	£2500	£4500	—
1680/79 — — 80 over 79	£850	£2500	—	—
1681 —	£300	£850	£3000	—
1681 — 1 over 0	£320	£900	£3100	—
1681/0 Elephant & Castle below bust	£2500	£8000	—	—
1682/1 — 2 over 1	£900	£2750	—	—
1683 —			Extremely rare	
1683 Fourth (Larger) bust	£200	£600	£2100	—
1684 —	£200	£600	£2100	—

JAMES II (1685–88)

1685	£160	£500	£1600	—
1685 Plume in centre rev. rev			Extremely rare	
1685 No stops on rev.	£200	£650	—	—
1686	£180	£550	£1750	—
1686/5 6 over 5	£225	£600	£1900	—
1687	£180	£600	£1800	—
1687/6 7 over 6	£180	£550	£1900	—
1688	£190	£600	£1900	—
1688/7 last 8 over 7	£180	£500	£1800	—

WILLIAM & MARY (1688–94)

1692	£175	£500	£2100	—
1692 inverted 1	£210	£550	£2200	—
1693	£175	£500	£2100	—

WILLIAM III (1694–1702)

Provincially produced shillings carry privy marks or initials below the bust:
B: Bristol. C: Chester. E: Exeter. N: Norwich. Y or y: York.

1695 First bust	£40	£120	£600	—
1696 —	£40	£100	£425	—
1696 — no stops on rev.	£60	£140	£750	—
1696 — MAB for MAG			Extremely rare	
1696 — 1669 error			Extremely rare	
1696 — 1669 various GVLELMVS errors			Extremely rare	
1696 — B below bust	£55	£150	£750	—
1696 — C	£55	£150	£750	—
1696 — E	£55	£160	£800	—
1696 — N	£45	£140	£700	—

DATE	F	VF	EF	UNC
1696 — y	£55	£130	£650	—
1696 — Y	£50	£130	£650	—
1696 Second bust		Only one known		
1696 Third bust C below	£160	£400	£1250	—
1696 — Y		Extremely rare		
1697 First bust	£50	£110	£400	—
1697 — GRI for GRA error		Extremely rare		
1697 — Scottish & Irish shields transposed		Extremely rare		
1697 — Irish arms at date		Extremely rare		
1697 — no stops on rev	£55	£180	£700	—
1697 — GVLELMVS error		Extremely rare		
1697 — B	£55	£150	£750	—
1697 — C	£55	£140	£750	—
1697 — E	£55	£140	£750	—
1697 — N	£55	£130	£725	—
1697 — — no stops on obv		Extremely rare		
1697 — y	£50	£150	£600	—
1697 — — arms of France & Ireland transposed		Extremely rare		
1697 — Y	£50	£140	£600	—
1697 Third bust	£45	£125	£550	—
1697 — B	£55	£140	£600	—
1697 — C	£55	£140	£600	—
1697 — — Fr.a error	£150	£425	—	—
1697 — — no stops on obv	£80	£275	—	—
1697 — — arms of Scotland at date		Extremely rare		
1697 — E	£55	£140	£700	—
1697 — N	£55	£140	£700	—
1697 — y	£55	£140	£650	—
1697 Third bust variety	£50	£130	£450	—
1697 — B	£55	£150	£700	—
1697 — C	£110	£525	—	—
1698 —	£70	£200	£750	—
1698 — Plumes in angles of rev.	£200	£500	£1500	—
1698 Fourth bust "Flaming hair"	£140	£475	£1650	—
1699 —	£110	£400	£1250	—
1699 Fifth bust	£100	£300	£1000	—
1699 — Plumes in angles on rev.	£150	£450	£1750	—
1699 — Roses in angles on rev.	£160	£500	£1750	—
1700 —	£65	£120	£525	—
1700 — Small round oo in date	£65	£120	£525	—
1700 — no stop after DEI		Extremely rare		
1700 — Plume below bust	£1800	£5000	—	—
1701 —	£80	£220	£700	—
1701 — Plumes in angles on rev.	£150	£525	£1650	—

William III First bust

ANNE (1702–14)

	F	VF	EF	UNC
1702 First bust (pre-Union with Scotland)	£80	£300	£700	—
1702 — Plumes in angles on rev.	£90	£275	£800	—
1702 — VIGO below bust	£70	£220	£650	—
1702 — — colon before ANNA		Extremely rare		
1703 Second bust, VIGO below	£65	£180	£600	—
1704 — Plain	£500	£1600	—	—
1704 — Plumes in angles on rev.	£80	£200	£750	—
1705 — Plain	£75	£200	£650	—
1705 — Plumes in angles on rev.	£70	£200	£650	—
1705 — Roses & Plumes in angles on rev.	£70	£200	£650	—
1707 — —	£60	£180	£600	—
1707 Second bust (post-Union) E below bust ..	£50	£125	£500	—
1707 — E* below bust	£70	£200	£700	—
1707 Third bust, Plain	£35	£100	£400	—
1707 — Plumes in angles on rev.	£50	£160	£750	—
1707 — E below bust	£40	£90	£450	—
1707 "Edinburgh" bust, E* below		Extremely rare		
1708 Second bust, E below	£50	£100	£450	—
1708 — E* below bust	£55	£165	£700	—
1708/7 — — 8 over 7		Extremely rare		
1708 — Roses & Plumes in angles on rev.	£80	£275	£650	—

Anne, VIGO below bust

DATE	MINTAGE	F	VF	EF	UNC
1708 Third bust, Plain		£40	£100	£350	—
1708 — Plumes in angles on rev.		£70	£200	£550	—
1708 Third bust, E below bust		£60	£175	£600	—
1708/7 — — 8 over 7		£100	£300	—	—
1708 — Roses & Plumes in angles on rev.		£70	£180	£550	—
1708 "Edinburgh" bust, E* below		£60	£170	£525	—
1709 Third bust, Plain		£50	£125	£500	—
1709 "Edinburgh" bust, E* below		£50	£170	£650	—
1709 — E no star (filled in die?)		£70	£160	£550	—
1710 Third bust, Roses & Plumes in angles		£60	£140	£600	—
1710 Fourth bust, Roses & Plumes in angles		£60	£150	£600	—
1711 Third bust, Plain		£70	£160	£425	—
1711 Fourth bust, Plain		£30	£75	£220	—
1712 — Roses & Plumes in angles on rev.		£60	£120	£400	—
1713 — —		£60	£120	£375	—
1713/2 — 3 over 2		£60	£200	—	—
1714 — —		£60	£100	£325	—
1714/3 —				Extremely rare	

GEORGE I (1714–27)

DATE	MINTAGE	F	VF	EF	UNC
1715 First bust, Roses & Plumes in angles on rev.		£80	£200	£800	—
1716 — —		£150	£500	£1800	—
1717 — —		£80	£250	£1100	—
1718 — —		£70	£225	£750	—
1719 — —		£120	£400	£1400	—
1720 — —		£70	£175	£450	—
1720/18 — —		£150	£500	£1400	—
1720 — Plain		£40	£100	£450	—
1721 — Roses & Plumes in angles on rev.		£100	£350	£1400	—
1721/0 — — 1 over 0		£70	£220	£850	—
1721 — Plain		£120	£450	£1250	—
1721/19 — — 21 over 19		£125	£350		—
1721/18 21 over 18 error, Plumes & Roses		£425	£1500	—	—
1722 — Roses & Plumes in angles on rev.		£80	£220	£900	—
1723 — —		£80	£220	£900	—
1723 — SSC rev., Arms of France at date		£100	£275	£750	—
1723 — SSC in angles on rev		£35	£110	£240	—
1723 Second bust, SSC in angles on rev.		£50	£160	£525	—
1723 — Roses & Plumes in angles		£90	£240	£1000	—
1723 — WCC (Welsh Copper Co) below bust		£500	£1500	£5000	—
1724 — Roses & Plumes in angles on rev.		£80	£200	£750	—
1724 — WCC below bust		£500	£1500	£5000	—
1725 — Roses & Plumes in angles on rev.		£80	£200	£900	—
1725 — — no stops on obv.		£90	£225	£950	—
1725 — WCC below bust		£550	£1600	£5250	—
1726 — — Roses & Plumes		£600	£1750	£6250	—
1726 — WCC below bust		£550	£1600	£5500	—
1727 — —				Extremely rare	
1727 — — no stops on obv.				Extremely rare	

GEORGE II (1727–60)

DATE	MINTAGE	F	VF	EF	UNC
1727 Young head, Plumes in angles on rev.		£75	£300	£950	—
1727 — Roses & Plumes in angles on rev.		£60	£180	£650	—
1728 — —		£65	£180	£650	—
1728 — Plain		£75	£220	£700	—
1729 — Roses & Plumes in angles on rev.		£60	£200	£700	—
1731 — —		£70	£200	£700	—
1731 — Plumes in angles on rev.		£75	£350	£1000	—
1732 — Roses & Plumes in angles on rev.		£65	£200	£750	—
1734 — —		£65	£200	£700	—
1735 — —		£65	£200	£700	—
1736 — —		£65	£200	£700	—
1736/5 — — 6 over 5		£70	£200	£800	—
1737 — —		£65	£200	£600	—
1739 — Roses in angles on rev.		£50	£150	£425	—
1739/7 — — 9 over 7				Extremely rare	
1741 — —		£50	£150	£425	—
1741/39 — — 41 over 39				Extremely rare	
1743 Old head, Roses in angles on rev.		£30	£80	£325	—
1745 — —		£30	£80	£325	—

*George II
Young head*

DATE	MINTAGE	F	VF	EF	UNC
1745 — — LIMA below bust		£28	£85	£310	—
1745/3 — — — 5 over 3		£60	£175	£400	—
1746 — — —		£50	£175	£650	—
1746/5 — — — 6 over 5		£100	£300	—	—
1746 — Plain, Proof		—	—	£1400	—
1747 — Roses in angles on rev.		£45	£100	£375	—
1750 — Plain		£35	£120	£350	—
1750/6 — — 0 over 6		£60	£150	£500	—
1751 — —		£100	£275	£750	—
1758 — —		£20	£50	£140	—

George II
Old head

GEORGE III (1760–1820)

	MINTAGE	F	VF	EF	UNC
1763 "Northumberland" bust		£450	£800	£1500	—
1787 rev. no semée of hearts in 4th shield		£15	£30	£80	—
1787 — No stop over head		£15	£30	£80	—
1787 — No stop at date		£15	£30	£80	—
1787 — No stops on obv		£18	£35	£85	—
1787 rev. with semée of hearts in shield		£15	£30	£80	—
1798 "Dorrien Magens" bust		—	—	—	£18000

NEW COINAGE—shield in garter reverse

	MINTAGE	F	VF	EF	UNC
1816	—	£8	£20	£50	£100
1817	3,031,360	£8	£20	£50	£100
1817 GEOE for GEOR	incl. above	£110	£250	£600	—
1818	1,342,440	£9	£22	£85	£150
1819	7,595,280	£8	£20	£50	£100
1819/8 9 over 8	incl. above	£15	£35	£80	—
1820	7,975,440	£8	£20	£50	£100

GEORGE IV (1820–30)

	MINTAGE	F	VF	EF	UNC
1821 First bust, first reverse	2,463,120	£10	£40	£150	£400
1821 — — Proof	incl. above	—	—	—	£900
1823 — Second reverse	693,000	£40	£75	£250	£550
1824 — —	4,158,000	£10	£40	£150	£375
1825 — —	2,459,160	£20	£50	£150	£500
1825/3 — — 5 over 3	incl. above		Extremely rare		
1825 Second bust, third reverse	incl. above	£6	£18	£60	£200
1825 — — Roman I	incl. above		Extremely rare		
1826 — —	6,351,840	£6	£18	£60	£200
1826 — — Proof	incl. above	—	—	—	£450
1827 — —	574,200	£30	£70	£200	£475
1829 — —	879,120	£20	£60	£175	£425

WILLIAM IV (1830–37)

	MINTAGE	F	VF	EF	UNC
1831 Proof only	—	—	—	—	£600
1834	3,223,440	£15	£35	£170	£400
1835	1,449,360	£15	£35	£170	£400
1836	3,567,960	£15	£35	£170	£400
1837	478,160	£20	£60	£200	£500

VICTORIA (1837–1901)

YOUNG HEAD ISSUES
First head

	MINTAGE	F	VF	EF	UNC
1838 WW on truncation	1,956,240	£15	£40	£175	£350
1839 —	5,666,760	£15	£40	£175	£350

Second head

	MINTAGE	F	VF	EF	UNC
1839 WW on truncation, Proof only	incl. above	—	—	—	£600
1839 no WW	incl. above	£18	£40	£160	£350
1840	1,639,440	£18	£40	£160	£350
1841	875,160	£20	£45	£160	£350
1842	2,094,840	£18	£40	£160	£350
1843	1,465,200	£18	£50	£180	£425
1844	4,466,880	£14	£40	£150	£325
1845	4,082,760	£14	£40	£150	£325
1846	4,031,280	£14	£40	£150	£325
1848 last 8 of date over 6	1,041,480	£70	£150	£550	£900

DATE	MINTAGE	F	VF	EF	UNC
1849	845,480	£25	£50	£170	£500
1850	685,080	£500	£1000	£2500	£5000
1850/49	incl. above	£550	£1100	£3000	—
1851	470,071	£40	£110	£400	£700
1852	1,306,574	£12	£30	£125	£300
1853	4,256,188	£12	£30	£125	£300
1853 Proof....................	incl. above	—	—	—	£850
1854	552,414	£150	£350	£1000	£2200
1854/1 4 over 1	incl. above	£170	£650	—	—
1855	1,368,400	£10	£30	£110	£250
1856	3,168,000	£10	£30	£110	£250
1857	2,562,120	£10	£30	£110	£250
1857 error F:G with inverted G ...	incl. above	£150	£400	—	—
1858	3,108,600	£10	£30	£110	£275
1859	4,561,920	£10	£30	£110	£275
1860	1,671,120	£10	£30	£110	£320
1861	1,382,040	£12	£40	£150	£425
1862	954,360	£40	£120	£275	£800
1863	859,320	£110	£300	£750	£1600
1863/1 3 over 1				Extremely rare	

Die no. added above date up to 1879

1864	4,518,360	£10	£30	£110	£225
1865	5,619,240	£10	£30	£110	£225
1866	4,984,600	£10	£30	£110	£225
1866 error BBITANNIAR	incl. above	£80	£220	£700	—
1867	2,166,120	£10	£35	£110	£260

Third head—with die no

1867	incl. above	£100	£400	—	—
1868	3,330,360	£10	£40	£110	£250
1869	736,560	£12	£45	£110	£275
1870	1,467,471	£10	£40	£100	£250
1871	4,910,010	£10	£40	£100	£250
1872	8,897,781	£10	£40	£100	£250
1873	6,489,598	£10	£40	£100	£250
1874	5,503,747	£10	£40	£100	£250
1875	4,353,983	£10	£40	£100	£250
1876	1,057,487	£10	£40	£100	£300
1877	2,989,703	£10	£40	£100	£250
1878	3,127,131	£10	£40	£100	£250
1879	3,611,507	£20	£55	£200	£500

Fourth head—no die no

1879 no Die no.	incl. above	£8	£25	£75	£185
1880	4,842,786	£8	£25	£75	£185
1881	5,255,332	£8	£25	£75	£185
1882	1,611,786	£20	£65	£200	£425
1883	7,281,450	£8	£25	£65	£170
1884	3,923,993	£8	£25	£65	£170
1885	3,336,526	£8	£25	£65	£170
1886	2,086,819	£8	£25	£65	£170
1887	4,034,133	£8	£25	£65	£170

JUBILEE HEAD ISSUES

1887	incl. above	£4	£8	£15	£40
1887 Proof....................	1,084	—	—	—	£170
1888.............................	4,526,856	£6	£10	£25	£60
1889.............................	7,039,628	£35	£90	£300	—
1889 Large bust (until 1892)........	incl. above	£6	£12	£45	£75
1890.............................	8,794,042	£6	£12	£45	£75
1891.............................	5,665,348	£6	£12	£45	£75
1892.............................	4,591,622	£6	£12	£45	£90

OLD HEAD ISSUES

1893.............................	7,039,074	£5	£10	£30	£65
1893 small lettering	incl. above	£5	£10	£30	£65
1893 Proof....................	1,312	—	—	—	£150
1894.............................	5,953,152	£9	£25	£60	£140
1895.............................	8,880,651	£9	£24	£55	£140
1896.............................	9,264,551	£7	£15	£40	£75
1897.............................	6,270,364	£7	£12	£40	£75
1898.............................	9,768,703	£7	£12	£40	£65
1899.............................	10,965,382	£7	£12	£40	£65
1900.............................	10,937,590	£7	£12	£40	£75
1901.............................	3,426,294	£7	£12	£40	£65

Victoria Jubilee head

Victoria Old or Veiled head

DATE	MINTAGE	F	VF	EF	UNC

EDWARD VII (1901–10)

DATE	MINTAGE	F	VF	EF	UNC
1902	7,809,481	£4	£15	£45	£75
1902 Proof matt	13,123	—	—	—	£75
1903	2,061,823	£10	£35	£140	£475
1904	2,040,161	£8	£35	£120	£440
1905	488,390	£80	£250	£900	£3000
1906	10,791,025	£5	£12	£40	£120
1907	14,083,418	£5	£12	£40	£125
1908	3,806,969	£10	£25	£150	£450
1909	5,664,982	£9	£22	£110	£350
1910	26,547,236	£4	£10	£45	£95

GEORGE V (1910–36)

First issue

DATE	MINTAGE	F	VF	EF	UNC
1911	20,065,901	£4	£8	£20	£55
1911 Proof	6,007	—	—	—	£75
1912	15,594,009	£5	£10	£25	£75
1913	9,011,509	£7	£20	£50	£140
1914	23,415,843	£4	£7	£25	£55
1915	39,279,024	£4	£7	£25	£55
1916	35,862,015	£4	£7	£25	£55
1917	22,202,608	£4	£7	£25	£60
1918	34,915,934	£4	£7	£25	£55
1919	10,823,824	£5	£8	£30	£65

Second issue — debased silver

DATE	MINTAGE	F	VF	EF	UNC
1920	22,825,142	£2	£4	£20	£45
1921	22,648,763	£2	£4	£20	£45
1922	27,215,738	£2	£4	£20	£45
1923	14,575,243	£2	£4	£20	£45
1924	9,250,095	£6	£12	£45	£140
1925	5,418,764	£6	£10	£40	£110
1926	22,516,453	£2	£7	£25	£100

George V First obverse

Third issue — Modified bust

DATE	MINTAGE	F	VF	EF	UNC
1926	incl. above	£2	£4	£25	£55
1927 —	9,247,344	£2	£4	£25	£55

Fourth issue — large lion and crown on rev., date in legend

DATE	MINTAGE	F	VF	EF	UNC
1927	incl. above	£2	£4	£20	£40
1927 Proof	15,000	—	—	—	£55
1928	18,136,778	£2	£4	£15	£40
1929	19,343,006	£2	£4	£15	£40
1930	3,172,092	£2	£4	£18	£45
1931	6,993,926	£2	£4	£15	£40
1932	12,168,101	£2	£4	£15	£45
1933	11,511,624	£2	£4	£15	£35
1934	6,138,463	£2	£4	£18	£50
1935	9,183,462	—	£4	£10	£22
1936	11,910,613	—	£4	£9	£20

GEORGE VI (1936–52)

George V Second obverse

E = England rev. (lion standing on large crown). S = Scotland rev. (lion seated on small crown holding sword and mace)

DATE	MINTAGE	F	VF	EF	UNC
1937 E	8,359,122	—	£2	£4	£6
1937 E Proof	26,402	—	—	—	£15
1937 S	6,748,875	—	£2	£4	£6
1937 S Proof	26,402	—	—	—	£15
1938 E	4,833,436	—	£3	£10	£20
1938 S	4,797,852	—	£3	£10	£20
1939 E	11,052,677	—	£2	£4	£6
1939 S	10,263,892	—	£2	£4	£6
1940 E	11,099,126	—	—	£4	£7
1940 S	9,913,089	—	—	£4	£7

DATE	MINTAGE	F	VF	EF	UNC
1941 E	11,391,883	—	—	£4	£6
1941 S	8,086,030	—	—	£4	£5
1942 E	17,453,643	—	—	£4	£5
1942 S	13,676,759	—	—	£4	£5
1943 E	11,404,213	—	—	£4	£6
1943 S	9,824,214	—	—	£4	£5
1944 E	11,586,751	—	—	£4	£5
1944 S	10,990,167	—	—	£4	£5
1945 E	15,143,404	—	—	£4	£6
1945 S	15,106,270	—	—	£4	£5
1946 E	16,663,797	—	—	£4	£5
1946 S	16,381,501	—	—	£4	£5
Cupro-nickel					
1947 E	12,120,611	—	—	—	£2
1947 S	12,283,223	—	—	—	£2
1948 E	45,576,923	—	—	—	£2
1948 S	45,351,937	—	—	—	£2
1949 E	19,328,405	—	—	—	£5
1949 S	21,243,074	—	—	—	£5
1950 E	19,243,872	—	—	—	£5
1950 E Proof	17,513	—	—	—	£18
1950 S	14,299,601	—	—	—	£5
1950 S Proof	17,513	—	—	—	£18
1951 E	9,956,930	—	—	—	£5
1951 E Proof	20,000	—	—	—	£18
1951 S	10,961,174	—	—	—	£6
1951 S Proof	20,000	—	—	—	£18

English reverse

Scottish reverse

ELIZABETH II (1952–)

E = England rev. (shield with three lions). S = Scotland rev. (shield with one lion).

1953 E	41,942,894	—	—	—	£1
1953 E Proof	40,000	—	—	—	£4
1953 S	20,663,528	—	—	—	£1
1953 S Proof	40,000	—	—	—	£4
1954 E	30,262,032	—	—	—	£2
1954 S	26,771,735	—	—	—	£2
1955 E	45,259,908	—	—	—	£2
1955 S	27,950,906	—	—	—	£2
1956 E	44,907,008	—	—	—	£10
1956 S	42,853,639	—	—	—	£10
1957 E	42,774,217	—	—	—	£1
1957 S	17,959,988	—	—	—	£10
1958 E	14,392,305	—	—	—	£10
1958 S	40,822,557	—	—	—	£1
1959 E	19,442,778	—	—	—	£1
1959 S	1,012,988	£1	£3	£10	£30
1960 E	27,027,914	—	—	—	£1
1960 S	14,376,932	—	—	—	£1
1961 E	39,816,907	—	—	—	£1
1961 S	2,762,558	—	—	—	£3
1962 E	36,704,379	—	—	—	£1
1962 S	17,475,310	—	—	—	£1
1963 E	49,433,607	—	—	—	£1
1963 S	32,300,000	—	—	—	£1
1964 E	8,590,900	—	—	—	£1
1964 S	5,239,100	—	—	—	£1
1965 E	9,216,000	—	—	—	£1
1965 S	2,774,000	—	—	—	£2
1966 E	15,002,000	—	—	—	£1
1966 S	15,604,000	—	—	—	£1

English reverse

Scottish reverse

SIXPENCES

DATE	F	VF	EF	UNC

OLIVER CROMWELL

1658 Patterns by Thos. Simon & Tanner
  Four varieties .... Extremely rare

CHARLES II (1660–85)

	F	VF	EF	UNC
1674..	£70	£300	£900	—
1675..	£70	£300	£900	—
1675/4 5 over 4	£80	£300	£925	—
1676..	£80	£300	£900	—
1676/5 6 over 5	£85	£300	£900	—
1677..	£70	£300	£900	—
1678/7	£70	£280	£900	—
1679..	£75	£300	£900	—
1680..	£90	£500	£1000	—
1681..	£70	£300	£900	—
1682/1	£80	£300	£1000	—
1682..	£95	£320	£950	—
1683..	£70	£300	£925	—
1684..	£75	£300	£900	—

JAMES II (1685–88)

	F	VF	EF	UNC
1686 Early shields	£120	£400	£1000	—
1687/6 — 7 over 6...	£125	£400	£1000	—
1687 Late shields	£120	£400	£975	—
1687/6 — 7 over 6	£120	£425	£1050	—
1688 —	£105	£425	£1050	—

WILLIAM & MARY (1688–94)

	F	VF	EF	UNC
1693	£120	£425	£950	—
1693 error inverted 3	£150	£500	£1050	—
1694..	£120	£450	£1050	—

WILLIAM III (1694–1702)

Provincially produced sixpences carry privy marks or initials below the bust:
B: Bristol. C: Chester. E: Exeter. N: Norwich. Y or y: York.

	F	VF	EF	UNC
1695 First bust, early harp in 4th shield on rev.	£35	£100	£400	—
1696 — —	£35	£100	£325	—
1696 — — French arms at date		Extremely rare		
1696 — — Scottish arms at date.....................		Extremely rare		
1696 — — DFI for DEI....................................		Extremely rare		
1696 — — No stops on obv.	£40	£110	£400	—
1696 — — B...	£40	£100	£400	—
1696 — — — B over E		Extremely rare		
1696 — — C...	£35	£100	£425	—
1696 — — E...	£50	£110	£425	—
1696 — — N...	£40	£100	£425	—
1696 — — y..	£40	£110	£475	—
1696 — — Y	£45	£200	£500	—
1696 — Later harp	£50	£175	£400	—
1696 — — B...	£70	£225	£500	—
1696 — — — no stops on obv..........................	£80	£275	£550	—
1696 — — C...	£80	£350	£850	—
1696 — — N...	£70	£325	—	—
1696 Second bust	£300	£800	—	—
1697 First bust, later harp	£30	£75	£300	—
1697 — — Arms of France & Ireland transposed		Extremely rare		

DATE	MINTAGE	F	VF	EF	UNC
1697 — — B		£50	£110	£425	—
1697 — — C		£70	£200	£475	—
1697 — — — Irish shield at date				Extremely rare	
1697 — — E		£70	£200	£450	—
1697 — — — error GVLIEMVS				Extremely rare	
1697 — — y		£60	£125	£450	—
1697 — — — Irish shield at date				Extremely rare	
1697 Second bust		£120	£400	£1200	—
1697 Third bust		£25	£70	£275	—
1697 — error GVLIEIMVS				Extremely rare	
1697 — B		£50	£110	£450	—
1697 — — IRA for FRA				Extremely rare	
1697 — C		£75	£220	£500	—
1697 — E		£75	£200	£550	—
1697 — Y		£60	£200	£500	—
1698 —		£60	£170	£450	—
1698 — Plumes in angles on rev.		£60	£200	£650	—
1699 —		£80	£250	£750	—
1699 — Plumes in angles on rev.		£60	£250	£700	—
1699 — Roses in angles on rev.		£70	£250	£700	—
1699 — — error G LIELMVS				Extremely rare	
1700 —		£40	£90	£350	—
1700 — Plume below bust	£2000	—	—	—	—
1701 —		£55	£120	£425	—

ANNE (1702–14)

1703 VIGO below bust Before Union with Scotland	£40	£130	£400	—	
1705 Plain	£60	£170	£500	—	
1705 Plumes in angles on rev.	£45	£150	£450	—	
1705 Roses & Plumes in angles on rev.	£60	£150	£425	—	
1707 Roses & Plumes in angles on rev.	£50	£150	£400	—	
1707 (Post-Union), Plain	£40	£80	£275	—	
1707 E (Edinburgh) below bust	£40	£80	£300	—	
1707 Plumes in angles on rev.	£45	£120	£325	—	
1708 Plain	£45	£100	£400	—	
1708 E below bust	£50	£100	£350	—	
1708 E* below bust	£60	£140	£400	—	
1708 "Edinburgh" bust E* below	£50	£140	£400	—	
1708 Plumes in angles on rev.	£55	£140	£450	—	
1710 Roses & Plumes in angles on rev.	£35	£110	£450	—	
1711 Plain	£25	£70	£200	—	

GEORGE I (1714–27)

1717 Roses & Plumes in angles on rev.	£90	£250	£700	—	
1717 Plain edge				Extremely rare	
1720 —	£80	£220	£600	—	
1723 SSC in angles on rev.	£30	£70	£200	—	
1723 Larger lettering	£30	£70	£200	—	
1726 Small Roses & Plumes in angles on rev.	£80	£225	£650	—	

GEORGE II (1727–60)

1728 Young head, Plain	£70	£240	£525	—	
1728 — Proof	—	—	£3000	—	
1728 — Plumes in angles on rev.	£40	£140	£400	—	
1728 — Roses & Plumes in angles on rev.	£35	£125	£300	—	
1731 — —	£35	£125	£300	—	
1732 —	£35	£125	£300	—	
1734 — —	£40	£140	£350	—	
1735 —	£35	£140	£350	—	
1735/4 5 over 4	£45	£150	£400	—	
1736 — —	£40	£140	£350	—	
1739 — Roses in angles on rev.	£30	£100	£275	—	
1741 —	£30	£100	£275	—	
1743 Old head, Roses in angles on rev.	£25	£75	£250	—	

DATE	MINTAGE	F	VF	EF	UNC
1745 — —		£25	£75	£250	—
1745 — — 5 over 3		£30	£85	£275	—
1745 — Plain, LIMA below bust		£30	£80	£260	—
1746 — — —		£30	£80	£260	—
1746 — — Proof		—	—	£925	—
1750 — —		£30	£120	£325	—
1751 — —		£35	£150	£350	—
1757 — —		£15	£30	£80	—
1758 — —		£15	£30	£80	—

GEORGE III (1760–1820)

	MINTAGE	F	VF	EF	UNC
1787 rev. no semée of hearts on 4th shield		£15	£35	£80	£110
1787 rev. with semée of hearts		£15	£35	£80	£110

NEW COINAGE

	MINTAGE	F	VF	EF	UNC
1816	—	£6	£15	£40	£95
1817	10,921,680	£7	£15	£40	£95
1818	4,284,720	£10	£25	£80	£175
1819	4,712,400	£7	£15	£40	£80
1819 very small 8 in date	incl. above	£7	£15	£40	£100
1820	1,488,960	£7	£15	£40	£100

GEORGE IV (1820–30)

	MINTAGE	F	VF	EF	UNC
1821 First bust, first reverse	863,280	£12	£25	£100	£300
1821 error BBRITANNIAR		£75	£250	£750	—
1821 — — Proof	incl. above	—	—	—	£600
1824 — Second (garter) reverse..	633,600	£10	£25	£100	£300
1825 —	483,120	£12	£25	£90	£275
1826 —	689,040	£30	£80	£200	£475
1826 Second bust, third (lion on crown) reverse	incl. above	£10	£25	£90	£200
1826 — — Proof	incl. above	—	—	—	£375
1827 — —	166,320	£25	£80	£240	£450
1828 — —	15,840	£16	£40	£125	£275
1829 — —	403,290	£12	£40	£110	£300

WILLIAM IV (1830–37)

	MINTAGE	F	VF	EF	UNC
1831	1,340,195	£15	£40	£125	£275
1831 Proof	incl. above	—	—	—	£400
1834	5,892,480	£15	£40	£125	£275
1835	1,552,320	£15	£40	£125	£275
1836	1,987,920	£15	£45	£250	£325
1837	506,880	£18	£40	£175	£425

VICTORIA (1837–1901)

YOUNG HEAD ISSUES
First head

	MINTAGE	F	VF	EF	UNC
1838	1,607,760	£10	£30	£80	£225
1839	3,310,560	£10	£30	£70	£225
1839 Proof	incl. above	—	—	—	£500
1840	2,098,800	£10	£30	£85	£240
1841	1,386,000	£10	£30	£80	£240
1842	601,920	£10	£30	£80	£240
1843	3,160,080	£10	£30	£80	£240
1844	3,975,840	£10	£25	£55	£240
1844 Large 44 in date	incl. above	£12	£40	£100	£275
1845	3,714,480	£10	£25	£65	£225
1846	4,226,880	£10	£25	£65	£225
1848	586,080	£40	£90	£275	£800
1848/6 final 8 over 6	incl. above	£40	£90	£300	—
1850	498,960	£10	£30	£80	£225
1850/3 0 over 3	incl. above	£15	£30	£90	£300
1851	2,288,107	£8	£25	£80	£225

DATE	MINTAGE	F	VF	EF	UNC
1852.........................	904,586	£8	£25	£90	£225
1853.........................	3,837,930	£8	£25	£90	£225
1853 Proof.................	incl above	—	—	—	£500
1854.........................	840,116	£100	£250	£700	£1400
1855.........................	1,129,684	£8	£25	£70	£175
1855/3 last 5 over 3...................	incl. above	£12	£40	£80	£225
1856.........................	2,779,920	£8	£25	£70	£200
1857.........................	2,233,440	£8	£25	£70	£200
1858.........................	1,932,480	£8	£25	£70	£200
1859.........................	4,688,640	£8	£25	£75	£200
1859/8 9 over 8	incl. above	£10	£30	£80	£250
1860.........................	1,100,880	£10	£25	£80	£225
1862.........................	990,000	£60	£150	£400	£900
1863.........................	491,040	£50	£100	£350	£800
Die no. added above date from 1864 to 1879					
1864.........................	4,253,040	£8	£25	£80	£200
1865.........................	1,631,520	£8	£25	£70	£200
1866.........................	4,140,080	£8	£25	£70	£200
1866 no Die no.	incl. above		Extremely Rare		

Jubilee head, shield reverse

Second head

1867.........................	1,362,240	£8	£20	£70	£220
1868.........................	1,069,200	£8	£20	£70	£160
1869.........................	388,080	£8	£20	£70	£160
1870.........................	479,613	£8	£20	£70	£160
1871.........................	3,662,684	£7	£20	£60	£150
1871 no Die no.	incl. above	£7	£20	£60	£150
1872.........................	3,382,048	£7	£20	£60	£150
1873.........................	4,594,733	£7	£20	£60	£150
1874.........................	4,225,726	£7	£20	£60	£150
1875.........................	3,256,545	£7	£20	£60	£150
1876	841,435	£7	£20	£60	£150
1877.........................	4,066,486	£7	£20	£60	£150
1877 no Die no	incl. above	£7	£20	£60	£150
1878.........................	2,624,525	£7	£20	£60	£140
1878 Dritanniar Error	incl. above	£60	£200	—	—
1879.........................	3,326,313	£7	£18	£60	£140
1879 no Die no	incl. above	£6	£18	£60	£140
1880 no Die no	3,892,501	£6	£20	£50	£140

Jubilee head, wreath reverse

Third head

1880	incl above	£7	£20	£50	£120
1881.........................	6,239,447	£7	£20	£50	£120
1882.........................	759,809	£12	£40	£125	£325
1883.........................	4,986,558	£7	£18	£40	£100
1884.........................	3,422,565	£7	£18	£40	£100
1885.........................	4,652,771	£7	£18	£40	£100
1886.........................	2,728,249	£7	£18	£40	£90
1887.........................	3,675,607	£7	£18	£40	£90

JUBILEE HEAD ISSUES

1887 Shield reverse	incl. above	£5	£8	£10	£25
1887 — Proof	incl. above	—	—	—	£100
1887 Six Pence in wreath reverse	incl. above	£3	£5	£15	£30
1888 —	4,197,698	£5	£8	£25	£45
1889 —	8,738,928	£5	£8	£25	£55
1890 —	9,386,955	£5	£8	£25	£55
1891 —	7,022,734	£5	£8	£25	£55
1892 —	6,245,746	£5	£10	£28	£65
1893 —	7,350,619	£400	£1000	£3000	—

OLD HEAD ISSUES

1893.........................	incl. above	£5	£10	£20	£45
1893 Proof.................	1,312	—	—	—	£75
1894.........................	3,467,704	£7	£14	£40	£80
1895	7,024,631	£6	£14	£35	£70
1896.........................	6,651,699	£5	£10	£30	£55
1897.........................	5,031,498	£5	£10	£30	£55
1898.........................	5,914,100	£5	£10	£30	£50
1899.........................	7,996,80	£5	£10	£30	£50
1900.........................	8,984,354	£5	£10	£30	£50
1901.........................	5,108,757	£5	£10	£28	£50

DATE	MINTAGE	F	VF	EF	UNC

EDWARD VII (1901–10)

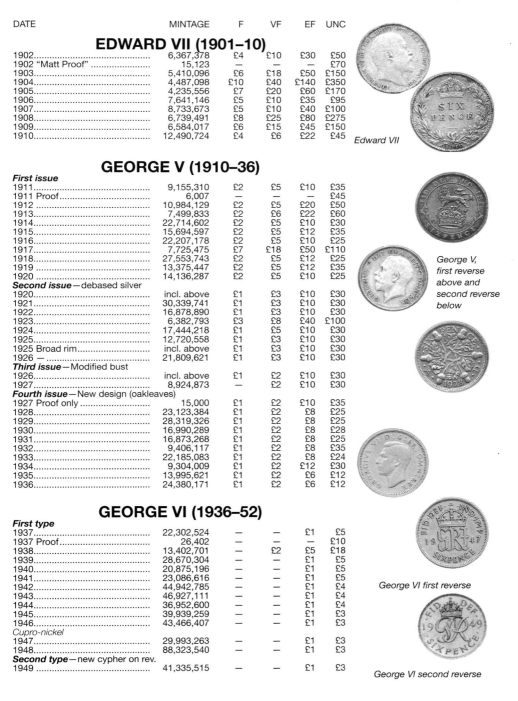

DATE	MINTAGE	F	VF	EF	UNC
1902	6,367,378	£4	£10	£30	£50
1902 "Matt Proof"	15,123	—	—	—	£70
1903	5,410,096	£6	£18	£50	£150
1904	4,487,098	£10	£40	£140	£350
1905	4,235,556	£7	£20	£60	£170
1906	7,641,146	£5	£10	£35	£95
1907	8,733,673	£5	£10	£40	£100
1908	6,739,491	£8	£25	£80	£275
1909	6,584,017	£6	£15	£45	£150
1910	12,490,724	£4	£6	£22	£45

Edward VII

GEORGE V (1910–36)

First issue

DATE	MINTAGE	F	VF	EF	UNC
1911	9,155,310	£2	£5	£10	£35
1911 Proof	6,007	—	—	—	£45
1912	10,984,129	£2	£5	£20	£50
1913	7,499,833	£2	£6	£22	£60
1914	22,714,602	£2	£5	£10	£30
1915	15,694,597	£2	£5	£12	£35
1916	22,207,178	£2	£5	£10	£25
1917	7,725,475	£7	£18	£50	£110
1918	27,553,743	£2	£5	£12	£25
1919	13,375,447	£2	£5	£12	£35
1920	14,136,287	£2	£5	£10	£25

Second issue—debased silver

DATE	MINTAGE	F	VF	EF	UNC
1920	incl. above	£1	£3	£10	£30
1921	30,339,741	£1	£3	£10	£30
1922	16,878,890	£1	£3	£10	£30
1923	6,382,793	£3	£8	£40	£100
1924	17,444,218	£1	£5	£10	£30
1925	12,720,558	£1	£3	£10	£30
1925 Broad rim	incl. above	£1	£3	£10	£30
1926 —	21,809,621	£1	£3	£10	£30

George V, first reverse above and second reverse below

Third issue—Modified bust

DATE	MINTAGE	F	VF	EF	UNC
1926	incl. above	£1	£2	£10	£30
1927	8,924,873	—	£2	£10	£30

Fourth issue—New design (oakleaves)

DATE	MINTAGE	F	VF	EF	UNC
1927 Proof only	15,000	£1	£2	£10	£35
1928	23,123,384	£1	£2	£8	£25
1929	28,319,326	£1	£2	£8	£25
1930	16,990,289	£1	£2	£8	£28
1931	16,873,268	£1	£2	£8	£25
1932	9,406,117	£1	£2	£8	£35
1933	22,185,083	£1	£2	£8	£24
1934	9,304,009	£1	£2	£12	£30
1935	13,995,621	£1	£2	£6	£12
1936	24,380,171	£1	£2	£6	£12

GEORGE VI (1936–52)

First type

DATE	MINTAGE	F	VF	EF	UNC
1937	22,302,524	—	—	£1	£5
1937 Proof	26,402	—	—	—	£10
1938	13,402,701	—	£2	£5	£18
1939	28,670,304	—	—	£1	£5
1940	20,875,196	—	—	£1	£5
1941	23,086,616	—	—	£1	£5
1942	44,942,785	—	—	£1	£4
1943	46,927,111	—	—	£1	£4
1944	36,952,600	—	—	£1	£4
1945	39,939,259	—	—	£1	£3
1946	43,466,407	—	—	£1	£3

Cupro-nickel

DATE	MINTAGE	F	VF	EF	UNC
1947	29,993,263	—	—	£1	£3
1948	88,323,540	—	—	£1	£3

Second type—new cypher on rev.

DATE	MINTAGE	F	VF	EF	UNC
1949	41,335,515	—	—	£1	£3

George VI first reverse

George VI second reverse

DATE	MINTAGE	F	VF	EF	UNC
1950	32,741,955	—	—	£1	£3
1950 Proof	17,513	—	—	—	£6
1951	40,399,491	—	—	£1	£3
1951 Proof	20,000	—	—	—	£6
1952	1,013,477	£5	£15	£40	£90

ELIZABETH II (1952–)

1953	70,323,876	—	—	—	£2
1953 Proof	40,000	—	—	—	£4
1954	105,241,150	—	—	—	£3
1955	109,929,554	—	—	—	£1
1956	109,841,555	—	—	—	£1
1957	105,654,290	—	—	—	£1
1958	123,518,527	—	—	—	£3
1959	93,089,441	—	—	—	£1
1960	103,283,346	—	—	—	£3
1961	115,052,017	—	—	—	£3
1962	166,483,637	—	—	—	25p
1963	120,056,000	—	—	—	25p
1964	152,336,000	—	—	—	25p
1965	129,644,000	—	—	—	25p
1966	175,676,000	—	—	—	25p
1967	240,788,000	—	—	—	25p

GROATS OR FOURPENCES

DATE	MINTAGE	F	VF	EF	UNC

The earlier fourpences are included in the Maundy oddments section as they are generally considered to have been issued for the Maundy ceremony.

WILLIAM IV (1831–37)

1836	—	£8	£16	£40	£85
1837	962,280	£8	£16	£40	£90

VICTORIA (1838–1901)

1837	Extremely Rare Proofs or Patterns only				
1838	2,150,280	£7	£15	£30	£80
1838 over last 8 on its side		£10	£20	£55	£110
1839	1,461,240	£7	£16	£40	£90
1839 Proof	incl. above				Rare
1840	1,496,880	£7	£15	£40	£85
1840 Small 0 in date	incl. above	£7	£15	£40	£85
1841	344,520	£7	£15	£40	£85
1842/1 2 over 1	incl. above	£7	£15	£40	£85
1842	724,680	£7	£15	£35	£80
1843	1,817,640	£8	£16	£40	£100
1843 4 over 5	incl. above	£7	£15	£40	£100
1844	855,360	£7	£15	£40	£90
1845	914,760	£7	£15	£40	£90
1846	1,366,200	£7	£15	£40	£90
1847 7 over 6	225,720	£15	£35	£110	—
1848	712,800	£7	£15	£40	£80
1848/6 8 over 6	incl. above	£30	£110	—	—
1848/7 8 over 7	incl. above	£8	£20	£50	£100
1849	380,160	£7	£15	£40	£85
1849/8 9 over 8	incl. above	£8	£20	£60	£125
1851	594,000	£30	£80	£200	£375
1852	31,300	£50	£120	£350	—
1853	11,880	£40	£100	£375	—
1853 Proof Milled Rim	incl. above	—	—	—	£550
1853 Plain edge Proof				Extremely rare	
1854	1,096,613	£7	£15	£40	£85
1855	646,041	£7	£15	£40	£85
1857 Proofs only				Extremely rare	
1862 Proofs only				Extremely rare	
1888 Jubilee Head	—	£8	£18	£40	£85

THREEPENCES

DATE	MINTAGE	F	VF	EF	UNC

The earlier threepences are included in the Maundy oddments section.

WILLIAM IV (1830–37)
(issued for use in the West Indies)

DATE	MINTAGE	F	VF	EF	UNC
1834		£7	£15	£60	£150
1835		£7	£15	£60	£150
1836		£7	£15	£60	£150
1837		£7	£20	£85	£170

VICTORIA (1837–1901)

YOUNG HEAD ISSUES

DATE	MINTAGE	F	VF	EF	UNC
1838 BRITANNIAB error			Extremely rare		
1838	—	£8	£20	£70	£140
1839	—	£8	£20	£70	£140
18t40	—	£8	£20	£70	£140
1841	—	£8	£20	£60	£160
1842	—	£8	£20	£60	£160
1843	—	£8	£20	£50	£135
1843/34 43 over 34	—	£8	£20	£80	£175
1844	—	£10	£20	£70	£160
1845	1,319,208	£9	£20	£60	£145
1846	52,008	£9	£25	£80	£200
1847	4,488		Extremely rare		
1848	incl. above		Extremely rare		
1849	131,208	£10	£24	£70	£170
1850	954,888	£10	£22	£40	£100
1851	479,065	£10	£24	£50	£130
1851 5 over 8	incl. above	£20	£40	£120	—
1852	4,488		Extremely rare		
1853	36,168	£20	£50	£100	£275
1854	1,467,246	£7	£20	£50	£130
1855	383,350	£7	£20	£50	£140
1856	1,013,760	£7	£20	£55	£130
1857	1,758,240	£7	£20	£60	£150
1858	1,441,440	£7	£20	£50	£130
1858 BRITANNIAB error	incl. above		Extremely rare		
1858/6 final 8 over 6	incl. above	£10	£30	£100	—
1858/5 final 8 over 5	incl. above	£10	£30	£100	—
1859	3,579,840	£6	£18	£50	£120
1860	3,405,600	£7	£20	£50	£130
1861	3,294,720	£7	£20	£50	£120
1862	1,156,320	£7	£20	£50	£120
1863	950,400	£10	£40	£100	£225
1864	1,330,560	£6	£20	£50	£120
1865	1,742,400	£6	£20	£50	£110
1866	1,900,800	£6	£20	£50	£110
1867	712,800	£6	£20	£50	£110
1868	1,457,280	£6	£20	£50	£110
1868 RRITANNIAR error	incl. above		Extremely rare		
1869	—	£35	£70	£175	£300
1870	1,283,218	£5	£16	£45	£90
1871	999,633	£5	£16	£40	£90
1872	1,293,271	£5	£16	£40	£90
1873	4,055,550	£5	£16	£40	£90
1874	4,427,031	£5	£16	£40	£90
1875	3,306,500	£5	£16	£40	£90
1876	1,834,389	£5	£16	£40	£90
1877	2,622,393	£5	£16	£40	£90
1878	2,419,975	£5	£16	£40	£90
1879	3,140,265	£5	£16	£40	£90
1880	1,610,069	£5	£16	£40	£75
1881	3,248,265	£5	£16	£40	£75
1882	472,965	£7	£22	£60	£140
1883	4,369,971	£5	£10	£30	£60

Victoria first type

DATE	MINTAGE	F	VF	EF	UNC
1884	3,322,424	£5	£10	£30	£60
1885	5,183,653	£5	£10	£30	£60
1886	6,152,669	£5	£10	£30	£60
1887	2,780,761	£5	£10	£30	£60

JUBILEE HEAD ISSUES

1887	incl. above	£2	£4	£10	£22
1887 Proof	incl. above	—	—	—	£60
1888	518,199	£2	£5	£20	£40
1889	4,587,010	£2	£5	£20	£40
1890	4,465,834	£2	£5	£20	£40
1891	6,323,027	£2	£5	£20	£40
1892	2,578,226	£2	£5	£20	£40
1893	3,067,243	£10	£30	£110	£240

Victoria
Jubilee head

OLD HEAD ISSUES

1893	incl. above	£1	£4	£15	£30
1893 Proof	incl. above	—	—	—	£45
1894	1,608,603	£2	£6	£24	£50
1895	4,788,609	£1	£5	£22	£50
1896	4,598,442	£1	£5	£18	£35
1897	4,541,294	£1	£5	£18	£35
1898	4,567,177	£1	£5	£18	£35
1899	6,246,281	£1	£5	£18	£35
1900	10,644,480	£1	£5	£18	£35
1901	6,098,400	£1	£5	£14	£30

Victoria
Old or Veiled
head

EDWARD VII (1901–10)

1902	8,268,480	£1	£2	£7	£15
1902 "Matt Proof"	incl. above	—	—	—	£20
1903	5,227,200	£1	£4	£20	£45
1904	3,627,360	£3	£10	£45	£90
1905	3,548,160	£1	£4	£25	£60
1906	3,152,160	£1	£5	£22	£55
1907	4,831,200	£1	£4	£20	£50
1908	8,157,600	£1	£3	£20	£50
1909	4,055,040	£1	£4	£20	£50
1910	4,563,380	£1	£4	£18	£35

GEORGE V (1910–36)

First issue

1911	5,841,084	—	—	£3	£10
1911 Proof	incl. above	—	—	—	£40
1912	8,932,825	—	—	£3	£12
1913	7,143,242	—	—	£3	£12
1914	6,733,584	—	—	£3	£12
1915	5,450,617	—	—	£3	£15
1916	18,555,201	—	—	£3	£10
1917	21,662,490	—	—	£3	£10
1918	20,630,909	—	—	£3	£10
1919	16,845,687	—	—	£3	£10
1920	16,703,597	—	—	£3	£10

Second issue—debased silver

1920	incl. above	—	—	£3	£12
1921	8,749,301	—	—	£3	£12
1922	7,979,998	—	—	£3	£40
1925	3,731,859	—	—	£5	£25
1926	4,107,910	—	—	£7	£28

Third issue—Modified bust

1926	incl. above	—	—	£8	£22

Fourth issue—new design (oakleaves)

1927 Proof only	15,022	—	—	—	£80
1928	1,302,106	£4	£9	£28	£65
1930	1,319,412	£2	£4	£10	£40
1931	6,251,936	—	—	£2	£7
1932	5,887,325	—	—	£2	£7
1933	5,578,541	—	—	£2	£7
1934	7,405,954	—	—	£2	£7
1935	7,027,654	—	—	£2	£7
1936	3,328,670	—	—	£2	£7

George V,
fourth issue
oak leaves
design reverse

DATE	MINTAGE	F	VF	EF	UNC

GEORGE VI (1936–52)

Silver

DATE	MINTAGE	F	VF	EF	UNC
1937	8,148,156	—	—	£1	£4
1937 Proof	26,402	—	—	—	£15
1938	6,402,473	—	—	£1	£4
1939	1,355,860	—	—	£4	£15
1940	7,914,401	—	—	£1	£3
1941	7,979,411	—	—	£1	£3
1942	4,144,051	£2	£5	£12	£35
1943	1,397,220	£2	£5	£12	£35
1944	2,005,553	£5	£12	£35	£80
1945	Only one known				

Brass — larger size, 12 sided, "Thrift" design

DATE	MINTAGE	F	VF	EF	UNC
1937	45,707,957	—	—	£1	£4
1937 Proof	26,402	—	—	—	£10
1938	14,532,332	—	—	£1	£18
1939	5,603,021	—	—	£3	£40
1940	12,636,018	—	—	£3	£30
1941	60,239,489	—	—	£1	£8
1942	103,214,400	—	—	£1	£8
1943	101,702,400	—	—	£1	£8
1944	69,760,000	—	—	£1	£8
1945	33,942,466	—	—	£3	£20
1946	620,734	£6	£25	£125	£400
1948	4,230,400	—	—	£5	£45
1949	464,000	£5	£25	£150	£475
1950	1,600,000	—	£2	£20	£110
1950 Proof	17,513	—	—	—	£15
1951	1,184,000	—	£2	£20	£100
1951 Proof	20,000	—	—	—	£15
1952	25,494,400	—	—	—	£10

*George VI "Thrift" design
of the brass 3d*

ELIZABETH II (1952–)

DATE	MINTAGE	F	VF	EF	UNC
1953	30,618,000	—	—	—	£1
1953 Proof	40,000	—	—	—	£6
1954	41,720,000	—	—	—	£5
1955	41,075,200	—	—	—	£5
1956	36,801,600	—	—	—	£6
1957	24,294,500	—	—	—	£6
1958	20,504,000	—	—	—	£9
1959	28,499,200	—	—	—	£6
1960	83,078,400	—	—	—	£2
1961	41,102,400	—	—	—	£1
1962	51,545,600	—	—	—	£1
1963	39,482,866	—	—	—	£1
1964	44,867,200	—	—	—	—
1965	27,160,000	—	—	—	—
1966	53,160,000	—	—	—	—
1967	151,780,800	—	—	—	—

TWO PENCES

It is generally accepted that earlier issues of the small silver twopences were only produced for inclusion with the Maundy sets, q.v., except for those listed below.

		F	VF	EF	UNC
1797 "Cartwheel"		£22	£45	£280	£800
1797 Copper Proofs	Many varieties from £500+				

VICTORIA (1837–1901)

For use in the Colonies

		F	VF	EF	UNC
1838		£4	£10	£18	£35
1848		£4	£12	£20	£40

THREE-HALFPENCES

DATE		F	VF	EF	UNC

WILLIAM IV (1830–37)

For use in the Colonies

		F	VF	EF	UNC
1834		£6	£16	£35	£80
1835		£9	£24	£70	£200
1835 over 4		£6	£16	£40	£90
1836		£8	£18	£40	£95
1837		£15	£35	£110	£300

VICTORIA (1837–1901)

For use in the Colonies

		F	VF	EF	UNC
1838		£6	£15	£35	£75
1839		£6	£15	£35	£75
1840		£8	£20	£60	£125
1841		£6	£15	£35	£80
1842		£6	£18	£40	£90
1843		£6	£15	£30	£70
1860		£9	£20	£70	£140
1862		£9	£20	£70	£140

PENNIES

DATE	MINTAGE	F	VF	EF	UNC

The earlier small silver pennies are included in the Maundy oddments section.

GEORGE III (1760–1820)

	MINTAGE	F	VF	EF	UNC
1797 "Cartwheel", 10 laurel leaves	8,601,600	£20	£50	£300	£900
1797 — 11 laurel leaves	incl. above	£20	£50	£300	£900
1806 Third type	—	£6	£15	£70	£240
1807	—	£6	£15	£70	£240
1808					Unique

GEORGE IV (1820–30)

	MINTAGE	F	VF	EF	UNC
1825	1,075,200	£12	£40	£240	£550
1826 (varieties)	5,913,600	£12	£40	£240	£550
1826 Proof	—	—	—	—	£450
1827	1,451,520	£170	£600	£2200	—

WILLIAM IV (1830–37)

	MINTAGE	F	VF	EF	UNC
1831 (varieties)	806,400	£20	£60	£350	£850
1831 Proof	—	—	—	—	£600
1834	322,560	£25	£70	£400	£1100
1837	174,720	£55	£170	£650	£2000

"Cartwheel" penny

VICTORIA (1837–1901)

YOUNG HEAD ISSUES

Copper

	MINTAGE	F	VF	EF	UNC
1839 Proof	unrecorded	—	—	—	£1250
1841	913,920	£7	£20	£140	£600
1841 No colon after REG	incl. above	£8	£20	£140	£550
1843	483,840	£75	£250	£1200	£3000
1844	215,040	£10	£25	£110	£340
1845	322,560	£15	£35	£180	£550
1846	483,840	£15	£25	£130	£450
1846 FID: DEF colon spaced	incl. above	£15	£25	£140	£450
1846 FID:DEF colon close	incl. above	£16	£25	£140	£500
1847	430,080	£8	£20	£120	£350

DATE	MINTAGE	F	VF	EF	UNC
1848	161,280	£8	£20	£100	£350
1848/7 final 8 over 7	incl. above	£7	£20	£100	£300
1848/6 final 8 over 6	incl. above	£20	£100	£450	—
1849	268,800	£175	£500	£1850	—
1851	268,800	£10	£30	£130	£500
1853	1,021,440	£7	£14	£75	£130
1853 Proof	—	—	—	—	£1000
1854	6,720,000	£8	£18	£80	£135
1854/3 4 over 3	incl. above	£12	£40	£150	—
1855	5,273,856	£8	£18	£80	£200
1856	1,212,288	£80	£200	£600	£2000
1857 Plain trident	752,640	£7	£18	£80	£230
1857 Ornamental trident	incl. above	£6	£18	£70	£220
1858/7 final 8 over 7	incl. above	£7	£18	£75	£240
1858/3 final 8 over 3	incl. above	£25	£90	£400	—
1858	1,599,040	£7	£16	£80	£220
1859	1,075,200	£8	£25	£100	£300
1860/59	32,256	£350	£1000	£2750	£5000

Prices of bronze pennies of Victoria bun head are for the common type, there are many varieties.

Bronze

1860 Beaded border	5,053,440	£25	£45	£150	£600
1860 Toothed border	incl. above	£6	£16	£55	£250
1860 — Piedfort flan	—		Extremely rare		
1861	36,449,280	£5	£12	£50	£200
1862	50,534,400	£5	£12	£50	£200
1862 8 over 6	incl. above		Extremely rare		
1863	28,062,720	£5	£12	£45	£200
1863 Die no below date	incl. above		Extremely rare		
1864 Plain 4	3,440,640	£25	£120	£500	£1800
1864 Crosslet 4	incl. above	£25	£110	£500	£2000
1865	8,601,600	£7	£16	£55	£300
1865/3 5 over 3	incl. above	£40	£125	£450	—
1866	9,999,360	£6	£18	£70	£350
1867	5,483,520	£7	£18	£85	£650
1868	1,182,720	£15	£70	£200	£700
1869	2,580,480	£120	£400	£1250	£3500
1870	5,695,022	£9	£35	£125	£500
1871	1,290,318	£35	£120	£450	£1750
1872	8,494,572	£6	£20	£60	£225
1873	8,494,200	£6	£20	£60	£225
1874	5,621,865	£7	£20	£60	£225
1874 H	6,666,240	£7	£22	£60	£225
1874 Later (older) bust	incl. above	£12	£30	£85	£350
1875	10,691,040	£7	£22	£75	£275
1875 H	752,640	£35	£110	£800	£2500
1876 H	11,074,560	£5	£12	£60	£220
1877	9,624,747	£5	£14	£55	£220
1878	2,764,470	£5	£14	£55	£220
1879	7,666,476	£4	£12	£55	£220
1880	3,000,831	£4	£12	£55	£220

Victoria
copper penny

(N.B. Prices for Victoria Bun head coins will be considerably higher in mint with full lustre)

DATE	MINTAGE	F	VF	EF	UNC
1881	2,302,362	£5	£12	£55	£220
1881 H	3,763,200	£5	£12	£55	£200
1882 H	7,526,400	£5	£12	£55	£200
1882 no H	—		Extremely Rare		
1883	6,237,438	£5	£14	£55	£190
1884	11,702,802	£5	£14	£55	£190
1885	7,145,862	£5	£14	£55	£190
1886	6,087,759	£5	£14	£55	£190
1887	5,315,085	£5	£14	£55	£190
1888	5,125,020	£5	£14	£55	£190
1889	12,559,737	£4	£14	£50	£200
1890	15,330,840	£4	£14	£50	£180
1891	17,885,961	£4	£12	£50	£180
1892	10,501,671	£4	£12	£60	£180
1893	8,161,737	£4	£12	£50	£175
1894	3,883,452	£8	£30	£100	£300

OLD HEAD ISSUES

	MINTAGE	F	VF	EF	UNC
1895 Trident 2mm from P(ENNY)	5,395,830	£10	£55	£160	£450
1895 Trident 1mm from P	incl. above	—	£2	£18	£75
1896	24,147,156	—	£2	£18	£65
1897	20,756,620	—	£2	£15	£60
1897 Raised dot after One (O·NE)		£125	£225	£650	—
1898	14,296,836	—	£3	£18	£60
1899	26,441,069	—	£3	£16	£50
1900	31,778,109	—	£3	£16	£40
1901	22,205,568	—	£3	£10	£30

EDWARD VII (1901–10)

	MINTAGE	F	VF	EF	UNC
1902	26,976,768	—	£1	£8	£25
1902 "Low tide" to sea line	incl. above	£4	£15	£60	£175
1903	21,415,296	—	£3	£15	£75
1904	12,913,152	—	£4	£25	£140
1905	17,783,808	—	£3	£15	£80
1906	37,989,504	—	£3	£15	£70
1907	47,322,240	—	£3	£15	£70
1908	31,506,048	—	£3	£18	£80
1909	19,617,024	—	£3	£20	£120
1910	29,549,184	—	£3	£15	£60

GEORGE V (1910–36)

	MINTAGE	F	VF	EF	UNC
1911	23,079,168	—	£3	£12	£50
1912	48,306,048	—	£3	£12	£45
1912 H	16,800,000	—	£4	£40	£200
1913	65,497,812	—	£3	£15	£70
1914	50,820,997	—	£3	£18	£70
1915	47,310,807	—	£3	£20	£80
1916	86,411,165	—	£3	£15	£60
1917	107,905,436	—	£3	£15	£50
1918	84,227,372	—	£3	£12	£50
1918 H	3,660,800	£1	£15	£100	£450
1918 KN	incl. above	£7	£70	£500	£2000
1919	113,761,090	—	£2	£15	£45
1919 H	5,209,600	£1	£15	£200	£700
1919 KN	incl. above	£10	£85	£650	£2500
1920	124,693,485	—	£2	£12	£30
1921	129,717,693	—	£2	£12	£30
1922	16,346,711	—	£2	£20	£80
1922 with reverse of 1927		£1000	£2500	—	—
1926	4,498,519	—	£6	£25	£110
1926 Modified effigy	incl above	£25	£140	£800	£2500
1927	60,989,561	—	£2	£10	£35
1928	50,178,00	—	£2	£10	£35
1929	49,132,800	—	£2	£10	£35
1930	29,097,600	—	£2	£18	£60
1931	19,843,200	—	£2	£10	£45
1932	8,277,600	—	£2	£12	£80
1933			Only 7 examples known		

DATE	MINTAGE	F	VF	EF	UNC
1934	13,965,600	—	£2	£25	£65
1935	56,070,000	—	—	£2	£10
1936	154,296,000	—	—	£2	£10

GEORGE VI (1936–52)

DATE	MINTAGE	F	VF	EF	UNC
1937	88,896,000	—	—	—	£4
1937 Proof	26,402	—	—	—	£10
1938	121,560,000	—	—	—	£6
1939	55,560,000	—	—	—	£12
1940	42,284,400	—	—	—	£18
1944 Mint Dark	42,600,000	—	—	—	£8
1945 Mint Dark	79,531,200	—	—	—	£8
1946 Mint Dark	66,855,600	—	—	—	£7
1947	52,220,400	—	—	—	£5
1948	63,961,200	—	—	—	£5
1949	14,324,400	—	—	—	£8
1950	240,000	£7	£15	£30	£50
1950 Proof	17,513	—	—	—	£25
1951	120,000	£18	£30	£50	£70
1951 Proof	20,000	—	—	—	£40

ELIZABETH II (1952–   )

DATE	MINTAGE	F	VF	EF	UNC
1953	1,308,400	—	—	£1	£4
1953 Proof	40,000	—	—	—	£7
1954	Only one known				
1961	48,313,400	—	—	—	£2
1962	143,308,600	—	—	—	50p
1963	125,235,600	—	—	—	50p
1964	153,294,000	—	—	—	50p
1965	121,310,400	—	—	—	50p
1966	165,739,200	—	—	—	50p
1967	654,564,000	—	—	—	—

Later issues are included in the Decimal section.

HALFPENNIES

DATE	F	VF	EF	UNC

CHARLES II (1660–85)

	F	VF	EF	UNC
1672	£60	£300	£1200	—
1672 CRAOLVS error		Extremely rare		
1673	£60	£300	£1150	—
1673 CRAOLVS error		Extremely rare		
1673 No rev. stop	£100	£600	—	—
1673 No stops on obv.		Extremely rare		
1675	£60	£500	£1250	—
1675 No stops on obv.	£80	£550	—	—
1675/3 5 over 3	£175	£600	—	—

JAMES II (1685–88)

	F	VF	EF	UNC
1685 (tin)	£225	£700	£3250	—
1686 (tin)	£250	£700	£3750	—
1687 (tin)	£300	£750	£3750	—

WILLIAM & MARY (1688–94)

Tin

	F	VF	EF	UNC
1689 Small draped busts, edge dated		Extremely rare		
1690 Large cuirassed busts, edge dated	£175	£700	£3000	—
1691 — date on edge and in exergue	£160	£650	£2800	—
1692 — —	£160	£650	£2800	—

DATE	F	VF	EF	UNC

Copper

	F	VF	EF	UNC
1694 Large cuirassed busts, date in exergue ..	£75	£275	£1000	—
1694 — — GVLIEMVS error		Extremely rare		
1694 — — MΛRIΛ error		Extremely rare		
1694 — No stops on rev.		Extremely rare		

WILLIAM III (1694–1702)

	F	VF	EF	UNC
1695 First issue (date in exergue)....................	£45	£175	£1000	—
1695 — No stop after BRITANNIA on rev.		Extremely rare		
1696 —	£35	£160	£900	—
1696 — TERTVS error		Extremely rare		
1697 —	£35	£150	£850	—
1697 — No stop after TERTIVS on obv.	£50	£275	—	—
1698 —	£45	£200	£1000	—
1698 Second issue (date in legend)	£45	£180	—	—
1698 — No stop after date..........................	£45	£180	—	—
1699 —	£50	£200	£900	—
1699 — No stop after date..........................	£225	—	—	—
1699 Third issue (date in exergue) (Britannia with right hand on knee)......................................	£40	£160	£850	—
1699 — No stop after date..........................		Extremely rare		
1699 — BRITΛNNIΛ error	£200	—	—	—
1699 — TERTVS error		Extremely rare		
1699 — No stop on rev................................		Extremely rare		
1699 — No stops on obv..............................	£90	£350	—	—
1700 —	£40	£150	£850	—
1700 — No stops on obv..............................	£100	£340	—	—
1700 — No stops after GVLIELMUS	£100	£340	—	—
1700 — BRITVANNIA error...........................		Extremely rare		
1700 — GVIELMS error................................	£100	£350	—	—
1700 — GVLIEEMVS error............................	£100	£350	—	—
1701 —	£40	£175	£850	—
1701 — BRITΛNNIΛ error	£70	£275	—	—
1701 — No stops on obv..............................		Extremely rare		
1701 — inverted As for Vs............................	£70	£300	—	—

GEORGE I (1714–27)

	F	VF	EF	UNC
1717 "Dump" issue	£40	£225	£750	
1718 —	£35	£200	£700	—
1719 "Dump" issue. Patterns...........................				Rare
1719 Second issue..	£40	£180	£800	—
1720 —	£30	£160	£575	—
1721 —	£30	£140	£550	—
1721 — Stop after date...................................	£40	£150	—	—
1722 —	£30	£140	£600	—
1722 — inverted A for V on obv.		Extremely rare		
1723 —	£30	£140	£600	—
1723 — No stop on rev....................................	£100	£375	—	—
1724 —	£30	£140	£600	—

GEORGE II (1727–60)

	F	VF	EF	UNC
1729 Young head	£25	£80	£400	—
1729 — No stop on rev.....................................	£25	£75	£400	—
1730 —	£20	£80	£375	—
1730 — GEOGIVS error...................................	£70	£225	£650	—
1730 — Stop after date....................................	£25	£100	£400	—
1730 — No stop after REX on obv.	£30	£140	£450	—
1731 —	£20	£100	£375	—
1731 — No rev. stop..	£25	£125	£425	—
1732 —	£20	£100	£375	—
1732 — No rev. stop..	£25	£125	£450	—
1733 —	£20	£80	£350	—

DATE	MINTAGE	F	VF	EF	UNC
1734/3 — 4 over 3		£35	£190	—	—
1734 — No stop on obv.		£35	£200	—	—
1735 —		£20	£80	£375	—
1736 —		£20	£80	£375	—
1737 —		£20	£85	£375	—
1738 —		£20	£80	£340	—
1739 —		£18	£70	£325	—
1740 Old head		£15	£70	£300	—
1742 —		£15	£70	£300	—
1742/0 — 2 over 0		£25	£125	£400	—
1743 —		£15	£70	£300	—
1744 —		£15	£70	£300	—
1745 —		£15	£70	£300	—
1746 —		£15	£70	£300	—
1747 —		£15	£70	£280	—
1748 —		£15	£70	£280	—
1749 —		£15	£70	£280	—
1750 —		£15	£70	£280	—
1751 —		£15	£70	£280	—
1752 —		£15	£70	£280	—
1753 —		£15	£70	£280	—
1754 —		£15	£70	£280	—

GEORGE III (1760–1820)

First type — Royal Mint

1770		£18	£50	£250	—
1770 No stop on rev.		£25	£65	£300	—
1771		£12	£50	£280	—
1771 No stop on rev.		£20	£65	£300	—
1772 Error GEORIVS		£60	£175	£600	—
1772		£12	£45	£200	—
1772 No stop on rev		£20	£65	£280	—
1773		£10	£45	£250	—
1773 No stop after REX		£25	£70	£350	—
1773 No stop on rev.		£20	£65	£280	—
1774		£12	£40	£220	—
1775		£12	£40	£220	—

Second type — Soho Mint

1799		£5	£12	£55	£120

Third type

1806		£5	£11	£60	£110
1807		£5	£11	£60	£110

George III second type

GEORGE IV (1820–30)

1825	215,040	£12	£45	£160	£300
1826 (varieties)	9,031,630	£12	£45	£160	£300
1826 Proof	—	—	—	—	£400
1827	5,376,000	£12	£45	£130	£260

WILLIAM IV (1830–37)

1831	806,400	£12	£30	£110	£300
1831 Proof	—	—	—	—	£350
1834	537,600	£12	£30	£110	£300
1837	349,440	£12	£30	£110	£300

VICTORIA (1837–1901)

YOUNG HEAD ISSUES

Copper

1838	456,960	£5	£16	£60	£180
1839 Proof	268,800	—	—	—	£300

DATE	MINTAGE	F	VF	EF	UNC
1841	1,075,200	£5	£16	£50	£150
1843	967,680	£25	£45	£170	£500
1844	1,075,200	£6	£18	£60	£175
1845	1,075,200	£80	£200	£950	—
1846	860,160	£8	£20	£65	£180
1847	725,640	£8	£18	£65	£175
1848	322,560	£8	£18	£60	£175
1848/7 final 8 OVER 7	incl. above	£10	£25	£70	£220
1851	215,040	£5	£15	£60	£175
1852	637,056	£8	£20	£60	£180
1853	1,559,040	£4	£8	£35	£100
1853/2 3 over 2	incl. above	£15	£30	£60	£200
1853 Proof	—	—	—	—	£500
1854	12,354,048	£4	£8	£40	£100
1855	1,455,837	£4	£8	£40	£100
1856	1,942,080	£8	£20	£60	£200
1857	1,820,720	£5	£15	£50	£100
1858	2,472,960	£4	£10	£45	£90
1858/7 final 8 over 7	incl. above	£4	£10	£45	£90
1858/6 final 8 over 6	incl. above	£4	£10	£45	£90
1859	1,290,240	£7	£20	£60	£180
1859/8 9 over 8	incl. above	£8	£25	£70	£220
1860	unrecorded	£1000	£2750	£6000	£8500

Victoria copper halfpenny

Bronze

1860 Beaded border	6,630,400	£3	£9	£50	£180
1860 Toothed border		£4	£12	£60	£250
1861	54,118,400	£4	£10	£40	£160
1862 Die letter A, B or C to left of lighthouse			Extremely rare		
1862	61,107,200	£3	£9	£40	£140
1863	15,948,800	£3	£9	£75	£140
1864	537,600	£3	£10	£45	£150
1865	8,064,000	£4	£18	£75	£250
1865/3 5 over 3	incl. above	£40	£100	£375	—
1866	2,508,800	£5	£15	£60	£200
1867	2,508,800	£5	£15	£50	£180
1868	3,046,400	£5	£14	£55	£200
1869	3,225,600	£15	£75	£200	£800
1870	4,350,739	£5	£15	£60	£220
1871	1,075,280	£75	£100	£350	£1000
1872	4,659,410	£4	£10	£50	£170
1873	3,404,880	£4	£10	£50	£200
1874	1,347,655	£5	£25	£110	£300
1874 H	5,017,600	£3	£10	£60	£210
1875	5,430,815	£3	£8	£60	£175
1875 H	1,254,400	£5	£12	£60	£200
1876 H	5,809,600	£4	£10	£60	£200
1877	5,209,505	£3	£10	£60	£175
1878	1,425,535	£5	£20	£100	£270
1878 Wide date		£100	£200	£400	—
1879	3,582,545	£3	£10	£40	£175
1880	2,423,465	£4	£12	£60	£190
1881	2,007,515	£4	£12	£50	£160
1881 H	1,792,000	£3	£10	£50	£175
1882 H	4,480,000	£3	£10	£50	£180
1883	3,000,725	£3	£10	£50	£160
1884	6,989,580	£3	£10	£45	£140
1885	8,600,574	£3	£10	£45	£140
1886	8,586,155	£3	£10	£45	£140
1887	10,701,305	£3	£10	£45	£110
1888	6,814,670	£3	£10	£45	£140
1889	7,748,234	£3	£10	£45	£140
1889/8 9 over 8	incl. above	£15	£40	£125	—

Victoria bronze halfpenny

DATE	MINTAGE	F	VF	EF	UNC
1890	11,254,235	£3	£10	£40	£110
1891	13,192,260	£3	£10	£35	£110
1892	2,478,335	£3	£10	£45	£140
1893	7,229,344	£3	£10	£35	£110
1894	1,767,635	£5	£10	£60	£200

OLD HEAD ISSUES

1895	3,032,154	£2	£6	£18	£55
1896	9,142,500	£1	£4	£10	£45
1897	8,690,315	£1	£4	£10	£45
1898	8,595,180	£1	£5	£12	£50
1899	12,108,001	£1	£4	£10	£45
1900	13,805,190	£1	£4	£10	£35
1901	11,127,360	£1	£2	£8	£20

EDWARD VII (1901–10)

1902	13,672,960	£2	£4	£8	£30
1902 "Low tide"	incl. above	£10	£40	£130	£325
1903	11,450,880	£2	£5	£20	£50
1904	8,131,200	£2	£6	£25	£70
1905	10,124,800	£2	£5	£20	£45
1906	16,849,280	£2	£5	£20	£50
1907	16,849,280	£2	£5	£20	£60
1908	16,620,800	£2	£5	£20	£56
1909	8,279,040	£2	£5	£20	£60
1910	10,769,920	£2	£5	£20	£50

GEORGE V (1910–36)

1911	12,570,880	£1	£4	£15	£35
1912	21,185,920	£1	£3	£15	£35
1913	17,476,480	£1	£3	£15	£40
1914	20,289,111	£1	£3	£15	£40
1915	21,563,040	£2	£3	£20	£50
1916	39,386,143	£1	£2	£15	£40
1917	38,245,436	£1	£2	£15	£35
1918	22,321,072	£1	£2	£15	£35
1919	28,104,001	£1	£2	£15	£35
1920	35,146,793	£1	£2	£15	£35
1921	28,027,293	£1	£2	£15	£40
1922	10,734,964	£1	£3	£20	£45
1923	12,266,282	£1	£2	£15	£35
1924	13,971,038	£1	£2	£15	£30
1925	12,216,123	—	£2	£15	£30
1925 Modified effigy	incl. above	£3	£8	£40	£75
1926	6,172,306	—	£2	£10	£40
1927	15,589,622	—	£2	£10	£35
1928	20,935,200	—	£2	£8	£30
1929	25,680,000	—	£2	£8	£30
1930	12,532,800	—	£2	£8	£30
1931	16,137,600	—	£2	£8	£30
1932	14,448,000	—	£2	£8	£30
1933	10,560,000	—	£2	£8	£30
1934	7,704,000	—	£2	£12	£35
1935	12,180,000	—	£1	£6	£18
1936	23,008,800	—	£1	£5	£15

GEORGE VI (1936–52)

1937	24,504,000	—	—	£1	£5
1937 Proof	26,402	—	—	£1	£10
1938	40,320,000	—	—	£1	£6
1939	28,924,800	—	—	£1	£5

DATE	MINTAGE	F	VF	EF	UNC
1940	32,162,400	—	—	£2	£9
1941	45,120,000	—	—	£1	£7
1942	71,908,800	—	—	£1	£4
1943	76,200,000	—	—	£1	£4
1944	81,840,000	—	—	£1	£4
1945	57,000,000	—	—	£1	£4
1946	22,725,600	—	—	£1	£5
1947	21,266,400	—	—	£1	£4
1948	26,947,200	—	—	£1	£3
1949	24,744,000	—	—	£1	£3
1950	24,153,600	—	—	£1	£4
1950 Proof	17,513	—	—	—	£10
1951	14,868,000	—	—	£1	£5
1951 Proof	20,000	—	—	—	£10
1952	33,78,400	—	—	£1	£3

ELIZABETH II (1952–   )

1953	8,926,366	—	—	—	£1
1953 Proof	40,000	—	—	—	£4
1954	19,375,000	—	—	—	£3
1955	18,799,200	—	—	—	£3
1956	21,799,200	—	—	—	£3
1957	43,684,800	—	—	—	£1
1957 Calm sea	incl. above8	—	—	£10	£30
1958	62,318,400	—	—	—	£1
1959	79,176,000	—	—	—	£1
1960	41,340,000	—	—	—	£1
1962	41,779,200	—	—	—	£1
1963	45,036,000	—	—	—	20p
1964	78,583,200	—	—	—	20p
1965	98,083,200	—	—	—	20p
1966	95,289,600	—	—	—	20p
1967	146,491,200	—	—	—	10p

Later issues are included in the Decimal section.

FARTHINGS

DATE			F	VF	EF	UNC

OLIVER CROMWELL

Undated (copper) Draped bust, shield rev. Variations   Extremely rare

CHARLES II (1660–85)

Copper

	F	VF	EF	UNC
1672	£40	£225	£700	—
1673	£45	£240	£725	—
1673 CAROLA for CAROLO error	£125	£500	—	—
1673 No stops on obv.			Extremely rare	
1673 No stop on rev.			Extremely rare	
1674	£45	£250	£750	—
1675	£40	£220	£675	—
1675 No stop after CAROLVS			Extremely rare	
1679	£55	£250	£800	—
1679 No stop on rev.	£60	£300		
Tin				
1684 with date on edge	£200	£650	—	—
1685 —			Extremely rare	

DATE	F	VF	EF	UNC

JAMES II (1685–88)

	F	VF	EF	UNC
1684 (tin) Cuirassed bust			Extremely rare	
1685 (tin) —	£170	£600	£2250	—
1686 (tin) —	£180	£600	£2250	—
1687 (tin) —			Extremely rare	
1687 (tin) Draped bust	£220	£800	—	—

WILLIAM & MARY (1688–94)

	F	VF	EF	UNC
1689 (tin) Small draped busts	£650	—	—	—
1689 (tin) — with edge date 1690			Extremely rare	
1690 (tin) Large cuirassed busts	£150	£600	£2750	—
1690 (tin) — with edge date 1689			Extremely rare	
1691 (tin) —	£160	£600	—	—
1692 (tin) —	£175	£650	£2750	—
1694 (copper) —	£70	£240	£850	—
1694 No stop after MARIΛ			Extremely rare	
1694 No stop on obv.			Extremely rare	
1694 No stop on rev.			Extremely rare	
1694 Unbarred As in BRITANNIA			Extremely rare	

WILLIAM III (1694–1702)

	F	VF	EF	UNC
1695 First issue (date in exergue)	£40	£200	£800	—
1695 — GVLIELMV error			Extremely rare	
1696 —	£40	£200	£800	—
1697 —	£40	£200	£750	—
1697 — GVLIELMS error			Extremely rare	
1698 —	£200	£650	—	—
1698 Second issue (date in legend)	£50	£250	£750	—
1699 First issue	£40	£200	£700	—
1699 Second issue	£40	£200	£700	—
1699 — No stop after date	£50	£275	—	—
1700 First issue	£35	£140	£600	—
1700 — error RRITANNIA			Extremely rare	

ANNE (1702–14)

	F	VF	EF	UNC
1714	£300	£550	£1050	—

GEORGE I (1714–27)

	F	VF	EF	UNC
1717 First small "Dump" issue	£200	£575	£1100	—
1718 1 Known				—
1719 Second issue	£30	£140	£450	—
1719 — No stop on rev.	£70	£350	—	—
1719 — No stops on obv.	£70	£300	—	—
1720 —	£30	£140	£475	—
1721 —	£25	£140	£475	—
1721/0 — Last 1 over 0	£40	£150	—	—
1722 —	£35	£125	£450	—
1723 —	£35	£125	£475	—
1723 — R over sideways R in REX			Extremely rare	
1724 —	£35	£140	£475	—

George I, first type

George I second type

GEORGE II (1727–60)

	F	VF	EF	UNC
1730 Young head	£15	£60	£275	—
1731 —	£15	£60	£275	—
1732 —	£15	£75	£325	—
1733 —	£15	£70	£325	—
1734 —	£15	£65	£325	—
1734 — No stop on obv.	£30	£110	£375	—

DATE	MINTAGE	F	VF	EF	UNC
1735 —		£15	£60	£275	—
1735 — 3 over 5		£20	£100	£375	—
1736 —		£12	£60	£275	—
1737 —		£12	£60	£275	—
1739 —		£12	£60	£275	—
1741 Old Head		£12	£50	£270	—
1744 —		£11	£50	£275	—
1746 —		£11	£50	£275	—
1746 — V over LL in GEORGIVS				Extremely rare	
1749 —		£15	£60	£250	—
1750 —		£15	£55	£240	—
1754 —		£9	£30	£175	—
1754 — 4 over 0		£25	£100	£300	—

GEORGE III (1760–1820)

	MINTAGE	F	VF	EF	UNC
1771 First (London) issue		£20	£60	£250	—
1773 —		£12	£40	£200	—
1773 — No stop on rev		£18	£50	£220	—
1773 — No stop after REX		£25	£75	£240	
1774 —		£10	£40	£180	—
1775 —		£10	£40	£180	—
1797 Second (Soho Mint) issue				Patterns only	
1799 Third (Soho Mint) issue		£2	£8	£40	£100
1806 Fourth (Soho Mint) issue		£2	£8	£40	£100
1807 —		£2	£8	£40	£100

George III, third (Soho Mint) issue

GEORGE IV (1820–30)

	MINTAGE	F	VF	EF	UNC
1821 First bust (laureate, draped), first reverse (date in exergue)	2,688,000	£3	£10	£60	£110
1822 —	5,924,350	£3	£10	£60	£110
1823 —	2,365,440	£4	£10	£60	£110
1823 I for 1 in date	incl. above	£20	£70	£250	£110
1825 —	4,300.800	£4	£10	£60	£120
1826 —	6,666,240	£4	£10	£60	£110
1826 Second bust (couped, date below), second reverse (ornament in exergue)	incl. above	£4	£10	£60	£110
1826 — Proof	—	—	—	—	£300
1827 —	2,365,440	£4	£10	£60	£140
1828 —	2,365,440	£4	£12	£60	£140
1829 —	1,505,280	£4	£12	£60	£140
1830 —	2,365,440	£4	£12	£60	£140

George III, fourth (Soho Mint) issue

WILLIAM IV (1830–37)

	MINTAGE	F	VF	EF	UNC
1831	2,688,000	£5	£12	£45	£120
1831 Proof	—	—	—	—	£300
1834	1,935,360	£5	£12	£50	£120
1835	1.720,320	£5	£12	£50	£120
1836	1,290.240	£5	£12	£55	£120
1837	3.010,560	£5	£12	£55	£135

VICTORIA (1837–1901)

FIRST YOUNG HEAD (COPPER) ISSUES

	MINTAGE	F	VF	EF	UNC
1838	591,360	£5	£15	£45	£140
1839	4,300,800	£5	£15	£45	£140
1839 Proof	—	—	—	—	£300
1840	3,010,560	£4	£15	£40	£120
1841	1,720,320	£4	£15	£40	£140
1841 Proof				Extremely rare	
1842	1,290,240	£10	£35	£100	£300

DATE	MINTAGE	F	VF	EF	UNC
1843	4,085,760	£5	£12	£40	£140
1843 I for 1 in date		£80	£375	—	—
1844	430,080	£65	£140	£700	£1800
1845	3,225,600	£6	£10	£40	£120
1846	2,580,480	£7	£20	£55	£170
1847	3,879,720	£5	£12	£50	£120
1848	1,290,240	£5	£12	£50	£120
1849	645,120	£40	£80	£300	£700
1850	430,080	£5	£10	£40	£110
1851	1,935,360	£8	£20	£70	£200
1851 D over sideways D in DEI ...	incl. above	£70	£100	£400	—
1852	822,528	£10	£20	£70	£180
1853	1,028,628	£4	£7	£30	£65
1853 Proof	—	—	—	—	£600
1854	6,504,960	£4	£10	£35	£60
1855	3,440,640	£4	£10	£35	£60
1856	1,771,392	£8	£20	£65	£200
1856 R over E in VICTORIA	incl. above	£20	£50	£200	—
1857	1,075,200	£4	£10	£35	£75
1858	1,720,320	£4	£10	£35	£75
1859	1,290,240	£10	£25	£65	£220
1860	unrecorded	£900	£2500	£5000	—

Victoria Young Head first (copper) issue

SECOND YOUNG OR "BUN" HEAD (BRONZE) ISSUES

1860 Toothed border	2,867,200	£2	£5	£40	£100
1860 Beaded border	incl. above	£3	£7	£40	£110
1860 Toothed/Beaded border mule	incl. above			Extremely rare	
1861	8,601,600	£2	£5	£35	£100
1862	14,336,000	£1	£5	£35	£100
1862 Large 8 in date	incl. above			Extremely rare	
1863	1,433,600	£20	£50	£200	£500
1864	2,508,800	£1	£5	£30	£100
1865	4,659,200	£1	£5	£30	£85
1865 5 over 2	incl. above	£10	£20	£60	—
1866	3,584,000	£1	£5	£25	£85
1867	5,017,600	£1	£5	£25	£85
1868	4,851,210	£1	£5	£25	£85
1869	3,225,600	£1	£8	£40	£135
1872	2,150,400	£1	£5	£25	£70
1873	3,225,620	£1	£5	£25	£70
1874 H	3,584,000	£1	£5	£25	£100
1874 H both Gs over sideways G	incl. above	£150	£300	£800	—
1875	712,760	£4	£12	£40	£125
1875 H	6,092,800	£1	£5	£20	£70
1876 H	1,175,200	£3	£12	£50	£130
1878	4,008,540	£1	£4	£20	£70
1879	3,977,180	£1	£4	£20	£70
1880	1,842,710	£1	£4	£20	£70
1881	3,494,670	£1	£4	£20	£70
1881 H	1,792,000	£1	£4	£20	£70
1882 H	1,792,000	£1	£5	£20	£70
1883	1,128,680	£5	£18	£60	£140
1884	5,782,000	£1	£4	£20	£40
1885	5,442,308	£1	£4	£20	£40
1886	7,707,790	£1	£4	£20	£40
1887	1,340,800	£1	£4	£20	£40
1888	1,887,250	£1	£4	£20	£40
1890	2,133,070	£1	£4	£20	£40
1891	4,959,690	£1	£4	£20	£40
1892	887,240	£2	£10	£50	£125
1893	3,904,320	£1	£4	£20	£40

Victoria Young Head second (bronze) issue

DATE	MINTAGE	F	VF	EF	UNC
1894	2,396,770	£1	£4	£20	£40
1895	2,852,852	£10	£25	£80	£220

OLD HEAD ISSUES

1895 Bright finish	incl. above	£1	£2	£16	£35
1896 —	3,668,610	£1	£2	£16	£25
1897 —	4,579,800	£1	£2	£16	£25
1897 Dark finish	incl. above	£1	£2	£16	£25
1898 —	4,010,080	£1	£2	£16	£25
1899 —	3,864,616	£1	£2	£16	£25
1900 —	5,969,317	£1	£2	£16	£25
1901 —	8,016,460	£1	£2	£10	£20

EDWARD VII (1901–10)

1902	5,125,120	50p	£1	£10	£15
1903	5,331,200	50p	£1	£12	£20
1904	3,628,800	£2	£5	£18	£45
1905	4,076,800	£1	£2	£12	£30
1906	5,340,160	50p	£1	£12	£25
1907	4,399,360	50p	£1	£10	£20
1908	4,264,960	50p	£1	£10	£20
1909	8,852,480	50p	£1	£10	£20
1910	2,298,400	£2	£8	£20	£60

GEORGE V (1910–36)

1911	5,196,800	25p	50p	£5	£12
1912	7,669,760	25p	50p	£8	£12
1913	4,184,320	25p	50p	£5	£12
1914	6,126,988	25p	50p	£4	£12
1915	7,129,255	25p	50p	£4	£14
1916	10,993,325	25p	50p	£4	£12
1917	21,434,844	25p	50p	£4	£10
1918	19,362,818	25p	50p	£4	£10
1919	15,089,425	25p	50p	£4	£10
1920	11,480,536	25p	50p	£4	£8
1921	9,469,097	25p	50p	£4	£8
1922	9,956,983	25p	50p	£4	£8
1923	8,034,457	25p	50p	£4	£8
1924	8,733,414	25p	50p	£4	£8
1925	12,634,697	25p	50p	£4	£8
1926 Modified effigy	9,792,397	25p	50p	£4	£8
1927	7,868,355	25p	50p	£4	£8
1928	11,625,600	25p	50p	£4	£8
1929	8,419,200	25p	50p	£4	£8
1930	4,195,200	25p	50p	£4	£8
1931	6,595,200	25p	50p	£4	£8
1932	9,292,800	25p	50p	£4	£8
1933	4,560,000	25p	50p	£4	£8
1934	3,052,800	25p	50p	£4	£8
1935	2.227,200	£1	£3	£10	£25
1936	9,734,400	25p	50p	£3	£6

GEORGE VI (1936–52)

1937	8,131,200	—	—	50p	£1
1937 Proof	26,402	—	—	—	£7
1938	7,449,600	—	—	£1	£6
1939	31,440,000	—	—	50p	£1
1940	18,360,000	—	—	50p	£1
1941	27,312,000	—	—	50p	£1
1942	28,857,600	—	—	50p	£1
1943	33,345,600	—	—	50p	£1

DATE	MINTAGE	F	VF	EF	UNC
1944	25,137,600	—	—	50p	£1
1945	23,736,000	—	—	50p	£1
1946	24,364,800	—	—	50p	£1
1947	14,745,600	—	—	50p	£1
1948	16,622,400	—	—	50p	£1
1949	8,424,000	—	—	50p	£1
1950	10,324,800	—	—	50p	£1
1950 Proof	17,513	—	—	50p	£8
1951	14,016,000	—	—	50p	£1
1951 Proof	20,000	—	—	50p	£8
1952	5,251,200	—	—	50p	£1

ELIZABETH II (1952–)

1953	6,131,037	—	—	—	£1
1953 Proof	40,000	—	—	—	£6
1954	6,566,400	—	—	—	£1
1955	5,779,200	—	—	—	£1
1956	1,996,800	—	£1	£2	£4

HALF FARTHINGS

DATE	MINTAGE	F	VF	EF	UNC

GEORGE IV (1820–30)

1828 (two different obverses) (issued for Ceylon)	7,680,000	£10	£20	£50	£140
1830 (large or small date) (issued for Ceylon)	8,766,320	£10	£20	£50	£135

WILLIAM IV (1830–37)

1837 (issued for Ceylon)	1,935,360	£20	£55	£140	£240

VICTORIA (1837–1901)

1839	2,042,880	£5	£10	£30	£80
1842	unrecorded	£4	£8	£25	£80
1843	3,440,640	£3	£6	£20	£50
1844	6,451,200	£3	£6	£15	£50
1844 E over N in REGINA	incl. above	£10	£45	£100	—
1847	3,010,560	£6	£12	£35	£75
1851	unrecorded	£5	£12	£35	£100
1851 5 over 0	unrecorded	£8	£20	£60	£135
1852	989,184	£5	£12	£40	£90
1853	955,224	£5	£15	£50	£120
1853 Proof	incl. above	—	—	—	£300
1854	677,376	£8	£25	£75	£175
1856	913,920	£8	£25	£75	£175
1868	unrecorded	—	—	—	Rare
1868	unrecorded	—	—	—	Rare

THIRD FARTHINGS

DATE	MINTAGE	F	VF	EF	UNC

GEORGE IV (1820–30)

1827 (issued for Malta)...............	unrecorded	£8	£18	£50	£125

WILLIAM IV (1830–37)

1835 (issued for Malta)................	unrecorded	£8	£18	£50	£140

VICTORIA (1837–1901)

1844 (issued for Malta)................	1,301,040	£10	£25	£75	£180
1844 RE for REG	incl. above	£30	£60	£250	—
1866...	576,000	£6	£15	£35	£70
1868...	144,000	£6	£15	£35	£65
1876...	162,000	£6	£15	£35	£80
1878...	288,000	£6	£15	£35	£70
1881...	144,000	£6	£15	£35	£75
1884...	144,000	£6	£15	£35	£75
1885...	288,000	£6	£15	£35	£75

EDWARD VII (1902–10)

1902 (issued for Malta)...............	288,000	£4	£8	£22	£40

GEORGE V (1911–36)

1913 (issued for Malta)...............	288,000	£4	£8	£22	£40

QUARTER FARTHINGS

DATE	MINTAGE	F	VF	EF	UNC

VICTORIA (1837–1901)

1839 (issued for Ceylon)..............	3,840,000	£25	£40	£80	£175
1851 (issued for Ceylon)..............	2,215,680	£25	£40	£80	£175
1852 (issued for Ceylon)..............	incl. above	£25	£40	£80	£175
1853 (issued for Ceylon)..............	incl. above	£25	£40	£80	£175
1853 Proof...................................	—	—	—	—	£600

EMERGENCY ISSUES

DATE		F	VF	EF	UNC

GEORGE III (1760–1820)

To alleviate the shortage of circulating coinage during the Napoleonic Wars the Bank of England firstly authorised the countermarking of other countries' coins, enabling them to pass as English currency. The coins, countermarked with punches depicting the head of George III, were mostly Spanish American 8 reales of Charles III. Although this had limited success it was later decided to completely overstrike the coins with a new English design on both sides — specimens that still show traces of the original host coin's date are avidly sought after by collectors. This overstriking continued for a number of years although all the known coins are dated 1804. Finally, in 1811 the Bank of England issued silver tokens which continued up to 1816 when a completely new regal coinage was introduced.

DOLLAR
Oval countermark of George III

	F	VF	EF	UNC
On "Pillar" type 8 reales	£175	£650	£1000	—
*On "Portrait" type.............	£200	£350	£750	—

Octagonal countermark of George III

	F	VF	EF	UNC
On "Portrait" type	£200	£600	£850	—

HALF DOLLAR
Oval countermark of George III

	F	VF	EF	UNC
On "Portrait" type 4 reales	£200	£400	£900	—

FIVE SHILLINGS OR ONE DOLLAR
These coins were overstruck on Spanish-American coins

	F	VF	EF	UNC
1804..................................	£110	£275	£500	—

— With details of original coin still visible add from 10%.

BANK OF ENGLAND TOKENS

THREE SHILLINGS

	F	VF	EF	UNC
1811 Draped bust..............	£35	£60	£185	—
1812 —	£35	£60	£210	—
1812 Laureate bust	£35	£60	£135	—
1813 —	£35	£60	£135	—
1814 —	£35	£60	£135	—
1815 —	£35	£60	£135	—
1816 —	£200	£400	£1250	—

ONE SHILLING AND SIXPENCE

	F	VF	EF	UNC
1811 Draped bust..............	£20	£45	£100	£175
1812 —	£20	£45	£100	£175
1812 Laureate bust	£20	£45	£100	£175
1812 Proof in platinum				Unique
1813 —	£20	£40	£70	£160
1813 Proof in platinum				Unique
1814 —	£20	£35	£75	£160
1815 —	£20	£35	£75	£160
1816 —	£20	£35	£75	£160

NINEPENCE

	F	VF	EF	UNC
1812 Pattern only	—	—		Very Rare

MAUNDY SETS

DATE	F	VF	EF	UNC

DATE	F	VF	EF	UNC

Sets in contemporary dated boxes are usually worth a higher premium. For example approximately £20 can be added to sets from Victoria to George VI in contemporary undated boxes and above £30 for dated boxes.

GEORGE I (1714–27)

	F	VF	EF	UNC
1723	£190	£370	£715	–
1727	£185	£360	£695	–

GEORGE II (1727–60)

	F	VF	EF	UNC
1729	£160	£275	£570	–
1731	£160	£280	£570	–
1732	£150	£275	£550	–
1735	£145	£265	£550	–
1737	£150	£270	£565	–
1739	£145	£265	£535	–
1740	£145	£260	£515	–
1743	£225	£360	£750	–
1746	£140	£255	£485	–
1760	£155	£265	£525	–

GEORGE III (1760–1820)

	F	VF	EF	UNC
1763	£135	£250	£415	–
1763 Proof	–	Extremely rare		
1766	£150	£245	£450	–
1772	£150	£250	£450	–
1780	£140	£260	£460	–
1784	£145	£265	£440	–
1786	£150	£250	£440	–
1792 Wire	£205	£350	£550	£700
1795	£100	£160	£250	£360
1800	£100	£150	£240	£340

New Coinage

	F	VF	EF	UNC
1817	£115	£175	£235	£380
1818	£110	£160	£230	£370
1820	£115	£170	£235	£375

GEORGE IV (1820–30)

	F	VF	EF	UNC
1822	–	£130	£205	£360
1823	–	£120	£215	£340
1824	–	£125	£215	£340
1825	–	£120	£210	£340
1826	–	£110	£190	£325
1827	–	£110	£210	£340
1828	–	£120	£210	£345
1828 Proof	–	–	–	£3100
1829	–	£115	£200	£340
1830	–	£115	£205	£340

WILLIAM IV (1830–37)

	F	VF	EF	UNC
1831	–	£135	£225	£375
1831 Proof	–	–	–	£1000
1831 Proof Gold	–	–		£29000
1832	–	£135	£335	£375
1833	–	£135	£225	£365
1834	–	£135	£235	£365
1835	–	£130	£225	£365
1836	–	£140	£235	£380
1837	–	£160	£240	£400

CHARLES II (1660–85)

	F	VF	EF	UNC
Undated	£200	£330	£700	–
1670	£185	£315	£675	–
1671	£175	£285	£640	–
1672	£175	£285	£650	–
1673	£175	£275	£640	–
1674	£180	£280	£650	–
1675	£175	£285	£640	–
1676	£190	£315	£660	–
1677	£160	£280	£625	–
1678	£225	£425	£775	–
1679	£180	£300	£660	–
1680	£175	£285	£640	–
1681	£200	£295	£685	–
1682	£180	£300	£640	–
1683	£185	£300	£650	–
1684	£210	£375	£700	–

JAMES II (1685–88)

	F	VF	EF	UNC
1686	£195	£325	£675	–
1687	£195	£325	£680	–
1688	£205	£350	£690	–

WILLIAM & MARY (1688–94)

	F	VF	EF	UNC
1689	£725	£1000	£1700	–
1691	£650	£700	£1600	–
1692	£600	£850	£1500	–
1693	£425	£700	£1300	–
1694	£400	£650	£1000	–

WILLIAM III (1694–1702)

	F	VF	EF	UNC
1698	£215	£400	£800	–
1699	£450	£575	£1300	–
1700	£220	£410	£810	–
1701	£205	£385	£780	–

ANNE (1702–14)

	F	VF	EF	UNC
1703	£185	£350	£675	–
1705	£180	£330	£650	–
1706	£165	£305	£585	–
1708	£505	£725	£1500	–
1709	£210	£375	£750	–
1710	£215	£385	£725	–
1713	£180	£350	£650	–

VICTORIA (1837–1901)

YOUNG HEAD ISSUES

DATE	MINTAGE	EF	UNC
1838	4,158	£165	£325
1838 Proof	unrecorded		£2200
1838 Proof Gold			£26000
1839	4,125	£200	£325
1839 Proof	unrecorded	£550	£950
1840	4,125	£240	£350
1841	2,574	£270	£450
1842	4,125	£270	£465
1843	4,158	£195	£315
1844	4,158	£250	£425
1845	4,158	£175	£295
1846	4,158	£450	£750
1847	4,158	£435	£700
1848	4,158	£425	£700
1849	4,158	£275	£425
1850	4,158	£185	£315
1851	4,158	£195	£315
1852	4,158	£475	£725
1853	4,158	£485	£750
1853 Proof	unrecorded		£1200
1854	4,158	£205	£335
1855	4,158	£215	£345
1856	4,158	£175	£275
1857	4,158	£205	£330
1858	4,158	£185	£280
1859	4,158	£170	£275
1860	4,158	£185	£315
1861	4,158	£160	£290
1862	4,158	£195	£300
1863	4,158	£215	£365
1864	4,158	£185	£275
1865	4,158	£190	£290
1866	4,158	£185	£290
1867	4,158	£175	£295
1867 Proof	unrecorded		−£2000
1868	4,158	£170	£255
1869	4,158	£205	£330
1870	4,458	£155	£235
1871	4,488	£155	£225
1871 Proof	unrecorded		−£1900
1872	4,328	£140	£225
1873	4,162	£140	£210
1874	4,488	£145	£210
1875	4,154	£140	£210
1876	4,488	£140	£200
1877	4,488	£140	£195
1878	4,488	£145	£195
1878 Proof	unrecorded		−£1900
1879	4,488	£145	£195
1879 Proof	unrecorded		−£2300
1880	4,488	£140	£195
1881	4,488	£140	£200
1881 Proof	unrecorded		−£1850
1882	4,146	£155	£230
1882 Proof	unrecorded		−£1850
1883	4,488	£125	£185
1884	4,488	£125	£185
1885	4,488	£125	£185
1886	4,488	£125	£185
1887	4,488	£150	£210

JUBILEE HEAD ISSUES

DATE	MINTAGE	EF	UNC
1888	4,488	£130	£195
1888 Proof	unrecorded		−£1700
1889	4,488	£125	£185
1890	4,488	£130	£190
1891	4,488	£125	£185
1892	4,488	£135	£195

OLD HEAD ISSUES

DATE	MINTAGE	EF	UNC
1893	8,976	£80	£135
1894	8,976	£90	£145
1895	8,976	£80	£135
1896	8,976	£80	£135
1897	8,976	£80	£135
1898	8,976	£80	£135
1899	8,976	£80	£135
1900	8,976	£80	£130
1901	8,976	£80	£130

EDWARD VII (1902–110)

DATE	MINTAGE	EF	UNC
1902	8,976	£70	£120
1902 Matt proof	15,123	−	£130
1903	8,976	£75	£125
1904	8,976	£85	£135
1905	8,976	£90	£135
1906	8,800	£80	£130
1907	8,760	£80	£130
1908	8,769	£80	£130
1909	1,983	£130	£210
1910	1,440	£150	£230

GEORGE V (1911–136)

DATE	MINTAGE	EF	UNC
1911	1,786	£110	£195
1911 Proof	6,007	−	£200
1912	1,246	£120	£195
1913	1,228	£110	£195
1914	982	£125	£205
1915	1,293	£115	£195
1916	1,128	£115	£195
1917	1,237	£115	£195
1918	1,375	£115	£195
1919	1,258	£115	£195
1920	1,399	£120	£200
1921	1,386	£120	£200
1922	1,373	£120	£205
1923	1,430	£120	£195
1924	1,515	£120	£195
1925	1,438	£120	£195
1926	1,504	£115	£195
1927	1,647	£125	£160
1928	1,642	£125	£200
1929	1,761	£125	£200
1930	1,724	£115	£185
1931	1,759	£115	£185
1932	1,835	£115	£185
1933	1,872	£115	£185
1934	1,887	£115	£185
1935	1,928	£130	£200
1936	1,323	£140	£225

GEORGE VI (1936–52)

DATE	MINTAGE	EF	UNC
1937	1,325	£110	£190
1937 Proof	20,900	£110	£190
1938	1,275	£125	£210
1939	1,234	£125	£210
1940	1,277	£125	£210
1941	1,253	£130	£215
1942	1,231	£125	£210
1943	1,239	£125	£210
1944	1,259	£125	£210

DATE AND PLACE OF ISSUE	MINTAGE	UNC
1945	1,355	£125 £210
1946	1,365	£125 £210
1947	1,375	£135 £220
1948	1,385	£135 £225
1949	1,395	£135 £225
1950	1,405	£140 £230
1951	1,468	£140 £230
1952	1,012	£150 £240

ELIZABETH II (1952–)

1953 St. Paul's Cathedral	1,025	—	£750
1953 Proof in gold	unrecorded	Ex. rare	
1953 Proof Matt		Very rare	
1954 Westminster Abbey	1,020	—	£165
1955 Southwark Cathedral	1,036	—	£165
1955 Proof Matt		—	£2200
1956 Westminster Abbey	1,088	—	£165
1957 St. Albans Cathedral	1,094	—	£165
1958 Westminster Abbey	1,100	—	£165
1959 St. George's Chapel, Windsor	1,106	—	£165
1960 Westminster Abbey	1,112	—	£165
1961 Rochester Cathedral	1,118	—	£165
1962 Westminster Abbey	1,125	—	£165
1963 Chelmsford Cathedral	1,131	—	£165
1964 Westminster Abbey	1,137	—	£165
1965 Canterbury Cathedral	1,143	—	£165
1966 Westminster Abbey	1,206	—	£165
1967 Durham Cathedral	986	—	£175
1968 Westminster Abbey	964	—	£175
1969 Selby Cathedral	1,002	—	£170
1970 Westminster Abbey	980	—	£170
1971 Tewkesbury Abbey	1,018		£170
1972 York Minster	1,026		£170
1973 Westminster Abbey	1,004		£170
1974 Salisbury Cathedral	1,042		£170
1975 Peterborough Cathedral	1,050		£170
1976 Hereford Cathedral	1,158		£170
1977 Westminster Abbey	1,138		£175
1978 Carlisle Cathedral	1,178		£170
1979 Winchester Cathedral	1,188		£170

DATE AND PLACE OF ISSUE	MINTAGE	UNC
1980 Worcester Cathedral	1,198	£170
1981 Westminster Abbey	1,178	£175
1982 St David's Cathedral	1,218	£175
1983 Exeter Cathedral	1,228	£175
1984 Southwell Minster	1,238	£175
1985 Ripon Cathedral	1,248	£175
1986 Chichester Cathedral	1,378	£175
1987 Ely Cathedral	1,390	£180
1988 Lichfield Cathedral	1,402	£180
1989 Birmingham Cathedral	1,353	£180
1990 Newcastle Cathedral	1,523	£180
1991 Westminster Abbey	1,384	£180
1992 Chester Cathedral	1,424	£180
1993 Wells Cathedral	1,440	£180
1994 Truro Cathedral	1,433	£180
1995 Coventry Cathedral	1,466	£180
1996 Norwich Cathedral	1,629	£180
1997 Birmingham Cathedral	1,786	£180
1998 Portsmouth Cathedral	1,654	£180
1999 Bristol Cathedral	1,676	£180
2000 Lincoln Cathedral	1,686	£180
2000 Silver Proof	13,180	£175
2001 Westminster Abbey	1,132	£185
2002 Canterbury Cathedral	1,681	£185
2002 Gold Proof	2,002	£2000
2003 Gloucester Cathedral	1,608	£185
2004 Liverpool Cathedral	1,613	£185
2005 Wakefield Cathedral	1,685	£190
2006 Guildford Cathedral	1,937	£190
2006 Silver Proof	8,000	£180
2007 Manchester Cathedral	1,822	£195
2008 St Patrick's Cathedral (Armagh)	1,833	£525
2009 St. Edmundsbury Cathedral	1,602	£525
2010 Derby Cathedral	1,617	£450
2011 Westminster Abbey		£500

Despite the decimalisation of the coinage in 1971, in keeping with ancient tradition the Royal Maundy sets are still made up of four silver coins (4p, 3p, 2p and 1p). The designs for the reverse of the coins are a crowned numeral in a wreath of oak leaves—basically the same design that has been used for Maundy coins since Charles II.

MAUNDY ODDMENTS
SINGLE COINS

DATE	F	VF	EF

FOUR PENCE
CHARLES II (1660–85)

	F	VF	EF
Undated	£55	£85	£155
1670	£50	£90	£165
1671	£45	£75	£145
1672/1	£45	£85	£145
1673	£50	£80	£150
1674	£45	£75	£145
1674 7 over 6	£55	£90	£165
1675	£45	£80	£145
1675/4	£50	£90	£165
1676	£45	£75	£160
1676 7 over 6	£55	£90	£170
1677	£40	£75	£140
1678	£40	£70	£135
1678 8 over 7	£45	£90	£155
1679	£40	£65	£130
1680	£45	£70	£145
1681	£40	£75	£150
1682	£40	£70	£155
1682/1	£50	£75	£160
1683	£45	£70	£155
1684	£45	£75	£155
1684 4 over 3	£50	£80	£160

JAMES II (1685–88)

	F	VF	EF
1686	£45	£85	£165
1686 Date over crown	£55	£90	£175
1687	£45	£80	£150
1687 7 over 6	£55	£85	£160
1688	£45	£85	£160
1688 1 over 8	£55	£90	£165

WILLIAM & MARY (1688–94)

	F	VF	EF
1689	£50	£85	£150
1689 GV below bust	£55	£90	£160
1689 GVLEELMVS	£100	£185	£290
1690	£55	£90	£180
1690 6 over 5	£70	105	£195
1691	£60	£100	£190
1691 1 over 0	£70	£110	£195
1692	£80	£125	£215
1692 Maria	£165	£215	£315
1692 2 over 1	100	£125	£225
1693	£85	£125	£220
1693 3 over 2	£70	£125	£220
1694	£65	£115	£190

WILLIAM III (1694–1702)

	F	VF	EF
1698	£60	£110	£185
1699	£50	£95	£170
1700	£55	£100	£180
1701	£60	£95	£180
1702	£65	£115	£180

ANNE (1702–14)

	F	VF	EF
1703	£50	£95	£165
1704	£45	£85	£150
1705	£65	£125	£200

It is nowadays considered that the early small denomination silver coins 4d–1d were originally struck for the Maundy ceremony although undoubtedly many subsequently circulated as small change—therefore they are listed here under "Maundy silver single coins".

DATE	F	VF	EF	UNC
1706....................................	£50	£90	£150	—
1708....................................	£505£90	£100	£175	—
1709....................................	£50	£95	£145	—
1710....................................	£45	£80	£135	—
1713....................................	£50	£90	£155	—

GEORGE I (1714–27)

	F	VF	EF	UNC
1717....................................	£50	£90	£150	—
1721....................................	£50	£95	£160	—
1723....................................	£55	£95	£165	—
1727....................................	£55	£90	£160	—

GEORGE II (1727–60)

	F	VF	EF	UNC
1729....................................	£45	£80	£130	—
1731....................................	£45	£80	£130	—
1732....................................	£40	£80	£125	—
1735....................................	£40	£75	£125	—
1737....................................	£45	£75	£125	—
1739....................................	£45	£75	£125	—
1740....................................	£45	£70	£115	—
1743....................................	£100	£150	£240	—
1743 3 over 0........................	£110	£160	£250	
1746....................................	£45	£65	£115	—
1760....................................	£50	£80	£120	—

GEORGE III (1760–1820)

	F	VF	EF	UNC
1763 Young head	£40	£75	£110	—
1763 Proof.............................	—	—	Extremely rare	
1765....................................	£385	£635	£1000	—
1766....................................	£45	£80	£120	—
1770....................................	£115	£185	£285	—
1772....................................	£60	£110	£150	—
1776....................................	£55	£100	£145	—
1780....................................	£40	£80	£115	—
1784....................................	£40	£75	£110	—
1786....................................	£50	£90	£130	—
1792 Older head, Thin 4........	£65	£105	£175	£270
1795....................................	—	£45	£75	£110
1800....................................	—	£40	£70	£100
1817 New coinage.................	—	£40	£60	£100
1818....................................	—	£40	£60	£95
1820....................................	—	£40	£65	£105

GEORGE IV (1820–30)

	F	VF	EF	UNC
1822....................................	—	—	£50	£105
1823....................................	—	—	£45	£95
1824....................................	—	—	£45	£95
1826....................................	—	—	£45	£90
1827....................................	—	—	£45	£90
1828....................................	—	—	£45	£90
1829....................................	—	—	£45	£90
1830....................................	—	—	£45	£90

WILLIAM IV (1830–37)

	F	VF	EF	UNC
1831–37................................	—	—	£55	£115
1831 Proof.............................	—	—	£215	£315

VICTORIA (1837–1901)

	F	VF	EF	UNC
1838 Proof.............................	—	—	—	£375
1839 Proof.............................	—	—	—	£290
1853 Proof.............................	—	—	—	£315
1838–87 (Young Head)	—	—	£25	£45
1841 & 1857	—	—	£35	£50
1888–92 (Jubilee Head)..........	—	—	£25	£40
1893–1909 (Old Head)............	—	—	£20	£35

DATE	F	VF	EF	UNC

EDWARD VII (1901–10)

DATE	F	VF	EF	UNC
1902–08	—	—	£25	£35
1909 & 1910	—	—	£35	£60
1902 Proof	—	—	£25	£40

GEORGE V (1910–36)

	F	VF	EF	UNC
1911–36	—	—	£35	£45
1911 Proof	—	—	£40	£50

GEORGE VI (1936–52)

	F	VF	EF	UNC
1937–52	—	—	£35	£55
1937 Proof	—	—	£30	£50

ELIZABETH II (1952–)

	F	VF	EF	UNC
1953	—	—	£130	£200
1954–85	—	—	£40	£60
1986–2007	—	—	£45	£65
2002 in Gold Proof	—	—	£475	£700
2008	—	—	£60	£115
2009	—	—	£60	£115
2010	—	—	£50	£100
2011	—	—	£60	£100

THREEPENCE

CHARLES II (1660–85)

	F	VF	EF	UNC
Undated	£50	£85	£170	—
1670	£45	£80	£130	—
1671	£45	£70	£130	—
1671 GRVTIA	£60	£95	£210	—
1672	£45	£75	£135	—
1673	£45	£75	£135	—
1674	£45	£75	£140	—
1675	£50	£80	£140	—
1676	£55	£100	£185	—
1676 ERA for FRA	£65	£110	£200	—
1677	£45	£70	£135	—
1678	£40	£65	£115	—
1679	£35	£65	£110	—
1679 O/A in CAROLVS	£85	£110	£215	—
1680	£45	£80	£145	—
1681	£45	£80	£145	—
1682	£45	£80	£145	—
1683	£45	£80	£145	—
1684	£45	£85	£145	—
1684/3	£50	£85	£150	—

JAMES II (1685–88)

	F	VF	EF	UNC
1685	£50	£85	£165	—
1685 Struck on fourpence flan	£95	£130	£250	—
1686	£45	£75	£145	—
1687	£40	£75	£140	—
1687 7 over 6	£45	£75	£140	—
1688	£50	£100	£175	—
1688 8 over 7	£55	£105	£185	—

WILLIAM & MARY (1688–94)

	F	VF	EF	UNC
1689	£45	£80	£160	—
1689 No stop on reverse	£50	£90	£170	—
1689 LMV over MVS (obverse)	£80	£110	£205	—
1690	£60	£95	£165	—
1690 6 over 5	£65	£110	£180	—
1691 First bust	£360	£560	£770	—
1691 Second bust	£265	£425	£550	—
1692	£65	£110	£195	—
1692 G below bust	£70	£120	£200	—

DATE	F	VF	EF	UNC
1692 GV below bust...............	£70	£120	£185	—
1692 GVL below bust.............	£65	£110	£210	—
1693..	£100	£165	£235	—
1693 3 over 2...........................	£110	£175	£240	—
1694..	£65	£95	£175	—
1694 MARIΛ	£100	£135	£240	—

WILLIAM III (1694–1702)

1698..	£55	£100	£165	—
1699..	£45	£90	£150	—
1700..	£55	£110	£170	—
1701..	£45	£80	£145	—
1701 GBA instead of GRA......	£55	£105	£165	—

ANNE (1702–14)

1703..	£50	£80	£160	—
1703 7 of date above crown...	£60	£100	£170	—
1704..	£45	£75	£130	—
1705..	£60	£100	£165	—
1706..	£50	£80	£135	—
1707..	£45	£80	£130	—
1708..	£45	£80	£140	—
1709..	£45	£90	£145	—
1710..	£40	£70	£115	—
1713..	£45	£90	£145	—

GEORGE I (1714–27)

1717..	£50	£80	£135	—
1721..	£50	£80	£145	—
1723..	£55	£90	£155	—
1727..	£55	£90	£155	—

GEORGE II (1727–60)

1729..	£45	£75	£120	—
1731..	£45	£75	£120	—
1731 Small lettering...............	£50	£90	£135	—
1732..	£45	£75	£120	—
1731 Stop over head..............	£45	£80	£125	—
1735..	£40	£70	£120	—
1737..	£45	£75	£130	—
1739..	£45	£70	£135	—
1740..	£45	£70	£120	—
1743 Small and large lettering	£45	£65	£125	—
1743 Stop over head..............	£45	£75	£135	—
1746..	£35	£60	£115	—
1746 6 over 3...........................	£45	£65	£120	—
1760..	£50	£70	£130	—

GEORGE III (1760–1820)

1762..	£25	£40	£55	—
1763..	£25	£40	£60	—
1763 Proof..............................	—	—	Extremely rare	
1765..	£300	£450	£725	—
1766..	£45	£75	£125	—
1770..	£45	£80	£130	—
1772..	£40	£65	£95	—
1780..	£40	£65	£95	—
1784..	£60	£85	£150	—
1786..	£60	£85	£145	—
1792..	£60	£100	£180	£275
1795..	—	£35	£60	£100
1800..	—	£40	£65	£100
1817..	—	£35	£65	£125
1818..	—	£35	£65	£120

DATE	F	VF	EF	UNC
1820	—	£40	£70	£135

GEORGE IV (1820–30)

DATE	F	VF	EF	UNC
1822	—	—	£60	£130
1823	—	—	£55	£120
1824	—	—	£55	£125
1825–30	—	—	£55	£120

WILLIAM IV (1830–37)

DATE	F	VF	EF	UNC
1831 Proof	—	—	£175	£350
1831–1836	—	—	£60	£140
1837	—	—	£80	£155

VICTORIA (1837–1901)

DATE	F	VF	EF	UNC
1838	—	—	£85	£170
1839	—	—	£90	£195
1840	—	—	£110	£220
1841	—	—	£155	£300
1842	—	—	£155	£280
1843	—	—	£100	£180
1844	—	—	£135	£250
1845	—	—	£65	£135
1846	—	—	£325	£600
1847	—	—	£300	£550
1848	—	—	£300	£550
1849	—	—	£170	£300
1850	—	—	£95	£185
1851	—	—	£100	£200
1852	—	—	£370	£600
1853	—	—	£370	£600
1854	—	—	£125	£225
1855	—	—	£130	£225
1856	—	—	£75	£200
1857	—	—	£115	£225
1858	—	—	£95	£185
1859	—	—	£80	£155
1860	—	—	£110	£200
1861	—	—	£95	£190
1862	—	—	£95	£190
1863	—	—	£120	£240
1864	—	—	£95	£200
1865	—	—	£100	£205
1866	—	—	£95	£195
1867	—	—	£95	£190
1868	—	—	£90	£170
1869	—	—	£115	£225
1870	—	—	£80	£155
1871	—	—	£80	£160
1872	—	—	£80	£150
1873	—	—	£75	£140
1874	—	—	£75	£140
1875	—	—	£65	£125
1876	—	—	£65	£130
1877	—	—	£65	£120
1878	—	—	£65	£125
1879	—	—	£70	£135
1880	—	—	£65	£125
1881	—	—	£65	£125
1882	—	—	£100	£190
1883	—	—	£65	£120
1884	—	—	£60	£115
1885	—	—	£60	£110
1886	—	—	£50	£95
1887	—	—	£65	£140
1888–1892 (Jubilee Head)	—	—	£45	£90

DATE	F	VF	EF	UNC
1893–1901 (Old Head)............	—	—	£35	£55

EDWARD VII (1901–10)

	F	VF	EF	UNC
1902..	—	—	£25	£45
1902 Proof..............................	—	—	—	£45
1903..	—	—	£35	£70
1904..	—	—	£45	£85
1905..	—	—	£45	£85
1906..	—	—	£45	£80
1907..	—	—	£40	£70
1908..	—	—	£35	£60
1909..	—	—	£50	£100
1910..	—	—	£55	£110

GEORGE V (1910–36)

	F	VF	EF	UNC
1911–34..................................	—	—	£30	£60
1911 Proof..............................	—	—	—	£65
1935..	—	—	£35	£65
1936..	—	—	£50	£85

GEORGE VI (1936–52)

	F	VF	EF	UNC
1937–52..................................	—	—	£40	£70
1937 Proof..............................	—	—	—	£65

ELIZABETH II (1952–   )

	F	VF	EF	UNC
1953..	—	—	£125	£210
1954–85..................................	—	—	£35	£55
1986–2007..............................	—	—	£40	£60
2002 In gold (proof)	—	—	—	£525
2008..	—	—	—	£120
2009..	—	—	—	£120
2010..	—	—	—	£100

TWOPENCE

CHARLES II (1660–85)

	F	VF	EF	UNC
Undated..................................	£45	£70	£130	—
1668..	£50	£70	£140	—
1670..	£40	£70	£120	—
1671..	£40	£65	£120	—
1672..	£40	£65	£120	—
1672/1	£45	£70	£130	—
1673..	£40	£65	£125	—
1674..	£40	£70	£125	—
1675..	£40	£70	£115	—
1676..	£50	£75	£130	—
1677..	£35	£65	£115	—
1678..	£30	£55	£110	—
1679..	£30	£50	£95	—
1680..	£40	£65	£115	—
1681..	£40	£60	£115	—
1682..	£35	£60	£120	—
1682/1 ERA for FRA	£50	£75	£175	—
1683..	£40	£70	£125	—
1684..	£40	£70	£130	—

JAMES II (1685–88)

	F	VF	EF	UNC
1686..	£45	£70	£135	—
1686 reads IACOBVS	£50	£90	£175	—
1687..	£45	£75	£135	—
1687 ERA for FRA	£55	£95	£180	—
1688..	£40	£65	£125	—
1688/7	£45	£70	£135	—

WILLIAM & MARY (1688–94)

	F	VF	EF	UNC
1689..	£45	£75	£145	—
1691..	£35	£65	£115	—

DATE	F	VF	EF	UNC
1692	£60	£110	£160	—
1693	£45	£80	£135	—
1693 GV below bust	£55	£85	£140	—
1693/2	£50	£80	£140	—
1694	£35	£65	£115	—
1694 MARLA error	£55	£100	£225	—
1694 HI for HIB	£50	£90	£170	—
1694 GVLI under bust	£45	£75	£150	—
1694 GVL under bust	£45	£75	£150	—

WILLIAM III (1694–1702)

1698	£45	£85	£140	—
1699	£40	£70	£110	—
1700	£45	£80	£135	—
1701	£45	£80	£130	—

ANNE (1702–14)

1703	£45	£75	£140	—
1704	£35	£60	£110	—
1704 No stops on obverse	£45	£70	£135	—
1705	£45	£75	£135	—
1706	£40	£75	£130	—
1707	£35	£60	£120	—
1708	£40	£60	£115	—
1709	£60	£90	£170	—
1710	£35	£60	£100	—
1713	£50	£80	£150	—

GEORGE I (1714–27)

1717	£35	£65	£105	—
1721	£40	£65	£100	—
1723	£45	£75	£130	—
1726	£40	£60	£110	—
1727	£40	£65	£120	—

GEORGE II (1727–60)

1729	£35	£55	£95	—
1731	£35	£55	£90	—
1732	£40	£60	£95	—
1735	£35	£55	£90	—
1737	£3	£55	£90	—
1739	£40	£60	£90	—
1740	£35	£55	£90	—
1743	£30	£50	£85	—
1743/0	£35	£65	£100	—
1746	£30	£50	£75	—
1756	£30	£50	£75	—
1759	£30	£55	£75	—
1760	£30	£55	£85	—

GEORGE III (1760–1820)

1763	£28	£50	£75	—
1763 Proof			Extremely rare	
1765	£305	£475	£700	—
1766	£30	£50	£75	—
1772	£28	£50	£70	—
1780	£28	£50	£70	—
1784	£28	£50	£70	—
1786	£35	£55	£70	—
1792	—	£60	£95	£150
1795	—	£25	£50	£70
1800	—	£25	£45	£60
1817	—	£25	£50	£70

DATE	F	VF	EF	UNC
1818....................................	—	£20	£50	£70
1820....................................	—	£20	£50	£70

GEORGE IV (1820–30)

1822–30................................	—	—	£35	£50
1825 TRITANNIAR	—	—	£55	£90

WILLIAM IV (1830–37)

1831–37................................	—	—	£35	£55
1831 Proof.............................	—	—	£60	£160

VICTORIA (1837–1901)

1838–87 (Young Head)	—	—	£30	£45
1859 BEITANNIAR	—	—	£60	£110
1861 6 over 1.........................	—	—	£35	£60
1888–92 (Jubilee Head).........	—	—	£30	£40
1893–1901 (Old Head............	—	—	£20	£35
1838 Proof.............................	—	—	—	£185
1839 Proof.............................	—	—	—	£175
1853 Proof.............................	—	—	—	£210

EDWARD VII (1901–10)

1902–08................................	—	—	£17	£30
1909....................................	—	—	£35	£60
1910....................................	—	—	£35	£60
1902 Proof.............................	—	—	£22	£35

GEORGE V (1910–36)

1911–34................................	—	—	£25	£40
1935....................................	—	—	£27	£45
1936....................................	—	—	£35	£50
1911 Proof.............................	—	—	£25	£50

GEORGE VI (1936–52)

1937–47................................	—	—	£25	£40
1948–52................................	—	—	£30	£50
1937 Proof.............................	—	—	£25	£40

ELIZABETH II (1952–)

1953....................................	—	—	£90	£150
1954–85................................	—	—	£30	£45
1986–2007............................	—	—	£30	£45
2002 Gold Proof	—	—	—	£4125
2008....................................	—	—	—	£85
2009....................................	—	—	—	£85
2010....................................	—	—	—	£65
2011....................................	—	—	—	£70

PENNY

CHARLES II (1660–85)

Undated................................	£60	£90	£165	—
1670....................................	£55	£90	£145	—
1671....................................	£55	£90	£140	—
1672/1	£55	£90	£140	—
1673....................................	£50	£85	£135	—
1674....................................	£50	£85	£135	—
1674 Gratia (error)	£65	£120	£220	—
1675....................................	£50	£90	£135	—
1675 Gratia (error)	£65	£120	£220	—
1676....................................	£60	£90	£150	—
1676 Gratia (error)	£75	£130	£230	—
1677....................................	£50	£80	£135	—
1677 Gratia (error)	£65	£110	£200	—
1678....................................	£130	£240	£325	—
1678 Gratia (error)	£160	£240	£375	—
1679....................................	£65	£100	£170	—
1680....................................	£50	£80	£145	—
1681....................................	£75	£120	£190	—

Charles II

DATE	F	VF	EF	UNC
1682..	£55	£85	£160	—
1682 ERA for FRA	£60	£120	£215	—
1683..	£55	£85	£160	—
1683/1	£60	£110	£190	—
1684..	£170	£240	£330	—
1684/3	£180	£250	£335	—

JAMES II (1685–88)

1685..	£50	£80	£130	—
1686..	£50	£80	£135	—
1687..	£55	£90	£150	—
1687/8	£55	£95	£155	—
1688..	£50	£75	£135	—
1688/7	£55	£85	£150	—

James II

WILLIAM & MARY (1688–94)

1689..	£425	£575	£850	—
1689 MARIΛ	£380	£575	£850	
1689 GVIELMVS (Error)	£390	£565	£815	—
1690..	£50	£110	£175	—
1691..	£50	£110	£175	—
1692..	£165	£290	£485	—
1692/1	£170	£300	£495	—
1693..	£70	£120	£195	—
1694..	£60	£95	£180	—
1694 HI for HIB......................	£75	£130	£225	—
1694 No stops on obverse	£70	£125	£210	—

WILLIAM III (1694–1702)

1698..	£65	£110	£165	—
1698 HI. BREX (Error)	£80	£135	£225	—
1699..	£250	£360	£570	—
1700..	£70	£110	£170	—
1701..	£65	£110	£165	—

ANNE (1702–14)

1703..	£55	£90	£150	—
1705..	£50	£85	£140	—
1706..	£45	£70	£125	—
1708..	£350	£420	£635	—
1709..	£45	£75	£125	—
1710..	£110	£175	£270	—
1713/0	£60	£95	£140	—

GEORGE I (1714–27)

1716..	£40	£70	£95	—
1718..	£40	£70	£95	—
1720..	£45	£75	£100	—
1720 HIPEX (Error)..................	£55	£85	£175	—
1723..	£50	£85	£135	—
1725..	£40	£70	£105	—
1726..	£40	£70	£100	—
1727..	£45	£90	£135	—

GEORGE II (1727–60)

1729..	£35	£70	£100	—
1731..	£35	£65	£100	—
1732..	£30	£50	£80	—
1735..	£30	£50	£75	—
1737..	£30	£50	£80	—
1739..	£35	£50	£75	—
1740..	£35	£55	£80	—
1743..	£30	£60	£80	—
1746..	£35	£65	£90	—
1746/3	£40	£70	£90	—
1750..	£25	£45	£65	—
1752..	£25	£45	£65	—
1753..	£25	£45	£65	—
1754..	£25	£45	£65	—
1755..	£25	£45	£65	—

George II

DATE	F	VF	EF	UNC
1756....................................	£25	£50	£65	—
1757....................................	£25	£50	£65	—
1757 No colon after Gratia	£35	£60	£80	—
1758....................................	£25	£45	£65	—
1759....................................	£25	£40	£65	—
1760....................................	£30	£55	£80	—

GEORGE III (1760–1820)

	F	VF	EF	UNC
1763....................................	£35	£50	£80	—
1763 Proof...........................	—	—	Extremely rare	
1766....................................	£30	£55	£70	—
1772....................................	£35	£55	£60	—
1780....................................	£55	£80	£130	—
1781....................................	£25	£40	£60	—
1784....................................	£30	£50	£70	—
1786....................................	£25	£45	£70	—
1792....................................	£30	£55	£75	£110
1795....................................	—	£20	£35	£50
1800....................................	—	£20	£30	£50
1817....................................	—	£20	£35	£40
1818....................................	—	£20	£35	£45
1820....................................	—	£20	£35	£40

George III

GEORGE IV (1820–30)

	F	VF	EF	UNC
1822–30................................	—	—	£30	£45

WILLIAM IV (1830–37)

	F	VF	EF	UNC
1831–37................................	—	—	£30	£50
1831 Proof...........................	—	—	—	£150
1838 Proof...........................	—	—	—	£180

VICTORIA (1837–1901)

	F	VF	EF	UNC
1838–87 (Young Head)	—	—	£25	£40
1888–92 (Jubilee Head)..........	—	—	£25	£35
1893–1901 (Old Head)............	—	—	£17	£28
1839 Proof...........................	—	—	—	£135
1853 Proof...........................	—	—	—	£170

EDWARD VII (1901–10)

	F	VF	EF	UNC
1902–08................................	—	—	£17	£25
1909	—	—	£30	£55
1910	—	—	£35	£70
1902 Proof...........................	—	—	£18	£30

GEORGE V (1910–36)

	F	VF	EF	UNC
1911–14................................	—	—	£30	£55
1915....................................	—	—	£30	£55
1916–19................................	—	—	£30	£55
1920....................................	—	—	£30	£60
1921–28................................	—	—	£30	£55
1929....................................	—	—	£30	£60
1930–34................................	—	—	£30	£55
1935....................................	—	—	£30	£60
1936....................................	—	—	£35	£65
1911 Proof...........................	—	—	£30	£55

GEORGE VI (1936–52)

	F	VF	EF	UNC
1937–40................................	—	—	£30	£60
1941....................................	—	—	£35	£65
1942–47................................	—	—	£30	£60
1948–52................................	—	—	£35	£70
1937 Proof...........................	—	—	£25	£55

ELIZABETH II (1952–   )

	F	VF	EF	UNC
1953....................................	—	—	£225	£330
1965–85................................	—	—	£35	£55
1986–2007............................	—	—	£35	£60
2002 Proof in gold	—	—	—	£425
2008....................................	—	—	£60	£90
2009....................................	—	—	£60	£90
2010....................................	—	—	£50	£75
2011....................................	—	—	£60	£100

DECIMAL COINAGE

Since the introduction of the Decimal system in the UK, many coins have been issued for circulation purposes in vast quantities. In addition, from 1982 sets of coins to non-proof standard, and including examples of each denomination found in circulation, have been issued each year. For 1982 and 1983 they were to "circulation" standard and described as "Uncirculated". Individual coins from these sets are annotated "Unc" on the lists that follow. From 1984 to the present day they were described as "Brilliant Uncirculated" (BU on the lists), and from around 1986 these coins are generally distinguishable from coins intended for circulation. They were from then produced by the Proof Coin Division of the Royal Mint (rather than by the Coin Production Room which produces circulation-standard coins). For completeness however, we have included the annotations Unc and BU back to 1982, the start year for these sets.

It is emphasised that the abbreviations Unc and BU in the left-hand columns adjacent to the date refer to an advertising description or to an engineering production standard, not the preservation condition or grade of the coin concerned. Where no such annotation appears adjacent to the date, the coin is circulation-standard for issue as such.

We have included the "mintage" figures for circulation coins down to Half Penny. Strictly speaking, these figures are for coins issued by the Royal Mint up to December 31, 2005. The figure given for the 1997 Two Pounds, for example, is considerably less than the actual quantity struck, because many were scrapped before issue due to failing an electrical conductivity test. Where a coin is available in uncirculated grade at, or just above, face value no price has been quoted.

Base metal Proof issues of circulation coinage (£2 or £1 to one or half penny) of the decimal series were only issued, as with Unc or BU, as part of Year Sets, but many of these sets have been broken down into individual coins, hence the appearance of the latter on the market.

The lists do not attempt to give details of die varieties, except where there was an obvious intention to change the appearance of a coin, e.g. 1992 20p.

2008 saw new reverses and modified obverses for all circulation denominations from the One Pound to the One Penny. All seven denominations were put into circulation dated 2008, all with both the old and the new reverses.

It is assumed that all circulation denominations will appear to circulation standard in due course for 2009 and 2010. The circulation standard mintage figures have, in general been kindly supplied by courtesy of the Head of Historical Services at The Royal Mint.

HUNDRED POUNDS AND BELOW
(Britannia and Olympic Gold series)

In 1987 the gold £100 coin was introduced, known as the Britannia. It contained one Troy ounce of fine gold, alloyed to 22 carat, and this has continued to the present day. At the same time, and also continuing, coins of face value £50, £25 and £10 appeared, containing a half ounce, quarter ounce and one tenth of an ounce of fine gold respectively. From 1987 to 1989 the alloy was of copper (Red Gold), whereas from 1990 to the present day the alloy has been of silver and copper (yellow gold).

Proof sets of these coins are listed in the "Proof and Specimen Sets" section. In addition, non-proof coins have been minted, it is believed for each of the four coins for every year. The one ounce £100 Britannia is primarily issued as a bullion coin in the non-proof standard, originally in competition with the South African Krugerrand. Its price is quoted daily on the financial pages of some newspapers.

There were five reverse designs by Philip Nathan:- 1987-1996 Standing Britannia, 1997 Chariot, 1998-2000 Standing Britannia, 2001 Una and the Lion, 2002 Standing Britannia, 2003 Britannia's Helmeted Head, 2004 Standing Britannia, 2005 Britannia seated, 2006 Standing Britannia. For 2007 the design is a Seated Britannia with lion at her feet, by Christopher Le Brun. The 2008 design is of Britannia standing and facing left, by John Bergdahl. The 2009 reverse is similar to that of 1997, Britannia on a chariot, while 2010 has Suzie Zamit's Britannia potrait with a Corinthian style helmet. The 2011 design is by David Mach, and portrays a seated Britannia with trident and shield, replicating the design on a 1937 penny, superimposed on a Union Flag. The rotation of the coin from left to right, or vice-versa, creates an illusion of Britannia moving with the ripple of the flag.

In general the proof coins have reverse features frosted, The proofs with Standing Britannia and Una and the Lion reverses include P NATHAN on the reverse, whereas the equivalent bullion coins include NATHAN. The other three reverses have PN on both proofs and bullion coins.

The issue of the second series of three coins in the Olympic Games gold proof series occurred in 2011, with the completion of the 9-coin series being expected in 2012. Reverses are summarised, along with known data, below:

DATE	FACE VALUE	FINE GOLD WEIGHT	FEATURED GOD	FEATURED PART OF OLYMPIC MOTTO
2010	£100 £25 £25	1 Troy oz 1/4 Troy oz 1/4 Troy oz	Neptune Diana Mercury	CITIUS
2011	£100 £25 £25	1 Troy oz 1/4 Troy oz 1/4 Troy oz	Jupiter Juno Apollo	ALTIUS
2012	£100 £25 £25	1 Troy oz 1/4 Troy oz 1/4 Troy oz	To be announced	FORTIUS

HUNDRED POUNDS AND BELOW
(Britannia Platinum series)

2007 saw the issue of four-coin proof sets in platinum, 0.9995 fine. The denomination and designs are similar to those of the Gold series of the same year. The issue was repeated in 2008, and again in 2009, above rule applies. It is understood that no bullion coins have been issued.

FIVE POUNDS (Sovereign series)

This series is all minted in gold, and, except where stated, have the Pistrucci St George and Dragon reverse. BU coins up to 2001 bear a U in a circle.

DATE	Mintage	UNC
1980 Proof	10,000	£950
1981 Proof	5,400	£950
1982 Proof	2,500	£975
1984 BU	15,104	£950
1984 Proof	8,000	£975
1985 New portrait BU	13,626	£950
1985 — Proof	6,130	£900
1986 BU	7,723	£950
1987 Uncouped portrait BU	5,694	£950
1988 BU	3,315	£950
1989 500th Anniversary of the Sovereign. Enthroned portrayal obverse and Crowned shield reverse BU	2,937	£1000
1989 — Proof	5,000	£1150
1990 Reverts to couped portrait BU	1,226	£900
1990 Proof	1,721	£950
1991 BU	976	£900
1991 Proof	1,336	£950
1992 BU	797	£900
1992 Proof	1,165	£950
1993 BU	906	£900
1993 Proof	1,078	£950
1994 BU	1,000	£900
1994 Proof	918	£950
1995 BU	1,000	£900
1995 Proof	1,250	£950
1996 BU	901	£900
1996 Proof	742	£950
1997 BU	802	£950
1997 Proof	860	£1000
1998 New portrait BU	825	£975
1998 Proof	789	£1000
1999 BU	991	£975
1999 Proof	1,000	£1000
2000 ("Bullion")	10,000	£900
2000 BU	994	£950
2000 Proof	3,000	£950
2001 BU	1,000	£900
2001 Proof	3,500	£950
2002 Shield rev. ("Bullion")	—	£900
2002 BU	—	£900
2002 Proof	3,000	£975
2003 BU	—	£950
2003 Proof	—	£1000
2004 BU	—	£950
2004 Proof	—	£975
2005 Noad's heraldic St George and Dragon BU	—	£1000
2005 — Proof	—	£1250
2006 BU	—	£900
2006 Proof	—	£950
2007 BU	—	£900
2007 Proof	—	£950
2008 BU	—	£120
2008 Proof	—	£900
2009 BU	—	£950
2009 Proof	—	£1250
2010 BU	—	—
2010 Proof	—	—
2011 BU	—	—
2011 Proof	—	—

NOTE: The prices quoted in this guide are set at August 2011 with the price of gold at £1,150 per ounce and silver £26 per ounce—market fluctuations will have a marked effect on the values of modern precious metal coins.

Pistrucci's famous rendering of St George and the Dragon.

The obverse of the 1989 gold coins portray HM the Queen enthroned

227

FIVE POUNDS (Crown series)

This series commenced in 1990 when the "Crown" was declared legal tender at £5, instead of 25p as all previous issues continued to be. Mintage is in cupro-nickel unless otherwise stated. BU includes those in individual presentation folders, and those in sets sold with stamp covers and/or banknotes.

DATE	Mintage	UNC
1990 Queen Mother's 90th Birthday.	2,761,431	£8
1990 — BU	48,477	£10
1990 — Silver Proof	56,800	£40
1990 — Gold Proof	2,500	£1200
1993 Coronation 40th Anniversary	1,834,655	£8
1993 — BU	—	£10
1993 — Proof	—	£15
1993 — Silver Proof	100,000	£45
1993 — Gold Proof	2,500	£1200
1996 HM the Queen's 70th Birthday	2,396,100	£8
1996 — BU	—	£10
1996 — Proof	—	£15
1996 — Silver Proof	70,000	£45
1996 — Gold Proof	2,127	£1200
1997 Royal Golden Wedding	1,733,000	£10
1997 — BU	—	£12
1997 — — with £5 note	5,000	£75
1997 — Proof	—	£20
1997 — Silver Proof	75,000	£45
1997 — Gold Proof	2,750	£1200
1998 Prince of Wales 50th birthday	1,407,300	£8
1998 — BU	—	£12
1998 — Proof	—	£20
1998 — Silver Proof	—	£50
1998 — Gold Proof	—	£1200
1999 Princess of Wales Memorial.	1,600,000	£10
1999 — BU	—	£12
1999 — Proof	—	£20
1999 — Silver Proof	350,000	£50
1999 — Gold Proof	7,500	£1200
1999 Millennium	3,796,300	£8
1999 — BU	—	£15
1999 — Proof	—	£22
1999 — Silver Proof	100,000	£45
1999 — Gold Proof	2,500	£1200
2000 —	3,147,092*	£8
2000 — BU	—	£15
2000 — — with special Millennium Dome mintmark	—	£20
2000 — Proof	—	£22
2000 — Silver Proof with gold highlight	50,000	£50
2000 — Gold Proof	2,500	£1200
2000 Queen Mother's 100th Birthday	*incl. above**	£7
2000 — BU	—	£12
2000 — Silver Proof	100,000	£55
2000 — — Piedfort	14,850	£150
2000 — Gold Proof	3,000	£1200
2001 Victorian Era.	851,491	£7
2001 — BU	—	£12
2001 — Proof	—	£20
2001 — Silver Proof	100,000	£45
2001 — — with frosted relief	—	£150
2001 — Gold Proof	3,000	£1200
2001 — — with frosted relief	750	£1400
2002 Golden Jubilee	3,687,882*	£7
2002 — BU	—	£12
2002 — Proof	—	£20
2002 — Silver Proof	75,000	£45
2002 — Gold Proof	5,502	£1200

DATE	Mintage	UNC
2002 Queen Mother Memorial...*incl. above**		£7
2002 — BU...	—	£12
2002 — Silver Proof	25,000	£45
2002 — Gold Proof...	3,000	£1200
2003 Coronation Jubilee 1,307,147		£7
2003 — BU...	—	£10
2003 — Proof..	—	£20
2003 — Silver Proof	—	£45
2003 — Gold Proof...	—	£1200
2004 Entente Cordiale Centenary 1,205,594		£6
2004 — Proof Reverse Frosting		£15
2004 — Silver Proof	—	£35
2004 — — — Piedfort	—	£150
2004 — Gold Proof...	—	£1200
2004 — Platinum Proof Piedfort..	501	£3750
2005 Trafalgar Bicentenary..................................... 1,075 516		£12
2005 — BU...	—	£14
2005 — Proof..	—	£20
2005 — Silver Proof	—	£45
2005 — — — Piedfort	—	£100
2005 — Gold Proof...	—	£1100
2005 Bicentenary of the Death of Nelson ....*incl. above**		£12
2005 — BU...	—	£14
2005 — Proof..	—	£22
2005 — Silver Proof	—	£50
2005 — — — Piedfort	—	£100
2005 — Gold Proof...	—	£110
2005 — Platinum Proof Piedfort..	200	£4000
2006 Queen's 80th birthday..	—	£10
2006 — BU...	—	£12
2006 — Proof..	—	£20
2006 — Silver Proof	—	£45
2006 — — — Piedfort, selective gold plating on reverse	—	£120
2006 — Gold Proof...	—	£120
2006 — Platinum Proof Piedfort..	250	£4000
2007 Queen's Diamond Wedding	—	£10
2007 BU...	—	£12
2007 — Proof..	—	£20
2007 — Silver Proof	—	£45
2007 — — — Piedfort	—	£100
2007 — Gold Proof...	—	£950
2007 — Platinum Proof Piedfort..	—	£4000
2008 Prince of Wales 60th Birthday	—	£10
2008 — BU...	—	£12
2008 — Proof..	—	£15
2008 — Silver Proof	—	£45
2008 — — — Piedfort	—	£100
2008 — Gold Proof...	—	£1100
2008 Elizabeth I 450th Anniversary of Accession	—	£12
2008 — BU...	—	£15
2008 — Proof..	—	£20
2008 — Silver Proof	—	£45
2008 — — — Piedfort	—	£100
2008 — Gold Proof...	—	£1100
2008 — Platinum Proof Piedfort..	—	£4000
2009 500th Anniversary of Henry VIII accession......................	30,000	£10
2009 — BU...	—	£15
2009 — Proof..	—	£25
2009 — Silver Proof	—	£45
2009 — — — Piedfort	—	£120
2009 — Gold Proof...	1,509	£1350
2009 — Platinum Proof Piedfort..	100	£4500
2009 Olympic Countdown (3 years) BU	—	£12
2009 — Silver Proof	—	£75
2009 — — — Piedfort	—	£120
2009 Olympic Celebration of Britain "The Mind" series (incl. green logo):		
Stonehenge Silver Proof	—	£65
Palace of Westminster/Big Ben Silver Proof..................	—	£65
— Cu Ni Proof...	—	£25

DATE	Mintage	UNC
Angel of the North Silver Proof	—	£65
Flying Scotsman Silver Proof	—	£65
Globe Theatre Silver Proof	—	£65
Sir Isaac Newton Silver Proof	—	£65
2010 350th Anniversary of the Restoration of the Monarchy	15,000	—
2010 — BU	—	—
2010 — Proof	—	—
2010 — Silver Proof	—	£50
2010 — — — Piedfort	—	£100
2010 — Gold Proof	—	£1350
2010 Olympic Countdown (2 years) BU	—	—
2010 — Silver Proof	—	—
2010 — — — Piedfort	—	—
2010 — Gold Proof	—	—
2010 Olympic Celebration of Britain, "The Body" series (incl. red logo):		
Coastline of Britain (Rhossili Bay) Silver Proof	—	£65
Giants Causeway Silver Proof	—	£65
River Thames Silver Proof	—	£65
British Fauna (Barn Owl) Silver Proof	—	£65
British Flora (Oak Leaves and Acorn) Silver Proof	—	£65
Weather Vane Silver Proof	—	£65
2010 Olympic Celebration of Britain "The Spirit" series (incl. blue logo):		
Spirit of London (Kind Hearts etc.) Silver Proof	—	£65
— CuNi Proof	—	£20
Humour Silver Proof	—	£65
Unity (Floral emblems of Britain) Silver Proof	—	£65
Music Silver Proof	—	£65
Anti-slavery Silver Proof	—	£65
2011 90th Birthday of the Duke of Edinburgh BU	—	£10
2011 — Silver Proof	—	£65
2011 — — — Piedfort		£115
2011 — Gold Proof	—	£1650
2011 — Platinum Proof Piedfort	—	£6350
2011 Royal Wedding of Prince William and Catherine Middleton BU	—	£10
2011 — Silver Proof	—	£56
2011 — Gold-plated Silver Proof	—	£85
2011 — Silver Proof Piedfort	—	£90
2011 — Gold Proof	—	£1550
2011 — Platinum Proof Piedfort	—	£5450
2011 Olympic Countdown (1 year) BU	—	£10
2011 — Silver Proof	—	£66
2011 — — — Piedfort	—	£125
2011 — Gold Proof	—	£1600

DOUBLE SOVEREIGN

As with the Sovereign series Five Pound coins, those listed under this heading bear the Pistrucci St George and Dragon reverse, except where otherwise stated, and are minted in gold. They are, and always have been, legal tender at £2, and have a diameter indentical to that of the base metal Two Pound coins listed further below under a different heading. The denomination does not appear on Double Sovereigns.

DATE	Mintage	UNC
1980 Proof	10,000	£550
1982 Proof	2,500	£550
1983 Proof	12,500	£500
1985 New Portrait Proof	5,849	£600
1987 Proof	14,301	£500
1988 Proof	12,743	£500
1989 500th Anniversary of the Sovereign. Enthroned portrayal obverse and Crowned shield reverse Proof	14,936	£600
1990 Proof	4,374	£600
1991 Proof	3,108	£600
1992 Proof	2,608	£600

1993 Proof..	2,155	£600
1996 Proof..	3,167	£600
1998 New Portrait Proof...	4,500	£525
2000 Proof..	2,250	£600
2002 Shield reverse Proof	8,000	£550
2003 Proof..	2,250	£600
2004 Proof..	—	£600
2005 Noad heraldic St George and Dragon Proof	—	£650
2006 Proof..	—	£575
2007 Proof..	—	£600
2008 Proof..	—	£600
2009 Proof..	—	£600
2010 Proof..	—	£600
2011 Proof	—	—

TWO POUNDS AND BELOW
(Britannia Silver Series)

This series commenced in 1997, and, as with the Gold Britannia series, sets of the coins are listed in the "Proof and Specimen Sets" section. Coins contain one Troy ounce of fine silver (£2) alloyed to Britannia standard, i.e. 95.8 per cent fine silver, or fractions of one ounce as follows: half ounce (£1), quarter ounce (50 pence) and one tenth of an ounce (20 pence). Reverses change anually, all four coins of any particular date being of the same design. The reverses by Philip Nathan appear as follows:

1997 Chariot, 1998 Standing Britannia, 1999 Chariot, 2000 Standing Britannia, 2001 Una and the Lion, 2002 Standing Britannia, 2003 Britannia's Helmeted Head, 2004 Standing Britannia, 2005 Britannia Seated, 2006 Standing Britannia, 2009 Chariot.

The 2007 design is by Christopher Le Brun, and features a seated Britannia with Lion at her feet. The 2008 is by John Bergdahl, and features a standing Britannia facing left.

Two pounds Britannia coins to BU or "bullion" standard have been issued as individual coins for each year from 1998 onwards. 2010 features Suzie Zamit's Britannia with a portrait with a Corinthian style helmet.

The 2011 coins feature a seated Britannia and Union Flag, as described in the Britannia gold series above.

Not shown to actual size

TWO POUNDS

This series commenced in 1986 with nickel-brass commemorative coins, with their associated base metal and precious metal BU and proof coins. From 1997 (actually issued in 1998) a thinner bi-metal version commenced with a reverse theme of the advance of technology, and from this date the coin was specifically intended to circulate. This is true also for the parallel issues of anniversary and commemorative Two Pound issues in 1999 and onwards. All have their BU and proof versions, as listed below.

In the case of Gold Proofs, a few have Certificates of Authenticity and/or green boxes of issue describing the coin as a Double Sovereign. All Gold Proofs since 1997 are of bi-metallic gold except for 2001 (red gold with the inner circle coated in yellow gold) and 2002 (Technology issue, uncoated red gold).

DATE	Mintage	UNC
1986 Commonwealth Games	8,212,184	£6
1986 — BU	—	£8
1986 — Proof	—	£12
1986 — Silver BU	—	£20
1986 — — Proof	—	£25
1986 — Gold Proof	—	£595
1989 Tercentenary of Bill of Rights.	4,392,825	£10
1989 — BU (issued in folder with Claim of Right)	—	£25
1989 — Proof	—	£15
1989 — Silver Proof (Pair as above)	—	£50
1989 — — Piedfort (Pair as above)	—	£85
1989 Tercentenary of Claim of Right (issued in Scotland)	381,400	£15
1989 — BU (see above)	—	£25
1989 — Proof (see above)	—	£15
1989 — Silver Proof (see above)	—	£50
1989 — — Piedfort (see above)	—	£85
1994 Tercentenary of the Bank of England	1,443,116	£5
1994 — BU	—	£8
1994 — Proof	—	£12
1994 — Silver Proof	—	£35
1994 — — Piedfort	—	£60
1994 — Gold Proof	—	£600
1994 — — — with Double Sovereign obverse (no denomination)	—	£675
1995 50th Anniversary of End of WWII.	4,394,566	£5
1995 — BU	—	£8
1995 — Proof	—	£12
1995 — Silver Proof	—	£35
1995 — — Piedfort	—	£60
1995 — Gold Proof	—	£650
1995 50th Anniversary of The United Nations	1,668,575	£5
1995 — BU	—	£6
1995 — Proof	—	£10
1995 — Silver Proof	—	£35
1995 — — Piedfort	—	£60
1995 — Gold Proof	—	£650
1996 European Football Championships.	5,195,350	£6
1996 — BU	—	£8
1996 — Proof	—	£10
1996 — Silver Proof	—	£35
1996 — — Piedfort	—	£60
1996 — Gold Proof	—	£650
1997	13,734,625	£4
1997 BU	—	£8
1997 Proof	—	£12
1997 Silver Proof	—	£35
1997 — — Piedfort	—	£60
1997 Gold Proof (red (outer) and yellow (inner) 22ct)	—	£600
1998 *New Portrait*	—	£3
1998 BU	91,110,375	£8
1998 Proof	—	£12
1998 Silver Proof	—	£35
1998 — — Piedfort	—	£60

DATE	Mintage	UNC
1999	33,719,000	£3
1999 Rugby World Cup	4,933,000	£5
1999 — BU	—	£6
1999 — Silver Proof (gold plated ring)	—	£40
1999 — — Piedfort (Hologram)	—	£95
1999 — Gold Proof	—	£650
2000	25,770,000	£3
2000 BU	—	£5
2000 Proof	—	£10
2000 Silver Proof	—	£40
2000 Gold Proof	—	£595
2001	34,984,750	£3
2001 BU	—	£4
2001 Proof	—	£10
2001 Marconi	4,558,000	£3
2001 — BU	—	£4
2001 — Proof	—	£10
2001 — Silver Proof (gold plated ring)	—	£40
2001 — — — Piedfort	—	£60
2001 — Gold Proof	—	£600
2002	13,024,750	£3
2002 BU	—	£4
2002 Proof	—	£10
2002 Gold Proof (red 22ct)	—	£650
2002 Commonwealth Games, Scotland	771,750	£3
2002 — Wales	558,500	£3
2002 — Northern Ireland	485,500	£3
2002 — England	650,500	£3
2002 — BU (issued in set of 4)	—	£20
2002 — Proof (issued in set of 4)	—	£25
2002 — Silver Proof (issued in set of 4)	—	£120
2002 — — — Piedfort (painted) (issued in set of 4)	—	£240
2002 — Gold Proof (issued in set of 4)	—	£650
2003	17,531,250	£3
2003 BU	—	£4
2003 Proof	—	£12
2003 DNA Double Helix	4,299,000	£3
2003 — BU	—	£4
2003 — Proof	—	£10
2003 — Silver Proof (Gold-plated ring)	—	£40
2003 — — — Piedfort	—	£65
2003 — Gold Proof	—	£600
2004	11,981,500	£3
2004 BU	—	£4
2004 Proof	—	£12
2004 Trevithick Steam Locomotive	5,004,500	£4
2004 — BU	—	£5
2004 — Proof	—	£12
2004 — Silver BU	—	£25
2004 — — Proof (Gold-plated ring)	—	£45
2004 — — — Piedfort	—	£65
2004 — Gold Proof	—	£600
2005	3,837,250	£3
2005 BU	—	£5
2005 Proof	—	£7
2005 Gunpowder Plot	5,140,500	£4
2005 — BU	—	£5
2005 — Proof	—	£6
2005 — Silver Proof	—	£35
2005 — — — Piedfort	—	£75
2005 — Gold Proof	—	£600
2005 End of World War II	10,191,000	£3
2005 — BU	—	£4
2005 — Silver Proof	—	£35
2005 — — — Piedfort	—	£70
2005 — Gold Proof	—	£650

233

DATE	Mintage	UNC
2006	16,715,000	£3
2006 Proof	—	£6
2006 Brunel, The Man (Portrait)	7,928,250	£3
2006 — BU	—	£4
2006 — Proof	—	£6
2006 — Silver Proof	—	£35
2006 — — — Piedfort	—	£70
2006 — Gold Proof..	—	£600
2006 Brunel, His Achievements (Paddington Station)	7,452,250	£3
2006 — BU	—	£4
2006 — Proof	—	£7
2006 — Silver Proof	—	£35
2006 — — — Piedfort	—	£70
2006 — Gold Proof..	—	£600
2007	10,270,000	£3
2007 Proof	—	£8
2007 Tercentenary of the Act of Union......................	7,545,000	£3
2007 BU	—	£4
2007 — Proof	—	£8
2007 — Silver Proof	—	£35
2007 — — — Piedfort	—	£70
2007 — Gold Proof..	—	£600
2007 Bicentenary of the Abolition of the Slave Trade .	8,445,000	£3
2007 — BU	—	£4
2007 — Proof	—	£7
2007 — Silver Proof	—	£35
2007 — — — Piedfort	—	£70
2007 — Gold Proof..	—	£600
2008..	—	£3
2008 BU	—	£4
2008 Proof	—	£12
2008 Centenary of 4th Olympiad, London	—	£3
2008 — BU	—	£4
2008 — Proof	—	£12
2008 — Silver Proof	—	£40
2008 — — — Piedfort	—	£85
2008 — Gold proof..	—	£600
2008 Olympic Games Handover Ceremony...............	—	£3
2008 — BU	—	£7
2008 — Silver Proof	—	£45
2008 — — — Piedfort	—	£75
2008 — Gold Proof..	—	£600
2009	—	£3
2009 BU	—	£4
2009 Proof	—	£10
2009 Silver Proof	—	£40
2009 250th Anniversary of birth of Robert Burns........	—	£3
2009 — BU	—	£8
2009 — Proof	—	£12
2009 — Silver Proof	—	£35
2009 — — — Piedfort	—	£75
2009 — Gold Proof..	—	£600
2009 200th Anniversary of birth of Charles Darwin.....	—	£3
2009 — BU	—	£8
2009 — Proof	—	£12
2009 — Silver Proof	—	£35
2009 — — — Piedfort	—	£70
2009 Gold Proof...	—	£600
2010..	—	£3
2010 BU	—	£8
2010 Proof	—	£12
2010 Silver Proof	—	£40
2010 Florence Nightingale 150 Years of Nursing	—	£4
2010 — BU	—	£10
2010 — Proof	—	£12
2010 — Silver Proof	—	£40

DATE	Mintage	UNC
2010 – — – Piedfort	—	£75
2010 — Gold Proof	—	£650
2011 —	—	£4
2011 BU	—	£5
2011 Proof	—	£12
2011 Silver Proof	—	£35
2011 500th Anniversary of the Mary Rose	—	£4
2011 — BU	—	£9
2011 — Proof	—	£12
2011 — Silver Proof	—	£40
2011 — — — Piedfort	—	£75
2011 — Gold Proof	—	£800
2011 400th Anniversary of the King James Bible	—	£4
2011 — BU	—	£9
2011 — Proof	—	£15
2011 — Silver Proof	—	£45
2011 — — — Piedfort	—	£75
2011 — Gold Proof	—	£800

ABBREVIATIONS COMMONLY USED TO DENOTE METALLIC COMPOSITION	
Cu	Copper
Cu/Steel	Copper plated Steel
Ag/Cu	Silver plated copper
Ae	Bronze
Cu-Ni	Cupro-Nickel
Ni-Ag	Nickel Silver (note-does not contain silver)
Brass/Cu-Ni	Brass outer, Cupro-Nickel inner
Ni-Brass	Nickel-Brass
Ag	Silver
Au/Ag	Gold plated silver
Au	Gold
Pl	Platinum

SOVEREIGN

All are minted in gold, bear the Pistrucci St George and Dragon reverse except where stated, and are legal tender at one pound.

DATE	Mintage	UNC
1974	5,002,566	£300
1976	4,150,000	£300
1978	6,550,000	£300
1979	9,100,000	£300
1979 Proof	50,000	£350
1980	5,100,000	£300
1980 Proof	91,200	£350
1981	5,000,000	£350
1981 Proof	32,960	£350
1982	2,950,000	£300
1982 Proof	22,500	£350
1983 Proof	21,250	£350
1984 Proof	19,975	£350
1985 New portrait Proof	17,242	£350
1986 Proof	17,579	£350
1987 Proof	22,479	£350
1988 Proof	18,862	£350
1989 500th Anniversary of the Sovereign—details as Five Pounds (Sov. Series). Proof	23,471	£650
1990 Proof	8,425	£350
1991 Proof	7,201	£350
1992 Proof	6,854	£350
1993 Proof	6,090	£350
1994 Proof	7,165	£350
1995 Proof	9,500	£350
1996 Proof	9,110	£350
1997 Proof	9,177	£350
1998 New Portrait Proof	11,349	£350
1999 Proof	11,903	£375
2000 (first Unc issue since 1982)	129,069	£300
2000 Proof	12,159	£350
2001	49,462	£300
2001 Proof	10,000	£350
2002 Shield Rev. ("bullion")	74,263	£300
2002 Proof	20,500	£350
2003 ("bullion")	43,208	£300
2003 Proof	—	£350
2004 ("bullion")	28,821	£300
2004 Proof	—	£350
2005 Noad heraldic St George and Dragon	—	£325
2005 — Proof	—	£450
2006 ("bullion")	—	£280
2006 Proof	—	£400
2007 ("bullion")	—	£300
2007 Proof	—	£350
2008 ("bullion")	—	£300
2008 Proof	—	£350
2009 ("bullion")	—	£300
2009 Proof	—	£350
2010 ("bullion")	—	£300
2010 Proof	—	£350
2011 ("bullion")	—	£350
2011 Proof	—	£400

NOTE: The prices quoted in this guide are set at August 2011 with the price of gold at £1,150 per ounce and silver £25 per ounce—market fluctuations will have a marked effect on the values of modern precious metal coins.

HALF SOVEREIGN

Legal Tender at 50 pence, otherwise the notes for the Sovereign apply.

DATE	Mintage	UNC
1980 Proof only	86,700	£160
1982	2,500,000	£160
1982 Proof	21,590	£175
1983 Proof	19,710	£175
1984 Proof	19,505	£175
1985 New portrait Proof	15,800	£175
1986 Proof	17,075	£175
1987 Proof	20,687	£175
1988 Proof	18,266	£175
1989 500th Anniversary of the Sovereign—details as Five Pounds (Sov. Series) Proof	21,824	£480
1990 Proof	7,889	£175
1991 Proof	6,076	£175
1992 Proof	5,915	£175
1993 Proof	4,651	£175
1994 Proof	7,167	£175
1995 Proof	7,500	£175
1996 New Portrait Proof	7,340	£180
1997 Proof	9,177	£175
1998 Proof	7,496	£175
1999 Proof	9,403	£175
2000	146,822	£145
2000 Proof	9,708	£175
2001	98,763	£145
2001 Proof	7,500	£175
2002 Shield reverse ("bullion")	61,347	£145
2002 Proof	—	£175

2003 ("bullion")	47,805	£145
2003 Proof	—	£175
2004 ("bullion")	32,479	£145
2004 Proof	—	£175
2005 Noad heraldic St George and Dragon	—	£185
2005 — Proof	—	£200
2006 ("bullion")	—	£145
2006 Proof	—	£180
2006 ("bullion")	—	£145
2007 Proof	—	£180
2008 ("bullion")	—	£150
2008 Proof	—	£180
2009 ("bullion")	—	£150
2009 Proof	—	£180
2010 ("bullion")	—	£170
2010 Proof	—	£190
2011 ("bullion")	—	£175
2011 Proof	—	£200

QUARTER SOVEREIGN

Minted in 22ct Gold, this new denomination was introduced in 2009, and follows on from two different patterns of 1853.

DATE	Mintage	UNC
2009 ("bullion")	—	£85
2009 Proof	—	£100
2010 ("bullion")	—	£85
2010 Proof	—	£100
2011 ("bullion")	—	£95
2011 Proof	—	£100

ONE POUND

Introduced into circulation in 1983 to replace the £1 note, all are minted in nickel-brass unless otherwise stated. The reverse changed yearly until 2008, and until 2008 the Royal Arms was the "definitive" version. 2008 also saw the introduction of the Matthew Dent Uncrowned Shield of the Royal Arms, a new "definitive", and this reverse appeared in 2008 and every year since then. 2010 and 2011 also saw the new Capital Cities series of four coins, although none of these has yet appeared in circulation. Collectors and others should be aware of the many different counterfeit £1 coin versions in circulation, a high proportion of which do not have matching obverses and reverses although many do.

DATE	Mintage	UNC
1983 Royal Arms	443,053,510	£5
1983 — Unc	1,134,000	£5
1983 — Proof	107,800	£6
1983 — Silver Proof	50,000	£32
1983 — — Piedfort	10,000	£125
1984 Scottish Thistle	146,256,501	£4
1984 — BU	199,430	£5
1984 — Proof	106,520	£6
1984 — Silver Proof	44,855	£30
1984 — — Piedfort	15,000	£50
1985 *New portrait.* Welsh Leek	228,430,749	£3
1985 — BU	213,679	£5
1985 — Proof	102,015	£6
1985 — Silver Proof	50,000	£30
1985 — — Piedfort	15,000	£50
1986 Northern Ireland Flax	10,409,501	£3
1986 — BU	—	£5
1986 — Proof	—	£6
1986 — Silver Proof	—	£30
1986 — — Piedfort	—	£55
1987 English Oak	39,298,502	£3
1987 — BU	—	£5
1987 — Proof	—	£6

1983, 1993, 1998, 2003
DECUS ET TUTAMEN

1984, 1989
NEMO ME IMPUNE LACESSIT

DATE	Mintage	UNC
1987 — Silver Proof	—	£30
1987 — — — Piedfort	—	£65
1988 Crowned Shield Of The Royal Arms	7,118,825	£2
1988 — BU	—	£5
1988 — Proof	—	£5
1988 — Silver Proof	—	£35
1988 — — — Piedfort	—	£65
1989 Scottish Thistle	70,580,501	£2
1989 — BU	—	£6
1989 — Proof	—	£9
1989 — Silver Proof	—	£30
1989 — — — Piedfort	—	£55
1990 Welsh Leek	—	£2
1990 — BU	97,269,302	£5
1990 — Proof	—	£6
1990 — Silver Proof	—	£30
1991 Northern Ireland Flax	38,443,575	£2
1991 — BU	—	£5
1991 — Proof	—	£6
1991 — Silver Proof	—	£32
1992 English Oak	36,320,487	£2
1992 — BU	—	£5
1992 — Proof	—	£7
1992 — Silver Proof	—	£32
1993 Royal Arms	114,744,500	£2
1993 — BU	—	£5
1993 — Proof	—	£7
1993 — Silver Proof	—	£34
1993 — — — Piedfort	—	£55
1994 Scottish Lion	29,752,525	£2
1994 — BU	—	£5
1994 — Proof	—	£7
1994 — Silver Proof	—	£34
1994 — — — Piedfort	—	£55
1995 Welsh Dragon	34,503,501	£2
1995 — BU	—	£5
1995 — (Welsh)	—	£5
1995 — Proof	—	£10
1995 — Silver Proof	—	£34
1995 — — — Piedfort	—	£60
1996 Northern Ireland Celtic Cross	89,886,000	£3
1996 — BU	—	£5
1996 — Proof	—	£7
1996 — Silver Proof	—	£35
1996 — — — Piedfort	—	£60
1997 English Lions	57,117,450	£3
1997 — BU	—	£5
1997 — Proof	—	£7
1997 — Silver Proof	—	£35
1997 — — — Piedfort	—	£60
1998 **New portrait.** Royal Arms. BU	—	£7
1998 — Proof	—	£8
1998 — Silver Proof	—	£32
1998 — — — Piedfort	—	£50
1999 Scottish Lion. BU	—	£6
1999 — Proof	—	£11
1999 — Silver Proof	—	£35
1999 — — — Reverse Frosting	—	£45
1999 — — — Piedfort	—	£55
2000 Welsh Dragon	109,496,500	£2
2000 — BU	—	£5
2000 — Proof	—	£7
2000 — Silver Proof	—	£35
2000 — — — Reverse Frosting	—	£45
2000 — — — Piedfort	—	£55
2001 Northern Ireland Celtic Cross.	63,968,065	£2
2001 — BU	58,093,731	£5
2001 — Proof	—	£6
2001 — Silver Proof	—	£35

1985, 1990
PLEIDIOL WYF I'M GWLAD

1986, 1991
DECUS ET TUTAMEN

1987, 1992
DECUS ET TUTAMEN

1988
DECUS ET TUTAMEN

1994, 1999
NEMO ME IMPUNE LACESSIT

1995, 2000
PLEIDIOL WYF I'M GWLAD

1996, 2001
DECUS ET TUTAMEN

DATE	Mintage	UNC
2001 — — — Reverse Frosting	—	£45
2001 — — — Piedfort	—	£50
2002 English Lions	77,818,000	£2
2002 — BU	—	£5
2002 — Proof	—	£8
2002 — Silver Proof	—	£35
2002 — — — Reverse Frosting	—	£45
2002 — — — Piedfort	—	£50
2002 — Gold Proof	—	£350
2003 Royal Arms	61,596,500	£2
2003 — BU	—	£5
2003 — Proof	—	£10
2003 — Silver Proof	—	£35
2003 — — — Piedfort	—	£50
2004 Forth Railway Bridge	39,162,000	£3
2004 — BU	—	£5
2004 — Proof	—	£10
2004 — Silver Proof	—	£35
2004 — — — Piedfort	—	£50
2004 — Gold Proof	—	£350
2005 Menai Bridge	99,429,500	£3
2005 — BU	—	£5
2005 — Proof	—	£10
2005 — Silver Proof	—	£35
2005 — — — Piedfort	—	£50
2005 — Gold Proof	—	£350
2006 Egyptian Arch	38,938,000	£3
2006 — BU	—	£5
2006 — Proof	—	£10
2006 — Silver Proof	—	£35
2006 — — — Piedfort	—	£55
2006 — Gold Proof	—	£350
2007 Gateshead Millennium Bridge	26,180,160	£3
2007 — BU	—	£6
2007 — Proof	—	£10
2007 — Silver Proof	—	£40
2007 — — — Piedfort	—	£55
2007 — Gold Proof	—	£350
2008 Royal Arms	3,910,000	£3
2008 — BU	—	£6
2008 — Proof	—	£8
2008 — Silver Proof	—	£35
2008 — Gold Proof	—	£350
2008 — Platinum Proof	—	£475
2008 A series of 14 different reverses, the 25th Anniversary of the modern £1 coin, Silver Proof with selected gold highlighting on the reverses. the latter being all those used since 1983, the coins being with appropriate edge lettering	—	£420
2008 The same as above, Gold Proof (the 2008 Royal Arms being already listed above)	—	—
2008 **New Rev.,** Shield of the Royal Arms, no border beads on Obv.	—	£3
2008 BU	—	£4
2008 Proof	—	£5
2008 Silver Proof	—	£35
2008 Silver Proof Piedfort	—	£50
2008 Gold Proof	—	—
2008 Platinum Proof	—	£575
2009	—	£3
2009 BU	—	£4
2009 Proof	—	£5
2009 Silver Proof	—	£35
2009 Gold Proof	—	£595
2010	—	£3
2010 BU	—	£4
2010 Proof	—	£5
2010 Silver BU	—	£30
2010 — Proof	—	£40
2010 City Series (London)	—	£3
2010 — BU	—	£4

1997, 2002
DECUS ET TUTAMEN

2004
PATTERNED EDGE

2005
PATTERNED EDGE

2006
PATTERNED EDGE

2007
PATTERNED EDGE

2008 (proof sets—silver and gold)
DECUS ET TUTAMEN

2008, 2009, 2010, 2011
DECUS ET TUTAMEN

2010 — Proof	—	£5
2010 — Silver Proof	—	£33
2010 — — — Piedfort	—	£55
2010 — Gold Proof	—	£620
2010 City Series (Belfast)	—	£3
2010 — BU	—	£4
2010 — Proof	—	£6
2010 — Silver Proof	—	£35
2010 — — — Piedfort	—	£55
2010 — Gold Proof	—	£600
2011	—	£2
2011 BU	—	£3
2011 Proof	—	£8
2011 Silver BU (in 21st and 18th Birthday cards)	—	£45
2011 — Proof	—	£55
2011 City Series (Cardiff)	—	£3
2011 — BU	—	£5
2011 — Proof	-	£7
2011 — Silver Proof	—	£40
2011 — — — Piedfort	—	£75
2011 — Gold Proof	—	£800
2011 City Series (Edinburgh)	—	£3
2011 — BU	—	£5
2011 — Proof	—	£8
2011 — Silver Proof	—	£45
2011 — — — Piedfort	—	£75
2011 — Gold Proof	—	£800

2011
**Y DDRAIG GOCH
DDYRY CYCHWYN**

2011
NISI DOMINUS FRUSTRA

FIFTY PENCE

Introduced as legal tender for 10 shillings to replace the banknote of that value prior to decimalisation, coins of the original size are no longer legal tender. Unless otherwise stated, i.e. for commemoratives, the reverse design is of Britannia. The reverse legend of NEW PENCE became FIFTY PENCE from 1982.

The description of "Unc" has been used against some 50 pence pieces dated 2009 and 2011 (for Olympic and Paralympic sports) to distinguish them from coins minted to circulation standard and BU standard, being a standard between the latter two. The uncirculated standard coins have a more even rim than the circulation standard examples, particularly observable on the obverse. Of the 29 different sports coins dated 2011, 16 have so far been put into circulation, and issue figures for these are give. The issue figures for Unc and Silver BU sports coins are the maxima authorised.

DATE	Mintage	UNC
1969	188,400,000	£5
1970	19,461,500	£5
1971 Proof	—	£7
1972 Proof	—	£7
1973 Accession to EEC	89,775,000	£5
1973 — Proof	—	£10
1973 — Silver Proof Piedfort	—	£2500
1974 Proof	—	£7
1975 Proof	—	£7
1976	43,746,500	£5
1976 Proof	—	£7
1977	49,536,000	£5
1977 Proof	—	£6
1978	72,005,000	£5
1978 Proof	—	£6
1979	58,680,000	£5
1979 Proof	—	£6
1980	89,086,000	£5
1980 Proof	—	£6
1981	74,002,000	£6
1981 Proof	—	£8
1982	51,312,000	£5
1982 Unc	—	£6
1982 Proof	—	£8
1983	62,824,000	£5
1983 Unc	—	£6

DATE	Mintage	UNC
1983 Proof	—	£8
1984 BU	—	£6
1984 Proof	—	£8
1985 **New portrait** .... estimated approx	3,400,000	£1
1985 BU	—	£5
1985 Proof	—	£6
1986 BU	—	£5
1986 Proof	—	£11
1987 BU	—	£4
1987 Proof	—	£11
1988 BU	—	£4
1988 Proof	—	£11
1989 BU	—	£4
1989 Proof	—	£11
1990 BU	—	£4
1990 Proof	—	£11
1991 BU	—	£5
1991 Proof	—	£10
1992 BU	—	£7
1992 Proof	—	£12
1992 Presidency of EC Council and EC accession 20th anniversary (includes 1993 date)	109,000	£15
1992 — BU	—	£10
1992 — Proof	—	£12
1992 — Silver Proof	—	£30
1992 — — — Piedfort	—	£65
1992 — Gold Proof	—	£500
1993 BU	—	£5
1993 Proof	—	£12
1994 50th Anniversary of the Normandy Landings	6,705,520	£5
1994 — BU (also in presentation folder)	—	£8
1994 — Proof	—	£12
1994 — Silver Proof	—	£35
1994 — — — Piedfort	—	£55
1994 — Gold Proof	—	£500
1995 BU	—	£8
1995 Proof	—	£12
1996 BU	—	£8
1996 Proof	—	£12
1996 Silver Proof	—	£25
1997 BU	—	£7
1997 Proof	—	£9
1997 Silver Proof	—	£25
1997 **New reduced size**	456,364,100	£4
1997 BU	—	£5
1997 Proof	—	£6
1997 Silver Proof	—	£25
1997 — — Piedfort	—	£35
1998 **New portrait**	64,306,500	£2
1998 BU	—	£5
1998 Proof	—	£7
1998 Presidency and 25th anniversary of EU entry ...	5,043,000	£3
1998 — BU	—	£5
1998 — Proof	—	£7
1998 — Silver Proof	—	£30
1998 — — — Piedfort	—	£45
1998 — Gold Proof	—	£400
1998 50th Anniversary of the National Health Service	5,001,000	£3
1998 — BU	—	£5
1998 — Silver Proof (believed not issued as Cu-Ni proof)	—	£30
1998 — — — Piedfort	—	£45
1998 — Gold Proof	—	£400
1999	24,905,000	£2
1999 BU	—	£5
1999 Proof	—	£9
2000	27,915,500	£1
2000 BU	—	£5
2000 Proof	—	£7
2000 150th Anniversary of Public Libraries	11,263,000	£5

DATE	Mintage	UNC
2000 — BU	—	£6
2000 — Proof	—	£9
2000 — Silver Proof	—	£30
2000 — — Piedfort	—	£45
2000 — Gold proof	—	£350
2001	84,998,500	£1
2001 BU	—	£5
2001 Proof	—	£7
2002	23,907,500	—
2002 BU	—	£5
2002 Proof	—	£7
2002 Gold Proof	—	£300
2003	23,583,000	—
2003 BU	—	£5
2003 Proof	—	£6
2003 Suffragette	3,124,030	—
2003 — BU	—	£6
2003 — Proof	—	£7
2003 — Silver Proof	—	£30
2003 — — Piedfort	—	£45
2003 — Gold Proof	—	£300
2004	35,315,500	—
2004 BU	—	£5
2004 Proof	—	£8
2004 Roger Bannister	9,032,500	—
2004 — BU	—	£5
2004 — Proof	—	£8
2004 — Silver Proof	—	£30
2004 — — Piedfort	—	£45
2004 — Gold Proof	—	£300
2005	25,363,500	£2
2005 BU	—	£6
2005 Proof	—	£8
2005 Samuel Johnson	17,649,000	£2
2005 — BU	—	£5
2005 — Proof	—	£8
2005 — Silver Proof	—	£30
2005 — — Piedfort	—	£45
2005 — Gold Proof	—	£300
2006	24,567,000	—
2006 Proof	—	£8
2006 Silver Proof	—	£30
2006 Victoria Cross, The Award	12,087,000	£2
2006 — BU	—	£5
2006 — Proof	—	£8
2006 — Silver Proof	—	£30
2006 — — — Piedfort	—	£45
2006 — Gold Proof	—	£300
2006 Victoria Cross, Heroic Acts	10,000,500	—
2006 — BU	—	£5
2006 — Proof	—	£8
2006 — Silver Proof	—	£30
2006 — — Piedfort	—	£45
2006 — Gold Proof	—	£350
2007	5,300,000	—
2007 BU	—	£6
2007 Proof	—	£8
2007 Centenary of Scout Movement	7,710,750	£5
2007 — BU	—	£6
2007 — Proof	—	£12
2007 — Silver Proof	—	£30
2007 — — Piedfort	—	£55
2007 — Gold Proof	—	£400
2008	700,000	—
2008 — BU	—	£5
2008 — Proof	—	£6
2008 — Silver Proof	—	£25
2008 — Gold Proof	—	£400
2008 Platinum Proof	—	£1500

DATE	Mintage	UNC
2008 **New Shield Rev.** Obv. rotated by approx.		
26 degrees	12,320,000	£5
2008 BU	—	£6
2008 Proof	—	£8
2008 Silver Proof	—	£25
2008 Silver Proof Piedfort	—	£45
2008 Gold Proof	—	£400
2008 Platinum Proof	—	£1500
2009 BU	—	£4
2009 Proof	—	£6
2009 Silver Proof	—	£20
2009 250th Anniversary of Kew Gardens	—	£3
2009 — BU	—	£4
2009 — Proof	—	£25
2009 — Silver Proof	—	£35
2009 — — Piedfort	—	£55
2009 — Gold Proof	—	£400
2009 Olympic and Paralympic Sports		
(Track & Field Athletics) UNC	100,000	£2
2009 16 different reverses from the past marking the		
40th Anniversary of the 50p coin. Proof	210,000	£225
2009 — Silver Proof	—	£475
2009 — Gold Proof	125	£7950
2009 — — — Piedfort	40	£19,950
2010 BU	—	£4
2010 Proof	—	£25
2010 Silver Proof	—	£35
2010 100 years of Girl Guiding UK	910,090	—
2010 — BU	—	£7
2010 — Proof	—	£20
2010 — Silver Proof	—	£35
2010 — — Piedfort	—	£55
2010 — Gold Proof	—	£575
2011 —	—	—
2011 BU	—	—
2011 Proof	—	—
2011 Silver Proof	—	£45
2011 50th Anniversary of the WWF	—	—
2011 — BU	—	£4
2011 — Proof	—	£25
2011 — Silver Proof	—	£45
2011 — — — Piedfort	—	£65
2011 — Gold Proof	—	£675
2011 Olympic & Paralympic Sports Issues:		
Aquatics		
— Unc	1,000,000	£3
— Silver BU	30,000	£35
Archery		
— Unc	800,000	£3
— Silver BU	30,000	£35
Track & Field Athletics		
— Unc	900,000	£3
— Silver BU	30,000	£35
Badminton		
— Unc	900,000	£3
— Silver BU	30,000	£35
Boccia		
— Unc	900,000	£3
— Silver BU	30,000	£35
Boxing		
— Unc	80,000	£3
— Silver BU	30,000	£35
Volleyball		
— Unc	1,000,000	£3
— Silver BU	30,000	£35
Canoeing		
— Unc	800,000	£3
— Silver BU	30,000	£35

DATE	Mintage	UNC
Cycling		
— Unc	400,000	£3
— Silver BU..	30,000	£35
Equestrian		
— Unc	—	£3
— Silver BU..	30,000	£35
Fencing...		
— Unc	1,000,000	£3
— Silver BU..	30,000	£35
Football		
— Unc	—	£3
— Silver Bu	30,000	£35
Goalball		
— Unc	900,000	£3
— Silver BU..	30,000	£35
Gymnastics		
— Unc	900,000	£3
— Silver BU..	30,000	£35
Handball		
— Unc	—	£3
— Silver BU..	30,000	£35
Hockey		
— Unc	1,000,000	£3
— Silver BU..	30,000	£35
Judo		—
— Unc	—	£3
— Silver BU..	30,000	£35
Modern Pentathlon		
— Unc	—	£3
— Silver BU..	30,000	£35
Rowing		—
— Unc	70,000	£3
— Silver BU..	30,000	£35
Sailing...		
— Unc	—	£3
— Silver BU..	30,000	£35
Shooting..		
— Unc	—	£3
— Silver BU..	30,000	£35
Taekwondo..		
— Unc	—	£3
— Silver BU..	30,000	£35
Table Tennis..		
— Unc	1,000,000	£3
— Silver BU..	30,000	£35
Tennis		
— Unc	—	£3
— Silver BU..	30,000	£35
Triathlon..		
— Unc	1,000,000	£3
— Silver BU..	30,000	£35
Basketball..		
— Unc	—	£3
— Silver BU..	30,000	£35
Weightlifting...		
— Unc	—	£3
— Silver BU..	30,000	£35
Wheelchair Rugby		
— Unc	—	£3
— Silver BU..	30,000	£35
Wrestling		
— Unc	—	£3
— Silver BU..	30,000	£35

TWENTY-FIVE PENCE (CROWN)

This series is a continuation of the pre-decimal series, there having been four crowns to the pound. The coins below have a legal tender face value of 25p to this day, and are minted in cupro-nickel except where stated otherwise.

DATE	Mintage	UNC
1972 Royal Silver Wedding	7,452,100	£2
1972 — Proof	150,000	£8
1972 — Silver Proof	100,000	£25
1977 Silver Jubilee	37,061,160	£2
1977 — in Presentation folder	Incl. above	£3
1977 — Proof	193,000	£8
1977 — Silver Proof	377,000	£20
1980 Queen Mother 80th Birthday	9,306,000	£2
1980 — in Presentation folder	Incl. above	£3
1980 — Silver Proof	83,670	£30
1981 Royal Wedding	26,773,600	£2
1981 — in Presentation folder	Incl. above	£3
1981 — Silver Proof	218,140	£30

TWENTY PENCE

The series commenced in 1982, some 11 years after the introduction of decimal coinage. Its presence from introduction date meant that there was no requirement for ten pence circulation—standard coins until the latter's size was reduced in 1992. Unlike the circulation coins on either side of it in face value, it's alloy is 84% copper and 16% nickel.

DATE	Mintage	UNC	DATE	Mintage	UNC
1982	740,815,000	£1	1991	35,901,250	£1
1982 Unc	incl. above	£3	1991 BU	incl. above	£3
1982 Proof	—	£5	1991 Proof	—	£5
1982 Silver Proof Piedfort	—	£35	1992	Est. approx. 1,500,000	£4
1983	158,463,000	£1	1992 *Enhanced effigy*		
1983 Unc	incl. above	£3		Est. approx. 29,705,000	£4
1983 Proof	—	£4	1992 BU	incl. above	£5
1984	65,350,000	£1	1992 Proof	—	£8
1984 BU	incl. above	£3	1993	123,123,750	£1
1984 Proof	—	£4	1993 BU	incl. above	£3
1985 *New portrait*	74,273,699	£1	1993 Proof	—	£5
1985 BU	incl. above	£3	1994	67,131,250	£1
1985 Proof	—	£4	1994 BU	incl. above	£3
1986 BU	incl. above	£4	1994 Proof	—	£5
1986 Proof	—	£5	1995	102,005,000	£1
1987	137,450,000	£1	1995 BU	incl. above	£3
1987 BU	incl. above	£3	1995 Proof	—	£5
1987 Proof	—	£5	1996	83,163,750	£1
1988	38,038,344	£1	1996 BU	incl. above	£3
1988 BU	incl. above	£3	1996 Proof	—	£5
1988 Proof	—	£5	1996 Silver Proof	—	£20
1989	132,013,890	£1	1997	89,518,750	£1
1989 BU	incl. above	£3	1997 BU	incl. above	£3
1989 Proof	—	£5	1997 Proof	—	£5
1990	88,097,500	£1	1998 *New portrait*	76,965,000	£1
1990 BU	incl. above	£3	1998 BU	incl. above	£3
1990 Proof	—	£5	1998 Proof	—	£5

DATE	Mintage	UNC
1999	73,478,750	£1
1999 BU	incl. above	£3
1999 Proof	—	£5
2000	136,428,750	£1
2000 BU	incl. above	£3
2000 Proof	—	£5
2000 Silver Proof	—	£25
2001	148,122,500	£1
2001 BU	incl. above	£3
2001 Proof	—	£5
2002	93,360,000	£1
2002 BU	incl. above	£3
2002 Proof	—	£5
2002 Gold Proof	—	£225
2003	153,383,750	£1
2003 BU	incl. above	£4
2003 Proof	—	£6
2004	120,212,500	£1
2004 BU	incl. above	£4
2004 Proof	—	£6
2005	124,488,750	—
2005 BU	incl. above	£4
2005 Proof	—	£6
2006	114,800,000	—
2006 BU	incl. above	£4
2006 Proof	—	£6
2006 Silver Proof	—	£15
2007	117,075,000	—
2007 BU	incl. above	£4

DATE	Mintage	UNC
2007 Proof	—	£6
2008	11,900,000	—
2008 BU	incl. above	£3
2008 Proof	—	£6
2008 Silver Proof	—	£15
2008 Gold Proof	—	£275
2008 Platinum Proof	—	£750
2008 **New Rev.,** date on Obv.	81,920,000	—
2008 — paired with old Obv. (thus no date).. Est. approx. 120,000 (?) .		£100
2008 BU	incl. above	£3
2008 Proof	—	£6
2008 Silver Proof	—	£15
2008 — — Piedfort	—	£30
2008 Gold Proof	—	£275
2008 Platinum Proof	—	£750
2009	—	—
2009 BU	—	£4
2009 Proof	—	£6
2009 Silver Proof	—	£15
2010	—	—
2010 BU	—	£4
2010 Proof	—	£6
2010 Silver Proof	—	£15
2011	—	—
2011 BU	—	—
2011 Proof	—	—
2011 Silver Proof	—	—

TEN PENCE

The series commenced before decimalisation with the legend NEW PENCE, this changed to TEN PENCE from 1982. These "florin-sized" coins up to 1992 are no longer legal tender. Cupro-nickel was replaced by nickel-plated steel from 2011.

DATE	Mintage	UNC
1968	336,143,250	£3
1969	314,008,000	£4
1970	133,571,000	£3
1971	63,205,000	£3
1971 Proof	—	£4
1972 Proof only	—	£5
1973	152,174,000	£3
1973 Proof	—	£4
1974	92,741,000	£3
1974 Proof	—	£4
1975	181,559,000	£3
1975 Proof	—	£4
1976	228,220,000	£3
1976 Proof	—	£4
1977	59,323,000	£4
1977 Proof	—	£4
1978 Proof	—	£5
1979	115,457,000	£2
1979 Proof	—	£4
1980	88,650,000	£2

DATE	Mintage	UNC
1980 Proof	—	£3
1981	3,487,000	£2
1981 Proof	—	£3
1982 BU	—	£4
1982 Proof	—	£6
1983 BU	—	£4
1983 Proof	—	£2
1984 BU	—	£4
1984 Proof	—	£6
1985 **New portrait** BU	—	£5
1985 Proof	—	£7
1986 BU	—	£4
1986 Proof	—	£6
1987 BU	—	£4
1987 Proof	—	£7
1988 BU	—	£5
1988 Proof	—	£7
1989 BU	—	£6
1989 Proof	—	£9
1990 BU	—	£6

DATE	Mintage	UNC	DATE	Mintage	UNC
1990 Proof	—	£9	2003 BU	—	£3
1991 BU	—	£6	2003 Proof	—	£5
1991 Proof	—	£9	2004	99,602,000	—
1992 BU	—	£5	2004 BU	—	£3
1992 Proof	—	£7	2004 Proof	—	£5
1992 Silver Proof	—	£12	2005	69,604,000	—
1992 **Size reduced (24.5mm)**	1,413,455,170	£3	2005 BU	—	£1
1992 BU	—	£4	2005 Proof	—	£4
1992 Proof	—	£5	2006	118,803,000	—
1992 Silver Proof	—	£12	2006 BU	—	£1
1992 — — Piedfort	—	£25	2006 Proof	—	£5
1993 BU	—	£2	2006 Silver Proof	—	£22
1993 Proof	—	£7	2007	72,720,000	—
1994 BU	—	£2	2007 BU	—	£4
1994 Proof	—	£7	2007 Proof	—	£5
1995	43,259,000	£1	2008	9,720,000	—
1995 BU	—	£3	2008 BU	—	£3
1995 Proof	—	£4	2008 Proof	—	£4
1996	118,738,000	£1	2008 Silver Proof	—	£25
1996 BU	—	£3	2008 Gold Proof	—	£250
1996 Proof	—	£4	2008 Platinum Proof	—	£350
1996 Silver Proof	—	£25	2008 **New Rev.**, no border beads		
1997	99,196,000	£1	on Obv.	53,900,000	—
1997 BU	—	£3	2008 BU	—	£3
1997 Proof	—	£4	2008 Proof	—	£5
1998 **New portrait** BU	—	£6	2008 Silver Proof	—	£25
1998 Proof	—	£9	2008 — — Piedfort	—	£35
1999 BU	—	£3	2008 Gold Proof	—	£250
1999 Proof	—	£11	2008 Platinum Proof	—	£350
2000	134,733,000	£1	2009	—	—
2000 BU	—	£3	2009 BU	—	£2
2000 Proof	—	£4	2009 Proof	—	£4
2000 Silver Proof	—	£15	2009 Silver Proof	—	£25
2001	129,281,000	£1	2010	—	—
2001 BU	—	£3	2010 BU	—	£2
2001 Proof	—	£4	2010 Proof	—	£5
2002	80,934,000	£1	2010 Silver Proof	—	£25
2002 BU	—	£3	2011 Nickel-plated steel	—	—
2002 Proof	—	£5	2011 — BU	—	—
2002 Gold Proof	—	£250	2011 — Proof	—	—
2003	88,118,000	—	2011 Silver Proof	—	—

FIVE PENCE

This series commenced simultaneously with the Ten Pence (qv). They were the same size and weight as their predecessor, the shilling, and such coins up to 1990 are no longer legal tender.

DATE	Mintage	UNC	DATE	Mintage	UNC
1968	98,868,250	£3	1975	141,539,000	£3
1969	120,270,000	£3	1975 Proof	—	£6
1970	225,948,525	£3	1976 Proof	—	£7
1971	81,783,475	£3	1977	24,308,000	£1
1971 Proof	—	£3	1977 Proof	—	£6
1972 Proof	—	£6	1978	61,094,000	£3
1973 Proof	—	£5	1978 Proof	—	£4
1974 Proof	—	£6	1979	155,456,000	£3

DATE	Mintage	UNC
1979 Proof	—	£4
1980	220,566,000	£3
1980 Proof	—	£4
1981 Proof	—	£6
1982 BU	—	£5
1982 Proof	—	£6
1983 BU	—	£4
1983 Proof	—	£6
1984 BU	—	£4
1984 Proof	—	£6
1985 *New Portrait*. BU	—	£2
1985 Proof	—	£6
1986 BU	—	£2
1986 Proof	—	£6
1987	48,220,000	—
1987 BU	—	£3
1987 Proof	—	£5
1988	120,744,610	—
1988 BU	—	£3
1988 Proof	—	£5
1989	101,406,000	—
1989 BU	—	£3
1989 Proof	—	£5
1990 BU	—	£2
1990 Proof	—	£5
1990 Silver Proof	—	£10
1990 *Size reduced (18mm)*	1,634,976,005	£2
1990 BU	—	£3
1990 Proof	—	£4
1990 Silver Proof	—	£12
1990 — — Piedfort	—	£15
1991	724,979000	—
1991 BU	—	£3
1991 Proof	—	£5
1992	453,173,500	—
1992 BU	—	£3
1992 Proof	—	£5
1993 BU BU	—	£3
1993 Proof	—	£5
1994	93,602,000	—
1994 BU	—	£3
1994 Proof	—	£6
1995	183,384,000	—
1995 BU	—	£3
1995 Proof	—	£6
1996	302,902,000	—
1996 BU	—	£3
1996 Proof	—	£6
1996 Silver proof	—	£20
1997	236,596,000	—
1997 BU	—	£1
1997 Proof	—	£3
1998 *New portrait*	217,376,000	—
1998 BU	—	£3
1998 Proof	—	£6
1999	195,490,000	—

DATE	Mintage	UNC
1999 BU	—	£3
1999 Proof	—	£6
2000	388,512,000	—
2000 BU	—	£4
2000 Proof	—	£6
2000 Silver Proof	—	£25
2001	337,930,000	—
2001 BU	—	£3
2001 Proof	—	£5
2002	219,258,000	—
2002 BU	—	£3
2002 Proof	—	£5
2002 Gold Proof	—	£120
2003	333,230,000	—
2003 BU	—	£3
2003 Proof	—	£5
2004	271,810,000	—
2004 BU	—	£3
2004 Proof	—	£5
2005	236,212,000	—
2005 BU	—	£3
2005 Proof	—	£5
2006	317,697,000	—
2006 BU	—	£3
2006 Proof	—	£5
2006 Silver Proof	—	£15
2007	246,720,000	—
2007 BU	—	£3
2007 Proof	—	£5
2008	86,400,000	—
2008 BU	—	£2
2008 Proof	—	£4
2008 Silver Proof	—	£15
2008 Gold Proof	—	£125
2008 Platinum Proof	—	£200
2008 *New Rev.,* no border beads on Obv	109,460,000	—
2008 BU	—	£3
2008 Proof	—	£5
2008 Silver Proof	—	£15
2008 — — Piedfort	—	£35
2008 Gold Proof		£125
2008 Platinum Proof		£220
2009		—
2009 BU		£3
2009 Proof		£4
2009 Silver Proof		£15
2010		—
2010 BU		£3
2010 Proof		£5
2010 Silver Proof		£15
2011 Nickel-plated steel	—	—
2011 — BU	—	—
2011 — Proof	—	—
2011 Silver Proof	—	—

TWO PENCE

Dated from 1971, and legal tender from Decimal Day that year, early examples are found in the blue Specimen decimal set wallets of 1968. They were minted in bronze up to 1991, and mainly in copper-plated steel from 1992. However details of where this rule does not totally apply (1992, 1996, 1998–2000 and 2002, 2006, 2008 and 2009) are given below. As with other denominations, "NEW" was replaced by the quantity of pence in word from 1982.

DATE	Mintage	UNC
1971	1,454,856,250	£2
1971 Proof	—	£3
1972 Proof	—	£5
1973 Proof	—	£5
1974 Proof	—	£6
1975	Est. approx. 273,145,000	£2
1975 Proof	—	£2
1976	Est. approx. 53,779,000	£2
1976 Proof	—	£2
1977	109,281,000	£2
1977 Proof	—	£2
1978	189,658,000	£2
1978 Proof	—	£2
1979	260,200,000	£2
1979 Proof	408,527,000	£2
1980	—	£1
1980 Proof	—	£2
1981	353,191,000	£2
1981 Proof	—	£3
1982 Legend changed to TWO PENCE	—	£2
1982 Proof	—	£4
1983	—	£2
1983 Error NEW instead of TWO	—	£475
1983 Proof	—	£3
1984	—	£1
1984 Proof		£4
1985 *New portrait*	107,113,000	£1
1985	—	£2
1985 Proof	—	£4
1986	168,967,500	50p
1986 BU	—	£2
1986 Proof	—	£4
1987	218,100,750	50p
1987 BU	—	£2
1987 Proof	—	£4
1988	419,889,000	50p
1988 BU	—	£2
1988 Proof	—	£4
1989	359,226,000	50p
1989 BU	—	£2
1989 Proof	—	£4
1990	204,499,700	50p
1990 BU	—	£2
1990 Proof	—	£3
1991	86,625,250	50p
1991 BU	—	£2
1991 Proof	—	£5
1992 Copper plated steel	102,247,000	£1
1992 Bronze BU	—	£2
1992 — Proof	—	£5
1993	235,674,000	50p
1993 BU	—	£2
1993 Proof	—	£3
1994	531,628,000	50p
1994 BU	—	£1
1994 Proof	—	£3
1995	124,482,000	—
1995 BU	—	£2
1995 Proof	—	£4
1996	296,278,000	—
1996 BU	—	£2
1996 Proof	—	£3
1996 Silver Proof	—	£20
1997	496,116,000	—
1997 BU	—	£2
1997 Proof	—	£4
1998 *New portrait*	Est. approx. 120,243,000	—
1998 BU	—	£2
1998 Proof	—	£4
1998 Bronze	Est. approx. 93,587,000	£1
1999	353,816,000	£1
1999 Bronze BU	—	£2
1999 — Proof	—	£4
2000	536,659,000	—
2000 BU	—	£2
2000 Proof	—	£4
2000 Silver Proof	—	£22
2001	551,880,000	—
2001 BU	—	£2
2001 Proof	—	£4
2002	168,556,000	—
2002 BU	—	£2
2002 Proof	—	£4
2002 Gold Proof	—	£120
2003	260,225,000	—
2003 BU	—	£2
2003 Proof	—	£4
2004	356,396,000	—
2004 BU	—	£2
2004 Proof	—	£4
2005	280,396,000	—
2005 BU	—	50p
2005 Proof	—	£2
2006	170,637,000	—
2006 BU	—	50p
2006 Proof	—	£2
2006 Silver Proof	—	£15
2007	254,500,000	—
2007 BU	—	£2
2007 Proof	—	£4
2008	10,600,000	—
2008 BU	—	£2
2008 Proof	—	£5
2008 Silver Proof	—	£20
2008 Gold Proof	—	£125
2008 Platinum Proof	—	—
2008 New Rev., no border beads on Obv	129,530,000	—
2008 — BU	—	£2
2008 — Proof	—	£4

DATE	Mintage	UNC	DATE	Mintage	UNC
2008 — Silver Proof	—	£20	2010	—	—
2008 — Silver Proof Piedfort	—	£45	2010 BU	—	£2
2008 — Gold Proof	—	£400	2010 Proof	—	£5
2008 — Platinum Proof	—	£800	2010 Silver Proof	—	£45
2009	—	—	2011	—	—
2009 BU	—	£2	2011 BU	—	—
2009 Proof	—	£4	2011 Proof	—	—
2009 Silver Proof	—	£45	2011 Silver Proof	—	—

ONE PENNY

The history of this coin is very similar to that of the Two Pence coin (qv) except that all 1998 examples were of copper-plated steel.

DATE	Mintage	UNC	DATE	Mintage	UNC
1971	1,521,666,250	£1	1989	658,142,000	—
1971 Proof	—	£2	1989 BU	—	£2
1972 Proof	—	£5	1989 Proof	—	£3
1973	280,196,000	£2	1990	529,047,500	£2
1973 Proof	—	£3	1990 BU	—	£3
1974	330,892,000	£2	1990 Proof	—	£4
1974 Proof	—	£3	1991	206,457,000	—
1975	221,604,000	£2	1991 BU	—	£2
1975 Proof	—	£4	1991 Proof	—	£4
1976	300,160,000	£1	1992 Copper-plated steel	253,867,000	£1
1976 Proof	—	£2	1992 Bronze BU	—	£3
1977	285,430,000	£2	1992 — Proof	—	£4
1977 Proof	—	£3	1993	602,590,000	—
1978	292,770,000	£2	1993 BU	—	£2
1978 Proof	—	£3	1993 Proof	—	£4
1979	459,000,000	£2	1994	843,834,000	£1
1979 Proof	—	£3	1994 BU	—	£2
1980	416,304,000	£2	1994 Proof	—	£4
1980 Proof	—	£3	1995	303,314,000	£1
1981	301,800,000	£2	1995 BU	—	£3
1981 Proof	—	£3	1995 Proof	—	£4
1982 Legend changed to ONE PENNY	100,292,000		1996	723,840,060	—
			1996 BU	—	£2
1982 Unc	—	£1	1996 Proof	—	£4
1982 Proof	—	£2	1996 Silver Proof	—	£20
1983	243,002,000	£1	1997	396,874,000	—
1983 Unc	—	£2	1997 BU	—	£2
1983 Proof	—	£4	1997 Proof	—	£4
1984	154,759,625	—	1998 New portrait	739,770,000	—
1984 BU	—	£2	1998 — BU	—	£2
1984 Proof	—	£3	1998 Proof	—	£4
1985 New portrait	200,605,245	—	1999	891,392,000	£2
1985 BU	—	£2	1999 Bronze BU	—	£2
1985 Proof	—	£3	1999 Bronze Proof	—	£4
1986	369,989,130	—	2000	1,060,420,000	—
1986 BU	—	£2	2000 BU	—	£2
1986 Proof	—	£3	2000 Proof	—	£4
1987	4999,946,000	—	2000 Silver Proof	—	£25
1987 BU	—	£2	2001	928,698,000	—
1987 Proof	—	£3	2001 BU	—	£2
1988	793,492,000	—	2001 Proof	—	£4
1988 BU	—	£2	2002	601,446,000	—
1988 Proof	—	£3	2002 BU	—	£2

DATE	Mintage	UNC
2002 Proof	—	£4
2002 Gold Proof	—	£120
2003	539,436,000	—
2003 BU	—	£2
2003 Proof	—	£3
2004	739,764,000	—
2004 BU	—	£2
2004 Proof	—	£4
2005	536,318,000	—
2005 BU	—	£2
2005 Proof	—	£3
2006	524,605,000	—
2006 BU	—	£2
2006 Proof	—	£4
2006 Silver Proof	—	£15
2007	548,002,000	—
2007 BU	—	£2
2007 Proof	—	£3
2008	180,600,000	—
2008 BU	—	£1
2008 Proof	—	£2
2008 Silver Proof	—	£15
2008 Gold Proof	—	£100
2008 Platinum Proof	—	£185

DATE	Mintage	UNC
2008 New Rev, no border beads on Obv	386,830,000	—
2008 — BU	—	£2
2008 — Proof	—	£3
2008 — Silver Proof	—	£15
2008 — Silver Proof Piedfort	—	£25
2008 — Gold Proof	—	£100
2008 — Platinum Proof	—	£185
2009	—	—
2009 BU	—	£1
2009 Proof	—	£3
2009 Silver BU, in "Lucky Baby Gift Pack"	—	£15
2009 — Proof	—	£15
2010	—	—
2010 BU	—	£1
2010 Proof	—	£2
2010 Silver BU, in "Lucky Baby Gift Card"	—	£15
2010 — Proof	—	£15
2011	—	—
2011 BU	—	£2
2011 Proof	—	£3
2011 Silver BU in "Lucky Baby Pack"	—	£18
2011 – Proof	—	£15

HALF PENNY

No longer legal tender, its history tracks that of the Two Pence and One Penny.

DATE	Mintage	UNC
1971	1,394,188,250	£2
1971 Proof	—	£3
1972 Proof	—	£5
1973	365,680,000	£2
1973 Proof	—	£3
1974	365,448,000	£2
1974 Proof	—	£3
1975	197,600,000	£2
1975 Proof	—	£3
1976	412,172,000	£2
1976 Proof	—	£3
1977	66,368,000	£1
1977 Proof	—	£3
1978	59,532,000	£1
1978 Proof	—	£4
1979	219,1322,000	£2

DATE	Mintage	UNC
1979 Proof	—	£4
1980	202,788,000	£2
1980 Proof	—	£3
1981	46,748,000	£2
1981 Proof	—	£4
1982 Legend changed to HALF PENNY	190,752,000	50p
1982 Unc	—	£2
1982 Proof	—	£3
1983	7,600,000	50p
1983 Unc	—	£1
1983 Proof	—	£4
1984	40,000	£4
1984 BU	—	£5
1984 Proof	—	£6

PROOF AND SPECIMEN SETS

NOTE: The prices quoted in this guide are set at August 2011 with the price of gold at £1,150 per ounce and silver £25 per ounce— market fluctuations will have a marked effect on the values of modern precious metal coins.

The following listings are an attempt to include all officially marketed products from the Royal Mint of two coins or more, but excluding those which included non-UK coins. It is appreciated that not all have been advertised as new to the public, but it is assumed that at some time they have been, or will be, available. In a few cases, therefore, the prices may be conjectural but are, nevertheless, attempts at listing realistic value, in some instances based on an original retail price. In the case of Elizabeth II sets, if no metal is stated in the listing, the coins in the sets are of the same metal as the circulation coin equivalent. In addition to the above we have excluded historical gold coin sets, such as sets of sovereigns from different mints, where the dates of the coins vary from one set to another.

DATE   FDC

GEORGE IV
1826 £5–farthing (11 coins) £30,000

WILLIAM IV
1831 Coronation £2–farthing (14 coins) £28,000

VICTORIA
1839 "Una and the Lion" £5–farthing (15 coins)..£65,000
1853 Sovereign–quarter farthing, including "Gothic"crown (16 coins) £40,000
1887 Golden Jubilee £5–3d (11 coins)...£15,000
1887 Golden Jubilee Crown–3d (7 coins)..£3,000
1893 £5–3d (10 coins) £15,000
1893 Crown–3d (6 coins)..£5,000

EDWARD VII
1902 Coronation £5–Maundy penny, matt proofs (13 coins) £5,500
1902 Coronation Sovereign–Maundy penny, matt proofs (11 coins) £3,500

GEORGE V
1911 Coronation £5–Maundy penny (12 coins)..£5,500
1911 Sovereign–Maundy penny (10 coins) £3,500
1911 Coronation Halfcrown–Maundy penny (8 coins) £1,000
1927 New types Crown–3d (6 coins)..£850

DATE	FDC

GEORGE VI

1937 Coronation £5–half sovereign (4 coins) £5500
1937 Coronation Crown–farthing including Maundy money (15 coins) £400
1950 Mid-century Halfcrown–farthing (9 coins) £175
1951 Festival of Britain, Crown–farthing (10 coins)...£185

ELIZABETH II

1953 Proof Coronation Crown–farthing (10 coins) £85
1953 Currency (plastic) set halfcrown–farthing (9 coins)..£15
1968 Specimen decimal set 10p, 5p and 1971-dated bronze in blue wallet (5 coins)................£2.50
1970 Proof Last £sd coins (issued from 1972) Halfcrown–halfpenny (8 coins)..............................£20
1971 Proof (issued 1973) 50p–half penny (6 coins)..£18
1972 Proof (issued 1976) 50p–half penny (7 coins including Silver Wedding crown) £24
1973 Proof (issued 1976) 50p–half penny (6 coins) £16
1974 Proof (issued 1976) 50p–half penny (6 coins) £18
1975 Proof (issued 1976) 50p–half penny (6 coins) £18
1976 Proof 50p–half penny (6 coins) £18
1977 Proof 50p–half penny (7 coins including Silver Jubilee crown) £22
1978 Proof 50p–half penny (6 coins) £16
1979 Proof 50p–half penny (6 coins) £18
1980 Proof gold sovereign series (4 coins) £2500
1980 — 50p–half penny (6 coins) £16
1981 Proof £5, sovereign, Royal Wedding Silver crown, 50p–half penny (9 coins) £800
1981 — 50p–half penny (6 coins) £18
1982 Proof gold sovereign series (4 coins) £2500
1982 — 50p–half penny (7 coins) £20
1982 Uncirculated 50p–half penny (7 coins)..£15
1983 Proof gold double-sovereign to half sovereign (3 coins) £1000
1983 — £1–half penny (8 coins) (includes H. J. Heinz sets)..£25
1983 Uncirculated £1–half penny (8 coins) (includes Benson & Hedges and Martini sets) £30
1983 — — (8 coins) (only Benson & Hedges and Martini sets) with "2 NEW PENCE" legend £1000
1983 — 50p–half penny (7 coins) (H. J. Heinz sets) £16
1984 Proof gold five pounds, sovereign and half-sovereigns (3 coins) £1000
1984 — £1 (Scottish rev.)–half penny (8 coins) £20
1984 BU £1 (Scottish rev.)–half penny (8 coins) £16
1985 New portrait proof gold sovereign series (4 coins) £1250
1985 Proof £1–1p in de luxe case (7 coins) £25
1985 — in standard case £20
1985 BU £1–1p (7 coins) in folder £15
1986 Proof gold Commonwealth Games £2, sovereign and half sovereign (3 coins)................£1000
1986 — Commonwealth Games £2–1p, de luxe case (8 coins) £30
1986 — — in standard case (8 coins) £25
1986 BU £2–1p in folder (8 coins) £20
1987 Proof gold Britannia set (4 coins) £2000
1987 — — — £25 and £10 (2 coins) £450
1987 — — double- to half sovereign (3 coins) £1000
1987 — £1–1p in de luxe case (7 coins) £35
1987 — £1–1p in standard case (7 coins) £25
1987 BU £1–1p in folder (7 coins) £20
1988 Proof gold Britannia set (4 coins) £2000
1988 — — — £25 and £10 (2 coins) £450
1988 — — double- to half sovereign (3 coins) £1000
1988 — £1–1p in de luxe case (7 coins) £35
1988 — £1–1p in standard case (7 coins) £30
1988 BU £1–1p in folder (7 coins) (includes Bradford & Bingley sets)..£18
1989 Proof gold Britannia set (4 coins) £2000
1989 — — — £25 and £10 (2 coins) £450
1989 — — 500th anniversary of the sovereign series set (4 coins) £2000
1989 — — double- to half sovereign (3 coins) £1000
1989 — Silver Bill of Rights £2, Claim of Right £2 (2 coins)..£65
1989 — — Piedfort as above (2 coins)..£100
1989 BU £2 in folder (2 coins) £25
1989 Proof £2 (both)–1p in de luxe case (9 coins) £35
1989 — in standard case (9 coins) £30
1989 BU £1–1p in folder (7 coins) £25
1990 Proof gold Britannia set (4 coins) £2000
1990 — — sovereign series set (4 coins) £2000

DATE	FDC
1990— — double- to half sovereign (3 coins)	£1000
1990 — silver 5p, 2 sizes (2 coins)	£28
1990 — £1–1p in de luxe case (8 coins)	£35
1990 — £1–1p standard case (8 coins)	£30
1990 BU £1–1p in folder (8 coins)	£20
1991 Proof gold Britannia set (4 coins)	£2000
1991 — — sovereign series set (4 coins)	£2000
1991 — — double- to half sovereign (3 coins)	£1000
1991 — £1–1p in de luxe case (7 coins)	£35
1991 — £1–1p in standard case (7 coins)	£28
1991 BU £1–1p in folder (7 coins)	£18
1992 Proof gold Britannia set (4 coins)	£2000
1992 — — sovereign series set (4 coins)	£2000
1992 — — double- to half sovereign (3 coins)	£1000
1992 — £1–1p including two each 50p and 10p in de luxe case (9 coins)	£38
1992 — £1–1p as above in standard case (9 coins)	£32
1992 BU £1–1p as above in folder (9 coins)	£16
1992 Proof silver 10p, two sizes (2 coins)	£25
1993 Proof gold Britannia set 1 (4 coins)	£2000
1993 — — sovereign series set (4 coins plus silver Pistrucci medal)	£2000
1993 — — double- to half sovereign (3 coins)	£1000
1993 — Coronation anniversary £5–1p in de luxe case (8 coins)	£38
1993 — — in standard case (8 coins)	£35
1993 BU £1–1p including 1992 EU 50p (8 coins)	£15
1994 Proof gold Britannia set (4 coins)	£2000
1994 — — sovereign series set (4 coins)	£2000
1994 — — £2 to half sovereign (3 coins)	£1000
1994 — Bank of England Tercentenary £2–1p in de luxe case (8 coins)	£38
1994 — — in standard case (8 coins)	£35
1994 BU £1–1p in folder (7 coins)	£18
1994 Proof gold 1992 and 1994 50p (2 coins)	£350
1994 — "Family silver" set £2–50p (3 coins)	£65
1995 Proof gold Britannia set (4 coins)	£2000
1995 — — sovereign series (4 coins)	£2000
1995 — — £2 to half sovereign (3 coins)	£850
1995 — 50th Anniversary of WWII £2–1p in de luxe case (8 coins)	£40
1995 — — as above in standard case (8 coins)	£35
1995 BU as above in folder (8 coins)	£16
1995 Proof "Family Silver" set £2 (two) and £1 (3 coins)	£90
1996 Proof gold Britannia set (4 coins)	£2000
1996 — — sovereign series set (4 coins)	£2000
1996 — — double- to half sovereign (3 coins)	£1000
1996 — Royal 70th Birthday £5–1p in de luxe case (9 coins)	£50
1996 — — as above in standard case (9 coins)	£45
1996 BU Football £2–1p in folder (8 coins)	£20
1996 Proof Britannia £10 and half-sovereign (2 coins)	£550
1996 — — sovereign and silver £1 (2 coins)	£250
1996 — — "Family silver" set £5–£1 (3 coins)	£85
1996 — silver 25th Anniversary of Decimal currency £1–1p (7 coins)	£150
1996 Circulation and BU 25th Anniversary of Decimalisation 2s 6d–halfpenny (misc.) and £1–1p in folder (14 coins)	£25
1997 Proof gold Britannia set (4 coins)	£2000
1997 — — sovereign series set (4 coins)	£2000
1997 — — — £2 to half sovereign (3 coins)	£1000
1997 — — Silver Britannia set (4 coins)	£150
1997 — Golden Wedding £5–1p in red leather case	£45
1997 — — as above in standard case (10 coins)	£35
1997 BU £2 to 1p in folder (9 coins)	£25
1997 Proof silver 50p set, two sizes (2 coins)	£45
1997/1998 Proof silver £2 set, both dates (2 coins)	£70
1998 Proof gold Britannia set (4 coins)	£2000
1998 — — sovereign series set (4 coins)	£2000
1998 — — — double- to half sovereign (3 coins)	£1000
1998 Proof silver Britannia set (4 coins)	£185
1998 — Prince of Wales £5–1p (10 coins) in red leather case	£45
1998 — — as above in standard case (10 coins)	£38
1998 BU £2–1p in folder (9 coins)	£16

DATE	FDC
1998 Proof silver European/NHS 50p set (2 coins)	£60
1998 BU Britannia/EU 50p set (2 coins)	£8
1999 Proof gold Britannia set (4 coins)	£2000
1999 — Sovereign series set (4 coins)	£2000
1999 — — — £2 to half sovereign (3 coins)	£1000
1999 — Princess Diana £5–1p in red leather case (9 coins)	£65
1999 — — as above in standard case (9 coins)	£45
1999 BU £2–1p (8 coins) in folder	£20
1999 Proof "Family Silver" set. Both £5, £2 and £1 (4 coins)	£150
1999 Britannia Millennium set. Bullion £2 and BU £5 (2 coins)	£30
1999/2000 Reverse frosted proof set, two x £1 (2 coins)	£75
2000 Proof gold Britannia set (4 coins)	£2000
2000 — — Sovereign series set (4 coins)	£2000
2000 — — — double- to half sovereign (3 coins)	£1000
2000 Millennium £5–1p in de luxe case (10 coins)	£50
2000 — — as above in standard case (10 coins)	£45
2000 — Silver set Millennium £5 to 1p plus Maundy (13 coins)	£225
2000 BU £2–1p set in folder (9 coins)	£20
2000 Millennium "Time Capsule" BU £5 to 1p (9 coins)	£30
2001 Proof gold Britannia set (4 coins)	£2000
2001 — Sovereign series set (4 coins)	£2000
2001 — — — £2–half sovereign (3 coins)	£1000
2001 — Silver Britannia set (4 coins)	£150
2001 — Victoria £5–1p in Executive case (10 coins)	£100
2001 — — as above in red leather case (10 coins)	£75
2001 — — as above in "Gift" case (10 coins)	£48
2001 — — as above in standard case (10 coins)	£40
2001 BU £2–1p in folder (9 coins)	£18
2002 Proof gold Britannia set (4 coins)	£2000
2002 — — Sovereign series set, all Shield rev. (4 coins)	£2000
2002 — — — double- to half sovereign (3 coins)	£1000
2002 — — Golden Jubilee set £5–1p plus Maundy (13 coins)	£3000
2002 — Golden Jubilee £5–1p in Executive case (9 coins)	£75
2002 — — as above in red leather de luxe case (9 coins)	£50
2002 — — as above in "Gift" case (9 coins)	£42
2002 — — as above in standard case (9 coins)	£40
2002 BU £2–1p (8 coins) in folder	£16
2002 Proof Gold Commonwealth Games £2 set (4 coins)	£2000
2002 — Silver Piedfort Commonwealth Games £2 set (4 coins)	£250
2002 — — Commonwealth Games £2 set (4 coins)	£125
2002 — Commonwealth Games £2 set (4 coins)	£30
2002 BU Commonwealth Games £2 set (4 coins) in folder	£25
2003 Proof gold Britannia set (4 coins)	£2000
2003 — — — £50–£10 (3 coins)	£1000
2003 — — — type set, one of each £100 reverse (4 coins)	£2500
2003 — — Sovereign series set (4 coins)	£2000
2003 — — — series £2–half sovereign (3 coins)	£1000
2003 — Silver Britannia set (4 coins)	£45
2003 — — type set (one of each £2 reverse) (4 coins)	£85
2003 — £5 to 1p, two of each £2 and 50p in Executive case (11 coins)	£80
2003 — — as above in red leather case (11 coins)	£55
2003 — — as above in standard case (11 coins)	£48
2003 BU £2 (two)–1p in folder (10 coins)	£22
2003 Proof silver Piedfort set. DNA £2, £1 and Suffragette 50p (3 coins)	£150
2003 Proof "Family Silver" set £5, Britannia and DNA £2, £1 and Suffragette 50p (5 coins)	£175
2003 Circ & BU "God Save the Queen" Coronation anniversary set 5s/0d to farthing (1953) and £5 to 1p (2003) in folder (19 coins)	£55
2003 Circulation or bullion "Royal Sovereign" collection, example of each Elizabeth II date (21 coins)	£3500
2004 Proof gold Britannia set (4 coins)	£2000
2004 — — — £50 to £10 (3 coins)	£1000
2004 — — Sovereign series set (4 coins)	£2000
2004 — — — Series £2-half sovereign (3 coins)	£1000
2004 (Issue date) Royal Portrait gold sovereign set, all proof except the first: Gillick, Machin, Maklouf and Rank-Broadley sovereigns, and the 2nd, 3rd and 4th of above half-sovereigns, various dates (7 coins)	£1500
2004 Proof silver Britannia set (4 coins)	£150

DATE	FDC
2004 — "Family Silver" set £5, Britannia and Trevithick £2, £1 and Bannister 50p (5 coins)	£165
2004 — Silver Piedfort set, Trevithick £2, £1 and Bannister 50p (3 coins)	£175
2004 — £2 to 1p, two each of £2 and 50p in Executive case (10 coins)	£75
2004 — — as above in red leather case (10 coins)	£45
2004 — — as above in standard case (10 coins)	£38
2004 BU £2 to 1p in folder (10 coins)	£22
2004 — "New Coinage" set, Trevithick £2, £1 and Bannister 50p (3 coins)	£10
2004 BU "Season's Greetings" £2 to 1p and Royal Mint Christmas medal in folder (8 coins)	£17
2005 Proof Gold Britannia set (4 coins)	£2000
2005 — — — £50 to £10 (3 coins)	£1000
2005 — — Sovereign series set (4 coins)	£2000
2005 — — — series, double to half sovereign (3 coins)	£1000
2005 — Silver Britannia (4 coins)	£135
2005 — Gold Trafalgar and Nelson £5 crowns (2 coins)	£2000
2005 — Silver, as above (2 coins)	£85
2005 — — Piedfort, as above (2 coins)	£135
2005 — Silver Piedfort set, Gunpowder Plot and World War II £2, £1 and Johnson 50p (4 coins)	£200
2005 — £5 to 1p, two of each of £5, £2 and 50p in Executive case (12 coins)	£80
2005 — — as above in red leather case (12 coins)	£58
2005 — — as above in standard case (12 coins)	£45
2005 BU Trafalgar and Nelson £5 crowns in pack (2 coins)	£25
2005 — £2 (two) to 1p in folder (10 coins)	£25
2005 — "New Coinage" set, Gunpowder Plot £2, £1 and Johnson 50p (3 coins)	£10
2005 — "Merry Xmas" £2 to 1p and Royal Mint Christmas medal in folder (8 coins)	£20
2006 Proof Gold Britannia set (4 coins)	£2000
2006 — — Sovereign Series set (4 coins)	£2000
2006 — — — series, double to half sovereign (3 coins)	£1000
2006 — Silver Britannia (4 coins)	£145
2006 — Silver Brunel £2 coin set (2 coins)	£75
2006 — — Piedfort Brunel £2 coin set (2 coins)	£125
2006 — Gold Brunel £2 coin set (2 coins)	£950
2006 — Silver VC 50p coin set (2 coins)	£58
2006 — Silver Piedfort VC 50p coin set (2 coins)	£115
2006 — Gold VC 50p coin set (2 coins)	£675
2006 — Silver proof set, £5 to 1p plus Maundy coins (13 coins)	£325
2006 — — Piedfort collection £5, with trumpets enhanced with 23 carat gold, both Brunel £2, £1, both VC 50p (6 coins)	£350
2006 — — Britannia £2 "Golden Silhouette" collection, five different reverses, all dated 2006 (5 coins)	£350
2006 — £5 to 1p, three of each £2 and 50p in Executive case (13 coins)	£80
2006 — as above in red leather case (13 coins)	£55
2006 — as above in standard case (13 coins)	£45
2006 BU £2 (two), £1, 50p (two) and to 1p in folder (10 coins)	£18
2006 Proof Brunel £2 in folder (2 coins)	£15
2006 — VC 50p in folder (2 coins)	£15
2006 — Gold Half-Sovereign set dated 2005 Noad and 2006 Pistrucci St George and the Dragon (2 coins)	£250
2007 — Gold Britannia set (4 coins)	£2000
2007 — — Sovereign Series set (4 coins)	£2000
2007 — — — series, double to half sovereign (3 coins)	£1000
2007 — — Sovereign and half-sovereign (2 coins)	£375
2007 — "Family Silver" set, Britannia, £5 crown, Union and Slavery £2, Gateshead £1 and Scouting 50p (6 coins)	£225
2007 Proof Silver Piedfort Collection, as "Family Silver" above but excluding a Britannia (5 coins)	£300
2007 — Silver £1 Bridge series coins, dated 2004 to 2007 (4 coins)	£135
2007 — Silver Proof Piedfort £1 Bridge Series, dated 2004 to 2007 (4 coins)	£275
2007 — Gold £1 Bridge series coins, dated as above (4 coins)	£1950
2007 — £5 to 1p, three £2 and two 50p in Executive case (12 coins)	£85
2007 — as above, Deluxe in red leather case (12 coins)	£65
2007 — as above, in standard case (12 coins)	£50
2007 BU £2 (two) to 1p (9 coins)	£18
2007 Proof Silver Britannia (four coins)	£145
2007 Proof Platinum Britannia (4 coins)	£5000
2007 Satin Proof Silver Britannia, 20th Anniversary Collection, six different reverses, all dated 2007 (6 coins)	£300
2007 50th Anniversary Sovereign set, 1957 circulation standard and 2007 Proof (2 coins)	£450
2008 Proof Gold Britannia set (4 coins)	£2000
2008 — Platinum Britannia set (4 coins)	£5000
2008 — Silver Britannia set (4 coins)	£150

DATE	FDC
2008 Gold Sovereign series set (4 coins)	£2000
2008 — — — double to half-sovereign (3 coins)	£1000
2008 — — Sovereign and half-sovereign (2 coins)	£500
2008 — "Family silver" set, 2x £5, Britannia £2, Olympiad £2 and Royal Arms £1 (5 coins)	£200
2008 — Silver Piedfort Collection, 2x £5, Olympiad £2 and Shield of Royal Arms £1 (4 coins)	£285
2008 — 2 x £5, 2 x £2, £1 to 1p in Executive case (11 coins)	£85
2008 — as above, Deluxe in black leather case (11 coins)	£55
2008 - as above, in standard back case (11 coins)	£45
2008 BU 2 x £2, Royal Arms £1 tp 1p (9 coins)	£18
2008 — "Emblems of Britain" ("old" Revs) Royal Arms £1 to 1p (7 coins)	£12
2008 — "Royal Shield of Arms" ("new" Revs) Shield of Royal Arms £1 to 1p (7 coins)	£12
2008 — Above two sets housed in one sleeve	£22
2008 Proof Base Metal "Royal Shield of Arms" set, £1 to 1p (7 coins)	£38
2008 — Silver Emblems of Britain" set, £1 to 1p (7 coins)	£160
2008 — — "Royal Shield of Arms" set, £1 to 1p (7 coins)	£160
2008 — — Above two sets in one black case	£325
2008 — Gold "Emblems of Britain" set, £1 to 1p (7 coins)	£3500
2008 — — "Royal Shield of Arms" set, £1 to 1p (7 coins)	£3500
2008 — — Above two sets in one oak-veneer case	£6750
2008 — Platinum "Emblems of Britain" set, £1 to 1p (7 coins)	£8500
2008 — — "Royal Shield of Arms" set, £1 to 1p (7 coins)	£8500
2008 — — Above two sets in one walnut veneer case	£15750
2008 — Silver Piedfort "Royal Shield of Arms" set, £1 to 1p (7 coins)	£325
2008 — Gold set of 14 £1 coins, one of each Rev used since 1983, all dated 2008 (25th anniversary) (14 coins)	£9500
2008 — Silver with gold Rev highlighting as above (14 coins)	£500
2008 — 2 x £2, Royal Arms £1 to 1p (9 coins) Christmas Coin Sets, two different outer sleeves, Father Christmas or Three Wise men	£20
2009 Proof Gold Britannia set (4 coins)	£2200
2009 — Platinum Britannia set (4 coins)	£4000
2009 — Silver Britannia set (4 coins)	£150
2009 — Gold Sovereign series set (5 coins)	£2500
2009 — — double to half-sovereign (3 coins)	£1000
2009 — — sovereign and half-sovereign (2 coins)	£450
2009 — "Family Silver" set, Henry VIII £5, Britannia £2, Darwin and Burns £2, £1 and Kew 50p (6 coins)	£225
2009 — Silver Piedfort collection, Henry VIII £5, Darwin and Burns £2 and Kew Gardens 50p (4 coins)	£275
2009 — Silver Set, £5 to 1p (12 coins)	£275
2009 — Base metal Executive set, £5 to 1p (12 coins)	£80
2009 — — — Deluxe set, £5 to 1p (12 coins)	£55
2009 — — — Standard set, £5 to 1p (12 coins)	£45
2009 BU Base metal set, £2 to 1p (11 coins)	£22
2009 — — —, £1 to 1p "Royal Shield of Arms" set (7 coins)	£12
2009 — — —, £2 to 1p (8 coins)	£15
2009 Proof set of 50p coins as detailed in FIFTY PENCE section, CuNi (16 coins)	£195
2009 — Silver (16 coins)	£425
2009 — Gold (16 coins)	£8200
2009 — Gold Piedfort (16 coins)	£19950
2009 "Mind" set of £5 coins, silver (6 coins)	£350
2010 Gold Britannia set (4 coins)	£2750
2010 — —, (£50 to £10 (3 coins)	£1500
2010 — Silver Britannia set (4 coins)	£140
2010 — Gold Olympic Series "Faster", £100 and £25 (2), (3 coins)	£2000
2010 — — Sovereign series set (5 coins)	£2750
2010 — — double to half (3 coins)	£1250
2010 — — sovereign to quarter (3 coins)	£550
2010 — "Silver Celebration" set, Restoration £5, Nightingale £2, London and Belfast £1 and Girlguiding 50p (5 coins)	£185
2010 Silver Piedfort set, coins as in "Silver Celebration" set (5 coins)	£300
2010 — Silver Collection, £5 to 1p (13 coins)	£300
2010 — Base Metal Executive Set, £5 to 1p (13 coins)	£80
2010 — — Deluxe set	£50
2010 — — Standard set	£40
2010 BU — Capital Cities £1 (2 coins)	£15
2010 — — Set, £2 to 1p (12 coins) £3	5

DATE	FDC
2010 — — Definitive pack, £2 to 1p (8 coins)	£20
2010 Proof "Body" Collection of £5 coins, silver (6 coins)	£300
2010 Proof "Spirit" Collection of £5 coins, silver (6 coins)	—
2010 Proof "Spirit" collection of £5 coins, silver (6 coins)	—
2011 Proof Gold Britannia set (4 coins)	£2750
2011 — — Premium set (3 coins)	£1500
2011 — Sovereign set (5 coins)	£3000
2011 — — double to half (3 coins)	£1200
2011 — — sovereign to quarter (3 coins)	£650
2011 — Silver Britannia set (4 coins)	£180
2011 — Olympic gold "Higher" set (3 coins)	£2650
2011 — — — "Faster" (2010) and "Higher" set (6 coins) in 9-coin case	£5300
2011 — Silver Collection, £5 to 1p (14 coins)	£400
2011 — — Celebration set, Duke of Edinburgh £5, Mary Rose and King James bible £, Cardiff and Edinburgh £1 and WWF 50p (6 coins)	£250
2011 — — — Piedfort, as above (6 coins)	£395
2011 Executive Proof Base metal set (14 coins)	£85
2011 De-luxe Proof Base metal set (14 coins)	£50
2011 Standard Proof Base metal set (14 coins)	£40
2011 BU set including £2, £1 and 50p commemoratives (13 coins)	£26
2011 BU set of Definitives (8 coins)	£25
2011 Proof gold Britannia set (4 coins`)	£2750
2011 — — Premium set (3 coins)	£1500
2011 — Sovereign set (5 coins)	£3000
2011 — — Double to half (3 coins)	£1200
2011 — — Sovereign to Quarter (3 coins)	£650
2011 — Silver Britannia set (4 coins	£180
2011 Olympic gold "Higher" set (s coins)	£2650
2011 — — — "Faster" (2010) and "Higher" set (6 coins) in 9-coin case	£5300
2011 — Silver collection, £5 to 1p (14 coins)	£400
2011 — — Celebration set, Duke of Edinburgh £5, Mary Rose and King James Bible £2, Cardiff and Edinburgh £1 and WWF 50p (6 coins)	£250
2011 — — — Piedfort, as above (6 coins)	£395
2011 Eexutive Proof Base metal set (14 coins)	£82
2011 De-luxe Proof Base metal set (14 coins)	£50
2011 Standard Proof Base metal set (14 coins)	£45
2011 BU set including £2, £1 and 50p commemoratives (13 coins)	£26
2011 BU set of Definitives (8 coins)	£20

In addition to the above the Royal Mint produce the BU sets detailed above in Wedding and in Baby gift packs each year. Also the following patterns have been made available:

1999 (dated 1994) Bi-metal £2, plus three unprocessed or part-processed elements	—
2003 — silver £1 as above (4 coins)	£150
2004 — gold £1 featuring heraldic animal heads, hall-marked on edge (4 coins)	£1000
2004 — silver £1 featuring heraldic animal heads, hall-marked on edge (4 coins)	£350

We have included above the incomplete Olympic proof gold set of 2010 and 2011, six coins out of nine. There are other series of Olympic coins which will form sets in the future, and for which appropriate cases or packaging have, or will become available:-

2011 BU Silver 50p of Sports (29 coins)	—
2011 INC CuNi 50p of Sports (29 coins)	£85
2009–2012 Olympic Countdown 4-coin £5 Proof sets in gold, silver, silver Piedfort, also BU in CuNi	—

SCOTLAND

The coins illustrated are pennies representative of the reign, unless otherwise stated.

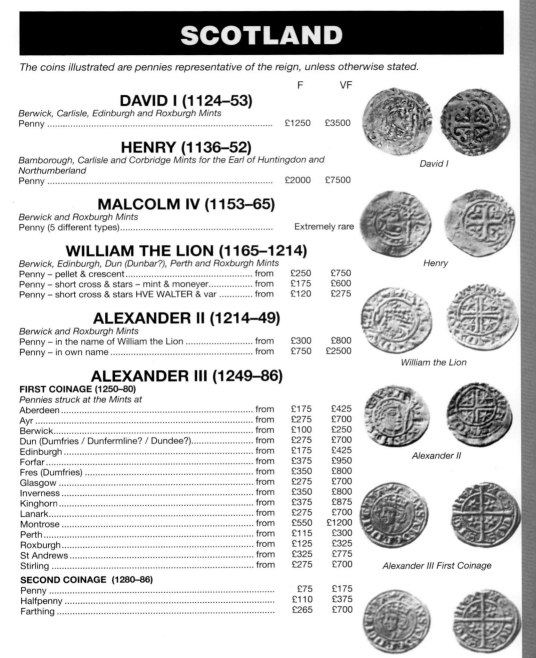

	F	VF

DAVID I (1124–53)
Berwick, Carlisle, Edinburgh and Roxburgh Mints

	F	VF
Penny	£1250	£3500

David I

HENRY (1136–52)
Bamborough, Carlisle and Corbridge Mints for the Earl of Huntingdon and Northumberland

	F	VF
Penny	£2000	£7500

Henry

MALCOLM IV (1153–65)
Berwick and Roxburgh Mints

Penny (5 different types)	Extremely rare

WILLIAM THE LION (1165–1214)
Berwick, Edinburgh, Dun (Dunbar?), Perth and Roxburgh Mints

	F	VF
Penny – pellet & crescent ... from	£250	£750
Penny – short cross & stars – mint & moneyer ... from	£175	£600
Penny – short cross & stars HVE WALTER & var ... from	£120	£275

William the Lion

ALEXANDER II (1214–49)
Berwick and Roxburgh Mints

	F	VF
Penny – in the name of William the Lion ... from	£300	£800
Penny – in own name ... from	£750	£2500

Alexander II

ALEXANDER III (1249–86)

FIRST COINAGE (1250–80)
Pennies struck at the Mints at

	F	VF
Aberdeen ... from	£175	£425
Ayr ... from	£275	£700
Berwick ... from	£100	£250
Dun (Dumfries / Dunfermline? / Dundee?) ... from	£275	£700
Edinburgh ... from	£175	£425
Forfar ... from	£375	£950
Fres (Dumfries) ... from	£350	£800
Glasgow ... from	£275	£700
Inverness ... from	£350	£800
Kinghorn ... from	£375	£875
Lanark ... from	£275	£700
Montrose ... from	£550	£1200
Perth ... from	£115	£300
Roxburgh ... from	£125	£325
St Andrews ... from	£325	£775
Stirling ... from	£275	£700

Alexander III First Coinage

SECOND COINAGE (1280–86)

	F	VF
Penny	£75	£175
Halfpenny	£110	£375
Farthing	£265	£700

Alexander III Second Coinage

	F	VF

JOHN BALIOL (1292–1306)

FIRST COINAGE *(Rough Surface issue)*

Penny .... from	£175	£475
Halfpenny .... from	£500	Ex. rare
Penny – St. Andrews .... from	£175	£475
Halfpenny – St. Andrews .... from	£1000	Ex. rare

SECOND COINAGE *(Smooth Surface issue)*

Penny .... from	£200	£475
Halfpenny .... from	£225	£550
Farthing	Extremely rare	
Penny – St. Andrews .... from	£350	£950
Halfpenny – St. Andrews	Extremely rare	

John Baliol

ROBERT BRUCE (1306–29)

Berwick Mint

Penny .... from	£550	£1500
Halfpenny .... from	£850	£2175
Farthing .... from	£1750	£4375

Robert Bruce

DAVID II (1329–71)

Aberdeen and Edinburgh Mints

Noble	Extremely Rare	
Groat (Edinburgh) .... from	£115	£300
Groat (Aberdeen) .... from	£375	£1100
Halfgroat (Edinburgh)... from	£125	£325
Halfgroat (Aberdeen) .... from	£525	£1250
Penny (Edinburgh) .... from	£85	£180
Penny (Aberdeen) .... from	£275	£750
Halfpenny .... from	£225	£800
Farthing .... from	£550	£1250

David II

ROBERT II (1371–90)

Dundee, Edinburgh and Perth Mints

Groat .... from	£100	£350
Halfgroat .... from	£100	£350
Penny .... from	£95	£250
Halfpenny .... from	£185	£375

Robert II

ROBERT III (1390–1406)

Aberdeen, Dumbarton, Edinburgh, Perth Mints

Lion or crown... from	£1250	£3750
Demy lion or halfcrown... from	£675	£2000
Groat .... from	£100	£275
Halfgroat .... from	£175	£350
Penny .... from	£225	£600
Halfpenny .... from	£300	£850

JAMES I (1406–37)

Aberdeen, Edinburgh, Inverness, Linlithgow, Perth, Stirling Mints

Demy .... rom	£950	£2500
Half demy .... from	£750	£2250
Groat .... from	£125	£350
Penny .... from	£250	£650
Halfpenny	Extremely rare	

JAMES II (1437–60)

Aberdeen, Edinburgh, Linlithgow, Perth, Roxburgh, Stirling Mints

Demy .... from	£950	£2500
Lion... from	£1250	£4500

Robert III Lion

	F	VF
Half lion	Extremely rare	
Early groats (fleur-de-lis).. from	£300	£800
Later groats (crown)... from	£225	£650
Halfgroat.. from	£500	£1200
Penny (billon) .... from	£250	£650

JAMES III (1460–88)
Aberdeen, Berwick and Edinburgh Mints

Rider..	£1750	£4500
Half rider	£1750	£4500
Quarter rider...	£2500	£7000
Unicorn..	£1250	£3500
Groat... from	£130	£375
Halfgroat... from	£225	£625
Penny (silver .... from	£500	Ex. rare
Plack (billon .... from	£175	£450
Half plack .... from	£195	£525
Penny (billon .... from	£130	£600
Farthing (copper	Extremely rare	
Penny – ecclesiastical issue.. from	£75	£200
Farthing – ecclesiastical issue... from	£125	£350

James III Groat, Berwick Mint

JAMES IV (1488–1513)
Edinburgh Mint

Unicorn..	£1250	£3500
Half unicorn	£850	£2750
Lion or crown..	Extremely rare	
Half lion	Extremely rare	
Groat... from	£400	£1375
Halfgroat... from	£650	£1750
Penny (silver .... from	£150	£400
Plack... from	£50	£125
Half plack .... from	Extremely rare	
Penny (billon .... from	£75	£200

JAMES V (1513–42)
Edinburgh Mint

Unicorn	£1450	£4500
Half Unicorn	Extremely rare	
Crown..	£1100	£3500
Ducat or Bonnet piece .... from	£1250	£5000
Two-thirds ducat...	£2500	£6500
One -third ducat	£3500	£9500
Groat... from	£195	£600
One-third groat... from	£225	£750
Plack... from	£75	£200
Bawbee .... from	£85	£250
Half bawbee .... from	£140	£325
Quarter bawbee..	Extremely rare	

James IV Unicorn

MARY (1542–67)
Edinburgh and Stirling Mints
FIRST PERIOD (1542–58)

Crown	£1325	£3500
Twenty shillings	Extremely rare	
Lion (Forty-four shillings)	£1250	£3500
Half lion (Twenty-two shillings)	£1000	£2750
Ryals (Three pounds..	£3500	£9500
Half ryal	£4500	£12500
Portrait testoon..	£3500	£10000

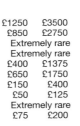

James V Ducat or Bonnet Piece

	F	VF
Non-portrait testoon...... from	£225	£700
Half testoon...... from	£250	£750
Bawbee...... from	£75	£195
Half bawbee...... from	£125	£325
Bawbee - Stirling......	£150	£425
Penny (facing bust)...... from	£250	£725
Penny (no bust)...... from	£175	£500
Lion...... from	£75	£215
Plack...... from	£95	£250

SECOND PERIOD (Francis and Mary, 1558–60)

Ducat (Sixty shillings)......	Extremely rare	
Non-portrait testoon...... from	£350	£1000
Half testoon...... from	£400	£1150
12 penny groat...... from	£80	£225
Lion...... from	£45	£125

THIRD PERIOD (Widowhood, 1560–65)

| Portrait testoon...... | £2750 | £8000 |
| Half testoon...... | £3000 | £8500 |

Mary Lion or Forty-Four Shillings

FOURTH PERIOD (Henry and Mary, 1565–67)

Portrait ryal......	£45000	£125000
Non-portrait ryal...... from	£300	£850
Two-third ryal...... from	£350	£950
One-third ryal...... from	£400	£1100

FIFTH PERIOD (Second widowhood, 1567)

Non-portrait ryal...... from	£325	£950
Two thirds ryal...... from	£275	£750
One-third ryal...... from	£550	£1250

JAMES VI (1567–1603)
(Before accession to the English throne)
FIRST COINAGE (1567–71)

Ryal...... from	£600	£1750
Two-thirds ryal...... from	£350	£950
One-third ryal...... from	£375	£1050

SECOND COINAGE (1571–80)

Twenty pounds......	£22500	£65000
Noble (or half merk)...... from	£200	£550
Half noble (or quarter merk)...... from	£150	£375
Two merks or Thistle dollar...... from	£1500	£3750
Merk...... from	£2500	£7250

THIRD COINAGE (1580–81)

Ducat......	£5000	£14500
Sixteen shillings......	£2500	£7250
Eight shillings......	£1950	£5750
Four shillings......	£4000	£9500
Two shillings......	Extremely rare	

James VI Fourth coinage
Ten Shillings

FOURTH COINAGE (1582–88)

Lion noble......	£5500	£15000
Two-third lion noble......	£4750	£13500
One-third lion noble......	Extremely rare	
Forty shillings......	£5000	£14500
Thirty shillings......	£450	£1300
Twenty shillings......	£425	£1250
Ten shillings......	£425	£1250

	F	VF

FIFTH COINAGE (1588)
Thistle noble £1700 £5250

SIXTH COINAGE (1591–93)
"Hat" piece £3500 £10000
"Balance" half merk.. from £275 £850
"Balance" quarter merk .... from £725 £2000

SEVENTH COINAGE (1594–1601)
Rider £850 £2250
Half rider £1200 £3500
Ten shillings .... from £200 £550
Five shillings .... from £175 £450
Thirty pence... from £225 £625
Twelve pence .... from £130 £375

EIGHTH COINAGE (1601–04)
Sword and sceptre piece .... from £575 £1500
Half sword and sceptre piece............................ from £425 £1250
Thistle-merk... from £120 £275
Half thistle-merk .... from £85 £225
Quarter thistle-merk .... from £75 £210
Eighth thistle-merk .... from £70 £200

BILLON AND COPPER ISSUES
Eightpenny groat .... from £50 £125
Fourpenny groat .... from £350 £1000
Twopenny plack.. from £130 £375
Hardhead.. from £45 £125
Twopence .... from £80 £230
Penny plack.. from £160 £750
Penny .... from £500 £1250

James VI Seventh Coinage Rider

JAMES VI (1603–25)
(After accession to the English throne)

Unit... from £850 £2150
Double crown .... from £1100 £3250
British crown.. from £550 £1550
Halfcrown .... from £750 £2150
Thistle crown .... from £650 £2050
Sixty shillings.. from £350 £1050
Thirty shillings... from £175 £500
Twelve shillings... from £175 £575
Six shillings .... from £500 Ex. rare
Two shillings .... from £50 £140
One shilling.. from £125 £350
Copper twopence... from £30 £80
Copper penny... from £85 £250

James VI Seventh Coinage 10 Shillings

CHARLES I (1625–49)
FIRST COINAGE (1625–36)
Unit £1050 £3250
Double crown £1000 £3150
British crown.. Extremely rare
Sixty shillings.. £750 £2150
Thirty shillings.. £150 £425
Twelve shillings.. £175 £575
Six shillings .... from £325 £950
Two shillings £60 £175
One shilling... £150 £495

James VI after accession thirty shillings

	F	VF

SECOND COINAGE (1636)
	F	VF
Half merk	£90	£260
Forty penny piece	£75	£210
Twenty penny piece	£70	£200

THIRD COINAGE (1637–42)
		F	VF
Unit	from	£825	£2500
Half unit	from	£950	£2950
British crown	from	£600	£1750
British half crown	from	£525	£1500
Sixty shillings		£575	£1500
Thirty shillings	from	£110	£350
Twelve shillings	from	£125	£350
Six shillings	from	£95	£275
Half merk	from	£95	£275
Forty pence	from	£50	£145
Twenty pence	from	£30	£85

*Charles I Third Coinage
Sixty Shillings*

FOURTH COINAGE (1642)
	F	VF
Three shillings thistle	£60	£150
Two shillings large II	£40	£110
Two shillings small II	£60	£155
Two shillings no value	£80	£225

COPPER ISSUES
(1629 Issue)
	F	VF
Twopence (triple thistle	£30	£85
Penny	£175	£500

(1632-39 Issue)
		F	VF
Twopence (Stirling turner	from	£30	£75

*Charles I Fourth Coinage
Two Shillings*

(1642-50 ISSUE)
	F	VF
Twopence (CR crowned	£25	£70

CHARLES II (1660–85)

FIRST COINAGE
Four merks
	F	VF
1664 Thistle above bust	£800	£2250
1664 Thistle below bust	£1250	£3500
1665	\multicolumn{2}{Extremely rare}	
1670 varieties from	£950	£2700
1673	£950	£2700
1674 F below bust varieties from	£800	£2250
1675	£800	£2250

Two merks
	F	VF
1664 Thistle above bust	£650	£1750
1664 Thistle below bust	£850	£2250
1670	£850	£2250
1673	£650	£1750
1673 F below bust	£750	£1950
1674	£850	£2250
1674 F below bust	£850	£2250
1675	£550	£1550

Charles II two merks

Merk
		F	VF
11664	varieties from	£250	£715
1665		£275	£780
1666		£230	£650
1668		£185	£520

		F	VF
1669	varieties from	£115	£325
1670		£160	£455
1671		£140	£390
1672	varieties from	£125	£360
1673	varieties from	£140	£390
1674		£230	£650
1674 F Below bust		£210	£585
1675 F below bust		£185	£520
1675		£210	£585
1674 F Below bust		£125	£350
1675 F below bust		£125	£500
1675		£125	£500

Half merk

1664		£250	£650
1665	varieties from	£200	£520
1666	varieties from	£225	£585
1667		£200	£520
1668		£125	£325
1669	varieties from	£150	£390
1670	varieties from	£150	£390
1671	varieties from	£150	£390
1672		£175	£455
1673		£175	£455
1675 F below bust		£150	£390
1675		£175	£455

SECOND COINAGE
Dollar

1676	£660	£1800
1679	£770	£2100
1680	£770	£2100
1681	£660	£1800
1682	£550	£1500

Half Dollar

1675	£330	£950
1676	£530	£1525
1681	£400	£1140

Quarter Dollar

1675		£225	£630
1676	varieties from	£125	£350
1677	varieties from	£125	£350
1678		£175	£490
1679		£200	£560
1680		£150	£420
1681		£150	£420
1682	varieties from	£150	£420

Eighth Dollar

1676	varieties from	£135	£295
1677		£160	£355
1678/7		£245	£530
1679		Extremely rare	
1680	varieties from	£160	£355
1682	varieties from	£245	£530

Sixteenth Dollar

1677		£75	£200
1678/7	varieties from	£120	£320
1679/7		£135	£360

Charles II Dollar

Charles II Sixteenth Dollar

Charles II Bawbee

	F	VF
1680.. varieties from	£135	£360
1681..	£75	£200

Copper Issues

Twopence CR crowned .... varieties from	£25	£70
Bawbees 1677-79 .... varieties from	£75	£250
Turners 1677-79 .... varieties from	£60	£150

JAMES VII (1685–89)

Sixty shillings

1688 proof only .... varieties from	—	£2300

Forty shillings

1687.. varieties from	£300	£750
1688.. varieties from	£350	£1000

Ten shillings

1687..	£150	£425
1688.. varieties from	£250	£700

WILLIAM & MARY (1689–94)

Sixty shillings

1691..	£295	£1100
1692..	£350	£1100

Forty shillings

1689.. varieties from	£325	£950
1690.. varieties from	£225	£650
1691.. varieties from	£250	£700
1692.. varieties from	£250	£700
1693.. varieties from	£250	£700
1694.. varieties from	£300	£875

James VII ten shillings

Twenty shillings

1693..	£450	£1300
1694..	Extremely rare	

Ten shillings

1689..	Extremely rare	
1690.. varieties from	£295	£750
1691.. varieties from	£125	£350
1692.. varieties from	£140	£400
1694.. varieties from	£250	£700

Five shillings

1691..	£200	£575
1694.. varieties from	£120	£350

William & Mary ten shillings

Copper Issues

Bawbees 1691–94 .... varieties from	£100	£275
Bodle (Turners) 1691–94.................... varieties from	£55	£180

WILLIAM II (1694–1702)

Pistole	£3000	£7500
Half pistole	£3750	£8500

Forty shillings

1695.. varieties from	£175	£450
1696..	£200	£495
1697..	£250	£550

1698	£200	£495
1699	£325	£650
1700	Extremely rare	

Twenty shillings

1695		£200	£550
1696		£200	£550
1697	varieties from	£250	£700
1698	varieties from	£175	£650
1699		£225	£625

Ten shillings

1695		£150	£375
1696		£150	£375
1697	varieties from	£150	£375
1698	varieties from	£150	£375
1699		£295	£750

Five shillings

1695		£95	£275
1696		£85	£250
1697	varieties from	£95	£275
1699		£95	£275
1700		£95	£275
1701		£125	£350
1702		£150	£425

Copper Issues

Bawbee 1695–97	varieties from	£85	£325
Bodle (Turners) 1695–97	varieties from	£50	£150

William II ten shillings

ANNE (1702–14)

Pre -Union 1702–7

Ten shillings

1705		£175	£450
1706	varieties from	£225	£650

Five shillings

1705	varieties from	£85	£225
1706		£85	£225

Anne five shillings

POST-UNION 1707–14
See listing in English section.

JAMES VIII (The Old Pretender) (1688–1766)

A number of Guineas and Crowns in various metals were struck in 1828 using original dies prepared by Norbert Roettiers, all bearing the date 1716. These coins are extremely rare and are keenly sought after.

Our grateful thanks go to David Stuart of ABC Coins & Tokens who has spent many hours updating the Scottish section for 2012

DATE	F	VF	EF	UNC

PENNY

	F	VF	EF	UNC
1709 Cast	£45	£125	£275	—
1709 Silver cast Proof	—	—	—	£1950
1709 Brass	£45	£110	£265	—
1733 "Quocunque"	£40	£55	£245	£360
1733 "Ouocunoue"	£40	£65	£260	£650
1733 Bath metal "Quocunque"	£30	£50	£220	—
1733 Silver Proof	—	—	—	£765
1733 Bronze Proof	—	—	—	£465
1733 Proof	—	—	—	£665
1733 Cap frosted	£30	£50	£250	£365
1733 Brass, cap frosted	£40	£60	£265	£520
1733 Silver Proof cap frosted	—	—	—	£575
1733 Bronze annulets instead of pellets	£50	£95	£350	£265
1758	£30	£45	£200	£425
1758 Proof	—	—	—	£630
1758 Silver Proof	—	—	—	£995
1786 Engrailed edge	£35	£50	£220	£450
1786 Engrailed edge Proof	—	—	—	£495
1786 Plain edge Proof	—	—	—	£990
1786 Pellet below bust	£35	£60	£275	£550
1798	£35	£60	£200	£430
1798 Proof	—	—	—	£390
1798 Bronze Proof	—	—	—	£390
1798 Copper-gilt Proof	—	—	—	£1770
1798 Silver Proof	—	—	—	£2470
1813	£40	£60	£185	£385
1813 Proof	—	—	—	£425
1813 Bronze Proof	—	—	—	£385
1813 Copper-gilt Proof	—	—	—	£2470
1839	£35	£50	£155	£320
1839 Proof	—	—	—	£470

HALF PENCE

	F	VF	EF	UNC
1709 Cast	£50	£125	£250	—
1709 Brass	£55	£185	£490	—
1723 Silver	£695	£1250	£3100	—
1723 Copper	£295	£580	£1750	£2470
1733 Copper	£35	£55	£225	£425
1733 Bronze	£35	£55	£225	£425
1733 Silver Proof plain cap	—	—	—	£595
1733 Silver Proof frosted cap	—	—	—	—
1733 Bronze Proof	—	—	—	£470
1733 Bath metal plain cap	£40	£50	£215	—
1733 Bath metal frosted cap	£40	£50	£215	—
1758	£40	£50	£215	£400
1758 Proof	—	—	—	£770
1786 Engrailed edge	£30	£45	£120	£340
1786 Proof engrailed edge	—	—	—	£425
1786 Plain edge	£40	£65	£250	£340
1786 Proof plain edge	—	—	—	£650
1786 Bronze Proof	—	—	—	£450
1798	£35	£45	£110	£345
1798 Proof	—	—	—	£400
1798 Bronze Proof	—	—	—	£395

DATE	F	VF	EF	UNC
1798 Copper-gilt Proof	—	—	—	£1500
1798 Silver Proof	—	—	—	£1475
1813	£30	£45	£125	£265
1813 Proof	—	—	—	£360
1813 Bronze Proof	—	—	—	£320
1813 Copper-gilt Proof	—	—	—	£1230
1839	£30	£45	£100	£225
1839 Bronze Proof	—	—	—	£395

FARTHING

	F	VF	EF	UNC
1839 Copper	£30	£45	£100	£235
1839 Bronze Proof	—	—	—	£385
1839 Copper-gilt Proof	—	—	—	£2275

The last issue of coins made in the Isle of Man had been in 1839 but in 1970 Spink & Son Ltd was commissioned to produce a modern coinage for the Isle of Man Government which was struck at the Royal Mint. From 1973 onwards the Pobjoy Mint took over the contract and has been a very prolific producer of definitive and commemorative issues. It is not proposed to give a complete listing of all these coins but the Crown and 25p, which from the collector's point of view are the most interesting in the series, have been selected. Additionally a special 50p coin is issued to celebrate Christmas each year.

The listings that follow are of the ordinary uncirculated cupro-nickel crown-size coins. The Island has also issued most of the coins listed in other metals, including silver, gold and platinum in non proof and proof form and in 1984 some were also issued in silver clad cupro-nickel in proof form.

DATE	UNC
1970 Manx Cat	£15
1972 Royal Silver Wedding	£15
1974 Centenary of Churchill's birth	£15
1975 Manx Cat	£15
1976 Bi-Centenary of American Independence	£15
1976 Centenary of the Horse Drawn Tram	£10
1977 Silver Jubilee	£10
1977 Silver Jubilee Appeal	£10
1978 25th Anniversary of the Coronation	£10
1979 300th Anniversary of Manx Coinage	£10
1979 Millennium of Tynwald (5 coins)	£20
1980 Winter Olympics	£15
1980 Derby Bicentennial	£15
1980 22nd Olympics (3 coins)	£20
1980 80th Birthday of Queen Mother	£10
1981 Duke of Edinburgh Award Scheme (4 coins)	£15
1981 Year of Disabled (4 coins)	£15
1981 Prince of Wales' Wedding (2 coins)	£15
1982 12th World Cup—Spain (4 coins)	£20
1982 Maritime Heritage (4 coins)	£20
1983 Manned Flight (4 coins)	£20
1984 23rd Olympics (4 coins)	£20
1984 Quincentenary of College of Arms (4 coins)	£20
1984 Commonwealth Parliamentary Conference (4 coins)	£20
1985 Queen Mother (6 coins)	£20
1986 13th World Cup—Mexico (6 coins)	£15
1986 Prince Andrew Wedding (2 coins)	£15
1987 200th Anniversary of the United States Constitution	£15

DATE	UNC
1987 America's Cup Races (5 coins)	£25
1988 Bicentenary of Steam Navigation (6 coins)	£30
1988 Australia Bicentennial (6 coins)	£30
1988 Manx Cat	£15
1989 Royal Visit	£10
1989 Bicentenary of the Mutiny on the Bounty (4 coins)	£20
1989 Persian Cat	£15
1989 Bicentenary of Washington's Inauguration (4 coins)	£20
1990 150th Anniversary of the Penny Black	£15
1990 World Cup—Italy (4 coins)	£20
1990 25th Anniversary of Churchill's Death (2 coins)	£15
1990 Alley Cat	£15
1990 Queen Mother's 90th Birthday	£10
1991 Norwegian Forest Cat	£10
1991 Centenary of the American Numismatic Association	£10
1991 1992 America's Cup	£15
1991 10th Anniversary of Prince of Wales' Wedding (2 coins)	£15
1992 Discovery of America (4 coins)	£20
1992 Siamese Cat	£15
1992 1992 America's Cup	£10
1993 Maine Coon Cat	£10
1993 Preserve Planet Earth—Dinosaurs (2 coins)	£15
1994 Preserve Planet Earth—Mammoth	£15
1994 Year of the Dog	£15
1994 World Football Cup (6 coins)	£30
1994 Japanese Bobtail Cat	£10
1994 Normandy Landings (8 coins)	£40
1994 Preserve Planet Earth—Endangered Animals (3 coins)	£20
1995 Man in Flight—Series i (8 coins)	£60
1995 Man in Flight—Series ii (8 coins)	£60
1995 Queen Mother's 95th Birthday	£15
1995 Year of the Pig	£15
1995 Turkish Cat	£15
1995 Preserve Planet Earth—Egret and Otter	£15
1995 America's Cup	£15
1995 Aircraft of World War II (19 coins)	£130
1995 Famous World Inventions—Series i (12 coins)	£120
1996 Year of the Rat	£15
1996 70th Birthday of HM the Queen	£20
1996 The Flower Fairies—Series i (4 coins)	£40
1996 Famous World Inventions—Series ii (6 coins)	£40
1996 Olympic Games (6 coins)	£35
1996 Preserve Planet Earth—Killer Whale and Razorbill	£15
1996 Burmese Cat	£15
1996 Robert Burns (4 coins)	£30
1996 King Arthur & the Knights of the Round Table (5 coins)	£35
1996 European Football Championships (8 coins)	£50
1996 Football Championships Winner	£15
1996 Explorers (2 coins)	£20
1997 Year of the Ox	£20
1997 The Flower Fairies—Series ii (4 coins)	£25
1997 Royal Golden Wedding (2 coins)	£20
1997 Explorers—Eriksson and Nansen (2 coins)	£15
1997 Long-haired Smoke Cat	£15
1997 10th Anniversary of the "Cats on Coins" series (silver only)	£45
1997 90th Anniversary of the TT Races (4 coins)	£35
1998 The Millennium (16 coins issued over 3 years)	£96
1998 Year of the Tiger	£20
1998 FIFA World Cup (4 coins)	£35
1998 Birman Cat	£20
1998 The Flower Fairies—Series iii (4 coins)	£30
1998 18th Winter Olympics, Nagano (4 coins)	£30
1998 Explorers—Vasco da Gama and Marco Polo (2 coins)	£25
1998 125th Anniversary of Steam Railway (8 coins)	£65
1998 International Year of the Oceans (4 coins)	£33
1999 50th Birthday of HRH the Prince of Wales	£15
1999 Year of the Rabbit	£15

DATE	UNC
1999 27th Olympics in Sydney (5 coins)	£40
1999 Rugby World Cup (6 coins)	£40
1999 Wedding of HRH Prince Edward and Sophie Rhys-Jones	£15
1999 Queen Mother's 100th Birthday (4 coins)	£35
1999 The Millennium (4 coins)	£35
1999 Titanium Millennium crown	£15
2000 Year of the Dragon	£15
2000 Scottish Fold cat	£15
2000 Millennium—own a piece of time	£15
2000 Explorers, Francisco Piarro and Wilem Brents (2 coins)	£15
2000 Life and times of the Queen Mother (4 coins)	£30
2000 Queen Mother's 100th Birthday	£15
2000 60th Anniversary of the Battle of Britain	£15
2000 BT Global Challenge	£15
2000 18th Birthday of HRH Prince William	£15
2001 Year of the Snake	£15
2001 The Somali cat	£15
2001 Life and times of the Queen Mother (2 coins)	£15
2001 Explorers, Martin Frobisher and Roald Amundsen (2 coins)	£15
2001 75th Birthday of HM the Queen	£15
2001 Joey Dunlop	£15
2001 Harry Potter (6 coins)	£80
2002 Year of the Horse	£15
2002 The XIX Winter Olympiad, Salt Lake City (2 coins)	£20
2002 World Cup 2002 in Japan/Korea (4 coins)	£35
2002 The Bengal Cat	£15
2002 The Queen's Golden Jubilee—i (1 coin)	£15
2002 Introduction of the Euro	£15
2002 The Queen's Golden Jubilee—ii (4 coins)	£60
2002 A Tribute to Diana Princess of Wales—5 years on	£30
2003 Year of the Goat	£15
2003 The Balinese Cat	£15
2003 Anniversary of the "Star of India"	£15
2003 Lord of the Rings (5 coins)	£60
2004 Olympics (4 coins)	£50
2004 100 Years of Powered Flight (2 coins)	£30
2005 Lord of the Rings: The Return of the King	£30
2005 Manx Hero Lt. John Quilliam and the Battle of Trafalgar (2 coins)	£30
2005 The Himalayan Cat with kittens	£20
2005 Bicentenary of the Battle of Trafalgar (6 coins)	£55
2005 60th Anniversary of D-Day (6 coins)	£65
2005 60th Anniversary of Victory in Europe	£30
2005 200th Anniversary of the Battle of Trafalgar	£30
2005 400th Anniversary of the Gun Powder Plot (2 coins)	£30
2005 Bicentenary of the Battle of Trafalgar and Death of Nelson	£30
2005 Italy and the Isle of Man TT races (2 coins)	£30
2005 Harry Potter and the Goblet of Fire (4 coins)	£35
2006 100 Years of Norwegian Independence	£25
2006 80th Birthday of Her Majesty the Queen (4 coins)	£35
2006 The Battles that Changed the World—Part II (6 coins)	£55
2006 150th Anniversary of the Victoria Cross (2 coins)	£30
2006 30th Anniversary of the first Translantic Flight	£25
2007 The Ragdoll Cat	£15
2007 Fairy Tales—Sleeping Beauty, The Three Little Pigs (2 coins)	£25
2007 The Graceful Swan	£15
2007 The Royal Diamond Wedding Anniversary	£15
2007 The Centenary of the TT races	£15
2007 The Centenary of the Scouting	£15
2008 50th Anniversary of Paddington Bear	£15
2008 Prince Charles 60th Birthday	£15
2008 Centenary of the Olympics	£15
2008 Burmilla Cat	£15
2008 Year of Planet Earth	£15
2008 The Adorable Snowman	£15
2008 UEFA European Football Championships	£15
2008 The Return of Tutankhamun	£30

DATE   UNC

GUERNSEY

DATE	F	VF	EF	UNC

TEN SHILLINGS

	F	VF	EF	UNC
1966	—	£5	£9	£12
1966 Proof	—	—	—	£20

THREEPENCE

	F	VF	EF	UNC
1956	70p	£4	£8	£10
1956 Proof	—	—	—	£15
1959	70p	£4	£8	£12
1966 Proof	—	—	—	£15

EIGHT DOUBLES

	F	VF	EF	UNC
1834	£10	£10	£50	£160
1858 5 berries	£6	£9	£50	£150
1858 4 berries	£6	£9	£50	£160
1864 1 stalk	£6	£4	£40	£70
1864 3 stalks	£6	£4	£30	£65
1868	£7	£8	£30	£65
1874	£4	£6	£15	£50
1885H	£4	£6	£15	£45
1889H	£3	£4	£15	£40
1893H small date	£3	£4	£15	£40
1893H large date	£3	£4	£15	£40
1902H	£3	£4	£15	£40
1903H	£3	£4	£15	£40
1910	£3	£4	£15	£40
1911H	£3	£4	£15	£45
1914H	£1	£3	£9	£30
1918H	£1	£3	£8	£25
1920H	£1	£3	£8	£25
1934H	£1	£3	£8	£32
1934H Proof	—	—	—	£140
1938H	£1	£3	£9	£23
1945H	—	£2	£8	£15
1947H	—	£2	£8	£15
1949H	—	£2	£9	£15
1956	—	£1	£7	£14
1956	—	£1	£5	£14
1959	—	£1	£5	£14
1966 Proof	—	—	—	£26

FOUR DOUBLES

	F	VF	EF	UNC
1830	£4	£9	£50	£120
1830 Mule with obv. St Helena 1/2 d	—	£750	—	—
1858	£6	£12	£50	£120
1864 Single stalk	£2	£6	£18	£57
1864 3 stalks	£2	£6	£20	£65
1868	£3	£7	£22	£70
1874	£2	£6	£22	£70
1885H	£2	£6	£20	£42
1889H	£2	£3	£13	£35
1893H	£2	£3	£13	£35
1902H	£2	£3	£9	£30
1903H	£2	£3	£13	£30
1906H	£2	£3	£9	£26
1908H	£2	£3	£9	£26
1910H	£2	£3	£9	£26
1911H	£2	£3	£8	£25
1914H	£2	£3	£13	£40
1918H	£2	£3	£12	£35
1920H	£2	£3	£9	£35
1945H	£2	£3	£9	£33
1949H	£2	£3	£12	£33
1956	£1	£2	£7	£14
1966 Proof	—	—	—	£14

DATE	F	VF	EF	UNC
TWO DOUBLES				
1858..	£6	£9	£50	£200
1868 Single stick	£6	£11	£55	£200
868 3 stalks	£7	£13	£80	£205
1874..	£4	£9	£50	£150
1885H...	£3	£6	£17	£35
1889H...	£3	£4	£17	£35
1899H...	£3	£5	£21	£42
1902H...	£3	£4	£19	£35
1902H...	£3	£4	£19	£35
1906H...	£3	£4	£19	£35
1908H...	£3	£5	£19	£35
1911H...	£3	£5	£22	£42
1914H...	£3	£5	£22	£42
1917H...	£7	£18	£80	£210
1918H...	£3	£4	£13	£30
1920H...	£3	£4	£13	£30
1929H...	£2	£3	£11	£18
ONE DOUBLE				
1830..	£3	£4	£22	£45
1868..	£4	£10	£33	£90
1868/30	£5	£7	£27	£85
1885H...	£2	£3	£8	£20
1889H...	60p	£2	£6	£20
1893H...	60p	£2	£6	£20
1899H...	60p	£2	£6	£20
1902..	60p	£2	£6	£20
1903H...	60p	£2	£6	£20
1911H...	60p	£2	£8	£20
1911 (new shield)	60p	£2	£6	£20
1914H	60p	£2	£8	£20
1929H...	60p	£2	£6	£20
1933H...	60p	£2	£6	£20
1938H...	60p	£2	£6	£20

DECIMAL COINAGE

Ordinary circulating coinage from 1986 onwards is usually available in uncirculated condition at a small premium above face value thus it is not listed here. The coins listed are cupro-nickel unless otherwise stated.

	UNC
ONE HUNDRED POUNDS—Gold	
1994 50th Anniversary of Normandy Landings. Proof	£1600
1995 Anniversary of the Liberation. Proof..	£1600
FIFTY POUNDS—Gold	
1994 50th Anniversary of Normandy Landings. Proof	£950
1995 Anniversary of the Liberation. Proof...	£950
1998 Queen Elizabeth and Queen Mother Gold Proof...........................	£1000
1999 Queen Elizabeth and Queen Mother Gold	£900
2004 Anniversary of D-Day	£1100
TWENTY-FIVE POUNDS—Gold	
1994 50th Anniversary of Normandy Landings......................................	£400
1994 — Proof	£400
1995 Anniversary of the Liberation. Proof...	£400
1995 Queen Mothers 95th Birthday	£400
1996 European Football Championships. Proof	£400
1997 Royal Golden Wedding. Proof..	£400
1998 Royal Air Force. Proof	£400
2000 Queen Mother 100th Birthday. Proof..	£400
2001 Queen Victoria centennial Proof..	£400
2001 Queen Victoria gold proof	£400
2001 HM the Queen's 75th Birthday. Proof...	£400
2002 Princess Diana memorial. Proof	£400
2002 Duke of Wellington. Proof..	£400
2002 Golden Jubilee. Proof..	£400
2002 Queen Mother. Proof	£400

DATE	UNC
2003 Golden Jubilee. Proof	£400
2004 Anniversary of D-Day. Proof	£400
2006 FIFA World Cup. Proof	£400

TEN POUNDS

1994 50th Anniversary of Normandy Landings. Gold proof	£200
1995 Anniversary of the Liberation. Gold proof	£200
2000 Century of Monarchy. Silver proof	£160
2000 Guernsey Gold Proof 'Nugget'	£200
2001 19th Century Monarchy. Silver proof	£160
2002 18th Century Monarchy. Silver proof	£160
2004 Anniversary of D-Day. Silver proof	£195

FIVE POUNDS

1995 Queen Mother's 95th birthday	£25
1995 — Silver proof	£55
1995 — Small size gold	£250
1996 HM the Queen's 70th birthday	£18
1996 — Silver proof	£55
1996 European Football Championships	£35
1996 — Silver proof	£55
1997 Royal Golden Wedding	£21
1997 — Silver proof	£55
1997 — Small size gold. BU	£180
1997 Castles of the British Isles—Castle Cornet, Guernsey	£18
1997 — Silver proof	£65
1997 Castles of the British Isles—Caernarfon Castle. Silver proof	£75
1997 Castles of the British Isles—Leeds Castle. Silver proof	£75
1998 Royal Air Force	£15
1998 Royal Air Force. Silver proof	£70
1999 Millennium. Brass	£25
1999 — Silver proof	£55
1999 Wedding of HRH Prince Edward and Sophie Rhys-Jones	£25
1999 — Silver proof	£55
1999 Queen Mother	£25
1999 — Silver proof	£80
1999 Winston Churchill	£15
1999 — Gold	£1200
2000 Queen Mother's 100th Birthday	£10
2000 — Silver proof	£85
2000 — Small size gold. Proof	£170
2000 Centuries of the British Monarchy	£45
2000 — Silver proof	£85
2000 — Small size gold. Proof	£180
2001 The Reign of Queen Victoria	£20
2001 — Gold proof	£360
2001 — Proof	£60
2001 — Silver proof	£60
2001 HM the Queen's 75th Birthday	£15
2001 — Silver proof	£60
2001 — Small size gold. Proof	£180
2001 19th Century Monarchy	£20
2001 — Silver proof	£60
2001 — Small size gold. Proof	£180
2002 Golden Jubilee (two types)	£15
2002 — Silver proof	£65
2002 Princess Diana Memorial	£15
2002 — Proof	£60
2002 — Gold proof	£1200
2002 Century of Monarchy	£15
2002 — Silver proof	£60
2002 — Small size gold. Proof	£180
2002 Queen Mother Memoriam	£20
2002 — Proof	£25
2002 — Silver proof	£65
2002 — Small size gold proof	£180
2002 — Large size gold proof	£1200

DATE	UNC
2003 Duke of Wellington	£15
2003 — Silver proof	£50
2003 — Small size gold proof	£160
2003 — Large size gold proof	£1200
2003 Prince William	£20
2003 — Silver proof	£60
2003 — Gold proof	£1150
2003 Golden Hind	£20
2003 17th Century Monarchy	£22
2003 History of the Royal Navy, Nelson	£20
2003 — Nelson with coloured flag. Proof	£30
2004 — Invincible. Silver proof	£50
2004 16th Century monarchs	£15
2004 History of the Railways, Mallard	£12
2004 — City of Truro	£15
2004 — The Boat Train	£12
2004 — The Train Spotter	£15
2004 History of the Royal Navy, Henry VIII	£15
2004 — Invincible	£15
2004 Anniversary of D-Day	£12
2004 — Silver proof	£50
2004 — Gold proof	£1150
2004 Anniversary of the Crimean War. Plain	£12
2004 — with colour	£15
2004 — Silver proof	£55
2004 — Gold proof with colour	£1200
2005 200th Anniversary of the Battle of Trafalgar	£25
2005 60th Anniversary of the Liberation of the Channel Islands	£25
2005 End of World War II. Silver proof	£55
2005 — Gold proof	£1200
2005 Anniversary of Liberation. Gold proof	£1250
2006 Royal 80th Birthday. Silver proof	£55
2006 FIFA World Cup. Silver proof	£55
2006 Great Britons—Sir Winston Churchill Silver. Issued as part of set	£60
2006 80th Birthday of Her Majesty the Queen	£25
2007 History of the Royal Navy—Henry VIII, The Golden Hind (2 coins)	£65
2007 Royal Diamond Wedding	£25
2011 350th Anniversary of the Crown Jewels. Silver proof	£95
2011 90th Anniversary of the British Legion (gold-plated copper)	£40
— Silver proof	£95
2011 40th Anniversary of decimalisation, proof	£20

TWO POUNDS

1985 40th anniversary of Liberation	£10
1985 — Proof	£27
1985 — Silver proof	£55
1986 Commonwealth Games, in plastic case	£12
1986 — in special folder	£12
1986 — .500 Silver	£45
1986 — .925 Silver proof	£55
1987 900th anniv. of death of William the Conqueror, in folder	£14
1987 — Silver proof	£55
1987 — Gold proof	£1300
1988 William II, in presentation folder	£14
1988 — Silver proof	£55
1989 Henry I, in presentation folder	£14
1989 — Silver proof	£55
1989 Royal Visit	£14
1989 — Silver proof	£55
1990 Queen Mother's 90th birthday	£14
1990 — Silver proof	£55
1991 Henry II, in presentation folder	£14
1991 — Silver proof	£55
1993 40th Anniversary of the Coronation	£14
1993 — Silver proof	£60
1994 Anniversary of the Normandy Landings	£14

DATE	F	VF	EF	UNC
1994 — Silver proof				£55
1995 50th Anniversary of Liberation				£14
1995 — Silver proof				£55
1995 — Silver Piedfort proof				£100
1997 Conserving Nature i				£10
1997 — Silver proof				£55
1997 Bimetallic Latent image				£5
1997 — Proof				£8
1998 Conserving Nature ii				£10
1998 Bimetallic Latent image				£5
2003 —				£6
2006 —				£8

ONE POUND

	F	VF	EF	UNC
1981				£10
1981 Gold proof				£145
1981 Gold piedfort				£345
1983 New specification, new reverse				£9
1985 New design (in folder)				£9
1995 Queen Mother's 95th Birthday. Silver proof				£50
1996 Queen's 70th Birthday. Silver proof				£55
1997 Royal Golden Wedding. Silver BU				£18
1997 — Silver proof				£55
1997 Castles of the British Isles—Tower of London. Silver proof only				£27
1998 Royal Air Force. Silver proof				£42
1999 Wedding of Prince Edward. Silver proof				£55
1999 Queen Mother. Silver proof				£55
1999 Winston Churchill. Silver proof				£55
2000 Millennium. Silver proof (gold plated)				£65
2000 Queen Mother's 100th Birthday. Silver proof				£42
2001				£2
2001 HM the Queen's 75th Birthday. Silver proof				£42
2002 William of Normandy. Silver				£20
2003				£2
2006				£2

FIFTY PENCE

	F	VF	EF	UNC
1969				£4
1970				£6
1971 Proof				£9
1981				£4
1982				£4
1985 New design				£4
2000 60th Anniversary of the Battle of Britain.				£4
2000 — Silver proof				£55
2000 — Silver piedfort				£55
2000 — Gold proof				£365
2003				£2
2006				£2
2008				£2

TWENTY-FIVE PENCE

	F	VF	EF	UNC
1972 Royal Silver Wedding				£12
1972 — Silver proof				£42
1977 Royal Silver Jubilee				£9
1977 — Silver proof				£42
1978 Royal Visit				£9
1978 — Silver proof				£42
1980 Queen Mother's 80th birthday				£9
1980 — Silver proof				£42
1981 Royal Wedding				£9
1981 — Silver proof				£42

JERSEY

DATE	F	VF	EF	UNC
FIVE SHILLINGS				
1966	—	£3	£7	£15
1966 Proof	—	£3	£9	£25
ONE QUARTER OF A SHILLING				
1957	—	£2	£5	£10
1960 Proof	—	—	£5	£14
1964	—	—	£4	£10
1966	—	—	£4	£10
ONE TWELFTH OF A SHILLING				
1877H	£2	£3	£18	£55
1877H Proof in nickel	—	—	—	£1275
1877 Proof only	—	—	—	£475
1877 Proof in nickel	—	—	—	£1265
1881	£3	£3	£14	£60
1888	£2	£3	£14	£48
1894	£2	£3	£17	£48
1909	£2	£3	£14	£35
1911	£2	£3	£7	£30
1913	£2	£3	£7	£30
1923 Spade shield	£2	£3	£7	£30
1923 Square shield	£2	£3	£7	£30
1926	£2	£3	£8	£42
1931	£2	£3	£5	£12
1933	£2	£3	£7	£12
1935	£2	£3	£7	£12
1937	£2	£3	£7	£12
1946	£2	£3	£7	£12
1947	—	£3	£7	£12
"1945" GVI	—	—	£1	£9
"1945" QE2	—	—	£1	£7
1957	—	—	£1	£7
1960 1660–1960 300th anniversary	—	—	£1	£7
1960 Mule	—	—	—	£150
1966 "1066–1966"	—	—	£1	£7

DATE	F	VF	EF	UNC
ONE THIRTEENTH OF A SHILLING				
1841	£4	£8	£40	£195
1844	£4	£9	£40	£195
1851	£5	£12	£60	£200
1858	£4	£9	£45	£195
1861	£5	£13	£60	£175
1865 Proof only	—	—	—	£700
1866 with LCW	£2	£5	£95	£145
1866 without LCW Proof only	—	—	—	£390
1870	£4	£8	£40	£110
1871	£4	£8	£42	£110

DATE	F	VF	EF	UNC
ONE TWENTY-FOURTH OF A SHILLING				
1877H	£3	£4	£11	£55
1877 Proof only	—	—	—	£300
1888	£3	£4	£11	£42
1894	£3	£4	£11	£42
1909	£3	£4	£11	£42
1911	£2	£3	£8	£42
1913	£2	£3	£8	£42

DATE	F	VF	EF	UNC
1923 Spade shield	£2	£3	£9	£33
1923 Square shield	£2	£3	£8	£35
1926	£2	£3	£8	£22
1931	£2	£3	£8	£22
1933	£2	£3	£8	£22
1935	£2	£3	£8	£22
1937	60p	£2	£6	£16
1946	60p	£2	£6	£19
1947	60p	£2	£6	£16

ONE TWENTY-SIXTH OF A SHILLING

	F	VF	EF	UNC
1841	£4	£7	£30	£90
1844	£4	£7	£25	£90
1851	£3	£6	£25	£90
1858	£4	£11	£48	£180
1861	£3	£6	£25	£65
1866	£3	£6	£27	£77
1870	£3	£6	£20	£55
1871	£3	£6	£20	£55

ONE FORTY-EIGHTH OF A SHILLING

	F	VF	EF	UNC
1877H	£6	£12	£57	£130
1877 Proof only	—	—	—	£400

ONE FIFTY-SECOND OF A SHILLING

	F	VF	EF	UNC
1841	£9	£25	£60	£195
1861 Proof only	—	—	—	£650

DECIMAL COINAGE

Ordinary circulating coinage from 1986 onwards is usually available in uncirculated condition at a small premium above face value thus it is not listed here.

ONE HUNDRED POUNDS
1990 50th Anniversary of the Battle of Britain. Gold Proof.	£1000
1995 50th Anniversary of Liberation. Gold proof	£1000

FIFTY POUNDS
1972 Silver Wedding. Gold proof	£850
1990 50th Anniversary of the Battle of Britain. Gold proof	£850
1995 50th Anniversary of Liberation. Gold proof	£820
2003 Golden Jubilee. Silver Proof (100mm)	£650

TWENTY-FIVE POUNDS
1972 25th Royal Wedding anniversary. Gold	£300
1972 — Gold proof	£380
1990 50th Anniversary of Battle of Britain. Gold proof	£350
1995 50th Anniversary of Liberation. Gold proof	£350
2002 Princess Diana memorial. Gold proof	£350
2002 Queen Mother. Gold proof	£350
2002 Golden Jubilee. Gold proof	£350
2002 Duke of Wellington. Gold proof	£350
2003 Golden Jubilee. Gold proof	£350
2003 History of the Royal Navy. Naval Commanders	£350
2003 — Francis Drake	£350
2003 — Sovereign of the Seas	£350
2004 60th Anniversary of D-Day. Gold proof	£350
2004 Charge of the Light Brigade. Gold proof	£350
2004 HMS Victory. Gold proof	£350
2004 John Fisher 1841–1920 Gold proof	£350
2004 The Coronation Scot. Gold proof	£350
2004 The Flying Scotsman. Gold proof	£350
2004 Golden Arrow. Gold proof	£350
2004 Rocket and Evening Star. Gold proof	£350

DATE	UNC
2005 Andrew Cunningham. Gold proof..	£350
2005 HMS Conqueror. Gold Proof	£350
2005 200th Anniversary of Nelson. Gold proof	£350
2009 500th Anniversary of Accession. Gold proof...................................	£350

TWENTY POUNDS

1972 Royal Wedding. The Ormer. Gold..	£300
1972 — Gold proof..	£300

TEN POUNDS

1972 25th Royal Wedding anniversary. Gold	£75
1972 — Gold proof..	£180
1990 50th Anniversary of the Battle of Britain. Gold proof	£180
1995 50th Anniversary of Liberation. Gold proof	£140
2003 Coronation Anniversary. Gold/silver proof......................................	£50
2004 Crimea. Silver proof..	£20
2205 Trafalgar. Silver proof...	£20
2005 — Silver/gold proof	£110
2005 End of World War II. Silver proof	£25
2007 Diamond Wedding. Platinum proof	£280
2008 History of RAF. Silver proof	£25
2008 — Silver/Gold proof..	£110
2011 Royal Wedding of HRH Prince William & Catherine Middleton, silver (65mm)£395	

(Enlarged)

FIVE POUNDS

1972 Gold proof	£65
1990 50th Anniversary of the Battle of Britain. Silver Proof (5 ounces)	£180
1997 Royal Golden Wedding..	£10
1997 — Silver proof...	£25
2000 Millennium. Silver proof..	£35
2002 Princess Diana memorial..	£12
2002 — Silver proof...	£30
2002 — Gold proof..	£820
2002 Royal Golden Jubilee	£25
2003 Golden Jubilee	£20
2003 — Silver proof...	£55
2003 — Gold proof..	£1100
2003 Prince William 21st Birthday	£15
2003 — Silver Proof	£55
2003 —Gold proof...	£1200
2003 Naval Commanders...	£15
2003 — Silver proof...	£55
2003 — Gold proof..	£1200
2003 Francis Drake	£15
2003 — Silver proof...	£55
2003 — Gold proof..	£1200
2003 Sovereign of the Seas	£15
2003 — Silver proof...	£55
2003 — Gold proof..	£1200
2004 60th Anniversary of 'D' Day..	£15
2004 — Silver proof...	£55
2004 — Gold proof..	£1200
2004 Charge of the Light Brigade	£15
2004 — Silver proof...	£50
2004 — Gold proof..	£1200
2004 HMS Victory	£15
2004 — Silver proof...	£55
2004 — Gold proof..	£1200
2004 John Fisher 1841–1920	£15
2004 — Silver proof...	£55
2004 —Gold proof...	£1200
2004 The Coronation Scot	£15
2004 — Silver proof...	£55

(Reduced)

(Enlarged)

DATE	UNC
2004 — Gold proof	£1200
2004 The Flying Scotsman	£15
2004 — Silver proof	£55
2004 — Silver/Gold proof	£500
2004 — Gold proof	£1200
2004 Golden Arrow	£15
2004 — Silver proof	£55
2004 — Gold proof	£1200
2005 Driver and Fireman	£15
2005 — Silver proof	£45
2005 — Gold proof	£1100
2005 Box Tunnel and King Loco	£15
2005 — Silver Proof	£45
2005 — Gold Proof	£1100
2005 Rocket and Evening Star	£15
2005 — Silver proof	£45
2005 — Silver/Gold proof	£500
2005 — Gold proof	£1200
2005 200th Anniversary of the Battle of Trafalgar	£30
2005 Andrew Cunningham	£20
2005 — Silver proof	£60
2005 — Gold proof	£1200
2005 HMS Conqueror	£15
2005 — Silver proof	£20
2005 — Gold proof	£1200
2005 Battle of Trafalgar	£15
2005 — Silver proof	£45
2005 — Gold proof (9mm)	£500
2005 — Gold proof (38.6mm)	£1200
2005 Returning Evacuees	£15
2005 — Silver proof	£45
2005 — Gold proof	£1200
2005 Searchlights and Big Ben	£15
2005 — Silver proof	£45
2005 — Gold proof	£1200
2006 60th Anniversary of the Liberation of the Channel Islands	£30
2006 80th Birthday of Her Majesty the Queen (3-coin set)	—
2006 Sir Winston Churchill	£15
2006 — Silver proof	£45
2006 — Gold proof	£1200
2006 Charles Darwin	£15
2006 — Silver proof	£45
2006 — Gold proof	£1200
2006 Bobby Moore	£20
2006 — Silver Proof	£55
2006 — Gold Proof	£1250
2006 Florence Nightingale	£20
2006 — Silver proof	£55
2006 — Gold proof	£1200
2006 Queen Mother	£20
2006 — Silver proof	£55
2006 — Gold proof	£1200
2006 Henry VIII	£15
2006 — Silver proof	£55
2006 — Gold proof	£1200
2006 Princess Diana	£20
2006 — Silver Proof	£60
2006 — Gold Proof	£1350
2006 Sir Christopher Wren	£15
2006 — Silver proof	£55
2006 — Gold proof	£1200
2006 HM the Queen's 80th Birthday—Streamers	£15
2006 — Silver proof	£55
2006 — Gold proof	£1200
2006 HM the Queen's 80th Birthday—Trooping colour	£20
2006 — Proof	£60

DATE	UNC
2006 — Silver proof	£1100
2006 — Silver/Gold proof	£650
2006 — Gold proof	£1200
2006 HM the Queen's 80th Birthday—Wembley Stadium	£20
2006 — Silver proof	£55
2006 — Gold proof	£1200
2006 Guy Gibson	£15
2006 — Silver proof	£55
2006 — Gold proof	£1200
2006 Eric James Nicholson	£15
2006 — Silver proof	£55
2006 — Gold proof	£1200
2006 Hook, Chard and Bromhead	£15
2006 — Silver proof	£55
2006 — Gold proof	£1200
2006 1st Lancs Fusiliers	£15
2006 — Silver proof	£55
2006 — Gold proof	£1200
2006 Noel Chavasse	£15
2006 — Silver proof	£55
2006 — Gold proof	£1200
2006 David Mackay	£15
2006 — Silver proof	£55
2006 — Gold proof	£1200
2006 Coronation Scot. Silver proof	£60
2006 Flying Scotsman. Silver proof	£60
2006 Fireman and Driver. Silver proof	£60
2006 Box Tunnel. Silver proof	£60
2007 Diamond Wedding balcony scene waving	£15
2007 — Silver proof	£60
2007 Diamond Wedding cake	£15
2007 — Silver proof	£60
2007 Diamond Wedding balcony scene waving	£15
2007 —Silver proof	£60
2007 Diamond Wedding HM the Queen and Prince Philip	£20
2007 — Silver proof	£60
2007 Diamond Wedding arrival at Abbey	£20
2007 — Silver proof	£55
2007 — Gold proof	£1200
2008 George & Dragon	£20
2008 Dambusters, Wallis, Chadwick, Gibson	£15
2008 — Silver/Copper proof	£30
2008 — Silver proof	£55
2008 Frank Whittle	£15
2008 — Silver proof	£55
2008 — Gold proof	£1200
2008 R. J. Mitchell	£15
2008 — Silver proof	£55
2008 — Gold proof	£1200
2008 Maj. Gen. Sir Hugh Trenchard	£15
2008 — Silver proof	£55
2008 — Gold proof	£1200
2008 Bomber Command	£15
2008 — Silver proof	£55
2008 — Gold proof	£1200
2008 Coastal Command	£20
2008 — Silver proof	£60
2008 — Gold proof	£1300
2008 Fighter Command	£20
2008 — Silver proof	£60
2008 — Gold proof	£1300
2008 Battle of Britain	£20
2008 — Silver proof	£60
2008 — Gold proof	£1300
2008 RBL Poppy	£20
2008 — Silver proof	£60

DATE	UNC
2008 — Gold proof..	£1300
2008 Flying Legends	£15
2008 — Silver proof...	£55
2008 — Gold proof..	£1200
2009 George & Dragon. Siver proof	£500
2009 Battle of Agincourt. Silver proof	£55
2009 Battle of the Somme. Silver proof	£55
2009 Capt. Cook and *Endeavour*. Silver proof....................................	£55
2009 500th Anniversary of Accession of Henry VIII. Silver proof..............	£55
2011 Landmark birthdays of HM the Queen & Prince Philip.....................	£9.95
2011 90th Anniversary of the British Legion (gold-plated copper).............	£40
— Silver proof...	£95

TWO POUNDS FIFTY PENCE

1972 Royal Silver Wedding	£22
1972 — Silver proof..	£33

TWO POUNDS
(note all modern Proof coins have frosted relief)

1972 Royal Silver Wedding. Silver...	£22
1972 — Silver proof..	£35
1981 Royal Wedding, nickel silver (crown size).....................................	£4
1981 — in presentation pack	£7
1981 — Silver proof..	£20
1981 — Gold proof..	£450
1985 40th Anniversary of Liberation (crown size).................................	£5
1985 — in presentation pack	£12
1985 — Silver proof..	£20
1985 — Gold proof..	£1365
1986 Commonwealth Games..	£6
1986 — in presentation case...	£8
1986 — .500 silver..	£12
1986 — .925 silver proof..	£20
1987 World Wildlife Fund 25th Anniversary	£80
1987 — Silver proof..	£25
1989 Royal Visit	£14
1989 — Silver proof..	£25
1990 Queen Mother's 90th Birthday	£14
1990 — Silver proof..	£25
1990 — Gold proof..	£600
1990 50th Anniversary of the Battle of Britain, silver proof........................	£30
1993 40th Anniversary of the Coronation..	£14
1993 — Silver proof..	£20
1993— Gold proof..	£600
1995 50th Anniversary of Liberation...	£14
1995 — Silver Proof	£25
1995 — — Piedfort..	£75
1996 HM the Queen's 70th Birthday	£14
1996 — Silver proof..	£25
1997 Bi-metal	£5
1997 — Silver proof..	£50
1997 — new portrait...	£5
1998 —	£5
2003 —	£5
2005 —	£5
2006 —	£5
2007 —	£5

ONE POUND

1972 Royal Silver Wedding	£15
1972 — Silver proof..	£20
1981..	£15

DATE	UNC
1981 Silver proof	£15
1981 Gold proof	£320
1983 New designs and specifications on presentation card (St Helier)	£4
1983 — Silver proof	£18
1983 — Gold proof	£395
1984 Presentation wallet (St Saviour)	£21
1984 — Silver proof	£45
1984 — Gold proof	£450
1984 Presentation wallet (St Brelade)	£20
1984 — Silver proof	£45
1984 — Gold proof	£490
1985 Presentation wallet (St Clement)	£25
1985 — Silver proof	£45
1985 — Gold proof	£490
1985 Presentation wallet (St Lawrence)	£25
1985 — Silver proof	£40
1985 — Gold proof	£490
1986 Presentation wallet (St Peter)	£16
1986 — Silver proof	£35
1986 — Gold proof	£490
1986 Presentation wallet (Grouville)	£18
1986 — Silver proof	£40
1986 — Gold proof	£490
1987 Presentation wallet (St Martin)	£18
1987 — Silver proof	£40
1987 — Gold proof	£490
1987 Presentation wallet (St Ouen)	£12
1987 — Silver proof	£40
1987 — Gold proof	£490
1988 Presentation wallet (Trinity)	£13
1988 — Silver proof	£40
1988 — Gold proof	£490
1988 Presentation wallet (St John)	£14
1988 — Silver proof	£40
1988 — Gold proof	£490
1989 Presentation wallet (St Mary)	£14
1989 — Silver proof	£40
1989 — Gold proof	£490

1991 Ship Building in Jersey Series

1991 "Tickler". Nickel-brass	£5
1991 "Tickler". Silver proof	£25
1991 — Gold proof Piedfort	£490
1991 "Percy Douglas". Nickel-brass	£5
1991 "Percy Douglas". Silver proof	£25
1991 — Gold proof Piedfort	£450
1992 "The Hebe". Nickel-brass	£5
1992 "The Hebe". Silver proof	£25
1992 — Gold proof Piedfort	£490
1992 "Coat of Arms". Nickel-brass	£5
1992 "Coat of Arms". Silver proof	£25
1992 — Gold proof Piedfort	£450
1993 "The Gemini". Nickel-brass	£5
1993 "The Gemini". Silver proof	£25
1993 — Gold proof Piedfort	£490
1993 "The Century". Nickel-brass	£5
1993 "The Century". Silver proof	£25
1993 — Gold proof Piedfort	£490
1994 "Resolute". Nickel-brass	£5
1994 "Resolute". Silver proof	£25
1994 — Gold proof Piedfort	£490
1997 — Nickel-brass	£5
1998 — — Nickel-brass	£5

DATE	UNC
2003 — — Nickel-brass	£5
2005 — — Nickel-brass	£5
2006 — — Nickel-brass	£5
2007 Diana Commem. Gold proof	£280

FIFTY PENCE

1969	£10
1972 Royal Silver Wedding. Silver	£11
1972 — Silver proof	£11
1980 —	£1
1980 Arms	£2
1980 — Proof	£5
1981 —	£1
1981 —	£5
1981 — Proof	£5
1983 Grosnez Castle	£10
1983 — Silver proof	£12
1984 —	£2
1985 40th Anniversary of Liberation	£3
1986	£5
1986	£5
1987	£5
1988	£5
1989	£5
1990	£5
1992	£5
1994	£5
1997	£5
1997 Smaller size	£4
1998 —	£3
2003	£3
2003 Coronation Anniversary (4 types)	£4
2003 — 4 types. Silver proof	£15
2005	£4
2006	£4
2009	£4
2011 Diamond Jubilee (full colour reverse, gold-plated)	£15

TWENTY-FIVE PENCE

1977 Royal Jubilee	£3
1977 — Silver proof	£20

TWENTY PENCE

1982 Corbiere Lighthouse (cased)	£8
1982 — Silver proof piedfort	£35
1983 — Obv. with date, rev. no date on rocks	£5
1983 — — Silver proof	£15
1984 —	£1
1986 —	£1
1987 —	£1
1989 —	£1
1992 —	£1
1994 —	£1
1996 —	£1
1997 —	£1
1998 —	£1
2002 —	£1
2003 —	£1
2005 —	£1
2006 —	£1
2007 —	£1
2009 —	£1

DATE   UNC

SOVEREIGN — Gold sovereign size
1999 The Millennium. King William on Throne £250
1999 — Gold proof £300

TEN PENCE
1968 Arms £1
1975 Arms £1
1979 (dated 1975 on thick flan) £2
1980 — £1
1980 — Proof £5
1981 - £1
1981 — Proof £5
1983 L'Hermitage £1
1983 — Silver proof £5
1984 — £1
1985 — £1
1986 — £1
1987 — £1
1988 — £1
1989 — £1
1990 — £1
1992 — £1
1997 — £1
2002 — £1
2003 — £1
2005 — £1
2006 — £1
2007 — £1

FIVE PENCE
1968 Arms £1
1980 — £1
1981 — £1
1981 — Proof £2
1983 Seymour Towers £1
1983 — Silver proof £5
1984 — £1
1985 — £1
1986 — £1
1987 — £2
1988 — £1
1990 — £1
1991 — £1
1992 — £5
1993 — £1
1997 — £4
1998 — £1
2002 — £1
2003 — £1
2005 — £5
2006 — £1
2008 — £1

Other denominations are generally available at face value or a small premium above.

ALDERNEY

DATE   UNC

ONE THOUSAND POUNDS
2003 Concorde. Gold proof..   —
2004 D-Day Anniversary. Gold proof..   —

ONE HUNDRED POUNDS
1994 50th Anniversary of D-Day Landings. Gold proof £280
2003 Prince Wiliam. Gold proof (100mm) ....   —
2005 Trafalgar Anniversary. Gold proof (100mm) ....   —

FIFTY POUNDS
1994 50th Anniversary of D–Day Landing. Gold proof............................. £500
2003 Anniversay of Coronation (4 types). Silver proof ea. (100mm) £500
2003 Prince William. Silver proof (100mm)................................. £500
2004 Anniversary of D-Day. Silver proof (100mm) £500
2005 200th Anniversary of the Battle of Trafalgar. Silver proof (100mm) ... £500

TWENTY FIVE POUNDS
1993 40th Anniversary of Coronation. Gold proof.................................... £160
1994 50th Anniversary of D-Day Landings. Gold proof £160
1997 Royal Golden Wedding. Gold proof £295
1997 — Silver proof £40
1999 Winston Churcill. Gold proof £350
2000 Queen Mother. Gold proof.. £325
2000 60th Anniversary of the Battle of Britain. Gold proof £275
2001 Royal Birthday. Gold proof £300
2002 Golden Jubilee. Gold proof £295
2002 Princess Diana. Gold proof £295
2002 Duke of Wellington. Gold proof £300
2003 Prince William. Gold proof.. £300
2003 HMS Mary Rose. Gold proof... £300
2004 D-Day Anniversary. Gold proof.. £395
2004 The Rocket. Gold proof.. £295
2004 Merchant Navy Class Locomotive. Gold proof £295
2005 Battle of SAints Passage. Gold proof.. £295
2006 World Cup 2006 (4 Coins). Gold ea................................. £350

TEN POUNDS
1994 50th Anniversary of D–Day Landing. Gold proof.................... £150
2003 Concorde. Silver proof (65mm) £280
2005 60th Anniversary of the Liberation of the Channel Islands (65mm)... £250
2007 80th Birthday of Her Majesty the Queen (65mm)............................ £180
2008 Concorde. Silver proof £180
2008 90th Anniversary of the end of WWI. Silver Proof £180
2009 50th Anniversary of the Mini—Silver with colour.............................. £180

FIVE POUNDS
1995 Queen Mother £15
1995 — Silver proof... £50
1995 — Silver piedfort... £155
1995 — Gold proof... £900
1996 HM the Queen's 70th Birthday £18
1996 — Silver proof... £60
1996 — Silver piedfort... £150
1996 — Gold proof... £895
1999 Eclipse of the Sun £25
1999 — Silver proof with colour centre.. £55
1999 Winston Churchill. Gold proof £895
2000 60th Anniversary of the Battle of Britain............................. £22
2000 — Silver proof... £55
2000 Queen Mother. 100th Birthday. Silver proof £50
2000 Millennium. Silver proof.. £35

289

DATE	UNC
2001 HM Queen's 75th Birthday.	£15
2001 — Silver proof.	£45
2002 Golden Jubilee. Silver proof	£50
2002 50 Years of Reign.	£15
2002 —Silver proof.	£50
2002 Diana memorial	£15
2002 — Silver proof.	£45
2002 — Gold proof.	£900
2002 Duke of Wellington	£20
2002 — Silver proof.	£50
2002 — Gold proof.	£900
2003 Prince William	£20
2003 — Silver proof.	£50
2003 — Gold proof.	£900
2003 Mary Rose	£18
2003 — Silver proof.	£120
2003 Alfred the Great. Silver proof	£150
2003 —Gold proof.	£300
2003 Last Flight of Concorde	£25
2003 — Silver proof.	£150
2003 — Gold proof.	£395
2004 Anniversary of D-Day	£20
2004 — Silver proof.	£75
2004 — Gold proof.	£395
2004 Florence Nightingale	318
2004 — Silver proof.	£45
2004 150th Anniversary of the Crimean War	£20
2004 — Silver proof.	£45
2004 — Gold proof.	£395
2004 The Rocket	£20
2004 — Silver proof.	£45
2004 — Gold proof.	£875
2004 Royal Scot	£20
2004 — Silver proof.	£45
2004 Merchant Navy Class Locomotive	£20
2004 — Silver proof.	£45
2005 End of WWII. Silver proof	£45
2005 — Gold proof.	£875
2005 200th Anniversary of the Battle of Trafalgar	£16
2005 — Silver proof.	£50
2005 History of the Royal Navy. John Woodward. Silver proof	£30
2005 Anniversary of Liberation. Gold proof	£780
2005 Anniversary of the Battle of Saints Passage	£15
2005 — Silver proof.	£45
2005 HMS Revenge 1591	£15
2005 — Silver proof.	£45
2006 80th Birthday of Her Majesty the Queen (3-coin set) ea	£20
2006 Gold plated portraits of Her Majesty the Queen	—
2006 80th Birthday of Her Majesty the Queen (3-coin set) ea	£16
2007 History of the Royal Navy—*Mary Rose* (2 coins) ea	£16
2007 150th Anniversary of the Victoria Cross (18 coin set). Silver proof	—
2007 Monarchs of England (12 coin set). Gold plated	—
2008 90th Anniversary of the end of WWI (3 coins). Gold proof	—
2008 Classic British Motorcars (18 coin set). Silver proof.	—
2008 Concorde. Gold proof.	£300
2009 50th Anniversary of the Mini (4 coins). Silver proof ea.	£25
2011 Royal Engagement gold proof.	£300
2011 — Gold plated silver proof	£150
2011 — Silver proof.	£55
2011 — Curpro Nickel	£15
2011 John Lennon Silver proof	£55
2011 Battle of Britain 70th Anniversary silver proof	£55

TWO POUNDS

1989 Royal Visit	£12
1989 — Silver proof.	£25

DATE	UNC
1989 — Silver piedfort	£45
1989 — Gold proof	£1200
1990 Queen Mother's 90th Birthday	£12
1990 — Silver proof	£25
1990 — Silver piedfort	£45
1990 — Gold proof	£1200
1992 40th Anniversary of Accession	£15
1992 — Silver proof	£35
1992 — Silver piedfort	£50
1992 — Gold proof	£1200
1993 40th Anniversary of Coronation	£15
1993 — Silver proof	£35
1993 — Silver piedfort	£50
1994 50th Anniversary of D-Day Landings	£15
1994 — Silver proof	£35
1994 — Silver piedfort	£50
1995 50th Anniversary of Return of Islanders	£15
1995 — Silver proof	£35
1995 — Silver piedfort	£50
1995 — Gold proof	£1200
1997 WWF Puffin	£18
1997 — Silver proof	£35
1997 Royal Golden Wedding	£20
1997 — Silver proof	£50
1999 Eclipse of the Sun. Silver	£20
1999 — Silver proof	£50
1999 — Gold proof	£1250
2000 Millennium. Silver proof	£50

ONE POUND

1993 40th Anniversary of Coronation Silver proof	£50
1995 50th Anniversary of VE Day Silver proof	£45
1995 — Gold proof	£500
2008 Concorde. Gold proof	£275
2009 50th Anniversary of the Mini. Gold proof	£375

Alderney's coinage is often issued as part of a set incorporating coins from other countries. Illustrated is the special set issued to mark the 90th Anniversary of the end of World War I which also included coins from the Cayman and Solomon Islands as well as Alderney.

IRELAND

As in the English hammered section (q.v.) the prices given here are for the most common coins in the series. For a more specialised listing the reader is referred to *Coincraft's Standard Catalogue of Scotland, Ireland, Channel Islands & Isle of Man*, or other specialised publications. Collectors should be aware that with most of the coins of the Irish series there are many varieties struck at different mints. The coins listed are all silver unless mentioned otherwise. Another important factor to consider when collecting early Irish coins is that few examples exist in high grades.

	F	VF
HIBERNO-NORSE ISSUES (995–1155)		
Penny, imitating English silver pennies, many various types	£210	£475

A typical Hiberno-Norse period example.

JOHN, Lord of Ireland (1185–99)

	F	VF
Halfpenny, profile		Extremely rare
Halfpenny, facing	£95	£250
Farthing	£360	£975

JOHN de COURCY, Lord of Ulster (1177–1205)

	F	VF
Halfpenny		Extremely rare
Farthing	£675	£2750

John Lord of Ireland halfpenny.

JOHN as King of England and Lord of Ireland (c. 1199–1216)

	F	VF
Penny	£65	£250
Halfpenny	£150	£385
Farthing	£650	£2000

HENRY III (1216–72)

	F	VF
Penny	£65	£275

EDWARD I (1272–1307)

	F	VF
Penny	£65	£275
Halfpenny	£65	£275
Farthing	£140	£385

Henry III penny.

No Irish coins were struck for Edward II (1307–27).

EDWARD III (1327–77)

Halfpenny	Extremely rare

No Irish coins were struck for Richard II (1377–99), Henry IV (1399–1413) or Henry V (1413–22).

HENRY VI (1422–61)

Penny	Extremely rare

Edward III halfpenny.

	F	VF

EDWARD IV (1461–83)

	F	VF
"Anonymous crown" groat	£650	£12500
— penny	£1100	—
"Titled crown" groat	£1600	—
— halfgroat		Extremely rare
— penny		Extremely rare
Cross on rose/Sun groat	£1750	—
Bust/Rose on sun double groat	£2250	£6500
— groat	£2250	—
— halfgroat		Extremely rare
— penny		Extremely rare
Bust/Cross & pellets groat—First issue	£125	£425
— halfgroat	£575	£1500
— penny	£75	£285
— halfpenny		Extremely rare
— Second (light) issue	£100	£375
— halfgroat	£575	£1400
— penny	£90	£200
— halfpenny		Extremely rare
Bust/Rose on cross groat	£475	£1250
— penny	£65	£165

Edward IV groat.
"Anonymous crown"
issue.

Billon/Copper issues

	F	VF
Small crown/Cross farthing (1460–61)	£1625	—
— half farthing ("Patrick")	£1050	—
Large crown/Cross farthing (1462)		Extremely rare
Patricius/Salvator farthing (1463–65)	£350	£1950
— half farthing		Extremely rare
Shield/Rose on sun farthing	£175	£800

Edward IV penny.
"Anonymous crown"
issue.

RICHARD III (1483–85)

	F	VF
Bust/Rose on cross groat	£1100	£3750
— halfgroat		Unique
— penny		Unique
Bust/Cross and pellets penny	£100	£2850
Shield/Three-crowns groat	£625	£2500

HENRY VII (1485–1509)

Early issues (1483–90)

	F	VF
Shield/Three crowns groat	£150	£450
— halfgroat	£260	£585
— penny	£625	£2200
— halfpenny		Extremely rare

Richard III bust/rose
on cross groat.

Later issues (1488–90)

	F	VF
Shield/Three crowns groat	£100	£345
— halfgroat	£200	£595
— penny	£500	£1200
Facing bust groat (1496–1505)	£125	£345
— halfgroat	£1100	—
— penny	£950	—

LAMBERT SIMNEL
(as EDWARD VI, Pretender, 1487)

	F	VF
Shield/Three crowns groat	£1150	£3950

Henry VII "three
crowns" half groat.

	F	VF

HENRY VIII (1509–47)

	F	VF
"Harp" groat	£90	£280
— halfgroat	£475	£2200

The "Harp" coins have crowned initials either side of the reverse harp,
e.g. HR (Henricus Rex), HA (Henry and Anne Boleyn), HI (Henry and Jane
Seymour), HK (Henry and Katherine Howard).

Posthumous (Portrait) issues
Sixpence	£140	£465
Threepence	£150	£500
Threehalfpence	£510	£1650
Threefarthings	£650	£1900

Henry VIII "harp" halfgroat.

EDWARD VI (1547–53)

Shilling (base silver) 1552 (MDLII)	£900	£3250
Brass contemporary copy	£90	£365

MARY (1553–54)

Shilling 1553 (MDLIII)	£850	£3200
Shilling 1554 (MDLIIII)		Extremely rare
Groat		Extremely rare
Halfgroat		Extremely rare
Penny		Extremely rare

Mary Tudor shilling.

PHILIP & MARY (1554–58)

Shilling	£350	£1325
Groat	£100	£325
Penny		Extremely rare

ELIZABETH I (1558–1603)

Base silver portrait coinage
Shilling	£350	£1300
Groat	£180	£650

Fine silver, portrait coinage (1561)
Shilling	£270	£850
Groat	£325	£1100

Third (base silver) shield coinage
Shilling	£200	£650
Sixpence	£150	£450

Copper
Threepence	£200	£650
Penny	£60	£175
Halfpenny	£100	£285

Reverse of a "fine" Elizabeth I shilling.

JAMES I (1603–25)

Shilling	£100	£365
Sixpence	£75	£225

Coins struck under Royal Licence from 1613

"Harrington" farthing (small size)	£55	£185
"Harrington" farthing (large size)	£50	£160
"Lennox" farthing	£50	£160

James I sixpence.

CHARLES I (1625–49)

During the reign of Charles I and the Great Rebellion many coins were struck under unusual circumstances, making the series a difficult but fascinating area for study. Many of the "coins" were simply made from odd-shaped pieces of plate struck with the weight or value.

	F	VF
Coins struck under Royal Licence from 1625		
"Richmond" farthing..............................	£45	£130
"Maltravers" farthing	£55	£185
"Rose" farthing	£45	£160

Charles I "Maltravers" farthing.

Siege money of the Irish Rebellion, 1642–49

"Inchiquin" Money (1642)		
Crown...	£2100	£5650
Halfcrown	£1800	£4800
Shilling...		Extremely rare
Ninepence		Extremely rare
Sixpence...		Extremely rare
Groat...		Extremely rare

"Dublin" Money (1643)		
Crown...	£890	£3200
Halfcrown	£600	£2500

"Ormonde" Money (1643–44)		
Crown...	£500	£1250
Halfcrown	£325	£920
Shilling...	£130	£435
Sixpence...	£130	£435
Groat...	£120	£320
Threepence...	£110	£275
Twopence	£450	£1250

Coinage of the Great Rebellion—a "Dublin Money" crown.

"Ormonde" gold coinage (1646)		
Double pistole. 2 known (both in museums)		Extremely rare
Pistole. 10 known (only 1 in private ownership		Extremely rare

"Ormonde" money threepence.

"Ormonde" Money (1649)		
Crown...		Extremely rare
Halfcrown	£1200	£3650

Dublin Money 1649		
Crown...	£2800	£7575
Halfcrown	£2200	£4500

Issues of the Confederated Catholics

Kilkenny issues (1642–43)		
Halfpenny	£265	£825
Farthing	£390	£1100

Rebel Money (1643–44)		
Crown...	£2500	£5200
Halfcrown	£2850	£5200

Kilkenny halfpenny.

	F	VF
"Blacksmith's" Money (16??)		
Imitation of English Tower halfcrown.....	£650	£3000

Local Town issues of "Cities of Refuge"

Bandon

Farthing (copper)		Extremely rare

Cork

Shilling..		Extremely rare
Sixpence...	£750	£1200
Halfpenny (copper)		Extremely rare
Farthing (copper)	£560	—

Kinsale

Farthing (copper)	£400	—

Youghal

Farthing (copper)	£490	£1650

"Cork" countermarked on a copper coin.

CHARLES II (1660–85)

	Fair	F	VF	EF
"Armstrong" coinage				
Farthing (1660–61).................................	£65	£235	—	—
"St Patrick's" coinage				
Halfpenny	£225	£465	—	—
Farthing	£65	£165	£500	£1350
Legg's Regal coinage				
Halfpennies				
1680 large lettering...............................	£35	£90	£275	—
1681 large lettering...............................	—	£195	£625	—
1681 small lettering		Extremely rare		
1682 small lettering	—	£195	£625	—
1683 small lettering	£30	£40	£375	
1684 small lettering	£40	£110	£620	—

"St Patrick" farthing of Charles II.

JAMES II (1685–88)

REGAL COINAGE

Halfpennies

1685..	£22	£75	£300	£675
1686..	£22	£60	£200	£575
1687..		Extremely rare		
1688..	£22	£75	£300	£1200

297

	Fair	F	VF	EF

EMERGENCY COINAGE

GUN MONEY
Most of these coins were struck in gun metal but a few rare specimens are also known struck in gold and in silver

Crowns

	Fair	F	VF	EF
1690 (many varieties)......................from	£45	£60	£520	—

"Gun Money" crown.

Large halfcrowns
Dated July 1689–May 1690

	Fair	F	VF	EF
Prices from	£35	£60	£195	—

Small halfcrowns
Dated April–October1690

Prices from	£35	£60	£195	—

Large shillings
Dated from July 1689–April 1690

Prices from	£35	£55	£120	£420

Small shillings
Dated from April–September 1690

Prices from	£25	£35	£120	£395

Sixpences
Dated from June 1689–October 1690

Prices from	£35	£60	£220	—

"Gun Money" shilling (large size).

PEWTER MONEY (1689–90)

	Fair	F	VF	EF
Crown...	£700	£1100	£2850	—
Groat..		Extremely rare		
Penny large bust....................................	£230	£650	—	—
— small bust	£165	£485	£1350	—
Halfpenny large bust	£130	£325	£700	—
— small bust	£110	£225	£675	—

LIMERICK MONEY (1690–91)

	Fair	F	VF	EF
Halfpenny, reversed N in HIBERNIA......	£35	£75	£245	—
Farthing, reversed N in HIBERNIA.........	£35	£75	£245	—
— normal N	£45	£100	£275	—

WILLIAM & MARY (1688–94)

Halfpennies

	Fair	F	VF	EF
1692...	£12	£40	£100	£575
1693...	£12	£40	£85	£575
1694...	£17	£45	£110	£645

Reverse of a "Pewter Money" penny.

WILLIAM III (1694–1702)

	Fair	F	VF	EF
1696 Halfpenny draped bust.................	£35	£65	£220	—
1696 — crude undraped bust	£45	£265	£800	—

No Irish coins were struck during the reign of Queen Anne (1706–11).

DATE	F	VF	EF	UNC

GEORGE I (1714–27)

Farthings

1722 D.G. REX Harp to left (Pattern)..............	£650	£1550	£2300	—
1723 D.G. REX Harp to right	£120	£225	£500	—
1723 DEI GRATIA REX Harp to right	£35	£65	£200	£550
1723 — Silver Proof	—	—	—	£2000
1724 DEI GRATIA REX Harp to right	£60	£130	£350	£800

Halfpennies

1722 Holding Harp left	£55	£130	£385	£900
1722 Holding Harp right	£45	£110	£350	£775
1723/2 Harp right	£50	£120	£350	£775
1723 Harp right	£25	£65	£200	£495
1723 Silver Proof..	—	—	—	£3250
1723 Obv. Rs altered from Bs	£35	£100	£265	—
1723 No stop after date	£25	£80	£265	£425
1724 Rev. legend divided	£40	£100	£300	—
1724 Rev. legend continuous........................	£40	£110	£375	—

Farthing of George I.

GEORGE II (1727–60)

Farthings

1737...	£35	£60	£175	£400
1737 Proof	—	—	—	£420
1737 Silver Proof..............................	—	—	—	£895
1738...	£35	£65	£165	£410
1744...	£35	£65	£165	£410
1760	£30	£45	£100	£320

Halfpennies

1736...	£25	£60	£200	£425
1736 Proof	—	—	—	£595
1736 Silver Proof..............................	—	—	—	£1200
1737...	£25	£45	£175	—
1738...	£30	£60	£200	—
1741...	£30	£60	£200	—
1742...	£30	£60	£200	—
1743...	£30	£60	£180	—
1744/3	£30	£60	£185	—
1744...	£30	£60	£300	—
1746...	£30	£60	£225	—
1747...	£30	£60	£225	—
1748...	£30	£60	£225	—
1749...	£30	£60	£225	—
1750...	£30	£60	£225	—
1751...	£30	£60	£225	—
1752...	£30	£60	£225	—
1753...	£30	£60	£225	—
1755...	£30	£100	£315	—
*1760	£25	£55	£195	—

Halfpenny of George II

GEORGE III (1760–1820)

All copper unless otherwise stated

Pennies

1805...	£17	£40	£180	£395
1805 Proof.......................................	—	—	—	£545
1805 in Bronze Proof.......................	—	—	—	£545
1805 in Copper Gilt Proof.................	—	—	—	£545
1805 in Silver Proof (restrike)...........	—	—	—	£3000
1822...	£17	£40	£180	£395

DATE	F	VF	EF	UNC
1822 Proof...	—	—	—	£545
1823..	£12	£25	£150	£365
1823 Proof...	—	—	—	£545

Halfpennies

	F	VF	EF	UNC
1766..	£30	£55	£165	—
1769..	£30	£55	£165	—
1769 Longer bust	£40	£75	£200	£575
1774 Pattern only Proof..............................	—	—	—	£1850
1775..	£30	£55	£200	£420
1775 Proof	—	—	—	£610
1776..	£55	£140	£400	—
1781..	£45	£60	£165	£395
1782..	£45	£60	£165	£395
1805..	£18	£45	£120	£395
1805 Copper Proof.....................................	—	—	—	£395
1805 in Bronze	—	—	—	£275
1805 in Gilt Copper	—	—	—	£410
1805 in Silver (restrike)	—	—	—	£1775
1822..	£18	£40	£120	£395
1822 Proof...	—	—	—	£595
1823..	£18	£40	£120	£395
1823 Proof...	—	—	—	£625

1806 farthing

NB Prooflike Uncirculated Pennies and Halfpennies of 1822/23 are often misdescribed as Proofs. The true Proofs are rare. Some are on heavier, thicker flans.

Farthings

	F	VF	EF	UNC
1806..	£18	£35	£75	£165
1806 Copper Proof.....................................	—	—	—	£320
1806 Bronzed Copper Proof	—	—	—	£220
1806 Copper Gilt Proof	—	—	—	£325
1806 Silver Proof (restrike)	—	—	—	£1000
1822 George IV (Pattern) Proof	—	—	—	£1650

TOKEN ISSUES BY THE BANK OF IRELAND
Five Pence in Silver

	F	VF	EF	UNC
1805..	£30	£45	£75	£320
1806..	£30	£65	£150	£345
1806/5	£55	£140	£450	£1250

Ten Pence in Silver

	F	VF	EF	UNC
1805..	£17	£35	£95	£210
1806..	£17	£60	£150	£250
1813..	£17	£35	£90	£245
1813 Proof...	—	—	—	£410

Thirty Pence in Silver

	F	VF	EF	UNC
1808..	£35	£95	£220	£550

Six Shillings

	F	VF	EF	UNC
1804 in Silver..	£95	£200	£400	£1675
1804 Proof...	—	—	—	£1700
1804 in Copper (restrike)	—	—	—	£700
1804 Copper Gilt	—	—	—	£1650
1804 in Gilt Silver	—	—	—	£2850

In this series fully struck specimens, with sharp hair curls, etc., are worth appreciably more than the prices quoted.

DATE	F	VF	EF	UNC

TEN SHILLINGS

	F	VF	EF	UNC
1966 Easter Rising	—	£12	£17	£35
1966 Cased Proof	—	—	—	£40
1966 special double case	—	—	—	£70

HALF CROWNS

	F	VF	EF	UNC
1928	£7	£12	£40	£80
1928 Proof	—	—	—	£85
1930	£12	£35	£130	£495
1931	£12	£35	£165	£530
1933	£12	£25	£165	£430
1934	£12	£12	£55	£250
1937	£60	£150	£600	£1600
1938				Unique
1939	£7	£17	£30	£95
1939 Proof	—	—	—	£635
1940	£8	£13	£35	£85
1941	£7	£17	£35	£85
1942	£7	£130	£35	£80
1943	£85	£200	£925	£3300
1951	£2	£3	£17	£50
1951 Proof	—	—	—	£500
1954	£2	£3	£9	£75
1954 Proof	—	—	—	£500
1955	£2	£3	£9	£45
1955	—	—	—	£590
1959	£2	£3	£12	£45
1961	£2	£3	£25	£55
1961 Obv as 1928, rev. as 1951	£30	£60	£300	—
1962	£2	£3	£6	£32
1963	£2	£3	£6	£25
1964	£2	£3	£6	£25
1966	£2	£3	£6	£25
1967	£2	£3	£6	£25

FLORINS

	F	VF	EF	UNC
1928	£3	£6	£25	£55
1928 Proof	—	—	—	£70
1930	£4	£12	£140	£445
1930 Proof				Unique
1931	£5	£19	£170	£445
1933	£4	£17	£140	£445
1934	£6	£110	£240	£695
1934 Proof	—	—	—	£3000
1935	£3	£12	£65	£190
1937	£6	£25	£140	£400
1939	£2	£6	£35	£75
1939 Proof	—	—	—	£650
1940	£3	£6	£30	£75
1941	£3	£6	£35	£70
1941 Proof	—	—	—	£800
1942	£6	£12	£30	£75
1943	£2675	£5250	£9500	£22200
1951	60p	£2	£12	£45
1951 Proof	—	—	—	£475
1954	60p	£2	£9	£40
1954 Proof	—	—	—	£375

DATE	F	VF	EF	UNC
1955..	—	£2	£6	£40
1955 Proof.....................................	—	—	—	£545
1959..	40p	£2	£6	£35
1961..	60p	£3	£13	£50
1962..	40p	£2	£6	£25
1963..	30p	£2	£6	£20
1964..	30p	£2	£6	£20
1965..	30p	£2	£6	£20
1966..	30p	£2	£6	£20
1968..	30p	£2	£6	£20

SHILLINGS

	F	VF	EF	UNC
1928..	£2	£6	£17	£40
1928 Proof.....................................	—	—	—	£70
1930..	£6	£25	£95	£445
1930 Proof.....................................	—	—	—	£845
1931..	£3	£17	£95	£430
1933..	£3	£17	£95	£425
1935..	£3	£13	£50	£150
1937..	£6	£60	£220	£1200
1939..	£2	£6	£25	£60
1939 Proof.....................................	—	—	—	£700
1940..	£2	£6	£17	£55
1941..	£2	£5	£17	£55
1942..	£2	£5	£12	£40
1951..	60p	£2	£6	£25
1951 Proof.....................................	—	—	—	£435
1954..	60p	£2	£6	£25
1954 Proof.....................................	—	—	—	£500
1955..	60p	£2	£6	£25
1959..	60p	£2	£6	£35
1962..	30p	£2	£3	£20
1963..	30p	£2	£3	£12
1964..	30p	£2	£3	£12
1966..	30p	£2	£3	£12
1968..	30p	£2	£3	£12

SIXPENCES

	F	VF	EF	UNC
1928..	60p	£2	£11	£40
1928 Proof.....................................	—	—	—	£50
1934..	60p	£3	£17	£90
1935..	85p	£3	£25	£125
1939..	60p	£2	£6	£50
1939 Proof.....................................	—	—	—	£635
1940..	60p	£2	£6	£50
1942..	60p	£2	£9	£60
1945	£3	£11	£35	£95
1946..	£3	£6	£65	£400
1947..	£2	£2	£22	£75
1948..	60p	£3	£13	£65
1949..	60p	£2	£8	£45
1950..	£2	£3	£25	£95
1952..	60p	£2	£4	£20
1953..	60p	£2	£4	£20
1953 Proof.....................................	—	—	—	£115
1955..	60p	£2	£4	£22
1956..	60p	£2	£3	£22
1956 Proof.....................................	—	—	—	£165
1958..	£2	£3	£11	£65
1958 Proof.....................................	—	—	—	£375
1959..	30p	60p	£3	£15
1960..	30p	60p	£2	£15

DATE	F	VF	EF	UNC
1961	—	£2	£3	£20
1962	£2	£6	£30	£70
1963	60p	£3	£6	£15
1964	60p	£2	£4	£10
1966	60p	£2	£4	£10
1967	60p	£2	£2	£8
1968	60p	£2	£2	£8
1969	£2	£3	£6	£15

THREEPENCES

	F	VF	EF	UNC
1928	£2	£3	£9	£30
1928 Proof	—	—	—	£40
1933	£3	£13	£70	£365
1934	70p	£3	£10	£75
1935	£2	£4	£30	£225
1939	£3	£7	£60	£365
1939 Proof	—	—	—	£1150
1940	£2	£3	£13	£60
1942	—	£2	£6	£45
1943	£2	£3	£13	£75
1946	—	£1	£6	£40
1946 Proof	—	—	—	£270
1948	£2	£3	£25	£75
1949	—	£2	£6	£35
1949 Proof	—	—	—	£235
1950	—	£2	£6	£20
1950 Proof	—	—	—	£225
1953	—	£2	£4	£15
1956	—	£2	£3	£8
1961	—	60p	£2	£5
1962	—	60p	£2	£8
1963	—	60p	£2	£8
1964	—	60p	£2	£5
1965	—	60p	£2	£5
1966	—	60p	£2	£5
1967	—	60p	£2	£5
1968	—	—	£2	£5

PENNIES

	F	VF	EF	UNC
1928	£2	£3	£11	£40
1928 Proof	—	—	—	£55
1931	£2	£4	£35	£115
1931 Proof	—	—	—	£950
1933	£2	£5	£50	£225
1935	60p	£2	£25	£70
1937	90p	£2	£35	£120
1937 Proof	—	—	—	£950
1938				2 known
1940	£6	£30	£140	—
1941	60p	£2	£9	£30
1942	—	60p	£4	£15
1943	—	£2	£6	£30
1946	—	£2	£4	£15
1948	—	£2	£4	£15
1949	—	£2	£4	£15
1949 Proof	—	—	—	£395
1950	—	£2	£6	£30
1952	—	£2	£4	£10
1962	—	£2	£4	£12
1962 Proof	—	—	—	£165
1963	—	—	£2	£10
1963 Proof	—	—	—	£100

DATE	F	VF	EF	UNC
1964..	—	—	£2	£8
1965..	—	—	60p	£5
1966..	—	—	60p	£4
1967	—	—	60p	£4
1968..	—	—	60p	£4
1968 Proof..............................	—	—	—	£245

HALFPENNIES

	F	VF	EF	UNC
1928..	£2	£3	£12	£32
1928 Proof..............................	—	—	—	£40
1933..	£6	£17	£65	£500
1935..	£3	£6	£30	£160
1937..	£2	£4	£12	£50
1939..	£3	£6	£35	£175
1939 Proof..............................	—	—	—	£850
1940..	£2	£4	£50	£180
1941..	60p	£2	£6	£25
1942..	60p	£2	£6	£25
1943..	60p	£2	£7	£30
1946..	£2	£3	£17	£70
1949..	60p	£2	£6	£25
1953..	—	£2	£3	£10
1953 Proof..............................	—	—	—	£495
1964..	—	—	60p	£3
1965..	—	—	90p	£4
1966..	—	—	60p	£3
1967..	—	—	60p	£3

FARTHINGS

	F	VF	EF	UNC
1928..	£3	£4	£9	£15
1928 Proof..............................	—	—	—	£45
1930..	£3	£4	£9	£30
1931..	£4	£6	£14	£35
1931 Proof..............................	—	—	—	£845
1932..	£4	£6	£17	£45
1933	£3	£4	£12	£30
1935..	£4	£6	£17	£35
1936..	£4	£6	£17	£35
1937..	£3	£4	£12	£30
1939..	£3	£4	£6	£15
1939 Proof..............................	—	—	—	£595
1940..	£4	£5	£8	£20
1941	£3	£4	£6	£12
1943..	£3	£4	£6	£12
1944	£3	£4	£6	£12
1946..	£3	£4	£6	£12
1949..	£4	£6	£8	£25
1949 Proof..............................	—	—	—	£450
1953..	£3	£4	£5	£8
1953 Proof..............................	—	—	—	£315
1959..	£3	£4	£5	£10
1966	£3	£4	£5	£10

For the 1928–50 copper issues it is worth noting that UNC means UNC with some lustre. BU examples with full lustre are extremely elusive and are worth much more than the quoted prices.

IRISH DECIMAL COINAGE

DATE	MINTAGE	BU

HALF PENCE

1971	100,500,000	£5
1975	10,500,000	£6
1976	5,500,000	£6
1978	20,300,000	£5
1980	20,600,000	£4
1982	9,700,000	£4
1985	2,800,000	Rare
1986. Only issued in the 1986 set	19,750,000	£325

ONE PENNY

1971	100,500,000	£3
1974	10,000,000	£10
1975	10,000,000	£15
1976	38,200,000	£5
1978	25,700,000	£8
1979	21,800,000	£10
1980	86,700,000	£3
1982	54,200,000	£5
1985	19,200,000	£8
1986	36,600,000	£5
1988	56,800,000	£5
1990	65,100,000	£5
1992	25,600,000	£6
1993	10,000,000	£6
1994	45,800,000	£5
1995	70,800,000	£3
1996	190,100,000	95p
1998	40,700,000	95p
2000	Unknown	95p

TWO PENCE

1971	75,500,000	£3
1975	20,000,000	£8
1976	5400,000	£10
1978	12,000,000	£10
1979	32,400,000	£8
1980	59,800,000	£6
1982	30,400,000	£5
1985	14,500,000	£6
1986	23,900,000	£6
1988	35,900,000	£5
1990	34,300,000	£5
1992	10,200,000	£8
1995	55,500,000	£5
1996	69,300,000	£2
1998	33,700,000	£2
2000	Unknown	95p

FIVE PENCE

1969 Toned	5,000,000	£5
1970	10,000,000	£5
1971	8,000,000	£6
1974	7,000,000	£8
1975	10,000,000	£8
1976	20,600,000	£5
1978	28,500,000	£5
1980	22,200,000	£5
1982	24,400,000	£4
1985	4,200,000	£8
1986	15,300,000	£5
1990	7,500,000	£5

DATE	MINTAGE	BU
Size reduced to 18.4mm		
1992	74,500,000	£5
1993	89,100,000	£5
1994	31,100,000	£5
1995	12,000,000	£5
1996	14,700,000	£2
1998	158,500,000	75p
2000	Unknown	75p

TEN PENCE

1969	27,000,000	£8
1971	4,000,000	£10
1973	2,500,000	£16
1974	7,500,000	£12
1975	15,000,000	£12
1976	9,400,000	£12
1978	30,900,000	£10
1980	44,600,000	£7
1982	7,400,000	£7
1985	4,100,000	£8
1986. Only issued in the 1986 set	11,280	£265

Size reduced to 22mm		
1993	80,100,000	£5
1994	58,500,000	£5
1995	16,100,000	£5
1996	18,400,000	£3
1997	10,000,000	£3
1998	10,000,000	£3
1999	24,500,000	£2
2000	Unknown	£1.50

TWENTY PENCE
1985. Only 600 minted and 556 melted down, only 3 known		Extremely rare
1986	50,400,000	£6
1988	20,700,000	£6
1992	14,800,000	£5
1994	11,100,000	£5
1995	18,200,000	£5
1996	29,300,000	£5
1998	25,000,000	£3
1999	11,000,000	£3
2000	Unknown	£2

FIFTY PENCE
1970	9,000,000	£7
1971	650,000	£6
1974	1,000,000	£55
1975	2,000,000	£55
1976	3,000,000	£45
1977	4,800,000	£55
1978	4,500,000	£45
1979	4,000,000	£45
1981	6,000,000	£25
1982	2,000,000	£25
1983	7,000,000	£25
1986. Only issued in the 1986 set	10,000	£295
1988	7,000,000	£5
1988 Dublin Millennium	5,000,000	£5
1988 — Proof	50,000	£25
1996	6,000,000	£7
1997	6,000,000	£7
1998	13,800,000	£5
1999	7,000,000	£4
2000	Unknown	£4

ONE POUND
1990	42,300,000	£5
1990 Proof	50,000	£25
1994	14,900,000	£5
1995	9,200,000	£5
1995 UN silver proof in case of issue	2,850	£175
1996	9,200,000	£5
1998	22,960,000	£4
1999	10,000,000	£5
2000	4,000,000	£5
2000 Millennium	5,000,000	£5
2000 – Silver Proof Piedfort	90,000	£35

OFFICIAL COIN SETS ISSUED BY THE CENTRAL BANK
1971 Specimen set in green wallet. 6 coins	£16
1975 6 coin set	£55
1978 6 coin set	£55
1978 6 coin set. Black cover, scarce	£75
1982 6 coin set. Black cover	£75
1986 Specimen set in card folder 1/2p to 50p, 7 coins. Very scarce. Most sets have glue problems	£600
1996 7 coin set	£55
1998 7 coin set	£50
2000 Millennium set. Last decimal set	£125
2000 — With 1999 instead of the 2000 £1 coin	£245

The world's only magazine devoted to Medals and Battles

Medal News

Subscribing is easy!

Call 01404 44166

Complete the order form and send it to—
Token Publishing Ltd,
Orchard House,
Duchy Road, Heathpark,
Honiton, Devon, EX14 1YD

Complete the order form and fax it to 01404 44788

log on to
www.tokenpublishing.com

Subscription Rates
UK £35,
Europe/World Surface £42,
Rest of World Airmail £52

Save money when you take out a subscription to *Medal News* for either yourself or a friend. Pay just £35 for 10 issues, or £17.50 for 5 issues, save money on the cover price and enjoy having the world's only magazine devoted to medals and battles delivered to your door before it goes on sale in the newsagents!

Subscriber Benefits

- **FREE** delivery before the magazine goes on sale in the newsagents
- **FREE** classified advertising for all non-trade subscribers
- **FREE** medal tracker for subscribers—find those missing medals
- Never miss an issue!
- **FREE** online version of Medal News to subscribers, with direct links to dealers websites!

(Digital version available separately—see below)

View your monthly magazine on-line at work, on the train, on your phone and never miss out on that bargain again!

OFFICIAL AND SEMI-OFFICIAL COMMEMORATIVE MEDALS

It is probably a strong love of history, rather than the strict disciplines of coin collecting that make collectors turn to commemorative medals. The link between the two is intertwined, and it is to be hoped that collectors will be encouraged to venture into the wider world of medallions, encouraged by this brief guide, originally supplied by Daniel Fearon (author of the *Catalogue of British Commemorative Medals)* and kindly updated again this year by Charles Riley.

DATE	VF	EF

JAMES I
1603 Coronation (possibly by
  C. Anthony), 29mm, Silver £1200   £1170

QUEEN ANNE
1603 Coronation, 29mm, AR.............................. £650   £1100

CHARLES I
1626 Coronation (by N. Briot), 30mm, Silver....... £750   £1000
1633 Scottish Coronation (by N. Briot), 28mm,
  Silver.. £450   £750
1649 Memorial (by J. Roettier). Struck after the
  Restoration, 50mm, Bronze £120   £275

James I Coronation, 1603

CHARLES II
1651 Scottish Coronation, in exile (from design
  by Sir J. Balfour), 32mm, Silver £800   £1500

CROMWELL
1651 Lord Protector (by T. Simon), 38mm,
  Silver.. £400   £900
— Cast examples.. £120   £275

CHARLES II
1661 Coronation (by T. Simon), 29mm
— Gold... £1800   £3000
— Silver... £350   £550
1685 Death (by N. Roettier), 39mm, Bronze........ £150   £325

Charles II Coronation, 1661

DATE	VF	EF

JAMES II
1685 Coronation (by J. Roettier), 34mm
— Gold £1900 £3500
— Silver £375 £800
MARY
1685 Coronation (by J. Roettier), 34mm
— Gold £1500 £2800
— Silver £300 £600

WILLIAM & MARY
1689 Coronation (by J. Roettier), 32mm
— Gold £1750 £2800
— Silver £350 £495
1689 Coronation, "Perseus" (by G. Bower),
 38mm, Gold £1750 £3000

MARY
1694 Death (by N. Roettier), 39mm, Bronze........ £95 £230

WILLIAM III
1697 "The State of Britain" (by J. Croker), 69mm,
 Silver £850 £1400

ANNE
1702 Accession, "Entirely English" (by J. Croker), 34mm
— Gold £1300 £2500
— Silver £95 £180
1702 Coronation (by J. Croker), 36mm
— Gold £1500 £2500
— Silver £200 £300
1707 Union with Scotland (by J. Croker, rev. by S. Bull), 34mm
— Gold £1500 £2750
— Silver £150 £250
1713 Peace of Utrecht (by J. Croker—issued in gold to Members
of Parliament), 34mm
— Gold £2500 £5000
— Silver £130 £300

GEORGE I
1714 Coronation (by J. Croker), 34mm
— Gold £1500 £3000
— Silver £195 £295
1727 Death (by J. Dassier), 31mm, Silver £120 £300

GEORGE II
1727 Coronation (by J. Croker), 34mm
— Gold £1500 £3000
— Silver £175 £350

QUEEN CAROLINE
1727 Coronation (by J. Croker), 34mm
— Gold £1750 £3000
— Silver £190 £400
1732 The Royal Family (by J. Croker), 70mm
— Silver £1500 £3000
— Bronze... £400 £700

Queen Anne, 1702–1713.

George I Coronation, 1714.

DATE	VF	EF

GEORGE III
1761 Coronation (by L. Natter), 34mm
- Gold £2250 £3500
- Silver £350 £550
- Bronze... £150 £250

QUEEN CHARLOTTE
1761 Coronation (by L. Natter), 34mm
- Gold £1750 £3500
- Silver £375 £600
- Bronze... £150 £295
1810 Golden Jubilee, "Frogmore", 48mm, Silver £150 £300
- Bronze... £95 £195

GEORGE IV
1821 Coronation (by B. Pistrucci), 35mm
- Gold £1500 £2950
- Silver £175 £395
- Bronze... £60 £110

WILLIAM IV
1831 Coronation (by W. Wyon; rev.shows
   Queen Adelaide), 33mm
- Gold £1500 £2500
- Silver £175 £325
- Bronze... £65 £100

QUEEN VICTORIA
1838 Coronation (by B. Pistrucci), 37mm
- Gold £1500 £3000
- Silver £150 £300
- Bronze... £45 £95

George III, Coronation, 1761

Queen Victoria Coronation, 1838

Queen Victoria Diamond Jubilee 1897

DATE	VF	EF
1887 Golden Jubilee (by J. E. Boehm, rev. by Lord Leighton)		
— Gold, 58mm	£2800	£3500
— Silver, 78mm	£250	£500
— Bronze, 78mm	£95	£180
1897 Diamond Jubilee (by T. Brock),		
— Gold, 56mm	£3000	£4000
— Silver, 56mm	£95	£125
— Bronze, 56mm	£45	£75
— Gold, 25mm	£350	£400
— Silver, 25mm	£35	£55

EDWARD VII
1902 Coronation (August 9) (by G. W. de Saulles)

	VF	EF
— Gold, 56mm	£3000	£3500
— Silver, 56mm	£95	£125
— Bronze, 56mm	£35	£60
— Gold, 31mm	£450	£500
— Silver, 31mm	£25	£45

Some rare examples of the official medal show the date as June 26, the original date set for the Coronation which was postponed because the King developed appendicitis.

GEORGE V
1911 Coronation (by B. Mackennal)

	VF	EF
— Gold, 51mm	£3000	£3500
— Silver, 51mm	£95	£250
— Bronze, 51mm	£30	£60
— Gold, 31mm	£450	£550
— Silver, 31mm	£25	£35

George V Silver Jubilee, 1935

1935 Silver Jubilee (by P. Metcalfe)

	VF	EF
— Gold, 58mm	£3500	£4000
— Silver, 58mm	£100	£150
— Gold, 32mm	£600	£750
— Silver, 32mm	£25	£40

PRINCE EDWARD
1911 Investiture as Prince of Wales (by W. Goscombe John)

	VF	EF
— Gold, 31mm	£1000	£1850
— Silver, 31mm	£45	£95

EDWARD VIII
1936 Abdication (by L. E. Pinches), 35mm

	VF	EF
— Gold	£750	£1500
— Silver	£45	£65
— Bronze	£20	£40

GEORGE VI
1937 Coronation (by P. Metcalfe)

	VF	EF
— Gold, 58mm	£3500	£4000
— Silver, 58mm	£60	£95
— Gold, 32mm	£600	£750
— Silver, 32mm	£35	£75
— Bronze, 32mm	£10	£15

Edward, Prince of Wales, 1911

DATE	VF	EF

ELIZABETH II

1953 Coronation (by Spink & Son)

	VF	EF
— Gold, 57mm	£3500	£4000
— Silver, 57mm	£75	£140
— Bronze, 57mm	£45	£95
— Gold, 32mm	£350	£550
— Silver, 32mm	£40	£65
— Bronze, 32mm	£10	£20

1977 Silver Jubilee (by A. Machin)

— Silver, 57mm	—	£100
— Silver, 44mm	—	£50

The gold medals are priced for 18ct—they can also be found as 22ct and 9ct, and prices should be adjusted accordingly.

PRINCE CHARLES

1969 Investiture as Prince of Wales (by M. Rizello)

— Silver, 57mm	—	£75
— Bronze gilt, 57mm	—	£40
— Silver, 45mm	—	£65
— Gold, 32mm	—	£400
— Silver, 32mm	—	£45
— Bronze, 32mm	—	£5

Prince Charles, Prince of Wales 1969.

QUEEN ELIZABETH THE QUEEN MOTHER

1980 80th Birthday (by L. Durbin)

— Silver, 57mm	—	£90
— Silver, 38mm	—	£50
— Bronze, 38mm	—	£20

N.B.—Official Medals usually command a premium when still in their original cases of issue.

The Half-crowns of Charles I
1625-1649 (Volume I-VolumeV) by Maurice Bull

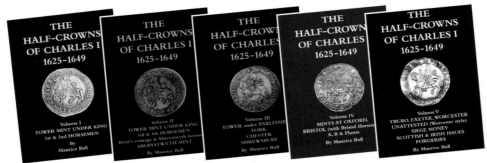

A well illustrated series of 5 volumes looking at the Half-crowns of Charles I.

Volume I
Tower Mint under the King.
1st and 2nd Horsemen

Volume II
Tower Mint under the King, 3rd and 4th horsemen, Aberystwyth horseman, Briot's coinage (English) and the Aberystwyth Mint.

Volume III
Tower Mint under Parliament, 3rd and 5th horsemen, the mints at York, Chester and Shrewsbury.

Volume IV
Mints at Oxford, Bristol (with Bristol Horseman) A, B & Plume

Volume V
Truro, Exeter, Worcester, Unattested (Worcester Style), Siege Money, Scottish & Irish Issues, Forgeries

Price per volume £85.00+ (+£5.00 p&p, UK/ Europe/World surface, Airmail £10.00)

Order two or more copies from 'The Half crown of Charles I' series and p&p is **FREE!**

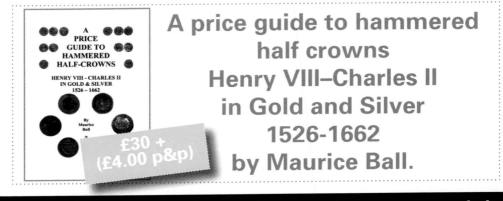
For a full selection of numismatic titles, please see our website:
www.tokenpublishing.com

DIRECTORY *section*

O N the following pages will be found the most useful names and addresses needed by the coin collector.

At the time of going to press with this edition of the YEARBOOK the information is correct, as far as we have been able to ascertain. However, people move and establishments change, so it is always advisable to make contact with the person or organisation listed before travelling any distance, to ensure that the journey is not wasted.

Should any of the information in this section not be correct we would very much appreciate being advised in good time for the preparation of the next edition of the COIN YEARBOOK.

BNTA

Dealers who display this symbol are Members of the

BRITISH NUMISMATIC TRADE ASSOCIATION

The primary purpose of the Association is to promote and safeguard the highest standards of professionalism in dealings between its Members and the public. In official consultations it is the recognised representative of commercial numismatics in Britain.

For free a Membership Directory please send a stamped addressed envelope to:
General Secretary, BNTA
PO Box 2, Rye, East Sussex TN31 7WE
Tel/Fax: 01797 229988
E-mail: bnta@lineone.net

www.bnta.net

The BNTA will be organising the following events:

COINEX 2012 28 & 29 September
COINEX 2013 27 & 28 September
at The Ballroom, Millennium Hotel, London Mayfair,
44 Grosvenor Square, London W1K 2HP

The BNTA is a member of the International Numismatic Commission.

BNTA MEMBERSHIPS
IN COUNTY ORDER
(Those members with a retail premises are indicated with an*)

LONDON AREA
*A.H. Baldwin & Sons Ltd
ATS Bullion Ltd
Beaver Coin Room
Keith Chapman
* Classical Numismatic
Group Inc / Seaby
Coins
*Philip Cohen
Numismatics
Andre de Clermont
Michael Dickinson
*Dix Noonan Webb
Christopher Eimer
Glendining's
Harrow Coin & Stamp
Centre
*Knightsbridge Coins
C. J. Martin (Coins) Ltd
Nigel Mills
Morton & Eden Ltd
Moruzzi Ltd
*Colin Narbeth & Son
Ltd
Numismatica Ars
Classica
*Pavlos S Pavlou
Physical Gold
Ltd Predecimal.
com incorporating
Rotographic
Publications
Roma Numismatics Ltd
Simmons Gallery
*Spink & Son Ltd
Surena Ancient Art &
Numismatic
The London Coin
Company Ltd
BEDFORDSHIRE
*Cambridge Coins and
Jewellery
Simon Monks
BERKSHIRE
Frank Milward
BRISTOL
Saltford Coins
BUCKINGHAMSHIRE
Charles Riley

CAMBRIDGESHIRE
*Den of Antiquity
International Ltd
CHESHIRE
A F BROCK & Co Ltd
CORNWALL
Richard W Jeffery
DEVON
Glenn S Ogden
DORSET
*Dorset Coin Co. Ltd
ESSEX
Time Line Originals
**ESSEX/HERTS/LONDON
BORDERS**
David Seaman
GLOUCESTERSHIRE
Silbury Coins Ltd
HAMPSHIRE
*SPM Jewellers
Studio Coins
*Victory Coins
West Essex Coin
Investments
HERTFORDSHIRE
DRG Coins and
Antiquities
K B Coins
David Miller
KENT
London Coins
*Peter Morris
LANCASHIRE
*Colin de Rouffignac
James Murphy
*Peter Ireland Ltd
MONMOUTHSHIRE
Anthony M. Halse
NORFOLK
*Roderick Richardson
Chris Rudd
BucksCoins
NORTHAMPTONSHIRE
*Giuseppe Miceli Coin &
Medal Centre
NORTHUMBERLAND
*Corbitt Stamps Ltd
NOTTINGHAMSHIRE
History in Coins

OXFORDSHIRE
*Richard Gladdle
SUFFOLK
*Lockdale Coins Ltd
Mike R. Vosper Coins
SURREY
Allgold Coins
Daniel Fearon
M. J. Hughes
KMCC Ltd
Mark Rasmussen
Numismatist
Nigel Tooley Ltd
SUSSEX
Tim Wilkes
WEST MIDLANDS
*Birmingham Coins
David Craddock
Paul Davis Birmingham
Ltd
*Format of Birmingham
Ltd
Mint Coins Ltd
WARWICKSHIRE
*Peter Viola
*Warwick & Warwick Ltd
WORCESTERSHIRE
J. Whitmore
YORKSHIRE
Airedale Coins
AMR Coins
Paul Clayton
Paul Davies Ltd
Weighton Coin Won-
ders*
WALES
Lloyd Bennett
*Cardiff Coins & Medals
*North Wales Coins Ltd
Colin Rumney
SCOTLAND
*Scotmint Ltd
IRELAND
Ormonde Coins

MUSEUMS
& libraries

Listed below are the Museums and Libraries in the UK which have coins or items of numismatic interest on display or available to the general public.

A

• Anthropological Museum, University of Aberdeen, Broad Street, **Aberdeen,** AB9 1AS (01224 272014).

• Curtis Museum (1855), High Street, **Alton,** Hants (01420 2802). *General collection of British coins.*

• Ashburton Museum, 1 West Street, **Ashburton,** Devon. *Ancient British and Roman antiquities including local coin finds.*

• Ashwell Village Museum (1930), Swan Street, **Ashwell,** Baldock, Herts. *Roman coins from local finds, local trade tokens, Anglo-Gallic coins and jetons.*

• Buckinghamshire County Museum (1862), Church Street, **Aylesbury,** Bucks (01296 88849). *Roman and medieval English coins found locally, 17th/18th century Buckinghamshire tokens, commemorative medals.*

B

• Public Library and Museum (1948), Marlborough Road, **Banbury,** Oxon (01295 259855). *Wrexlin Hoard of Roman coins.*

• Museum of North Devon (1931), The Square, **Barnstaple,** EX32 8LN (01271 46747). *General coin and medal collection, including local finds. Medals of the Royal Devonshire Yeomanry.*

• Roman Baths Museum, Pump Room, **Bath,** Avon (01225 461111 ext 2785). *Comprehensive collection of Roman coins from local finds.*

• Bagshaw Museum and Art Gallery (1911), Wilton Park, **Batley,** West Yorkshire (01924 472514). *Roman, Scottish, Irish, English hammered, British and foreign coins, local traders' tokens, political medalets, campaign medals and decorations.*

• Bedford Museum (1961), Castle Lane, **Bedford** (01234 353323). *Collections of the Bedford Library and Scientific Institute, the Beds Archaeological Society and Bedford Modern School (Pritchard Memorial) Museum.*

• Ulster Museum (1928), Botanic Gardens, **Belfast** BT9 5AB (01232 381251). *Irish, English and British coins and commemorative medals.*

• Berwick Borough Museum (1867), The Clock Block, Berwick Barracks, Ravensdowne, **Berwick**. TD15 1DQ (01289 330044). *Roman, Scottish and medievial coins.*

• Public Library, Art Gallery and Museum (1910), Champney Road, **Beverley,** Humberside (01482 882255). *Beverley trade tokens, Roman, English, British and foreign coins.*

• Bignor Roman Villa (1811), **Bignor,** nr Pulborough, West Sussex (017987 202). *Roman coins found locally.*

• City Museum and Art Gallery (1861), Chamberlain Square, **Birmingham** B3 3DH (0121 235 2834). *Coins, medals and tokens (special emphasis on the products of the Soho, Heaton, Birmingham and Watt mints.*

• Blackburn Museum, Museum Street, **Blackburn,** Lancs (01254 667130). *Incorporates the Hart (5,000 Greek, Roman and early English) and Hornby (500 English coins) collections, as well as the museum's own collection of British and Commonwealth coins.*

• Museum Collection, Town Hall, **Bognor Regis,** West Sussex. *Roman, English and British coins and trade tokens.*

• Museum and Art Gallery,(1893), Civic Centre, **Bolton,** Lancashire (01204 22311 ext 2191). *General collection of about 3000 British and foreign coins, and over 500 British medals. Numismatic library.*

• Art Gallery and Museum, Central Library, Oriel Road, **Bootle,** Lancs. *Greek, Roman, English, British and some foreign coins, local trade tokens.*

• Roman Town and Museum (1949) Main Street, **Boroughbridge,** N. Yorks. YO2 3PH (01423 322768). *Roman coins.*

• The Museum (1929), The Guildhall, **Boston,** Lincs (01205 365954). *Small collection of English coins.*

- Natural Science Society Museum (1903), 39 Christchurch Road, **Bournemouth,** Dorset (01202 553525). *Greek, Roman and English hammered coins (including the Hengistbury Hoard), local trade tokens.*

- Bolling Hall Museum (1915), Bolling Hall Road, **Bradford,** West Yorkshire BD4 7LP (01274 723057). *Some 2,000 coins and tokens, mostly 18th–20th centuries.*

- Cartwright Hall Museum and Art Gallery (1904), Lister Park, **Bradford,** West Yorkshire BD9 4NS (01274 493313). *Roman coins found locally.*

- Museum and Art Gallery (1932), South Street, **Bridport,** Dorset (01308 22116). *Roman coins, mainly from excavations at Claudian Fort.*

- The City Museum (1820), Queen's Road, **Bristol** BS8 1RL (0117 9 27256). *Ancient British, Roman (mainly from local hoards), English hammered coins, especially from the Bristol mint, and several hundred local trade tokens.*

- District Library and Museum (1891), Terrace Road, **Buxton,** Derbyshire SK17 6DU (01298 24658). *English and British coins, tokens and commemorative medals. Numismatic library.*

C

- Segontium Museum (1928), Beddgelert Road, **Caernarfon,** Gwynedd (01286 675625) *Roman coins and artifacts excavated from the fort.*

- Fitzwilliam Museum (1816), Department of Coins and Medals, Trumpington Street, **Cambridge** (01223 332900). *Ancient, English, medieval European, oriental coins, medals, plaques, seals and cameos.*

- National Museum & Galleries of Wales, Cathays Park, **Cardiff** (029 20397951). *Greek, Celtic, Roman and British coins and tokens with the emphasis on Welsh interest. Also military, civilian and comm. medals.*

- Guildhall Museum (1979), Greenmarket, **Carlisle,** Cumbria (01228 819925). *General collection of coins and medals.*

- Tullie House (1877), Castle Street, **Carlisle,** Cumbria (01228 34781). *Roman, medieval and later coins from local finds, including medieval counterfeiter's coin-moulds.*

- Gough's Caves Museum (1934), The Cliffs, **Cheddar,** Somerset (01934 343). *Roman coins.*

- Chelmsford and Essex Museum (1835), Oaklands Park, Moulsham Street, **Chelmsford,** Essex CM2 9AQ (01245 615100). *Ancient British, Roman, medieval and later coins mainly from local finds, local medals.*

- Town Gate Museum (1949), **Chepstow,** Gwent. *Local coins and trade tokens.*

- Grosvenor Museum (1886), Grosvenor Street, **Chester** (01244 21616). *Roman coins from the fortress site, Anglo-Saxon, English medieval and post-medieval coins of the Chester and Rhuddlan mints, trade tokens of Chester and Cheshire, English and British milled coins.*

- Public Library (1879), Corporation Street, **Chesterfield,** Derbyshire (01246 2047). *Roman coins from local finds, Derbyshire trade tokens, medals, seals and railway passes. Numismatic library and publications.*

- Red House Museum (1919), Quay Road, **Christchurch,** Dorset (01202 482860). *Coins of archaeological significance from Hampshire and Dorset, notably the South Hants Hoard, ancient British, Armorican, Gallo-Belgic, Celtic and Roman coins, local trade tokens and medals.*

- Corinium Museum (1856), Park Street, **Cirencester,** Glos (01285 655611). *Roman coins.*

- Colchester and Essex Museum (1860), The Castle, **Colchester,** Essex (01206 712931/2). *Ancient British and Roman coins from local finds, medieval coins (especially the Colchester Hoard), later English coins and Essex trade tokens, commemorative medals.*

D

- Public Library, Museum and Art Gallery (1921), Crown Street, **Darlington,** Co Durham (01325 463795). *Coins, medals and tokens.*

- Borough Museum (1908), Central Park, **Dartford,** Kent (01322 343555). *Roman, medieval and later English hammered coins, trade tokens and commemorative medals.*

- Dartmouth Museum (1953), The Butterknowle, **Dartmouth,** Devon (01803 832923). *Coins and medals of a historical and maritime nature.*

- Museum and Art Gallery (1878), The Strand, **Derby** (01332 255586). *Roman coins, English silver and copper regal coins, Derbyshire tradesmen's tokens, British campaign medals and decorations of the Derbyshire Yeomanry and the 9/12 Royal Lancers.*

- Museum and Art Gallery (1909), Chequer Road, **Doncaster,** South Yorkshire (01302 734293). *General collection of English and foreign silver and bronze coins. Representative collection of Roman imperial silver and bronze coins, including a number from local hoards. English trade tokens, principally of local issues, medals.*

- Dorset County Museum(1846), **Dorchester,** Dorset (01305 262735). *British, Roman, medieval and later coins of local interest.*

- Central Museum (1884), Central Library, St James's Road, **Dudley,** West Midlands (01384 453576). *Small general collection of coins, medals and tokens.*

- Burgh Museum (1835), The Observatory, Corberry Hill, **Dumfries** (01387 53374). *Greek, Roman, Anglo-Saxon, medieval English and Scottish coins, especially from local hoards. Numismatic library.*

- Dundee Art Galleries and Museums (1873). Albert Square, **Dundee** DD1 1DA (01382 23141). *Coins and medals of local interest.*

- The Cathedral Treasury (995 AD), The College, **Durham** (0191-384 4854). *Greek and Roman coins bequeathed by Canon Sir George Wheeler (1724), Renaissance to modern medals, medieval English coins, especially those struck at the Durham ecclesiastical mint.*

- Durham Heritage Centre, St Mary le Bow, North Bailey, **Durham** (0191-384 2214). *Roman, medieval and later coins, mainly from local finds.*

E

- Royal Museum of Scotland (1781), Queen Street, **Edinburgh** EH1 (0131 225 7534). *Roman, Anglo-Saxon, English and Scottish coins, trade tokens, commemorative medals and communion tokens. Numismatic library. Publications.*

• Royal Albert Memorial Museum (1868), Queen St, **Exeter** EX4 3RX (01392 265858). *Roman and medieval. Coins of the Exeter Mint.*

G

• Hunterian Museum (1807), Glasgow University, University Avenue, **Glasgow** G12 8QQ (0141 339 8855). *Greek, Roman, Byzantine, Scottish, English and Irish coins, Papal and other European medals, Indian and Oriental coins, trade and communion coins.*

• Art Gallery and Museum (1888), Kelvingrove, **Glasgow** G3 (0141 357 3929). *General collection of coins, trade tokens, communion tokens, commemorative and military medals.*

• Museum of Transport (1974), Kelvin Hall, Bunhouse Road, **Glasgow** G3 (0141 357 3929). *Transport tokens and passes, commemorative medals, badges and insignia of railway companies and shipping lines.*

• City Museum and Art Gallery (1859), Brunswick Road, **Gloucester** (01452 524131). *Ancient British, Roman, Anglo-Saxon (from local finds), early medieval (from local mints), Gloucestershire trade tokens.*

• Guernsey Museum and Art Gallery, St Peter Port, **Guernsey** (01481 726518). *Armorican, Roman, medieval and later coins, including the coins, medals, tokens and paper money of Guernsey.*

• Guildford Museum (1898), Castle Arch, **Guildford,** Surrey GU1 3SX (01483 444750). *Roman and medieval coins and later medals.*

H

• Gray Museum and Art Gallery, Clarence Road, **Hartlepool,** Cleveland (01429 268916). *General collection, including coins from local finds.*

• Public Museum and Art Gallery (1890), John's Place, Cambridge Road, **Hastings,** East Sussex (01424 721952). *General collection of English and British coins, collection of Anglo-Saxon coins from Sussex mints.*

• City Museum (1874), Broad Street, **Hereford** (01432 268121 ext 207). *Coins from the Hereford mint and local finds, Herefordshire trade tokens, general collection of later coins and medals.*

• Hertford Museum (1902), 18 Bull Plain, **Hertford** (01992 582686). *British, Roman, medieval and later English coins and medals.*

• Honiton and Allhallows Public Museum (1946), High Street, **Honiton,** Devon (01404 44966). *Small general collection, including coins from local finds.*

• Museum and Art Gallery (1891), 19 New Church Road, **Hove,** East Sussex (01273 779410). *English coins, Sussex trade tokens and hop tallies, campaign medals, orders and decorations, comm. medals.*

• Tolson Memorial Museum (1920), Ravensknowle Park, **Huddersfield,** West Yorkshire (01484 541455). *Representative collection of British coins and tokens, Roman and medieval coins, mainly from local finds.*

• Hull and East Riding Museum (1928), 36 High Street, **Hull** (01482 593902). *Celtic, Roman and medieval coins and artifacts from local finds. Some later coins including tradesmen's tokens.*

I

• The Manx Museum, Douglas, **Isle of Man** (01624 675522). *Roman, Celtic, Hiberno-Norse, Viking, medieval English and Scottish coins, mainly from local finds, Manx traders' tokens from the 17th to 19th centuries, Manx coins from 1709 to the present day.*

J

• Jersey Museum, Weighbridge, St Helier, **Jersey** (01534 30511). *Armorican, Gallo-Belgic, Roman, medieval English and French coins, coins, paper money and tokens of Jersey.*

K

• Dick Institute Museum and Art Gallery (1893), Elmbank Avenue, **Kilmarnock,** Ayrshire (01563 26401). *General collection of coins and medals, and the Hunter-Selkirk collection of communion tokens.*

L

• City Museum (1923), Old Town Hall, Market Square, **Lancaster** (01524 64637). *Roman, Anglo-Saxon, medieval English coins, provincial trade tokens, medals of the King's Own Royal Lancashire Regiment.*

• City Museum (1820), Municipal Buildings, The Headrow, **Leeds,** West Yorkshire (01532 478279). *Greek, Roman, Anglo-Saxon, English medieval, Scottish, Irish, British, Commonwealth and foreign coins. Several Roman and Saxon hoards. The Backhouse collection of Yorkshire banknotes, the Thornton collection of Yorkshire tokens, British and foreign commemorative medals.*

• Leicester Museum and Art Gallery (1849), New Walk, **Leicester** (01533 554100). *Roman, medieval and later coins, mainly from local finds, tokens, commemorative medals, campaign medals and decorations.*

• Pennington Hall Museum and Art Gallery, **Leigh,** Lancashire. *Roman and British coins and medals.*

• Museum and Art Gallery (1914), Broadway, **Letchworth,** Herts (01462 65647). *Ancient British coins minted at Camulodunum, Roman, medieval and English coins, Hertfordshire trade tokens, commemorative and campaign medals.*

• City Library, Art Gallery and Museum (1859), Bird Street, **Lichfield,** Staffs (01543 2177). *Roman, medieval and later English coins, Staffordshire trade tokens and commemorative medals.*

• Liverpool Museum(1851), William Brown Street, **Liverpool** L3 8EN (0151 207 0001). *General collection of Roman, medievaland later British coins, tokens.*

• Bank of England Museum, Threadneedle Street, **London** EC2 (020-7601 5545). *Exhibits relating to gold bullion, coins, tokens and medals, the design and manufacture of banknotes, and a comprehensive collection of bank notes dating from the 17th century to the present day.*

• British Museum(1752), HSBC Coin Gallery, Great Russell Street, **London** WC1 (020-7636 1555). *Almost a million coins, medals, tokens and badges of all period from Lydia, 7th century BC to the present time. Extensive library of books and periodicals.*

• British Numismatic Society (1903), Warburg Institute, Woburn Square, **London** WC1. *Library containing over 5,000 volumes, including sale catalogues, periodicals and pamphlets. Open to members only.*

• Cuming Museum (1906), Walworth Road, **London** SE17 (020-7703 3324/5529). *Some 8,000 items, including Greek, Roman, medieval English and modern British coins, English tokens and commemorative medals.*

• Gunnersbury Park Museum (1927), Acton, **London** W3. *Ancient British, Greek, Roman, medieval English, British and some foreign coins, tradesmen's tokens and commemorative medals, including local finds.*

• Horniman Museum and Library (1890), London Road, Forest Hill, **London** SE23 (020-7699 2339). *General collection, primitive currency, some tokens.*

• Imperial War Museum, Lambeth Road, **London** SE1 6HZ (020-7416 5000). *Emergency coinage of two world wars, occupation and invasion money, extensive collection of German Notgeld, commemorative, propaganda and military medals, badges and insignia.*

• Sir John Soane's Museum (1833), 13 Lincoln's Inn Fields, **London** WC2 (020-7405 2107). *Napoleonic medals and medallic series of the late 18th and early 19th centuries.*

• National Maritime Museum, Romney Road, Greenwich, **London** SE10 (020-8858 4422). *Commemorative medals with a nautical or maritime theme, naval medals and decorations.*

• Victoria and Albert Museum (1852), South Kensington, **London** SW7 (020-7938 8441). *Byzantine gold and medieval Hispano-Mauresque coins (Department of Metalwork), large collection of Renaissance and later medals (Department of Architecture and Sculpture). Numismatic books.*

• Ludlow Museum (1833). The Assembly Rooms. Castle Square, **Ludlow** (01584 873857). *Roman and medieval coins from local finds.*

• Luton Museum and Art Gallery (1927), Wardown Park, **Luton**, Beds (01582 36941). *Coins, tokens and medals.*

M

• Museum and Art Gallery (1858), **Maidstone**, Kent (01622 754497). *Ancient British, Roman, Anglo-Saxon and medieval coins found in Kent, modern British coins, Kent trade tokens, banknotes, hop tallies and tokens, primitive currency, collections of Kent Numismatic Society.*

• The Manchester Museum (1868), The University, **Manchester** M13 (0161-275 2634). *Very fine collections of Greek and Roman coins, comprehensive collections of English, European and Oriental coins, over 30,000 in all.*

• Margate Museum (1923), The Old Town Hall, Market Place, **Margate**, Kent (01843 225511 ext 2520). *Small collection of coins, including Roman from local finds.*

• Montrose Museum and Art Gallery (1836). Panmure Place, **Montrose**, Angus DD10 8HE (01674 73232). *Scottish and British coins.*

N

• Newark-on-Trent Museum (1912), Appleton Gate, **Newark**, Notts (01636 702358). *Siege pieces, trade tokens and coins from local finds and hoards.*

• Newbury District Museum, The Wharf, **Newbury**, Berkshire (01635 30511). *Ancient British, Roman and medieval coins and artifacts, later coins and tokens.*

• The Greek Museum, Percy Building, **Newcastle-upon-Tyne** (0191 2226000 ext 7966). *Ancient coins.*

O

• Heberden Coin Room, Ashmolean Museum (1683), **Oxford** (01865 278000). *Extensive collections of all periods, notably Greek, Roman, English and Oriental coins, Renaissance portrait and later medals, tokens and paper money. Large library. Numerous publications.*

P

• Peterborough Museum (1881), Priestgate, **Peterborough**, Cambs (01733 340 3329). *Roman (mainly from local hoards and finds), Anglo-Saxon, medieval English, British and modern European coins, English and British commemorative medals and tokens.*

• City Museum and Art Gallery (1897), Drake Circus, **Plymouth**, Devon (01752 264878). *General collections of British and Commonwealth coins and tokens, Devon trade tokens and Plymouth tradesmen's checks, Ancient British and Roman coins from local sites.*

• Waterfront Museum, 4 High Street, **Poole**, Dorset (01202 683138). *General collection of British and foreign coins, medals and tokens (view by appointment).*

• City Museum (1972), Museum Road, Old **Portsmouth** PO1 (023 80827261). *Roman, medieval and later coins mainly from local finds and archaeological excavation, British coins, trade tokens of Hampshire, commemorative medals.*

• Harris Museum and Art Gallery (1893), Market Square, **Preston**, Lancashire (01772 58248). *English and British coins, tokens and medals.*

R

• The Museum of Reading (1883), Blagrave Street, **Reading**, Berks (0118 939 9800). *British, Roman and medieval English coins, many from local finds, tradesmen's tokens and commemorative medals.*

• Rochdale Museum (1905), Sparrow Hill, **Rochdale**, Lancs (01706 41085). *Roman and medieval coins from local finds, Rochdale trade tokens, miscellaneous British and foreign coins and medals.*

• Municipal Museum and Art Gallery (1893), Clifton Park, **Rotherham** (01709 382121). *Collection includes Roman coins from Templeborough Forts, medieval English coins from local hoards and a general collection of British coins.*

S

• Saffron Walden Museum (1832) (1939), Museum Street, **Saffron** Walden, Essex (01799 522494). *Ancient British, Roman, medieval and later coins, mainly from local finds and archaeological excavation, trade tokens and commemorative medals.*

• Verulamium Museum, St Michael's, **St Albans**, Herts (01727 819339). *Coins and artifacts excavated from the Roman town.*

• Salisbury and South Wiltshire Museum (1861), The Cathedral Close, **Salisbury,** Wilts (01722 332151). *Collection of coins minted or found locally, including finds of Iron Age, Roman, Saxon and medieval coins, as well as 18th and 19th century tradesmen's tokens.*

• Richborough Castle Museum (1930), **Sandwich,** Kent (0304 612013). *Roman coins of 1st–5th centuries from excavations of the Richborough site.*

• Scarborough Museum (1829), The Rotunda, Vernon Road, **Scarborough**, North Yorkshire (01723 374839). *Collection of over 4,000 Roman coins, 1,500 English and 600 coins from local finds, siege pieces and trade tokens.*

• Shaftesbury and Dorset Local History Museum (1946), 1 Gold Hill, **Shaftesbury**, Dorset (01747 52157). *Hoard of Saxon coins.*

• City Museum (1875), Weston Park, **Sheffield** (0114 2 768588). *Over 5,000 coins of all periods, but mainly English and modern British. European coins, imperial Roman (including three hoards of about 500 coins each), Yorkshire trade tokens, British historical medals, campaign medals. Library.*

• Rowley's House Museum, Barker Street, **Shrewsbury**, Salop (01743 361196). *Coins minted at Shrewsbury 925-1180, Civil War coinage of 1642, Shropshire tradesmen's tokens, English coins and medals.*

• Museum of Archaeology (1951), God's House Tower, Town Quay, **Southampton**, Hants (023 8022 0007). *Main emphasis lies in Ancient British, Roman and medieval English coins from local archaeological excavations. General collection of later coins and medals.*

• Atkinson Art Gallery (1878), Lord Street, **Southport,** Lancs (01704 533133). *Roman coins.*

• Botanic Gardens Museum, Churchtown, **Southport,** Lancs (01704 87547). *English and British coins and medals, military medals and decorations.*

• Southwold Museum (1933), St Bartholomew's Green, **Southwold**, Suffolk (01502 722375). *General collection of coins, specialised Suffolk trade tokens.*

• Stamford Museum (1961), Broad Street, **Stamford**, Lincs (01780 66317). *General collection of coins, medals and tokens, including a selection from the Stamford mint.*

• Municipal Museum (1860), Vernon Park, Turncroft Lane, **Stockport**, Cheshire (0161 474 4460) *Miscellaneous general collection of coins, tokens and medals.*

• Stroud Museum (1899), Lansdown, **Stroud**, Glos (01453 376394). *Ancient British, Roman, Saxon, Norman, later medieval English, British coins and Gloucestershire trade tokens.*

• Museum and Art Gallery (1846), Borough Road, **Sunderland**, Tyne & Wear (0191 514 1235). *Roman imperial, medieval and later English, including examples of the pennies minted at Durham, modern British and foreign coins, 17th-19th century tradesmen's tokens, local medallions and campaign medals.*

• Swansea Museum (1835), Victoria Road, **Swansea**, W. Glamorgan, SA1 1SN (0792 653765). *Coins and medals of local interest.*

T

• Tamworth Castle and Museum (1899), The Holloway, **Tamworth**, Staffs (01827 63563). *Anglo-Saxon coins, medieval English including coins of the Tamworth mint, later English and British coins, tokens, commemorative medallions and medals.*

• Somerset County Museum, Taunton Castle, **Taunton**, Somerset (01823 255510/320200). *Celtic, Roman, Anglo-Saxon, early Medieval, tokens, medallions and banknotes. Strong emphasis on locally-found items.*

• Thurrock Local History Museum (1956), Civic Square, **Tilbury**, Essex (01375 390000 ext 2414). *Roman coins.*

• Royal Cornwall Museum (1818), River Street, **Truro,** Cornwall (01872 72205). *Coins, tokens and medals pertaining principally to the county of Cornwall.*

W

• Wakefield Museum (1919), Wood Street, **Wakefield,** West Yorkshire (01924 295351). *Roman and medieval English silver and copper coins.*

• Epping Forest District Museum, 39/41 Sun Street, **Waltham Abbey**, Essex EN 9. *Ancient British, Roman and medieval coins, Essex tradesmen's tokensof local interest.*

• Warrington Museum and Art Gallery (1848). Bold Street, **Warrington**, Cheshire, WA1 1JG (01925 30550). *Coins, medals and tokens.*

• Worcester City Museum (1833), Foregate Street, **Worcester** (01905 25371). *Roman, medieval and later coins and tokens. Coins of the Worcester mint.*

• Wells Museum (18903), 8 Cathedral Green, **Wells,** Somerset (01749 3477). *Ancient and modern British and world coins, local trade tokens and medals.*

• Municipal Museum and Art Gallery (1878), Station Road, **Wigan**, Lancashire. *British, Commonwealth and foreign coins from about 1660 to the present. Roman coins from local sites, commemorative medals.*

• City Museum (1851), The Square, **Winchester**, Hants (01962 848269). *Roman and medieval coins chiefly from local hoards and finds. Hampshire tradesmen's tokens and commemorative medals. Small reference library.*

• Wisbech and Fenland Museum (1835), Museum Square, **Wisbech,** Cambridgeshire (01945 583817), *British Roman, medieval and later coins, medals and tokens.*

Y

• The Museum of South Somerset (1928), Hendford, **Yeovil,** Somerset (01935 24774). *Roman coins from local sites, medieval English, modern British coins and medals and a fine collection of tokens (particularly 17th century Somerset).*

• Castle Museum (1938), **York** (01904 653611). *English and British coins, campaign medals, orders and decorations, commemorative medals.*

• Jorvik Viking Centre (1984), Coppergate, **York** (01904 643211). *Coins and artefacts pertaining to the Viking occupation of York.*

• The Yorkshire Museum (1823), **York** (01904 629745). *Roman imperial, medieval English and later coins, about 12,000 in all.*

CLUB *directory*

Details given here are the names of Numismatic Clubs and Societies, their date of foundation, and their usual venues, days and times of meetings. Meetings are monthly unless otherwise stated. Finally, the telephone number of the club secretary is given; the names and addresses of club secretaries are withheld for security reasons, but full details may be obtained by writing to the Secretary of the British Association of Numismatic Societies, Keith Sugden, Honorary Curatorial Assistant, Department of Numismatics, Manchester Museum, Oxford Road, Manchester M13 9PL or visiting the website at www.coinclubs.freeserve.co.uk.

Banbury & District NS (1967). St John's Social Club, St John's Church, Oxford Road, Banbury 2nd Mon (exc Jul & Aug), 19.45. (01295 275128).

Bath & Bristol Numismatic Society (1950). Fry's Club, Keynsham, Bristol. 2nd Thu, 19.30. (0117 968 7259).

Bedfordshire Numismatic Society (1966). Dave Allen, Secretary (01234 870645).

Bexley Coin Club (1968). St Martin's Church Hall, Erith Road, Barnehurst, Bexleyheath, Kent. 1st Mon (exc Jan & Aug), 19.30. (020 8303 0510).

Birmingham Numismatic Society (1964). Friend's Meeting House, Bull Street. (0121 308 1616).

Matthew Boulton Society (1994). PO Box 395, Bir-mingham B31 2TB (0121 781 6558 fax 0121 781 6574).

Bradford & District Numismatic Society (1967). East Bowling Unity Club, Leicester Street, Bradford, West Yorkshire. 3rd Mon, 19.00. (01532 677151).

British Cheque Collectors' Society (1980). John Purser, 71 Mile Lane, Cheylesmore, Coventry, West Midlands CV3 5GB.

British Numismatic Society (1903). Warburg Institute, Woburn Square, London WC1H 0AB. Monthly (exc Aug & Dec), 18.00. (020 7323 8585)

Cambridgeshire Numismatic Society (1946). Friends' Meeting House, 12 Jesus Lane (entrance in Park Street), Cambridge, CB5 8BA. 3rd Mon, Sept–June, 19.30. (01480 210992).

Chester & North Wales Coin & Banknote Society (1996). Liver Hotel, 110 Brook Street, Chester. 4th Tue, 20.00. (0151 478 4293)

Essex Numismatic Society (1966). Chelmsford Museum, Moulsham Street, Chelmsford, Essex. 4th Fri (exc Dec), 20.00. (01277 656627).

Glasgow & West of Scotland Numismatic Society (1947). Woodside Halls, 26 Glenfarg Street, Glasgow, G3. 2nd Thu, Oct-May, 19.30. (0141 9424776).

Harrow Coin Club (1968). Telephone for details of venue. 2nd and 4th Mon, 19.30. (020 8952 8765).

Havering Numismatic Society (1967). Fairkytes Arts Centre, Billet Lane, Hornchurch, Essex. 1st Tue, 19.30. (07910 124549).

Horncastle & District Coin Club (1963). Bull Hotel, Bull Ring, Horncastle, Lincs. 2nd Thu (exc Aug), 19.30. (01754 2706).

Huddersfield Numismatic Society (1947). Huddersfield Library, Princess Alexandra Walk, Huddersfield, West Yorkshire. 1st Mon (exc Jul & Aug), 19.30. (01484 866814).

Hull & District Numismatic Society (1967). The Young People's Institute, George Street, Hull. Monthly (exc Aug & Dec), 19.30. (01482 441933).

International Bank Note Society (1961). Victory Services Club, 63–79 Seymour Street, London W1. Website: www.ibns.org.uk. Last Thu (exc Dec), 18.00. (www.ibnslondon.org.uk).

International Bank Note Society (East Midlands Branch), Wollaton Park Community Association, Wollaton Park, Nottingham. (0115 928 9720).

International Bank Note Society, Scottish Chapter (1995). West End Hotel, Palmerston Place, Edinburgh. Last Sat (exc Dec), 14.30.

Ireland, Numismatic Society of (Northern Branch). Denman International, Clandeboye Road, Bangor or Shaws Bridge Sports Assoc.123 Milltown Road, Belfast. 1st Fri 19.30. (028 9146 6743)

Ireland, Numismatic Society of. (Southern Branch). Ely House, 8 Ely Place, Dublin. Third Fri, 20.00. (0035 3 283 2027).

Ipswich Numismatic Society (1966). Ipswich Citizens Advice Bureau, 19 Tower Street, Ipswich, Suffolk. Monthly meetings, 19.30. (01473 728653).

Kent Towns Numismatic Society (1913). (Mr. R. Josland, 01634 721187).

Kingston Numismatic Society (1966). King Athel-stan's School, Villiers Road, Kingston-upon-Thames, Surrey. 3rd Thu (exc Dec & Jan), 19.30. (020-8397 6944).

Lancashire & Cheshire Numismatic Society (1933). Reception Room, 2nd Floor, Manchester Central Library, St Peter's Square, Manchester. Monthly, Sep-June, Sat (14.00). Manchester Museum (May & Dec only). (0161 275 2661).

Lincolnshire Numismatic Society (1932). Grimsby Bridge Club, Bargate, Grimsby, South Humberside. 4th Wed (exc Aug), 19.30.

London Numismatic Club (1947). Warburg Institute, Woburn Square, London WC1H 0AB. First Tuesday of month (except January and August), 1830. (01223 332918).

Loughborough Coin & Search Society (1964). Wallace Humphry Room, Shelthorpe Community Centre, Loughborough, Leics. 1st Thu, 19.30. (01509 261352).

Mid Lanark Coin Circle (1969). Hospitality Room, The Civic Centre, Motherwell, Lanarkshire. 4th Thu, Sep–Apr (exc Dec), 19.30. (0141-552 2083).

Morecambe & Lancaster Numismatic Society. Monthly, 19.30. (01524 411036).

Newbury Coin & Medal Club (1971). Monthly, 20.00. (01635 41233).

Northampton Numismatic Society (1969). Old Scouts RFC, Rushmere Road, Northampton.
Norwich Coin & Medal Society, The White Horse, Trowse, Norwich. (01603 408393).

Norwich Numismatic Society (1967). Assembly House, Theatre Street, Norwich, Norfolk. 3rd Mon, 19.30. (01603 408393).

Nottinghamshire Numismatic Society (1948). The Cecil Roberts Room, County Library, Angel Row, Nottingham NG1 6HP. 2nd Tue (Sep-Apr), 18.45. (0115 9257674).

Nuneaton & District Coin Club (1968). United Reformed Church Room, Coton Road, opposite Council House, Nuneaton, Warwickshire. 2nd Tue, 19.30. (01203 371556).

Orders & Medals Research Society (1942). National Army Museum, Royal Hospital Road, Chelsea, London SW3. Monthly, 14.30 (020-8680 2701).

Ormskirk & West Lancashire Numismatic Society (1970).The Eagle & Child, Maltkiln Lane, Bispham Green L40 1SN. 1st Thu, 20.15. (01704 531266).

Peterborough & District Numismatic Society (1967). Belsize Community Centre, Celta Road Peter-borough, Cambs. 4th Tue (exc July & Aug), 19.30. (01733 562768 or 567763).

Plymouth Numismatics Society (1970). Mutley Conservative Club, Mutley Plain, Plymouth, Devon. 2nd Wed (exc Dec), 19.30. (01752 490 394).

Preston & District Numismatic Society (1965). Eldon Hotel, Eldon Street, Preston, Lancs. 1st and 3rd Tue, 20.00. (012572 66869).

Reading Coin Club (1964). Abbey Baptist Church, Abbey Square, Reading. 1st Mon, 20.00. (0118 933 2842).

Romsey Numismatic Society (1969). Romsey WM Conservative Club, Market Place, Romsey, Hants SO5 8NA. 4th Fri (exc Dec), 19.30. (01703 253921).

Rotherham & District Coin Club (1982). Rotherham Art Centre, Rotherham, South Yorkshire. 1st Wed, 19.00. (01709 528179).

Royal Mint Coin Club, PO Box 500, Cardiff CF1 1HA (01443 222111).

Royal Numismatic Society (1836). Warburg Institute, Woburn Square, London, WC1H 0AB. (some meetings held at British Museum). Third Thursday of monthly (Oct-June), 18.00. Joe Cribb, Coins and Medals, British Museum, London WC1B 3DG (020-7323 8175).

Rye Coin Club (1955). Rye Further Education Centre, Lion Street, Rye, East Sussex. 2nd Thu (Oct-Dec, Feb-May), 19.30. (01424 422974).

St Albans & Hertfordshire Numismatic Society (1948). St Michael's Parish Centre, Museum Entrance, Verulamium Park, St Albans, Herts AL3 4SL. 2nd Tue (exc Aug), 19.30. (01727 824434).

South East Hants Numismatic Society. The Langstone Conservative Club, Havant. Second Fri. Contact: Tony Matthews, (01292 389419)

South Manchester Numismatic Society (1967). Nursery Inn, Green Lane, Heaton Mersey, Stockport. 1st & 3rd Mondays of each month (excl. Public hols), 20.15. (0161-476 3184).

South Wales & Monmouthshire Numismatic Society (1958). 1st Mon (except Bank Holidays when 2nd Mon, 19.30. (For location tel: 029 20561564).

Thurrock Numismatic Society (1970). Stanley Lazell Hall, Dell Road, Grays, Essex. 3rd Wed, 19.00.

Tyneside Numismatic Society (1954). RAFA Club, Eric Nelson House, 16 Berwick Road, Gateshead, Tyne & Wear. 2nd Wed, 19.30. (01661 825824).

Wessex NS (1948). Edward Wright Room, Beaufort Community Centre, Southbourne, Bournemouth, Dorset. 2nd Thurs (exc Aug), 20.00. (020 7731 1702).

Wiltshire Numismatic Society (1965). The Village Hall, Poulshot, Nr. Devizes, Wiltshire. 3rd Mon, March -Dec, 20.00. (01380 828453).

Worthing & District Numismatic Society (1967). Berkeley Hotel, Marine Parade, Worthing, West Sussex BN11 3QQ. 3rd Thu, 20.00. (01634 260114).

Yorkshire Numismatic Society (1909). Swarthmore Institute, Woodhouse Square, Leeds. 1st Sat (exc Jan, Aug & Dec) (0113 3910848).

Information correct at time of going to press

Important Notice to Club Secretaries:

If your details as listed are incorrect please let us know in time for the next edition of the **COIN YEARBOOK.**

Amendments can be sent via post or email to: abbey@tokenpublishing.com

IMPORTANT ORGANISATIONS

ADA
The Antiquities
Dealers Association

Secretary: Susan Hadida, Duke's Court, 32 Duke Street, London SW1Y 6DU

ANA
The American
Numismatic Association

818 North Cascade Avenue, Colorado Springs, CO 80903-3279, USA

BNTA
The British Numismatic
Trade Association

Secretary: Mrs R. Cooke, General Secretary, BNTA, PO Box 2, Rye, East Sussex TN31 7WE

IAPN
International Association of
Professional Numismatists

Secretary: Jean-Luc Van der Schueren, 14 Rue de la Bourse, B–1000, Brussels.

IBNS
International
Bank Note Society

Membership Secretary:
Clive Rice, 25 Copse Side, Binscombe, Godalming, Surrey, GU7 3RU

RNS
Royal Numismatic Society

Dept of Coins & Medals, British Museum, London WC1B 3DG.

BAMS
British Art Medal Society

Philip Attwood, Dept of Coins & Medals, British Museum, London WC1B 3DG.

BNS
British Numismatic Society

Dr K. Clancy, The Royal Mint, Llantrisant, Pontyclun, Mid Glamorgan CF72 8YT

Society activities are featured every month in the "Diary Section" of COIN NEWS—available from all good newsagents or on subscription.
Telephone 01404 44166 for more details or log onto www.tokenpublishing.com

DIRECTORY
of auctioneers

Listed here are the major auction houses which handle coins, medals, banknotes and other items of numismatic interest. Many of them hold regular public auctions, whilst others handle numismatic material infrequently. A number of coin companies also hold regular Postal Auctions—these are marked with a ❷

Baldwin's Auctions Ltd
11 Adelphi Terrace, London WC2N 6BJ.
(020 7930 6879 fax 020 7930 9450,
auctions@baldwin.sh, www.baldwin.sh).

Banking Memorabilia
PO Box 14, Carlisle CA3 8DZ. (016974 76465).

Birmingham Auctions
Units 17-18, Station Yard South, Worcester Road, Leominster, Herefordshire, HR6 8TW. (01885 488871, barryfaulkner@btopenworld. com, www.birmauctions.co.uk).

Blyth & Co
7/9 Market Square, Ely, Cambs, CB7 4NP. (01353 668320, auctions@fenlord.com).

Bonhams (incorporating Glendinings)
Montpelier Street, Knightsbridge, London SW7 1HH. (020 7393 3914, www.bonhams.com).

A. F. Brock & Company
269 London Road, Hazel Grove, Stockport, Cheshire SK7 4PL. (0161 456 5050 fax 0161 456 5112, info@afbrock. co.uk, www.afbrock.co.uk).

Bushey Auctions
(020 8386 2552, enquiries@busheyauctions. com, www.busheyauctions.com).

Christie, Manson & Wood Ltd
8 King Street, St James's, London SW1Y 6QT. (020 7839 9060).

Classical Numismatic Group Inc (Seaby Coins)
14 Old Bond Street, London W1X 4JL. (020 7495 1888 fax 020 7499 5916, cng@historicalcoins.com, www.historicalcoins.com). ❷

Coins4u.net
38 Livingstone Place, Galashiels, Scotland TD1 1ED. On-line coin auction.

Corbitts
5 Moseley Street, Newcastle upon Tyne NE1 1YE. (0191-232 7268, fax 0191-261 4130).

Croydon Coin Auctions
PO Box 201, Croydon, CR9 7AQ. (020 8656 4583, www.croydoncoinauctions.co.uk).

Dix Noonan Webb (IAPN)
16 Bolton Street, Piccadilly, London. (020 7016 1700, auctions@dnw.co.uk, www.dnw.co.uk).

Dublin Coin Auction
5 St. Assam's Park, Raheny, Dublin 5. (00 353 868 714 880).

Edinburgh Coin Shop
11 West Crosscauseway, Edinburgh EH8 9JW. (0131 668 2928 fax 0131 668 2926). ❷

Jean Elsen & ses Fils s.a.
Avenue de Tervueren 65, B–1040, Brussels. (0032 2 7346356, www.elsen.eu).

Fellows & Sons
Augusta House, 19 Augusta Street, Hockley, Birmingham B18 6JA. (0121-212 2131). www.fellows.co.uk).

B. Frank & Son
3 South Avenue, Ryton, Tyne & Wear NE40 3LD. (0191 413 8749 fax 0191 413 2957, bfrankandson@aol.com).

T. Gillingham
42 Highbury Park, Warminster, Wilts BA12 9JF. (01985 216486).

Goldberg Coins & Collectibles
350 South Beverly Drive, Ste. 350, Beverly Hills CA 90212. (001 310.432.6688, fax: 001 310.551.2626, www.goldbergcoins.com).

Graves, Son & Pilcher Fine Arts
71 Church Road, Hove, East Sussex BN3 2GL. (01273 735266, fax 01273 723813).

Helios Numismatik
Ottostrasse 5, D–80333, München, Germany (+49 089 5527949 0, www.helios-numismatik. de).

Heritage World Coin Auctions
3500 Maple Avenue, 17th Floor, Dallas, Texas 75219–3941, USA. (001 214 528 3500, fax 001 214 443 8425, www.heritagecoins.com).

International Coin Exchange
Charter House, 5 Pembroke Row, Dublin 2. (+353 (0) 868493353, email: auctionice@gmail.com).

Kleeford Coin Auctions
1 Parkhall House, 42b Shop Lane, Nether Heage, Belper, Derbyshire DE56 2AR. (01773 856900). **℗**

Fritz Rudolf Künker
Gutenbergstrasse 23, 49076, Osnabrück, Germany. (0049 541 962020, fax: 0049 541 96 20222, www.kuenker.com).

Lakeland Coin Auctions
The Riverside Hotel, Penrith, Cumbria (venue). (01946 832693, www.lakelandcoinauctions.co.uk).

W. H. Lane & Son
65 Morrab Road, Penzance, Cornwall TR18 2QT. (01736 61447 fax 01736 50097).

Lawrence Fine Art Auctioneers
South Street, Crewkerne, Somerset TA18 8AB. (01460 73041).

Lockdale Coins
Shops at: 37 Upper Orwell Street, Ipswich IP4 1BR.(01473 218588, www.lockdales.com).

London Coins
4–6 Upper Street South, New Ash Green, Kent DA3 8JJ. (01474 871464, email: info@londoncoins.co.uk, www.londoncoins.co.uk).

Morton & Eden Ltd
45 Maddox Street, London W1S 2PE. (020 7493 5344 fax 020 7495 6325, info@mortonandeden.com, www.mortonandeden.com).

Mowbray Collectables
Private Bag 63000, Wellington New Zealand. (+64 6 364 8270, www.mowbraycollectables.co.nz).

Neales
192–194 Mansfield Road, Nottingham NG1 3HU. (0115 9624141, fax 0115 9856890).

Noble Numismatics
169 Macquire Street, Sydney, Australia. (+61 2 9223 4578, www.noble.com.au).

Numismatica Ars Classica NAC AG
3rd Floor, Genavco House, 17 Waterloo Place, London SW1Y 4AR (020 783 97270, email: info@arsclassicacoins.com).

Penrith, Farmers' & Kids PLC
Skirsgill Saleroom, Penrith, Cumbria, CA11 0DN. (01768 890781, www.pfkauctions.co.uk)

R & W Coin Auctions
307 Bretch Hill, Banbury, Oxon OX16 0JD (01295 275128).

Regency Auctions
Unit 1, The Capricorn Centre, Cranes Farm Road, Essex SS14 3JA. (0871 423 8871, www.regencyauctions.co.uk).

Simmons Gallery
PO Box 104, Leytonstone, London. (Tel: 0207 8989 8097. info@simmonsgallery.co.uk, www.simmonsgallery.co.uk). **℗**

Sovereign Auctions
Golden Cross House, 6–8 Duncannon Street, Charing Cross, London WC2N 4JF. (07890 764452/07854 547351, info@sovereignauctions.co.uk).

Spink & Son Ltd
69 Southampton Row, Bloomsbury, London WC1B 4ET. (020 7563 4000, fax 020 7563 4066, info@spink.com, www.spink.com).

Spink Coins & Medals
47 The Shambles, York, YO1 7XL. (01904 654769, info@spink.com, www.spink.com).

Stacks, Bowers and Ponterio
118061 Fitch, Irvine, California 92614, USA. (001 949 253 0916, www.stacksbowers.com).

St James's Auctions
43 Duke Street, St James's, London SW1Y 6DD. (020 7930 7597/7888/8215, www.sixbid.com).

Tennants Auctioneers
The Auction Centre, Leyburn, North Yorkshire DL8 5SG. (01969 623780, www.tennants.co.uk).

The-saleroom.com
115 Shaftesbury Avenue, London WC2H 8AF. Live bidding in real-time auctions from around the world. (www.the-saleroom.com).

Thomson Roddick & Metcalf
Coleridge House, Shaddongate, Carlisle CA2 5TU. (01228 528939, www.thomsonroddick.com).

Timeline Auctions
PO Box 193, Upminster RM14 3WH. (01708 222824, www.timelineauctions.com).

Mavin International
20 Kramat Lane, #01-04/05 United House, Singapore 228773. (+65 6238 7177, fax: +65 6238 7077, mail@mavininternational.com).

Warwick & Warwick
Chalon House, Scarbank, Millers Road, Warwick CV34 5DB. (01926 499031 fax 01926 491906, richard.beale@warwickandwarwick.com, www.warwickandwarwick.com).

Westminster Auctions
PO Box 199, Dereham, Norfolk, NR19 9BU. (01362 638045, info@westminsterauctions.com, www.westminsterauctions.com).

DIRECTORY *of fair*

Listed below are the names of the fair organisers, their venue details where known along with contact telephone numbers. Please call the organisers direct for information on dates etc.

Aberdeen
Jarvis Amatola Hotel, Great Western Road, also venues in **Glenrothes** and **Glasgow.** *Cornucopia Collectors Fairs (01382 224946).*

Birmingham
National Motor Cycle Museum, Bickenhill, Birmingham. *Midland Stamp & Coin Fair (01694 731781, www.midlandfair.co.uk).*

Birmingham
Collingwood Centre, Collingwood Drive, Great Barr, Birmingham. *Dave Burnett Fairs (0776 5792998).*

Bristol
Patchway High School, Hempton Lane, Almondsbury, Bristol. *Avemart Fairs (01626 859350, avemart@btopenworld.com).*

Britannia Medal Fair
Carisbrooke Hall, The Victory Services Club, 63/79 Seymour Street, London W2 2HF. *Token Publishing Ltd (01404 46972).*

Colchester
Stanway Football Club, New Farm Road, Colchester. *ClickCollect Fairs (01485 578117).*

Cardiff
City Hall, Cardiff. *M. J. Promotions. (01792 415293).*

Dublin
Serpentine Hall, RDS, Ballsbridge, Dublin 4. *Mike Kelly (00353 86 87 14 880).*

Eastleigh
The Pavilion, Southampton University, Wide Lane Sports GroundEastleigh, Hants. *South Coast Coin Fair (07890 764452).*

East Grinstead
Large Parish Hall, De La Warr Road, East Grinstead. *John Terry Fairs (01342 326317).*

Ely
The Maltings, Ship Lane, Ely. *ClickCollect (01485 578117).*

Exeter
The America Hall, De La Rue Way, Pinhoe, Exeter. *Phoenix Fairs (01761 414304).*

Harrogate
Old Swan Hotel, Swan Road, Harrogate HG1 2SR. *Simon Monks* (01234 270260).

Lichfield
Civic Hall, Castle Dyke, City Centre. *C. S. Fairs (01562 710424).*

London
Holiday Inn, Coram St., Bloomsbury, London WC1. *London Coin Fair. (01694 731781).*

London
Jury's Hotel, 16-22 Great Russell Street, London WC1 3NN. *Linda Monk Fairs (020 8656 4583).*

Plymouth
Lower Guildhall. *Bruce Stamps* (01749 813324).

Stowmarket
Stowmarket Football Club, Bury Road, Stowmarket. *ClickCollect (01485 578117).*

Suttton Coldfield
Fellowship Hall, South Parade. *C. S. Fairs (01562 710424).*

Newcastle upon Tyne
The Park Hotel, Tynemouth, Newcastle upon Tyne. *B. Frank & Son* (0191 413 8749).

Wakefield
Cedar Court Hotel, Denby Dale Road, Calder Grove, Wakefield *Eddie Smith (01552 684681).*

West Bromwich
Town Hall, High Street. *C. S. Fairs (01562 710424).*

York
The Grandstand, York Race Course. *York Coin Fair (01793 513431, 020 8946 4489 or 01425 656459).*

Important annual events — The B.N.T.A. (Coinex), Tel: 01797 229 988 for details
The I.B.N.S. (World Paper Money Fair), Email: enquiries@wpmf.info for details

THE LONDON COIN FAIR

HOLIDAY INN

London, Bloomsbury, Coram Street, WC1N 1HT

2011 dates: 19th November

2012 dates: 11th February, 26th May, 3rd November

THE MIDLAND COIN FAIR

NATIONAL MOTORCYCLE MUSEUM

Bickenhill, Birmingham, B92 0EJ

(Opposite the NEC on the M42/A45 junction)

2011 dates: 14th August, 11th December

2012 dates: 8th January, 12th February, 11th March, 8th April,
13th May, 10th June, 12th August, 9th September, 14th October,
11th November, 9th December

BLOOMSBURY COIN FAIR

BLOOMSBURY HOTEL

16-22 Great Russell Street

London WC1 3NN

2011 dates: 3rd September, 3rd December

2012 dates: 7th January, 3rd March, 5th May,
7th July, 1st September, 1st December

For more information please contact:
Lu Veissid, Hobsley House, Frodesley, Shrewsbury SY5 7HD
Tel: 01694 731781

www.coinfairs.co.uk

DEALERS *directory*

The dealers listed below have comprehensive stocks of coins and medals, unless otherwise stated. Specialities, where known, are noted. Many of those listed are postal dealers only, so to avoid disappointment always make contact by telephone or mail in the first instance, particularly before travelling any distance.

Abbreviations:
ADA— — Antiquities Dealers Association
ANA — American Numismatic Association
BADA — British Antique Dealers Association
BNTA — British Numismatic Trade Association
IAPN — International Association of Professional Numismatists
IBNS — International Bank Note Society
P — — Postal only
L — — Publishes regular lists

ABC Coins & Tokens
PO Box 52, Alnwick, Northumberland NE66 1YE. (01665 603851, email: d–stuart@d–stuart.demon. co.uk, www.abccoinsandtokens.com).

A. Ackroyd (IBNS)
62 Albert Road, Parkstone, Poole, Dorset BH12 2DB. (Tel/fax 01202 739039, www.AAnotes.com). **P L** *Banknotes and cheques*

Airedale Coins (ANA, BNTA)
PO Box 7, Bingley, West Yorkshire, BD16 1XU. (01535 272754 fax 01535 275727, email: info@airedalecoins.com, www.airedalecoins. co.uk). **P L** *British and modern coins of the world.*

Joan Allen Electronics Ltd
190 Main Road, Biggin Hill, Kent TN16 3BB. (01959 571255). Mon–Sat 09.00–17.00.
Metal detectors.

Allgold of Sevenoaks
P.O Box 260, Wallington, SM5 4H. (0844 5447952, email: sales@allgoldcoins.co.uk, www.allgoldcoins. co.uk). *Quality Sovereigns.*

A. J. W. Coins
Taunton, Somerset. (0845 6708072, email: andrewwide@ajw-coins.co.uk, www.ajw-coins. co.uk). **P** *Sovereigns and CGS-UK specialist.*

AMR COINS
(07527 569308, www.amrcoins.com). *Quality English coins specialising in rare hammered and milled coins.*

Ancient & Gothic
PO Box 5390, Bournemouth, BH7 6XR. (01202 431721). **P L** *Greek, Roman, Celtic and Biblical coins. English hammered coins & antiquities.*

Otavio Anze
Avenida Oaula Ferreira, 2159 Vila Bonilha. Pirtuba. Sao Paulo. SP. Brazil.
Coins, Antiques and collectables.

Argentum Coins
Row Foot, SowerbyRow, Carlisle, Cumbria CA4 0QG. (01697 476990, www.argentumandcoins. co.uk).
British milled coins from 1662 to date.

Arghans
Unit 9, Callington Business Park, Tinners Way Moss side, Callington PL17 7SH. (01579 382405, email: keithp44@waitrose.com). *British banknotes.*

ARL Collectables
(www.litherlandcollectables.com).
Coins, banknotes, medallions and paper emphemera.

ATS Bullion (BNTA)
2, Savoy Court, Strand. London WC2R 0EZ. (020 7240 4040, email: bullion@atslimited.fsnet. co.uk). *Bullion and modern coins.*

Keith Austin (IBNS)
10A-12-2 Pearl View Condo, Jalan Bunga Pudak, 1200, Tanjang Bunga, Penang, Malaysia. (0060 84890 7830).
L *Banknotes.*

Mark Bailey
120 Sterte Court, Sterte Close, Poole, Dorset BH15 2AY. (01202 674936). **P L** *Ancient, modern, world coins and antiquities.*

A. H. Baldwin & Sons Ltd (ANA, BADA, BNTA, IAPN)
11 Adelphi Terrace, London WC2N 6BJ. 09.00–17.00 weekdays.
(email: coins@baldwin.sh) *Coins, tokens, commemorative medals, war medals and decorations, numismatic books.*

Banking Memorabilia (IBNS)
PO Box 14, Carlisle, Cumbria. (016974 76465). 09.00–18.00 (not Sun). *Cheques, banknotes, related ephemera.*

G. Barrington Smith
Cross Street, Oadby, Leicestershire LE2 4DD. (01533 712114). 08.30–17.15 weekdays. *Albums, catalogues and accessories.*

Bath Stamp and Coin Shop
Pulteney Bridge, Bath, Avon BA2 4AY.
(01225 463073). Mon–Sat 09.30–17.30. *British.*

Michael Beaumont
PO Box 8, Carlton, Notts NG4 4QZ. (0115 9878361).
🅟 *Gold & Silver English/Foreign Coins.*

Beaver Coin Room (BNTA)
57 Philbeach Gardens, London SW5 9ED.
(020 7373 4553). 🅟 *European coins and medals.*

R. P. & P. J. Beckett
Maesyderw, Capel Dewi, Llandyssul, Dyfed
SA44 4PJ. (Fax only 01559 395631, email:
becket@xin.co.uk). 🅟 *Coin sets and banknotes.*

Lloyd Bennett (BNTA)
PO Box 2, Monmouth, Gwent NP5 3YE. (01600
890634). Abergavenny Market (Tue), Monmouth
Market (Fri–Sat) 09.00–16.00. *English hammered,
milled and coins of the world.*

Berkshire Coin Centre
35 Castle Street, Reading, Berkshire RG1 7SB.
(0118 957 5593). 0630–15.00 W, Th, Fri & Sat.
Sat. *British British and world coins and militaria.*

Beron Coins
64 Rosewood Close, Glascote, Tamworth, Staffs
B77 3PD. (01827 54541).🅟 🅛*British & world
coins.*

Stephen J. Betts
4 Victoria Street, Narborough, Leics LE9 5DP.
(0116 2864434).🅟 🅛*Medieval and modern coins,
counters, jetons and tokens, countermarks and
medals.*

Bigbury Mint
River Park, Ermington Mill, Ivybridge, Devon
PL21 9NT. (01548 830717. *Specialists in
reproductionhammered coins*

Birchin Lane Gold Coin Company
6 Castle Court, St Michael's Alley (off Cornhill),
London EC3V 9DS. (020 7621 0370/020 7263 3981).
Mon–Fri 10.00–16.30. *Gold and bullioncoins.*

Barry Boswell
24 Townsend Lane, Upper Boddington, Daventry,
Northants NN11 6DR. (01327 261877, fax 01327
261391, email: Barry.Boswell@btinternet.com).
🅟 🅛*British and world banknotes.*

James & C. Brett
17 Dale Road, Lewes, East Sussex BN7 1LH.
🅟 🅛*British and world coins.*

J. Bridgeman Coins
129a Blackburn Road, Accrington, Lancs
(01254 384757). 09.30–17.00 (closed Wednesday).
British & World coins.

Brighton Coin Company (ANA, BNTA)
The Hove Coin Shop, Church Road, Hove, (01273
737537) Mon–Fri 9.45–17.30, Sat 9.45–15.30
(closed alternate Wednesdays and Saturdays).
World coins.

Britco
23 Orkney Close, Stenson Fields, Derby DE24
3LW. (Tel: 01332 760189. http://stores.ebay.
co.uk/britcoins). *18th to 20th Century British coins.*

BRM Coins
3 Minshull Street, Knutsford, Cheshire WA16 6HG.
(01565 651480 and 0606 74522). Mon–Fri 11.00–
15.00, Sat 11.00–1.00 or by appt. *British coins.*

A. F. Brock & Company
269 London Road, Hazel Grove, Stockport,
Cheshire SK7 4PL. (0161 456 5050/5112, email
info@afbrock.co.uk, www.afbrock.co.uk).
Auctioneers and valuers.

Bucks Coins
Jordan House, Jordan Lane, Whitwell, Norfolk
NR10 4RQ. (07825 440085). *English milled coins.*

Iain Burn
2 Compton Gardens, 53 Park Road, Camberley,
Surrey GU15 2SP. (01276 23304).
Bank of England & Treasury notes.

BBM Coins
8–9 Lion Street, Kidderminster, Hereford &
Worcester, DY10 1PT. (01562 515007). Wed, Th, Fri.
10.00–14.00 or by appointment.
World coins.

Cambridge Coins
52 High Street, Biggleswade SG18 0LJ. 01767
6003000/07787 358689. Email: shop@cambridge
coins.co.uk, www.cambridgecoins.co.uk). *Coins,
medals, banknotes, bullion and jewellery.*

Cambridgeshire Coins
355 Newmarket Road, Cambridge CB5 8JG.
(01223 503703, info@cambridgeshirecoins.com,
www.cambridgeshirecoins.com).
Coins, banknotes and accessories.

Cambridge Stamp Centre Ltd
9 Sussex Street, Cambridge CB4 4HU.
(01223 63980). Mon–Sat 09.00–17.30.
British coins.

Castle Galleries
81 Castle Street, Salisbury, Wiltshire SP1 3SP.
(01722 333734). Tue, Thu Fri 09.00–17.00,
Sat 09.30–16.00. *British coins, medals and tokens.*

Cathedral Coins
23 Kirkgate, Ripon, North Yorkshire HG4 1PB.
(01765 701400). Mon–Sat 10.00–17.00.

Cathedral Court Medals
First Floor Office, 30A Market Place, West Ripon,
North Yorks HG4 1BN. (01765 601400). *Coin and
medal sales. Medal mounting and framing.*

David L. Cavanagh
49 Cockburn Street, Edinburgh EH1 1BS.
(0131 226 3391). Mon–Sat 11.00–17.00. *British coins.*

Central Bank of Ireland
Currency Centre, Sandyford Road, Dublin 16,
Ireland. Issuer of *new coin and banknote issues of
Ireland.*

Certified Coin Investment
PO Box 83, Longfield DA3 9AX.
(01474 874895). *English milled coins.*

C. G. S.
4-6 Upper Street South, New Ash Green, Longfield,
Kent DA3 8JJ. (01474 874895, email: info@cgs-uk.
biz). *Coin grading service.*

Lance Chaplin
17 Wanstead Lane, Ilford, Essex IG1 3SB.
(020 8554 7154. www.shaftesburycoins.com).
P L*Roman, Greek, Celtic, hammered coins and antiquities.*

Chard (BNTA)
521 Lytham Road, Blackpool, Lancs FY4 1RJ.
(01253 343081. www.chards.co.uk).
Mon–Sat 09.00–17.00. *British, and world coins.*

Nigel A. Clark
28 Ulundi Road, Blackheath, London SE3 7UG. (020 8858 4020, email: nigel.a.clark@btinternet.com).**P L**
Tokens (Mainly 17th century) and British Farthings.

Classical Numismatic Group (IAPN)
14 Old Bond Street, London W1X 4JL. (020 7495 1888 Fax 020 7499 5916, email cng@cngcoins.com, www.cngcoins.com). **P***Ancient and world coins. Publishers of the Classical Numismatic Review.*

Paul Clayton (BNTA)
PO Box 21, Wetherby, West Yorkshire LS22 5JY.
(01937 72441). *Modern gold coins.*

André de Clermont (BNTA)
PO Box 3615, London, SW10 0YD. (020 7351 5727, Fax 020 7352 8127). *World coins, especially Islamic & Oriental coins, Latin America.*

M. Coeshaw
PO Box 115, Leicester LE3 8JJ. (0116 287 3808). **P**
Coins, banknotes, coin albums and cases.

Philip Cohen Numismatics (ANA, BNTA)
20 Cecil Court, Charing Cross Road, London WC2N 4HE. (020 7379 0615). Mon–Sat 11.00–17.30.

Coin & Collectors Centre
PO Box 22, Pontefract, West Yorkshire WF8 1YT. (01977 704112, email sales@coincentre.co.uk, www.coincentre.co.uk). **P***British coins.*

Coincraft (ANA, IBNS)
44/45 Great Russell Street, London, WC1B 3JL.
(020 7636 1188 and 020 7637 8785 fax 020 7323 2860, email: info@coincraft.com). Mon–Fri 09.30–17.00, Sat 10.00–14.30. **L**(newspaper format). *Coins and banknotes.*

Coinote Services Ltd
74–74a Elwick Road, Hartlepool TS26 9AP. (01429 890894).**P L***Coins & banknotes 1615 to date. Accessories, & books. Also at Stockton Market, Wednesdays. Chester Le Street Market, Saturdays.*

Coinswap.co.uk
Swap, sell or trade coins.

Coins Historic
PO Box 5043, Lower Quinton, Stratford Upon Avon, Warks CV37 8WH. (01789 721117). *Celtic, Roman, Greek and English hammered coins.*

Coins of Beeston
PO Box 19, Beeston, Notts BG9 2NE.**P L**
Tokens, medals and paranumismatics.

Coins of Canterbury
PO Box 47, Faversham, Kent ME13 7HX.
(01795 531980). **P** *English coins.*

Collectors' World (Mark Ray)
188 Wollaton Road, Wollaton, Nottingham NG8 1HJ.
(01159 280347). *Coins, Tokens, Banknotes, Accessories.*

Constantia CB
15 Church Road, Northwood, Middlesex HA6 1AR. **P** *Roman and medieval hammered coins.*

Colin Cooke
P.O. Box 602, Altrincham, WA14 5UN. (0161 927 9524 fax 0161 927 9540, email coins@colin cooke.com, www.colincooke.com).
L*British coins.*

Colonial Coins & Medals
218 Adelaide Street, Brisbane, QLD 4001.
(Email:coinshop@bigpond.net.au).
Auctions of World coins

Corbitts (BNTA)
5 Mosley Street, Newcastle Upon Tyne NE1 1YE.
(0191 232 7268 fax: 0191 261 4130). *Dealers and auctioneers of all coins and medals.*

David Craddock
PO Box 3785, Camp Hill, Birmingham B11 2NF.
(0121 733 2259) **L***Crown to farthings. Copper and bronze specialist. Some foreign.*

Roy Cudworth
8 Park Avenue, Clayton West, Huddersfield HD8 9PT. *British and world coins.*

Mark Davidson
PO Box 197, South Croydon, Surrey, CR3 0ZD.
(020 8651 3890). *Ancient, hammered coinage.*

Paul Davis
PO Box 418, Birmingham, B17 0RZ.
(0121 427 7179). *British and World Coins.*

R. Davis
(01332 862755 days/740828 evenings). *Maker of traditional coin cabinets.*

Linda Monk Fairs
PO Box 201, Croydon, Surrey CR9 7AQ. (020 8656 4583). Organiser of fairs at the Jury's Hotel, 16–22 Great Russell Street, London, WC1 3NN.

Paul Davies Ltd (ANA, BNTA, IAPN)
PO Box 17, Ilkley, West Yorkshire LS29 8TZ.
(01943 603116 fax 01943 816326). **P**
World coins.

Ian Davison
PO Box 256, Durham DH1 2GW (0191 3750808).**L**
English hammered and milled coins 1066–1910.

Decus Coins
The Haven, Brockweir, Chepstow, Gwent NP6 7NN. (01291 689216). **P**

Dei Gratia
PO Box 3568, Buckingham MK18 4ZS (01280 848000).**P L** *Pre–Roman to modern coins, antiquities, banknotes.*

Den of Antiquity
(01223 863002, www.denof antiquity.co.uk.)
Ancient and medieval coins.

Clive Dennett (BNTA)
66 St Benedicts Street, Norwich, Norfolk NR2 4AR.
(01603 624315). Mon–Fri 09.00–17.30, Sat 09.00–16.00 (closed 1.00–2.00 & Thu).**L** *Specialising in paper money.*

C. J. Denton (ANA, BNTA, FRNS)
PO Box 25, Orpington, Kent BR6 8PU (01689 873690).**P** *Irish coins.*

Detecnicks
3 Orchard Crescent, Arundel Road, Fontwell. West Sussex BN18 0SA. (01243 545060 fax 01243 545922) *Retail shop. Wide range of detectors.*

Michael Dickinson (ANA, BNTA)
Ramsay House, 825 High Road Finchley, London N12 8UB. (0181 441 7175). **P**
British and world coins.

Dorset Coin Co Ltd (BNTA)
193 Ashley Road, Parkstone, Poole, Dorset BH14 9DL. (01202 739606, fax 01202 739230. www.dorsetcoincompany.co.uk). **P** **L**
Separate coin and banknote lists.

Douglassaville.com
(0118 918 7628). *Out of print, second-hand and rare coin and medal books.*

Dyas Coins & Medals
30 Shaftmoor Lane, Acocks Green, Birmingham B27 7RS. (0121 707 2808). Fri 10.30–18.30, Sun 10.30–13.00. *World coins and medals.*

Eagle Coins
Winterhaven, Mourneabbey, Mallow, Co. Cork, Ireland. (010 35322 29385). **P** **L** *Irish coins.*

Early World Coins
7–9 Clifford Street, York, YO1 9RA. (08454 900724).

Eden Coins
PO Box 77, Brierley Hill, West Midlands DY5 2GS. (01384 834648). **P**
English coins, tokens and medals.

Edinburgh Coin Shop (ANA)
11 West Crosscauseway, Edinburgh EH8 9JW. (0131 668 2928 fax 0131 668 2926). Mon–Sat 10.00–17.30. **L**
World coins and medals. Postal auctions.

Educational Coin Company
Box 892, Highland, New York 12528, USA. (+ 845 691 6100.) *World banknotes.*

Christopher Eimer (ANA, BNTA, IAPN)
PO Box 352 London NW11 7RF. (020 8458 9933 fax 020 8455 3535, email: art@christophereimer.co.uk). **P** *Commemorative medals.*

Malcolm Ellis Coins
Petworth Road, Witley, Surrey, GU8 5LX. (01428 685566, email: malcolm.ellis@wizardvideo.co.uk, www.malcolmelliscoins.co.uk). *Collectors and dealers of British and foreign coins and medals.*

Elm Hill Stamps & Coins
27 Elm Hill, Norwich, Norfolk NR3 1HN. (01603 627413). Mon. 09.00–17.00, Tues–Wed. 09.00–17.00, Thur. 0900–13.00, Sat. 09.30–15.00. *Mainly stamps, occasionally coins.*

Europa Numismatics (ANA, BNTA)
PO Box 119, High Wycombe, Bucks HP11 1QL. (01494 437307). **P** *European coins.*

Evesham Stamp & Coin Centre
Magpie Antiques, Paris House, 61 High Street, Evesham, Worcs WR11 4DA (01386 41631). Mon–Sat 09.00–17.30. *British coins.*

Michael E. Ewins
Meyrick Heights, 20 Meyrick Park Crescent, Bournemouth, Dorset BH3 7AQ. (01202 290674). **P**
World coins.

I. Fine & Son Ltd
Victoria House, 93 Manor Farm Road, Wembley, Middlesex HA10 1XB. (020 8997 5055). **P** *British & World coins.*

Robin Finnegan Stamp Shop
83 Skinnergate, Darlington, Co Durham DL3 7LX. (01325 489820/357674). Mon–Sat 10.00–17.30 (closed Wed). *World coins.*

Richard N. Flashman
54 Ebbsfleet Walk, Gravesend, Kent, DA11 9EW. **L** **P** *British banknotes.*

David Fletcher (Mint Coins) (ANA, BNTA)
PO Box 64, Coventry, Warwickshire CV1 5YR. (024 7671 5425, Fax 024 7601 0300). **P**
World new issues.

Format of Birmingham Ltd (ANA, BNTA, IAPN, IBNS)
2nd Floor, Burlington Court, Lower Temple Street, Birmingham, B2 4JD. (0121 643 2058 fax 0121 643 2210). Mon–Fri 09.30–7.00. **L** *Coins, tokens and medals.*

B. Frank & Son (ANA, IBNS)
3 South Avenue, Ryton, Tyne & Wear NE40 3LD. (0191 413 8749. www.b–frank–and–son.co.uk). **P** **L** *Banknotes and cheques, coins of the world. Organiser of the North of England fair.*

Galata Coins Ltd (ANA)
The Old White Lion, Market Street, Llanfylin, Powys SY22 5BX. (01691 648 765). **P** *British and world coins.*

G. B. Gold Coins
PO Box 1515, Kingston Upon Thames KT1 9UE. (07917 160308, www.gbgoldcoins.co.uk). *British and World coins specialising in sovereigns and krugerands.*

G. Gant
Glazenwood, 37 Augustus Way, Witham, Essex CM8 1HH. **P** *British and Commonwealth coins.*

A. & S. Gillis
59 Roykilner Way, Wombwell, Barnsley, South Yorkshire S73 8DY. (01226 750371, email: catalogues@gilliscoins.com. www.gilliscoins.com). **P** **L** *Ancient coins and antiquities.*

G. K. Coins
17 Hanover Square, London W1S 1HU (020 7518 0383, fax: 020 7518 0302, email: george@gkcoins.com, www.gkcoins.com). *Rare and common sovereigns. British and world coins.*

Richard Gladdle – Northamptonshire
(01327 858511, email: gladdle@plumpudding.org). *Tokens.* **P** **L**

Glance Back Books
17 Upper Street, Chepstow, Gwent NP6 5EX. (01291 626562). 10.30–17.30. *Coins, banknotes.*

Glendining's (Bonhams) (ANA, BNTA)
101 New Bond Street, London W1Y 9LG (020 7493 2445). Mon–Fri 08.30–17.00, Sat 08.30–13.00. *Auctioneers.*

Glenely Coins
73 Ladymead, Cricklade, Swindon, Wiltshire SN6 6EP. (01793 750307, email: chris kellow@hotmail.com). *British coins.*

GM Coins
(01242 701144, email: gmcoins@blueyonder.co.uk, www.gmonlinecoins.co.uk/gmcoins). *Hammered and milled coins.*

Goulborn
PO Box 122, Rhyl LL18 3XR. (Tel: 01745 338112). *Coins and banknotes.*

Ian Gradon
PO Box 359, Durham DH7 6WZ. (0191 3719 700, email: igradon960@aol.com, www.worldnotes. co.uk). 🅛 *World banknotes.*

Grantham Coins (BNTA)
PO Box 60, Grantham, Lincs. (01476 870565).🅟🅛 *English coins and banknotes.*

Eric Green—Agent in UK for Ronald J. Gillio Inc
1013 State Street, Santa Barbara, California, USA 93101. (020 8907 0015, Mobile 0468 454948). *Gold coins, medals and paper money of the world.*

Philip Green
Suite 207, 792 Wilmslow Road, Didsbury, Manchester M20 6UG. (0161 440 0685). G*old coins.*

R. I. Groves
8 Catherine Street, Dumfries DG1 1JA. (01387 266617, email: richard@I-groves.demon.co.uk, www. worldcoins.biz). 🅟 *British & world coins.*

Ian Haines
PO Box 45, Hereford, HR2 7YP. (01432 268178). 🅟 🅛*British and foreign coins and banknotes.*

Anthony Halse
PO Box 1856, Newport, Gwent NP6 2JN. (01633 413238).🅟🅛*English and foreign coins and tokens.*

A. D. Hamilton & Co (ANA)
7 St Vincent Place, Glasgow G1 5JA. (0141 221 5423, email jeffineman@hotmail.com, www.ad hamilton.co.uk). *Mon–Sat 10.00–17.00. British and World coins.*

Peter Hancock
40–41 West Street, Chichester, West Sussex PO19 1RP. (01243 786173). *Tues–Sat. World coins, medals and banknotes.*

Munthandel G. Henzen
PO Box 42, NL – 3958ZT, Amerogngen, Netherlands. (0031 343 430564 fax 0031 343 430542, email: info@henzen.org, www.henzen.org). 🅛*Ancients, Dutch and foreign coins.*

History In Coins.com
(01949 836988, www.historyincoins.com). *World coins.*

Craig Holmes
6 Marlborough Drive, Bangor, Co Down BT19 1HB.🅟 🅛*Low cost banknotes of the world.*

R. G. Holmes
11 Cross Park, Ilfracombe, Devon EX34 8BJ. (01271 864474). 🅟🅛
Coins, world crowns and banknotes.

John L. Homan
Oxford Grange, Marsh Lane, Barrow Haven, Barrow–on–Humber, South Humberside DN19 7ER. (01469 32109). 🅟 *Greek, Roman and Byzantine.*

Homeland Holding Ltd (IBNS)
Homeland, St John, Jersey, Channel Islands JE3 4AB. (01534 65339). Mon–Fri 09.00–2.00. *World coins.*

HTSM Coins
26 Dosk Avenue, Glasgow G13 4LQ.🅟🅛
British and foreign coins and banknotes.

T. A. Hull
15 Tangmere Crescent, Hornchurch, Essex RM12 5PL.🅟🅛 *British coins, farthings to crowns, tokens.*

J. Hume
107 Halsbury Road East, Northolt, Middlesex UB5 4PY. (020 8864 1731).🅟 🅛 *Chinese coins.*

D. A. Hunter
(Email: coins@dahunter.co.uk, www.dahunter.co.uk/ coins).🅟🅛
UK and World Coins.

D. D. & A. Ingle
380 Carlton Hill, Nottingham. (0115 9873325). Mon–Sat 09.30–17.00. *World coins.*

R. Ingram Coins
206 Honeysuckle Road, Bassett, Southampton, Hants SO16 3BU. (023 8032 4258, email: info@ ringramcoins.com, www.ringramcoins.com).🅟🅛
Dealers in UK coins.

Intercol London (ANA, IBNS)
43 Templars Cresent, London N3 3QR. (020 8349 2207) 🅟 *Paper money of the World.*

Isle of Wight Mint
PO Box 195, Cowes, Isle of Wight, PO30 9DP. (www.iowmint.org). *Producer of Isle of Wight bullion.*

J. B. J. Coins
(www.jbjcoins.dk). *World coins and banknotes.*

F. J. Jeffery & Son Ltd
Haines Croft, Corsham Road, Whitley, Melksham, Wilts SN12 8QF. (01225 703143).🅟
British, Commonwealth and foreign coins.

Richard W. Jeffery
Trebehor, Porthcurno, Penzance, Cornwall TR19 6LS. (01736 871263). 🅟 *British and world coins. Banknotes.*

Jersey Coin Co Ltd
26 Halkett Street, St Helier, Jersey, Channel Islands. (01534 25743). Mon–Sat 09.00–17.00.
World coins.

J. G. Coins
PO Box 206, Southshore, Blackpool FY1 6GZ. (01253 349138).🅟🅛*British Coins.*

Robert Johnson Coin Co
Zeilerviertel 6, 8232, Grafendorf, Steiermark, Austria (06644 882 301, email: rjcoinco@aol.com). *British and world coins.*

Jumbo Coins
22 Woodend Lane, Stalybridge, Cheshire SK15 2SR. (0161 338 5741). Fri–Sat 14.00–19.00. *World coins, medals and tokens.*

Kates Paper Money
Kate Gibson, PO Box 819, Camberley, Surrey, GU16 6ZU. (01276 64181, www.katespapermoney.co.uk). *Banknotes.*

KB Coins (BNTA)
50 Lingfield Road, Martins Wood, Stevenage, Herts SG1 5SL. (01438 312661, fax 01438 311990). 09.00–18.00 by appointment only. 🅛
Mainly British coins.

K&M Coins
PO Box 3662, Wolverhampton WV10 6ZW.
(0771 2381880/079719 50246,
email: M_Bagguley@hotmail.com). *Englishmilledcoins.*

Knightsbridge Coins (ANA, BNTA, IAPN, PNG)
43 Duke Street, St James's, London SW1Y 6DD.
(020 7930 8215/7597 Fax 020 7930 8214). Mon–Fri
10.00–17.30. *Quality coins of the world.*

Lancashire Coin & Medal Co
31 Adelaide Street, Fleetwood, Lancs FY7 6AD .
(01253 779308). 🅟 *British coins and medals.*

Lennox Gallery Ltd
K12/13, 4 Davies Mews, London, W1Y 1AR. (020
7629 9119 fax 020 7629 9119). Ancient coins.
Lighthouse Publications (Duncannon Partnership)
4 Beaufort Road, Reigate, Surrey RH2 9DJ (01737
244222 Fax 01737 224743. www.duncannon.
co.uk). 🅛 *Manufacturers and stockists of coin
albums, cabinets and numismatic accessories.*

Lindner Publications Ltd
3a Hayle Industrial Park, Hayle, Cornwall TR27 5JR.
(01736 751914 fax: 01736 751911, email
lindner@prinz.co.uk). Mon–Fri 09.00–13.00.
🅛 *Manufacturers of coin albums, cabinets and
accessories.*

Jan Lis (BNTA)
Beaver Coin Room, 57 Philbeach Gardens, London
SW5 9ED. (020 7373 4553 fax 020 7373 4555).
By appointment only. *European coins.*

Keith Lloyd
45 Bramblewood, The Beeches, Ipswich, Suffolk
IP8 3RS. (01473 603067). 🅟 🅛 *Greek, Roman and
ancient coins.*

Lockdale Coins (BNTA)
Shops at: 37 Upper Orwell Street, Ipswich IP4
1BR. (01473 218588), 168 London Road South,
Lowestoft NR33 0BB. (01502 568468) & 23
Magdalene Street, Cambridge, CB3 OAF. (01223
361163). 🅛 (Shops open 9.30–4.30 Mon–Sat).
World coins, medals, banknotes and accessories.

Stephen Lockett (BNTA)
4–6 Upper Street, New Ash Green, Kent, DA3 8JJ.
(01474 871464). *British and world coins.*

The London Coin Company
(0800 085 2933, 020 8343 2231, email:
sales@thelondoncoincompany.com,
www.thelondoncoincomany.com).
Modern gold and silver coins.

Mike Longfield Detectors
83 Station Road, Balsall Common, nr Coventry,
Warwickshire CV7 7FN. (01676 533274).
Mon–Sat 09.30–17.00. *Metal detectors.*

Don MacRae Coins
PO Box 233, Uxbridge, Middlesex UB9 4HY.
(01895 832625). 🅟 *British and world coins.*

MA Shops
(www.mashops.com). On-line coin mall. *Coins,
medals, banknotes and saccessories.*

Mannin Collections Ltd
5 Castle Street, Peel, Isle of Man, IM5 1AN. (01624
843897, email: manncoll@advsys.co.uk). Mon–Sat
10.00–16.00. Closed Thu. *IOM coins, tokens, etc.*

Manston Coins of Bath
Bartletts St. Antique Centre, Bath. (01761 416133.
Coins, tokens and medals.

I. Markovits
1–3 Cobbold Mews, London W12 9LB.
(020 8749 3000). *Enamelled coins.*

C. J. Martin Coins (BNTA)
85 The Vale, Southgate, London N14 6AT. (020 8882
1509, www.ancientart.co.uk). 🅟 🅛 Bi–monthly
catalogue. *Greek, Roman & English hammered coins.*

M. G. Coins & Antiquities
12 Mansfield, High Wych, Herts CM21 0JT. (01279
721719). 🅛
Ancient and hammered coins, antiquities.

M&H Coins
PO Box 10985, Brentwood, CM14 9JB. (07504
804019, www.mhcoins.co.uk). 🅛 *British hammered
and milled coins.*

Giuseppe Miceli
204 Bants Lane, Duston, Northampton NN5 6AH.
(01604 581533). 🅛 *British coins and medals.*

Michael Coins
6 Hillgate Street, London W8 7SR. (020 7727 1518).
Mon–Fri 10.00–17.00. *World coins and banknotes.*

David Miller Coins & Antiquities (ANA, BNTA)
PO Box 711, Hemel Hempstead, HP2 4UH. (Tel/fax
01442 251492).
Ancient and hammered English coins.

Timothy Millett
PO Box 20851, London SE22 0YN.
(Tel: 020 8693 1111, fax: 020 8299 3733,
www.historicmedals.com). 🅛
Historical medals.

Nigelmills.net
(020 8504 2569. email: nigelmills@onetel.com,
www.nigelmills.net). *Coins and antiquities.*

Frank Milward (ANA, BNTA)
2 Ravensworth Road, Mortimer, Berkshire RG7
3UU. (01734 322843). 🅟 *European coins.*

Mis–struck World Coins
Storhojdgstan 17, 416 71 Gothenburg, Sweden.
(Email: mawett@hotmail.com). *Gold coins.*

Graeme & Linda Monk (ANA, BNTA)
PO Box 201, Croydon, Surrey, CR9 7AQ.
(020 8656 4583 fax 020 8656 4583). 🅟
Fair organisers.

Moore Antiquities
Unit 12, Ford Lane Industrial Estate, Ford, nr.
Arundel, West Sussex BN18 0AA. (01243 824 232,
email moore.antiquities@virgin.net).
Coins and artefacts up to the 18th Century.

Mike Morey
19 Elmtrees, Long Crendon, Bucks HP18 9DG. 🅟 🅛
British coins, halfcrowns to farthings.

Peter Morris (BNTA, IBNS)
1 Station Concourse, Bromley North Station,
Bromley, BR1 1NN or PO Box 223, Bromley,
BR1 4EQ (020 8313 3410 fax 020 8466 8502,
email: info@petermorris.co.uk, www.petermorris.
co.uk). Mon–Fri 10.00–18.00, Sat 0900–14.00 or
by appointment. 🅛 *British and world coins, proof
sets and numismatic books.*

James Murphy
PO Box 122, Chorley, Lancashire PR7 2GE. (01257 274 381). 🅟 🅛 *Ancient coins and antiquities.*

N3 Coins—London
(07768 795575, email: mail@n3coins.com, www.n3coins.com). *High quality Roman and Ancient coins.*

Colin Narbeth & Son Ltd (ANA, IBNS)
20 Cecil Court, Leicester Square, London WC2N. 4HE (020 7379 6975 fax 01727 811 244, www.colin–narbeth.com). Mon–Sat 10.30–17.00. *World banknotes.*

New Forest Leaves
Bisterne Close, Burley, Ringwood, Hants BH24 4BA. (014253 3315). *Publishers of numismatic books.*

John Newman Coins
(01903 239867, email: john@newmancoins.co.uk, www.johnnewmancoins.co.uk). *English hammered coins, British milled coins and British tokens.*

Peter Nichols
2 Norman Road, St Leonards on Sea, East Sussex TN37 6NH. (01424 436682, email: orders@coin cabinets.com, www.coincabinets.com).

Wayne Nicholls
PO Box 44, Bilston, West Midlands. (01543 45476). 🅛 *Choice English coins.*

Northeast Numismatics (BNTA)
10 Concord Crossing Suite 220, Concord MA 01742, USA (001 978 369 9155, fax: 001 978 369 9619, www.northeastcoin.com). *British and world coins.*

North Wales Coins Ltd (BNTA)
1b Penrhyn Road, Colwyn Bay, Clwyd. (01492 533023/532129). Mon–Sat (closed Wed) 09.30–17.30. *British coins.*

NP Collectables
9 Main Street, Gedney Dyke, Spalding, Lincs PE12 0AJ. (01406 365211Ireland (010 35322 29385). 🅟 🅛 *English Hammered and Milled coins.*

Notability Notes (IBNS)
(Email: info@notability-banknotes.com, www.notability-banknotes.com). *Quality banknotes from British Isles, Commonwealth and world.*

Glenn S. Ogden
53 Chestnut Crescent, Culver Green, Chudleigh, Devon TQ13 OPT. (01626 859350 or 07971 709427, www.glenogdencoins.com). 🅟 🅛 *English milled coins.*

John Ogden Coins
Hodge Clough Cottage, Moorside, Oldham OL1 4JW. (0161 678 0709) 🅟 🅛 *Ancient and hammered.*

Michael O'Grady (IBNS)
PO Box 307, Pinner, Middlesex HA5 4XT. (020 428 4002). 🅟 *British and world paper money.*

Colin James O'Keefe
5 Pettits Place, Dagenham, Essex RM10 8NL. 🅟 *British and European coins.*

Don Oliver Gold Coins
Stanford House, 23 Market Street, Stourbridge, West Midlands DY8 1AB. (01384 877901). Mon–Fri 10.00–17.00. *British gold coins.*

Onewebby.com
PO Box 6219, Basildon, Essex, SS14 0AS. *World and British copper and silver.*

Ongar Coins
14 Longfields, Marden Ash, Ongar, Essex IG7 6DS. 🅟 *World coins.*

Orpington Coins and Medals
242 High Street, Orpington, Kent BR6 0LZ. (01689 890045). Wed–Sat 09.45–17.30).
Coins, medals, banknotes, badges, militaria etc.

Roger Outing
PO Box 123, Huddersfield HD8 9WY. (01484 60415, email: rogerandlizbanknotes4u.co.uk, www.banknotes4u.co.uk). *World banknotes.*

Tim Owen Coins
63 Allerton Grange Rise, Leeds 17, West Yorkshire. 🅟 🅛 *Quality hammered coins.*

P&D Medallions
PO Box 269, Berkhampstead, Herts HP4 3FT. (01442 865127, www.pdmedallions.co.uk). 🅟 *Historical and Commemorative medals.*

Del Parker
PO Box 998, Mercer Island, WA 98040, USA. (+ 1 206 232 2560. Email: Irishcoins2000@ hotmail.com). *Irish and American Coins. Irish Art medals and banknotes.* 🅛

Kleeford Coins
Parkhall House, 42b Shop Lane, Nether Heage, Belper, Derbyshire, DE56 2AR. (01773 856900, Email: info@parkhallcoins.co.uk, www.parkhallcoins.co.uk). *Buying and selling British coins.*

www.paulspapermoney.com
Selling and buying high quality and rare UK banknotes.

Pavlos S. Pavlou
Stand L17, Grays Antique Market, 1–7 Davies Mews, Mayfair, London W1Y 2LP. (020 7629 9449, email: pspavlou@hotmail.com). *Ancient, Medieval & Modern Coins.*

PCGS
(+33 (0) 140200994, email:info@pcgsglobal.com, www.pcgs.com). *Coin grading and authentication service.*

www.pennycrowncoins.co.uk
Specialising in British milled coins 1662–1970.

Penrith Coin & Stamp Centre
37 King Street, Penrith, Cumbria CA11 7AY. (01768 64185). Mon–Sat 09.00–17.30. *World coins.*

Pentland Coins (IBNS)
Pentland House, 92 High Street, Wick, Caithness KW14 L5. 🅟 *British and world coins and world banknotes.*

John Phillimore
The Old Post Office, Northwood, Shropshire SY4 5NN. 🅛 *Foreign coins 1600–1950.*

Philip. P. Phipps
PO Box 139, Tiverton, Devon EX16 0AU. (07850 864554, email p.p.phipps@tesco.net). 🅟 🅛 *World and German banknotes.*

B. C. Pickard
1 Treeside, Christchurch, Dorset BH23 4PF. (01425 275763, email: bcpickard@fsmail.net). 🅟 *Stone Age, Greek, Roman items (inc. coins) for sale.*

David C. Pinder
20 Princess Road West, Leicester LE1 6TP. (0116 2702439). 🅟 *Greek, Roman and Byzantine coins.*

Pobjoy Mint Ltd (ANA)
Millennium House, Kingswood Park, Bonsor Drive, Kingswood, Surrey KT20 6AY. (01737 818181 fax 01737 818199). Mon–Fri 09.00–17.00. Europe's largest private mint. *New issues.*

David Pratchett
UCCE, PO Box 57648, Mill Hill, London NW7 0FE. (07831 662594, fax 020 7930 1152, email: uccedcp@aol.com, www.coinsonline.co.uk). Mon–Fri 10.00–7.30. *Gold and silver world coins.*

Pykerleys Collectables
PO Box 649, Whitley Bay NE26 9AF. (Email: pykereley@yahoo.co.uk, www.pykerley.worldonline.co.uk). *Western European and US coins.*

George Rankin Coin Co Ltd (ANA)
325 Bethnal Green Road, London E2 6AH. (020 7729 1280 fax 020 7729 5023). Mon–Sat 10.00–18.00 (half-day Thu). *World coins.*

The Rare Coin Company
111 Princes Highway, Kogarah, NSW 2217. (+02 9588 7111, www.therarecoincompany.com). *Specialists in Australian coins and banknotes.*

Mark Rasmussen (BNTA, IAPN)
PO Box 42, Betchworth RH3 7YR. (01737 84100, Email: mark.rasmussen@rascoins.com, www.rascoins.com). 🅛 *Hammered and milled coins.*

Mark T. Ray (see Collectors World)

Rhyl Coin Shop
12 Sussex Street, Rhyl, Clwyd. (01745 338112). Mon–Sat 10.00–17.30. *World coins and banknotes.*

Chris Rigby
PO Box 181, Worcester WR1 1YE. (01905 28028). 🅟 🅛 *Modern British coins.*

Roderick Richardson (BNTA)
The Old Granary Antiques Centre, King's Staithe Lane, King's Lynn, Norfolk. (01553 670833, www.roderickrichardson.com) 🅛 *English, Hammered and early milled coins.*

Charles Riley (BNTA)
PO Box 733, Aylesbury HP22 9AX. (01296747598, charles.riley@virgin.net, www.charlesriley.co.uk). *Coins, medals and medallions.*

F. J. Rist
PO Box 4, Ibstock, Leics LE67 6ZJ. (01530 264278). 🅟 🅛 *Ancient and medieval coins.*

Robin–on–Acle Coins
Parkeston House, Parkeston Quay, Harwich, Essex CO12 4PJ. (01255 554440, email: enquiries@robin–on–acle.coins.co.uk). *Ancient to modern coins and paper money.*

S. J. Rood & Co Ltd
52–53 Burlington Arcade, London W1V 9AE. (0171 493 0739). Mon–Sat 09.30–17.00. *World gold coins.*

Royal Australian Mint
(www.ramint.gov.au). *New coin issues.*

Royal Gold
PO Box 123, Saxonwold, 2132, South Africa. (+27 11 483 0161, email: royalg@iafrica.com). *Gold coins.*

Royal Mint Coin Club
PO Box 500, Cardiff CF1 1YY. (01443 623456). 🅟 *Updates and special offers of new issues struck by the Royal Mint.*

Colin de Rouffignac (BNTA)
57, Wigan Lane, Wigan, Lancs WN1 2LF. (01942 237927). *P. English and Scottish hammered.*

R. P. Coins
PO Box 367, Prestwich, Manchester, M25 9ZH. (07802 713444, www.rpcoins.co.uk). *Coins, books, catalogues and accessories.*

Chris A. Rudd (IAPN, BNTA)
PO Box 222, Aylsham, Norfolk, NR11 6TY. (01263 735007 fax 01263 731777, www.celticcoins.com). 🅟 🅛 *Celtic coins.*

Colin Rumney (BNTA)
PO Box 34, Denbighshire, North Wales, LL16 4YQ. (01745 890621). *All world including ancients.*

R & J Coins
21b Alexandra Street, Southend-on-Sea, Essex, SS1 1DA. (01702 345995). *World coins.*

Safe Albums (UK) Ltd
16 Falcon Business Park, 38 Ivanhoe Road, Finchampstead, Berkshire RG40 4QQ. (0118 932 8976 fax 0118 932 8612). *Accessories.*

Saltford Coins
Harcourt, Bath Road, Saltford, Bristol, Avon BS31 3DQ. (01225 873512, email: info@saltfordcoins.com, www.saltfordcoins.com). 🅟 *British, Commonwealth and world coins.*

Satin Coins
PO Box 63, Stockport, Cheshire SK4 5BU. (07940 393583 answer machine).

David Seaman
PO Box 449, Waltham Cross EN9 3WZ. (01992 719723, email davidseamancoins@lineone.net). 🅟 🅛 *Hammered, Milled, Maundy.*

Patrick Semmens
3 Hospital Road, Half Key, Malvern, Worcs WR14 1UZ. (0886 33123). 🅟 *European and British coins.*

Mark Senior
553 Falmer Road, Woodingdean, Brighton, Sussex (01273 309359). By appointment only. 🅟 🅛 *Saxon, Norman and English hammered.*

S. E. Sewell
PO Box 149, Stowmarket, IP14 4WD. (01449 782185 or 07739 071822, email: sewellmedals@hotmail.com, www.sewellmedals.co.uk). *Mainly British milled.*

Shepshed Coins & Jewellery
24 Charnwood Road, Shepshed, Leics LE12 9QF. (01509 502511). Mon, Wed–Sat 09.15–16.30. *British coins.*

Silbury Coins
PO Box 281, Cirencester, Gloucs GL7 9ET (info@silburycoins.com, www.silburycoins.com). (info@silburycoins.com, www.silburycoins.com). *Iron Age, Roman, Saxon, Viking, medieval coins and later.*

Simmons Gallery (ANA, BNTA, IBNS)
PO Box 104, Leytonstone, London E11 1ND (020 8989 8097, www.simmonsgallery.co.uk). 🅛 *Coins, tokens and medals.*

E. Smith (ANA, IBNS)
PO Box 348, Lincoln LN6 0TX (01522 684681 fax 01522 689528). Organiser of the Morley, Leeds, monthly coin fair. 🅟 *World coins and paper money.*

J. Smith (BNTA)
47 The Shambles, York YO1 2LX. (01904 654769).
Mon–Sat 09.30–17.00. *World coins.*

Neil Smith
PO Box 774, Lincoln LN4 2WX. (01522 522772 fax
01522 689528). *GB and World Gold coins 1816 to
date, including modern proof issues.*

Jim Smythe
PO Box 6970, Birmingham B23 7WD. (Email:
Jimdens@aol.com). 🅿🅛 *19th/20th century British
and world coins.*

S&B Coins
Suite 313, St Loyes House, 20 Loyes Street, Bedford
MK40 1ZL. (01234 270260). 🅿🅛 *Medallions.*

SCoin Shop
Unit 1143b, Ground Floor, Westfield Shopping Mall,
London. (020 8749 8450, email: london@sagoldcoin.
com, www.scoinshop.com). Gold coins.

Spink & Son Ltd (ANA, BNTA, IAPN, IBNS)
69 Southampton Row, Bloomsbury, London.
WC1B 4ET. (020 7563 2820, fax 020 7563 4066,
email: info@spinkandson.com, www.spink.com).
*Ancient to modern world coins, orders, medals,
banknotes and books.*

SPM Jewellers (BNTA)
112 East Street, Southampton, Hants SO14 3HD.
(023 80 223255/020 80 227923, fax 023 80 335634,
email: user@spm.in2home.co.uk, www.spm
goldcoins.co.uk). Tue–Sat 09.15–17.00,
Sat 09.15–16.00. *World coins and medals.*

Stamford Coins
65–67 Stamford Street, Bradford, West Yorkshire
BD4 8SD. (07791 873595, email: stamfordcoins@
hotmail.co.uk).

Stamp & Collectors Centre
404 York Town Road, College Town, Camberley,
Surrey GU15 4PR. (01276 32587 fax 01276 32505).
World coins and medals.

St Edmunds Coins & Banknotes
PO Box 118, Bury St Edmunds IP33 2NE.
(01284 761894).

Sterling Coins & Medals
2 Somerset Road, Boscombe, Bournemouth, Dorset
BH7 6JH. (01202 423881). Mon–Sat 09.30–16.30
(closed Wed). *World coins and medals.*

Studio Coins (ANA, BNTA)
16 Kilham Lane, Winchester, Hants SO22 5PT.
(01962 853156 fax 01962 624246). 🅿 *English coins.*

Time Line Originals
PO Box 193, Upminster, RM14 3WH. (01708
222014/ 07775 651218, email: sales@time–lines.
co.uk).

Stuart J. Timmins
Smallwood Lodge Bookshop, Newport, Salop.
(01952 813232). *Numismatic literature.*

R. Tims
39 Villiers Road, Watford, Herts WD1 4AL. 🅿🅛
Uncirculated world banknotes.

D. A. Travis
8 Cookridge Drive, Leeds LS16 7LT. 🅿🅛 *US coins.*

Michael Trenerry
PO Box 55, Truro, Cornwall TR1 2YQ. (01872
277977 fax 01872 225565, email veryfinecoins@aol.
com). By appointment only. 🅛 *Roman, Celtic and
English hammered coins and tokens.*

Vera Trinder Ltd
38 Bedford Street, Strand, London WC2E 9EU. (020
7257 9940). 🅛 *Coin accessories.*

Robert Tye
7–9 Clifford Street, York, YO1 9RA. (0845 4 900 724,
email: orders@earlyworldcoins.com. 🅿*European
and Oriental hammered coins.*

Universal Currency Coin Exhange
PO Box 57648, Mill Hill, London, NW7 0FE.
(07831 662594, email: uccedcp@aol.com.)
German, Canadian and American Coins.

Valda Coins
80 Aberfan Road, Aberfan, Mid Glamorgan CF48
4QJ. (01443 690452). 🅿🅛

Vale (ADA)
21 Tranquil Vale, Blackheath, London SE3 0BU.
(020 8852 9817. *British coins and medals.*

Van der Schueren, John-Luc (IAPN)
14 Rue de la Borse, 1,000 Bussels, Belgium. (Email: iapnsecret@compuserve.com, www.coins.be.) Mon–Fri 1100–1800 hrs. Coins and tokens of the world and of the low countries.

Tony Vaughan Collectables
PO Box 364, Wolverhampton, WV3 9PW. (01902 27351). **P L** *World coins and medals.*

Victory Coins (BNTA)
184 Chichester Road, North End, Portsmouth, Hants PO2 0AX. (023 92 751908/663450). Thurs–Sat 09.00–17.00. *British and world coins.*

Viking Metal Detectors
1 angela Street, Mill Hill, Blacburn, Lancashire BB2 4DJ. (01254 55887 fax 01254 676901, email viking@metaldetectors.co.uk).

Mark J. Vincenzi (BNTA)
Rylands, Earls Colne, Essex CO6 2LE. (01787 222555). **P** *Greek, Roman, Hammered.*

Vista World Banknotes
5 Greenfields Way, Burley-in-Wharfedale, Ilkley, W. Yorks LS29 7RB. (Email: vistabanknotes @barclays.net).

Mike Vosper
PO Box 32, Hockwold, Brandon IP26 4HX. (01842 828292, email: mikevosper@vosper4coins.co.uk. www.vosper4coins.co.uk).

Weighton Coin Wonders
(01430 879740, www.weightoncoin.co.uk). *Modern gold, silver proofs and sets.*

John Welsh
PO Box 150, Burton–on–Trent, Staffs DE13 7LB. (01543 73073 fax 0543 473234). **P L** *British coins.*

Pam West (IBNS, BNTA)
PO Box 257, Sutton, Surrey SM3 9WW. (020 8641 3224, email: pamwestbritnotes@aol.com, www. brishnotes.co.uk,). **P L** *English banknotes*

West Essex Coin Investments (BNTA, IBNS)
Croft Cottage, Station Road, Alderholt, Fordingbridge, Hants SP6 3AZ. (01425 656 459). *British and World coins and paper money.*

West Wicklow Coins
Blessington, Co Wicklow, Ireland. (00353 45 858767, email: westwicklowcoins@hotmail.com). Irish and *World coins.*

Whitmore (BNTA)
Teynham Lodge, Chase Road, Upper Colwall, Malvern, Worcs WR13 6DT. (01684 50651). **P** *World coins, tokens and medals.*

T. Wilkes (IAPN)
PO Box 150, Battle, East Sussex TN33 0FA. (01424 773352, www.wilkescoins.com). *English Hammered, European Medieval, Crusader coins, Islamic/Indian.*

World Coins
35–36 Broad Street, Canterbury, Kent CT1 2LR. (01227 768887). Mon–Sat 09.30–17.30 (half–day Thu). World & British coins, tokens & banknotes.

Worldwide Coins (IBNS)
PO Box 11, Wavertree, Liverpool L15 0FG. (Email: sales@worldwidecoins.co.uk,www.worldwidecoins. co.uk. *World coins and paper money.*

World Treasure Books
PO Box 5, Newport, Isle of Wight PO30 5QE. (01983 740712). **L** *Coins, books, metal detectors.*

Barry Wright
54 Dooley Drive, Bootle, Merseyside. L3O 8RT. **P L** *World banknotes.*

I. S. Wright (Australia Numismatic Co)
208 Sturt Street, Ballarat, Vic. Australia 3350. (0061 3 5332 3856 fax 0061 3 5331 6426, email: ausnumis@netconnect.comau). **P** *Coins, banknotes, medallions, tokens.*

D. Yapp
PO Box 4718, Shrewsbury Mail Centre SY1 9EA. (01743 232557, www.david-yapp.com). **L** *World and British Banknotes.*

York Coins
PO Box 160, Red Hook, New York 12571. (Tel/fax: (718) 544 0120 email: antony@yorkcoins.com). *Ancient coins.*

York Coin and Stamp Centre
Cavendish Antique & Collectors Centre, 44 Stone gate, York, YO1 8AS. *Retail shop. Coins and medals.*

BUREAUX *of the World*

Many national banks and mints operate numismatic bureaux and sales agencies from which coins, medals and other numismatic products may be obtained direct. The conditions under which purchases may be made vary considerably. In many cases at the present time bureaux will accept orders from overseas customers quoting their credit card number and its expiry date; but in others payment can only be made by certified bank cheque, or international money order, or by girobank. Cash is seldom, if ever, acceptable. It is best to write in the first instance to enquire about methods of payment.

A

National Mint, Baghe Arg, Kabul, Afghanistan

Bank Mille Afghan, Kabul, Afghanistan

Banque d'Algerie, Sucursale d'Alger, 8 Boulevard Carnot, Alger, Algeria

Banco de Angola, Luanda, Daroal, Angola

Casa de Moneda de la Nacion, Avenida Antartica, Buenos Aires, BA, Argentina

Royal Australian Mint, Department of the Treasury, Canberra, ACT, Australia

GoldCorp Australia, Perth Mint Buildings, GPO Box M924, Perth, Western Australia 6001

Oesterreichsiches Hauptmunzamt, Am Heumarkt 1, A-1031 Wien, Postfach 225, Austria

Oesterreichische Nationalbank, A-1090 Wien, Otto Wagner-platz 3, Austria

B

Treasury Department, PO Box 557, Nassau, Bahamas (*coins*)

Ministry of Finance, PO Box 300, Nassau, Bahamas (*banknotes*)

Bank of Bahrain, PO Box 106, Manama, Bahrain

Eastern Bank, PO Box 29, Manama, Bahrain

Monnaie Royale de Belgique, Avenue de Pacheco 32, B-1000 Bruxelles, Belgium

Banque Nationale de Belgique SA, Caisse Centrale, Bruxelles, Belgium

Banque de Bruxelles SA, 2 Rue de la Regence, Bruxelles 1, Belgium

Casa de la Moneda, Potosi, BoliviaBanco Central de Bolivia, La Paz, Bolivia

Casa da Moeda, Praca da Republica 173, Rio de Janeiro, Brazil

Hemus FTO, 7 Vasil Levski Street, Sofia C-1, Bulgaria

Banque de la Republique, Bujumbura, Burundi

C

Banque Centrale, Douala, Boite Postale 5.445, Cameroun

Royal Canadian Mint, 320 Sussex Drive, Ottawa 2, Ontario, Canada K1A 0G8

Casa de Moneda, Quinta Normal, Santiago, Chile

Casa de Moneda, Calle 11 no 4-93, Bogota, Colombia

Numismatic Section, The Treasury, Avarua, Rarotonga, Cook Islands

Banco Centrale de Costa Rica, Departamento de Contabilidad, San Jose, Costa Rica, CA

Central Bank of Cyprus, PO Box 1087, Nicosia, Cyprus

Artia, Ve Smekach 30, PO Box 790, Praha 1, Czech Republic

D

Den Kongelige Mønt, Amager Boulevard 115, København S, Denmark

Danmarks Nationalbank, Holmens Kanal 17, 1060 København K, Denmark

Banco Central de Santo Domingo, Santo Domingo, Dominican Republic

E

Banco Central, Quito, Ecuador

Mint House, Abbassia, Cairo, Egyptian Arab Republic

Exchange Control Department, National Bank of Egypt, Cairo, Egyptian Arab Republic

Banco Central de la Republica, Santa Isabel, Equatorial Guinea

Commercial Bank of Ethiopia, Foreign Branch, PO Box 255, Addis Ababa, Ethiopia

F

Currency Board, Victoria Parade, Suva, Fiji

Suomen Rahapaja, Katajanokanlaituri 3, Helsinki 16, Finland

Suomen Pankki, PO Box 10160, Helsinki 10, Finland

Hotel de Monnaie, 11 Quai de Conti, 75-Paris 6e, France

G

Banque Centrale Libreville, Boite Postale 112, Gabon

Verkaufstelle fur Sammlermunzen, D-638 Bad Homburg vdH, Bahnhofstrasse 16–18, Germany

Staatliche Munze Karlsruhe, Stephanienstrasse 28a, 75 Karlsruhe, Germany

Staatliche Munze Cannstatt, Taubenheimerstrasse 77, 7 Stuttgart-Bad, Germany

Bayerisches Hauptmunzamt, Hofgraben 4, 8 Munich, Germany

Hamburgische Munze, Norderstrasse 66, 2 Hamburg 1, Germany

Bank of Ghana, PO Box 2674, Accra, Ghana

Pobjoy Mint, Millennia House, Kingswood Park, Bonsor Drive, Kingswood, Surrey KT20 6AY

Royal Mint, Llantrisant, Mid Glamorgan, Wales, CF7 8YT

Royal Mint Coin Club, PO Box 500, Cardiff, CF1 1HA

Bank of Greece, Treasury Department, Cash, Delivery & Despatch Division, PO Box 105, Athens, Greece

Casa Nacional de Moneda, 6a Calle 4-28, Zona 1, Ciudad Guatemala, Republica de Guatemala CA

States Treasury, St Peter Port, Guernsey, Channel Islands

Bank of Guyana, PO Box 658, Georgetown, Guyana

H

Banque Nationale de la Republique d'Haiti, Rue Americaine et Rue Fereu, Port-au-Prince, Haiti

Banco Central de Honduras, Tegucigalpa DC, Honduras CA

State Mint, Ulloi utca 102, Budapest VIII, Hungary

Artex, PO Box 167, Budapest 62, Hungary

Magyar Nemzeti Bank, Board of Exchange, Budapest 54, Hungary

I

Sedlabanki Islands, Reykjavik, Iceland

Indian Government Mint, Bombay 1, India

Arthie Vasa, Keabajoran Baru, Djakarta, Indonesia

Perum Peruri, Djakarta, Indonesia

National Mint, Tehran, Iran

Bank Markazi Iran, Tehran, IranCentral Bank of Iraq, PO Box 64, Baghdad, Iraq

Central Bank of Ireland, Dublin 2, Republic of Ireland

The Treasury, Government Buildings, Prospect Hill, Douglas, Isle of Man

Israel Stamp and Coin Gallery, 4 Maze Street, Tel Aviv, Israel

Istituto Poligraphico e Zecca dello Stato, Via Principe Umberto, Roma, Italy

J

Decimal Currency Board, PO Box 8000, Kingston, Jamaica

Mint Bureau, 1 Shinkawasakicho, Kita-ku, Osaka 530, Japan

Numismatic Section, Treasury Department, St Helier, Jersey

Central Bank of Jordan, Amman, Jordan

Banque Nationale du Liban, Rue Masraf Loubnan, Beirut, Lebanon

K

Central Bank, PO Box 526, Kuwait

L

Bank of LatviaK. Valdemara iela 2A, LV-1050, Riga, Latvia

Bank of Lithuania, Cash Department, Gedimino av. 6, 2001 Vilius, Lithuania

Caisse Generale de l'Etat, 5 Rue Goethe, Luxembourg-Ville, Grande Duche de Luxembourg

M

Institut d'Emission Malgache, Boite Postale 205, Tananarive, Madagascar

Central Bank of Malta, Valletta 1, Malta

Casa de Moneda, Calle del Apartado no 13, Mexico 1, DF, Mexico

Le Tresorier General des Finances, Monte Carlo, Principaute de Monaco

Banque de l'Etat du Maroc, Rabat, Morocco

Banco Nacional Ultramarino, Maputo, Republica de Mocambique

British Bank of the Middle East, Muscat

N

Royal Mint, Dharahara, Katmandu, Nepal

Nepal Rastra Bank, Katmandu, Nepal

Rijks Munt, Leidseweg 90, Utrecht, Netherlands

Hollandsche Bank-Unie NV, Willemstad, Breedestraat 1, Curacao, Netherlands Antilles

Central Bank of Curacao, Willemstad, Curacao, Netherlands Antilles

New Zealand Post Stamps Centre, Private Bag 3001, Wanganui 4540, New Zealand

Banco de Nicaragua, Departamento de Emison, La Tresoria, Apartada 2252, Managua, Nicaragua

Nigerian Security Printing and Minting Corporation, Ahmadu Bello Road, Victoria Island, Lagos, Nigeria

Central Bank of Nigeria, Tinubu Square LB, Lagos, Nigeria

Norges Bank, Oslo, Norway

Den Kongelige Mynt, Hyttegaten, Konigsberg, Norway

P

Pakistan State Mint, Baghban Pura, Lahore 9, Pakistan

National Development Bank, Asuncion, Paraguay

Casa Nacional de Moneda, Calle Junin 791, Lima, Peru

Central Bank of the Philippines, Manila, Philippines

Bank Handlowy w Warszawie, Ul. Romuald Traugutta 7, Warsaw, Poland

Desa Foreign Trade Department, Al. Jerozolimskie 2, Warszawa, Poland

Casa da Moeda, Avenida Dr Antonio Jose de Almeida, Lisbon 1, Portugal

R

Cartimex, 14-18 Aristide Briand St, PO Box 134-135, Bucharest, Roumania

Bank of Foreign Trade, Commercial Department, Moscow K 16, Neglinnaja 12, Russian Federation

Banque Nationale du Rwanda, Boite Postale 351, Kigali, Republique Rwandaise

S

Numismatic Section, Box 194, GPO, Apia, Samoa

Azienda Autonoma di Stato Filatelica-Numismatica, Casalla Postale 1, 47031 Repubblica di San Marino

Banque Internationale pour le Commerce, 2 Avenue Roume, Dakar, Senegal

Bank of Yugoslavia, PO Box 1010, Belgrade, Serbia

The Treasury, PO Box 59, Victoria, Seychelles

Bank of Sierra Leone, PO Box 30, Freetown, Sierra Leone

The Singapore Mint, 20 Teban Gardens Crescent, Singapore 608928

South African Mint, PO Box 464, Pretoria, South Africa

Government Printing Agency, 93 Bukchang Dong, Chungku, Seoul, Republic of South Korea

Fabrica Nacional de Moneda y Timbre, Jorge Juan 106, Madrid 9, Spain

Bank of Sri Lanka, PO Box 241, Colombo, Sri Lanka

Hong Kong and Shanghai Banking Corporation, PO Box 73, Colombo 1, Sri Lanka

Sudan Mint, PO Box 43, Khartoum, Sudan

Bank of Sudan, PO Box 313, Khartoum, Sudan

Bank of Paramaribo, Paramaribo, Suriname

Kungelige Mynt och Justeringsverket, Box 22055, Stockholm 22, Sweden

Eidgenossische Staatskasse, Bundesgasse 14, CH-3003, Berne, Switzerland

Central Bank of Syria, Damascus, Syrian Arab Republic

T

Central Mint of China, 44 Chiu Chuan Street, Taipei, Taiwan, ROC

Royal Thai Mint, 4 Chao Fah Road, Bangkok, Thailand

Numismatic Section, The Treasury, Nuku'alofa, Tonga

Central Bank of Trinidad and Tobago, PO Box 1250, Port of Spain, Trinidad

Banque Centrale de Tunisie, Tunis, Tunisia

State Mint, Maliye Bakanligi Darphane Mudurlugu, Istanbul, Turkey

U

Bank of Uganda, PO Box 7120, Kampala, Uganda

Numismatic Service, US Assay Office, 350 Duboce Avenue, San Francisco, CA, 94102, USA

Office of the Director of the Mint, Treasury Department, Washington, DC, 20220, USA

Philadelphia Mint, 16th and Spring Garden Streets, Philadelphia, PA, 19130, USA

Franklin Mint, Franklin Center, Pennsylvania, 19063, USA

Banco Central del Uruguay, Cerrito 351, Montevideo, RO del Uruguay

V

Ufficio Numismatico, Governatorato dello Stato della Citta de Vaticano, Italy

Banco Central de Venezuela, Caracas, Venezuela

Y

Yemen Bank, Sana'a, Yemen.

Z

Bank of Zambia, PO Box 80, Lusaka, Zambia

Chief Cashier, Reserve Bank, PO Box 1283, Harare, Zimbabwe

TREASURE *and the Law*

Until the introduction of the new Treasure Act, the legal position regarding articles of gold, silver or bullion, found long after they were hidden or abandoned, was not as simple and straightforward as it might be supposed. Furthermore, this was a case where the law in England and Wales differed fundamentally from that in Scotland.

Treasure Trove was one of the most ancient rights of the Crown, deriving from the age-old right of the monarch to gold, silver or bullion treasure whose owner was not known. In England and Wales, the law applied only to objects made of, or containing, gold or silver, whether in the form of coin, jewellery, plate or bullion. Moreover, the object had to be shown to have been deliberately hidden with intent to retrieve and the owner could not be readily found. The English law therefore excluded precious stones and jewels set in base metals or alloys such as bronze or pewter. It also took no account of artifacts in pottery, stone, bone, wood or glass which might be of immense antiquarian value.

In recent years, as a result of the rise in metal-detecting as a hobby, the archaeological lobby brought pressure to bear on Parliament to change the law and bring it into line with Scotland where the rules on Treasure Trove were far more rigorously interpreted. In Scotland the Crown is entitled to *all* abandoned property, even if it has not been hidden and is of little value. This applies even to objects dumped in skips on the pavement. Strictly speaking you would be committing a criminal offence if you removed an old chair from a skip without the owner's permission, although in practice such helping oneself rarely proceeds to a prosecution. In 1958 an archaeological expedition from Aberdeen University found several valuable artifacts on St Ninian's Isle, Shetland. These included silver vessels and ornaments, as well as a porpoise bone which had incised decoration on it. The archaeologists challenged the rights of the Crown to this treasure, arguing that the Crown would have to prove that the articles had been deliberately hidden, and that a porpoise bone was in any case not valuable enough to count as treasure. The High Court, however, decided that as long as the property had been abandoned, it belonged automatically to the Crown. Its value, intrinsic or otherwise, or whether or not it was hidden, did not make any difference. Since then, as a result of this decision in case law, the criteria for Treasure Trove have been very strictly applied in Scotland. It would have only required a similar test case in England or Wales to result in a similar tightening of the rules. This has been resisted, mainly by the detectorist lobby, but inevitably the government considered legislation to control the use of metal detectors, if not to ban them altogether.

A rather worn denarius of Commodus, minted in Rome approximately 180s AD. This coin was one of many coins found in a Worcestershire field close to a deserted medieval village site.

In England and Wales a find of gold or silver coins, artifacts or ornaments, or objects which contain some of these metals, which appears to have been concealed by the original owner, was deemed to be Treasure Trove. It was not even necessary for the articles to be buried in the ground; objects concealed in thatched roofs or under the floorboards of buildings have been judged to be Treasure Trove. Such finds had to be notified immediately to the police who then informed the district coroner. He then convened an inquest which decided whether all or part of the find was Treasure Trove. Establishing the gold or silver content was straightforward, but the coroner's inquest had to decide whether the material was hidden deliberately and not just lost or abandoned, and that the owner could not be located. A gold coin found on or near a country footpath might reasonably have been dropped by the original possessor through a hole in pocket or purse and in such cases it was very unlikely that it would be deemed Treasure Trove, even if the coin turned out to be very rare. In this instance the coroner would then have had to determine who was the lawful owner of the find: the actual finder, the owner of the land where it was found or even the tenant of the land. As a rule, however, it was left to the finder and landowner to decide between them who the owner of the coin should

be, and in some cases the matter could only be resolved by referring to a civil court. For this reason it was vital that metal detectorists should secure permission *in writing* from landowners before going on to their land, defining rights and obligations on both sides, in order to determine the disposal or share-out of any finds or proceeds from the sale of finds, *beforehand*.

If the coroner decided that the articles were deliberately concealed, and declared them to be Treasure Trove, the find automatically reverted to the Crown. In practice the find was considered by the Treasure Trove Reviewing Committee of the Treasury. They might decide that although the articles, *invariably coins,* were gold or silver, they were so common that they were not required by the British Museum or one of the other great national collections, and would return them to the finder to dispose of at their discretion. If some or all of the coins were deemed vital for inclusion in a national collection the finder was recompensed with the full market value of the material. On the other hand, if someone found gold or silver which might be Treasure Trove and failed to declare it at the time, that person was liable to prosecution under the Theft Act 1968 should the find subsequently come to light. Not only could they face a heavy fine but the articles would be forfeit to the Crown,

Detectorist Marjorie Dandy was delighted when she found the remains of a pot with about 1,500 coins in a potato field.

Once a hoard has been reported great care is taken in excavating the site to ensure no important historical details are destroyed.

and of course no reward or recompense was then payable either.

The anomalies and inconsistencies of existing law on Treasure Trove were eliminated and the position considerably tightened up by the passage, on July 5, 1996, of the Treasure Act.

Announcing that the Treasure Act had received the Royal Assent, Lord Inglewood, National Heritage Minister, said, "This represents the first legislation on Treasure Trove to be passed in England and Wales and will replace Common Law precedents and practices dating back to the Middle Ages. The Act, which offers a clearer definition of treasure and simplified procedures for dealing with finds, will come into force after a code of practice has been drawn up and agreed by both Houses of Parliament". The Act came into force in England, Wales and Northern Ireland on September 24, 1997, replacing the Common Law of Treasure Trove.

The act was introduced as a Private Member's Bill by Sir Anthony Grant, after the failure of an earlier attempt by Lord Perth. For the first time, it would be a criminal offence to fail to report within 14 days the discovery of an item which could be declared Treasure Trove. Finders will continue to be rewarded for reporting their discoveries promptly, while landowners and occupiers will also be eligible for rewards for the first time.

The Treasure Act covers man-made objects and defines treasure as objects other than coins which are at least 300 years old and contain at least 10 per cent by weight of gold or silver; coins more than 300 years old which are found in hoards (a minimum of two coins if the precious metal content is more than 10 per cent, and a minimum of 10 coins if the precious metal content is below 10 per cent). The act also embraces all objects found in clear archaeological association with items which are treasure under the above definitions. It also covers any object which would have been Treasure Trove under the previous definitions (e.g. hoards of 19th century gold or silver coins).

An extension to The Act from January 1992 provides that groups of prehistoric bronze implements are also deemed to be Treasure.

The maximum penalty for failing to report the discovery of treasure within 14 days will be a fine of £5,000 or three months imprisonment, or both.

In Scotland the police pass the goods on to the procurator fiscal who acts as the local representative of the Queen's and Lord Treasurer's Remembrancer. If the articles are of little value, historically or intrinsically, the finder will usually be allowed to keep them. If they are retained for the appropriate national collection then a reward equal to the market value is payable.

A favourite haunt of metal-detectorists these days is the beach, and many hobbyists make quite a lucrative living by sweeping the beaches especially just after a Bank Holiday. It's surprising how much loose change gets lost from pockets and handbags over a holiday weekend. Technically the coins recovered from the beach are lost property, in which case they ought to be surrendered to the police, otherwise the finder may be guilty of theft. In practice, however, the law turns a blind eye to coins, on the sensible grounds that it would be impossible to prove ownership. On the other hand, banknotes are treated as lost property since someone could in theory at least identify a note as his by citing the serial number.

In the case of other objects, such as watches and jewellery, of course the law governing lost property is enforced, and the old adage of "finders keepers" does not apply. Any object of value, identifiable as belonging to someone, that is washed up on the foreshore or found in territorial waters is known technically as "wreck". This includes not just a wrecked ship, but any cargo that was being carried by a ship.

If wreck is not claimed by its owner, it falls to the Crown. In this case it is not necessary to prove deliberate concealment, as in the case of Treasure Trove. This law has a specific numismatic application in the case of the gold and silver coins washed up after storms around our shores, from Shetland to the Scillies. Such coins, emanating from wrecks of Spanish treasure ships and Dutch East Indiamen in particular, are well documented, and any such finds ought to be reported immediately to the police.

Stray finds of coins, as well as other objects of value, on public places, such as the street, a public park or a sports ground, are also subject to law. In this case the finder must take all reasonable steps to locate the owner. Anyone who keeps a coin without making reasonable effort to find the owner could be prosecuted for theft. As with the beach, however, such "reasonable effort" would clearly be impractical. Finding coins on private premises is another matter. In this case large

bodies, such as the Post Office, British Rail, the British Airports Authority, bus companies, municipal authorities, hospitals, the owners of department stores, theatre and cinema proprietors and the like, may have bye-laws, rules and regulations for dealing with lost property found within their precincts, or in their vehicles. If you found a purse or wallet on a bus or train, or in a telephone kiosk or a shop, common sense (and your conscience) would tell you to hand it over to the driver, conductor, shopkeeper or official in charge. As a rule, unclaimed lost property reverts eventually to the finder, but not always; British Rail and some other organisations have a rule that in such cases the property reverts to the organisation. In any event, failure to disclose the find immediately might render you liable to prosecution for stealing by finding.

The oldest Roman coin found in the UK is a silver denarius which formed part of a hoard of 5,000 Iron Age and Roman coins found in Hallaton, Leicestershire in 2000. It dates from 211 BC.

A hoard of 206 Roman denarii dating from the 2nd century BC to the 1st century AD was discovered by detectorists Norman Howard and John Halles in Suffolk. Known as the North Suffolk Hoard, the men reported the find to the local museum. An inquest declared the hoard to be Treasure and the British Museum acquired nine of the coins for the National Collection. The remainder were sold at auction by Morton & Eden.

TREASURE ACT
Code of Practice

For easy reference a summary of the main points of the new law is reproduced here. Further information will be found in the Code of Practice on the Treasure Act, which can be obtained free of charge from the Department for Culture, Media and Sport (telephone: 020 7211 6200, email enquiries@culture.gov. uk). Metal detectorists are strongly advised to obtain a copy of the Code of Practice which, among other things, contains guidance for detectorists, sets out guidelines on rewards, gives advice on the care of finds and has lists of useful addresses.

What is the definition of treasure?

The following finds are treasure under the Act (*more detailed guidance is given in the Code of Practice*):

1. *Objects other than coins:* any object other than a coin provided that it contains at least 10 per cent of gold or silver and is a least 300 years old when found (objects with gold or silver plating normally have less than 10 per cent of precious metal).

2. *Coins:* all coins from the same find provided they are at least 300 years old when found (but if the coins contain less than 10 per cent of gold or silver there must be at least 10 of them; there is a list of these coins in the Code of Practice).

An object or coin is part of the same find as another object or coin if it is found in the same place as, or had previously been left together with, the other object. Finds may have become scattered since they were originally deposited in the ground.

Only the following groups of coins will normally be regarded as coming from the "same find":

(a) hoards that have been deliberately hidden;

(b) smaller groups of coins, such as the con
tents of purses, that may have been dropped
or lost and

(c) votive or ritual deposits.

Single coins found on their own are not treasure and groups of coins lost one by one over a period of time (for example those found on settlement sites or on fair sites) will not normally be treasure, but two coins over 300 years old found together can be deemed to be treasure.

3. *Associated objects:* any object, whether it is made of, that is found in the same place as, or that had previously been together with, another object that is treasure.

4. *Objects that would have been treasure trove:* any object that would previously have been treasure trove, but does not fall within the specific categories given above. These objects have to be made substantially of gold or silver; they have to have been buried with the intention of recovery and their owner or his/her heirs cannot be traced. The following types of find are not treasure:

(a) objects lost whose owners can be traced;

(b) unworked natural objects, including human and animal remains, even if they are found in association with treasure;

(c) objects from the foreshore, which are wreck.

If you are in any doubt, it will probably be safest to report your find.

What about objects found before the Act came into force?

You should report objects that come into any of the four categories just described (if found after September 23, 1997). There is no need to report any objects found before that date unless they may be treasure trove (see 4 above).

What should I do if I find something that may be treasure?

You must report all finds of treasure to the coroner for the district in which they are found *either* within 14 days after the date on which you made the find *or* within 14 days after the day on which you realised that the find might be treasure (for example, as a result of having it identified). The obligation to report finds applies to everyone, including archaeologists.

How do I report a find of treasure?

Very simply. You may report your find to the coroner in person, by letter, telephone or fax. The coroner or his officer will send you an acknow-ledgement and tell you where you should deliver your find. The Code of Practice has a list of all coroners' addresses, telephone and fax numbers.

There are special procedure for objects from a few areas for which treasure franchises exist, but they should be reported to the coroner in the usual way. The main franchise-holders (the Duchies of Lancaster and Cornwall, the Corporation of London and the City of Bristol) have confirmed that they will pay rewards for finds of treasure from their franchises in the normal way.

Where will I have to take my find?

You will normally be asked to take your find to a local museum or archaeological body. Local agreements have been drawn up for each coroner's district in England and Wales to provide the coroner with a list of such museums and archaeological organisations. The Department is publishing a series of leaflets, roughly one for each county of England and one for Wales, listing the relevant coroners, museums and archaeological services in each area.

The body which receives the find on behalf of the coroner will give you a receipt. Although they will need to know where you made the find, they will keep this information confidential if you or the landowner wish—and you should do so too.

The body receiving the find will notify the Sites and Monuments Record as soon as possible (if that has not already happened), so that the site where the find was made can be investigated by archae-ologists if necessary. A list of Sites and Monuments Records is in Appendix 3 of the Code of Practice.

What if I do not report a find of treasure?

If you fail to report a find that you believe or have reasonable grounds for believing to be treasure without a reasonable excuse you may be imprisoned for up to three months or receive a fine of up to level 5 on the standard scale (currently £5,000) or both. You will not be breaking the law if you do not report a find because you do not initially recognise that it may be treasure, but you should report it once you do.

What happens if the find is not treasure?

If the object is clearly not treasure, the museum or archeological body will inform the coroner, who may then decide to give directions that the find should be returned without holding an inquest.

What happens if the find is treasure?

If a museum curator or archaeologist believes the find may be treasure, they will inform the British Museum or the National Museums & Galleries of Wales. The museums will then decide whether they or any other museum may wish to acquire it.

If no museum wishes to acquire the find, the Secretary of State will be able to disclaim it. When this happens, the coroner will notify the occupier and landowner that he intends to return the object to the finder after 28 days unless he receives an objection. If the coroner receives an objection, the find will be retained until the dispute is settled.

What if a museum wants to acquire my find?

If a museum wants to acquire part or all of a find, then the coroner will hold an inquest to decide whether it is treasure. The coroner will inform the finder, occupier and landowner and they will be able to question witnesses at the inquest. Treasure inquest will not normally be held with a jury.

If the find is declared to be treasure, then it will be taken to the British Museum or the National Museums & Galleries of Wales, so that it can be valued by the Treasure Valuation Committee.

How do I know I will receive a fair price for my find?

Any find of treasure that a museum wishes to acquire must be valued by the Treasure Valuation Committee, which consists of independent experts. The Committee will commission a valuation from one or more experts drawn from the trade. You, together with the museum that wishes to acquire the find and any other interested party, will have an opportunity to comment on the valuation and to send in a separate valuation of your own, before the Committee makes its recommendation. If you are dissatisfied you can appeal to the Secretary of State.

What if the coroner or museum loses or damages my find?

They are required to take reasonable steps to ensure that this does not happen; but, if it does, you should nonetheless be compensated.

Who will receive the reward?

This is set out in detail in the Code of Practice. To summarise:

— where the finder has permission to be on the land, rewards should continue to be paid in full to him or her (the burden of proof as to whether he or she has permission will rest with the finder). If the finder makes an agreement with the occupier/landowner to share a reward, the Secretary of State will normally follow it;
— if the finder does not remove the whole of a find from the ground but allows archaeologists to excavate the remainder of the find, the original finder will normally be eligible for a reward for the whole find;
— rewards will not normally be payable when the find is made by an archaeologist;
— where the finder has committed an offence in relation to a find, or has trespassed, or has not followed best practice as set out in the Code of Practice, he or she may expect no reward at all or a reduced reward. Landowners and occupiers will be eligible for rewards in such cases.

How long will it take before I receive my reward?

The Code of Practice states that you should receive a reward within one year of you having delivered your find, although this may take longer in the case of very large finds or those that present special difficulties. If no museum wants to acquire the find it should be disclaimed within six months or within three months if it is a single object.

ADVERTISERS Directory

Dealer Directory

See our website at tokenpublishing.com for up-to-date dealer entries, with hyperlinks taking you directly to their websites.